SUCCESS IS ALL THAT WAS EXPECTED

Also by Robert M. Browning, Jr.

From Cape Charles to Cape Fear: The North Atlantic Blockading Squadron during the Civil War

U.S. Merchant Vessel War Casualties of World War II

SUCCESS IS ALL THAT WAS EXPECTED

ROBERT M. BROWNING, JR.

The South Atlantic Blockading Squadron during the Civil War

Potomac Books, Inc.
Washington, D.C.

Library of Congress Cataloging-in-Publication Data

Browning, Robert M., 1955–
    Success is all that was expected : the South Atlantic blockading
  squadron during the Civil War / Robert M. Browning, Jr. —
  1st ed.
      p. cm.
    ISBN 1-57488-514-6 (cloth : alk. paper)
    1. United States—History—Civil War, 1861–1865—Blockades.
  2. United States—History—Civil War, 1861–1865—Naval operations
  3. United States. Navy. South Atlantic Blockading Squadron (1861–
  1865).   4. Atlantic Coast (U.S.)—History, Naval—19th century.
  5. United States. Navy—History—Civil War, 1861–1865.   6. United
  States. Army—History—Civil War, 1861–1865.   7. Confederate States
  of America. Navy—History.   8. United States—Politics and
  government—1861–1865.   I. Title.
  E600.B87   2002
  973.7'5—dc21

                                                            2002008674

ISBN 1-57488-705-X (paper)

Printed in Canada on acid-free paper that meets the
American National Standards Institute Z39-48 Standard.

Potomac Books, Inc.
22841 Quicksilver Drive
Dulles, Virginia 20166

First Edition

10 9 8 7 6 5 4 3 2 1

For Susan

CONTENTS

LIST OF MAPS

ACKNOWLEDGMENTS

Clergyman and poet John Donne wrote, "No man is an island, entire of itself." This statement can not be truer for authors that write history. Assistance, encouragement, and support from a large number of colleagues, friends, and institutions are necessary for the final product. The staff of the National Archives and in particular John and Angie Van De Dereedt and Rick Peuser all helped tremendously with many of the primary documents. Mike Musick was extremely helpful in locating Army records. Thanks go to the staffs of the Library of Congress, the South Carolina Historical Society, the Massachusetts Historical Society, the Southern Historical Collection, and local and regional libraries too numerous to mention. I would like to thank Richard Fraser of the New-York Historical Society, Alan Jutzi of the Huntington Library, Pat Webb and William Erwin of the Duke University Manuscript Collection, Talley Kirkland Jr. of the Fort Pulaski National Monument, David Keough of the U.S. Army Military History Institute, Willis J. Keith of the South Carolina Department of Resources, Allen Stokes of the South Caroliniana Library, Skip Theberge from NOAA, and Richard Hatcher of the Fort Sumter National Monument. All these people provided cheerful assistance and have materially added to my research. Dr. John Coski of the Museum of the Confederacy in Richmond, Beverly B. Allen of Special Collections, Robert W. Woodruff Library, Emory University, Judy Wood of the Savannah Office U.S. Army Corps of Engineers, Marjorie G. McNinch of the Hagley Museum and Library, Margaretha Talerman of the American Swedish Historical Museum, and Carol Texley of the Lincoln Museum also provided important documents and information. Bob Holcombe of the Port Columbus Civil War Naval Center deserves special mention. He not only provided me many documents from the museum's collection, but also offered his invaluable and indispensable insight on the manuscript and answers to my many questions. I would also like to thank Ray Morton, Dennis Noble, Bill Roberts, Mel Melton, Kevin Foster, Marty Davis, James Legg, Don Canney, and Glenn Knight for their contributions. I would like to give special thanks to Bob Schneller and Steve Wise for their careful review of the manuscript and for providing documentation and guidance. Similarly I owe a debt to Robert Johnson, Scott Price, Chris Havern, and Bill Still for their comments and advice on the manuscript. Lastly, I would like to thank my family, and especially my wife, who not only created the maps in the book but also makes most of my writing possible by her patience, love and support.

INTRODUCTION

The War Begins in Charleston

On Thursday 20 December 1860, when the bells of St. Michael began to peal, Charlestonians knew what it meant. The Ordinance of Secession had passed. A wild frenzy seemed to grip the whole city. Huzzas filled the air as the Stars and Stripes fell to the South Carolina State flag. Citizens carried Palmetto branches in triumph along the streets proclaiming their new freedom. Some even strung bales of cotton on ropes between the houses. Slogans decorated these bales, one of which stated "THE WORLD WANTS IT." As bands played "Dixie" into the night, bonfires lit the sky with a glare never witnessed in the city's past. Against this light the ground "fairly shook beneath the double-quick of all the young men of the city under arms and apparently eager for the fray."[1]

Six days later, in the darkness of 26 December, the garrison of Fort Moultrie escaped, rowed across the harbor and occupied Fort Sumter. When the flag of the United States rose over the fort the next day it became a symbol that the entire city could see. This single piece of bunting represented the sole Union presence left in the Charleston area. As it was isolated from the world by the harbor, state authorities speculated it would be only a short time before the federal government tried to reinforce the fort's garrison. President James Buchanan outfitted an expedition in New York at the same time South Carolina authorities began preparing for this eventuality. The President considered sending the screw sloop *Brooklyn*, but instead sent the little side-wheel steamer *Star of the West* hoping she might slip into the harbor without much notice. Southern sympathizers in New York, however, learned of her destination and sent telegrams of the steamer's intentions, thereby spoiling this covert mission.

On the morning of 9 January 1861, the *Star of the West* lay bobbing outside Charleston Harbor awaiting daylight. Captain John McGowan,

1

late of the Revenue Marine, had on board about 250 men to augment the beleaguered garrison in Fort Sumter. McGowan managed to get his bearings shortly after the first rays of light flickered over the horizon. Immediately he turned his vessel into the channel. All seemed well as the small steamer continued down the channel to within two miles of Fort Sumter. Forewarned of McGowan's intentions, a masked battery on Morris Island sent a shot arcing toward the harbor's entrance at 7:15. The shot fell ahead and short of the surging steamer. This did not deter McGowan and, to show his determination, he had a large United States flag hoisted on the ship's fore.

A second round from the masked battery also fell short, but ricocheted and bounded over the vessel. With this near miss, other gun crews began testing their aim. The fourth shot hit the *Star of the West* in the fore chains, but McGowan remained steady and continued toward the harbor. As the steamer stood farther down the channel, larger guns opened fire. These shots continued to pass over and strike nearby but close enough that McGowan realized his ship would never arrive safely. With much regret McGowan conceded that he could not relieve the fort and turned his vessel back to sea.

Cut off from the outside, the garrison of Fort Sumter could not remain indefinitely. For three months the tensions increased as Anderson and his men held the fort. The leaders on both sides remained indecisive and uncompromising. The situation worsened as the fort and the garrison became, for both sides, a distinct symbol of the rift between the North and South.

On 4 March, Abraham Lincoln became the new president. After a month of indecision, he ordered a naval expedition to relieve the garrison and notified South Carolina authorities that he would do so. Confederate President Jefferson Davis determined to prevent it. On 12 April, after Major Robert Anderson, the commander of Fort Sumter, refused an ultimatum for surrender, the nearby forts in the harbor began a bombardment—the first shell bursting over the fort at 4:30 A.M. During the bombardment the revenue cutter *Harriet Lane*, the supply vessel *Baltic*, and the gunboat *Pawnee*, sent to relieve Fort Sumter, lay helplessly outside the harbor. The ships remained as spectators and only brought off Anderson and his garrison after the surrender. Again the powerful forts ringing the harbor turned back a naval expedition.[2]

Because the war began at Fort Sumter, Charleston became a larger symbol of rebellion. The public's attention, in both regions, remained focused on everything that happened there. Charleston, the cradle of se-

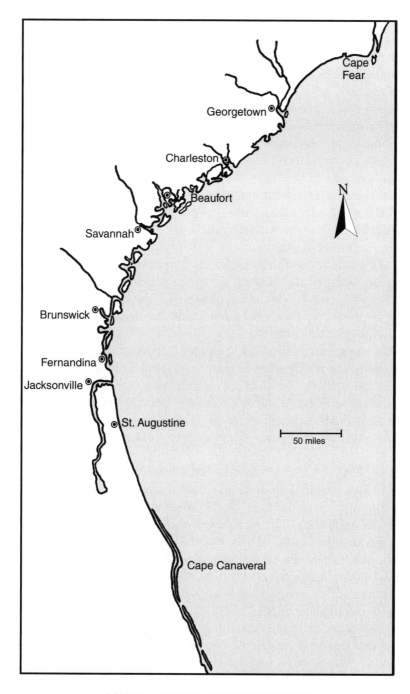

MAP I.   SOUTH ATLANTIC COAST

cession, could not boast of important industries or other attributes that would make it essential to the Confederate government, but it had enormous political value. The politicians on both sides realized this fact and coordinated their war efforts accordingly. The tremendous political value similarly caused the politicians and the public to scrutinize every operation there. The views and actions often reflected a skewed vision of the military importance of Charleston. Under such scrutiny, the military officers in this theatre often met undue criticism.

Much of the focus on Charleston by the Union navy was due to Assistant Secretary of the Navy Gustavus Vasa Fox. From the *Baltic*, Fox had led the aborted expedition to relieve the fort in April. He never forgot his failure. This disappointment distorted his perspective and throughout the war he actively promoted the capture of the city and sought retribution on those whom he felt had started the war. Fox even viewed the officers and ships under his command as an "avenging arm" to "inflict act[s] of retribution" on the South. Fox firmly believed that the "Fall of Charleston is the fall of Satan's Kingdom." For Fox and the Navy Department, this retribution could be best accomplished by a naval victory at this port.[3]

The engagements between ships and forts certainly tell only part of the story in the South Atlantic theatre of the war. It is also a narrative of ironclad actions, the blockade, amphibious operations, and underwater warfare. Despite the wide-ranging activity of the armed forces along the South Atlantic coast, their focus remained at Charleston throughout most of the war. The capture of the city remained the ultimate goal.

The South Atlantic Blockading Squadron was established in the fall of 1861 and operated along an expanse of over 500 miles of coastline, from the northern boundary of the state of South Carolina to Cape Canaveral in Florida. The activities of this squadron, in effect, defined the war along the South Atlantic coast. This squadron was, for much of the conflict, the largest of the four coastal blockading squadrons. The squadron made a significant contribution to all the combined operations in this area and its role was both important and essential.

The accomplishments of the squadron, however, might have been more significant had the leaders in Washington developed a clear strategy for this theatre. Many of the combined operations undertaken along the South Atlantic coast had defective goals based on flawed or nonexistent strategy. The lack of guidance from Washington complicated matters for the Union army and naval commanders who were expected to succeed. Despite the fact that the leaders in Washington failed to express clearly their strategic vision, they remained disappointed that the armed forces never secured Charleston. The story that relates to the military actions along the South Atlantic Coast is full of bravery, sacrifice, and victory, as well as unfulfilled expectations, lost opportunities, and failure.

– 1 –

"The Blockade Is a Farce"

The Navy Enters the War

A week after the first shots fell on Fort Sumter and amid the confusion in the nation's capital, President Abraham Lincoln declared his intention to blockade the southern states. At the time of this proclamation, the U.S. Navy consisted of ninety vessels—only forty-two of these in commission. The navy designed and built most of its ships for deep-water operations, and most of them would find it difficult to carry out a close blockade of the shallow southern coast. For example, the main strength of the U.S. Navy was its five steam frigates. Although formidable warships, they could not perform effectively as blockaders because of their deep draft. In addition, naval appropriations had languished for several years and the navy was not in a state of readiness to fight a war. At the outbreak of war the navy had only three vessels ready for service on the Atlantic coast. The vast majority of the naval vessels lay in ordinary, were on foreign stations, or patrolled the Gulf of Mexico. It would be some time before the navy could assign to stations any significant number of warships to make a blockade effective.[1]

Winfield Scott, General in Chief of the U.S. Army, envisioned the navy and armies acting in unison. He proposed to defeat the South by a massive blockading effort and pressure by a huge army from many points. The press dubbed it the Anaconda Plan, because it reminded the press of a large snake that kills its victim by constriction. The navy, however, was in no way ready to participate in this comprehensive plan. In

1861, the navy would be hard pressed to provide the requisite blockading force for a plan named after a garter snake.

The situation for the navy worsened as the other southern states left the fold of the Union and events uncontrollably rushed headlong toward a broader war. Only one day after Lincoln's proclamation of the blockade, the United States Navy suffered the shattering loss of the Norfolk Navy Yard. The fall of Norfolk included the loss of not only the Navy's largest yard and logistical base, but about $8,000,000 in property. This included 3,000 pieces of ordnance, of which 300 were the navy's most modern—Dahlgren guns. This weakened a navy that was already far from strong.[2]

The initial responsibility to blockade the entire length of the Atlantic coast fell on the shoulders of Captain Garrett J. Pendergrast. Pendergrast entered the service in 1812 and served on board a dozen different ships in a naval career that spanned nearly forty years. Flag Officer Pendergrast commanded the Home Squadron, whose jurisdiction stretched from the Chesapeake Bay to the Florida Keys. Flag Officer Pendergrast directed the movements of the Home Squadron and the blockade of the entire Atlantic Coast from his flagship, the frigate *Cumberland*, anchored off Fort Monroe. His major concern was the blockade of the major port cities. Despite the small number of vessels at his disposal and no logistical base between the outer points, he believed he could maintain an efficient blockade.[3]

Even when large numbers of vessels comprised the Union squadron, later commanders would find that the geography of the southern shoreline complicated the implementation and maintenance of the blockade. Along the entire southern seaboard, and particularly from Charleston to Fernandina, a series of low swampy islands stretched along the coast. Narrow rivers separated the islands and at intervals large estuaries lay at the river mouths. Behind the islands lay an intricate network of waterways that allowed shallow-draft vessels to keep communications open north and south without the need to enter the Atlantic.[4]

The major commercial entrances along the South Atlantic coast lay within a 300-mile stretch from Georgetown, South Carolina to Fernandina, Florida. About fifty miles above Charleston lies Winyah Bay, the dual entrance to the Santee River, and Bull Bay. Winyah Bay is the outlet of the Pee Dee and Waccamaw rivers. Schooners and light draft steamers used these waterways to carry cotton, lumber, rice, and naval stores to Georgetown and Charleston. Georgetown, without rail connections, had ceased being used for overseas commerce. Shallow-draft schooners and steamers carried rice to Charleston to be shipped abroad. Six miles southeast of Winyah Bay lies the North Santee River; this served as the chief passage of vessels carrying rice to Charleston from the interior down the Santee River. Bull Bay stretched over six miles and was about one and a half miles wide. Considered a "Noble Harbor of Refuge," it had no developed commerce, but did connect with Charleston and the Santee River by shallow water interior routes. Prices, Capers, Dewees and Breach inlets above Charleston also offered access to the interior.[5]

Between Charleston and Savannah are the large estuaries of Stono Inlet, North and South Edisto, St. Helena, and Port Royal. These sounds offered vessels easy access to the interior. A complex series of waterways connected them all. Vessels drawing less than ten feet of water could travel north and south without venturing into the ocean. Port Royal Sound stood out as the most important roadstead for the Union planners. The port of Beaufort, South Carolina, on the Beaufort River, was one of the most accessible ports on the coast but had little to offer the Confederacy with its limited facilities and the absence of rail connections.[6]

South of Beaufort lay Savannah, Georgia. Savannah served the South as the second most important port on the East coast after Charleston. The city lay about sixteen miles above the mouth of the Savannah River. Merchants shipped rice and cotton from the interior, carried to the city, in part, by three railroad lines. The Savannah River's narrow channel could accommodate vessels with a fifteen-foot draft to the city's docks. The city also had water connections to Florida via shallow interior waterways. These allowed steamers not drawing more than five feet, smooth water navigation for about 100 miles.

Below Savannah are six important sounds: Wassaw, Ossabaw, St. Catherine's, Sapelo, Doboy, and Altamaha. None of these sounds had been developed, but all had potential as entrances for shallow-draft blockade runners. Their connections with each other by interior routes would only complicate the efforts of the Union navy. South of these bodies of water was St. Simon's Sound, also in Georgia, which allowed access to the town of Brunswick. The two remaining sounds in Georgia, St. Andrew's Sound and Cumberland Sound on the Georgia–Florida state boundary, both admitted vessels to travel to Fernandina, Florida.[7]

Only three towns of any size lay on the east coast of Florida: Fernandina, Jacksonville, and St. Augustine. Fernandina seemed the most desirable as a potential logistical base for the Union navy. The main ship channel over the St. Mary's Bar into Fernandina could accommodate vessels with a twenty-foot draft at high tide. This would permit all but the largest vessels to use this port. Both Fernandina and Jacksonville had rail connections and gave them commercial value and potential for further development. St. Augustine and the small harbors farther south on the Florida Peninsula, such as Mosquito and Indian River inlets, had little merit because only the most shallow-draft vessels and steamers could use these waterways.

Even apart from its political and psychological importance, Charleston stood out as the major port on the South Atlantic seaboard and the most crucial to blockade. The harbor had several unique features. The city lay on a peninsula formed by the meeting of the Ashley and Cooper rivers and formed a wide and deep harbor, one of the best in the south. The bar lay as far as five miles from the harbor entrance and four main channels offered access into the harbor. Even if the navy closed the four channels, navigation along the interior waterways allowed communication both north and south. When Bermuda and Nassau became the major points of transshipment of blockade goods, the port of Charleston with its well-developed rail connections became a prime port. The depth of the Charleston bar also made this port important early in the war. The ships running the blockade in 1861 were usually larger and had not evolved into the special shallow-draft vessels that ran the blockade later in the war. Only about 780 miles from Bermuda and just over 500 miles from Nassau, Charleston offered a quick trip for blockade runners. Savannah lay only about 850 miles from Bermuda and 500 miles from Nassau, while St. Augustine was just less than 900 miles from Bermuda and only about 370 from Nassau.[8]

In the midst of this national crisis, Secretary of the Navy Gideon Welles began to organize the navy for the conflict. He appointed his senior officers to ready the warships that lay in ordinary. On 1 May, realizing that the current naval organization would not suffice, he appointed Captain Silas Stringham to flag rank and instructed him to report to the Boston Navy Yard. Here he prepared the frigate *Minnesota* for sea. Stringham, having served fifty years in the navy and nearly twenty as captain, hoisted his flag on the foremast of the frigate as Commander of the Coast Blockading Squadron. Pendergrast, meanwhile, became the flag officer of the West India Squadron under the direction of Stringham. The squadrons divided officially on 14 May, and Stringham's command became the Atlantic Blockading Squadron. Stringham had only fourteen vessels to watch the entire East Coast. The West India Squadron comprised the brig *Bainbridge*, the sloop of war *Vandalia*, the old sloop *Macedonian*, and the screw frigate *Roanoke*. This situation created a somewhat awkward command structure. The West Indian Squadron's operational area overlapped the southern portion of the Atlantic Blockading Squadron's and Pendergrast, while reporting to Welles, also made reports to Stringham who had responsibility for the entire Atlantic coast. This confusing chain of command was a symptom of the general confusion in the Navy Department and in Washington during the first months of the war.[9]

On the morning of 11 May 1861, the steam frigate *Niagara* arrived off Charleston to formalize the blockade of that port. For three weeks after Lincoln's blockade announcement, commerce had continued at this port as if no war existed. When the *Niagara* steamed over the horizon on 11 May, the situation changed but little. According to international law, all vessels in port had two weeks to clear without fear of capture. The blockaders would warn off others bound to Charleston. As the blockaders cruised along the coast and met vessels, they inserted a notification of the blockade on the register and muster roll and also noted the time and the longitude and latitude. As the war progressed and an adequate time had elapsed for knowledge of the blockade, Union naval officers no longer gave warnings and began capturing suspicious vessels without notice.[10]

The *Niagara*'s second day on station was eventful. *Niagara* could take station only in the main channel because her draft of more than twenty-four feet prevented her from using the other three. This situation allowed the bark *A and A* from Belfast, running close to the shore, to slip over the bar. The *Niagara* could do little but watch her flight, and the *A and A* became the first ship to run the blockade of Charleston. Also on the 12th, the British ship *General Parkhill* from Liverpool, bound to Charleston, hove to and men from the *Niagara* boarded her and warned her master of the blockade. Instead of leaving, unexpectedly the *General Parkhill* began to edge toward shore and tried to communicate with signal flags. Feeling that the merchant vessel had violated the blockade, the *Niagara* seized her, whereby she became the first prize taken off the port of Charleston.[11]

For weeks the screw steamer *Seminole*, the steam frigate *Wabash*, the sloop *Vandalia*, and the revenue cutter *Harriet Lane*, and other blockaders of both the Atlantic Blockading Squadron and West India Squadron made occasional appearances off Charleston. Due to a lack of warships, Pendergrast kept them moving along the coast and stopping at different ports. While keeping as close to shore as their drafts would admit, they kept their fires banked to conserve coal. The steamers spent most of their time plying to Hampton Roads, Virginia, or Pensacola, Florida, for coal, and burning most of it on the passage back to Charleston. Daniel Ammen of the *Roanoke* wrote "it never occurred . . . that a deck-load of coal might enable them to reach Charleston with full bunkers."[12]

The logistical difficulties became more evident as the vessels began to take their stations and attempted to keep a close blockade. Welles realized that getting coal to the blockaders would be a vital concern. In April he called a meeting of the chiefs of the bureaus to discuss this critical topic. Stringham recognized the logistical problems and tried to keep his vessels plying back and forth to perform a "coast guard" type duty. This allowed a greater coverage of area but left fewer warships at each post. Illustrative of the inadequacy of the blockade is the fact that after reaching her station on 11 May, *Niagara* remained only four days before proceeding to Pensacola for coal. By 19 May, the *Harriet Lane* was the only vessel off Charleston until the *Minnesota* carrying Flag Officer Stringham stood in toward the bar on the twenty-eighth. Steamers with large coal capacities could remain on station for longer periods of time and could use their ample bunkers to supply other gunboats. Welles noted the difficulty of supplying the squadron and asked Stringham if there existed some point between the Chesapeake and Key West, Florida, that he could use as a depot.[13]

With so few vessels and the logistical handicap of no base on the Atlantic coast south of Washington, D.C., Pendergrast managed to keep usually only a single vessel off the major ports. But this satisfied international law because it was somewhat vague on the concept of a legitimate blockade. It only had to be maintained by a force sufficient to prevent access by the enemy. One officer considered the blockade at this time "rather nominal than real." This laxity concerned Robert Bunch, the British consul at Charleston. He felt the Union navy had, thus far, done a poor job implementing and maintaining the blockade. After *Niagara* left her station six vessels slipped into Charleston. He noted to Lord Richard Lyons, the British Minister in Washington, that fifty-one vessels ran the blockade between 28 May and 25 July.[14] The blockade, however, would remain substantially weak for several months as the Navy Department recalled warships from foreign stations and hastened to buy vessels. The navy yards remained crowded converting and fitting out merchantmen for war purposes. Sometimes this conversion process required nearly three months.

The laxity in the blockade prompted Gideon Welles to remind Stringham of the "necessity of a rigid blockade of the port of Charleston."

Welles realized that in thick weather and at night some of the smaller craft might run the blockade, but reminded Stringham that it was his duty to "prevent it." Welles suggested the flag officer keep one large vessel and two lighter draft vessels off each major port. Stringham posted vessels off Charleston, Savannah, and Fernandina along the South Atlantic coast, but at the other entrances he could only have his cruising vessels watch as they passed to their more permanent stations. Stringham, though, inherited a group of unfamiliar vessels. Others in his command were unfit for sea or were reliable for the relatively calm waters of the Chesapeake. In May Stringham predicted that he would need about fifteen more vessels for the ports on the South Atlantic seaboard to make the blockade "perfect and strict." Meanwhile, he decided to sail to Charleston in the *Minnesota* to observe the blockade in person. By mid-June there were four vessels lying off this port.[15]

Stringham had to sail back to Hampton Roads to oversee the naval operations along the entire Atlantic coast. In July Pendergrast shifted his flag to the *Roanoke* and sailed for Charleston to oversee blockading operations there. Off Charleston, he found the *Vandalia* and the *Wabash* at anchor, two less than the month before. The overlapping and redundant command situation lasted until 29 August when Welles relieved Pendergrast of command. He gave him a two-month leave of absence. Pendergrast was later given command of the Philadelphia Navy Yard but died two days later.[16]

It was evident that blockading only the major southern ports along the nearly 900 miles stretch of coastline from the Chesapeake to Key West was difficult at best. The early strategy did not change for some months, because one or two of the squadron's warships were constantly steaming north to Hampton Roads for coal and supplies. The navy could never maintain a "strict" blockade in this fashion. Only the addition of more warships and more convenient bases could make the blockade effective.

Washington Formulates a Strategy

While the flag officers worked to build their commands and to implement an efficient blockade, Gideon Welles worked in Washington to forge a navy from the limited resources at hand. His full beard gave him a patriarchal look and earned him the name "King Neptune." A native of Glastonbury, Connecticut, Welles had an extensive background in politics and journalism. He served as editor of the *Hartford Times* and later as the head of the navy's Bureau of Provisions and Clothing. Well connected politically, Welles marshaled support for Lincoln during his election and Lincoln appointed him as his Secretary of the Navy. Some considered Welles peculiar, but wise, patient, intelligent, and strong-willed. Charles A. Dana wrote of the Secretary, "There was nothing decorative about him; there was no noise in the street when he went along; but he understood his duty, and did it efficiently, continually, and unvaryingly."[17]

Welles's alter ego, and Assistant Secretary of the Navy, was Gustavus Vasa Fox. Born in Saugus, Massachusetts, in 1821, Fox had a naval background. He had received a midshipman's appointment in 1838 and served in the navy until 1856, when he resigned his lieutenant's commission to accept a position with a textile mill in Massachusetts. Fox married the daughter of Levi Woodbury, a former Secretary of the Navy, Secretary of the Treasury and Associate Justice of the Supreme Court. Another of Woodbury's daughters was married to Montgomery Blair, who served as Lincoln's Postmaster General, which made Blair and Fox brothers-in-law. During the Fort Sumter crisis, Blair arranged for Fox to lead the relief expedition. Lincoln later recognized Fox's talents and appointed him Chief Clerk of the department. Fox later filled the newly created post of Assistant Secretary of the Navy. Welles and Fox complemented each other. Each contributed assets to the partnership and each man's strengths reinforced the other's weaknesses.[18]

In an attempt to devise an overall strategy and to offer solutions to a range of potential problems, Welles created a "Commission of Conference," often referred to as the "Blockade Strategy Board." Before this board met, the Navy Department had no strategic plan and addressed every problem as it arose. The Blockade Strategy Board was the only board that met during the war that approached in character that of a general staff. The idea for the creation of this board originated with Professor Alexander Dallas Bache, the superintendent of the United States Coast Survey. Organized on 27 June 1861, the board consisted of Bache, Chief Engineer of the Army Department of Washington, John G. Barnard, and two naval officers, Captain Charles H. Davis, who acted as recorder and secretary, and Captain Samuel Francis Du Pont, who served as chair.[19]

The Strategy Board met frequently at the Smithsonian Institution from July to September. Poring over charts and studying hydrographic, topographic, and geographic information, its members developed strategies and devised methods to render the blockade more effective. The board accumulated the information necessary to establish logistical bases on the Atlantic coast. In six major reports and four supplementary ones, the board recommended points the navy could seize as coaling stations and naval bases. The board also prepared a general guide for all blockading operations that the Navy Department followed closely throughout the war.[20]

After thorough discussion and debate among the board members, they hammered out strategy and organizational changes. Throughout the deliberations, logistical matters continued to receive the board's attention. The president, the cabinet, and the General in Chief, U.S. Army, Winfield Scott discussed and modified the recommendations. Although the board's confidential proceedings were not intended for the public, accounts of the meetings began to appear in Northern newspapers in July, undermining the effectiveness of its strategic deliberations.[21]

To plan for the blockade and for future military operations, the Strategy Board divided the South Atlantic Coast into three subsections, from Cape Romain to Tybee Island, from Tybee Island to Cumberland Sound, and from Fernandina to Cape Florida. The board discussed the attributes of the harbors of Port Royal, Bull Bay, and St. Helena, but considered Charleston and Savannah the major ports to watch on the Atlantic coast. The latter two's excellent rail connections north, south, and west gave them added importance to the Confederacy. The harbor at Port Royal received consideration due to its spaciousness and deep water.[22]

On 13 July, the board made a special report on the most important secondary bays and harbors of the South Atlantic coast. All were on the coast of South Carolina—Bull Bay, St. Helena Sound, and Port Royal. Bull Bay lay only fifteen miles from Cape Romain and about twenty-two from the main bar off Charleston. The board suggested that Bull Island be secured. It felt that the occupation of Bull Bay would virtually secure four other inlets to the south (Prices, Capers, Dewees and Breach inlets). By fortifying Bull Island with 4,000 troops, the board believed Union forces could hold the bay. Possession of this bay would allow the navy to build wharves for coaling and meet other logistical concerns. No other point north of Charleston would serve as well.[23]

St. Helena Sound held an advantage because it lay midway between Charleston and Savannah. The Blockade Strategy Board considered capturing two separate anchorages in the sound, one at Otter Island and the other near Trinity Island. These lay far enough apart that the navy could use them as independent roadsteads. The Ashepoo, Combahee, Bull,

Coosaw, and lesser rivers emptied into the sound and offered interior communication south from Charleston to Fernandina. Over the years these rivers developed into a complex and important series of interior lines of trade. These waterways would also allow enemy troops to move up and down the coast outside the reach of naval vessels. St. Helena Sound also had an excellent spot for a coaling depot off Hunting Island. The board agreed that four thousand men could hold this island.[24]

Between St. Helena and Port Royal sounds lay four inlets: Fripp, Skull, Pritchards and Trenchards. Only the first and last of these inlets concerned the board. But it was Port Royal Sound that intrigued the members of the board the most. They considered this harbor the finest south of Chesapeake Bay. Three channels allowed access to the harbor, one with seventeen feet and the other two providing nineteen feet at mean low water. The whole Union navy could easily ride at anchor in the bay, including the deep draft steam frigates. The entrance stretched over two miles and a fine anchorage at Bay Point would allow the navy to build a commodious logistical station. To hold Port Royal, the board felt that union forces should capture and occupy Hilton Head, Parry's (now Parris Island) and Phillip's islands. They projected that 6,000 men could capture Port Royal, but to hold the harbor would take 10,000–12,000 troops in addition to a naval force.[25]

In its report, the board suggested the capture of Bull Bay over Port Royal. The former was more accessible; Union forces could hold it by capturing a single point, and it had a safe anchorage. The other two sounds left "room for doubt" in the minds of the men. St. Helena lay in a more central location between Charleston and Savannah, but Port Royal commanded more of the enemy's interior communications and trade networks. Thinking the enemy would not expect an attack farther north, the board suggested the seizure of St. Helena Sound rather than Port Royal.[26]

About two weeks later, the board considered the strategic situation farther south along the Georgia coast where the exterior chain of islands provided protected waterways and allowed interior communications. Concerned with this, the four men discussed at some length the major inlets. They felt that each of these offered varying degrees of access to the interior but they made no recommendations for their capture. The coast of Florida received little attention due to the fact that the state had a small and sparse population and held little strategic importance early in the war.[27]

The insights of the board laid out an important framework for the early strategy of the navy. The department used its advice with great advantage. The board discontinued its deliberations in September after discussing the most important and pressing issues. Unfortunately, the board never broached any future strategy. Had the board reconvened, possibly with retired officers sitting in these positions, it may have played a significant role in formulating a continuing strategy for the Union navy.[28]

The Problems of the Blockade Continue

In order to implement the Strategy Board's recommendations, the Navy Department had to procure ships capable of blockading the coast. The department tried to meet this need quickly by converting and chartering vessels for naval service. Some of the early charters proved troublesome while others worked well. The screw steamer *Union* serves as a good example. The navy chartered her on 24 April, and by July her charter had nearly expired. She proved to be a successful blockader, capturing three blockade runners, but she had serious drawbacks. Not built as a warship, and with only a few months of service, the weight of her ordnance caused her planking to pull loose and in moderate seas she shook and trembled. Another converted warship, the ex-merchant screw steamer *Penguin*, required boiler and engine repairs. Her battery became unmanageable in a seaway, her upper deck leaked, and her propeller came out of the water in heavy seas. While some vessels proved to be underpowered and strained their engines in a seaway, others served well as warships. The purchased screw steamer *Flag* had by 19 July, been under steam continuously for fifty-three days. With minor adjustments to her armament and the repair of a leak, she remained in service. The commanding officers complimented her good speed and the fact that she carried her battery of 8-inch guns well.[29]

But even the conversion of ships was slow, causing the navy to play a "shell game" with their blockading vessels alternately going for coal, repairs, and refueling. At times, however, this left the blockade off Charleston with a small number of warships. Captain Samuel Mercer of the *Wabash* lamented, "Now Flag-Officer, you know as well as I do that to blockade this port efficiently with this ship alone is next door to an impossibility." Yet by 10 September over one third of the squadron's vessels lay in yards for repairs.[30]

Because of the small number of ships available off all the ports, the early tactics called for vessels to be ready to move but to anchor with their topsails loosed during the day. The blockading vessels usually maintained their stations at the main ship channels only. Utilizing the interior waterways in conjunction with the numerous inlets, the shallow-draft vessels attempting to evade the blockade had easy access to open water. It complicated the enforcement of the blockade particularly when so few ships were available. Naval vessels might check the shallower inlets north and south of the main channels only when several vessels lay off the port or when cruising for coal and repairs and travelling back to their stations. The Confederates complicated the enforcement of the blockade when they began building earthworks at many of these entrances. This kept the gunboats at a respectable distance and gave an added advantage to blockade runners. With so few ships, the Union blockade was minimal at best. British ships cruised from Virginia to Texas to observe the deficiencies of the blockade. Commodore Algernon Lyons of the British HMS steam sloop *Racer* noted that during a July trip from Cape Florida to Cape Fear he found only Charleston and Savannah blockaded.[31]

A similar visit by a British warship off Charleston nearly caused an international incident. On 28 September, Commander Samuel Phillips Lee, commanding the *Vandalia*, sighted a suspicious vessel that fit the description of a blockade runner. Lee quickly had his crew beat to quarters. Following set procedures, he fired a shot well ahead of the steamer and then put out a boat with a boarding officer. As the stranger hove to, she proved to be the British steam gunboat HMS *Steady* sent to Charleston to communicate with the British Consul there. Lee apologized to her commanding officer for the incident. He explained that the *Steady*'s appearance "was questionable." He also commented that "A smart steamer moving under false colors . . . bent on running the blockade, can slip by a sailing vessel lying to, without steam and near the bar." Fortunately, the British did not take offense and it only strengthened the Union claims of an effective blockade.[32]

During the first few months of the war, and despite the fact that at least one vessel lay off the major ports, the blockade was not even slightly effective. In the six weeks after the bombardment of Fort Sumter, nearly 30,000 bales of cotton left the port of Charleston alone. From June to December 1861, 150 vessels, mainly small coasting vessels, arrived at Charleston through the interior waterways. This laxity had the Atlanta *Daily Intelligencer* boasting that "contempt for Lincoln's blockade must prevail even at Timbucktoo!"[33]

The British did not protest this apparent laxity because international law required only that "an adequate force" be stationed at all times at the entrance to a port to prevent communication. Interpreted broadly, this concept remained virtually undefined by international law and the

British, who had the largest navy in the world, were not ready to redefine this. By the widest interpretation of the law, one vessel could qualify as an adequate force. With a navy second to none, it was in the best interest of the British to keep the law vague. But adequate force did not include warships cruising up and down the coast. The Union ships had to establish the blockade of each port by notification. Once the navy instituted the blockade of a port, at least one vessel had to remain on station; otherwise, they would have to reinstate the blockade.[34]

The Confederate Foe

A growing threat to the strict enforcement of the blockade was the Confederate vessels that comprised the "Mosquito Fleet." This motley collection of warships included passenger vessels, tugs, side wheel steamers, and included vessels from the Lighthouse Service, Coast Survey, and the U.S. Revenue Cutter Service. Hastily converted and with guns added, they could not hope to break the blockade, but still caused concern. Shortly after secession, most of the seceded states formed their own navies. The state of South Carolina, for example, established a Coast and Harbor Police and placed Captain James H. North in command.[35]

The state of Georgia chose one of its sons to head its state navy. One of the most senior officers to resign his commission in the United States Navy, Josiah Tattnall, accepted an appointment as senior flag officer in the Georgia Navy. Once the state navies transferred to Confederate service, he became a commodore in charge of defending the coasts of South Carolina and Georgia. Tattnall's contemporaries described him as the *beau idéal* of a naval officer. He was a "striking looking man" nearly six feet in height with a ruddy complexion and "deep-sunk blue eyes." His fellow officers considered him chivalrous, genial, unassuming and heroic.[36] Tattnall's small piebald force, however, could offer only feeble resistance to the Union naval force that lay off the coast. The shallow waterways that connected Savannah and Charleston allowed him to move his force north and south without venturing into open water.

Another great embarrassment to the efficiency of the blockade were the numerous privateers that operated off the South Atlantic coast during the early months of the war. These warships operated under a Letter of Marque. This commission, granted by the Confederate Government, allowed civilians to make prizes of enemy shipping. Some of these bold adventurers captured United States merchant vessels under the nose of the blockaders and then scurried back into port with their prizes. The brisk business of the privateers prompted a committee of the New York Board of Underwriters to demand a resolution of the problem.

While fewer than a dozen privateers operated out of the South Atlantic ports, they occupied the full attention of naval authorities. At first these private warships had some limited success. The most successful and notorious was the brig *Jefferson Davis* commanded by Louis M. Coxetter. During a seven-week foray in the summer of 1861, the privateer captured nine vessels. The Charleston papers proclaimed that the vessel's name had "become a word of terror to the Yankees." As the number of naval vessels off the coast increased, the privateers' chances of success greatly diminished and their prizes sharply declined until they no longer ventured from southern ports. The success of the *Jefferson Davis* represented the height of privateering activity and her total loss after running aground on a bar off St. Augustine in August signaled the decline.[37]

The Union effort to keep the privateers from sailing became an early challenge to the efficiency of the blockade and weighed heavily upon the shoulders of the commanding officers. By September, despite the pleas from the insurance underwriters and merchants, the Navy Department could muster only five vessels to watch the coast from Georgetown to Savannah. The following month the blockade of the South Atlantic coast consisted of only seven vessels. Two of these lay off Charleston while one vessel each watched Georgetown, Bull Bay, Savannah, St. Simon's Sound, and Fernandina. Stringham seemed exasperated by the privateers and blockade runners regularly darting in and out of the shallow southern inlets. Stringham lamented that he had "labored night and day" with the vessels at his disposal in an attempt to both blockade the coast and perform the other duties required by the department. An officer on the screw sloop *Iroquois* off Savannah wrote, "The blockade is a perfect farce . . . we can see steamers run up and down the coast every day . . ."[38]

The deliberations of the Blockade Strategy Board advised that the blockade would become more effective with the capture of points along the coast. Not only did seizing ports deny their use to privateers and blockade runners, but those ports could also serve the navy's needs. Following the board's recommendations, the department instructed Flag Officer Stringham to assemble a fleet for the capture of Hatteras Inlet, and on 3 August, Gideon Welles ordered Captain Samuel Francis Du Pont to New York to begin preparing and organizing an expedition to capture another anchorage farther south. Du Pont, who was knowledgeable about the deliberations of the Blockade Strategy Board, knew he had several possibilities. His fellow board members had recently identified Fernandina, Florida, as a desirable depot for provisions, coal, and a harbor or refuge for the squadron. The inlet had twenty feet of water at high tide and the anchorage in the Amelia River provided protected waters that could accommodate a fleet. Fernandina also had wharves that would be useful and the town served as the terminus of the Florida Railroad Company. The area had no large populace and its isolation by surrounding marshes would simplify the defense of the town. The board had also considered the capture of Bull Bay, St. Helena Sound, and Port Royal important. The Strategy Board ended its discussions with the knowledge that a superior naval force must control the coast.[39]

On August 27th, only weeks after the Union army's debacle at Bull Run, Stringham's expedition arrived off Hatteras. After a naval bombardment and the landing of infantry, the forts surrendered without being stormed. Stringham thus won a significant victory at Hatteras Inlet virtually without the aid of the army. Yet rather than congratulating him on his victory, both the press and the Navy Department criticized his actions. The department questioned his inability to maintain the blockade while the press wondered why he did not follow up his victory and attack into the sounds.[40]

The first major Union victory of the war did not turn out well for Stringham, who had to weather the unwarranted attacks. He became disgusted with the department's criticism of his conduct of the blockade and the public's castigation of the Hatteras Expedition. Sensing that he had fallen from the department's favor, Stringham offered his resignation on 16 September 1861. It came at an opportune time, for the department, acting under the advice of the Strategy Board, had considered a division of the Atlantic Blockading Squadron. The board realized that the extent of the coast, the augmented forces, and the complicated nature of the geography of the southern coast would require more than one man's supervision. A reduction in Stringham's command likely would have injured his dignity and compelled him to resign.[41]

The department created two new East Coast squadrons, the North Atlantic and the South Atlantic Blockading Squadrons. When Welles received Stringham's letter of resignation, he offered command of one of the two squadrons to Captain Samuel Francis Du Pont, who was then preparing a naval expedition to strike somewhere on the South Atlantic seaboard. Du Pont's new command, the South Atlantic Blockading Squadron, stretched from the boundary of North and South Carolina to Key West. Frank Du Pont continued with his preparations, spending weeks planning and arranging his southern expedition. Du Pont remained much too busy to oversee a blockade as well as ready this expeditionary force. Therefore, Flag Officer Louis M. Goldsborough, the commander of the North Atlantic Blockading Squadron, directed affairs along the whole East Coast for five weeks until Du Pont and his force sailed south.[42]

Du Pont inherited a squadron at a time when confusion reigned in the Navy Department. Additionally, the naval victory at Hatteras had inspired Welles to push for another lodgment on the southern coast. President Lincoln also yearned for another success and stressed to Welles that he not abandon any plans for a joint movement farther south. The President also expected the forces to be ready by early October. Du Pont urged his subordinates to meet the President's expectations. The new flag officer would find that it required a great deal of effort to pull together the widely disparate forces needed to carry out the department's wishes.[43]

– 2 –

"The Success Is All
That Was Expected"

Preparation for the Southern Expedition

Before sunrise on 29 October 1861, Commodore Samuel Francis Du Pont watched from the bridge of the frigate *Wabash* as fifty warships and transports formed into a convoy. This group of vessels represented the largest United States naval expedition ever assembled. Just over five weeks earlier Gideon Welles had given command of the South Atlantic Blockading Squadron to Du Pont.[1]

The new flag officer stood at the top of his profession and had an extremely distinguished family background. He was the youngest son of Victor Marie du Pont, a French consul in Charleston, South Carolina, and later a businessman. His paternal grandfather was a distinguished French statesman, writer, and economist. Born in 1803, at Bergen Point, New Jersey, he began his long naval career at the age of twelve when he received a midshipman's warrant from President James Monroe. Frank Du Pont made his first cruise on the ship-of-the-line *Franklin* in 1817. In 1833, he married his cousin Sophie Madeleine, the youngest daughter of his father's brother Irénée. The navy promoted Du Pont to commander in 1841 and he obtained the rank of captain in 1855. Between these years he commanded the *Grampus, Warren, Perry, Columbia,* and *Congress.* During the Mexican War, he blockaded the coast of southern California while in command of the sloop of war *Cyane.* After the war Du Pont served on naval boards until 1857, when he received command

23

of the newly commissioned frigate *Minnesota*. He took her on a diplomatic cruise to China and remained in Chinese waters for about two years, not returning until January 1861. At the outbreak of the Civil War, Du Pont commanded the Philadelphia Navy Yard. Du Pont was urbane, had an aristocratic bearing, inspired admiration and trust from his men, and thus, got the best from his subordinates. One of his officers thought him brave, energetic, cheerful, intelligent, and, at over six feet tall, graceful and commanding in appearance. David Dixon Porter felt that no officer in the navy had more friends or admirers.[2]

As president of the Blockade Strategy Board, Du Pont had supported a lodgment on the South Atlantic coast, and on 3 August Welles placed Du Pont in charge of organizing the expedition. For its part, the War Department agreed to furnish 13,000 men in three brigades all under the command of Brigadier General Thomas W. Sherman. Sherman's brigades were led by Brigadier Generals Egbert L. Viele, Isaac I. Stevens, and Horatio G. Wright.[3]

On 18 September, Du Pont assumed command of the South Atlantic Blockading Squadron. Flag Officer Louis M. Goldsborough, however, directed the blockading operations along the entire Atlantic coast until Du Pont left Hampton Roads on October 29th. Welles insisted on this arrangement because he believed that the planning of a southern naval expedition was so important and arduous that he did not want the demanding duties of administering the blockade to interfere. To further the chance of success, Welles permitted Du Pont to select most of his officers for the squadron and for the expedition.[4]

Gathering the warships for his fleet became one of Du Pont's greatest challenges. The navy purchased a number of merchant vessels for conversion into men of war. Though the navy yards feverishly worked to add shell rooms, magazines, batteries, and heavier supporting frames and timbers to make them serviceable for war purposes, Du Pont remained skeptical of the value of the converted merchant ships. Due to their light scantlings, he did not think them capable of withstanding gunfire and initially did not even want them to go into battle. He also felt he would be lucky if one in five of the vessels being converted would be ready in time. After examining three of them Du Pont commented, "But, alas! it is like altering a vest into a shirt to convert a trading steamer into a man-of-war."[5]

Without knowing the final destination of the expedition, Du Pont nevertheless feared that the draft of his larger vessels would be too deep for some of the potential targets. He asked for smaller gunboats armed with heavier 11-inch guns. He also had to secure small boats for the landing of troops. For this, Du Pont sought the advice of the constructor in the Philadelphia Navy Yard, Thornton A. Jenkins, who advised Du Pont to use whaleboats that had shallow drafts and broad beams. The army also secured ferryboats to carry men and guns ashore.[6]

At the end of July, the planning of the expedition began in earnest. General Scott called meetings attended by Du Pont, the Quartermaster General, Brigadier General Montgomery Meigs, and generals Sherman and Wright. They met about five times and used the Strategy Board deliberations for their discussions. The committee concluded that the expedition should capture two harbors. They initially decided to occupy Bull Bay, South Carolina, and Fernandina, Florida. With this decision made, they divided the expedition into two separate striking forces. The army would send 8,000 men to Bull Bay and 4,000 men to Fernandina.[7]

By mid-September, as the fleet assembled in New York, reservations began surfacing concerning the expedition's objectives. Once again the planners opened further discussion concerning the expedition's destination. The Assistant Secretary of the Navy, Gustavus Fox, now became an integral part of the planning. Du Pont and Fox dined together in mid-September to continue their deliberations. Du Pont noted that Fox liked the planning more than the execution. Charles Henry Davis likewise noticed that the assistant secretary changed his mind frequently, giving him "serious anxiety" about the entire project.[8]

Abraham Lincoln also became personally involved. Eager to follow up the success at Hatteras Inlet and fretting over the delay, he reminded the secretary not to abandon the proposed move south and insisted that the expedition must be ready to move by the first of October or shortly thereafter. The army, meanwhile, began planning for a joint movement to strike in the sounds of North Carolina. Fox initially feared that Lincoln would cancel the South Atlantic expedition and asked for a conference with the President. Du Pont did not hear of the meeting and accidentally met Fox as he left the Navy Department for the meeting at Secretary of State William Seward's house. At Seward's they found the Secretary of State and the President sitting on a sofa. Lincoln did not recognize Du Pont until someone in the room reminded him that he commanded the naval portion of the expedition. Fox sat down on the sofa and began smoking a cigar, and to Du Pont's amazement blew smoke into Lincoln's face. The discussion did not proceed immediately because of the absence of key members. A "desperate hunt" went on to round up Secretary of War Simon Cameron, Major General George

B. McClellan, and General Sherman. Cameron and Sherman appeared, but they could not find McClellan. The meeting therefore began without him.[9]

Fox opened the discussion with an inquiry about the impending amphibious expedition to the sounds of North Carolina. Brigadier General Ambrose E. Burnside promoted this expedition, which directly competed for the resources of the combined army-navy operation farther south. According to Du Pont, Lincoln then became exasperated. He did not have any knowledge of the Burnside project and chastised all those present for the lack of coordination. Du Pont reminded the president that his project had been in motion for two months and suggested that it would be "wise to handle one at a time and to get this one off first." After a short discussion everyone agreed, but when McClellan walked in, Lincoln changed his mind. After more debate they decided to put Burnside's project second. In the "haste of ignorance," however, the group decided Du Pont should leave in four days.[10]

With all dispatch Du Pont hurried to New York to oversee some of the final preparations. He lamented to his brother that the expedition had grown "like a mushroom," much beyond the original intentions. Despite earlier considerations and the fact that Du Pont had heard that as many as 200 guns defended Port Royal Sound, he now proposed a possible attack there. It was the only harbor south of Chesapeake Bay with room to accommodate all the vessels of the fleet. Furthermore, its central position between Charleston and Savannah would be a convenient staging area for future operations. He argued that such a move would be like "driving a wedge into the flanks of the rebels" between Charleston and Savannah. Du Pont, however, left New York "fairly oppressed" by the public's and the department's expectations of his success.[11]

When Du Pont hoisted his flag on the *Wabash* on 10 October, he remained uncertain about the destination of the attacking force. Welles gave Du Pont flexible instructions four days earlier, only specifying that the flag officer capture two points along the coast. He specifically mentioned Bull Bay, St. Helena, and Port Royal, South Carolina, as well as Fernandina, Florida. Fox, meanwhile, urged the expedition to take Port Royal. With reservations still bothering Du Pont, the fleet sailed from the battery at New York at one o'clock on 16 October to rendezvous in Hampton Roads. On the way down, the flag officer met with his flag captain Charles H. Davis and Commander John Rodgers to get their views. By this time he believed that Port Royal was the most important and desirable target for the expedition. In Hampton Roads, Du Pont met with General Sherman to reconsider their earlier deliberations. Despite the flag officer's thorough knowledge of the coast, he remained uncommitted. Du Pont believed the president and the Navy Department had rushed the entire expedition without the proper preparation. In a letter to his wife, he displayed doubts about the success of the expedition.[12]

On 21 October the army transports finished loading in Annapolis, Maryland, to rendezvous with the navy in Hampton Roads. The delays in preparing the army transports were "embarrassing." After the final supplies were stowed the men came to the docks to board the ships. Amidst the singing of hymns, the infantry clumsily attempted to clamber over the sides into the transports, a spectacle that thoroughly entertained the old tars. Then, after the passage of about a day, the transports arrived in Hampton Roads only to find bad weather. The gale-force winds forced the fleet and the transports to remain there for a week as the ships tossed at anchor. This delay only added to the burgeoning logistical requirements of the expedition as the men of the expedition consumed 19,000 gallons of water each day. Orders went to Baltimore for an additional 200,000 gallons of water to follow the expedition south.[13]

The delay did offer one advantage. It allowed time for Du Pont and the army commanders to make final arrangements. Conferences among Sherman, his three brigade commanders, Du Pont, Charles Davis, and John Rodgers and his cousin Raymond on board the flagship *Wabash* commenced on the twenty-third. They discussed the potential ports to attack, but made no decision. They met again the next day until the "small hours" but still did not commit to a final destination. Du Pont remained cautious and insisted on the input of Charles Boutelle of the Coast Survey, before making a decision.[14]

Boutelle had worked for six years to survey thoroughly the area from the Cape Fear to the St. Marys River. His insight was critical because Du Pont feared he might not be able to get the *Wabash* over the Port Royal Bar. This warship represented a large percentage of his fleet's firepower and Du Pont felt that Boutelle's opinions were critical before making the final decision. Deliberations began again at 9 A.M. on the twenty-fifth and fortunately, Boutelle arrived to share his knowledge. The group focused its discussions on the merits of Port Royal over Bull Bay. As the group pondered their options, they concluded that Bull Bay was "too insignificant" and that Port Royal would serve all the future needs of the army and navy. They finally all agreed to attack Port Royal, but only after Du Pont had satisfied personally every contingency that he could imagine.[15]

The Expedition Sails

When Du Pont made the signal to get the fleet underway on the morning of the twenty-ninth, he felt uneasy. He believed the army troops were too raw and had been in the transports too long. Amidst the shrill whistle of bosun pipes, the anchors rose under the tramp of feet and of song as the men marched around the capstans. The fifty ships of this "heterogeneous squadron" belched forth plumes of smoke as they left their anchorages. Ferryboats, tugs, river steamboats, improvised gunboats, frail transports, and other vessels "without shape before known to the maritime world" moved seaward. The twenty-four coal and powder vessels had left the anchorage the day before escorted by the *Vandalia* and the bark *Gem of the Sea.* In order not to divulge the final destination, the masters received sealed instructions to open only if they became separated. These instructions did not reveal any of the plans and merely ordered them to rendezvous off Savannah.[16]

After noon, the vessels cruised south of Cape Henry and a signal from the *Wabash* to the fleet ordered them to form a double echelon line (V-shaped formation). This maneuver took some time to perform as the commanders of vessels without experience wasted a good deal of time. A strong headwind also slowed the ships and the sea rose to such an extent that the vessels gave Cape Henry a berth of six miles. It was thirty-six hours before the six-mile line of ships rounded Cape Hatteras. On the trip around this cape, however, one of the transports struck on the outer shoal and the fleet hauled farther off to the southeast. This angered Du Pont, who believed there was enough room for the careful and attentive but he later wrote scornfully, it was obviously "too close for careless, stupid skippers or second- and-third [sic] class merchant captains." After the fleet rounded Hatteras, the wind gradually rose, the sky turned gray, and the barometer began to fall. With rough weather and a southeast gale approaching at 2:30, Du Pont hoisted a signal to disregard the order of sailing.[17]

Morning daylight revealed a widely scattered fleet. By noon of 1 November, a dull sky and southeastern wind gradually settled into a heavy gale. The rain increased and fell "like sleet" and phosphorescent seas broke over the ships. The *Wabash*, the largest ship in the fleet, rolled and wallowed "like a pig." Lieutenant John Sanford Barnes on board the flagship believed it "utterly incomprehensible to all seafaring men" that the frail craft attached to the expedition managed to weather the gale.[18]

In Washington Welles chafed with uncertainty as he worried about how the storm might have imperiled the expedition. On Saturday the second, lookouts on the *Wabash* could see only about a half dozen sails. Over the next few days, however, the scattered fleet began to show up as the flagship arrived off Port Royal on the afternoon of the third. On the fourth, *Wabash* anchored off the bar, in company with twenty-five other vessels, and later that day others began to heave into sight.[19]

The men on board scanned the enemy coast. They could see only a low flat shore with long green masses of pine trees beyond the sandbanks. From the sea the forts looked inconspicuous and "would certainly fail to attract the attention of a person not on the lookout for them."[20]

As the ships' commanders reported to the flagship, each had a story to tell and Du Pont fretted as he heard the losses. The little screw steamer *Isaac Smith* had thrown her battery overboard to stay afloat. Others such as the side-wheel steamer *Florida* had returned north for repairs. More important to the expedition was the loss of some of the quartermaster supplies. Some of the transports jettisoned their equipment to save the troops. Three ships carrying food and supplies—the *Union, Osceola,* and *Peerless*—were lost.[21]

One of the great stories of the storm is the rescue of the Marine battalion from the sinking transport *Governor*. On 1 November the fury of the gale swept over the transport, causing the *Governor* to lose her port and starboard hog braces and most of the stack. Shortly afterwards a steam pipe on board burst, rendering the bilge pumps inoperative, and water began to fill the ship. With great human effort the Marine battalion held ropes to secure the hog braces and over 100 men bailed to keep ahead of the encroaching water. Every lurch of the vessel reminded all hands that death could arrive at any moment.[22]

The next morning the *Isaac Smith* and screw bark *Young Rover* spied the Union Jack upside down and at half-mast. They stood by the foundering transport and the *Isaac Smith* managed to pass a hawser to the stricken vessel. Before 2:00 the frigate *Sabine*, Captain Cadwalader Ringgold commanding, came over the horizon and anchored. The *Governor* anchored close aboard and that night the crews passed a hawser between the two ships. Ringgold then had his anchor cable paid out to allow the *Sabine*'s stern to drift down on the transport's bow. They whipped about thirty men onto the frigate and another forty jumped across. While alongside, *Sabine* struck the port bow of the *Governor* and carried away about twenty feet of the hurricane deck. This event convinced the commanding officers to wait until the next day.[23]

The *Sabine* stood by the battered transport during the night. At daybreak on the third, the *Governor* was still afloat but gaining water rapidly. Due to the frailty of the transport, Ringgold could not risk the frigate striking her again. Since the whipping lines had failed to quickly bring the men to safety, Ringgold put out his boats. The boats pulled close to the *Governor* and the men began to jump into the sea, allowing the *Sabine*'s tars to haul the men into the boats. This spared them from being crushed between the ships. Of the 365 men in the Marine Battalion, only 7 perished. The Life-Saving Benevolent Association of New York recognized this tremendous effort and later awarded Ringgold a gold lifesaving medal for this feat. Du Pont barely acknowledged Ringgold's achievement and seemed jealous of Ringgold's award. He stated to his wife that the captain had "made more capital out of an ordinary act of humanity than has yet been accorded to any human being in this war . . ."[24]

The storm delayed the beginning of the attack for several days as the ships slowly gathered off the South Carolina coast. There were no recent coastal charts of this area, therefore Du Pont and the army leaders remained anxious about whether they could get the larger ships and transports over the Port Royal Bar. On the fourth, Boutelle, in the little Coast Survey vessel *Vixen*, led a survey mission accompanied by the screw gunboats *Ottawa*, *Seneca*, *Pembina*, and *Penguin*. Under the command of Commander Charles H. Davis, they stood in toward the bar to sound it for the fleet. Under the watchful eye of Boutelle, they felt their way with the lead and surveyed the bar, which lay ten miles from the harbor. The difficult task of getting the *Wabash* over the two-mile-long bar began. With only about two feet of water to spare, the *Wabash* cleared the bottom. At 3:00 P.M. that afternoon Du Pont began sending all the vessels with drafts under eighteen feet over the bar to anchor. By dark they all lay securely in the roadstead about five miles off the headlands. The masts of all the transports and gunboats at anchor gave the illusion to one soldier of a "forest in the ocean . . ."[25]

A feeble Confederate naval force commanded by Flag Officer Josiah Tattnall watched as the Union vessels arrived. Du Pont knew that Tattnall was an officer to be reckoned with. He earned a reputation for being aggressive in China in 1859 when he assisted the British fleet in their fight with the Chinese. During this struggle he violated American neutrality on the grounds that "blood is thicker than water." He had at his disposal, however, only a hodgepodge of frail steamboats and tugs improvised into lightly armed gunboats. At Port Royal his naval force comprised his flagship, the ex-coastwise steamer *Savannah*, and three converted tugs, the *Lady Davis, Resolute,* and *Sampson.*[26]

Tattnall watched helplessly as the Union vessels gathered off shore. He assembled his small squadron at the mouth of Skull Creek, and weighed his options, hoping the Union forces would put themselves in a vulnerable position. On the fourth, as they sounded and crossed over the bar, he determined to attack the Union vessels. Three of the Confederate steamers sortied toward the Union gunboats at about 5:00 P.M. At a distance of about a mile and a half, the Confederate gunboats opened fire. The *Seneca, Pembina,* and *Ottawa* got underway and stood toward the Confederate steamers. In a cannonade that lasted forty minutes the Union vessels' heavier guns drove Tattnall's steamers back to the safety of the harbor. The Union vessels then withdrew and anchored across the channel to protect the transports from a second enemy sortie.[27]

At daylight on Tuesday, 5 November, Commander John Rodgers took the ninety-day gunboat *Ottawa* in toward the enemy batteries to draw their fire and reveal their strength. On board was his old friend General Wright. Before the warships could get near enough to draw fire, the Confederate steamers attacked again. This time the *Seneca, Pembina, Curlew, Isaac Smith,* and *Pawnee* accompanied the *Ottawa* and stood toward the rebel steamers. In a ninety-minute fight, the Union gunboats again drove the enemy back into the harbor and pursued them until they came under a crossfire from the forts on Hilton Head and Bay Point. The gunboats accurately and frequently put shells into Fort Beauregard and one shot struck a caisson, causing it to explode. John Rodgers found this engagement exciting and admired the "beautiful firing upon both sides." When one shot splashed close aboard *Ottawa,* he exclaimed, "Well done rebel . . ."[28]

Before noon the rebel steamers ventured out once more. The flagship *Savannah,* under command of John Newland Maffitt, took the van and *Seneca* stood toward them. As soon as *Savannah* came into range, Lieutenant Commander Daniel Ammen personally sighted *Seneca*'s 11-inch gun and fired on Tattnall's flagship. The shot "skimmed along the water like a duck" and struck just abaft the starboard wheelhouse. Overmatched, the Confederate steamers withdrew to Bay Point. Tattnall, ashore during the fight, suspended Maffitt from command for disobedience of orders. He maintained that the gunboats were to remain at anchor. Maffitt, on the other hand, asserted that Tattnall had given him the order to allow no soundings and when he saw the Union vessels, he "went at them." Both men eventually set their differences aside and Tattnall approved Maffitt's transfer to General Robert E. Lee's staff as a naval aide.[29]

Later that day, Du Pont summoned his captains to the wardroom of the *Wabash* to discuss the order of battle. Most felt that the main squadron should stand down the mid-channel and first engage Fort Beauregard, the weaker of the two works. If Fort Beauregard fell it would cut communications with Charleston and cut off the retreat of the fort's defenders. They also discussed an attack on Fort Walker so that they could utilize the entire strength of the fleet.[30]

Complicating the tactical planning for the attack was the fact that landing the army forces would be problematic. These men arrived in no condition to disembark efficiently. Therefore, the sole responsibility for landing the troops fell onto the navy. The surfboats had all arrived safely but the storm had driven back north some of the small steamers needed to put the troops ashore. More critical than the debarkation and deployment of the troops was the fact that the transports were not combat-loaded. Freight sat on top of the ammunition in many of the transports. The ammunition needed for the landing could not be used without unloading entire ships. Other key supplies were not shared among several ships but loaded in single transports. The army transport *Ocean Express*, for example, carried the entire expedition's cargo of small ammunition and heavy ordnance. Due to the storm, she would not arrive at Port Royal until after the attack. Sherman refused to commit his men until this vessel arrived or he could replace her cargo. Unfortunately, the planners had stripped the arsenals in order to get the expedition underway. It now appeared that Du Pont and Sherman might abandon the attack. Du Pont became frantic. He recommended that his vessels be stripped of their guns and to send the guns ashore. He even suggested that maybe the "bayonet could supply the absence of small ammunition." Sherman acquiesced and agreed not to postpone the attack. Du Pont, therefore, passed the order that the attack would begin the next day. This unexpected situation whereby the navy had to reduce the forts before landing the troops put the burden of the attack on the navy—a position Du Pont had feared.[31]

The geography of this roadstead presented the Confederates with a defensive challenge. Two navigable rivers flowed into Port Royal: the Broad and Beaufort rivers. A maze of small waterways connected the nearby islands, which formed the agricultural center of the production

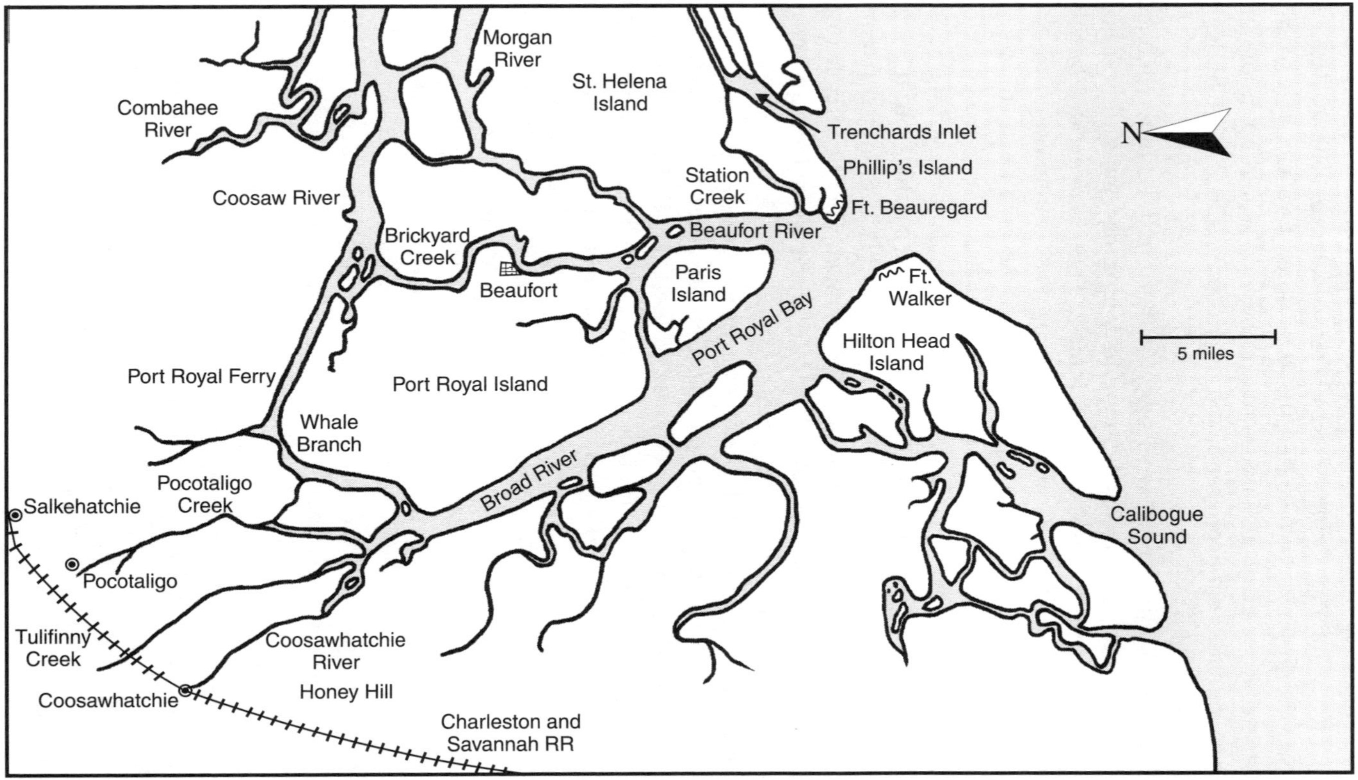

MAP 2.   PORT ROYAL TO POCOTALIGO

33

of Sea Island cotton. Two and a half miles separated the headlands of Hilton Head and Bay Point. General Pierre Gustave Toutant Beauregard, who earlier had commanded the provisional forces in South Carolina, felt that the great distance between the forts would not allow his troops to defend them properly or put an attacking naval force under a crossfire.[32]

Work on two defensive works began there in July, but remained largely unfinished. A lack of heavy and long-range guns diminished both forts' powers to resist a naval attack. The Confederates hastily constructed the earthworks and did not provide bombproofs for the men or traverses between the guns to protect the men from enfilading gunfire. The workers had also laid the guns out too close together, making the guns and crews easy targets for the naval gunfire. More importantly, the flanks of the forts lay unprotected from assault from the sea. When the navy arrived, Fort Walker on Hilton Head mounted twenty guns, but only thirteen guns bore on the channel. Fort Beauregard on Bay Point mounted nineteen guns, thirteen on the water face, and only seven that faced the fleet in the channel.[33]

When Du Pont met with Davis and the Rodgers cousins to talk over the final plan, he posed an essential question. He asked if the naval vessels should attack at long range or close to short range. With the loss of key army transports and their critical supplies, Du Pont now knew they could not count on the army to land with any certainty or to remain ashore. Fire at long range might take two days to reduce the works, so all agreed that, despite the danger of grounding, they should attack at short range. This would allow them to use with advantage the firepower of the *Wabash* and her two 10-inch, twenty-eight 9-inch, and fourteen 8-inch guns. They felt that a "shower of iron hail, or iron hell, dropped in the briefest time" would make victory more certain.[34]

At 3:30 on the afternoon of 5 November, Du Pont ordered his signalman to hoist the preparatory signal to get underway and the squadron began forming for the attack. Du Pont planned to bombard the batteries on Hilton Head just before sunset so that he could see the outline of the forts. As the *Wabash*, drawing over twenty-two feet, stood toward the forts, she and the side-wheel frigate *Susquehanna* grounded on Fishing Rip Shoals. Freeing *Wabash* from the bottom consumed about two hours and Du Pont cancelled the attack for the day. The whole fleet anchored for the night, but the following day the wind picked up and became "too fresh" and the flag officer postponed the attack until the seventh.[35]

During the delay Du Pont and his staff continued to discuss the most effective way to attack the forts. With the knowledge gained by the reconnaissance on the fifth, Du Pont decided to attack Fort Walker in close, at a range that would allow the fleet to avoid the fire of Fort Beauregard. This plan, however, was altered just before the battle began. When Charles Henry Davis awoke the morning of the seventh, he began to review the attack plans in his mind. Suddenly he perceived a more effective way to attack the forts. He hurried to Du Pont's stateroom without dressing to tell the flag officer. He proposed that instead of attacking Fort Walker directly by engaging it on its strongest side, they should enter the bay in mid-channel. The warships could fire on both forts as they stood down the channel and then the main column could turn back toward Fort Walker from the north, enfilading its water batteries. They could then repeat this pattern until the fort surrendered. This circular motion was similar to that used by Flag Officer Stringham at Hatteras. Du Pont concurred.[36]

The Battle of Port Royal

The seventh of November dawned "with unusual splendor in a cloudless sky; no breath of wind marred the smooth surface of the ocean and it shone like a thousand mirrors." As the crews prepared their warships for battle, the flagship sent a signal for the men to "go to breakfast." At 8:15 the flagship hoisted the preparatory signal for the fleet to get underway, followed by "form line of battle" and "prepare for action."[37]

At 8:30 the *Wabash*'s anchor was hove up and the vessels formed in two lines of battle. The main attacking column consisted of *Wabash* in the van, followed by the *Susquehanna*, the sloops *Mohican*, *Seminole*, and *Pawnee*, the ninety-day gunboats *Unadilla*, *Ottawa*, and *Pembina* and the steamer *Isaac Smith* towing the sailing sloop-of-war *Vandalia*. The flanking column steamed to starboard with the side-wheel gunboat *Bienville* in the van, followed by the gunboats *Seneca*, *Penguin*, *Curlew* and *Augusta*. The plan agreed upon on the flagship had the two columns passing into the harbor together. As the ships steamed past the enemy, the attacking column was to direct its fire against Fort Beauregard as it passed into the harbor, then to concentrate on the stronger of the two works, Fort Walker on Hilton Head. The five warships of the flanking column would position themselves to prevent the enemy vessels from raking the main column as it turned back up the sound. These ships would also keep the enemy from making a sortie toward the transports. Once the flanking column neutralized Tattnall's force it would take up a position north of Fort Walker and enfilade the batteries. The *R. B. Forbes*, *Mercury*, and *Penguin* formed a third division and protected the transports that remained anchored at a safe distance.[38]

As the vessels stood into the harbor on the flood tide, Fort Walker shattered the silence from long range at 9:26. As an omen of things yet to come for the defenders, the shell from this 9-inch Dahlgren gun exploded harmlessly near the muzzle. The next shot, however, came screaming across the bow of the *Wabash* from Fort Beauregard. Acting Master Roswell H. Lamson replied with *Wabash*'s forward pivot gun, and before the smoke could clear the ship, the frigate fired a broadside at each fort. *Susquehanna* was the next warship to join the fray and the rest of the fleet opened fire as they steamed into range. About thirty minutes elapsed before the *Wabash* reached the point where she would turn toward Fort Walker. As she turned, her broadsides bore on Tattnall's fleet. *Wabash* delivered a broadside at 800 yards, but only one shell struck Tattnall's flagship. Tattnall knew his fleet was outgunned and he ordered them to the safety of Skull Creek. Regretting that he could not return Du Pont's fire, Tattnall had his blue flag dipped three times as an acknowledgment to his old messmate.[39]

Du Pont's carefully planned attack went awry shortly after the ships completed the first turn. As the *Wabash* began her southward turn, Commander Sylvanus W. Godon of *Mohican*, in Nelsonian fashion, pulled his vessel out of line and steered her into a position to enfilade the fort. This unexpected movement confused the commanding officers of all the vessels behind Godon and they followed him. Commander Charles Steedman of the *Bienville* watched for ten minutes as the other vessels of the attacking column (except for *Susquehanna*) failed to support the flagship in line of battle as prescribed. To this point, *Bienville*, the leading vessel in the flanking column, had kept up a brisk fire on the enemy vessels. Instead of pursuing Tattnall and taking an enfilading position north of the fort, Steedman, wishing to support Du Pont, ordered his ship at full steam to pass into the attacking line ahead of the *Mohican*.[40]

As the ships closed to flank the fort, the *Vandalia*, attached by a long hawser in tow of the *Isaac Smith*, "swept in a long, graceful" arc past and among the vessels. The ninety-day gunboat *Unadilla* drifted through the other vessels with a disabled engine. Lieutenant Napolean Collins hailed and requested the other warships to get out of the way as "he could not stop." These vessels took up a position about 1,200 yards or more from the fort and received from the Confederate batteries little gunfire, but what they did receive was accurate. One shot struck the 389-ton screw steamer *Penguin*'s port side tiller chain, and at 10:45 another struck the steam drum. These shots effectively took her out of the action. The ex-merchant steamer *Augusta*, however, passed her a line and towed her back into action. Acting Lieutenant Thomas Budd, the commanding officer of the *Penguin*, commended the *Augusta* for keeping his ship "under fire upon every favorable occasion."[41]

When *Wabash* made her turn toward Fort Walker, Du Pont observed that not all the ships in his attacking column followed his movement. He ordered a general signal hoisted for the ships to "close action," then "follow the motions of the commanding officer," and "close order." From 10:20 until 11:35, he had these signals flown and repeated the signal to close order at 12:30 with no results. In front of the fort, he hailed over to Captain James L. Lardner of the *Susquehanna*, "I can't get my signals obeyed, I can't get the ships to come up."[42]

Godon, who was an old friend of Du Pont, must have felt that he could take the initiative to break the line. His unauthorized maneuver led the attacking ships into a position to severely damage Fort Walker, and do so from an infilading position relatively safe from the enemy's fire. *Wabash*, meanwhile, followed by the *Susquehanna* and *Bienville*, steamed against the tide and at 800 yards off Fort Walker began delivering a devastating fire on the fort.[43]

Shortly after the *Bienville* dropped out of line, *Seneca* "shaped a course directly up stream for the rebel fleet" and boldly attacked. *Seneca* pursued Tattnall's fleet until they reached the safety of Skull Creek. Nearby a crowd of people had come on an excursion to witness the struggle. Seven large steamers crowded with onlookers peered through the smoke for a glimpse at the battle. One steamer displayed the French flag and another a British flag, indicating that the consuls of these nations had come to witness the destruction of the Union fleet. Later during the battle, the rebel warships again appeared as if they might venture out. *Seneca*, though, chased Tattnall's warships for nearly two miles, sending ricochet fire after them, before returning to enfilade the batteries at Hilton Head.[44]

John Rodgers witnessed the battle from the bridge of the flagship. He recalled that initially the enemy shells "flew thick over our heads—the shells screaming like fiends." Through the long glass he observed shells "bursting in the fort as fast as you could move your fingers in playing upon the piano." John Sanford Barnes also on the flagship commented about the "constant roar of the guns" as the naval gunners fired as rapidly as possible, causing many of the shots to burst ineffectively over the fort or to fall beyond the target. The smoke from the ships blew toward the fort, obscuring the vision of the rebels. The naval gunfire struck so rapidly and effectively that "great volumes of sand were hurled into the air, nearly burying . . . the gunners in its fall." The tremendous firepower of the warships began to dismount guns and the Confederate defenders managed to return a withering fire only after the initial stages of the fight. One shot from the 10-inch Columbiad mounted at Fort Walker, however, went clear through the mainmast of the *Wabash*, barely missing Du Pont and his staff on the bridge and showering them with splinters.[45]

The initial pass of the Union fleet did not satisfy Du Pont, and he turned his ships around for a second pass into the harbor. As the main column passed beyond the guns of Fort Walker, at 10:40 the ships majestically turned and headed back toward the harbor for a third pass by the forts. This time they closed to within 600 yards. As the *Wabash* and the other warships steamed against the flood tide, the slow speed allowed the naval gunners to pour accurate, effective, and devastating fire into Fort Walker. An eyewitness described the *Wabash* as "a destroying angel" as she steamed close to shore, slowing her engines just enough to give steerageway. The response from the fort slackened further as the two frigates and *Bienville* passed. It was the warships on the flank, however, that continued to do most of the damage to the enemy's batteries.[46]

Brigadier General Thomas Drayton commanded the defenses of Port Royal. He was not prepared for such a devastating attack and, shortly after the vessels appeared, he began calling for reinforcements. He remained in Fort Walker watching for a Union landing and directed the defense for most of the battle. Defending Fort Walker were two companies of the First Regiment Artillery, South Carolina Militia, three companies of the Ninth Regiment of South Carolina Volunteers, and four companies of the Twelfth Regiment, South Carolina Volunteers, for a total of 622 men in the fort and on the island. The thirteen guns that bore on the channel could not match the firepower of the Union ships. The defenders had only three other usable guns on the flanks that they occasionally fired at the warships as they reached the end of their elliptical maneuvers.[47]

The rebel gunners encountered troubles almost at once. They found that the shells would not fit down the barrels of two of their largest guns.

Soon after the 9-inch Dahlgren gun's first shot exploded near the muzzle, the gunners found they could not ram home the other shells provided for this gun. The fourth shot from the fort's other heavy gun, a 10-inch Columbiad, caused the gun to jump over its limber and become useless. While the warships kept up a "vigorous attack" other guns dropped from the action as a result of naval fire or other malfunctions. Without traverses to protect the men, the fire from ships on the flanks proved devastating. Before the battle the rebels did not have an opportunity to mount many of the guns on the northern part of the works. This proved disastrous because of the effectiveness of the flanking column's fire.[48]

The Union fleet kept up its vigorous attack. During the battle, however, the *Wabash* hove to. Steedman brought the *Bienville* under the stern of the flagship and ordered a boat lowered. Passing to the *Wabash*, Steedman boarded the flagship and asked if the frigate was aground. Du Pont told Steedman that he had stopped his ship to give his men biscuit and grog at the guns. According to Steedman, Du Pont then asked, "How is it that I can't get my signal obeyed and my orders carried out?" And Steedman replied, "I can't tell . . . but I hope I have done my duty." Whereby Du Pont reportedly said, "Yes Steedman, you have done just what I expected of you."[49]

At about 11:00 General Drayton ordered into the fort some men from a battery on the other side of the island to give relief to his fatigued gunners. Despite the fact that much of the Union navy's fire sailed over the targets, the sheer volume and rapidity of gunfire from the warships made the difference. During the battle the *Wabash* and *Susquehanna* alone fired over 1,700 shot and shell in five passes between the forts. The men in the fort stood by their guns until all but three on the water face of the fort lay disabled and only 500 pounds of powder remained in the magazines.[50]

Delayed by the storm, the screw steamer *Pocahontas* arrived just after 12:00 to take part in the battle. South Carolina native Commander Percival Drayton commanded *Pocahontas*. His brother, Thomas Drayton, commanded the Confederate forces ashore. Despite his family ties, Drayton brought his vessel into action, engaging both forts as he stood down the harbor. Drayton, who had a "humorous twinkling eye," reportedly told his men, "now boys, my brother is in that battery, and I want you to drive him out of it." He then placed the *Pocahontas* in position off Fort Walker and engaged the batteries there. Du Pont later commended Drayton on bringing his vessel into the most exposed position and for firing the best shots.[51]

At 1:15, before the warships could make a sixth pass by the forts, *Ottawa* hoisted a signal that the enemy was abandoning the works on Hilton Head. *Pembina* repeated this signal a few minutes later. After four hours of suffering under a deadly fire, the Confederates began streaming out of Fort Walker. The naval gunners continued to fire without realizing the enemy was retreating. The men therefore had to quickly cross about one mile of open ground to the safety of nearby woods. They carried their wounded, but left their camp equipment and their dead—many buried under sand and guns. Northern accounts labeled this a panic, but with as many as sixty shells bursting each minute in their midst, the Confederate gunners had no choice but to cover the ground quickly.[52]

Fort Beauregard, across the sound on Bay Point, did not receive the same pounding as Fort Walker. Nevertheless, Union gunfire had knocked twelve of the fort's nineteen guns out of the fight. The 619 men in the garrison stood by their guns bravely and witnessed the abandonment of Fort Walker, after which the fort's commander, Colonel Richard G. M. Dunovant, fearful that the naval vessels would cut off his retreat, ordered his men out of the works. They left without their camp equipment, stores, or heavy baggage and without destroying the property.[53]

When the fire from Fort Walker ceased, Du Pont ordered Raymond Rodgers to prepare a party of sailors and Marines to debark and take possession of the fort. Raymond Rodgers' cousin, John, asked permission to take a flag of truce ashore and to raise the Union flag. Du Pont assented and the latter Rodgers had a boat hoisted out from the *Wabash* and rowed ashore carrying a white flag. At 2:25 he hoisted the Union flag over the fort on South Carolina soil. With the raising of this flag, Du Pont hoisted the signal to cease fire.[54]

Shortly after the flag rose over Fort Walker, the sailors of the fleet manned the rigging and gave three cheers. The soldiers on the transports also joined the cheering, but had watched the entire battle merely as spectators. The bands on board the transports struck up martial tunes as the ships began to move into the harbor to land the troops. At dusk John Sanford Barnes watched as the "dilatory soldiers commenced to land amidst the wildest confusion, & in most beautiful disorder." After dispatching the Rodgers cousins to Fort Walker, Du Pont sent a small squadron to Fort Beauregard to reconnoiter. Daniel Ammen found this fort also abandoned and hauled down the Confederate flag. It was not until the following day at sunrise that the Union flag rose on the flagstaff of Fort Beauregard.[55]

Victory

After the battle Du Pont mustered the captains on board *Wabash* for a victory toast. The flag officer wrote his wife, "The victory was complete and attended with circumstances which gave it a glare of brilliancy I never looked forward to . . . The victory was quick, complete, relatively bloodless, and solely a naval affair." The navy had suffered only eight killed and twenty-three wounded. The injuries to the warships were overall, minor—shots in the hulls and damage to the masts, spars, and rigging accounted for most of the damage. Confederate losses mounted to only sixty-six. After hearing of the victory, an extremely relieved Welles wrote Du Pont, "The success is all that was expected, and more than we ought to have asked."[56]

This victory had significant consequences for the war along the Southern seaboard. Du Pont captured an excellent port for future naval and logistical operations. The capture of Port Royal would prove essential to the maintenance of the blockade and for future military operations. The victory came on the heels of the Hatteras expedition, giving the navy a second victory before the Union armies had won a single major battle. The victory also heaped praise upon the navy. Favorable public opinion swelled and Du Pont earned a congressional vote of thanks.[57]

The fall of Port Royal threw Charleston into a panic. Rumors of traitors and of an advancing enemy began to circulate among the city's inhabitants. This, however, was far from the truth. Du Pont admitted to Gustavus Fox that he had not prepared to follow up the victory with another movement, writing, "I never thought I could carry it out so fast . . ."[58]

This easy victory, however, did have long-term consequences, not all of which were positive for the Union navy. Forts had rarely fallen so easily to ships. The naval victories at Hatteras and Port Royal planted a seed in the mind of Welles and Fox that ships were superior to fortifications. Both Welles and Fox would later assume that steam vessels could successfully attack forts—an important tenet in subsequent naval strategy.

This victory also reassured Fox that the navy could be victorious without army assistance. The rivalry between the army and the navy became more focused and divisive. At the battle of Port Royal, the Union forces completely outmatched the Confederates. The *Wabash* alone likely could have driven the fort's defenders from their guns. The army, however, did not come prepared to land quickly because the deep-draft transports could not get near the shore to land troops rapidly. The troops might have gotten ashore, but their supplies were not prepared to follow. Had it been necessary for the army to land to take the forts, it may have been both a comic and a tragic scene. One could hardly imagine a worse-planned expedition. It was a blessing that the army did not have to take the forts by assault.

Du Pont's limitations as a flag officer began to surface. The victory obscured Du Pont's failure to effectively communicate his battle plan to the officers in the attacking force. While Godon's maneuver effectively placed the Union warships where they could do the most damage, the officers who left the attacking column and took a position to enfilade the Confederate fort would have never disobeyed orders as a group. Instead they acted as if they did not fully comprehend their responsibilities nor understood Du Pont's plan of attack. Yet, the ease of the victory allowed Du Pont to bury this issue.

Expecting to find the enemy better prepared, neither Du Pont nor Sherman had a continuing strategy once Port Royal fell so quickly. Both Du Pont and Sherman had orders to take several anchorages; however, neither had discussed with the other any details or decided on the next target. The army, in fact, did not send with Sherman the necessary cavalry force or field artillery to make an attack inland. The lack of shallow-draft steamers for transportation of troops and supplies would also be a problem. The federal forces also failed to make contingency plans and the necessary logistical arrangements to follow up this initial success. They therefore likely missed an opportunity to capture more significant places in both South Carolina and Georgia that lay virtually undefended at this time. Du Pont's base of operations would lie between Savannah and Charleston, but the Union forces would not quickly attack either of these cities. The capture of Port Royal did put a strong naval force between them and threatened them both. This situation may have allowed a subsequent joint operation to capture either one of these cities, since the Confederates had their resources divided between the two. Unprepared to follow up this quick success, the expeditionary force virtually ground to a halt. The flag officer would later gain a greater understanding of the difficulty of attacking prepared defenses.[59]

— 3 —

"Flying about Like Moths around a Lamp"

Probing the Confederate Defenses

The fall of Port Royal caused widespread panic in the South. The *Charleston Mercury* advanced the theory that the Union forces landed in South Carolina solely for revenge and avarice. The paper even suggested that its citizens destroy all valuables that they could not carry out of the range of the Union soldiers. The press in Georgia, however, remained much more pragmatic. It generally sought to rally the state's people to the defense. The small Sandersville paper wrote, "Shall one of Lincoln's vandals set foot upon Georgia's soil? Let it not be so."[1]

The capture of Port Royal, however, left the navy in no condition to follow up the victory. During the battle Du Pont's naval forces had fired away over half of their ammunition and could not commit to another large attack. They would wait about three weeks before the next shipment arrived. Du Pont, though, quickly followed up his Port Royal victory by probing the Confederate defenses. On 7 November, shortly after the capture of Port Royal, the *Seneca* steamed two miles up the Beaufort River with General Sherman on board. She then returned to Port Royal Sound and steamed into Skull Creek looking for batteries and enemy vessels. On the ninth, Du Pont sent the *Unadilla* up the Broad River. Meanwhile the *Seneca*, the *Pembina*, and the small screw steamer *Curlew* forged up the Beaufort River looking for the two lightships

43

seized by the rebels. They approached to within a half mile of the town of Beaufort and sent a flag of truce ashore.[2]

Beaufort was a town of stately homes situated on broad avenues. Many of the houses had large verandas and impressive formal gardens. As the sailors approached shore in several armed boats, they observed a scene of complete chaos. The white inhabitants had fled, leaving the town in the hands of their former slaves. Unrestrained, the blacks had broken into the houses, and parties of them were loading scows and boats with their newfound loot. The naval landing parties did their best to stop the vandalism and to restore order. Captain John P. Bankhead nailed a notice to the principal house in Beaufort stating that the navy had made every effort to stop the looting. He pointed out that if the owners had stayed this would not have occurred.[3]

The restoration of order by the navy, however, did not stop the vandalism. Shortly after the capture of the town and the landing of troops, men from the army transports and the coal vessels came ashore in the Port Royal area to join in the plundering. They broke into houses on Parris Island and destroyed property for amusement. Du Pont wrote Fox, "our army here are depredators & freebooters—they are robbing . . . in all directions, & robbing the poor negroes too, for all sheep, poultry, sweet potatoe patches, etc. belonging to them . . ." Afraid this would force the locals to respond adversely, Du Pont required passes be issued to boats landing on shore to prevent this activity.[4]

On the twelfth, Du Pont and Sherman came ashore to visit Beaufort. The *Unadilla* and *Pembina*, there since the ninth, remained at the wharves to keep order and to allow the inhabitants to return. Neither the inhabitants nor the army, however, showed any interest. Sherman told Du Pont that he did not feel the town was strategically valuable and without a presence ashore Du Pont decided to withdraw his vessels.[5]

The decision to withdraw only accentuated the fact that the federal forces did not come prepared to follow up their victory at Port Royal and that neither Sherman nor Du Pont came with a continuing strategy. Sherman though felt restrained by a lack of transportation, both land and water. He also believed it important to fortify his position on Hilton Head before moving farther. Sherman believed strengthening the defenses would allow 2,000 men to defend the island against anything the Confederates could muster for an attack. This would make available the majority of his forces for offensive operations. A week after the capture of the forts, General Sherman laid out two alternatives for future movements. The first option he considered was to open another harbor with naval cooperation—part of his original instructions. The second option he considered was to use Beaufort as a base to operate on a line from Port Royal Island to Pocataligo in order to cut the Charleston and Savannah Railroad. This reversed his earlier decision to abandon the town, but by operating from this line, he could threaten both Charleston and Savannah via the railroad or through the interior waterways.[6]

Sherman, however, did not urge a move until a month after the fall of Port Royal. During this intervening time he continually requested more troops and transportation. He blamed his lack of initiative on the loss of the ferryboats initially slated for his command and the fact that Du Pont had not supplied him oarsmen for his boats. He also blamed Du Pont for bringing along only enough boats to land troops, but not enough to transport his men through the intricate system of marshes and waterways. Thus, he maintained that he could not follow up the victory at Port Royal. In an effort to diminish the contributions of the navy, Sherman informed his superiors that he had not relied on the navy for the victory at Port Royal. He also claimed that his force could have reduced the works, as well as captured the garrisons of the forts.[7]

On 6 December Sherman officially reversed his earlier decision and decided to occupy Beaufort. He informed Du Pont and asked for a couple of gunboats for support. He wrote the flag officer of his intentions, almost as an afterthought, as his transports left the docks in Port Royal. Sherman also continued to write his superiors complaining that he was chafing to take Fernandina, but blamed the navy for the delays. The navy, however, was still suffering from a shortage of powder and of 11-inch shells after the Port Royal fight. Sherman, however, never made any specific plans for a movement and at no time discussed or relayed in writing any of his plans or his concerns to Du Pont. This was the beginning of a series of poor relationships between the army and the navy. These command problems would eventually create a rift so wide that interservice cooperation would be difficult.[8]

Sherman's thoughts, though, increasingly turned to the capture of Charleston, and he relied on the knowledge of Captain Quincy A. Gillmore, his chief engineer, to formulate his proposals. Gillmore suggested two plans. The first plan called for a landing on Morris and Sullivan's Islands. Siege artillery could then reduce Fort Sumter by bombardment. With the fort no longer a threat, the fleet would have access to the city. The second plan projected the capture of James Island. In this move, the navy would operate against the batteries on the Stono River. The occupation of James Island would allow the army to control the harbor and place the remaining Confederate forts in a weak position. Sherman's plan, however, called for an increase in guns and men.[9] Du Pont, though, only knew of his plans to strike at Fernandina. While Sherman planned the other operation, there was no indication that he communicated his ideas to the navy. It is difficult to take the general's grumbling to his superiors seriously since he never pressured nor approached Du Pont for any naval assistance. This lack of coordination between the army and navy manifested itself frequently during the war. It would throughout the war create divisiveness, and mistrust and would hamper all the joint operations along the South Atlantic seaboard.

Probing Southward

Du Pont pushed forward while the army vacillated, awaiting transportation and directions from Washington. During the aftermath of the battle for Port Royal, sailors found a coastal chart at General Drayton's headquarters with the Confederate defensive positions marked with red pencil. Using this as a guide, Du Pont sent all his available force to visit these places, hoping to capture the guns, but his men found most of them already removed.[10]

Coastal defense for the state of Georgia received scant attention in the early months of the war. Poor cooperation between the provisional governments of the seceded states hampered the early efforts to prepare the defenses. After the capture of Port Royal, Savannah became a priority for defense in Georgia. State troops obstructed the Savannah River with piles and cribs and erected batteries to command the obstructions. The people of the state, nevertheless, still felt extremely insecure about the inadequate defenses available. After Port Royal fell, the Georgia legislature remained indecisive on appropriating money for defense. Interestingly, the states rights champion Governor Joseph E. Brown even felt the need of defenses so great that he uncharacteristically asked the Confederate Government for help to fund them.[11]

Du Pont, though, moved vessels south in order to "cork up Savannah like a bottle." Additionally, Commander John Rodgers in the *Flag* conferred with Commander John S. Missroon of the ship *Savannah* to determine the best place, if necessary, to obstruct the bar off the Tybee entrance. Du Pont also instructed Rodgers to "push his reconnaissance," to get an estimate of the force on Tybee Island and to ascertain the possibility of getting over the bar and holding the river by anchoring inside.[12]

Tybee Island was a key position for control of the Savannah River. The island was almost due east of Fort Pulaski on Cockspur Island. It was a low barren expanse of sand hills eight miles long and six miles wide. Situated on the island was an abandoned earthen battery and a circular fort or Martello Tower, but the Confederates used the latter only as a lookout tower. With control of this island, the Union forces, without a blockade, could stop all vessels coming and going down the main ship channel. Early on the morning of the twenty-fourth, all commanding officers off the river repaired on board *Savannah* to discuss a landing. Around 10:30 the steamers got underway and found the bar rough and the navigation difficult because the rebels destroyed the ranges. The *Flag*, *Pocahontas*, *Augusta*, and *Seneca* carefully stood over the bar and began to fire at the Martello Tower. Rodgers sent a landing party onto the island at 3:00 P.M. and found no enemy. He hoisted a United States flag on both the tower and the Tybee Island lighthouse. Rogers left a small party of men on the island to give the enemy the impression that it was occupied.[13]

Two days later the frigate *Savannah* passed over the bar and moored so that her heavy battery controlled the approaches to Tybee Island. Du Pont learned that the rebels, afraid the Union warships intended to steam up the river, had laid down obstructions near Fort Pulaski. On the morning of 27 November, Du Pont hoisted his flag on the side-wheel steamer *Florida* to observe personally the situation off Tybee Island. With the *Ottawa* and the screw steamer *R. B. Forbes* he landed men and Marines on Tybee Island. The sailors found the island deserted and marched to secure the Martello Tower. He transferred his flag to the *Savannah* and then took about thirty boats ashore to reconnoiter Tybee Island. The *Ben Deford* brought down 200 army troops to take possession and to hold this important island. The army forces landed and made a complete reconnaissance. Sherman concurred with the navy's assessment that he should occupy the island because a battery here could control the channel and be used to reduce Fort Pulaski.[14]

Du Pont anticipated the need to reconnoiter the fortifications on Wassaw Island that lay across Wassaw Sound, south of Tybee Island. He sent Raymond Rodgers in command of the *Ottawa*, *Seneca*, and *Pembina* to determine the nature of the works. Rodgers found them abandoned. He also probed the area near the mouth of the Wilmington River and around Little Tybee Island.[15]

Additionally, Du Pont ordered a reconnaissance into St. Helena Sound. On 25 November, at 3:0 A.M., the *Pawnee*, *Unadilla*, and *Pembina* left Port Royal under the command of Percival Drayton, guided by

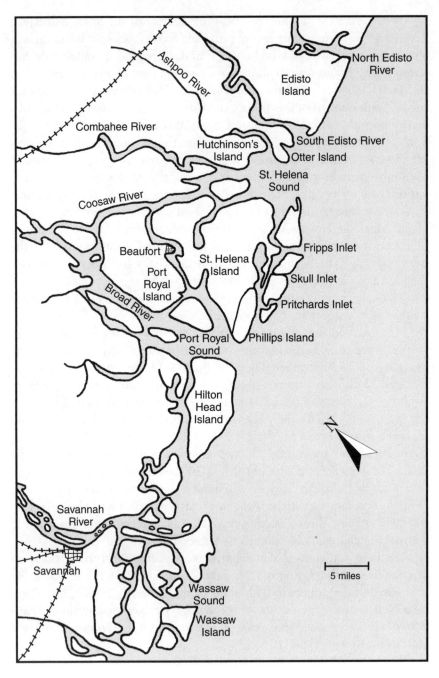

MAP 3. COAST NORTH OF SAVANNAH

Charles Boutelle in the *Vixen*. The steamers entered St. Helena Sound and steamed up the Coosaw River. The gunboats fired several rounds into fortifications as they reconnoitered around Otter Island. Sending small boats ashore, the landing parties discovered abandoned fortifications. On the twenty-seventh, the *Vixen*, *Pembina*, and *Unadilla* steamed up the Ashepoo River leaving the deeper drafted *Pawnee* behind. These three steamers found additional abandoned fortifications and obsolete and old ordnance that they destroyed. They continued as far as the vessels could go—to Hutchinson's Island, twelve miles above Otter Island. Drayton returned finding little evidence of the rebels' sustained intent to contest the waterways. Drayton reported that the fort on Otter Island commanded the approaches to South Edisto and Ashepoo rivers and could be a potential problem if armed and manned by the enemy.[16]

Drayton went ashore on 29 November to persuade General Sherman to occupy the fort on Otter Island. He argued that possession of this fort would allow complete control of St. Helena Sound, as well as the Ashepoo and Combahee rivers. It would therefore close one of the navigable back doors to Charleston. During the meeting, Drayton could not convince Sherman that occupying this position would be advantageous. He left Sherman's headquarters with the impression that Sherman was "a mighty slow coach."[17]

The Confederate forces, though, were powerless to stop this naval activity. The overall Confederate commander of the military department comprising the coasts of South Carolina, Georgia and eastern Florida was General Robert E. Lee. After the defeat at Port Royal, Lee initially strengthened his general defenses in the low country in an effort to contain a Union advance. He found the defensive work slow, the guns to arm the works scarce, and the troops to man them hard to obtain. His defensive efforts along the coast earned him the nickname "King of Spades." Lee could not muster many resources in order to stop a joint army and navy attack. Lee, however, did not panic. He wrote General Samuel Cooper that "The farther we can be withdrawn from his floating batteries the weaker he will become . . ." Lee knew that he could oppose the fleet only with fixed batteries and he used this principle to select the areas to defend. He withdrew guns from numerous points to strengthen more important points farther from the coast. He felt the Union forces would seize the Charleston and Savannah Railroad near the head of the Broad River; exactly as Sherman proposed. Had the Union forces struck this strategic point, they would have severed the critical communications between Charleston and Savannah.[18]

The Confederate naval forces under Flag Officer Tattnall also faced a bleak situation. He had no real force to stop the advancing Union vessels. The largest ship the flag officer had under his command was the *Savannah* (ex-*Everglade*), a 122-foot, 383-ton paddle-wheel steamer. This former inland passenger vessel became his flagship and mounted two smoothbore cannon. Other vessels attached to his flotilla were the *Sampson* the *Lady Davis*, and the *Resolute*, tugs that became warships merely by the addition of guns. Tattnall also had at his disposal the side-wheel steamer *Huntress*. She was virtually worthless as a warship, having both her engine and boilers on the main deck. Having only contempt for his squadron, he reportedly issued "holy vows that he will yet sink each and all those d____d old tubs off the bar."[19]

At noon on the twenty-sixth, Tattnall steamed downriver to test the range of a new rifled gun with hopes of luring the Union warships into Fort Pulaski's range. Flying his pennant from the steamer *Savannah* with a hulk lashed alongside, he sortied toward the Union vessels lying off the fort. With the *Resolute* and the *Sampson* along, he stood down the sound a short distance and opened fire at the *Pocahontas* at long range. The shot fell nearly one-half mile short while the fire of the Union vessels burst over the *Savannah*. After an hour's cannonade and discovering the poor quality of his new gun, Tattnall fled to his former anchorage under the protection of Fort Pulaski.[20]

Du Pont had no intention of allowing the Confederate forces to relax. He wrote Fox that he intended to drive the rebels from their coastal defenses whenever possible. Sherman likewise indicated a desire to move, but neither Sherman nor Du Pont seemed to know the intentions of the other. The general changed his mind and reversed an earlier decision not to occupy Otter Island. Du Pont, meanwhile, grew concerned about losing possession of St. Helena Sound and the command of a number of large rivers that controlled the interior water communications of the state. He, therefore, sent Commander Drayton to visit the area again; this time with instructions to hold Otter Island until Sherman could put a force there. On 5 December, Drayton took *Pawnee*, *Unadilla*, *Isaac Smith*, and *Vixen* and steamed up the Ashepoo River to the entrance of Mosquito Creek.[21]

The next morning the ship *Dale* appeared and Drayton sent the *Isaac Smith* to tow her over the bar. The *Dale*, however, went aground about halfway over the bar and could not be refloated until 11:00 P.M. The following day the *Unadilla*, *Isaac Smith*, and *Vixen* examined the river up to Hutchinson's Island. On the eighth, the gunboats explored the Coosaw

River and, when the *Unadilla*'s engine failed, Drayton left her behind and pushed up river with the other two steamers. Farther along, he left the *Isaac Smith* behind and continued up river in the *Vixen* until he reached Brickyard Creek. After reconnoitering this area, he then stood back down the river, reaching Port Royal after dusk on the ninth.[22]

Drayton remained active and, under orders from Du Pont, planned a reconnaissance in force into St. Helena Sound and the adjacent waters. He prepared to leave Port Royal at daylight on 16 December with the *Pawnee*, the *Seneca* and *Vixen*, but a heavy northeaster kept his command in the harbor. The following day he reached the North Edisto River and *Vixen* guided the vessels over the bar. The enemy fortifications, a mile and a half ahead, reportedly had a garrison and Drayton instructed the bow guns of both the *Pawnee* and the *Seneca* to fire slowly into the works as they approached. The vessels received no reply and found the earthworks abandoned. Lieutenant Commander Daniel Ammen proceeded five miles upriver in the *Seneca* while Drayton examined the fort. Ammen's reconnaissance prompted the local landowners to burn their cotton houses and outbuildings. At daylight on the seventeenth, Drayton took *Vixen* and some Marines and the boats from *Seneca* and *Pawnee* and landed at Rockville, a little over a mile up Bohicket Creek. Here he captured a schooner laden with cotton and provisions. The local infantry fled their camp on the approach of the gunboats and left their provisions and equipment. At 2:00 A.M. the following morning, Drayton continued up the North Edisto River and found *Seneca* on a mud bank unable to get free. The *Seneca* floated free the following day at noon and Drayton returned with a couple of prisoners and about 150 former slaves. On the nineteenth Drayton steamed down the South Edisto with the *Vixen* and found the fortifications on Edisto Island deserted.[23]

Farther south, Raymond Rodgers began probing Confederate positions to determine if the gunboats might reach Savannah through waterways that connected with the Savannah River above Fort Pulaski. On 5 December before daylight the gunboats *Ottawa*, *Seneca*, and *Pembina* left Tybee Roads and approached Wassaw Island. They found the fortifications on the island abandoned and their armament removed. Steaming to the mouth of the Wilmington River, they could see enemy encampments and fortifications. A few days later Du Pont sent the *Henry Andrew* to augment Rodgers' forces with instructions to visit Ossabaw Inlet and the Vernon and Great Ogeechee rivers. Rodgers crossed the bar at Ossabaw on the morning of 11 December and passed up the Vernon River, where he observed a well-placed fort on Green Island. This fort, on the eastern end of the island, commanded Vernon, Little Ogeechee, Hell Gate, and the passage from Vernon River to Great Ogeechee. The fort fired two rifled shells at the naval force, one falling aft of the *Seneca* and the other well short of the *Pembina*. Passing back down and crossing Ossabaw Sound, the vessels steamed four miles up the Great Ogeechee River to within sight of Vernonburg. Observing no fortifications, Rodgers brought his gunboats back to Tybee Roads.[24]

These reconnaissance missions by the squadron accomplished several goals. They allowed the Union forces to keep the Confederates guessing their intentions and denied them the opportunity to defend the areas immediately adjacent to the coast. They likewise prevented the rebel forces from concentrating to strike at the Union forces. The army, meanwhile, remained virtually inactive, perhaps missing an opportunity to strike at the unprepared Confederates. Yet Sherman continued his complaints and wrote Washington that the occupation of such a vast area of the coast had confirmed that they had accomplished the main object of the expedition. He also inexplicably changed his mind on the immediate need to capture Fernandina. He wrote the War Department that he felt the city's capture "is now of so secondary a character" that it was insignificant compared with the capture of other places.[25]

The Stone Fleet

Du Pont found he had an inadequate number of naval vessels to blockade the extensive coastline, to perform reconnaissance missions, and to participate in combined operations. The Blockade Strategy Board had proposed closing some of the southern inlets with stone-filled hulks to alleviate having to watch them. The Navy Department, following advice of the Strategy Board, obstructed channels off North Carolina. They also decided to block some of the channels off Charleston and Savannah, hoping to free up part of the blockading fleet for other activities. While the Strategy Board had discussed the idea of sinking hulks, it was Fox who promoted and championed the effort. Du Pont called it a "hobby of Fox's which nothing could put out of his head."[26]

Beginning on 17 October, Welles instructed his brother-in-law, George D. Morgan, to purchase twenty-five obsolete vessels. Welles authorized him to obtain vessels of at least 250 tons and to have them filled with granite blocks to use as obstructions for Savannah. Several weeks later the department purchased twenty additional ships to sink off the Charleston Bar. The ships cost the government an average of just under

$15,000 a piece. They were to have minimal sails and ground tackle and instructions called for workmen to fit the ships with valves to allow them to sink quickly. Most of the vessels, however, simply carried a 5-inch knockout plug backed by a hand brace. In most of the vessels cheaper fieldstones from New England meadows replaced the cargoes of granite.[27]

On 20 November the ships and barks bound for Savannah began their trip. The other twenty vessels followed three weeks later and remained separate. The first ship reached Savannah on 3 December, and the remaining vessels staggered in over the next ten days. Many exhibited "fiji ports"—the broad white stripes running fore and aft along the sides of the ships, broken at regular intervals by black squares. Tradition held that these false gun ports originally served to give South Pacific islanders the impression that the ship carried guns. It had a similar effect on the Confederates. The sight of the vessels created excitement in Savannah and the local papers broadcast the arrival of the hulks as the "Vandal Blockade" and called the effort a "dastardly act of vandalism."[28]

Several of the ancient hulks arrived in sinking condition. One ran aground off Tybee Island and another parted her cable and drifted ashore on the south edge of the channel. The ship *Phoenix* struck the bar while crossing and began to leak. Unable to staunch the flow of water, the naval vessels towed her to the beach and sank her as a breakwater. Here she sheltered the landing of the troops that Sherman later sent from Port Royal. They also added three other hulks thought to be unlikely to remain afloat to this jetty.[29]

As the Savannah papers decried the efforts of the United States Navy, Union observations and intelligence gathering confirmed that the Confederates panicked and sank vessels across the channel below the fort to keep the Union warships from ascending the river. Du Pont wrote the department that the enemy had effectively closed the channel. The flag officer faced a decision of whether to sink any of the ships as obstructions. He suggested to Fox that they should supply Tattnall "with a half dozen vessels to help his obstructions off Pulaski." With the news that the Confederates had blocked the channel and the fact that the Union forces held Tybee Island, the stone fleet became an "elephant" to Du Pont. With no real use for the hulks at Savannah, he decided to send the seaworthy vessels back to Port Royal to augment the second contingent of twenty vessels then en route to Charleston.[30]

The flag officer placed Captain Charles Henry Davis, his Chief of Staff, in charge of sinking the stone laden vessels at Charleston. Davis had a special knowledge of the Charleston area, having surveyed these waters some ten years earlier. Du Pont, however, could not have chosen a more unenthusiastic officer. Davis thought that this was a "mania" of Fox and had a "special disgust for this business . . ." He personally objected to this method of interrupting Confederate trade and believed that it would only be a temporary situation.[31]

With the hulks from Savannah on hand, Davis began the operation off Charleston on 17 December. In good weather he sank the first vessels on the eastern and western edge of the Main Ship Channel to mark the boundaries of the field. Small steamers began towing sixteen hulks on and inside the bar and placed them in a checkerboard pattern stretching for just over two hundred yards. Davis arranged the hulks in this fashion to obstruct the channel enough to make navigation "hazardous and uncertain," but not to stop the flow of water. Davis' crews removed the last plug at 10:30 A.M. and after they settled on the bottom, his men began removing the masts.[32]

The second contingent of hulks began to arrive before Davis even finished preparing the vessels brought from Savannah. Much like the first group, some wrecked before the naval crews could sink them. They considered others too valuable to sink and diverted these for logistical and station use. As the vessels lay off Charleston a northeast gale caused some to veer out of line and four lost their anchors and drifted away. One of these vessels, the *Peri*, they did not get back and placed down in the channel until 13 February. In another effort on 25 and 26 December, the navy prepared thirteen hulks for sinking across Maffitt's Channel. When the final vessel struck bottom, some considered the channels effectively closed. The New York *Times* claimed that the hulks presented "unconquerable obstacles." General Robert E. Lee called the whole act an "abortive expression of the malice and revenge of a people . . ." Like Davis, Charles Boutelle of the Coast Survey believed, however, that the obstructions would be only "ephemeral" and he proved to be right. A survey of the Main Ship Channel four months later found that the currents had scoured a twenty-one-foot channel at low water—a deeper channel than had existed originally.[33]

Keeping the Confederates Vigilant

Since the sinking of the stone fleet occupied the naval forces, joint operations with the army had to wait until the end of December. While the navy probed the Confederate defenses and worked to lay down the hulks, the army continued to fortify Hilton Head, picketed all of Port Royal Island, and established posts along the coast. The Confederates realized they could not stop this activity and withdrew most of their forces to interior lines.[34] Du Pont's forces remained active and continued to probe the interior lines. Small expeditions kept the Confederate forces guessing where the navy might strike next. Illustrative of this are two reconnaissance expeditions made in the North and South Edisto rivers.

In late December Lieutenant Commander William T. Truxtun sent a launch and the first cutter from the *Dale* in command of Acting Master William Ottiwell and a contingent of Marines up the South Edisto River. Ottiwell had instructions to reconnoiter and to capture or destroy a schooner seen cruising in the river. Leaving on the morning of 27 December, Ottiwell's party encountered pickets from the Fourth South Carolina Regiment. Two officers asked for the surrender of Ottiwell and his men, and when they refused, the rebels fired a volley at the boats and a skirmish ensued. Ottiwell unlimbered the boat howitzer and began firing canister shot and shells into a house sheltering the troops. Gunfire from the boat howitzer and the Marines drove the rebels back and Ottiwell returned down river without a casualty.[35]

Du Pont also sent a steamer into the North Edisto River. On 2 January, Acting Lieutenant Thomas Budd took the little screw steamer *Penguin* on a reconnaissance up the North Edisto River. As the gunboat ascended the river, he fired a few shots at rebel pickets and withdrew down the river. Two days later he returned to check out a story concerning a storage site of corn at Bear Bluff. He dispatched a flatboat and howitzer with two officers and twenty-five men. As the flatboat approached the landing, about two dozen enemy soldiers fired on the boat and Budd dispersed them with small arms and grapeshot. The tars landed, raised the United States flag on the house, and then allowed the local ex-slaves to fill their boats with corn before setting fire to the buildings and retiring back down stream.[36]

These small expeditions did little to satisfy General Sherman, who continued to chafe at his inactivity as the army languished at Hilton Head. The War Department never answered Sherman concerning his earlier proposal to capture Savannah. This is important because on 1 November, General George B. McClellan succeeded Winfield Scott as the General-in-Chief of the Armies of the United States. McClellan ignored Sherman's request because he was, at this time, putting together an expedition to the sounds of North Carolina. He planned to allow his old friend, Major General Ambrose E. Burnside, to command the army forces. This expedition took precedent over other projects.

In late December, Sherman submitted Gillmore's two proposals to attack Charleston. Sherman's project, however, required more men and guns, which the War Department could not spare. The navy also was not in the position to offer the assistance required at Charleston. The stone fleet had closed, at least temporarily, the main channel into Charleston. The other channels were too shallow to allow the larger vessels into the harbor.[37]

With this operation uncertain, Du Pont and Sherman agreed to strike at the Confederates elsewhere. The rebels had begun to strengthen their position above Port Royal by obstructing the Coosaw River and Whale Branch with piles. Additionally, they built heavy batteries at the crossings of the Port Royal Ferry and at Seabrook. Both Sherman and Du Pont felt the Confederates might decide to close the river completely, isolate Port Royal, and cross over the Coosaw in force. With the navy stretched thin, Du Pont scraped together gunboats to probe up the narrow and shallow Coosaw River. They could approach either of these enemy earthworks from Hilton Head by water from the western side by traveling up the Broad River and then into Whale Branch. The eastern route passed through Beaufort River and then into Brickyard Creek to enter the Coosaw River. Du Pont put Raymond Rodgers in overall command of the expedition, and he took the eastern route with the gunboats *Ottawa* and *Pembina*, the tug *E. B. Hale* and four boats from *Wabash* armed with howitzers. Lieutenant Commander Ammen took the *Seneca* and tug *Ellen* up the Broad River to approach the batteries at Seabrook and Port Royal Ferry by the way of Whale Branch.[38]

Rodgers readied his gunboats, having the topmasts housed and the rigging "snaked down." He concealed the approach of his warships by leaving Beaufort after dark on 31 December, then ascended the river and anchored for the remainder of the night about two miles from the Coosaw. At 4:00 A.M. he moved on with launches and joined Brigadier General Isaac I. Stevens' brigade strengthened by two New York regiments in flats, launches, and boats. In a thick fog, the craft steered across the river and at 8:00 A.M. the first group landed under the cover of two howitzers from the *Wabash*'s boats. At sunrise the *Ottawa* successfully sounded through the difficult Brickyard Channel passage and passed up the narrow river. *Pembina* and the *E. B. Hale* arrived shortly thereafter. The remaining troops disembarked that morning and the gunboats anchored at 10:00 A.M. to cover the advancing column. Rodgers took the

Hale to within range of the battery at Port Royal Ferry and fired at the earthwork, but received no reply.[39]

At 1:30 the army was ready to move. With army signalmen on board to communicate with the troops ashore and to direct the gunfire, Rodgers' gunboats began shelling the woods. The shells fell in advance of the skirmishers moving towards Port Royal Ferry. The gunboats threw a rapid fire into the fort effecting "a perfect concert of action afloat and ashore." At 2:40 the vessels lay anchored with kedge anchors in front of the fort. Rodgers entered the works and found them abandoned and only one gun and some ammunition inside.[40]

Earlier that morning Ammen brought the *Seneca* and the *Ellen* into Whale Branch and embarked the Seventy-Ninth New York Infantry. A mile farther up stream the river narrowed and an earthwork at Seabrook guarded the river where the ferry once crossed. The two warships anchored and shelled the work without a reply. Meanwhile a force of three hundred men debarked into scows and landed at the earthwork and found it unfinished with a single gun mounted. The troops destroyed the works.[41]

That afternoon Ammen's force passed into Broad River and came within signal distance of the other naval force. Low tide prevented Ammen's gunboats from joining Rodgers until later that afternoon and the *Seneca* did not arrive until the next morning. On the second, the enemy appeared in the woods in force and the five gunboats opened a "hot fire" on these men and drove them back into the woods. Each time the Union infantry advanced beyond the cover of the gunboats, the rebels drove them back. Additionally, each time the enemy troops advanced, the large guns of the naval vessels laid down a deadly barrage, forcing the Confederates back to the safety of the woods. An aide on General Stevens staff wrote, "The facts is [sic] the frightful effects of the explosions of the 11-inch shell which some of our gunboats carry have produced a great panic among the land forces of South Carolina." Most of the Confederate casualties resulted from the naval gunfire. By noon the Union soldiers recrossed the ferry under the covering fire of the warships and the Confederate forces withdrew to the interior. At 2:00 P.M. Rodgers signaled the gunboats to move back down the Coosaw River, but low water compelled them to wait for the morning tide to pass through the Brickyard Channel.[42]

The naval vessels made this entire operation possible. The Confederate forts never fired a shot and the naval vessels kept the enemy troops from concentrating to attack the Union troops. Despite this contribution,

General Sherman belittled the navy's efforts in his report to Washington. He claimed the naval vessels had served merely as reserves, remaining in the rear of the storming parties. Yet the army never stormed any works. This successful joint operation ensured that the Coosaw River remained the dividing line between the Union and Confederate pickets. It also ended the Confederates' attempt to control this part of the interior rivers and quelled a potential move against Port Royal Island.[43]

Operations Against Savannah

One of the two ports initially discussed as desirable along the South Atlantic coast was Fernandina, Florida. After the capture of Port Royal, Du Pont and Sherman discussed a move on this town. The operations against the Confederates, however, had succeeded so well along the whole coast that both men felt that Fernandina's capture was now less crucial. Du Pont was anxious to attack Fernandina just after the fall of Port Royal, fearing that the soldiers would "absorb the fleet" with other projects. But the Confederates' virtual abandonment of the coast from North Edisto to Ossabaw Sound made it prudent for the Union forces to occupy this broader area rather than push on farther south. Sherman, however, blamed the delay on the "want of readiness" of the navy. Sherman also felt that a major problem was the lack of unified command. He remarked that if either he or Du Pont had had sole responsibility for joint operations that they would have accomplished more.[44]

Since Fernandina was no longer as attractive, General Sherman began promoting an attack on Savannah. The fall of this city would cause the enemy to abandon all the forts south of St. Simon's Sound and Brunswick. Near the end of December, both Sherman and Du Pont agreed to launch a powerful coup de main against Savannah. Savannah was one of the South's largest and most important cities. With a population of about fourteen thousand, the city's commercial activities occupied most of its inhabitants. Before the war, the city exported nearly twenty million dollars worth of cotton and lumber.[45]

There were three main approaches to Savannah. The major route, up the Savannah River, would require bypassing Fort Pulaski. To do this, the navy faced a "narrow and difficult" Savannah River Channel. They could also attack Savannah from the rear by two routes. The first included a passage through Wassaw Sound, up the Wilmington River and then into Tybee Creek, which connected to the Savannah River about four miles below the city. The second route passed through Ossabaw

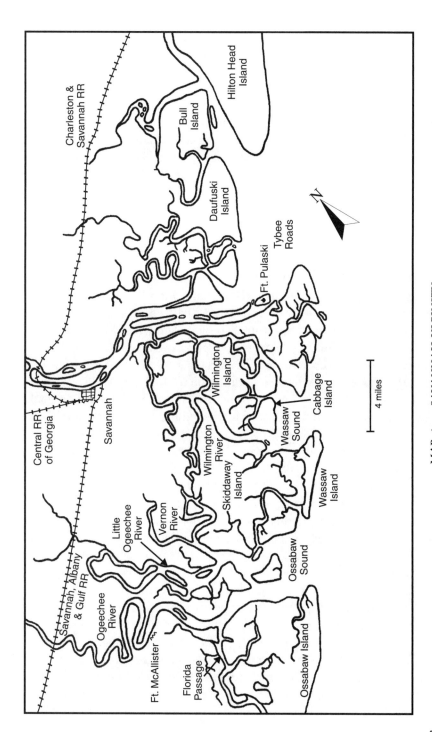

MAP 4. SAVANNAH VICINITY

Sound and then up the Vernon River, the same thoroughfare the French took during the American Revolution. The Confederates had defended all three of these passages well. Should the Union forces capture the city, Fort Pulaski would fall without a fight. Sherman did not feel he could bypass Fort Pulaski and believed the only feasible plan included the reduction of the fort. The War Department approved of the siege, but did not answer Sherman until late February and then sanctioned only a coup de main. Reconnaissance missions and intelligence data gained from local contrabands encouraged both Du Pont and Sherman that they could isolate and bypass the fort and starve its garrison out rather than bombarding it into submission.[46]

While Sherman waited for his siege material, Du Pont sent John Rodgers to find out if they could operate in the shallow waterways above Pulaski. General Sherman hoped that the naval vessels could enter the Savannah River above Fort Pulaski and protect disembarking troops at the rear of Fort Jackson. In early January, John Rodgers and Captain Quincy Gillmore made an examination of Freeborn's Cut, also called Wilmington Narrows. This waterway connected the Wilmington and Tybee rivers and ran parallel to the Savannah River with an outlet into the latter about seven miles above Fort Pulaski. Access via this waterway would give the naval vessels admission to the Savannah River above Fort Pulaski and might allow the navy to land troops behind Fort Jackson. Rodgers and Gillmore also interviewed black pilots thoroughly familiar with these channels.[47]

Ten days later Rodgers surveyed the northern side of the Savannah River, north of Fort Pulaski. In this "labyrinth of mud banks," an artificial channel that connected New and Wright's rivers, named Wall's Cut, appeared to be a promising route to get above Fort Pulaski. The Confederates obstructed this passage with rows of large pilings and a sunken bark. An army expedition clandestinely sawed the pilings off near the bottom and dragged the wreck out of the channel, leaving a passage sixty feet wide with about fourteen feet of water at high tide. The Confederates discovered this too late and Tattnall managed to come down only once with three steamers to disrupt the work.[48]

While the army removed the obstructions in Wall's Cut, John Rodgers, John Sanford Barnes, and Sherman's chief topographical engineer, Lieutenant James H. Wilson, performed a night survey of this area. Rodgers considered this channel too shallow to risk running the gunboats through until he could buoy or stake the channel. Mud River, for example, had only eighteen inches of water at extreme low tide. Should

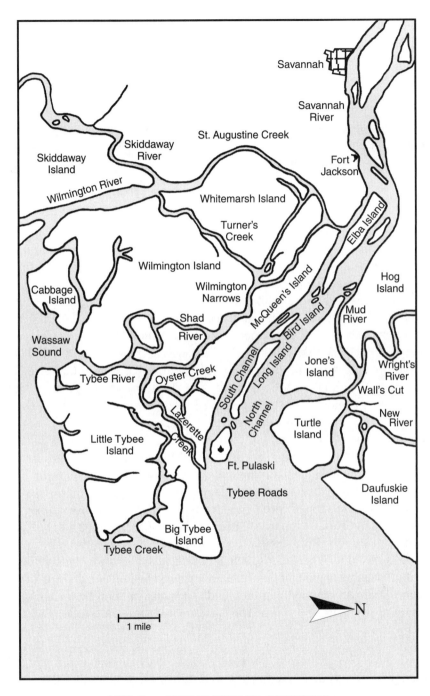

MAP 5.   APPROACHES TO SAVANNAH

one of the vessels get aground they would be vulnerable to the enemy's guns for as long as twelve hours. The army officers viewed this as a delay on the part of the navy. One officer wrote, "The Navy will not venture into the Savannah till they are reinforced, and we can do nothing about them." He continued, "We are all disgusted with the navy. They have detained us in everything we have yet undertaken." Both John Sanford Barnes and Wilson disagreed with Rodgers' assessment of the channel. But Du Pont trusted Rodgers' "skill and judgement." He wrote that Rodgers has more "knowledge of such things than all of them put together . . ." He thus implicitly would not offer Sherman any of his vessels for such a move. Du Pont realized that this decision would leave the army feeling that he was "uncooperative."[49]

Both Fox and Welles remained anxious about attacking the enemy farther south. For weeks Sherman got no response from the War Department and without orders would not commit to any operation. Du Pont, meanwhile, continued "pushing reconnaissances." Fox, in particular, pressed the flag officer to strike south. Du Pont had to remind Fox that he had already accomplished more than the original plan of the department by taking seven ports and holding five. He had not lost interest in the "Florida business," but it was a question of not having enough ships. After all, he could not abandon places they had already captured. Du Pont could sense that the operation was shaping up, but he did not always share this with Welles lest he "might raise expectations . . . which could not be realized."[50]

Sherman and Du Pont and their staffs met on the *Wabash* to discuss the expedition. Sherman had still not received the light-draft steam transports the War Department promised. Instead, when the War Department earlier diverted these steamers and a large number of small boats to the Hatteras Expedition, it constrained the later movements on the South Atlantic seaboard. On board *Wabash* Sherman and Du Pont discussed using sailing vessels to transport the men that the transports could not carry. The dearth of light draft steamers and boats to land troops was an obstacle too great, at least in Du Pont's mind, to overcome. Sherman claimed that if he had the transportation he would have attacked without the navy. The absence of these resources and the tremendous responsibilities of the squadron caused Du Pont to later change his mind about a sudden strike on Savannah. He also felt that naval vessels could not attack Fort Jackson from the river and learned the rebels had prepared fire rafts. He believed the risk to his vessels too great with so little to gain. Sherman blamed the failure on a "want of cooperation of the navy." Despite the impasse, Sherman and Du Pont turned their proposed coup de main on Savannah into an elaborate feint on the city. They did this in an attempt to pull enemy troops away from Fernandina, their next objective.[51]

The Feint

Both Du Pont and Sherman agreed that they had to accomplish something while they awaited the siege train. They agreed to make a "strong demonstration" on Savannah in order to alarm the city and then move on to Fernandina. The feint comprised two squadrons of warships. A force under Fleet Captain Davis would probe up the south side of the Savannah River; the force under Rodgers would operate north of the Savannah River. On 26 January, Davis and Raymond Rodgers readied their warships. Davis' command included *Ottawa* and *Seneca* and the *Isaac Smith*, the screw steamers *Potomska* and *Western World*, and the side-wheel steamer *Ellen* as well as the armed launches of the *Wabash*. The army transports *Boston, Delaware,* and *Cosmopolitan* carried three regiments to give the feint more realism. The army forces commanded by Brigadier General Horatio G. Wright followed the naval vessels and anchored in Wassaw Sound. Davis' gunboats proceeded, but the shallowness of the bar prevented the vessels from entering Tybee River until 8:30 A.M. the next day. They did not pass above Fort Pulaski until that afternoon. Heavy piles blocked Davis' progress and he launched boats from all his warships to make a reconnaissance in the nearby creeks and tributaries. On the morning of 28 January, John Rodgers and the *Unadilla*, the *Pembina*, and the small screw steamer *Henry Andrew* meanwhile steamed into Wright's River to Wall's Cut on the north side of the river. *Unadilla* and *Henry Andrew* passed through at high tide, but the *Pembina* grounded.[52]

The sight of the Union warships convinced the Confederates that this was a major assault on Fort Pulaski. With provisions and ammunition low, and afraid the Union forces would cut communications with the fort, Flag Officer Tattnall mounted an expedition to carry a six-month's stock of ammunition and provisions to Pulaski. On 27 January Tattnall prepared his flotilla of five steamers and steamed down the river. Flagship *Savannah* and the armed steamers *Resolute* and *Sampson* escorted the transport *Ida* and the steamer *Bartow* with scows of supplies in tow. They moved downriver and came to anchor off Elba Island in the South Channel.[53]

Davis could see Tattnall's vessels in the river, but heavy pilings blocked his way into the Savannah River. While boats examined the channels looking for deeper water, Lieutenant Commander Ammen observed a telegraph wire connecting Fort Pulaski with Savannah. Davis directed a junior officer to cut the wire but he returned an hour later, unsuccessful. Disgusted with this unenthusiastic attempt, Ammen called for his gig and poled along the marsh and then waded, knee deep in mud, to cut the wire personally in several places.[54]

At 11:15 on the morning of the twenty-eighth, Tattnall's flotilla tried to pass down the Savannah River to Fort Pulaski. John Rodgers' vessels in Wall's Cut and Davis' in Little Tybee River (Wilmington Narrows) lay on either side of the river and only about four miles separated the two Union forces. Tattnall had to run between the two Union forces to resupply the fort and placed his transports in advance. When Tattnall did this, Union officers may have felt they had an opportunity to let Tattnall's fleet get below them and then cut him off from the city. Tattnall, however, let *Sampson*, *Ida*, and *Bartow* run down the river, and *Savannah* and *Resolute* remained behind. When the Union officers realized what had happened, both sides fought a spirited engagement from three different rivers for less than an hour. Through the cannonade *Sampson*, *Ida*, and *Barstow* successfully passed to the fort.[55]

At 2:00 the firing resumed as Tattnall, with his flag at the fore, brought *Savannah* and *Resolute* back up the river. Low tide aided the Confederate vessels because the banks of the river protected them. By this time, both 90-day gunboats *Unadilla* and *Pembina* were aground. Both sides kept up a terrific fire, but not a single shot struck during the afternoon skirmish. Only the *Sampson* claimed an injury during the day's fights. Four shells struck her during the morning engagement as she passed down the river. Two passed through her, a third struck the deck, and the last exploded in the ship's storeroom, but did little damage.[56]

This encounter proved several things. The navy could not prevent communication with Fort Pulaski from these points in the river. The warships could only do so by controlling points farther up the river. Both Du Pont and Sherman also realized that in order to approach Savannah from this direction, they should occupy Wilmington Island with a strong force. Lastly, the shallow and narrow rivers would certainly complicate all the movements of the naval vessels.[57]

John Rodgers kept some of his vessels near Wall's Cut to continue probing the area. In early February Rodgers ran into the New River with *Unadilla*, *Pembina*, *Ottawa*, *Hale*, and *Henry Andrew*. They found a fortification and a heavy boom with a chain cable. They cut this obstruction and passed above it. Again they ran into narrow passages and the *Henry Andrew* damaged her rudder trying to turn. About two weeks later while operating in Wright's River, Rodgers discovered five electric torpedoes stretched across the entrance to the Savannah River. This weapon created immediate concerns among the Union officers. The mere threat of torpedoes would later complicate the operations of the squadron, and keep the naval forces cautious when moving into enemy waters.[58]

General Sherman meanwhile wished to stop rebel communications along the Savannah River and ordered the erection of a battery on Jones Island. He also hoped that this would make the feint look more realistic. By 11 February, army engineers placed six siege guns on Venus Point overlooking the Savannah River between Elba and Long islands. This army position, however, required gunboats to remain in Mud River to protect the batteries from being taken in reverse.[59]

The enemy quickly put the battery on Venus Point to the test. On the thirteenth the *Ida*, coming down the South Channel under full steam, successfully ran past the battery. The Union gunners fired nine shots and all but one of the guns recoiled off their platforms. The following day she attempted to return up river and four rebel steamers from Savannah joined her. In an engagement that lasted an hour, the Union gunners drove off the Confederate steamers. They managed to disable the *Savannah* and her consorts towed her out of danger. On the sixteenth the *Ida* returned to the fort and during an unusually high tide she steamed back to Savannah by way of Lazaretto Creek and Wilmington River. Unsure of continuing naval support and realizing the vulnerability of the battery, Sherman asked Du Pont for hulks to block Lazaretto Creek.[60]

Instead of consolidating and strengthening his positions, however, Sherman began putting troops ashore on Jones, Bird, and Daufuskie islands. These deployments gave the navy an additional responsibility— the protection and support of these positions. These detached posts could not be easily supported if the enemy attacked. This worried Brigadier General Egbert L. Viele and he regularly called for the protection of light-draft gunboats. Army officers began to imagine the presence of an ironclad in the Savannah River causing Sherman to plead for the protection of Viele's rear.[61]

Sherman had not yet received word from Washington concerning any of the operations. The delays occurred due to a long illness of General McClellan. During his incapacity he did not read any of Sherman's dispatches for weeks. When he finally digested them, the general had other problems in the Western Theatre and had troops and assets tied up in the Burnside Expedition. McClellan answered the dispatches for the first time on 12 February and decided to send the surfboats that Sherman had requested. With the opportunity for a coup de main lost, McClellan began looking for future opportunities. Two days after his initial letter, he suggested that Sherman plan to reduce Pulaski by bombardment. The War Department did not consider the city of Savannah to be worth putting under siege and instructed Sherman to concentrate his forces on Pulaski, Fernandina, and maybe St. Augustine. He felt, however, that the reduction of Charleston and its defenses would be "worthy of our greatest efforts and considerable sacrifices" as well as a moral victory for the North. On the fourteenth, he promised to send a siege train of heavy guns to accomplish the reduction of Fort Pulaski. The plans to capture Fernandina still pleased the department and about the time the equipment for the siege began to arrive, the expedition to capture the town was assembling.[62]

Despite the cancellation of the coup de main movement on Savannah, the feint had accomplished its goal of unnerving the Confederate forces. Du Pont felt positive about his accomplishments. He wrote Fox that the Union's combined operations had the enemy so unsettled that they were "flying about like moths around a lamp." Du Pont and Sherman for some time had planned to capture Fernandina but they had aborted the move several times. Late in February both the army and navy finally made the commitment to an expedition. Many believed Fernandina to be the most important port on the eastern coast of Florida. It lay only 430 miles from Nassau and served as the eastern terminus of the Florida Railroad that ran 155 miles across to Cedar Keys on the west coast of the state.[63]

The Capture of Fernandina

The defenses of Florida never received serious attention by the Confederate government. Given the sparse population of the state and the relative unimportance of the coastal towns, the leaders in Richmond did not consider its defense a high priority. When Forts Henry and Donelson in Tennessee fell on 6 and 16 February, respectively, Confederate leaders felt it necessary to draw their defensive lines tighter. This meant the abandonment of all the seaboard forts of Florida. On 19 February, General Lee ordered all the coastal forces to secure their artillery and to

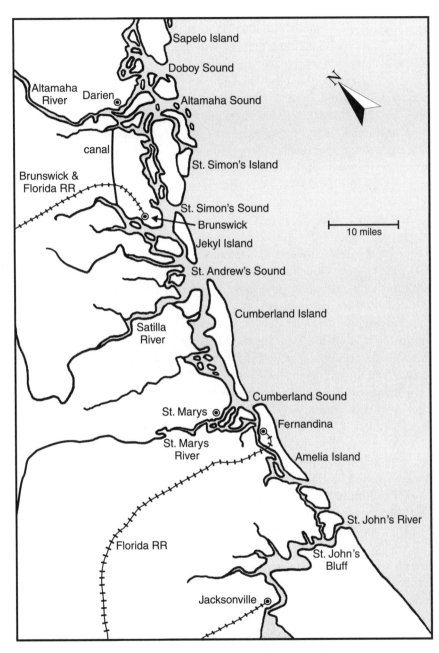

MAP 6. SOUTHEAST GEORGIA AND
NORTHERN FLORIDA COASTLINE

withdraw. The Confederates began to remove their ordnance, but a lack of transportation caused them to leave nearly half behind.[64] The Union forces did not know about the Confederate withdrawal, which left the route to Fernandina virtually undefended.

The most direct route to the city was by steaming into Cumberland Sound and up the Amelia River. Initially, General Sherman proposed that the navy enter the channel at Cumberland Sound and cut off the retreat of the troops in Fort Clinch, which guarded the entrance. Du Pont objected to this approach. His vessels would have to steam two miles up a narrow channel, under a raking fire, and without knowing the armament of the fort. By 24 February, the flag officer convinced Sherman that they should attack by moving the vessels through the sound behind Cumberland Island. Pilots believed the inside passage had sixteen feet of water and all but the *Susquehanna* and *Wabash* could pass through. This plan avoided any enemy batteries until the ships reached the flank and rear of Fort Clinch. The Confederates also believed that the western approach behind Cumberland Island was the most likely approach but had little to stop such an effort.[65]

Bad weather initially delayed the expedition, but on 28 February, a starlit night, a coston flare signaled the naval gunboats and army transports to get underway. On 2 March the vessels anchored off St. Andrew's Sound, twenty miles north of the Cumberland Sound entrance. Du Pont hoisted his flag on the screw steamer *Mohican* to direct the squadron through the inside passage to Cumberland Sound.[66]

Seventeen armed vessels and seven army transports felt their way behind Cumberland Island. The final plan agreed upon called for the naval vessels to steam to the southern end of Cumberland Island. Here, under a naval bombardment, Du Pont could put naval howitzers and seamen ashore to capture Confederate batteries on this island and prevent the escape of their garrisons. The remaining vessels would steam on toward Fort Clinch on Amelia Island and attack the batteries bearing on the Amelia River. After taking this fort, they planned to push up the river in order to get control of the railroad bridge where it crossed Kingsly's Creek. Troops meanwhile would land and capture the town. If the Confederates retreated before the gunboats could accommodate the army landing, the vessels would pursue the retreating enemy from the ocean and fire at them across the island.[67]

With *Ottawa* in the van, followed by Du Pont in the *Mohican*, the remaining gunboats and the revenue cutter *Henrietta* followed in line ahead. The seven transports brought up the rear on the journey through the inside passage. At 10:30 A.M. on 2 March, the vessels anchored so that they could examine the channel and wait for a higher tide. A black man approached the fleet in a small boat and informed Du Pont that the Confederates were hastily abandoning the works and withdrawing from Fernandina. Du Pont immediately detached the steamers that drew less than eleven feet and placed them under command of Percival Drayton in the steam sloop *Pawnee*. Du Pont instructed Drayton to advance to Fernandina as quickly as possible and to save the public property from destruction. He also sent instructions to Captain James L. Lardner of the *Susquehanna* to cut off any retreating force by sea. Du Pont left with the heavier ships by sea to Fernandina.[68]

Drayton left at daylight on 3 March with the *Pawnee* and eight other gunboats. In addition, three launches from the *Wabash* commanded by Raymond Rodgers, two army transports, and the cutter *Henrietta* accompanied Drayton. The navigation proved difficult and only *Pawnee*, *Ottawa*, and *Huron* managed to cross the shoals that divided Cumberland Sound. Drayton pushed these three vessels toward Fort Clinch but at 3:00 P.M., when only three miles from the fort, both the *Huron* and the *Pawnee* grounded. Not wishing to wait, Drayton and Rodgers boarded the *Ottawa* and continued with the three armed launches.[69]

As they approached Fort Clinch they found the works abandoned. Lieutenant George B. White cast off in an armed boat and pulled ashore to plant the American flag. Drayton insisted on forging ahead and the *Ottawa* continued her advance toward Fernandina. When the gunboat came to the outskirts of Old Fernandina, north of the main town, some of the town's inhabitants displayed a white flag. Drayton continued upriver, and just as he arrived at Fernandina a few rifle shots broke the silence. At the same moment lookouts spotted a train attempting to escape. Drayton directed Lieutenant Commander Thomas H. Stevens to take the *Ottawa* in pursuit. Under full steam the *Ottawa* began the chase and fired several shots at two locomotives and cars, but the train escaped across the railroad bridge at Kingsley's Creek.[70]

Raymond Rodgers pushed on toward the bridge in the one of the *Wabash*'s launches. Here he captured the steamer *Darlington* trying to escape upriver carrying women, children, military wagons, mules and forage. At 8:00 P.M. the *Ottawa* dropped back down the river to Fernandina. Rodgers then took the *Ottawa* and two cutters of the *Wabash* ten miles up river to the town of St. Marys and occupied the town just after midnight. The *Isaac Smith* arrived at St. Marys, and Lieutenant Commander Stevens took *Ottawa* on a reconnaissance fifty miles farther up the river, reaching a point called Woodstock Mills. Here, Confederate infantry attacked from both sides of the river. The *Ottawa*'s battery opened with grape and canister and drove the enemy away. While passing down the river, the *Ottawa* engaged cavalry and more infantry, but easily drove them away.[71]

On the morning of 4 March, both the *Huron* and the *Pawnee*, having come up during the night, anchored off the town of Fernandina. The *Pawnee* landed her Marines and a landing party from the *Wabash* to garrison the town. The beautiful homes with their gardens, flowers, and verandas impressed the naval officers. Only a few of the citizens remained behind, the rest having fled inland. The naval forces immediately secured the town to protect the public property and to assure the inhabitants that they meant no harm. Meanwhile, Drayton sent midshipman Mortimer L. Johnson up the rail line. Johnson managed to return with the two locomotives and three cars they had chased earlier along with stores of rosin, turpentine, and cotton.[72]

The naval officers felt that the Confederates had shown poor judgement by abandoning their forts and earthworks. The defenses included twenty-two masked batteries and the navy captured thirty-seven guns of heavy caliber. The officers considered the defenses of the area "formidable." Raymond Rodgers believed that the navy might have encountered heavy casualties trying to cross the unmarked bar under the fire of well-handled batteries at Fort Clinch. Drayton agreed and wrote, "they ought to have been able to keep out all the fleets of the Union combined, the bar being a very difficult one, and its turns bringing vessels directly under batteries almost end on for miles." Another participant wrote, "If the *Wabash* and large ships had attempted to pass them, I believe that they would have been blown out of the water." The navy's movement to the rear of the forts, however, made the positions less tenable.[73] Brigadier General Wright entered Fernandina Harbor on the fifth and landed his brigade, relieving the navy of its occupation duties.

On to Jacksonville, Brunswick, and St. Augustine

This easy conquest convinced Du Pont that he should press on toward Jacksonville, the portal to Eastern Florida, about thirty miles from the bar up the narrow and twisting St. John's River. On 7 March, Du Pont shifted his flag from the *Mohican* to the *Pawnee*. He instructed the commanding officers of *Ottawa*, *Seneca*, *Pembina*, *Huron*, *Isaac Smith*, and *Ellen* to cross the bar at the St. John's River and steam to Jacksonville. The vessels had difficulty crossing the bar because of the rough state of the sea. Only the *Ellen*, having a draft of eight feet, managed to quickly cross the bar. She took the *Wabash*'s launches and proceeded up river. On 11 March *Seneca*, *Pembina* and *Ottawa* managed to get across at 4:00 P.M. with "no water to spare" under their keels. These three steamers anchored at Mayport Mills, three miles upriver. The vessels stopped here to land troops and to secure the guns ashore. They waited until the next day to ascend the river. To avoid turning over valuable property to the approaching federal troops, the Confederates torched eight sawmills and over four million board feet of lumber as well as an iron foundry, ironwork shops, and a gunboat under construction.[74]

On the twelfth, the *Ellen* steamed to St. John's Bluff, about five miles above Mayport Mills, to capture the guns and munitions there. She accomplished this and then hurried on to Jacksonville. The local authorities in Jacksonville greeted the naval officers with a flag of truce. About a week later both the *Ellen* and *Ottawa* ventured about eighty miles up the St. John's River to Orange Mills. At Dunn's Creek they succeeded in raising the yacht *America* and towed her back down river.[75]

While the warships of the squadron secured the St. John's River, Du Pont also learned that the Confederates had abandoned Brunswick, Georgia. On 7 March, he immediately sent *Mohican*, *Pocahontas*, and *Potomska*, under the command of Godon, to hold that town. The gunboats entered St. Simon's Sound on the eighth and at sundown anchored within two miles of the forts below Brunswick. The following morning they steamed toward the forts and sent an armed launch ashore to take possession of St. Simon's Island. The enemy had abandoned two strong earthworks with twelve embrasures and well-constructed magazines. Additionally, they withdrew from two other batteries on Jekyll Island that the naval officers considered even stronger. These included a bomb-proof of palmetto logs, sandbags, and railroad iron.[76]

On the ninth, after examining the works, Commander Godon in the *Potomska* passed up the Brunswick River toward Brunswick. The capture of this town denied the Confederates another valuable logistical connection since it served as the terminus of the Brunswick and Florida Railroad. When the naval vessels hove into sight, the retreating Confederates set the wharf and the railroad depot on fire and retreated by train. Since Godon had the only pilot on board *Potomska*, he stood back down the river to bring up the *Mohican* and *Pocahontas*. The three ships steamed up opposite Brunswick and launches armed with howitzers landed Marines, a naval landing party, and two 12-pounder guns. Godon posted proclamations urging the inhabitants to come back and promised to protect their property.[77]

Godon left the *Mohican* at Brunswick and, on the thirteenth, proceeded with the *Potomska* and *Pocahontas* with the armed launch from the *Mohican* in tow. They steamed up the Altamaha River toward Darien in order to capture two rebel steamers. He found a double row of piles blocking the channel and after a few hours' work removed enough of the piles to proceed. At midnight, five miles upriver, he came to a second row of similar pilings. He managed to pass through these obstructions at about noon the following day and, just as he arrived off Darien, witnessed the flight of the steamers up the Altamaha River.[78]

On 11 March, in order to augment his holdings, Du Pont ordered the *Wabash* south to St. Augustine to reconnoiter. Lying off the bar in *Wabash*, he sent Raymond Rodgers in a boat to the town with a flag of truce. After crossing the bar with difficulty, Rodgers found a white flag flying over Fort Marion, and the city officials met Rodgers and placed the city under his control. The capture of this town had no strategic implications as the town served as a resort for invalids. The navy's interests, however, lay in its use by a couple of blockade runners and the privateer *Jefferson Davis* who had sent her prizes into this port. Knowing the Union forces would soon come, General Lee had suggested the rebel troops abandon the town. The night before Du Pont arrived, they sailed south to New Smyrna along with twenty percent of the town's inhabitants.[79]

These conquests had come much quicker and easier than anticipated. Both Sherman and Du Pont made limited arrangements to consolidate and protect this unexpected sweep of the coast of southern Georgia and northern Florida. Du Pont's instructions from Welles included a provision to hold Fernandina after its capture. Sherman sent extra troops and Du Pont sent more gunboats and the battalion of Marines under the command of Major John G. Reynolds.[80]

St. Augustine, however, was another matter. Sherman was "disappointed" at the navy's capture of the town and the flag officer found the General "lukewarm about holding Jacksonville . . . " Du Pont observed that Sherman seemed disturbed that he intended to use his Marine battalion to garrison St. Augustine. Du Pont felt that the army had unnecessarily sent troops on the expedition when the gunboats alone could have taken the town. Du Pont wrote that Sherman "flies about like a shuttlecock, imagining great things about Savannah and Charleston." Greater friction began to appear between the two after the initial strike at Fernandina. This might have resulted because Sherman had no specific orders after the capture of this town. Sherman's command had no prescribed limits whereas Du Pont's command stretched to Cape Canaveral and within his domain he had carte blanche to capture anything. Du Pont commented, "I conceive I could not only take St. Augustine—of course without asking him [Sherman] if I please—but hold it too."[81]

The garrisoning of St. Augustine with Marines was more than Sherman could take. Shortly after learning that Du Pont had disembarked his battalion, he sent two companies of the Fourth New Hampshire Regiment, under the command of Lieutenant Colonel Louis Bell, to garrison the town. Since Bell outranked Major Reynolds, Du Pont felt no need to keep the Marines there and sent them back to Washington. Raymond Rodgers believed that Sherman's actions were "the most unhandsome thing he has done."[82]

Fifty miles farther south the navy continued to probe Confederate positions. Thinking that Mosquito Inlet served as a base for small shallow-draft blockade runners, Du Pont instructed the *Henry Andrew* and *Penguin* to cross the Mosquito Inlet bar, buoy the river, and blockade the river from the inside. Also in his instructions he asked the crews to secure a large quantity of live oak timber on shore near Smyrna, Florida.[83] On 21 March Acting Lieutenant Commander Thomas A. Budd and Acting Master S. W. Mather organized an expedition with about five small boats and just over forty men. They made a reconnaissance some fifteen miles upriver and returned on the twenty-second. Within sight of the *Henry Andrew*, Mather and Budd, in advance of the other boats, landed at an earthwork to reconnoiter. Concealed by a dense thicket, a large number of enemy troops opened fire on the party. The initial volley killed Budd instantly, and mortally wounded Mather. The other boats came under fire as they passed down river. Some of the men had to hide ashore until dark before returning to the ships. The Confederates managed to kill two officers and six men and wounded seven more. They also took three prisoners. Budd's and Mather's death upset Du Pont who wrote his wife, "How sorry I feel for both!"[84]

The Blockade

Du Pont's naval forces had made great strides in capturing the ports along the South Atlantic coast. Despite diminishing the number of ports, the flag officer had not been able to show a real improvement of the blockade's efficiency. When the *Nashville* cleared Charleston Harbor as a warship on 29 October 1861, it struck a major blow at the prestige of Du Pont's blockade. This sortie also caused the department to scrutinize closely the blockade of the South Atlantic coast. On 12 November, days after the gunboats moved to capture Beaufort, South Carolina, the *Fingal* steamed into the Savannah River in a thick fog. The passing of this steamer through the blockade was another blow to both Du Pont and the blockade. This vessel carried an entire cargo of military supplies for the South including 14,000 Enfield rifles; 1,000,000 cartridges; 2,000,000 percussion caps; thousands of sabers, rifles, bayonets, and revolvers; 10 rifled cannon and ammunition; 400 barrels of powder; medical supplies; blankets; coats; and shoes. Just over a week after the *Fingal* ran into Savannah, Welles admonished Du Pont for the laxity of the blockade at both Savannah and Charleston. The timing of this event could not have been worse for Du Pont. With the riverine operations at Savannah underway, the flag officer had only two vessels to watch each of these ports.[85]

The early blockade of the South Atlantic coast suffered from a want of gunboats more than from any other symptom. The squadron patrolled the South Atlantic coast from South Carolina to Key West, covering a distance of 700 miles. Du Pont lamented to his wife that the "most difficult part of my command has been the blockade." He frequently asked for more warships to augment the squadron. Despite the numerous activities of the squadron, Welles continued to stress vigilance and the need of a "rigorous blockade." While he confided in Du Pont's knowledge and expertise, he insisted that Du Pont spread his vessels along the coast and not concentrate them at one point. He conceded that some ships may run the blockade on dark nights or bad weather and concluded by telling Du Pont he would reinforce his command.[86]

Early in the war Du Pont placed his steamers in and near the major channels leading to the ports. The smaller vessels often changed position while the larger vessels, which consumed great amounts of fuel, remained anchored. The smaller warships remained as close to shore as their drafts would permit. A single vessel, the *Mohican*, cruised between Savannah and Fernandina until December when Du Pont could spare the side-wheel steamer *Bienville* to lay off the latter port.[87]

Because of the geography of the coastline, and the fact that the Confederates lacked ordnance and men to defend the numerous inlets, Du Pont was able to maintain a close or inside blockade. The capture of Tybee Island, Fernandina, St. Augustine, Jacksonville, and Brunswick altered the blockade greatly. This allowed even greater access with little to fear from the enemy. His small and shallow draft vessels anchored directly in the fairways of the inlets. In most cases even a lightly armed gunboat could control the approaches and effectively close or constrict the trade. Du Pont felt that vessels like the *Mohican* were particularly valuable. By April 1862 Du Pont could boast that eight major waterways had an inside blockade—this virtually stopped any potential trade at these points.[88]

This type of blockade, however, required that the anchorages and channels be well marked. The Union vessels had to move about in these shallow and confined waters to maintain a vigilant watch. An almost unsung hero was Charles Boutelle of the United States Coast Survey, who systematically surveyed and marked all the major sounds and harbors along the South Atlantic seaboard. The Lighthouse Board also sent buoy tenders and lightships to tend the aids to navigation in the ports. This allowed the gunboats to safely maintain their presence in these waters.[89]

While Du Pont kept most of these vessels directly in the fairways and as close to shore as possible, he did use steamers farther at sea. In the first months the frigate *Savannah*, blockading the Savannah River, kept her station about ten miles off shore and later anchored closer to Fort Pulaski. Because of her large size, however, she could not expect to catch a blockade runner. Nontheless, her guns, controlled a large expanse of water and her commanding officer, Commander John S. Missroon, directed the movement of the other blockaders from the frigate. At night the two other vessels on blockade here remained close to shore. They showed no lights, kept up their boarding nettings, and anchored outside the range of the *Savannah*'s guns to avoid being mistaken for a blockade runner.[90]

The types of ships in the squadron influenced both the effectiveness of the blockade and the positioning of the ships. The large frigates *Savannah*, *St. Lawrence*, and *Wabash* drew too much water to be useful as blockaders. Off Charleston they served as beacons—the *Wabash*'s "huge hull and lofty spars made her a conspicuous object day or night." Du Pont later considered them "obsolete" and returned all but *Wabash* north. Since the deep-drafted ships could not serve well close off the southern coast, Du Pont began sending them to sea. In December, the flag officer instructed Captain Hugh Y. Purviance in the frigate *St. Lawrence* to cruise on an outside track between Georgetown and Savannah Sound, a line of about 130 miles. In good weather he was to communicate with all the vessels blockading the inlets between these two points. This gave Du Pont coverage between the major inlets and a vessel to watch enemy activity at the points of entrance. Du Pont grew tired of the frigates, not only because their deep drafts did not allow them to patrol close to shore, but also because they used many more supplies than the smaller warships. While Du Pont had only a few sailing vessels attached to his command, he was "painfully impressed with the worthlessness of sailing vessels" for both the blockade and military operations.[91]

Du Pont actively involved himself with the details of the numerous military operations, but on blockade matters he gave to his senior officers present (SOP) great discretion and latitude to make decisions. The flag officer's presence at Port Royal, though, allowed him to adjust the blockade constantly to meet the specific challenges. The early procedures of the blockade of the South Atlantic coast were somewhat formal. Off Charleston, where the largest concentration of ships lay, the SOP kept the vessels in the main channels and, when possible, lying off the coast north and south. Only the warship wearing the "guard flag" chased unidentified vessels. When lookouts spotted a suspicious vessel they sent a signal to the senior officer, who in turn instructed this ship to give chase. The other vessels remained at anchor about four miles off the coast and moved only when necessary.[92]

Orders prescribed that the commanding officers observe rigid and formal rules to maintain the blockade. Vessels anchoring or getting underway had to get the permission, by signal, of the SOP. Commanding officers also had to report if they sent down yards or loosed sail. They even had to signal if the ship lay moored or dropped a single anchor. The captain of an arriving ship had to report to the SOP immediately. If a lookout spotted a blockade runner, the captain had to go through the formality of signaling the SOP to ask permission to chase. At night the ships did not strike bells and used coston flares or flashing lights to signal the other vessels. Often at night the SOP's vessel wore a lantern at her peak, but this only provided the blockade runners the whereabouts of the blockaders.[93]

The blockade of Charleston, more than any other port, received great scrutiny from foreign governments, politicians, naval administrators and the press. In December 1861 the British felt the blockade of both Savannah and Charleston ineffective for small vessels but adequate to keep large vessels from evading the blockade. In February 1862 the Philadelphia *Daily Evening Bulletin* printed an article that claimed sixty-five vessels had run out of Charleston since the war began. This caused Senator John P. Hale, the chairman of the Committee on Naval Affairs, to call for an investigation. The fact is that many small sailing vessels had run the blockade, but only seven steam vessels had arrived or cleared during this period. In April the New York *Times* reported that fifty-four vessels had arrived at Nassau from South Atlantic ports since June 1861. Most of these, however, were sloops and schooners, and thirty-five of these types had successfully eluded the blockaders since 1 January. Thirty-two of these vessels had run out of Charleston. Du Pont felt it necessary to remind Commander John R. Goldsborough, the senior officer off Charleston, that he commended his zeal but that he trusted that he would be "able effectually to close up Charleston . . ."[94]

Logistical Concerns

Steam propulsion revolutionized the navy, but it also brought with it unique logistical problems. Repairs to steam machinery required special knowledge and tools. Major repairs required a visit to a navy yard with a machine shop. The navy provided Du Pont a mixture of regular and converted naval ships. He believed that the purchased vessels in his squadron had "turned out remarkably well" and were useful. Several "lame ducks" constantly needed repairs and their engines overhauled, causing the engineers to be "tinkering all the time" to keep them running. Most of the gunboats had not seen a shipyard for months. The absence of vessels and the need to keep a certain number of warships deployed left the flag officer constantly playing a shell game. With some of the vessels constantly "lame ducks," it required shifting these ships to less vulnerable stations or to stations where they likely would not have to move. The flag officer wrote his wife, "My vessels are coming in all the time broken down, the truth is they have been tried to the utmost." During the first months of his command, Du Pont had the capability to have minor repairs made to woodwork and to engines at Port Royal, but most of the major repair work still required travel to a northern shipyard.[95]

When Du Pont sailed south with his invasion fleet, he had a fair idea of the logistical requirements of his newly formed squadron. As the former commandant of the Philadelphia Navy Yard, he had experienced these situations. He was able to discern problems and offer solutions. Within a week of his capture of Port Royal, Du Pont wrote Fox suggesting that they fit out a floating machine shop in Port Royal. He cited the British use of one in the Crimean War and mentioned that he had earlier visited a French floating machine shop in Hong Kong. He related their "remarkable advantages" because they had all the convenience of those on shore and vessels were always coming and going for repairs.[96]

Initially the Bureau of Construction and Repair made provisions to prefabricate two buildings to serve as a machine shop ashore similar to the one at Fort Monroe. The bureau planned to send them to Port Royal along with eleven artisans to perform the work. Fate intervened with the arrival of the Stone Fleets. Instead of sinking the most valuable whalers for obstructions, Du Pont had seven of them saved to serve as logistics hulks for the squadron.[97]

The two most important were the 366-ton ship *India* and the 340-ton bark *Edward*. The *India* was the most expensive ship per ton that sailed with the Stone Fleet. When the prefabricated buildings arrived, Du Pont instead used these structures to cover over the ships themselves. Chained together, both ships remained moored in Station Creek to serve the repair needs of the squadron. All the material to outfit these vessels as shops arrived in Port Royal in the winter of 1861. William B. Cogswell, a master mechanic, supervised the work. Master mechanic W. S. Kimball supervised the entire operation.[98]

These whalers became indispensable to the squadron. They transformed the *India* into a blacksmith's shop. By 1863 she employed nearly 100 men with several furnaces on board. She also stored her coal for the furnaces on board and served as a storage facility and barracks. The *Edward* served as a machine shop and five compartments divided the second deck. In the bow was a shop where craftsmen made patterns and molds for castings. The workmen also slept here in hammocks. The next compartment aft was the brass foundry, iron furnaces, and the coppersmith's room. Aft of this compartment was a blacksmith's and boilermaker's shop. It contained a large furnace for forging important items such as grate bars for the boilers, and heavy objects such as shafts and cranks weighing as much as one thousand pounds. The shop could also make castings here that weighed upwards of five hundred pounds. Near the other end of the bark they placed a machine shop with steam engines. The engines ran five lathes, the largest of which could turn a casting thirty-six inches in diameter. Here workmen also used planing machines, bolt cutters, and punches to cut holes in boiler iron. The aftermost compartments contained an office and another berthing area. Between decks accommodated berthing, mess rooms, and storerooms. The hold stored coal for the operation of the furnaces and steam machinery.[99]

These hulks served the squadron well for nearly two years. They handled many repairs without sending the vessels north, where delays could keep a ship awaiting repairs for months. Once the squadron grew, however, these facilities could not handle all of the necessary work. By the fall of 1863, Cogswell wanted to move part of the foundry work ashore and requested a thousand-square-foot building and the necessary boiler, engines, and castings to start work. Eventually, they built a foundry and quarters for the workmen ashore along with a wharf to expedite repair work.[100]

Repairs to woodwork were also vital. Ships strained their hulls in the rough weather, opening the planking to major leaking. In addition, vessels hurriedly constructed with green timber later suffered leaks. Many of the squadron's vessels operated in shallow water, where contact with the bottom tore copper off the bottom, strained timbers, and tore away rudders. Du Pont therefore employed carpenters to perform the necessary woodwork. Initially, the carpenter's mates lived on the old ship of the line, *Vermont*, but eventually, the carpentry work increased to such an extent that the *Vermont* no longer could accommodate the work. Du Pont therefore had the 341-ton side-wheel steamer *Ellen* converted to a carpenter's shop and by April 1864 this shop employed thirty-five men who lived on board. By this time she was no longer afloat and lay beached; at high tide water flowed through her open bottom. Despite this inadequacy, she continued to serve the squadron.[101]

The use of Port Royal as a logistical base worked well because it was central to the entire command and reduced the travel time necessary to make repairs or obtain coal or supplies. The largest number of warships in the command lay on the Charleston blockade, only hours away from the depot. When the facilities at Port Royal could not make the repairs, the blockaders traveled north to the navy or private yards. This usually meant an absence for a long period. The yards were overtaxed with work and never showed improvement in making repairs during the war. These facilities handled an average of three vessels before the war and were now working on dozens. Du Pont noted that the navy yards needed improved facilities as well as better direction and supervision.[102]

The private yards performed work when the navy yards were full. Baltimore could handle smaller vessels, but the naval officers almost universally condemned the work there. Du Pont could never remember any work "decently done for the Government in Baltimore." Poor work, delays, and overcharging were common. The *Flag* stayed there for ninety-six days and left the yard not much better than she had arrived. In one incident, the government spent $40,000 in repairs on a ship worth only $96,000. Du Pont complained that the repairs would have been finished in thirty days in a navy yard, even as slow as they worked there. Instead the government gave money "to some pretended Union men of Baltimore." The squadron also sent warships for minor repairs to Jacksonville, where local mechanics and carpenters performed the work.[103]

Du Pont found one practice of repairing vessels seriously flawed. When the warships arrived to receive repairs, the crew went on leave. If the repairs were to take some time, the crew transferred to other ships awaiting men. Du Pont suggested that only half the crew be allowed to take leave or transfer and that the other half remain behind on the ship to move guns, work on the masts, and help with the repairs. He believed this would expedite the repairs and improve morale. The navy was short of men and not ships and therefore did not adopt Du Pont's recommendation.[104]

The warships suffered numerous maladies that made them less efficient and sometimes endangered the vessel and the crews. Du Pont remarked, "One disease is chronic in all the ships: broken engines." The need of boiler repairs constituted the main complaint. The constant use of the machinery denied the engineers sufficient time for maintenance and repairs. Repairs to leaking boiler tubes required drawing the fires, which was often not practicable. This particular ailment decreased the speed of the vessel and had an impact on her efficiency as a blockader. The *Flag*, though judged a useful ship, had been "almost useless" for some time. Her repairs waited for so long that the bottom of her boiler "dropped out" and it had to be supported by blocks of wood. All the commanding officers, however, were still learning about the long-term and constant use of steam machinery. Du Pont lamented that "not to haul fires for seventy-five and eighty days, then only for two or three days, to be immediately followed up by a repetition of long service, has never before been attempted."[105]

In addition to engine breakdowns, the competency of the engineers was a common source of discussion. Du Pont decided early that he would not send ships north for repairs unless a survey pronounced them entirely broken down. Du Pont claimed they had to make repairs daily, not only when the ships lay in the Northern yards. He found the volunteer engineers could not "compare in respectability with a half dozen of our firemen, nor in knowledge . . ." Nevertheless, because of the dearth of qualified individuals, it was necessary to keep the positions in the ships filled.[106]

The logistical concerns regarding coal supplies kept Du Pont looking for ways to improve the system. Coal consumption had a direct impact on operations and affected the blockading procedure. Du Pont instructed his officers early in the war that, generally, the blockaders "should not chase far off the coast, as it consumes coal . . . ." Du Pont found it necessary to conserve coal whenever possible and at times found it necessary to borrow large amounts from the army. The dearth of coal had officers anxious to conserve fuel and caused them to be "inactive." Because of a lack of storage facilities, the 314-ton bark *Harvest*, the 243-ton bark *Garland* and the 330-ton bark *Margaret Scott* were all kept as coal storage hulks. The squadron also used the 554-ton store ship *Courier* for a while.[107]

Upon his arrival on the South Atlantic Coast, Du Pont realized that his squadron would also need a depot ship to store supplies and house supernumeraries. The *Vermont*, which arrived in February 1862, served in this capacity. The ship's first commanding officer, Commander Augustus S. Baldwin, and Du Pont did not work well together. Du Pont complained to Paymaster Horatio Bridge, the Chief of the Bureau of Provision and Clothing, "Oh! What an elephant that ship has been!" He found Baldwin incompatible with the job. He believed that Baldwin had some "sort of delusion, fostered by the Department when it put a battery on the ship, that she was a *man-of-war* and sent out as such; of course, to him, the storekeeper and his stores are there on sufferance."[108]

After only four months of Baldwin's mismanagement, the *Vermont* became overburdened with more than she could handle. Baldwin failed to resolve many of the problems he might have easily corrected. Du Pont wrote Baldwin, "While I fully appreciate and commend what I infer is your desire to keep the *Vermont* efficient as a vessel of war or guardship in this harbor, I have to repeat that this laudable spirit on your part must yield to a safe and convenient disposition of the public stores and property, to their accessibility day or night." Du Pont wrote that he had looked for other ships to relieve the *Vermont* of her burden with no results. He concluded, saying he would look at ways to fit the vessel to accommodate storekeeper's supplies.[109]

Within three months of this letter, Du Pont transferred Baldwin and the *Vermont* received a new commanding officer. Commander William Reynolds, the brother of General John F. Reynolds, replaced Baldwin. Reynolds would be a perfect match for this job. Reynolds had received an appointment as midshipman at age fifteen in 1831. He left the navy for a nine-year period before again being employed as a naval storekeeper in Honolulu in 1857. Reynolds was an extremely competent and conscientious officer. He served not only as the commanding officer of the *Vermont*, but also commanded the naval depot at Port Royal. Since these facilities were subordinate to the squadron, Reynolds had more authority and rarely had to communicate with Washington, receiving his orders from the flag officer. As senior officer present, he received all signals, directed the anchorages, gave permission to get underway, received visits from other officers, approved requisitions, and signed correspondence. He oversaw all the repairs, and the chief engineer, machinists, and carpenters reported to him directly. Yet, a confusing situation arose every time an officer senior to Reynolds came into the harbor. The roles then changed, forcing Reynolds to relinquish his duties to an officer not familiar with the command.[110]

Because of the continuous growth of the squadron, even Reynolds' efficient management could not transform the *Vermont* into the sole storeship. The *Vermont* served in some capacity virtually every ship that came into Port Royal. The ship stowed paymasters' and storekeepers' supplies, ordnance, and fresh water for the squadron. She received the drafts of men and provided berthing for the officers in transition to other commands. She also housed the many refugees, served as a prison for deserters, POWs, and captured crews from blockade runners. The *Vermont*, likewise, had on board a bakery and a hospital. As a result of a lack of equipment at the machine shops they used her main yards as derricks to hoist heavy guns, boilers, and anchors in and out of the other ships. The *Vermont* served the squadron until 29 July 1864, when *New Hampshire* arrived to replace her.[111]

The storage of the ordnance posed the most serious problem on *Vermont*. The demands for ordnance were "so numerous and constant that to observe the usual precautions of the service in receiving and delivering such is to seriously interrupt and interfere with the daily wants of the ship herself." *Vermont* handled the shells and powder and had powder filling rooms to fuse shells. Reynolds feared an accident would destroy the ship, a risk too great given the large number of officers and men she housed. Because of this, he asked that this duty be moved ashore.[112]

The *Vermont* continued to serve as the ordnance depot for the squadron during the first part of the war, yet the squadron did not have an ordnance officer and the *Vermont* did not even have a single gunner on board. Schooners stored most of the overflow of the ordnance stores. Schooners made good storage facilities because they could be moved if necessary and, as they had shallow hulls, it was not difficult to hoist the cargoes in and out. When the monitors began supporting the operations on Morris Island, the needs became so great that the usage could not be predicted. Just six months earlier, Du Pont had sent the ammunition back north rather than to pay to store it afloat.[113]

The storage needs of the squadron quickly outgrew the *Vermont.* Fortunately, Du Pont had reserved some of the Stone Fleet whalers and saved them for use as store hulks. The 402-ton ship *Valparaiso* served as another warehouse for storekeepers' and paymasters' supplies, described as a "department store on a small scale, being stocked with many kinds of goods to eat, drink, or wear." Soon she also was too small to accommodate the squadron's needs. The *Valparaiso* did not have copper sheathing on her hull and by July 1863 she was so badly worm-eaten that pumps could not keep her afloat much longer. The department delayed improving the accommodations afloat, hoping to move into the new logistical facilities being built on Bay Point for the squadron. The delays in this project, though, caused the floating facilities to become overburdened.[114]

The inadequacy of the *Vermont* and other hulks required the navy to pay substantial demurrage charges. The supply vessels arrived from the north and anchored for long periods of time waiting to be unloaded. The squadron later acquired the 200-ton bark *Ironsides Jr.* at $1,800 per month to relieve the *Vermont.* The squadron used her to receive and issue other stores.[115]

For better morale and the benefit of the men's health, the Navy Department early in the war made plans to purchase side-wheel steamers with good speed to supply fresh provisions to the ships at their stations. The system of supply evolved during the war from a haphazard distribution to that of a fairly systemized one. Early in the war, the Navy Department intended to use *Rhode Island* and *Connecticut*, alternately, to run regularly between New York and Texas, communicating with every vessel from Cape Hatteras to the Gulf of Mexico. This system worked well until the blockading squadrons increased in size.[116] These steamers became an important auxiliary to the blockade because they enabled the warships to obtain fresh food, which helped them to remain longer at their stations. Inaugurated by the Bureau of Provisions and Clothing, this system provided large fast steamers fitted with spacious icehouses. Some of these ships would hold fifty thousand pounds of fresh beef and three hundred tons or more of ice and could also carry livestock.[117]

The navy's implementation of regularly scheduled supply steamers with chill rooms on board was a new venture. The first step taken to provide the vessels along the East coast came in mid-July 1861. Welles instructed Bridge to send the steamer *Rhode Island* to New York and load her with fresh beef, vegetables, and other supplies for the gunboats south of Cape Hatteras.[118]

Initially three ships, *Supply*, *Rhode Island*, and *Connecticut* supplied the Atlantic coast squadron. In the fall of 1861, the Navy Department experimented with a new method of preserving beef on board one of the new fast steamers, the USS *Connecticut*. The usual method of preservation consisted of alternating a layer of ice and layer of meat. The new method used a "chill room," something in the style of a refrigerator on shore. *Connecticut* carried 400 quarters of beef hung on hooks and stowed together as close as possible. She carried 59,000 pounds of beef with 125 tons of ice, about a four-to-one ratio of ice to beef. The *Connecticut*'s captain, Commander Maxwell Woodhull, found the chill room inefficient and suggested that the previous method be used.[119]

The supply steamers loaded in New York, Boston, Philadelphia, and Baltimore. Not only did they perform the duties of supplying fresh foods, but they also carried other supplies to the ships and carried out many other important responsibilities as well. At times they "assisted the blockade in several instances by laying by certain steamers while they scaled their boilers and repaired them, besides keeping open the communication between the flag officers and the commanders of the . . . individual vessels composing their commands." The supply steamers became the major links in communication with the home front for the officers and seamen. They brought packages, boxes, trunks, and bundles that contained food, clothes, books, and news from home. *Connecticut* at times, in addition to her regular cargo, would carry hundreds of thousands of letters and packages.[120]

The supply steamers also carried sutlers, who sold various items that added greatly to the comfort of the officers and seamen. The navy regulated the sutlers so that they could not take advantage of the men. They could only charge a price twenty-five percent above what they paid for foodstuffs and other articles, such as tobacco, cigars, paper collars, and so forth. They could make no more than a forty-five percent profit on all other goods.[121]

On to Charleston

As the end of first year of the war neared, the South Atlantic Blockading Squadron stood on the threshold of control of the entire South Atlantic seaboard. The Port Royal Expedition had set as a goal the capture of two towns or anchorages. But, despite poor coordination, Du Pont and Sherman managed to capture or control most of the coastline from South Carolina to northern Florida. The only two major goals remaining were Charleston and Savannah.

Success is attributable, mainly, to the weaknesses of the Confederate defenses. Du Pont felt that "harmonious counsels and cordial cooperation" existed between the two branches of the service. In truth, the relationship never seemed symphonic. Both branches of the service merely tolerated each other to reach common goals. The relationship, as it existed, became more strained after the failure of the planned coup de main on Savannah. The army pointed the finger at the navy, blaming them for being dilatory. The Navy Department, on the other hand, felt that the army had relied too much on naval power that did not exist. The key to the whole operation seemed to be the lack of small boats and proper transportation. These boats never arrived and it caused the cancellation of the expedition.[122]

The army never managed to project its power far beyond the realm of the supporting fire of the naval vessels. The army failed to make use of the large number of troops at Hilton Head. It also did not utilize the superior naval firepower and greater mobility to strike at strategic points. The Confederates did not waste time. They built strong earthworks to guard the interior waterways and thereby made combined movements more difficult. Sherman might have struck at the Confederates, but instead remained overly cautious and waited for the approval of the War Department before moving. Percival Drayton summed up the navy's view when he said " . . . our great army has got to fight . . . not in mere skirmishes and under cover of gunboats behind which they retire after a few shots . . ."[123]

4

"Our Troops Will Not Fight if Gunboats Are within Their Reach"

The Siege of Fort Pulaski

Spring 1862 found both the army and the navy once again working toward a common objective: the reduction and capture of Fort Pulaski. The previous month's expeditions effectively gave the Union forces control over most of the South Atlantic seaboard. Both Savannah and Charleston remained the major exceptions to this sweep. Yet, the capture of Fort Pulaski would hermetically seal the Savannah River. In February, about the same time Sherman and Du Pont abandoned their coup de main attack on Savannah, the War Department committed to a siege operation against the fort.

Fort Pulaski, situated on Cockspur Island, guarded the main channels into Savannah. Southern forces gained control on 3 January 1861 when three companies of local militia embarked in Savannah on the steamer *Ida* to the airs of martial music. After disembarking at the fort, the militia met a single ordnance sergeant, who surrendered his keys without an argument. By noon, the state flag flew over the fort's masonry walls, signaling one of the first aggressive acts of the Civil War. The armament of the fort consisted of twenty 32-pounder guns mounted on rusty iron carriages. The Confederates labored for months to convert the fort into a strong work and by the beginning of 1862 believed it safe from attack. Storming the works in small boats would be suicidal. Furthermore, smoothbore guns could not breach the seven-and-one-half-foot-thick walls at a distance of over 900 yards. By March 1862, four companies of the First Regiment Georgia Infantry garrisoned the fort. The armament now included 8- and 10-inch Columbiads, a 42-pounder, two 24-pounder Blakely rifled guns, and two 10-inch mortars.[1]

The fort protected both the north and the south channels of the river. It was shaped like an irregular pentagon; two faces guarded each channel. The naval vessels blockading the river kept at a respectable distance, just out of the range of the fort. At night they kept boarding pikes ready and the watch remained alert in case soldiers from the fort mounted a boat attack. The screw gunboat *Wyandotte*, one of the first vessels off the fort, made herself look more menacing to the rebels. Her crew filled two of her empty gun ports with Quaker guns made of small casks covered with muzzle bags. Despite the posturing of both sides, the first shot fired in anger toward the fort did not occur until Christmas Day 1861. This Christmas present to the rebels fell five hundred yards short.[2]

The naval forces actively probed the areas around the fort as the Union siege train arrived. With great energy Captain Quincy Gillmore and First Lieutenant Horace Porter directed the building and placement of the batteries. The soldiers carried the building materials, sand bags, planks, and equipment to the various sites under cover of darkness. Once they completed the platforms, they also transported the guns after dark. The Confederates could hear the activity, but never saw the enemy. They knew, however, that the Union forces were building siege batteries. Exasperated, one Confederate wrote, ". . . the cowardly retches have no desire, to meet us face to face in a fair & equal contest."[3]

Before the main siege guns arrived, the army built batteries on Venus Point and Bird Island as part of the coup de main effort. They built these batteries upriver and isolated from the main Union lines to cut the enemy's river communications between the fort and the city. These batteries, in conjunction with the naval forces invested in the surrounding waterways, virtually stopped the rebel's river communications. Near the end of February, Flag Officer Tatnall made plans to attack the battery on Bird Island to relieve the fort. On 28 February, General Lee met in council with Tatnall on board *Savannah* to discuss the plan. Tatnall proposed storming these remote works at night with his entire force in boats, supported by the vessels in the squadron and a detachment of two hundred men from the army. The discussion revealed the truly desperate nature of the attack. The officers shared the opinion that the heavy fire of grape and canister at short range supported by the Union gunboats would cause a great loss of life. They concluded that, even if the attack carried the battery, it would only allow the spiking of the guns and a slight pause in the advance. All involved eventually agreed to abandon this expedition.[4]

In an attempt to further isolate the fort, Gillmore placed three guns on board the Stone Fleet hulk *Montezuma* in Lazaretto Creek. This creek ran above Tybee Island and connected the Tybee River and the South Channel of the Savannah River just below Fort Pulaski. A small guard boat with a navy six-pounder also patrolled the river to intercept messengers en route to the fort. On 31 March, a rebel scouting party surprised the guard boat and captured eighteen men and the boat. Du Pont later stationed the gunboat *Norwich* here to keep them from repeating this effort.[5]

Without the navy's presence, the army may have found it difficult to build the breaching batteries. The gunboats served as a mobile force multiplier and, as the batteries neared completion, the army's need for gunboats never ceased. The gunboats faced limitations and operated in many cases with abandon. Only at high tide could they freely move; often at low tide their bottoms rested on the mud. Du Pont continued to increase his support of the siege operations. By the first week in April, he had four vessels in Wright's and Mud rivers in addition to those off the mouth of the river.[6]

While the federal army forces worked to complete the batteries, the navy remained active in the shallow channels north of the fort. On 25 March the side-wheel tug *O. M. Pettit*, the small side-wheel steamer *Mercury*, and two launches from *Susquehanna*, carrying 250 men of the Sixth Connecticut Volunteers, probed up the New River. The following day they ascended Wright's River. During this reconnaissance Lieutenant James H. Gillis spotted what appeared to be a rebel ironclad. When Generals Sherman and Viele heard the news they panicked. Viele wrote Sherman expressing the opinion that unless the Savannah River was immediately closed by sinking a hulk, that the navy "will lose the greater portion of the blockading fleet." Du Pont did not seem concerned since he could merely withdraw them from danger. Du Pont told Sherman that he never considered that the army would require the gunboats to protect the batteries after completion. Since the gunboats were aground nearly all the time, he felt that it might be his "duty to withdraw every one of them." Du Pont reminded Sherman that he had established the naval blockade at Tybee Roads and that the vessels in Wright's and Mud rivers served there "to assist the batteries . . . having them [the batteries] there formed no part of a plan of mine."[7]

The Confederates were indeed building three ironclads and several gunboats in Savannah. The ironclads, *Georgia*, *Savannah*, and *Atlanta* all had similar designs with sloping casemates that protected the crew and batteries. The *Georgia*, however, never received an engine capable of moving her. Her inability to move earned her the nickname "mud tub." The Union naval leaders knew the limitations of the *Georgia* through information from deserters and scouts. *Atlanta*, commissioned in November, spanned 204 feet, had a 41-foot beam, and a draft of about 17 feet. The third ironclad, *Savannah*, did not become operational until the summer of 1863. The Confederates began building a fourth ironclad named the *Milledgeville*; she had a shortened casemate with six inches of iron plate, but the rebels never finished her.[8]

The navy learned of the possibility of an ironclad from a native German living on Whitmarsh Island, just above Wilmington Island on the Wilmington River. A boat reconnaissance near Elba Island confirmed the existence of a vessel 120 feet in length with the appearance of an ironclad. Nevertheless, this was much too short to be any of the ironclads being built in the city. The possibility of an ironclad in the river and Du Pont's suggestion of withdrawing his gunboats alarmed the army leaders and changed the whole perspective of the Union forces. Suddenly they took a defensive posture. Du Pont warned his vessels in Wassaw that the illusive ironclad might come down the Wilmington River. He considered obstructing this river but did not have the hulks or other means to do so. Instead, he pleaded with Welles for more ships. On 5 April, he sent the heavily armed sloop *Vandalia* to lie across the river responding to an army request for support. He wrote, "I will strain every nerve to give you all the aid just now I can, but I have not vessels enough, and particularly of light draft." General Viele, whom Du Pont considered "selfish" and who denigrated the navy, wanted to sink hulks in the Savannah River and asked for naval tugs to accomplish the task. Du Pont did not like the idea of his two tugs "against all of Tattnall's fleet, whether there be an ironclad or not." Sherman even admitted that the enemy could turn the batteries on the Savannah River from the rear without gunboats in Mud, Wright's, and New rivers. This whole business began to irritate Du Pont. The newspaper reporters also castigated Du Pont's lack of "cooperating with the land forces." He wrote his wife that he "felt a sense of oppression, caused by the position of my gunboats . . . and the panic of Viele and his disingenuousness combined." He concluded that, "All these annoyances would vanish if the bombardment of Pulaski would commence— but the delays are *fairly painful* . . ."[9]

Consumed by fear, the army officers decided to prepare for an enemy sortie and devised a desperate plan to deal with the threat of a Confederate ironclad. Using numerous rowboats, each with an officer and six oarsmen, they planned to board the ironclad should it come downriver. The army armed these men with revolvers, hand grenades, cold chisels, sledgehammers, grappling irons, and ropes. They hoped to keep the rebel gunners at bay while men cut through the armored casemate in order to capture the crew and the warship. This foolhardy and ridiculous scheme fortunately never needed implementation.[10]

The construction of the siege batteries went quickly, and Du Pont and Sherman continued to work together on this project with relatively little friction. Sherman, however, had not progressed as quickly with this project as the War Department wished. At the end of March, Major General David Hunter, a favorite of Lincoln, arrived to replace Sherman as the commander of the newly created Department of the South. Sherman reluctantly briefed Hunter on the progress of the siege before he sailed north. Du Pont commented about Sherman's removal, ". . . he ploughed, harrowed, sowed, and it does seem hard that when the crop was about being harvested he is not even allowed to participate in a *secondary* position." Hunter, nearly sixty years old, graduated from West Point in 1822. He served in the army on the frontier and then resigned his commission to speculate in real estate. He rejoined the army six years later and through correspondence with Lincoln received an appointment as the fourth ranking volunteer general. He had a reputation for being calm, urbane, and dignified, but also reticent and "independent in thought and action." Du Pont, though, found that "Everyone is charmed with the urbanity of General Hunter; the new brigadier is peculiar, fussy, interfering, *coarse*, although energetic and anxious to please the Navy."[11]

During the preceding two months, the army erected eleven batteries armed with 13- and 10-inch mortars, 10- and 8-inch Columbiads, 30-pounder Parrott rifles, and 24-, 32-, and 42-pounder rifles. Finally, at dawn on 10 April, with the siege batteries ready to fire, Hunter asked for Fort Pulaski's surrender. The fort's commanding officer, Colonel Charles Olmstead, declined, replying to Hunter that he was there "to defend the fort, not to surrender it." At 8:15, the Union batteries opened fire and the first shell burst high in the air above the Confederates. The naval vessels did not participate because all the light draft vessels except *Unadilla* lay in Wright's River and in Wassaw Sound supporting Brigadier Generals Viele and Henry Benham.[12]

On the ninth, General Hunter suggested that the navy take part in the bombardment. Du Pont instructed Lieutenant John Irwin to report to Raymond Rodgers for the men. Rodgers detailed one hundred men from the *Wabash* to participate. On the morning of the tenth, they landed before the batteries opened fire only to learn the army did not need them. The sailors spent the day and night on the beach as a reserve force. During the tenth, however, Gillmore relieved Colonel Rudolph Rosa, commanding Battery Sigel, for failing to obey orders and not controlling his men. When Gillmore relieved him of command his "German" Regiment also left. Gillmore assigned a detachment of the Eighth Maine to serve two of the guns and the men of the *Wabash* manned the remaining four.[13]

The Wabashes, the only experienced artillerists in any of the batteries, kept a "steady and well-directed fire." Gillmore wrote that the navy gunner's "skill and experience were applied with telling effect." While the first day's bombardment had been somewhat inaccurate, on the second day the Columbiads and rifled guns began pounding large holes in the fort's masonry walls. Between one and two o'clock, after about thirty hours of constant bombardment, one of these shells passed through a traverse built to protect the magazine. When this shell exploded in the passageway leading to the magazine, Colonel Olmstead realized that if this occurred again, the whole fort would be in danger. Just before 2:00 P.M. the fort's defenders hoisted a white flag and then slowly lowered the Confederate ensign.[14]

"Pulaski is ours, Sumter is avenged!" wrote Horace Porter, who supervised the building of the siege batteries. The siege proved to be nearly a bloodless victory. It cost the lives of only one man on either side. The quick surrender of the fort surprised many of the Confederate leaders and greatly alarmed the people of Savannah. As it was built before the invention of rifled shells, the designers of the fort did not build the walls to withstand their destructive power. This defeat stimulated the preparations for the defenses of the entire state of Georgia and greatly accelerated those under construction around Savannah. The state called up militia units, began feverishly working on obstructions and fire rafts, planting torpedoes and building and finishing the ironclads and gunboats.[15]

The fall of the fort opened the main channels of the Savannah River to the larger warships. Despite the fact that the river now served as a thoroughfare directly to the city of Savannah, the Union forces did not push up the river. Furthermore, Du Pont and Hunter really had no plans to exploit this situation. Instead, Du Pont had to move with caution caused by the possibility of an ironclad. This situation worried Du Pont for some time because he had no ironclad or warship to contend with this class of vessel. His regular gunboats were no match for such an enemy. He suggested strengthening some of his ships at the bow with "iron ties" for ramming, but this would only be a last resort for defense. Du Pont was likewise not enthusiastic about sacrificing his warships to protect the Union army's hold on the fort. As a result of the army's previous record of abandoning conquests, Du Pont had no faith that the army would even hold Fort Pulaski. With all the demands on the squadron and the large numbers of ships under repair, he felt that should an ironclad sortie down the river she "could play Jack the Giant killer with a vengeance . . ."[16]

Occupation Issues

Du Pont was uncertain of the army's commitments to many of the recently captured positions. The flag officer's fears of the army abandoning Fort Pulaski had merit. Before the fall of the fort, and despite the success of the earlier combined operations, General Hunter felt that he had overextended his positions and ordered the withdrawal of troops from Jacksonville. The absence of troops in Jacksonville, however, would also force the navy to abandon both the town and the river and compel the gunboats to take station at the mouth of the St. John's River. This decision drove Du Pont and his officers to despair. He wrote Fox that this action was counter to all the instructions from the Navy Department and the pressure put on the flag officer to capture as many points as possible. He felt that the Union forces would have been better served by leaving "Florida and the lower coast of Georgia alone, than to show an inability to keep what we have captured."[17]

The abandonment of Jacksonville hurt the inhabitants who had "committed themselves to the Union cause . . ." The number of Unionists in the area that would participate in forming a new government had been overestimated, and many, instead of flocking to the flag, instead offered resistance. Guerrilla bands also formed and roamed the area, posing a danger to those who cooperated with the Yankees. The majority of the Union sympathizers remaining in Jacksonville were the merchants, real estate operators, and lumbermen who stayed to protect their investments. These men tried to influence Union leaders to remain in the town but to no avail. After the announcement of a withdrawal, a substantial number of inhabitants decided to leave with the few possessions they could load on the transports and the naval vessels. The wharves in the town became crowded with those trying to escape. Trunks, carpet-bags, and furniture all made their way to the docks on small ponies and carts to be stowed in the ships. The "haste and bustle" added a "humane and praiseworthy ludicrousness to the melancholy scene."[18]

Du Pont remained concerned for these individuals and assumed the responsibility of removing any women and children who wished to leave. The navy, not able to control the river without an army garrison in Jacksonville, tried to strike a bargain with the local Confederate authorities. They told the Confederates that if they would not erect a battery within one mile of the town and did not deploy a large number of men there, then the naval vessels would not fire in the immediate vicinity of the town. An agreement would mean the removal of people would not be necessary. The rebels realized that they controlled the town and would not acquiesce. This obliged the Union vessels to visit at their peril. The Federal garrison left on 9 April and the Confederate forces immediately entered the town.[19] The Union vessels continued to visit Jacksonville despite the absence of garrison troops.

Farther south, the Union leaders believed St. Augustine more important to the war effort and strengthened its garrison. Only about twenty percent of the inhabitants of St. Augustine fled before the Union occupation. Yet the remaining citizens were no more loyal than those at Jacksonville and kept their sense of rebellion. The women of the town chopped down the public flagstaff so that it would not bear the Union flag. They then cut the staff into many pieces as mementos. Raymond Rodgers felt that the women seemed "to mistake treason for courage." The lack of food in this small town would be a problem and forged a unique relationship between the locals and the occupying forces. When Federal troops arrived, the citizens were on the brink of starvation and many lived largely on a subsistence diet for the rest of the war. The fact that the Union troops opened their commissary to keep some of the citizens from starving was an extra bitter pill for them to swallow.[20]

Another large group of individuals cared for by the navy along the South Atlantic coast was the free blacks. As the Confederates abandoned the coastal areas and as the Union army and naval forces seized control, the ex-slaves flocked to the protection of the Yankees. On 25 September 1861, the Navy Department initially authorized Du Pont to utilize the blacks by enlisting them. They could sign on board the ships as boys at a salary of ten dollars a month and one ration a day. This satisfied only a small number of the freed blacks and did not help the displaced women and children now within Union lines. The free blacks became so numerous that they established several colonies. By December 1861, a colony on the southeastern end of Edisto Island at Botany Bay had reached one thousand persons, most destitute of both clothing and food. As these groups gathered along the coast, the navy had several fears—that supplies to feed these people would fall short, that disease would appear, and that the rebels would attack the colonies.[21]

By May 1862, many ex-slaves remained on the Sea Islands unable to reach the established contraband camps on Hilton Head and St. Helena Islands. There were by some estimates twelve thousand blacks, perhaps as many as one-third of them children, within the Union lines. Du Pont proved to be extremely sympathetic to the plight of these refugees. The naval forces fed them, protected them, and later embarked them to consolidate the colonies. With the numbers growing daily, Du Pont also became anxious to employ the men on his warships. Then on 9 May, the abolitionist General Hunter "startled" everyone by proclaiming all the slaves within the Military Department of the South to be free. Hunter, who wanted to raise black regiments, did not have the authority to set any slaves free, much less all those in South Carolina, Georgia, and Florida, and Lincoln voided his proclamation on 19 May. The early efforts to protect the blacks could not have been made without the navy's presence. The navy's work with the free blacks, however, was made less critical as the Union lines became more defined. In addition, the Treasury Department sent agents and missionaries called "Gideonites" south to help the blacks adjust to their newfound freedom.[22]

Operations up the Stono

As the Confederate military authorities continued their consolidation of the coastal defenses by withdrawing farther up the rivers to better defensive positions, the gunboats enjoyed greater access to the tidal and interior waters. The Union warships continued to invest the waterways around Pulaski and probed Confederate positions. Combined operations in the North and South Edisto and Dawho rivers, as well as Sapelo and Doboy sounds, all kept the enemy off guard.[23]

These missions accentuated the inadequacies of the small steamers. In the narrow and shallow rivers these vessels proved to be especially vulnerable to gunfire and ran aground frequently. On 29 April, the diminutive *E. B. Hale* steamed up the Dawho River to destroy an enemy battery near the confluence of the Pon Pon, Dawho, and South Edisto rivers. As she moved upstream, an enemy battery opened fire in the turn of the river. When the *Hale* closed the distance, the enemy fled. Lieutenant Alexander Rhind and a landing party of twenty men spiked and destroyed two 24-pounders and then he reembarked his men. Expecting the enemy to attack from a bluff on the way back down the Dawho River, he kept his men under cover. When the *Hale* came abreast of a bluff in a narrow part of the stream, the enemy opened with a terrific fire. After the initial volley, Rhind called the men to their battle stations, but they would not budge. Finally, he "'howled' them up, by shaming them" and they returned grape, canister and shells, and passed by the enemy with little damage and no casualties. The *Hale* typified the small vessels converted for the war effort. Built for carrying stone on the North River, she displaced 220 tons and measured only 117 feet in length. More remarkable is the fact that she went into battle with the greater part of her machinery and her boiler exposed to enemy fire.[24]

Potential operations to probe Confederate defenses always included the Stono River. This artery served as a back door thoroughfare into the heart of the enemy's defenses protecting Charleston. In the spring of 1862, the Union leaders considered a combined operation up this river. Rebel batteries on Cole's Island, however, prevented operations up the Stono River before May. In March, Major General John C. Pemberton, following a directive from Robert E. Lee, ordered the guns removed from this island to defend the inner harbor of Charleston.[25] This might have gone unnoticed for some time had it not been for the actions of Robert Smalls and thirteen other slaves, who escaped to the Union lines in the Confederate steamer *Planter*.

On 12 May the small light draft steamer *Planter* departed Cole's Island with the four-gun battery from the island on board. The *Planter* steamed back to Charleston and tied up at her usual berth at the city wharf. Against regulations, all the officers disembarked and left Smalls in charge of the black crew. At three o'clock the next morning, Smalls, who had planned to escape for weeks, realized that his opportunity was here. Smalls took the steamer to another wharf and to pick up family and friends. They boarded the *Planter* and got her underway. Smalls moved the *Planter* away from the wharf, and with the customary whistle signal, the little steamer stood down the channel and passed Fort Ripley and Fort Sumter unchallenged. The sentinel at Fort Sumter never thought to challenge the vessel, thinking she was the guard ship headed for the bar. Smalls steamed out the main ship channel and was out of range before anyone in the forts realized what happened.[26]

As the steamer approached the blockaders, Smalls now realized that his vessel risked being mistaken for a blockade runner or a warship and he hauled down the Confederate flag and hoisted a white one. Met by the Union ship *Onward*, the Union officers interviewed Smalls and then took him and the *Planter* to Du Pont in Port Royal. Smalls told the flag officer that the rebels were abandoning the defenses in the lower Stono River. With this information, Du Pont wanted confirmation and instructed Commander John Marchand to make a reconnaissance.[27]

The removal of the guns on Cole's Island made it necessary for the Confederates to construct a long line of works to defend James Island. The abandonment of the positions on Cole's Island, though, occurred before the Confederates completed the defensive works on James Island. This left most of James Island open to landings. This weak point now invited an approach on the city of Charleston via the Stono River. With the defenses withdrawn, Marchard quickly grasped the possibility of an offensive movement on Charleston using the Stono as the route to transport the army. A survey made by the gunboats *Unadilla*, *Ottawa*, and *Pembina* on 17 May confirmed the absence of enemy batteries and a good depth of water. The following day Charles Boutelle buoyed the channel. On the nineteenth, Marchand visited Du Pont and laid out a plan to transport troops up the Stono, land on James Island, and take Fort Johnson. The capture of this fort would prevent communication by water between Charleston and forts Sumter and Moultrie, giving the Union forces control of Charleston Harbor.[28]

While the navy probed the Stono River, discussions between Du Pont and Hunter's staff began in earnest regarding a combined operation. Coincidentally, as Marchand pitched his plans, Du Pont received a message from the department that suggested a move on Charleston. Welles wrote the letter two days after the Confederates destroyed the ironclad *Virginia* off Craney Island and Welles optimistically felt that a quick naval move up the James River would cause the fall of Richmond. Should this happen, Welles promised the ironclads *Monitor* and *Galena* for a Charleston attack. He also instructed Du Pont to work closely with Hunter unless the move "should be purely naval . . ."[29]

Harmonious cooperation between the army and navy began to appear doubtful, despite the fact that the army leadership had similar ideas of a move up the Stono River. The army still had a dearth of shallow draft steamers to transport the troops in an offensive movement. Any large operation, therefore, relied on the navy for both fire support and transportation. Additionally, there was little communication between

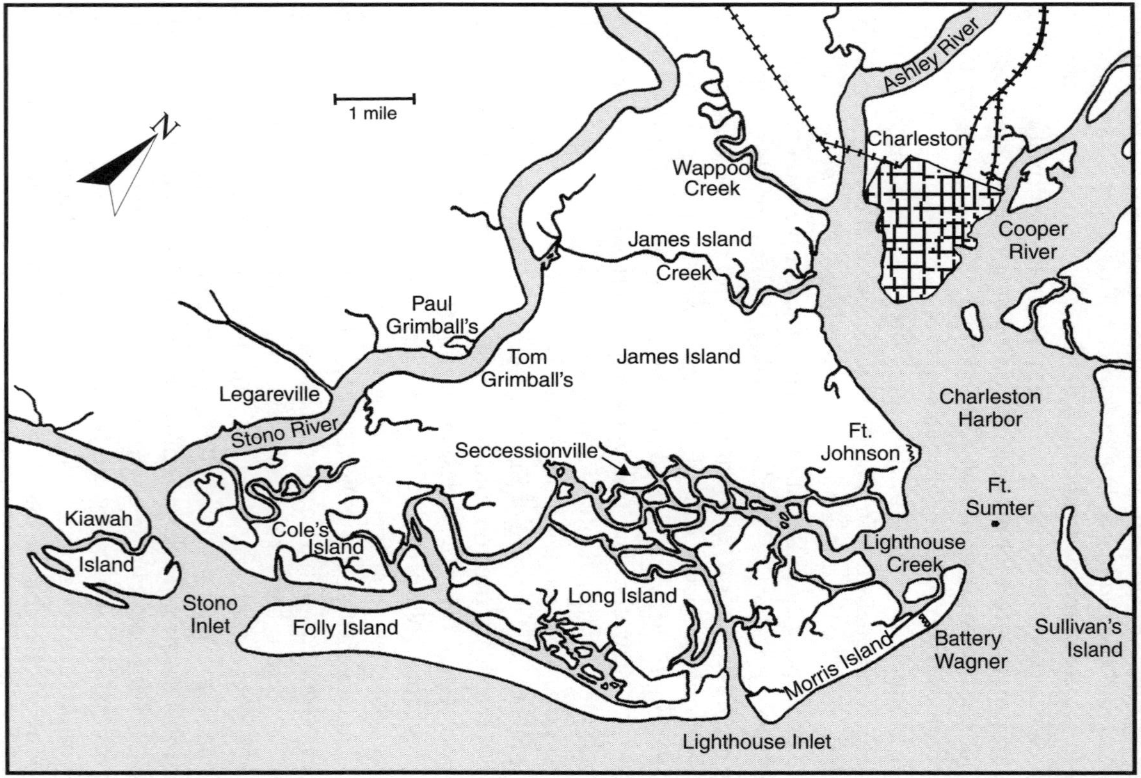

MAP 7. CHARLESTON VICINITY

the branches since Hunter had arrived and the communication that did occur was not constructive. Brigadier General Henry Benham created much of the animosity. Some considered him rough and rude and he did not impress Du Pont. The flag officer thought him "restless, energetic with courage but no conduct—anxious to do right, but wasting himself on details." His own officers felt he had an "unfortunate talent for blundering." Benham treated the navy as a subservient branch, which won him no friends among the naval officers. In a note to Raymond Rodgers, for example, he blamed the navy for delays in moving up the Stono. Rodgers reminded the general that a couple of weeks earlier he had communicated a plan to Du Pont. Benham's message, however, told the flag officer that he did not have Hunter's consent for an operation. Du Pont, meanwhile, assisted the army as the weather allowed, but heard nothing and considered the move canceled. Information from the defection of Robert Smalls caused Hunter to change his mind. On 16 May, Benham promised to confer with Hunter and give the flag officer an answer the next morning. Du Pont waited until the eighteenth, and when Benham failed to show, the flag officer sailed to Charleston.[30]

Benham immediately blamed the navy for being non-cooperative and uncommunicative. Rodgers wrote that although he felt "savage" he responded to Benham's charges with courtesy. "Pardon me my dear General for saying to you that it was most natural for the flag officer to suppose that if you were actively preparing a plan of operations which would require a very large cooperation by the wholly independent force under his command that you would lose no time in consulting him and stating distinctly what you desired." Rodgers further stated that the flag officer waited for two days and that failure was attributable only to the general for not informing the flag officer of the army's needs.[31]

The lack of army transports continued to be an obstacle that delayed the implementation of the operation. In order to prevent a cancellation of the movement or further delays, the army asked the navy to commit steamers to serve as transports. Yet, when Du Pont began to gather the vessels, Benham, who had requested two gunboats to lay off Jones and Wassaw islands, became uneasy over the withdrawal of gunboats for this operation. Benham expressed his concerns and wrote that this operation would put the rebels on the defensive. He felt that the occupation of the Stono would likely be a "difficult and bloody operation, perhaps impossible." Rodgers wrote to Du Pont that this seemed to be an "extraordinary hallucination." Benham, in a breach of protocol, asked for naval assistance without going through Du Pont. Du Pont followed this missive with a critical letter to Hunter about Benham's tone and request. He asked that further plans and intentions be addressed solely to him.[32]

With the gunboats over the bar at the Stono, the Confederate leadership realized that the next move against their defenses would likely be from this river. Benham continued to show indecisiveness and the Union army gave Du Pont no indication that they had any real interests. Du Pont waited for days at Port Royal for communications from the army and by the twenty-eighth, had still heard nothing. Rodgers feared that the army had begun the movement prematurely and warned the enemy of their intentions. He added that should the navy withdraw "there would be no end to the outcry from the Army." Yet, if the plan failed "it would be attributed to the shortcoming of the Navy."[33]

On 25 May, the two sides traded the first shots of the approaching campaign when a Confederate vessel ventured into range of the Union vessels. The 204-ton side-wheel steam transport *Chesterfield* towed a floating battery off James Island to protect the interior routes to Charleston Harbor. As the *Chesterfield* began to position the battery in one of the creeks south of James Island, the *Pembina* and *Unadilla* spotted it and attacked. Struck by one of the first shells, the *Chesterfield* steamed back up river to Secessionville. The battery, commanded by Acting Master Francis N. Bonneau, carried three guns, one a heavy rifled gun. Bonneau ordered his guns into action and fired fifteen shots at the Union warships, who replied with only six. When the rebel shells passed over the *Pembina* and the *Unadilla*, and their shells fell harmlessly short, Lieutenant Napoleon Collins of the *Unadilla* decided it best to withdraw. The *Chesterfield* returned that evening to tow the floating battery back to Morris Island.[34]

On the twenty-eighth, the *Huron* crossed the bar to join *Unadilla*, *Pembina*, *Ottawa*, and *Ellen*. The next day, *Pawnee* joined the other five warships. Du Pont made the large side-wheel gunboat *Alabama*; the converted gunboats *Bienville*, *Henry Andrew*, *Hale*, *Planter*, and the tugs *Pettit* and *Mercury* available to the army to serve as troop transports. Du Pont instructed Drayton, the senior officer present, to send his vessels to search for the floating battery. A flotilla consisting of *Pawnee* and the ninety-day gunboats *Pembina*, *Huron* and *Ottawa* probed above Legareville and up river to within sight of Wappoo Cut, about twelve miles above the Stono's mouth. On the twenty-ninth, they opened fire on a small steamer they spotted in the river. The following day they removed pile obstructions and passed through Newton's Cut, a thoroughfare that connected to James Island Creek. Here they traded shots with a fortification until sunset and then returned back downstream to Legareville. Drayton boasted that the navy had complete control of the Stono and could land and protect the army wherever it wished to operate. Du Pont, weary of the delayed movement of Hunter, wrote his wife sardonically ". . . our troops will not fight if gunboats are within their reach."[35]

On the night of the twenty-eighth, the army issued orders by telegram for the joint movement. While the Union forces prepared, General Stevens left on a diversion to cut the Charleston and Savannah Railroad about fifteen miles above Beaufort. The railroad served as a vital line of communications and crossed many rivers. Burning any one of the trestles might have disrupted railroad traffic for some time. Benham, instead of sending a large force, consented only to a demonstration. Stevens' troops, under the command of Colonel Benjamin C. Christ, assembled on the twenty-eighth and pushed across the Coosaw River on the twenty-ninth. One regiment, strengthened by two additional companies, two pieces of artillery and some cavalry, met a small but resolute Confederate force. The rebels managed to slow the Union troops during the early morning and the delays spoiled the surprise. Despite coming close to the railroad bridge, they withdrew.[36]

By 2 June, the army finished its final preparations to move up the Stono River. That morning, about 7,500 men of General Stevens's command departed Port Royal and that afternoon began landing on the southwestern end of James Island. The *Henry Andrew* and *Bienville* worked with General Wright to cross his troops from Edisto Island to John's Island. The men then had to march twenty-five miles to the Stono River and cross it to reach James Island. Commander Drayton, the senior officer in the Stono River, had under his command *Pawnee, Unadilla, Alabama, Bienville, Pembina, Ottawa, Huron, Ellen,* and the *Henry Andrew* to transport and cover the landing of the troops. Du Pont instructed Lieutenant Commander Rhind to take the screw gunboat *Crusader*, the *E. B. Hale* and the *Planter*, and join the army forces, making twelve vessels there. Commander Marchand expressed "deep mortification" to Du Pont over his decision to send Drayton, who superseded him in command of the operations. Du Pont, however, reminded Marchand that he had asked for more light draft vessels and that *Pawnee* was the only gunboat with a "formidable armament" that could cross the bar. He then asked Marchand "was I to take her commander out before sending her there?"[37]

With no tradition of interservice cooperation, tensions continued to run high between the army and navy, this being due to a lack of transports and shallow-draft vessels. Four days after Stevens's troops landed, the army made a desperate plea for reinforcements, ammunition, and gunboats when reports reached army headquarters that rebels had begun crossing at Port Royal Ferry "in force." Du Pont dispatched the *Pettit, Mercury,* and *Western World,* only to find out that "not a rebel had landed nor been seen." Livid, he wrote to his wife, "The whole thing was a lie from beginning to end . . ."[38]

As the Union troops advanced from their beachhead on the Stono River, they came under a harassing fire from Confederate batteries. Four thousand rebel soldiers defended the island behind approximately five miles of unfinished earthworks. Naval gunfire from the *Unadilla,* directed by an army signal officer, helped drive off the enemy and allowed the Union forces to capture three enemy guns. A signal officer remained at the river and worked with *Unadilla, Pembina, Henry Andrews, Hale,* and *Ellen* to direct their gunfire ashore.[39]

Hunter stalled for over a week after his troops landed. His forces never moved much beyond the beachhead, but did construct a number of forward artillery positions. Hunter claimed his presence was necessary in Hilton Head and, thinking his forces outnumbered, turned over command to General Benham. Hunter issued Benham strict orders not to attack, only allowing him to protect the Union positions on James Island. The Confederates, meanwhile, used their artillery to annoy the Union troops and the naval vessels in the Stono. The gunfire soon convinced Benham that his position was untenable because there was not enough dry land above high water to secure his forces outside the range of the Confederate guns. In addition to the land batteries, the Confederates also brought up Bonneau's floating battery and placed it in shallow water to flank the line of entrenchments. Drayton and his naval vessels could do nothing to negate the gunfire of this barge. He took the shallow-draft steamer *Ellen* to examine it and could not get within a mile before shallow water stopped the little Union steamer.[40]

General Benham decided it necessary to silence the Confederate batteries. He requested five gunboats, two to support operations on the right and two more to take a position above the camp and shell the woods beyond. The fifth naval vessel he requested to take a position to command the road at Newton's Cut to prevent or harass enemy reinforcements. Naval support was crucial. The Confederate guns still could reach the Union camps, leaving the Union positions indefensible without the naval support. When Du Pont considered recalling the *Unadilla,*

General Wright objected "strenuously." He believed that thirty thousand rebel troops opposed his men and knew that the naval vessels insured their safety.[41]

The navy continued to remind the Confederates of their presence. The gunboats kept up a tremendous fire on Confederate positions, firing hundreds of shells at enormous ranges. Using compass bearings, they fired at objects they could not even see. This practice consumed large amounts of ammunition to give the army moral support. A telegraph connected the *Pawnee* to General Benham's forward command post to help direct the gunfire. This made little difference in the accuracy. Drayton equated the naval gunfire with "shooting at a person with your eyes shut." Excessive firing caused the gun's vents to wear out and ammunition began to run short. Since they could not spare the absence of the ships to refuel, they had to get coal to the front. Getting coal into the Stono River was difficult because many of the coal vessels had drafts too deep to get over the bar. Du Pont became exasperated by the entire expedition and called the army operations a "dead failure."[42]

On the evening of 15 June, generals Benham, Wright, and Stevens met to discuss a reconnaissance in force toward the fort at Secessionville. The next day Benham sent about one-third of his men against this position. His men unfortunately struck at the strongest point in the overall weak Confederate line. On the morning of the sixteenth, the *Ellen* and the *Hale* steamed up the twisting channel of Lighthouse Creek and into Big Folly Creek within sight of the enemy fortifications. At a range of over two miles, army signal officers directed their gunfire. When it fell short, they had to cease fire. In a sharp and confused fight the Confederates threw back Stevens's and Wright's first assault at 4:00 A.M. Benham, leading Wright's troops, attempted two more assaults, but could not carry the fortifications, and Benham ordered a retreat at about 9:45. General Beauregard considered his forces lucky to have held, being saved, he thought, by the "skin of our teeth." The *Ellen* and the *Hale* covered the withdrawal, but the gunfire did not effectively cover the retreat. Drayton, however, believed they had done their best given the "vague and unintelligible" firing directions.[43]

Drayton received praise from both Du Pont and Hunter for the naval operations. Needing a scapegoat for the defeat, Hunter relieved Benham of command and later had him arrested for disobedience of orders. Drayton expressed to Du Pont that Benham's dismissal actually relieved everyone. He wrote, "I have never met anyone who appears more disliked by everyone than he seems to be."[44]

This defeat convinced Hunter to withdraw his forces from James Island. Hunter, however, never discussed or notified Du Pont about the evacuation. Du Pont learned this news from an officer on shore at Hilton Head. The officer overheard a conversation in the Quartermaster's office concerning the dispatching of transports to reembark the troops. This withdrawal confounded and upset the officers in the navy. The quick abandonment of the campaign gave the appearance that the whole effort had been just a whim of the army. The naval officers generally believed that Hunter was "crazy" and felt the evacuation "unfortunate" and "injurious." Du Pont realized that the Union forces missed a real opportunity to take Charleston. He wrote Fox, "Oh those soldiers I put them nearly on *top* of the house in Charleston, but I did not push them into the windows and they came back." Drayton, intimately involved in the whole campaign, also felt the army had abandoned the best route to take Charleston. Du Pont lamented to Fox that all the worrying, the month of work, and the loss of life had all been invested "for no earthy reason, perhaps a mere fret, or the desire for a quiet summer, on the part of the Comdg. General." He added, "It seems almost like a joke, but I really can see no reason why Fernandina and Pulaski should not be next . . ."[45]

The Blockade

While Du Pont scraped together the naval force necessary to support army operations in the Stono River, the department pressured him to keep the blockade as strict as possible. In February, Du Pont complained to Welles that his forces watched three states and that he needed more ships to effectively guard about seven hundred miles of coastline. On 17 April Welles effectively aided Du Pont by reducing the limits of his command. The secretary extended the East Gulf Blockading Squadron's boundary to Cape Canaveral, 150 miles southeast of the Georgia State line.[46]

With all the blockading operations under intense scrutiny, the department pressured Du Pont to keep it strict. Welles instructed the flag officer to hold a court of inquiry to investigate each successful evasion of the blockade. With this much interest in the success of his blockading force, Du Pont felt compelled to take a special interest in its details. This required him to relegate some of the squadron's administrative duties. Du Pont relied on his fleet captain, Raymond Rodgers, and Flag Lieutenant Samuel William Preston to process most of the correspondence and orders to and from the flagship. Du Pont believed that Rodgers did a more thorough job and had a better understanding of the squadron's needs than did Charles Henry Davis.[47] While Du Pont left most of the details to his senior officers off Charleston, he often interceded and micromanaged logistical and tactical matters when he believed it necessary.

Du Pont and his officers struggled to implement an efficient blockade with vessels not particularly suited for this duty. Du Pont complained to Fox that he had only nine true men-of-war in his squadron and pleaded for more warships like the *Mohican*. The Navy Department did send Du Pont vessels to augment the blockade. In all he had thirty-six vessels to watch the coast and rivers. He established an inner blockade of St. Catherine's, Sapelo, Doboy, and St. Simon's sounds as well as Fernandina, the St. John's River, St. Augustine and Mosquito Inlet.[48]

The blockade of Charleston still received most of the squadron's attention. By the end of April, six steamers and two sailing vessels watched this port. They remained, however, in an arc thirteen miles long. Despite their separation, the large number of vessels off Charleston worried the flag officer. He wrote his wife that they would "be firing into each other on the first night alarm." Yet, four days later, he wrote Welles that he needed additional vessels with better armament to contend with the ironclad gunboats reportedly being built in Europe for the South. Du Pont protested the recall of the side-wheel steamer *Susquehanna*. He believed this the only vessel, with an armament heavy enough, that might contend with an ironclad attack and protect his "weak vessels" off the port of Charleston. He appealed to Welles not to reduce his force at this time. He pointed to the "stringent directions" from the department and the recent congressional inquiries that had questioned the blockade's effectiveness. The scrutiny from Congress he felt reflected on himself and his officers.[49]

Before Fort Pulaski fell Congress passed a resolution made by Senator John P. Hale, the chairman of the Committee on Naval Affairs, to determine the effectiveness of the blockade of the South Atlantic states. The committee showed particular interest in the blockade at the port of Charleston. Welles pressured Du Pont to answer Hale and the committee quickly and completely. Du Pont felt the issue originated with an article in the New York *Tribune* on 31 March. The article's author gave a detailed description of running the blockade—information courtesy of Lieutenant John H. Upshur, the commanding officer of the *Flambeau*. This disclosure upset Du Pont, who wrote, "A more extraordinary case of furnishing a man with a stick to break your own head with is not now within reach of my memory."[50]

While the *Tribune* had negatively reported the state of the blockade, the New York *Times* ran an article pointing to the vigilance and readiness that the Union warships exhibited. The *Times* article wrote of lookouts at the masthead, yardarms, catheads, gangways, and on the paddleboxes. It spoke of how the crews remained always in readiness to slip the anchors and kept a forward gun cast loose to fire on blockade runners. This article, unfortunately, did not capture the attention of Congress.[51]

On 9 May, Welles answered the inquiry from the Senate Committee on Naval Affairs. He admitted to a "laxity" of the blockade of the South Atlantic coast and particularly off Charleston. He answered that there were reasons for this. He insisted that the flag officer, as well as the officers and men of the squadron, had "acquitted themselves in a manner eminently satisfactory" to the department. Welles admitted that violations of the blockade had occurred, but insisted that the double coastline and foreign interests complicated the enforcement of a strict blockade. Welles added that the "extraordinary demands" for warships to participate in expeditions along the South Atlantic coast and elsewhere forced the flag officer to detach these ships at the expense of the effectiveness of the blockade.[52]

Du Pont, though, did not fine tune the blockade to any great degree to offset his constantly changing resources. Most of the vessels lay at anchor off Charleston Harbor and guarded the main channels. The Senior Officer, Commander John B. Marchand, placed a steamer four to five miles outside the main line under steam to intercept and watch for blockade runners farther at sea. They tried to make Cape Romain Lighthouse in the afternoon and take their bearings for a final run into Charleston. The blockade runners at this time usually lay off the coast until dark, and often tried to pass north of Rattlesnake Shoal at high tide and inside the stone fleet obstructions. Hugging the breakers, they passed Dewees and Breech inlets and then steered into the harbor. Vessels escaping often took this route in reverse during the night. Vessels with light drafts sometimes steered out of Charleston heading south, passing through the breakers near the shore on Morris Island for four or five miles before heading to sea.[53]

In early May 1862 ten vessels lay along the thirty miles of coastline from Stono Inlet to Bull Bay. When weather permitted, a launch from the blockaders patrolled farther into the harbor to warn of blockade runners coming out. The commanders of the ships were vigilant and a "spirit of rivalry" existed between them. The vessels often grouped together during the day when visibility was good, but weighed anchor at dark to take up night stations and to prevent bearings being taken on them from the harbor. Du Pont realized that his small number of vessels could not effectively cover the coastline. He wrote to Welles on the same day that the secretary answered Hale's resolution. In his letter, Du Pont fretted about new negative newspaper coverage in the New York *Times*. He wrote that unsuitable blockading vessels weakened further his small force and greatly limited his chances of maintaining a strict blockade. He bluntly asked Welles if he wished "the blockade should be more stringent and effective I trust it will supply me with more vessels for that purpose."[54]

Du Pont hoisted his flag on the steamer *Keystone State* and, on 18 May, sailed to make a personal visit to the blockade from Georgetown to Fernandina. Raymond Rodgers convinced the flag officer not to carry any of the squadron's business with him. Du Pont took a break from his daily routine and left the administrative burden of the squadron behind. Meeting with his senior officers he discussed the needs of the blockade and arrived back in Port Royal six days later.[55]

The visit seemed to spawn new activity. Within weeks, the blockading vessels off Charleston shifted to cover the areas more north and east of the harbor. The senior officer off Charleston, Commander Marchand, instructed his steamers on dark nights to anchor as close to shore as safety permitted and in bad weather to shift their berths farther from shore. At dawn vessels on the northeast end of the line, off Dewees Inlet, got underway to intercept vessels attempting to enter or leave. In order for vessels not to mistake each other at night, Marchand ordered the blockaders to hoist lights while underway. The blockaders remained between four and five miles off the harbor and continued to lie mostly at anchor. A marked increase in cruising by the warships accentuated Du Pont's visit and now Marchand kept a fast steamer cruising all night.[56]

The new dispositions made by Marchand effectively kept the *Thomas L. Wragg* (ex-*Nashville*) out of Charleston Harbor. Three months earlier she successfully ran into Charleston and cleared the harbor five days later. On the morning of 23 June, lookouts on *Keystone State* spotted the notorious ex-cruiser bound into the port and a long chase began. Initially the *Flag* and the *James Adger* also pursued the *Wragg* but gave up due to their slow speed. Commander William Le Roy knew that he would need to increase the *Keystone State*'s speed to have any chance to catch his prey. He began by dumping the ship's drinking water overboard and then old chain cable. Next he shifted his quarterdeck guns forward, sent down the fore and fore topsail yards, and housed the fore topmast. By noon, the *Keystone State* had gained a mile, but in the next three hours during thick rain squalls, the *Thomas L. Wragg* increased the distance. The *Keystone State* again began to gain during the late afternoon but at nightfall, in the darkness, the blockade runner escaped after a chase of over three hundred miles.[57]

The escape of the *Thomas L. Wragg* prompted Du Pont to write the department again for more and better vessels. He pointed out that he had only twelve ships off Charleston and four of these propelled by sails. Du Pont also lamented that they lay too far apart to be effective. He judged that it required at least twenty vessels to blockade this port effectively. He considered his sailing vessels far from useful because they served as "beacons to the enemy, being seen so much farther than steamers."[58]

The successful escape of the *Thomas L. Wragg* also pointed to the deficiencies of his steamers for this duty. Du Pont instructed Marchand to send down the light spars of the blockaders in order to diminish their profiles and prevent them from being spotted so readily at a distance. Marchand also asked permission to paint the vessels a light color, like the blockade runners, to further reduce their visibility.[59]

Du Pont realized that steam brought a new variable into blockade running. He wrote to his friend Benjamin Gerhard that "it is all in favor of the runner. He chooses his time, makes his bound, and rushes through, his only danger a chance shot." The blockaders, on the other hand, had "banked fires, his chain to slip, his guns to point, and requires certainly fifteen minutes to get full way on his ship." Those running out had an added advantage by being able to drop down toward the throat of the harbor to look at the disposition of the Union ships before running out. Should anything not look promising, they could wait for a more favorable time. Yet, despite the advantages of steam both for blockade runners and the naval vessels, small sailing ships still managed to run the blockade successfully. By mid-1862, the larger sailing vessels had all but stopped their attempts and the steam blockade runners began to monopolize the trade. Each violation brought greater scrutiny upon Du Pont and his officers. Welles wrote encouraging letters to the flag officer, complimenting him on his achievements, but he also reminded him that "Great success has brought great responsibility."[60]

Whenever the senior officer off Charleston changed, each new commander had his own ideas for a stricter blockade. They continually shifted vessels to determine the best positioning of ships to keep the blockade strict. The Union sailing ships usually occupied positions close to shore, whereas the steamers lay inside them near each channel. The blockading vessels kept launches and boats armed with 12-pound howitzers toward the entrance of the harbor, but there was a real need for small shallow-draft vessels, such as tugs, for this work. At the end of August, Du Pont sought to gain more coverage of the coast. He instructed the *Keystone State* to cruise on a line outside the usual line of blockading vessels from Tybee and St. Andrews to Charleston.[61]

The blockade of Charleston remained difficult because of natural factors. By July the Stone Fleet, laid down only several months earlier, no longer blocked the channels. Daniel Ammen, on one of his surveying missions, found a new channel scoured by the strong tides and superior to the old channel. The squadron thus still had multiple channels to watch. Thick weather, fog, and poor visibility also helped the blockade runners elude the federal ships. During many of the nights the lookouts could not see more than three hundred yards distant and sometimes the noise of the paddlewheels was the only thing that betrayed the presence of a blockade runner. In order for the blockading vessels to avoid firing at each other, they had a rather elaborate, but always changing series of rockets, lights, and whistles. These signals identified themselves to other Union ships and directed their consorts in the direction of a suspicious vessel.[62]

The success of the blockade runners had a detrimental effect on the psyche of the officers and men. Lieutenant John Downes of the *Huron* considered the entire Union effort a "trifling impediment" to steamers entering the harbor. He wrote that he found it hard to impress others of the "discouraging" and "disgusting" nature of the naval service. The "anxieties of riding out a black, rainy, windy night in 3 or 3½ fathoms water, with our senses all on the alert for sound of paddles or sight of a miscreant violator of our blockade" took much out of the men. But it became extremely discouraging ". . . when morning comes to behold him lying there placidly inside Fort Sumter as if his getting there was the most natural thing in the world and the easiest."[63]

Du Pont continually begged for more and better ships to augment his forces. He was more fortunate than other squadron leaders in having the fine repair and logistical facilities in Port Royal. These concerns drove other flag officers to despair. The flag officer's machine shop kept returning his ships to their stations quicker. Many of the vessels of the squadron had not seen a repair facility, other than the one at Port Royal, since they steamed south. In July, with five vessels broken down, Du Pont wrote that "it was evident the war was intended to end in July so far as the steamers in the squadron were concerned . . ." The situation, however, never did get better. Despite Du Pont's pleas for more ships, the department committed some of its best gunboats for operations in the James River. At the beginning of August, seven steamers lay in Port Royal under repair. By the third week in August, every vessel off Charleston with the exception of the *Huron*, the *Bienville*, and the sailing vessels needed repairs. Du Pont lamented that he sent three "lame ducks" to his Port Royal repair facility each week. This problem became serious enough for Welles to intercede and instruct Rear Admiral Hiram Paulding, the Commandant of the New York Navy Yard, to have the work for the squadron "executed without delay . . ."[64]

Logistics and the Blockade

Keeping the warships on their stations was critical to the success of the blockade. By January, the increase in the numbers of vessels in the coastal squadrons began to burden the supply vessels. Du Pont felt that the time between visits was too long. He suggested relieving the supply steamers of carrying beef. He thought it more practical to purchase a cattle boat and set up a corral on shore.[65]

In April 1862, the *Rhode Island* and *Connecticut* were assigned duty with the Gulf blockading squadrons leaving the *Massachusetts* to supply both Atlantic squadrons. *Massachusetts* went only as far as Cape Canaveral. By mid-1862, with the vast increase in the number of blockaders, the need for more supply vessels became apparent. Since the large supply steamers carried ordnance, gun crews, and ammunition, such ships as *Rhode Island* (1,517 tons) could only carry 1,200 barrels—less than a ship of 350 tons. The navy gradually began using chartered schooners to supplement the supply steamers and eventually ordered *Connecticut* and *Rhode Island* to supply the Gulf Coast squadron only, adding *Massachusetts* as the only regular steamer from Virginia to the Florida Keys. To remedy some of the problems the department allowed Du Pont to "control" the movements of the supply steamer *Blackstone*. Du Pont could direct her movements at his discretion.[66]

Other supply vessels also touched at Port Royal to deliver supplies. After delays with communications going north, the supply ships returning from the Gulf Squadron were instructed to touch at Port Royal for mail, sick and wounded men, and passengers going north. Between the different supply vessels plying back and forth, most of the needs of the squadron were met. There were instances when provisions had to be borrowed from the army. At other times, the squadron was completely "bare" of certain stores. Du Pont commented that the supply ships "tantalize" the men at times. *Hope, Donegal, Arkansas, Union,* and *Circassian* also provided sustenance. One visit by the *Circassian* had Du Pont angry because she left in "great confusion, she brought no fresh provisions, lost things, and gave . . . [the squadron] neither comfort nor satisfaction in any way. . . ."[67]

By March 1863, only the *Massachusetts* served the South Atlantic Squadron. In August, the *Arkansas* was added. The former now supplied just the South Atlantic Squadron rather than both squadrons on the East coast. In January 1864, in order to put regularity in her schedule, the *Massachusetts* was asked to leave the Philadelphia Navy Yard every third Saturday, taking three weeks to make her rounds and return.[68]

The squadron also operated its own store ships. The 554-ton ship *Courier*, the 438 ton brig *Relief*, and the 327-ton bark *Release* all served the squadron. These vessels plied back and forth to the naval depots to supply the needs of the warships. Additionally, the vessels that went north for repairs might also bring back additional supplies and coal to share with the other warships. This, however, did not always happen. The bark *Kingfisher* sailed from the Boston Navy Yard in December 1862 and upon her arrival in Port Royal requisitioned canvas, stores, rigging, and clothing. Du Pont lamented to Welles, "I think it is to be regretted that a vessel direct from a navy yard should have to be supplied immediately from our resources here, which resources must be necessarily limited . . ."[69]

Once the supplies arrived at Port Royal, they then had to be redistributed to the vessels of the squadron as needed. This duty fell on the shoulders of William Reynolds, who managed the supply vessels coming south, both those of the navy and the private ones. He made every effort to have the private vessels unloaded as quickly as possible to avoid demurrage. The proper paperwork and officers who could sign the receipts were ordered to attend the delivery to expedite the unloading. Reynolds also used small vessels attached to the squadron to move the supplies from Port Royal to the extremities of the command. Vessels such as the *Oleander, Mary Sanford,* and various chartered vessels performed this duty. This procedure kept the vessels at their stations without having to leave them for supplies. The *Oleander* made trips southward on the average of about every ten days with supplies. When necessary, she also performed blockading duty, towed vessels for repairs, and carried men to and from the blockade.[70]

The storekeeper and his clerks on board the *Vermont* and later *New Hampshire* handled the requests for supplies. The senior officers generally collected requisitions from the vessels under their command and forwarded them in duplicate to Port Royal. Some ships forwarded their requisitions directly with the mail. The requisitions were checked with what was on hand and any deficiencies were forwarded to the respective bureaus to be filled. Those supplies to be issued and ordered were approved by either the flag officer or Reynolds—usually the latter. Later Reynolds administered all the vessels south of Port Royal. This required him to make any necessary revisions to the returns and send duplicates to the flag officer. Vessels leaving Port Royal for their stations were obliged to take "at least" two months of provisions and six months of stores.[71]

Despite Reynold's good management, the system was not perfect. The regular supply vessel from the north often did not bring many of the needed supplies and left the squadron in a great deal of "inconvenience and embarrassment." The attempts to make intermediate supply trips with the vessels of the squadron did not remedy the problems either. Many supply ships also waited for long periods to be unloaded. Demurrage expenses on these vessels were exorbitant, costing the government sometimes twice the cost of the entire cargo. Additionally, the stores were by necessity kept in different places. Despite the size of the various hulks, they could not stow all the supplies for the squadron. Much of it remained afloat and ashore at Station Creek, some at Bay Point. Vessels, therefore, might have to visit each location to receive all their wants.[72]

The tugs carried some of the stores, coal, and dispatches from place to place. They towed the supply schooners to the extremities of the squadron and in and out of Port Royal. These were the "life's blood" of the squadron. This class of vessel was continually requested by the flag officers. They did so much work running back and forth that without a sufficient number the squadron was considered "like an army without wagons." Generally, the screw tugs were preferred because they could come alongside other vessels without being damaged. The side-wheel tugs had an advantage in having shallower drafts, a greatly desired feature in carrying dispatches.[73]

Bricks without Straw

Like coal and stores, manpower was an important factor in the running of a ship. A shortage of officers and men, sickness, poor morale, or a combination of these and other factors could influence not only the operation of a single vessel, but in a larger context affect the squadron. The manpower problems of the navy were so severe during the Civil War that it made insignificant, by comparison, the problems of getting the ships constructed and outfitted. The lack of recruits, which plagued the service from the beginning until the end of the war, meant that ships lay at their berths, unmanned, awaiting crews. This was one logistical problem that became one of the most debilitating factors that weakened the navy during the war. One of the first measures of the president was to direct the enlistment of 18,000 men in addition to the number allowed by law. Furthermore, he authorized an increase of 1,000 in the Marine Corps. The navy increased from 7,600 men in March 1861 to 22,000 that December. Two years later, in December 1863, the navy had 38,000 enlisted men and at the end of the war over 51,000. The number of officers increased from 1,300 in 1861 to 6,700 in 1865. A total of 118,044 men enlisted in the navy from March 1861 to May 1865.[74]

Naval enlistments lagged behind the needs of the service for most of the war. Even though the average number of enlistments in the navy during 1862 amounted to over 1,500 a month, and in 1863 it was over 2,000 a month, the navy continued to suffer from a lack of men. The slow rate of enlistment was aggravated by the lack of a naval bounty payment and the high bounties paid by the army. In addition, the states did not push naval enlistments because men who shipped in the navy were not counted toward the states' draft quotas.[75]

In addition to finding enlisted men, a shortage of officers also plagued the navy. The officer corps was crippled by a loss of twenty-four percent to the Confederacy. A large number of those remaining had served in the navy for years because the system of seniority filled the ranks with older men, as there was no provision for retirement. This situation left a deficiency in the junior grade officers. As a result of this shortage, the upper three classes of the Naval Academy were ordered into active service and produced nineteen-year-old lieutenants.[76]

The navy also promoted many of its regular officers and commissioned men from the merchant service. The navy advanced master's mates to acting masters and promoted crew members to master's mates. The department sometimes rushed those promoted from the merchant service to sea without gunnery practice. To enter naval service these men had to pass an examination on seamanship, navigation, and gunnery. The service offered only five grades of line officers to volunteers: Acting Masters Mates, Acting Ensigns, Acting Masters, Acting Volunteer Lieutenants, and Acting Volunteer Lieutenant Commanders. As a rule, most regular officers found the volunteer officers far from adequate for sea duty.[77]

The shortage of regular officers became so acute that in some vessels all of the officers except the captain were volunteers. By mid-1863 almost ninety-eight percent of all the naval vessels had volunteer officers on board and nearly half of the ships had all volunteer officers or only one regular officer. In December 1863, the squadron's regular officers numbered twenty-seven percent of the total. Only eight percent of the total were regular "sea officers." One officer lamented, "How is it possible to give military consistence and coherence to a command . . . with so large a number of officers who are unpracticed in the experience of vessels of war?"[78]

As the navy commissioned more ships, the need for these officers increased. After fifteen months Du Pont had only two officers in his command that had originally sailed with him. Illnesses also incapacitated a substantial number of officers forced to spend long months at sea. The flag officers were left with officers they variously described as "ignoramuses," "too infirm," "useless," and "wholly incompetent."[79]

Furthermore, the squadron's gunboats usually operated with less than the authorized complement of officers. Shortages of this nature made it difficult to keep the watches, hold courts-martial and courts of inquiry, and command the guns when in action. Charles Henry Davis wrote to the Commandant of the Philadelphia Navy Yard: ". . . I have become like the gambler who is reduced to his last stake. The number of available officers is now so very, very small, that when I am asked to officer a ship I am somewhat in the condition of the Egyptians who were required to make bricks without straw."[80]

The enlistment of escaped slaves, probably more than any other factor, helped to alleviate the shortages. At the beginning of the war the navy had no plans to use these men. Large numbers escaped to the gunboats or into Union lines, forcing the Union to formulate some policy. In July 1861, Stringham asked Welles what he should do with them and asked if he could use them on board the storeships. Welles answered, "You will do well to employ them."[81]

In September 1861, the Navy Department authorized their employment. Captains could ship blacks at a rating no higher than "boys" and could pay them ten dollars a month and one ration a day. The navy went a step further. In December 1862, it allowed "contrabands" to be enlisted as landsmen and permitted advancement to the rank of seaman, ordinary seaman, fireman, or coal heaver. The department did not permit them to transfer from one vessel to another with a rating higher than landsman unless their vessel went out of commission.[82]

There were large numbers of blacks displaced by the war along the South Atlantic seaboard. Commanding officers were encouraged to enlist "acclimated persons" as boys and later as firemen and coal heavers. The contrabands from this area were thought to be able to "relieve in hot climates the whites of ships' companies . . ." Yet with the army also actively recruiting in the area contrabands were "scarce."[83]

Foreigners also filled many of the vacancies in the ships. British seamen were preferred, but the men of all countries joined the service. One officer remarked that there were so many foreigners in the service that "When I get into a boat it seems as if the English language had changed."[84]

Diseases and other physical ailments aggravated the already grave problem of manpower and decreased further the efficiency of the squadron. The doctors treated a variety of diseases and ailments that kept the small medical staffs busy. An extremely small number of seamen went ashore to hospitals for treatment. Surgeon Samuel Pellman Boyer had a unique way of keeping his binnacle list small. He gave some of his men harsh treatments, causing the men to fear the cure more than the illness or faking an illness.[85]

When the number of sick became too large to handle, several ships accommodated the sick. The *Valparaiso* was used for smallpox cases, but by 1864 was "foul with bilge water, leaking and worm eaten and altogether a most uncomfortable hospital." The *Mohawk* was also used. *Vermont* and *Wabash* also served as hospitals since neither had anywhere near a full complement on board. The staff on *Valparaiso* consisted of one steward and five contraband attendants.[86]

Coal for the Warships

The facilities at Port Royal remained busy and served the entire war as the major logistical base of the squadron. Importantly, it provided a convenient and smooth water anchorage for coaling. Chartered colliers brought the coal to this port and the naval vessels coaled directly from the colliers. Initially, Du Pont had asked for a thousand-ton hulk with hoisting machinery to serve the warships. As early as December 1862, Du Pont had surveys made to place a coal depot at Bay Point. He planned a rather sophisticated wharf with a railway and steam hoisting equipment to lift iron buckets that could discharge coal directly into the ships. This facility might have served the squadron well, but the project, unfortunately, was long delayed and was not complete until the war was nearly over.[87]

Reynolds was the man who administered the ordering and movement of the coal. One of his largest challenges was to get the coal to the vessels without them leaving their stations. Reynolds worked with Captain Henry Adams in Philadelphia, who coordinated all coal shipments for the navy. The vessels coming from Philadelphia were "liable to proceed to any point within the limits of the South Atlantic Blockading Squadron." About half sailed to Port Royal and a large portion traveled to Charleston. Colliers traveling to locations other than Port Royal received an extra compensation. When cleared for Port Royal, the masters usually balked when Reynolds asked them to travel to other ports because it voided their war risk policies. Reynolds, though, felt that if the coal were required at other ports and the masters would not agree to change their destination, then the government should seize the collier or assume the marine and war risks for the trip. This solution, however, required the navy to send officers and men with the ships.[88]

The size of the arriving colliers often had important ramifications. Du Pont specifically asked that Adams send only schooners that drew no more than eight feet. He made this request so that they could enter any port from Georgetown to the St. John's River. Adams sometimes found it necessary to send larger barks and brigs to satisfy the tremendous coal needs of the squadron. The larger vessels presented several problems. The tugs could not handle them easily when steaming against tides and wind. The yards were always in the way when coming alongside or shoving off. The holds were naturally deep and the bulwarks high. This meant it required extra time to deliver the coal because hoisting the coal from the hold took longer. Lastly, they could not go away unballasted and had to load about one hundred tons of rock or sand before they could sail north.[89]

Trying to coal off Charleston was problematical. The rough weather caused the ships to "knock each other to pieces." Even with the colliers at the station, it usually took at least twelve hours, but usually the better part of a day, to transfer coal. Off Charleston, Du Pont usually sent brigs rather than the more lightly framed schooners to perform this task. With constant damage to the colliers, combined with the raft of the complaints from the masters, Du Pont gave up this practice.[90]

Keeping the squadron furnished with a regular supply of coal required constant vigilance and planning. Prior to the winter of 1862, the squadron's coal was furnished on a "standing order for a certain number of tons a week." But this policy could either cause the coal to run short or accumulate to excess, depending on the activity of the warships. Navy agents working through the Bureau of Construction and Repair handled the requisitions until November 1862, when the department ordered Captain Henry Adams to Philadelphia to coordinate coal shipments under the new Bureau of Equipment and Recruiting. Requisitions for coal went directly to the bureau, with duplicates forwarded to Adams for his action. As the squadron grew the coal needs also expanded. In March 1862, the squadron used about 1,100 tons a week.[91]

The shortages for the squadron became critical several times during the war. These deficiencies threatened the continuance of operations and the blockade. In February 1862, the navy exhausted its supply and the army loaned coal to keep the ships operational. By the end of March, Du Pont had become agitated and had four steamers laid up waiting for coal. Without fuel, he reminded Welles, that the blockade of Charleston would be "seriously impaired." He wrote his wife, ". . . coal, my squadron is crippled for want of it. I am almost crazy, for a steam fleet without coal is like a sailing squadron dismasted. They ask me how much I require a week instead of sending it out—it never spoils like beef."[92]

The squadron suffered another shortage in September 1862, but a shortage in March 1863 affected all the squadrons. In 1863, a striking mob closed all the mines in Schuylkill County, Pennsylvania. Using violence, the mob kept the mines closed for four weeks. They retained the coal colliers and shut the pumps off, which allowed water to run into the mines, destroying sections of the shafts. Other strikes at the collieries and striking locomotive coal heavers further slowed the delivery. With this strike, Henry Adams suggested that Du Pont lend no more coal to the army.[93]

Again that August coal was at a premium when another event caused an unexpected lapse in the coal shipments. When the Confederate army invaded Pennsylvania in June and July 1863, it caused so much fear that the coal trade stopped for one month. Naval officers must have wondered why General Lee did not destroy the Reading Railroad, a major spur in the delivery of coal. The severing of this logistical artery would have affected every squadron. Again, operations had to be suspended. It became so grave that the blockaders began sending crews ashore to cut wood. This particular shortage lasted until the third week in August.[94]

Brown Water Operations

The Union navy's presence along the southern coast continued to be a threat to Confederate positions throughout the war. The commanders of blockading vessels acted under "definite but not compulsory instructions" to make reconnaissance missions and reconnoiter enemy defenses. On 21 May Commander George A. Prentiss in the screw steamer *Albatross*, along with Lieutenant Commander James M. Duncan in the screw gunboat *Norwich*, steamed into Winyah Bay, the portal to Georgetown, South Carolina. They encountered deserted works and "quaker" guns on both South and Cat islands. The next day they passed into the Sampit River to Georgetown. On their approach, the rebels torched a brig loaded with turpentine to block the Union vessels below the town. Both warships passed the brig with difficulty. The *Albatross* and the *Norwich* slowly worked their way along the wharves and passed within thirty yards of the houses of the town. After passing above Georgetown, they turned in the narrow channel and dropped back down the river. A few Union sympathizers appeared at the wharf, but Prentiss cautioned the men not to demonstrate too enthusiastically since he could not help them. A woman appeared from a belfry and spread a rebel flag over the bell, tempting action by Prentiss, but he decided against sending a landing party ashore.[95]

Interior operations such as this occupied the time and the assets of the squadron. In the upper St. John's River, interior blockade running required the presence of several gunboats. Most of the duty was mundane and without event, but tragedy could strike without warning. Concealed infantry was always a threat and in places the river was so narrow that in order to turn, the steamers had to use kedge anchors. A local band of men known as the "Regulators" operated near Black Creek, about twenty miles up the St. John's from Jacksonville. One of this band's leaders, George Huston, boasted of killing the black pilot captured when the rebel band ambushed the boats of the *Penguin* and *Henry Andrew*. On 8 June Lieutenant Commander Ammen sent his executive officer Lieutenant John G. Sprotson, two other officers, and seventy men in three boats to apprehend Huston. Landing at daylight, Sprotson and his men caught Huston at his home and called for his surrender. Huston opened the door bearing two pistols, a double-barreled

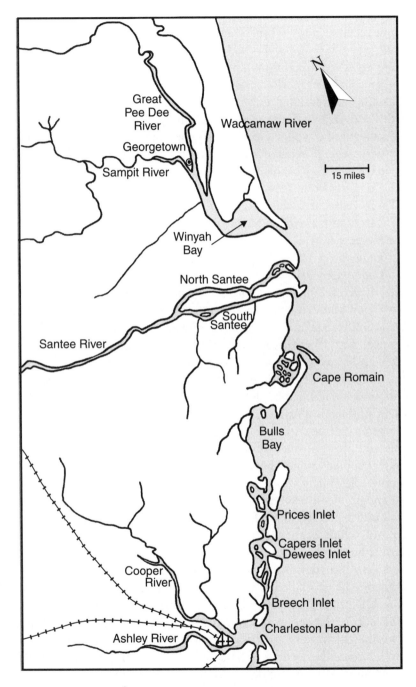

MAP 8. COAST NORTH OF CHARLESTON

shotgun, and a bowie knife. Huston's first shot killed Sprotson instantly. Huston received four wounds and died on board *Seneca* eleven days later.[96]

Brown water operations up the North Edisto and into Wadmelaw River on 21 June sparked a short engagement between Confederate troops and the *Crusader* and *Planter*, carrying seventy men of the Fifty-fourth Pennsylvania Volunteers. When the naval vessels neared a bluff, the enemy fired a volley of musketry, but the naval guns drove them away with several broadsides. The *Planter* landed the troops who destroyed the quarters of the Marion Artillery and the Sixteenth Regiment South Carolina Volunteers and then reembarked.[97]

Three days later the *E. B. Hale*, *Western World*, *Albatross*, and *Henry Andrew* passed the bar at the North Santee to destroy a bridge of the Northeastern Railroad seventy miles upstream. Only the tug *Hale* could maneuver well in the narrow and twisting river. While passing a plantation, enemy artillery, riflemen, and cavalry fired on the *Henry Andrew*—the vessel taking up the rear. The other warships stood back downstream and drove the enemy into the woods. Commander George Prentiss landed Marines and a party of seamen who burned a mill, some dwellings, and 100,000 bushels of rice. The rebels, meanwhile, reorganized and attacked in force. They drove the Marines and seamen back to the gunboats along with about four hundred slaves who boarded the Union vessels and escaped downriver.[98]

During July and August, while the army remained inactive, the navy continued to probe enemy defensive positions. Calls to support army positions and actions aimed at counter guerrilla operations kept the naval vessels occupied along the whole length of the coast. Illustrative of the navy's flexibility was a call for support by Brigadier General John M. Brannan. He sent word that the rebels planned to attack Port Royal Island and asked a gunboat to protect his positions along the Broad River and Whale Branch. Du Pont sent the light draft *Paul Jones* to aid the army, but the flag officer fretted over the possibility of guerrilla warfare and the "greater absorption" of his gunboats.[99]

On 14 August, the navy made a reconnaissance twenty-five miles up the Black River, a branch of the Pee Dee River above Georgetown. During this sortie, the captured Confederate tug *Treaty* and screw steamer *Pocahontas* drew more attention by the enemy. The senior officer, Lieutenant Commander George B. Balch, was one of Du Pont's favorites. He wrote about him, "a more devoted officer our Navy does not possess— with the greatest amount of energy and *pluck*, and skill in handling guns,

he is *always ready*, overcomes difficulties and is ever genial and cheerful
—he is a great favorite of mine." Balch protected the little tug by sheathing her with two inches of pine planking and placing the crews' hammocks behind this barrier. The vessels steamed twenty-two miles up the
river before nearing the enemy fortifications. The *Pocahontas* anchored
and tried to deliver a broadside by making her stern hawser fast to a tree.
The tide, however, caused Balch to change position and bring his vessel
to within five hundred yards of the fieldwork. At 9:25, he beat his crew
to quarters. Firing shells and grape shot, Balch found the enemy fortification abandoned, and he proceeded up the river with the two vessels for
several more miles. On the way back down the river rebel troops "kept
up a spirited fire" on the ships. For twenty miles the two vessels ran the
gauntlet to safety, twice running aground under the fire of riflemen. At
sunset they reached Georgetown and anchored below the city.[100]

By the summer of 1862, the Confederate forces in the St. John's
River began to exert more pressure on the naval forces that patrolled the
river. Guerrillas operated up and down the St. John's and they attempted
to close the upper portion of the river to the Union navy. The gunboats
maintained their inside blockade of the river by keeping a force at the
river's mouth. The Confederates made a determined attempt to close
the river to the naval forces by erecting a well-placed battery of seven
8-inch guns and two smaller rifled guns on the south bank of St. John's
Bluff seven miles above the mouth of the river. On 11 September the
screw steamers *Uncas* and *Patroon* exchanged fire for four hours with
the batteries. Because of the elevated position and the strong construction of the works, naval fire alone could not silence the guns.[101]

On 17 September the side-wheel gunboats *Paul Jones* and *Cimarron*, and the warships *E. B. Hale*, *Uncas*, and *Patroon* steamed up the
St. John's to attack the fortifications. The *Paul Jones* and the *Cimarron*
attacked from 1,600 yards and the other three, because of a misunderstanding, considered it necessary to attack in line ahead. Attacking in
this fashion, their firing "was of little, if any, service." For five hours the
gunboats kept up a cannonade but did little damage to the batteries and,
after expending half of their ammunition, withdrew.[102]

Commander John Steedman suggested a joint force might capture the
enemy fortifications. Major General Ormsby M. Mitchel, commanding
the Department of the South, detached General Brannon and sent him to
capture the fortifications. Brannon detached part of the First Brigade and
took along the entire Second Brigade with parts of other units, comprising 4,500 men. The side-wheel gunboat *Water Witch*, *Cimarron*, *Uncas*,

Paul Jones, Patroon and *E. B. Hale* accompanied the army transports *Neptune, Boston, Cosmopolitan* and *Ben De Ford*. On 1 October, the transports arrived off the St. John's River bar at dawn. By 1:00 P.M. the transports passed over the bar and anchored near Mayport Mills. Brannon landed 450 soldiers and the navy put ashore the boat howitzers from the *Paul Jones* and the *Cimarron* as well as a detachment of Marines to man them. While the boats put the force ashore the *Cimarron, Water Witch*, and *Uncas* proceeded upriver to St. John's Bluff. They opened fire on the enemy batteries there and, after a ninety-minute engagement, Steedman hoisted the recall signal. The vessels then dropped back downstream. On the afternoon of the third, before Brannon had disembarked all his troops, artillery, and calvary, the *Uncas* and *E. B. Hale* steamed upriver to reconnoiter. As they came into range they threw shells into the fortifications, but received no response. Steaming abreast the batteries, they discovered that the Confederates had abandoned the fortification, realizing that the advancing Union soldiers would flank their position. Lieutenant Alfred T. Snell took a boat ashore from the *E. B. Hale* and raised the American flag. The army troops later took possession of the fort, carried off the guns, and destroyed the works.[103]

The *Cimarron, Hale,* and *Water Witch* proceeded toward Jacksonville on the fourth destroying between two hundred and three hundred boats and flats on the way upriver. Arriving at Jacksonville, they found the town nearly deserted. On the fifth, the Union forces occupied the town for the second time during the war, but the troops remained only several days before departing again. The *E. B. Hale* then proceeded to Palatka, leaving both the *Water Watch* and the *Cimarron* behind. She anchored there on the sixth and after firing a few shells at rebel horsemen, dropped back downriver and anchored at Orange Mills that evening.[104]

On the sixth Lieutenant Commander Edward P. Williams proceeded up the St. John's in the side-wheel steam gunboat *Darlington* with the *E. B. Hale* covering her movements and destroying small boats along the way. The *Hale*'s draft did not permit her into Lake George and she remained behind while the *Darlington* steamed farther up the river. At Hawkinsville, 168 miles above Jacksonville, a landing party scoured the town looking for evidence of the steamer *Governor Milton*. Finding evidence that the steamer had been there, eight seamen and fourteen soldiers proceeded up a creek in a boat and a canoe. Here they found the vessel and cut her out as a prize and proceeded back downriver on the eighteenth.[105]

The navy continued to strike at the Confederate commercial infrastructure. Operating up the St. John's throughout the remainder of the year, they fought guerrilla groups and destroyed saltworks. Naval expeditions also wrecked as many as one thousand small boats in an effort to keep the river clear and restrict the movement of supplies and agricultural products. Destruction of the boats and the saltworks clearly struck a blow at the economic infrastructure of the this part of the coast. Throughout the remaining months of 1862, the Union naval forces also destroyed and seized other property. In an expedition up the Doboy River, a combined army and naval force seized about two hundred fifty thousand board feet of lumber, saws, corn mills, and other property. While the seizure of Confederate property included virtually anything of value, agricultural products were the most frequent targets. Cotton agents from the Treasury Department administered the confiscations. The sailors called them the "forty thieves" and Du Pont also had few kind words for these government men. He wrote his wife, "They managed to slip into their instructions at Washington, besides cotton, the words 'other property,' which I presume they construe into meaning pianos and organs out of churches!"[106]

While the gunboats actively operated in the rivers, Steedman and Brannan arranged another combined operation, this time to destroy railroad trestles of the Charleston and Savannah Railroad. No one consulted Du Pont about this expedition because he had traveled north on a visit to the Navy Department. The most senior naval officer present, who was much junior in rank to Brannan, felt compelled to assist the army. The expedition had three separate objectives, the trestles over Pocotaligo and Tulifinny creeks, and that over the Coosawhatchie River. The naval officers assembled on the *Vermont* and received instructions for times of sailing and other details, after which the 4,448 men attached to the expedition boarded eight gunboats and seven transports.[107]

At sunset on 21 October, the expedition started from Hilton Head. The vessels steamed to the mouth of the Broad River and four armed launches, carrying 100 troops towed by a tug, advanced ahead to make preliminary landings and capture Confederate pickets at the landing site. A signal prompted the remaining vessels to get underway after midnight. In the darkness confusion prevailed and the operation lost its cohesion. The *Paul Jones* and transport *Ben De Ford* started up the river, not realizing that no other vessels followed. The side-wheel steam gunboat *Conemaugh* never received any sailing instructions, missed the channel, and grounded. This threw the vessels in line astern into confusion. The screw steamer *Marblehead* and the *Water Witch* collided, and none of the steamers left the Broad River before daylight.[108]

The transports arrived on the morning of the twenty-second and the troops began to disembark at 10:00. The *Uncas* moved to support the troops up the Pocataligo while the *Patroon* and Coast Survey steamer *Vixen* steamed up the Coosawhatchie River to cover troops landing from the *Planter*. Three 12-pound boat howitzers and gun crews from *Wabash*, under the command of Lieutenant Lloyd Phoenix, traveled with Brannan's forces. Swamps, thickets, and burned bridges delayed the movement of the Union forces. After landing, the naval crews dragged the howitzers five miles inland and immediately met the enemy. Opening up a rapid fire, the naval gun crews advanced with the army forces until they fired away most of their ammunition. At this point, Coxswain Edward Ringold of the *Wabash* ran back two miles, filled his shirt with fixed ammunition, slung it over his back and ran back to the front under a heavy fire. He arrived in time to check the enemy's advance. This gallantry earned him the Medal of Honor.[109]

The uncoordinated Union forces allowed the Confederate pickets to warn of the landings. Since surprise was an important element in the campaign, when the Union forces failed to quickly reach their objectives, the momentum shifted in favor of the rebels. Despite facing an inferior foe, the general believed the expedition was now too risky and at 5:00 P.M. he recalled his troops. On the twenty-third the troops reembarked on the transports and the naval vessels. The *Marblehead* and *Vixen* covered the withdrawal and brought up the rear. By 10:00 P.M. the entire expeditionary force lay in the safety of its anchorage in Hilton Head.[110]

Brannan praised the navy and the cooperation between the two branches of the service, but Du Pont "regretted" the whole operation. Du Pont blamed the army's "restlessness" and believed that burning the railroad bridge was no more useful than "burning a pile of wood." He, likewise, pointed out that the operation gained nothing and that it was a "complete failure" because the troops "ventured out of reach of the gunboats and . . . were thrashed by an inferior force . . ." Corresponding with Fox, he expressed annoyance that the expedition was arranged in his absence. He, however, did not blame the senior naval officer present, who did not refuse the general's request for cooperation. The expedition also irritated him because it diverted vessels from the blockade.[111]

This latter expedition reveals the almost unquestionable and frequent cooperation given by the navy to army operations. Yet, the army officers often grumbled about the navy's lack of cooperation. Despite the fact that little strategic planning for joint operations occurred, the army officers never understood or tried to comprehend the limitations of the ships, specifically that their movements were, in many cases, tied to weather and tides. The army leadership also never fully appreciated the vast commitment that the blockade represented to the naval forces. These operations show clearly that the navy allowed the army forces to move about the coast with ease. The Union leadership, however, failed to exploit this advantageous situation.

By the fall of 1862, Du Pont had commanded the squadron for about a year. During this time, his naval forces had actively carried out operations along the entire coast. Not once, however, had he and Welles discussed at any length the continuing strategy of the war. Beginning in the spring of 1862, Fox began with regularity to hint at operations against Charleston. Fox, though, never pressed Du Pont on this matter before the summer, waiting for the completion of the campaign against Richmond. The Navy Department's enormous commitment of resources in the Peninsular Campaign would not allow any concentrated effort on Charleston until it ended. At the beginning of September, however, the eyes of the department began to look south.

— 5 —

"The Ironclads Are Not
Formidable Monsters"

Du Pont Travels North

On the morning of 9 August 1862, Du Pont climbed into his barge along-side the *Vermont*. In the highest form of respect, the men of the *Vermont* manned the yards to salute the flag officer. As Du Pont's barge passed the other ships in Port Royal, all the crews cheered and the barge's crew answered each in turn. When the barge approached the *Wabash*, the crew of the frigate also "laid out" on the yards. Additionally the men had sent aloft the upper yards and manned these as well, producing a "very thrilling effect" according to Du Pont. The boatswain piped Du Pont on board, and as he reached the deck, he observed the Marine guard at attention, and the officers of the squadron there to greet him. Du Pont shook hands with his officers as he strolled aft. Du Pont then stood in an elevated position as the gunners on the *Wabash* began firing a salute. When the last gun fired, the men "laid in," and climbed down from the yards. The square flag officer's pennant was hauled down from the mizzenmast and hoisted at the mainmast, denoting Du Pont's promotion to the newly created rank of Rear Admiral. In honor of this promotion the other ships of the squadron, as well as the fort at Hilton Head, also saluted Du Pont.[1]

By the fall of 1862, the Union war effort had not enjoyed abundant success. The recent withdrawal of the Union forces from the Virginia peninsula seemed to encapsulate the character of the military operations

127

for the Union. Now, nearly eighteen months into the conflict, the North craved another victory. On 29 August, the army suffered a crushing defeat at the Second Battle of Bull Run and Confederate General Braxton Bragg's move into Kentucky threatened Louisville. Yet, the fortunes shifted quickly after Lincoln restored McClellan to command. He mauled Lee's army at Antietam that September and Bragg's forces retreated to southeastern Tennessee. With these army successes stealing the headlines, Welles and Fox both felt that a naval victory at Charleston would give the service the prestige that it once had, and again deserved. Fox, in particular, had a complete disdain for the army. He wrote Du Pont that, "The crowning act of this war ought to be [carried out] by the navy. I feel that my duties are two fold: first, to beat our southern friends; second, to beat the Army." The Assistant Secretary of the Navy began an unrelenting campaign to attack Charleston because Fox believed "the Fall of Charleston is the fall of Satan's Kingdom." The focus on Charleston by the Navy Department would be the turning point in the war in the South Atlantic Theater of operations. Once the forces engaged, there would be no turning back.[2]

In spite of the department's growing interest in Charleston, Du Pont never discussed future operations at any length with Welles. Raymond Rodgers had for some time urged the flag officer to go north to do this. By September Du Pont finally acquiesced, but only after Welles instructed him to come to the capital. The flag officer left Port Royal on 27 September and traveled directly to Wilmington, Delaware. He then proceeded with his wife to Washington. Arriving at the department on 2 October, Du Pont met with Welles and Fox for several days. He escorted his spouse home and stopped by Philadelphia to see some of his ships being repaired. He traveled to his home in Delaware for a short respite and then returned to the capital.[3]

During the meetings at the department, Fox dominated the discussions and Du Pont patiently listened. Fox firmly believed that if the new *Passaic* class monitors made an attack on the Charleston forts, that even without other naval support, they alone could carry the works. Fox was so single-minded that Du Pont rarely spoke. When he did speak, he asked that the army and naval forces be augmented for a joint attack, though he never pressed Fox or Welles for this or insisted that the department adopt this strategy. Instead, both Fox and Welles interpreted his silence as acquiescence. This silence spoke volumes to Welles and Fox, who believed that the flag officer concurred with their views.

Du Pont, however, knew that Fox, who so forcefully argued for a naval attack, would not listen to a suggestion of combined operations due to his dislike of the army. He felt that trying to change Fox's views would be virtually impossible and that he would instead appear timid. Despite the days of meetings, the men never discussed the operations in detail or formulated a plan. Du Pont understood that he was to act quickly because the entire nation was anxious for the capture of Charleston. Extensive discussions on the use of ironclads in the attack seemed premature, since none of the new *Passaic* class monitors were complete at this time, but the conference was fatal because it bred misunderstandings on both sides that produced huge complications later.[4]

An imponderable question is why Du Pont did not show any real opposition to the department. Du Pont claimed that he hoped the circumstances would change before the attack could begin. He also might have felt that if he did not accept the concept of a purely naval attack, he risked losing his command. The cause of much of this anxiety was Captain John A. Dahlgren. On 1 October, Dahlgren, the Chief of the Bureau of Ordnance, applied directly to Welles to lead an attack on the city. Welles, though, would not replace Du Pont, knowing that the flag officer had earned the right to lead this attack. Undeterred, Dahlgren went over the secretary's head to President Lincoln. He also appealed directly to Du Pont and approached Andrew Foote and Henry Wise, as well, to take up his cause. Foote even visited Du Pont at his home to convince him to allow Dahlgren to lead the ironclads into Charleston. Fox also explained to Du Pont that "Dahlgren frets under the war bugles . . ." and had advised Dahlgren to take a monitor or go as Du Pont's ordnance officer. Du Pont offered to take him as one of his ironclad captains but believed Dahlgren "a diseased man on the subject of preferment and position . . ."[5]

Welles denied Dahlgren's request for command of the attacking force, telling the Chief of Ordnance that he could not rob Du Pont of this honor. He gave Dahlgren a chance to participate, however, and offered him command of an ironclad or the position of ordnance officer in the fleet. Du Pont, "astounded" by this offer, wrote Fox that he did not want Dahlgren as his ordnance officer afloat. Welles realized that Dahlgren sought this command only to make himself eligible for promotion to rear admiral. Welles's offer, though, insulted the highly sensitive Dahlgren and he countered by asking the secretary to relieve him of his bureau job and to promote him to the rank of rear admiral. Welles denied both requests and Dahlgren turned down both of the positions, only to continue his promotion campaign through other means.[6]

While in Washington Du Pont also reestablished his political and social ties by meeting with Lincoln, cabinet members, generals and naval officers. Before leaving the capital, Du Pont, Fox, and Raymond Rodgers visited the Washington Navy Yard to witness a test of Dahlgren's new 15-inch gun. Du Pont came away impressed at the gun's offensive capabilities believing that "a sufficient number of these . . . would tear away, I believe, the walls of forts." Yet, with Fox's enthusiasm weighing on his mind, Du Pont worried that the department might hurry him into attacking Charleston with an insufficient force.[7]

On 18 October Du Pont sailed south and stopped in Hampton Roads before continuing on to rejoin his squadron. Two days later in a meeting on board the *Keystone State* lying off Fort Monroe, he, Fox, and Rodgers held their final discussion concerning the attack. For a brief time he felt he had changed Fox's view on Charleston. That afternoon he realized that he had not managed to make his concerns known to the department and left without having discussed any real plan of attack. He expressed his concerns to his wife, claiming that the department did not consider all the difficulties. He also had warned Fox of the "undue influence of the political sentiment in hastening operations on Charleston." He sailed with instructions to attack quickly and that public sentiment considered six weeks a long time to do so. The admiral was never able to convince Fox or Welles of his concerns, nor did he grasp the department's political needs for a quick victory. The admiral left knowing he could not discard an attack on the cradle of secession no matter what complications might arise. Before Du Pont even left Washington, word reached General Beauregard that the enemy would attack Charleston. This message spurred the on-going improvement of the defenses in the Charleston area. Beauregard wrote Secretary of War George W. Randolph, "We will endeavor to give Commodore Du Pont as warm a reception as circumstances will permit."[8]

While the department expressed its desires for a quick naval attack on Charleston, several issues complicated a timely assault. A timetable of six weeks was simply not possible. The Charleston attack depended entirely on the use of ironclads and the next generation of these warships, the improved *Passaic* class, would not be complete for some months. In addition to the Charleston operation, the department had at the same time proposed attacking the forts at the mouth of the Cape Fear. The latter attack was to precede a move on Charleston, yet both plans relied on the impregnable attributes of the monitors for success.[9]

Fort McAllister

On the afternoon of 22 October, Du Pont passed through the Charleston fleet and arrived at Port Royal after sunset the next day. When he boarded the *Wabash*, he discovered his gunboats away on the ill-fated expedition up the Pocotaligo River. According to the flag officer, the whole expedition was a feint to draw off troops so that Fort McAllister, farther south, might be attacked. While the attack never developed, the capture of Fort McAllister had important strategic significance. The fort sat on top of a bluff on the south bank of the Ogeechee River about eighteen miles from the river's mouth. Here it protected an important bridge of the Savannah, Albany, and Gulf Railroad, twenty-two miles upstream. This earthwork fort anchored the defensive works south of the city and mounted five 32-pounders, a 42-pounder, one 8-inch Columbiad and a 10-inch mortar. Pilings driven across the river just below the fort kept naval vessels at a respectable distance during an attack.[10]

Initially, Fort McAllister appeared no stronger than many of the other river fortifications. In early July Du Pont instructed Commander Steedman to make a reconnaissance up the Ogeechee River without risking his vessels. Two weeks later the flag officer learned that the *Nashville* was lying near the fort. He immediately asked Steedman to make a "reconnaissance in force" and to destroy the fort, if possible. On 29 July, Steedman took the *Paul Jones*, *Unadilla*, *Huron*, and the screw steamer *Madgie* up river. At 10:00 A.M. they came within range of the fort's guns. Both sides kept up a "spirited fire" for ninety minutes. This attack convinced Steedman that wooden vessels could not advance without losing one or more ships. The piles across the river kept the vessels at an unfavorable distance and convinced him that naval vessels could not ascend the river without "great sacrifice of life . . ."[11]

The naval vessels had their next encounter with Fort McAllister on the morning of 19 November. The ninety-day gunboat *Wissahickon*, the screw steamer *Dawn* and mortar schooner *No. 5* moved up the Ogeechee River and opened fire on the batteries. During the naval bombardment, the guns of Fort McAllister remained silent. Thinking the rebels might have deserted their guns; the *Dawn* and *Wissahickon* advanced to a bend in the river about five hundred yards closer to the fort. At 9:45, when about three thousand yards away from the enemy, the rebel gunners opened fire and the first shot struck the *Wissahickon* four feet below the waterline abreast her 11-inch gun. The shot opened a large hole in her hull and the pumps could not keep the vessel clear of water. Lieutenant Commander John L. Davis, fearing he would have to run ashore or sink, dropped down the river to stop the leak. At 2:30 Davis signaled a cease fire and the vessels returned to their anchorage in the Vernon River, having rediscovered the fort's strength.[12]

Du Pont pondered his options and waited for the department to strengthen his command for operations against Charleston. Meanwhile, Rear Admiral Samuel Phillips Lee, commanding the North Atlantic Blockading Squadron, set in motion a plan to attack one or both forts guarding the Cape Fear River. The Navy Department committed a number of heavily armed warships and three monitors to this enterprise. The department hoped to capture these forts quickly and then take up operations against Charleston. The Wilmington forts, though, proved to be more difficult to attack because of the shallow channels that led to the river entrances. When the *Monitor* foundered on her trip to Beaufort, North Carolina, Welles cancelled the attack and decided to send the ironclads to Charleston.[13]

Parts of the attacking force began to arrive at Charleston less than three weeks after the *Monitor* sank. The trip of one of the new *Passaic* class monitors, *Montauk*, caused some concern. With the loss of the *Monitor* fresh in many minds, she encountered a storm off Hatteras. Waves began pounding the vessel, shaking her from stem to stern. Green seas crested to within six inches of her turret top but she managed to weather the storm. On 18 January the monitor *Montauk* and the seagoing *New Ironsides* arrived at Port Royal. The arrival of ironclads and the promise of others opened new vistas for Du Pont. These warships would enable the squadron to project the Union navy's power as never before imagined. These warships came, as he would later learn, with high expectations of both decisive action and success.[14]

The Confederates, meanwhile, had busied themselves converting the *Nashville* into a privateer they renamed the *Rattlesnake*. As a blockade runner, her escape would only cause embarrassment. A privateer, however, was a more viable threat to the blockade. This annoyed Du Pont and occupied his attention. His greatest fear was that the rebels would finish fitting her as a privateer and get her past the blockading vessels in Ossabaw Sound. Should she successfully raid Union shipping, it would damage Du Pont's credibility and would no doubt provoke probing questions from Welles and perhaps Congress. Captain Joseph Green passed on "reliable information" that the rebels planned to rescue the *Rattlesnake* and help her escape by using a shallow draft ironclad or the *Atlanta*. Green suggested sinking a stone-filled hulk to block the channel, but Du Pont did not overreact and merely sent another gunboat to watch Ossabaw Sound.[15]

Since Fort McAllister protected the anchorage of the *Rattlesnake*, Du Pont felt he might use his new weapon. He had in mind a "test" of both the offensive and defensive qualities of the monitors. The flag officer in particular wished to determine if 15-inch shells would effectively destroy well-built, casemented, earthwork fortifications. On 20 January, Du Pont ordered Commander John Worden, the former skipper of the *Monitor*, to take the *Montauk* up the Ogeechee River and capture Fort McAllister, destroy the *Rattlesnake*, and burn the railroad trestle upriver. They did not consider taking *New Ironsides*, because her draft exceeded the *Montauk*'s by more than four feet.[16]

On 24 January the *Montauk* left Port Royal in tow of the side-wheel warship *James Adger*. She arrived off the bar at Ossabaw Sound that afternoon, but a thick fog prevented the ironclad from immediately moving up the river. The fog lifted for nearly two hours and allowed the pilot to bring her into the river and anchor. The next day dense fog again prevented *Montauk* from moving any farther. Poor visibility on the morning of the twenty-sixth prompted Worden to call the commanding officers of *Seneca*, *Wissahickon*, *Dawn* and the mortar schooner *C. P. Williams* on board *Montauk* for a conference to discuss the attack. When the fog lifted that afternoon, the vessels proceeded upriver. The *Dawn* towed the schooner *C. P. Williams* and they anchored in line astern just outside the range of Fort McAllister's guns.[17]

At 8:00 P.M. a boat from each *Seneca* and *Wissahickon*, in the charge of Lieutenant Commander John Davis, pulled upriver to reconnoiter and to destroy any range markers placed in the river by the Confederates. Near Harvey's Cut, Davis and his men destroyed range markers made with rags placed on poles in the water. Davis also checked out the obstructions and found torpedoes attached to them. The party arrived back to report to Worden just before midnight.[18]

At 7:00 on the morning of 27 January, the vessels weighed anchor and got underway. The *Dawn* took the *C. P. Williams* in tow. The *Montauk*, in the van, steamed to a position 150 yards below the obstructions at a point designated by Lieutenant Commander Davis. The remaining vessels anchored starting 2,200 yards astern. The *Seneca* took the for-

wardmost position, and the *Wissahickon, Dawn*, and *C. P. Williams* anchored in line of battle astern. At 7:35, two shots from the *Montauk*
broke the silence. The fort answered with a brisk fire and most of the
Confederate shots either struck the *Montauk* or fell within fifteen feet.
None struck farther than forty feet away from the ironclad. Those striking the water nearby sent columns of water into the turret like "show-
ers of rain." The gunners on the *Montauk* did not find the fort's range
until sometime before 8:30. The *Montauk* expended all her shells by
11:15 and Worden, observing that the monitor's solid shot did no damage to the fort, ordered a cease-fire. The naval vessels retired downstream to their former anchorage.[19]

The warships had fired nearly two-thirds of their ammunition—370
shot and shells—at the fort without silencing the guns. Fort McAllister's
gunners concentrated their fire on *Montauk* and struck the ironclad
fourteen times, but did no serious harm. The *Montauk* added little to
the attack because her firing was not accurate. She managed to hit the
fort only about ten percent of the time. The other warships' fire also inflicted little or no injury to the earthworks. The fort's defenders suffered
no casualties and escaped injury by taking cover in the bomb proofs at
each shot.[20]

The citizens of Savannah heard the bombardment and the city council asked Tattnall to take *Atlanta* down to assist the fort. The commodore realized that this would be both risky and difficult. He hesi-
tantly agreed to run by *Montauk* and attack the wooden vessels below,
despite his conviction that his ironclad would not be a match for a monitor. To operate in these shallow waters would also require him to
lighten his warship, exposing portions under the knuckle, which was
only plated with two inches of iron. Tattnall believed he could avoid an
engagement and with superior speed run by the *Montauk*, but getting
by the monitor a second time in order to get back up the river could have
been problematic. The attack never occurred and within days two monitors lay in Ossabaw Sound.[21]

This initial attack on Fort McAllister by the *Montauk* began to shape
Du Pont's visions about the practicality of using the monitors against the
Charleston fortifications. The admiral believed that further attacks on
McAllister would be pointless unless troops accompanied the naval
force. Du Pont also told Worden that unless he could remove the obstructions, he saw no reason to renew the attack. Du Pont immediately
wrote Welles expressing his reservations about the monitors. He wrote
that despite their ability to withstand enemy fire, their slow rate of fire

had "no corresponding quality of aggression or destructiveness . . ." Du Pont also mentioned to Welles the near impossibility of removing obstructions while under fire.[22]

The Confederates Take the Offensive

Before the Union officers could thoroughly discuss and analyze the initial bombardments of Fort McAllister, the Confederates took the war to the Union forces. They attacked the blockading fleet off Charleston as well as the warships in the Stono River. These bold attacks shook the confidence of Du Pont and his officers and demonstrated that, despite numerical superiority, the blockading vessels did face grave risks.

Even as the Union warships approached Fort McAllister, the Confederates were completing plans to strike back. Both the 532-ton ex-ferry boat *Commodore McDonough* and the 453-ton screw steamer *Isaac Smith* made routine reconnaissance trips up the Stono River, shelling Confederate positions and watching for enemy movements. Rebel scouts reported this regular and predictable activity, and the Confederates organized a secret expedition to attack the two Union gunboats. Under the cover of darkness, the rebels constructed three gun platforms. The uppermost battery consisted of three rifled 24-pound guns. It lay on the east bank of the river at Thomas Grimball's plantation on James Island. Just downstream at Paul Grimball's plantation on John's Island, the rebels placed another battery. Situated about one-and-one-half miles farther down stream at Legare's Place, also on John's Island, was the third battery of two 24-pound rifled guns and fifty sharpshooters.[23]

About 4:00 on the afternoon of 30 January, the *Isaac Smith* steamed upriver as usual with the quartermaster at the masthead and others on lookout. She passed up the river over four miles and steamed by the lower two batteries at Legare's and Paul Grimball's. She came to anchor about five hundred yards off Thomas Grimball's plantation on James Island. The Confederates waited for twenty minutes hoping she might steam farther up the river toward the uppermost battery. At 4:25, when she failed to move any farther, the rebel gunners at Thomas Grimball's plantation opened fire.[24]

The *Isaac Smith*'s commanding officer, Acting Lieutenant Francis S. Conover, ordered his warship to get underway at once. The crew cleared the deck for action and returned fire in less than two minutes. The *Smith*, a former cattle boat, had a heavy armament of one 30-

pounder and eight 8-inch smoothbore guns. Despite the crew's quick reaction, they could not bring her guns to bear on the rebel positions in the narrow river. She managed to drop down the river and, as she came into range, the second Confederate battery opened fire and caught the *Smith* in a crossfire. For about a mile the Union gunboat received a raking fire from the Confederate artillery and sharpshooters.[25]

The men on the *Commodore McDonough* heard the firing at 4:40 and Lieutenant Commander George Bacon ordered his vessel upriver. Just before the *McDonough* came into sight, a shot struck the *Isaac Smith*'s boiler near the funnel, causing her to lose steam pressure. With no wind or tide, and his boats and upper works shot to pieces, Conover felt he had no other choice and ordered his men to strike the colors and hoist a white flag. The lower battery at Legare's Place prevented the *McDonough* from steaming to the *Smith*'s assistance and the Confederates quickly towed their prize upstream beyond reach. The crew of 117 suffered, 9 killed and 16 wounded. The loss was a blow to Du Pont's prestige and she became a constant reminder of failure when the Confederates renamed the gunboat *Stono* and she served as a picket boat in Charleston Harbor.[26]

Worse was to come. The very next day, two Confederate ironclads sortied from Charleston Harbor to break the blockade. This attack was the culmination of a year of planning. In an effort to negate the Union navy's numerical superiority, early in 1862, the State of South Carolina appropriated $300,000 to start an ironclad construction program. Workers laid the keel of the first ironclad in Charleston in January 1862 and the second that March. Both builders used the design and specifications of John L. Porter's *Richmond* class ironclads. The *Chicora*, built by James M. Eason, had an overall length of 172 feet, had a width of 45 feet, and a draft of about 13 feet. By June, the ironclads awaited their armor, but the army refused to allow the railroads to ship the metal. The Treasury Department's failure to pay the bills delayed their progress further. Eventually, two layers of two-inch iron plating, fastened perpendicular to each other with a backing of twenty-two inches of oak and pine, protected the gun crews in the casemate. The plating extended five feet below the waterline—a total of five hundred tons of armor. The *Palmetto State*, built by James G. Marsh and Son, had dimensions similar to the *Chicora*. She deviated from the original plan and her casemate was octagonal rather than rectangular in shape. The *Palmetto State* went by the nickname "Ladies Gunboat" because the women of South Carolina had raised money for her construction.[27]

The Confederates provided these ironclads with heavy armament. The *Palmetto State* carried a rifled and banded 42-pounder (7-inch) forward and a rifled and banded 32-pounder (6.4-inch) aft that fired 80- and 60-pound projectiles, respectively, and probably 2-VIII inch shell guns in broadsides. The Confederates armed the *Chicora* with two 9-inch smoothbores and two banded and rifled 32-pounders that fired a 60-pound projectile. Both these warships suffered from slow speed because the builders provided them secondhand and insufficient power plants. They finished *Chicora* first and launched her on 23 August. The *Palmetto State* slid into the water exactly seven weeks later.[28]

The Confederates did not wait long to try their new warships. General Beauregard and Flag Officer Duncan M. Ingraham, commander of the Charleston Squadron, discussed a night attack on the wooden blockaders off Charleston. They felt they might raise the blockade and at least damage a number of Union vessels. During the fall of 1862, this particular threat worried Du Pont. He felt that the ironclads could steam from the protection of the forts at both Pulaski and Charleston and could "do great harm" to his wooden ships, particularly the smaller and lighter armed vessels. As the ironclads neared completion, he admitted that he had a little "ram anxiety." With so many of his gunboats needing repairs, and despite the slow speed of the enemy ironclads, he felt that the Confederate ironclads might easily cripple or destroy one of his warships. By January 1863, he felt less apprehensive because intelligence gathering yielded the impression that the Charleston ironclads could not go to sea.[29]

The Confederate leaders acted on their idea of a night attack and, at 10:00 P.M. on 30 January, Commodore Ingraham boarded the *Palmetto State*, commanded by Lieutenant Commander John Rutledge, and hoisted his broad pennant. Ingraham, a Charleston native, had entered naval service as a midshipman in 1812 at the age of nine. As a lieutenant, he commanded the brig *Somers* during the Mexican War. From 1850 to 1852, he served as Commandant of the Philadelphia Navy Yard and then joined the Mediterranean Squadron. In 1855, he became Chief of the Bureau of Ordnance and Hydrography. In August 1860, he took command of the frigate *Richmond*, flagship of the Mediterranean Squadron. He returned to the United States in January 1861, resigned his commission, and accepted command of the naval forces in South Carolina. He served briefly as the Chief of the Bureau of Ordnance and Hydrography before he took command of the Charleston Squadron in November 1861.[30]

The commanding officer of *Chicora*, John Randolph "Handsome Jack" Tucker, a thirty-five-year veteran of the United States Navy, had sided with his native state of Virginia in April 1861. He began his career in the Virginia Navy as the captain of the *Patrick Henry*. In charge of the small flotilla of gunboats in the James River, he participated in the battles of Hampton Roads and Drewry's Bluff. Tucker took command of the *Chicora* in September 1862. Only a few months later, Mallory would appoint him to command the Charleston Squadron.[31]

The Confederate ironclads cast off from the wharf and got underway at 11:30. They planned to reach the bar at 4:00 A.M. at high tide on 31 January. Because of their deep drafts they could not cross until high tide and *Chicora* passed over the bar with only eighteen inches to spare. Ingraham also ordered three side-wheel steamers, the *General Clinch*, *Etiwan*, and *Chesterfield* with fifty soldiers to serve as tenders to the ironclads. These transports got underway and steamed toward the mouth of the harbor, but inexplicably they never crossed the bar. The moon had just set as the bluish gray ironclads, with their armor greased, steamed toward the fleet. A thick haze helped to obscure them but their funnels belched smoke that trailed after them for several miles like a "huge black serpent." The ironclads approached the Union blockaders with their port shutters closed, not showing any light to the outside. Inside, the battle lanterns "cast a pale, weird, light on the gun deck" as the men stood quietly at their stations.[32]

The *Palmetto State* and the *Chicora* stealthily approached the positions of the blockaders. Closest by, and just off the bar near the main ship channel, lay the *Mercedita* at anchor. Her commanding officer, Captain Henry S. Stellwagen, had just laid down for the night when lookouts saw smoke and the "faint appearance" of a vessel. At about 4:30 Acting Master Thomas J. Dwyer shouted, "That's black smoke, where's the night glass? There is a steamer standing this way." Lieutenant Commander Trevett Abbot, the executive officer and officer of the deck, called out, "Watch, man the guns, spring the rattle, call all hands to quarters!" Dwyer ran below to inform Stellwagen, who quickly slipped on his trousers and peacoat and climbed to the main deck. At one hundred yards the vessel was still unrecognizable in the haze and Stellwagen ordered the guns trained on the approaching vessel. Stellwagen peered through the haze at the approaching vessel and believed her to be a tug. He hailed, "Steamer ahoy! Stand clear of us and heave to! What steamer is that? . . . You will be into us!" Initially, the only answer that came back from the *Palmetto State*, however, was "Halloo."[33]

With a collision imminent, Stellwagen then got the truthful answer when across the water he heard the answer, "This is the Confederate States steam ram *Palmetto State.*" A moment later the ironclad's prow struck the *Mercedita* on the starboard side, abaft the aftermost 32-pounder gun. The tremendous impact caused her to heel to port. After contact, the *Mercedita*'s gun crews could not depress any of their nine guns to defend the ship, while the high freeboard of the Union steamer made an easy target for the Confederates. As the ironclad's prow passed into the *Mercedita*, the Confederate crew dropped the forward port shutter and fired the 7-inch bow gun into the blockader. This shot passed through the starboard side, through the condenser and the steam drum, and exploded on the port side at the waterline of the ship, tearing a huge hole in the hull. This single shot left the *Mercedita* critically wounded. The blockader immediately filled with steam. Water flooding into the ship from both sides put the fires out and left her in a sinking condition. Two men lay dead and others lay dying from scalding steam.[34]

After critically wounding *Mercedita*, the *Palmetto State* backed and swung under the blockader's starboard counter with her prow against the hapless gunboat. Stellwagen heard the words, "Surrender, or I'll sink you!" shouted across the water from the ironclad. Without any motive power and no way to depress his guns, Stellwagen decided to surrender his ship. Lieutenant Commander Abbot ordered a boat put over the side to offer the surrender to the enemy. The crew had trouble launching the whale boat and nearly ten minutes elapsed before Abbot reached the ironclad. During this time, calls from the ram continually inquired whether they intended to surrender. The Union sailors presented quite a sight to the Confederate tars. They rowed over dressed in "scant fashion," having been called to their battle stations from their sleep. When Abbot arrived, Lieutenants George S. Shryock and William H. Parker guided him to the captain to surrender the *Mercedita*. Abbot informed Lieutenant Commander Rutledge that the *Mercedita* was in a sinking condition. Rutledge conferred with Ingraham and the flag officer decided to receive the surrender of the Union ship, but not to take the vessel in tow as a prize. The delay of Abbot arriving on board the ironclad had cost the Confederates valuable time. Ingraham also took a considerable time deciding what to do with the Union crew. Anxious to continue his fight with the blockaders, but not able to take the crew on board, he paroled the officers and crew. This prevented them, on their word of honor, not to serve against the Confederate States until regularly exchanged. Had the three steam tenders followed the ironclads they might have taken the *Mercedita* in tow.[35]

When the *Palmetto State* struck the *Mercedita*, the *Chicora* passed to her starboard to locate another Union warship. The *Chicora*, however, did not find a target until about thirty minutes after her consort had fired her first shot. Lookouts on the ram spotted the side-wheel steamer *Keystone State*. Gunfire from the direction of the *Mercedita* failed to alarm the other blockading vessels and they remained at their stations. On deck, Commander William E. Le Roy, as well as the other officers on the blockaders not engaged, believed the gunfire was aimed at a blockade runner that had attempted to escape. Le Roy, appointed a midshipman in 1832, had an active prewar career that earned him promotion to commander in July 1861. He was one of Du Pont's favorite officers. Du Pont called Le Roy "thoroughly well-bred" and a "model Christian officer and gentleman."[36]

Soon after 5:00 A.M., lookouts on the *Keystone State* spotted a suspicious object and Le Roy ordered the cable slipped. The engineers spread the fires to generate steam "as fast as possible" and the Union vessel made for the suspicious craft. The *Keystone State*, armed with seven guns, steamed abreast of the mysterious steamer. Le Roy hailed "What steamer is that?" Le Roy, however, received the same reply as Stellwagen on the *Mercedita*— "Halloo." Finding this reply unacceptable, the *Keystone State*'s starboard bow gun fired at the ironclad. Le Roy then had his ship swung hard aport in order to fire the whole starboard battery when the guns came to bear.[37]

The *Chicora* answered with her bow gun, then rounded to and gave the blockader a broadside. She finished with a shot from the after gun. One of the first shots to penetrate the *Keystone State* passed forward under the spar deck. Traveling along a line of hammocks, it decapitated three men and cut the feet off a fourth. The latter man had just come off duty and turned in with his head facing the wrong way. Another shell entered the berth deck and exploded amidships, ripping a hole in the hull several feet in diameter. Another grazed a cabin boy's head and then entered the armory. All but one of the shells exploded. A fire started in the forehold and Le Roy had the helmsman steer north. Once the crew had the fire subdued, he turned his ship around and ordered full throttle to run the ironclad down. At 6:17 A.M. a shell fired from the *Chicora* entered the port side, struck both steam drums, and emptied their contents. This caused the ship to heel nearly to her guards. Steam enveloped the engine room and the forward part of the ship and prevented men from reaching the forward magazines. With the ship critically wounded, the officers met at the rail on the hurricane deck. Le Roy stood there "nervous and excited" getting reports from his subordinates. With his ship on fire and likely sinking and with every discharge of the *Chicora*'s guns killing and wounding his crew, Le Roy chose to strike the flag.[38]

The *Chicora* ceased fire when the Union tars hauled the flag down. The escaping steam had driven the black gang and the engineers from the engine room, and they escaped through the coal bunkers to the deck. In their flight they failed to secure the engines. The steam pressure remaining in the boilers continued to power the ship for twenty minutes. Due to her heel, the *Keystone State*'s starboard wheel remained buried deep in the water and took her slowly away from the ironclad. Lieutenant William T. Glassell requested permission to fire on the Union vessel, but Tucker replied, "No; she has lowered her flag and surrendered." When the executive officer of the *Keystone State*, Lieutenant Thomas Eastman, realized that someone had struck the flag, he asked who did it. Le Roy replied, "I ordered it down. We are disabled and at the mercy of the Ram who can rake and sink us. It is a useless sacrifice of life to resist further." Eastman, exasperated by this decision, reportedly threw his sword on the deck exclaiming, "God D____n it. I will have nothing to do with it." Le Roy asked Eastman if he would take responsibility and Eastman replied, "yes sir I'll take responsibility." He picked up his sword and had the flag hoisted again. At long range, the *Keystone State* began firing at the ironclad.[39]

The nearby *Memphis*, hearing the continued gunfire, steamed to the sounds and discovered the crippled *Keystone State*. Her crew passed her disabled consort a hawser and towed her out of danger. The escape of the *Keystone State* after striking her flag and Le Roy's actions, were viewed by the Confederates as "faithless" and "beyond the pale of civilized and honorable warfare." Le Roy escaped with his vessel shot up, twenty killed and a like number wounded, at least three mortally.[40]

The *Chicora* and *Palmetto State* now looked for other quarry. Despite the gunfire, most of the blockaders on station still assumed that it was the result of a vessel's attempt to run the blockade. Gradually, however, the continued firing alarmed some of the other vessels and they began slipping their anchors and steamed through the fog to determine the cause. Eventually the *Quaker City*, *Memphis*, *Augusta*, and *Housatonic* all entered the fray. The *Memphis* stumbled into both ironclads and fired a few shots, but did not remain to fight. She steamed eastward to escape and found the *Keystone State*. The *Quaker City* also advanced toward the gunfire and received a shot in her engine. The *Housatonic* and *Augusta* both exchanged shots with the rebel rams at long range and a shot struck *Augusta* just above the boiler. Not a single shot fired by the Union vessels hit its mark except for a random shot that severed the *Palmetto State*'s flag staff. At 7:30, believing they had done all the damage they could, the Confederate ironclads began steaming northeast back toward the harbor completely unscathed.[41]

The ironclads stood into Charleston at Beach Channel, leaving the Union blockade in chaos. The Confederate vessels met the three transports that helped guide them through the channel and they anchored at 8:45. They remained there for seven hours for high tide. The ironclads then stood down the harbor and received salutes from the Confederate forts. They arrived back in Charleston to a hero's welcome. The citizens of Charleston lined the banks and wharves to cheer. The Charleston papers' headlines read "Brilliant Naval Victory."[42]

The Union vessels, on the other hand, had suffered a humiliating defeat. The ironclads left two blockaders severely damaged, and the *Quaker City* received a shell in her engine room that left her machinery partially disabled. At least twenty-seven men died—twenty-three on the *Keystone State* and four on the *Mercedita*. Another twenty lay wounded, some seriously.[43]

Shortly after the ironclads steamed to their berths, Ingraham reported to Richmond that he had broken the Union blockade. The Confederate Government accepted this statement and General Beauregard and Confederate Secretary of State Judah P. Benjamin forwarded this information to the British, Spanish, and French Consuls. This statement carried important international and legal implications regarding the legitimacy of the blockade. If the ironclads had indeed broken the blockade, by international law it would be necessary to issue new notices of the blockade before the Union warships could legally reestablish it. They would need to observe a grace period of fifteen days before the blockade would be enforceable again.[44]

General Beauregard provided the steamer *General Clinch* to take the foreign consuls stationed in Charleston to observe personally the absence of blockading vessels. The British consul in Charleston, Robert Bunch, instead boarded the HMS *Petrel* to confirm that the ironclads broke the blockade. The French and Spanish consuls also went to observe the fleet to substantiate the claim. Much to the dismay of the Confederate State Department, all these men reacted with extreme caution, and none of the consuls accepted Beauregard's claim.[45]

The Union officers reacted to the Confederate proclamations with indignity and declared the statements "false in every particular." They claimed that the hazy day had added to the confusion of distance. They pointed out that even the vessels attacked by the ironclads did not withdraw. The others had supposed the firing was at a blockade runner and thus did not leave their stations until the battle ended. The executive officer of the *Palmetto State*, William Parker, admitted years later that the blockaders only withdrew slightly to the north, but kept the ironclads under observation. The misunderstanding was a case where "distance lent enchantment to the view."[46]

Many in the South celebrated this naval battle, and it boosted Confederate morale. Others closely associated with both sides, however, realized that this represented only a minor victory for the Confederacy and a small setback for the Union navy. The *Chicora*'s second assistant engineer best summed this when he wrote, "They say we raised the blockade, but we all felt we would have rather raised h__l and sunk the ships."[47]

Both Stellwagen and Le Roy requested a court of inquiry to clear them of any transgressions. Du Pont, though, declared a court of inquiry unnecessary for Le Roy. While waiting for the outcome of Stellwagen's court of inquiry, Du Pont "scrupulously avoided" making any changes to the *Mercedita*. He did not remove anything or change her armament in case the court ruled her a prize of war. He did have her repaired in Philadelphia in hopes the board would find in the United States Navy's favor.[48]

An initial court met and determined that it could not rule on portions of the case and that further proceedings were necessary. The court did conclude that the parole given by Lieutenant Commander Abbot should be binding, but also determined that the parole did not include the *Mercedita* and her equipment. The Navy Department convened a second board, consisting of Rear Admirals William B. Shubrick and Charles H. Davis, and Brigadier General Joseph G. Totten, to reexamine the findings of the first board. This board met and concluded that the paroles given were valid. It ruled that Stellwagen sanctioned Abbot to ask for surrender and that Abbot had "assumed the responsibility" of giving the parole for the men on the *Mercedita*.[49]

Du Pont now had an added concern; he knew that the Confederates would use their ironclads offensively. The attack on the blockaders showed the vulnerability of Du Pont's wooden and lightly built ex-merchant vessels, particularly the crippled ones. The attack, however, seemed not to concern the Navy Department. Fox believed the Union forces had learned more from the attack than they had disclosed. This attack also showed the extreme limitations of the Confederate ironclads—they did not have good speed. The attack did have one positive outcome in Du Pont's mind. He believed the attack "stirred up the Department which nothing else could have done . . ." His plans to attack Charleston would now be augmented with more monitors.[50]

Fort McAllister and the *Nashville*

To attack Charleston the department promised to send the monitors *Passaic*, *Montauk*, *Nahant*, and *Weehawken* and the ironclad *New Ironsides*. Welles also promised that the War Department would send ten thousand men to Port Royal. With these forces in the theatre, Welles felt confident that Du Pont's fleet could enter the harbor. He believed Du Pont should "demand the surrender" of the defenses or make the Confederates "suffer the consequences of a refusal." At the beginning of January, after Welles postponed the proposed attack on Wilmington, the eyes of the department now glanced south in earnest for operations against the cradle of secession. In his optimism, Welles suggested that after successful operations at Charleston, Du Pont might then capture Savannah while the city was still under a panic caused by the fall of Charleston. In addition, the extra warships could go to Pensacola, should Du Pont require only part of the ironclad force for the capture of Savannah.[51]

Neither the Navy Department nor Du Pont had given any considerable thought to, nor had they begun any detailed planning of, the attack on Charleston. The flag officer communicated with Fox almost exclusively on this topic but never discussed any details. Du Pont shared his reservations concerning the monitors with Fox. While he confirmed the defensive capabilities of these warships, he found their lack of offensive firepower a real concern. Even more shocking, particularly to Fox, was Du Pont's belief that operations against forts required troops. This is because Fox still saw the army as a *rival*, not a *partner*. On the twenty-fourth, after some thought, the flag officer pressed the department for more ironclads for the Charleston attack. In his letter to the secretary, he also showed hesitancy and shared reservations concerning the offensive abilities of the monitors. Du Pont faithfully kept Fox informed of his reservations on the monitors. Evidently, the Assistant Secretary of the Navy did not pass these concerns along to Welles. Surprised at the tone of Du Pont's letter, Welles immediately wrote the flag officer that the department had provided him for the Charleston operations all the monitors then complete on the Atlantic Coast.[52]

With the reservations mounting, Du Pont felt a need to again test the ironclads' offensive capabilities and limitations and he proposed to make this test in another attack on Fort McAllister. The *Montauk* still lay in Ossabaw Sound, below the fort, after the 27 January attack. On 21 January, the *Passaic* arrived at Port Royal under the command of Percival Drayton. *Passaic* also experienced a storm on her way south. Needing more reserve buoyancy, Drayton had the crew lighten her by heaving overboard her entire load of four hundred shot and shells. After she arrived at Port Royal, Du Pont dispatched her to Wassaw Sound to watch the *Atlanta*.[53]

In addition to testing the offensive power of the monitors, Du Pont increasingly worried about the presence of the *Rattlesnake*. The Confederates' progress in fitting her out as a privateer annoyed and somewhat embarrassed him. But the enemy's obstructions kept his monitors from approaching the fort to destroy her. Du Pont wrote his friend Benjamin Gerhard that she was is "a thorn in my flesh . . ."[54] Since July 1862, the Union navy kept the 1,221-ton *Rattlesnake* bottled up in the Ogeechee River. Although she was a fast side wheel steamer, her chances of escaping through the blockade had never looked more than marginal since the Union forces discovered her in the river. Her presence there continued to be a threat and guaranteed that extra ships would watch her to keep her from escaping to sea. The cruiser *Alabama*'s great successes continued to focus the attention of Du Pont and the department on this particular vessel.

Despite Du Pont's readiness to again test the ironclad's offensive powers against Fort McAllister and to destroy the *Rattlesnake*, other matters preempted the commencement. The *Montauk* remained unable to renew the attack on Fort McAllister effectively because of a shortage of ammunition. *Passaic*'s loss of her ammunition on the trip south only aggravated the situation further. The *Passaic* class monitors could carry only 170 15-inch shells and 230 11-inch shot or shells, and keeping the supply of ammunition in these vessels required a great deal of planning. Du Pont lamented to his wife, "these ironclads soon get out of ammunition, for they have not as much pouch as an oppossum [sic]." On the morning of 31 January, the steam tug *Daffodil* brought down the last load of ammunition needed for the *Montauk*. That evening, after the *Dawn* arrived, Commander Worden called the commanding officers together to discuss a plan of attack.[55]

At 6:40 the following morning the *Montauk* weighed anchor and moved up the Ogeechee followed by the *Seneca, Wissahickon, Dawn,* and *C. P. Williams.* About 7:30 the vessels steamed into position in-line, as they had during the earlier attack on the twenty-seventh. Worden anchored *Montauk* about seven hundred yards below the fort on the right bank of the river, in water as shoal as he dared. The wooden gunboats remained at a safer distance, about three thousand yards below the fort.[56]

The battle began at 7:45 with a shot fired from the *Montauk.* A mist hanging over the fort complicated the rebel gunner's aim. Once the battle began, the smoke from the Confederate guns added to the veil and neither side could clearly see the other. The Confederate gunners, who began the battle with a rapid fire, eventually settled for a more deliberate rate of fire. The Confederate gunners aimed almost exclusively at the *Montauk* and the first shot struck her turret at 7:53.[57]

Through the pilot house slit, Worden had a difficult time observing the effects of his fire. He directed the gunners to spend most of their fire on the fort's 8-inch Columbiad. The explosions caused by 11- and 15-inch shells displaced great quantities of sand and all but buried the rebel gun crews. By 8:30 the *Montauk*'s fire effectively demolished the parapet in front of the Columbiad, leaving the gun crew exposed. The monitor demonstrated the destructive power of the 15-inch shell when one passed through a parapet seventeen feet thick. Despite the danger, the Confederate gunners remained at their posts. The mortar shells fired by the *C. P. Williams* added to the danger by bursting directly over the fort. One shot from the *Montauk* disabled one of the 32-pounders and killed the gun crew's commanding officer.[58]

At 8:45 Worden called for a sounding and found only fourteen feet of water. Knowing the tide would fall five more feet, he ordered the anchor up to find deeper water for his ironclad. The *Montauk* dropped downstream to a position about fourteen hundred yards from the fort. As she shifted position, a breeze pushed away the mist and smoke hanging over the fort. After anchoring, the monitor renewed her fire with great accuracy and Worden observed the shells demolishing the rebel traverses. Despite the damage to the fort, the gunfire never effectively silenced the enemy's guns. At 11:53, with his supply of shells depleted and the cored shot doing little damage, Worden ordered the warships to cease fire. The vessels stood down the river and at 12:40, they anchored about three miles below the fort.[59]

The *Montauk* once again received the brunt of the enemy fire. The other vessels sustained little or no damage. New York *Herald* correspondent Bradley S. Osbon, on board during the attack, remarked that the shells hitting the turret sounded like the "cracking of gigantic nuts." Enemy shells struck the *Montauk* forty-eight times during the two engagements: sixteen times on the turret, three on the pilot house, and seven through the smokestack; fifteen struck the side and deck armor, and the remaining shots hit the boats, flag staffs, and spare anchor. The ironclad, however, suffered no major damage. The shots merely dented the plates between one and two inches, broke bolt heads, and sprung and split some plates.[60]

Fort McAllister's commanding officer, Colonel Robert H. Anderson, praised his "heroic garrison." He believed that earthworks could stand against ironclads when manned by "stout and gallant hearts." The *Montauk*'s concentrated fire on the single parapet did little permanent damage and the Confederates made most of the repairs within hours. After this battle the Confederates reported the 15-inch gun a "partial failure" because of its slow rate of fire. They believed concentrated fire by a smaller number of guns might have inflicted more damage. They may have been correct, for although the Union vessels hurled several hundred shells at the Confederate batteries, they inflicted only eight casualties— one dead and seven wounded.[61]

This knowledge gained from the attack on Fort McAllister did not satisfy Du Pont, and he determined that he should make yet another test of his monitors against forts. This time he planned to use four monitors to attack McAllister. But on the evening of 27 February, before Worden could assemble the monitors for another attack on the fort, he observed the *Rattlesnake* drop down the river. Worden immediately ordered a reconnaissance up the Ogeechee. The Union boat party observed the rebel steamer aground in a reach above the fort. Worden now did not hesitate, and at daylight moved up river in the *Montauk* followed by the *Wissahickon*, *Seneca*, and *Dawn*.[62]

As the warships came within sight, they found the *Rattlesnake* still aground around a bend in the river. Worden moved the *Montauk* close to the obstructions and to within twelve hundred yards of the raider and anchored. A few minutes after 7:00 A.M., the monitor fired a few ranging shots over land at the *Rattlesnake*. The gunners in the fort knew the raider was in trouble and maintained a heavy fire on *Montauk*. The other vessels entered the fray firing at both the fort and the Confederate steamer at long range. After establishing the range, the *Montauk* began striking the Confederate vessel with 15- and 11-inch shells and set the *Rattlesnake* afire within twenty minutes. The *Montauk* fired her last shot at *Rattlesnake* at 8:03. At 9:20 the raider's pivot gun amidships exploded, ten minutes later her stack fell, and at 9:55 the magazine exploded, leaving little but scattered wreckage.[63]

Shortly after 8:30, satisfied that the *Rattlesnake* was finished, *Montauk* weighed anchor and stood down river. During the short engagement, rebel guns had struck the ironclad only five times and had caused little damage. Then at 9:35 the monitor struck a torpedo and a violent concussion shook the monitor from stem to stern. Dust, debris, and smoke filled the engine room. The engineer raced up to the bridge and exclaimed, "That was a torpedo, Sir! It has blown a hole in her hull under the boilers, and the water is within three inches of her fires." The explosion started and fractured plates, broke piping and rivets, bent frames, and caused some leaking. The commanding officer of Fort McAllister believed that the *Montauk* had "passed and repassed with impunity" over the torpedoes, and never observed the explosion. Boats from the other vessels came with men and buckets to help keep the ironclad afloat. A damage control crew drove pine plugs covered with gutta-percha into the opening. While the engineers worked to repair the damage, the pilot beached the vessel. After shoring up the sagging frames with braces and wedges, Worden determined that the damage was not fatal and he took her under her own power downriver to Ossabaw Sound.[64]

Du Pont exuberantly wrote his wife, "The *Nashville* is destroyed! A thorn in my flesh—an idea or myth in the public mind . . ." The destruction of the raider made Du Pont more enthusiastic to test several monitors against the fort. The monitors *Nahant, Weehawken*, and *Patapsco* had all recently arrived at Port Royal and all three survived rough weather on their way south. These monitors received positive marks on their behavior and their capabilities in gale force weather. The *Weehawken*, however, suffered an engine breakdown, and could not participate in the planned attack.[65]

Du Pont placed Percival Drayton in *Passaic* in charge of the next attack. He sent the monitor *Nahant* to Ossabaw in tow of the *Flambeau* and the *Sebago* towed the *Patapsco*. Du Pont decided to use only the *Patapsco, Nahant* and *Passaic*, keeping the *Montauk* in reserve during the battle. Keeping the *Montauk* in reserve seemed necessary due to the fact that John Dahlgren, the Chief of the Bureau of Ordnance, did not believe that the 15-inch guns could withstand more than three hundred firings before wearing out. Three mortar schooners accompanied the expedition to fire on the fort from a distance.[66]

At 7:30 on 3 March, the beginning of the ebb tide, Drayton ordered the monitors to weigh anchor. At 8:00 they steamed upriver, the *Passaic* in the van followed by the *Patapsco, Nahant,* and *Montauk.* The *Wissahickon* towed the mortar schooner *Para* upriver; the *Seneca* towed the mortar schooner *C. P. Williams*; and the *Dawn* towed the mortar schooner *Norfolk Packet.* Below the fort, the mortar schooners dropped their tow lines. The *Wissahickon* remained just below the *Montauk* with the three mortar schooners anchored next in line. The *Seneca, Dawn,* and other vessels dropped farther down the river, but remained in signal distance to give assistance if necessary.[67]

At 8:30 the *Passaic* steamed to within 1,200 yards of the fort and dropped her anchor. The *Patapsco* anchored just below *Passaic,* but the *Nahant* ran aground about 1700 yards from the fort. The mortar vessels anchored at 9:00 and remained at a distance of 4,000 yards. Fort McAllister immediately opened fire and established the range rather quickly, relying on range markers placed along the river. The monitors opened fire just before 9:00. The *Nahant* joined the fight while aground, but eventually freed herself and moved to a range of 1,500 yards from the fort.[68]

After an hour of firing, Drayton observed that his shells were not striking the parapets. In order to improve the fall of the shot, he ventured on deck to direct personally the monitor's fire. From this exposed position he corrected each shot. Unexpectedly, a round from Fort McAllister struck the ironclad's deck and exploded, driving iron splinters into Drayton's face and forcing him to hurry back inside his ironclad.[69]

For almost eight hours both the monitors and the fort maintained a deliberate fire. The three mortar schooners also kept up a slow rate of fire. The monitors fired about every ten minutes and the mortar boats about every five. During the battle the monitors fired 87 shells from their 15-inch guns and 127 from their 11-inch guns. Around 3:30 a flag signal and whistle recalled the monitors, and they ceased fire at 4:15. During the day they managed to fire away most of the long fused ammunition that could reach the fort. The *Nahant* and *Passaic* immediately moved down the river, but the *Patapsco* ran aground and did not get off for about thirty minutes. Despite the fact that the *Passaic*'s guns had effectively blown huge amounts of sand from the parapets, the fire from the mortar ships had been ineffective. As in the earlier attack, the shells caused only slight injury to the earthworks, damage the enemy could repair overnight. Three of the fort's guns received minor damage, but the defenders had suffered little, taking cover each time the monitors swung their turrets around to fire.[70]

During the fight the Confederates concentrated their fire on the *Passaic*. Struck thirty-four times, she suffered damage to her deck and side armor. Most of the shells managed to dent and crack iron plates or pop the heads off rivets. One of the shots that struck the deck nearly passed through. Neither of the other ironclads suffered any effects from the fire. Small mechanical problems with the guns plagued the gun crews. They found that during the day they had to reduce their volume of fire. After returning to Port Royal, some of the repairs to *Passaic* took a week. This engagement educated Drayton, who felt fortunate that the navy discovered these shortcomings before attacking Charleston Harbor.[71]

This fight also enlightened a number of officers on the practicality of monitors attacking sand fortifications. Du Pont reported his observations to the Navy Department. He judged the 15-inch guns to be almost a liability. Though rated to fire only three hundred rounds before being replaced, these guns might fire this many times in several days during a siege. Du Pont also lamented to Fox that the guns usually needed repairs after a day's firing. An attack on Charleston might take a week. The flag officer also pointed out to Fox that these problems had shown themselves against an eight-gun fort.[72]

Du Pont's subordinates mirrored his concerns. Drayton concluded that to reduce heavy earthworks with the monitors they would need to attack them by continuous fire. Bombardment during the day would destroy the works and firing at night would disrupt the repairs. He also believed it impossible to reduce Fort McAllister "no matter how many ironclads were in the river." John Rodgers wrote, "I am less sanguine of taking Charleston than I was, the monitors have proved by practice . . . to be far less formidable in an attack than was anticipated." Rodgers also noted that the rate of fire was too slow and the monitors could not sustain themselves in a fight for long without breaking down. With this in mind, it appeared that the number of monitors provided for the attack on Charleston would not be sufficient. Only a portion of the attacking force would remain battle ready after a substantial fight with the forts near the throat of the harbor. This would leave too few available to take the city.[73]

Du Pont's concerns about the deficiencies of the ironclads grew with each day. He reiterated to his wife his fundamental concern that while the monitors could resist shot, their rate of fire was much too slow to damage enemy forts. Du Pont felt certain that Alban C. Stimers, the Chief

Engineer of the Navy, who witnessed the latest attack, would pass these concerns to the department. Du Pont believed that "Ericsson's high priest" would "enlighten them more at the Department than fifty letters from me would do . . ."[74]

Stimers did return to Washington quickly on board the steamer *Ericsson*. By telegram, Stimers pressed Welles for more monitors to operate against Charleston. Not wishing to be the bearer of bad news, he merely told Welles what he wanted to hear about the monitors and did not let the Secretary know Du Pont's concerns about the guns. Stimers merely reported that "[e]verything worked admirably." Even with this news Welles remained unsatisfied that Du Pont had not pressed forward the plan to attack Charleston. Within the next couple of months, this project would receive both the department's and Du Pont's full attention.[75]

Welles feared that the Confederates now knew the capabilities of the ironclads and would strengthen their works at a tremendous rate. He was almost prophetic. The rebels did recognize the monitors' potential abilities against masonry walls. But they also noted that their fire, while not rapid, was also not accurate, and that against sand fortifications they were no real threat. The Chief Engineer of the District of Georgia, Major David B. Harris, was "comfortable" with the defensive capabilities of earthwork forts against monitors. After a visit to McAllister, he wrote, "It would appear that the ironclads are not formidable monsters after all . . ."[76]

Secretary of the Navy
Gideon Welles. *Library
of Congress*

Assistant Secretary of the
Navy Gustavus Vasa Fox.
U.S. Naval Historical Center

Rear Adm. Samuel Francis Du Pont, July
1863. *U.S. Naval Historical Center*

The bombardment of Port Royal, South Carolina, August 1861. The
transport fleet is in the distance. *U.S. Naval Historical Center*

The screw gunboat USS *Unadilla* was an example of a class of quickly built warships popularly known as the "90-day gunboats." They served well as gun platforms for attacking fortifications along Southern rivers and coastlines. *U.S. Naval Historical Center*

The USS *Rhode Island* was employed early in the war as a supply ship for the blockading squadrons. *U.S. Naval Historical Center*

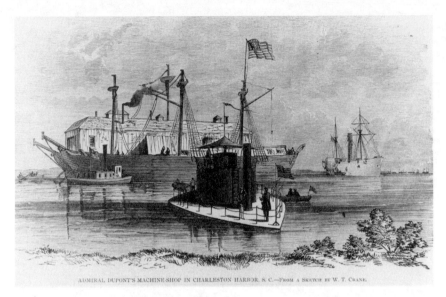

Pictured here side by side are the 340-ton bark *Edward* and the 366-ton ship *India* in Station Creek. These hulks were used by Admiral Du Pont as his machine shop. The *India* served as the blacksmith shop, a storage facility, and a barracks. The *Edward* had furnaces, forging equipment, and lathes on board. *U.S. Naval Historical Center*

The "90-day gunboat" USS *Huron* served with distinction in the blockade off Charleston, capturing five blockade-runners and helping to destroy two others. *U.S. Naval Historical Center*

THE CONFEDERATE STEAMER "ANGLIA," CAPTURED OFF BULL'S BAY, TWENTY-FIVE MILES FROM CHARLESTON, S. C.,
BY THE U. S. GUNBOATS "RESTLESS" AND "FLAG," SUNDAY, OCTOBER 19TH, 1862.

Anglia, captured off Bull's Bay, South Carolina, had many of the attributes of a typical blockade-runner. Note the low profile, light color, reduced masts, and the turtle-backed deck to help her drive through heavy seas.
U.S. Naval Historical Center

The monitor USS *Passaic. U.S. Naval Historical Center*

A depiction of the interior of the monitor USS *Passaic*.
U.S. Naval Historical Center

The USS *New Ironsides* ready for action off Charleston.
U.S. Naval Historical Center

The ironclad CSS *Palmetto State* in Charleston Harbor.
U.S. Naval Historical Center

The USS *Catskill*. Note the damage to the armor on the turret.
U.S. Naval Historical Center

Brig. Gen. Pierre
Gustave Toutant
Beauregard,
commander of
the Confederacy's
Department of
South Carolina,
Georgia, and East
Florida. *U.S. Naval
Historical Center*

Maj. Gen. David
Hunter, commanding
general of the Union's
Department of the South.
National Archives

Union Brig.
Gen. Thomas
W. Sherman.
*Library of
Congress*

Capt. John Rodgers
circa 1863. Rodgers
was one of Du Pont's
most trusted officers.
Library of Congress

Union Maj.
Gen. Quincy
A. Gillmore.
National Archives

South
Carolina native
Capt. Percival
Drayton. He was
considered one of
the best officers in
the Union navy.
*U.S. Naval
Historical Center*

Bombardment of Fort McAllister, Georgia, March 1863.
U.S. Naval Historical Center

Panoramic view of the Union ironclads advancing into Charleston Harbor on
7 April 1863. *U.S. Naval Historical Center*

Sketch of the obstruction remover attached to the USS *Weehawken* during the 7 April 1863, attack on Charleston. *U.S. Naval Historical Center*

USS *Keokuk* sinking off Charleston on 8 April 1863, the day after the ironclad attack on Fort Sumter. From *U.S. Naval Historical Center*

The Union monitor USS *Weehawken* engages the CSS *Atlanta* on 17 June 1863 in Wassaw Sound, Georgia. *U.S. Naval Historical Center*

Rear Adm. John A. Dahlgren standing beside the gun that bore his name, in a photo taken off Charleston in April 1865. *U.S. Naval Historical Center*

Capt. Stephen
C. Rowan, circa
1862. Rowan,
a native of Ireland,
was the highest-
ranking foreign-born
officer in the Union
navy. *U.S. Naval
Historical Center*

A CSS *David* torpedo boat aground in Charleston Harbor in a photo circa
1865. *U.S. Naval Historical Center*

The submarine CSS *Hunley* at Charleston 6 December 1863.
U.S. Naval Historical Center

The screw sloop USS *Housatonic*. This was one of the more heavily armed
warships off Charleston. She was attacked and sunk by the
CSS *Hunley* in February 1864, making her the first warship
sunk by a submarine. *U.S. Naval Historical Center*

INCIDENT ON THE OGEECHEE RIVER, NEAR FORT McALLISTER — OPENING COMMUNICATION BETWEEN ADMIRAL DAHLGREN AND GENERAL SHERMAN, DECEMBER 13TH, 1861.

Opening communications with Maj. Gen. William Tecumseh Sherman's army on 13 December 1864, near Fort McAllister, Georgia.
U.S. Naval Historical Center

HARPER'S WEEKLY.

[MARCH 18, 1865.

The landing of Brig. Gen. Edward E. Potter's troops at Bull's Bay, South Carolina, in February 1865. Engraving from *Harper's Weekly*.
U.S. Naval Historical Center

— 6 —

"You Have Not Turrets Enough
. . . You Have Not Guns Enough"

Union Chaos and Confederate Preparations

Since the fall of Fort Pulaski there had been little interservice cooperation and almost no dialogue or long range plans made for future movements against Confederate positions along the South Atlantic coast.
The Navy Department, and especially Fox, urged Du Pont to capture
Charleston with his ironclad fleet, despite Du Pont's pleas for army cooperation. In September the War Department, in order to infuse new life
in the command, sent Major General Ormsby M. Mitchel to replace the
inactive General Hunter as the commander of the Department of the
South. The early relationship between Mitchel and Du Pont seemed cordial and the general immediately launched a probing attack against the
railroad at Pocataligo. But Mitchel soon contracted yellow fever and
died about six weeks after his arrival. General Hunter returned as the
commander of the Department of the South where activity languished
again.[1]

The War Department also sent Brigadier General Truman Seymour,
a West Point graduate with considerable military experience. Considered an aggressive commander, he arrived at the department before
Hunter replaced Mitchel. He reconnoitered the area and concluded that
a landing on Morris Island, the capture of Battery Wagner, and the establishment of breeching batteries would cause Fort Sumter to fall and
allow the naval vessels into the harbor. Once Hunter returned he made

Seymour his Chief of Staff and Chief of Artillery, effectively silencing him and his ideas.[2]

In February, the War Department agreed to transfer ten thousand men into the department to operate against Charleston. They were under the command of Major General John G. Foster, an aggressive and competent officer, who, like Seymour, personally reconnoitered Charleston Harbor to determine if combined operations could capture the city. He proposed using a plan drawn up a year earlier by Gillmore whereby simultaneous landings on Morris and Sullivan's islands would allow breaching batteries to silence Fort Sumter. The plan assumed that with this fort removed, the navy could then steam into the harbor. Hunter, however, considered Foster's initiative insubordinate and Foster, not willing to take this abuse, asked to leave the department. By the time the navy was ready to attack, the army was in such disorder that it would not be prepared to participate.[3]

The Confederates, meanwhile, remained extremely active. The state of South Carolina took an early interest in coastal fortifications and committed many resources to prepare Charleston's defenses as a point of honor. Beauregard was an excellent engineer and spent most of his time and energy perfecting his defenses. At the end of September 1862, Commodore Ingraham and Beauregard met with other high-ranking naval officers, army engineers, and members of their staffs for a conference to discuss the issue of harbor defense. They analyzed the synergies between the forts, their armament, the obstructions, and the Confederate ironclads to determine the best use of all these elements to protect the city. They also projected the likely scenario should the Union naval forces attack.[4]

In the fall of 1862, the defenses contained many light guns, but only three 10-inch guns, a few 8-inch Columbiads, and about a dozen rifled but unbanded 32-pounders. By the spring of 1863, however, Beauregard could boast of many improvements. He shortened his defensive lines and heavily armed the forts in the harbor and created probably the most heavily fortified port in the Western Hemisphere. In addition to new heavy guns, he had two ironclads, obstructions, torpedoes, and fire rafts.[5]

Under Beauregard's scheme, naval vessels forcing an entrance into the harbor would face three interlocking circles of fire. Fort Sumter lay approximately in the center of the first line. The southern portion of the circle included Battery Gregg and Battery Wagner on Morris Island, and the north side of the circle stretched along Sullivan's Island and included the heavily armed Battery Bee, Battery Marion, Fort Moultrie, Battery

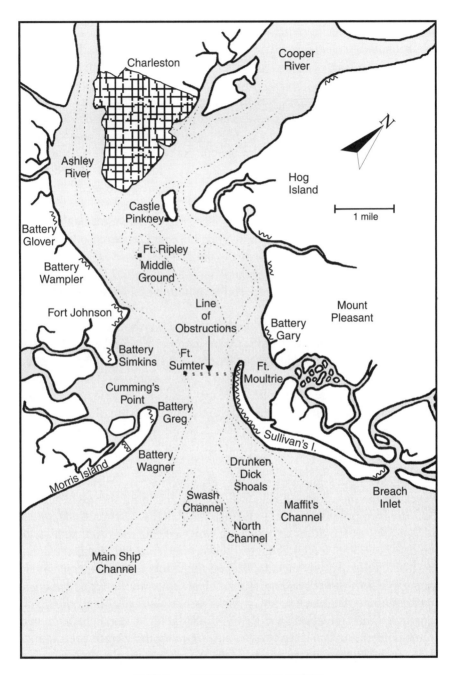

MAP 9. CHARLESTON HARBOR

Rutledge, Fort Beauregard, four small-detached batteries, and Fort Marshall. The second circle included Fort Johnson, Battery Cheves, Battery Wampler, Battery Glover, other minor works on James Island, Fort Ripley, and Castle Pinckney, a battery on Hog Island, and two small batteries on Mount Pleasant. The third circle comprised the fortifications of the city and those on the banks of the Cooper and Ashley rivers. Many of these guns ringing the harbor were 8- and 10-inch Columbiads, and the remaining mainly 32-pounders. The Confederates made their gunfire much more accurate by placing range buoys throughout the harbor.[6]

Fort Sumter and Fort Moultrie, the two most heavily armed forts, protected the throat of the harbor. Fort Sumter, with five faces, had two tiers of casemated guns and one in barbette. Its eighty-five guns, forty in casemate and forty-five in barbette, clearly made this a powerful stronghold. But only thirty-seven of these guns bore on the throat of the channel. Across the harbor on Sullivan's Island, Fort Moultrie lay atop the palmetto fort that had repulsed the British fleet in 1776. This brick fort "filled in with sand" had been greatly strengthened by the Confederates and mounted twenty-four heavy guns.[7]

Beauregard believed that Union forces might choose to attack Fort Sumter at long range and particularly against the weakest sides—the gorge, the southeast angle, and the east face. If the Union Navy attacked from this angle, the guns on Sullivan's Island could not support Fort Sumter's defense. He also believed that breeching batteries firing from Morris Island would be a real danger to Sumter. He strengthened both of these areas to prevent the Union forces from taking quick advantages of these perceived weaknesses. Beauregard felt that the enemy's best tactic would be to dash by the obstructions into the harbor without halting to engage or reduce the batteries. His greatest fear, however, was a night attack by the monitors. During a dark night, Union ironclads could get near the fort and take a position nearby to damage it severely. The gunners in the fort would have a difficult time sighting the small profiles of the monitors, which could change their position after each shot.[8]

The Confederate ironclads, despite their inherent weaknesses, were an integral part of the harbor defenses. They were not designed as seagoing craft and could reach speeds of only three to five miles per hour. Confederate leaders realized that their ironclads could not fight on equal terms with the Union monitors, but these warships were more than an equal match for wooden vessels. The ironclads kept the wooden gunboats at a respectable distance and posed a threat to the smaller craft making reconnaissance trips into the harbor. In early 1863 the Confederates fitted the ironclads with spar torpedoes carrying sixty pounds of powder. Despite their other weaknesses, if deployed properly, these weapons would pose a definite threat to the monitors. The limitations of the Confederate ironclads spawned other plans to neutralize the Union monitors. By the spring of 1863, Beauregard had plans for as many as six steam rams armed with torpedoes. The State of South Carolina appropriated $50,000 for their construction. It would be these craft in the latter part of the war that would most concern the Union naval officers.[9]

During a Union attack, the rams, by instruction, would remain with steam up just behind a line drawn from Fort Sumter to Cummings Point. Commodore Ingraham's instructions allowed him to attack the Union warships only if the monitors passed Sumter and Morris Island or advanced beyond the obstructions. Should the ironclads be unable to sink or damage the monitors severely or drive them back, the Confederates had outfitted twelve pulling boats armed with spar torpedoes and kept them ready to attempt to sink the monitors.[10]

The Confederate defenses also comprised passive weapons. The harbor obstructions greatly concerned the Union naval authorities. In early 1862, the Confederates had laid down a double row of pine timber piles across the middle ground. These piles stretched from a point due north of Fort Johnson across the harbor and ended 650 yards east of Fort Ripley. These piles decayed quickly and storms and tides left wide gaps to compromise their effectiveness. In May, the rebels began their most important obstruction. It consisted of a floating boom of heavy timber logs weighted and coupled together by iron. The sections, 12' × 12' and 20' long, stretched between Fort Sumter and Fort Moultrie and lay in water about thirty-five feet deep. To the dismay of the defensive planners it broke twice. The Confederate leaders considered this boom too costly to maintain, too fragile, and unreliable as a barrier to the Union vessels. It was abandoned with a few sections left intact. This heavy boom was replaced by a rope obstruction that formed a nearly continuous line stretching across the harbor from Fort Sumter to Battery Marion. It consisted of three cables fastened together like the ratlines of a ship. Secured to beer barrels, the upper portion of the line remained afloat in order to foul the wheels and propellers of ships. The Confederates anchored the lower edge of the connected cables and left an opening three hundred yards wide near Fort Sumter. With other cribs and booms to protect various portions of the harbor, the rebels hoped to keep any attacking vessels close together and within the easy range of the nearby guns. Despite the preparations, General Beauregard and Brigadier General Roswell

J. Ripley never believed the obstructions a "formidable" or serious barrier to the entrance of enemy vessels, and therefore mainly relied prima-
rily on the strength of the fortifications at the entrance to the harbor.[11]

The other passive weapon available in the spring of 1863 was the
torpedo. Along with the obstructions, this weapon created real apprehension for the Union officers. By March 1863, fixed torpedoes in the
Cooper and Ashley rivers protected the south side of the city. General
Ripley placed a large electrically fired torpedo in the ship channel, one
mile off Fort Sumter. Made of a boiler, eighteen feet long and three feet
in diameter, it contained three thousand pounds of powder and was held
in place by four anchors each weighing as much as the powder. Ripley's
men readied a second similar torpedo, but did not get it deployed before
the Union attack. The Confederates might have placed dozens of contact torpedoes near the throat of the harbor, but realized that contact
torpedoes would be largely useless at this point with the tremendous
amount of timber that drifted in and out of the harbor on every tide.[12]

Du Pont commented that Charleston Harbor was "a good deal like
a porcupine's hide and quills turned outside in and sewed up at one
end." Du Pont's limited knowledge of the defenses came from night
soundings, observations, and statements made by deserters and escaped
slaves. He knew that the obstructions existed and had a good idea of
their extensiveness, but he did not know exactly how reliable the information was.[13] Despite the pleas from the department and the importance of this knowledge before attacking the defenses, Du Pont failed to
reconnoiter the defenses thoroughly. He would never really know the
capabilities of the guns at the throat of the harbor or the extent or exact
character of the obstructions.

On to Charleston

By the Spring of 1863 Fox's obsession of a naval attack on Charleston
had not waned. Du Pont had repeatedly cautioned him not to underrate
the works, warning the assistant secretary, "Do not go in half cocked
about Charleston—it is a bigger job than Port Royal . . . Loss of life is
nothing, but *failure* now at Charleston is ten times the failure elsewhere—." Charles Henry Davis observed Fox's obsession and admitted
he had spent many "anxious hours in cogitation growing out of this
weakness of his." He wrote, "He has a fancy for planning, rather than
executing, so that while he is always ready to consider any scheme, he
is equally ready to postpone any step towards execution of a plan how-

ever maturely ripened and deliberately adopted . . ."[14] This was one plan, however, that despite the difficulties encountered, he would not terminate. Fox believed that a naval victory at Charleston would give the navy tremendous prestige and the propaganda value outweighed any of the risks involved.

As fall ended and winter arrived, the attack against Wilmington was still alive and scheduled to take place before an operation against Charleston. Welles pushed to have some of the new *Passaic* class ironclads complete by November. Fox even kept the Mississippi Squadron's commander, Rear Admiral David Dixon Porter, believing that his operations took precedence. He wrote Porter that this was the "imperative act to be considered above even the capture of Charleston." The assistant secretary, however, never lost sight of his pet Charleston project. Fox's expectation to have four *Passaic* class monitors at Charleston by November began to slip as strikes and shortages of material delayed their completion. A sense of urgency prevailed in Washington by December 1862. The crushing defeat of the Union army at Fredericksburg in mid-December hastened the administration's resolve to "strike a blow" somewhere.[15]

Northern leaders wanted a quick victory to offset this debacle. Anxious to get an expedition in motion, Fox continued to promise both Du Pont and flag officer Samuel P. Lee the same *Passaic* class monitors, as they became ready. It seems that Fox planned to give them to Lee to use at Wilmington in order to attack the forts at the Cape Fear, then he would send them south. The plans at Wilmington relied on too many contingencies, the most difficult being the shallow water and the lack of knowledge of the bars there. The Wilmington plan called for the reduction of the forts by monitors and gunboats. The success or failure of this enterprise would certainly affect how Du Pont approached his attack on Charleston. The plan to attack Wilmington ended on 31 December, when the *Monitor* foundered off Cape Hatteras. Without the most shallow draft ironclad for the attack, the department cancelled this operation, and began looking farther south. Welles wrote in his diary, "It is best, therefore to push on to Charleston and strengthen Du Pont."[16]

On 6 January, Fox wrote Du Pont that the *New Ironsides*, *Passaic*, *Montauk*, *Patapsco*, and *Weehawken* would be sent immediately. Possibly, in an effort to prod Du Pont into action, the admiral was told he could keep them only a short while before they sailed to attack other ports of the Confederacy. Du Pont's notice that these five ironclads were on their way south also came with language from Welles that must have made Du Pont uneasy. Welles wrote that these ironclads would enable him "to enter the harbor of Charleston and demand the surrender of all the defenses or suffer the consequences of the refusal." Furthermore, although Hunter's command was to be increased by ten thousand men, Du Pont was told, "The capture of this most important port, however, rests solely upon the success of the naval force . . ."[17]

Du Pont's reservations about the monitors remained. His concerns about a successful attack on Charleston became firmer after the ironclads' poor performance against the earthworks at Fort McAllister. He continued to be unsure of the qualities of the monitors, their strength, and at what angle the armor would deflect shot. He knew that the department did not grasp the "magnitude" and that Fox "overrates the monitors as much as he underrates the defenses . . ."[18]

On 24 January, Du Pont wrote Welles with doubts about the success of an attack. The flag officer pointed out that in his communications with Fox he discussed, at length, the character and extent of the rebel defenses as well as the weakness of the monitors and the difficulties of removing obstructions under fire. He let Welles know that he assumed all responsibility, but that the success or failure of this expedition had dire consequences to the Navy Department and the country. He concluded by asking for additional ironclads beyond the five promised.[19]

This letter took Welles completely by surprise. He had no idea that Du Pont had any reservations about the proposed attack because Fox had not passed along the concerns. Du Pont, on the other hand, felt that his detailed reports from the attacks on Fort McAllister should have sufficiently warned the department of the limitations of the monitors. Welles might have been critical of both Fox and Du Pont, but instead he forged a compromise that briefly settled Du Pont's misgivings and preserved Fox's pride and kept the attack on track. Welles wrote Du Pont on the thirty-first and gave him the authority to abandon the attack if he felt that he could not capture the port. Welles tried to build the admiral's confidence by stating that if he could pass the obstructions, then he would be successful. He reminded Du Pont that Confederate cruisers on the high seas had weakened the blockade and that the department had supplied all the ironclads he would get—no more would be ready for at least six weeks. Within the letter, Welles stated that the capture of Charleston was "imperative." When Du Pont read this, he interpreted it to mean that the project could not be abandoned. When the department later added additional ironclads for the attack, the flag officer realized the department had neglected his earlier judgment about his needs for more force. It confirmed in his mind that the department expected an attack regardless of his reservations. Lastly and most importantly, Welles wrote, "the Department will share the responsibility imposed upon the commanders who make the attempt." This statement indicated that should Du Pont fail, the department would support him. These words would later create a rift between the two that could not be closed.[20]

This letter was written on the day that the Confederate ironclads sortied to attack the blockading vessels off Charleston. Despite the setbacks elsewhere in the country, particularly the capture of Galveston, Texas, this letter convinced Du Pont that the department's resolve to forge ahead with an attack could not be altered. It now seemed that any plans to attack other ports along the coast would wait until Du Pont had his shot at Charleston.[21]

Fox Pushes His Agenda

On Sunday, 15 February, President Lincoln, Welles, Fox, Secretary of War Edwin M. Stanton, General in Chief Henry Halleck, and Major General Foster met to discuss the overall progress of the war. As the conversation progressed, the men began discussing the projected Charleston attack. During the meeting, Foster pitched a plan to capture Charleston by landing troops on Morris Island under the protection of the ironclads. In a manner similar to that of Seymour's earlier plan, the army would erect siege batteries and reduce Sumter. Fox, who could not endure the thought of sharing a victory with the army, belittled the idea. He afterwards wrote Du Pont that "such an idea was so insignificant and so characteristic of the army that I could not help expressing myself to that effect." Politics also entered the equation. During the discussion, the President expressed his concern that a siege would take too long and that the politicians needed a victory before Congress adjourned, so that they could "shape legislation." From earlier discussions, Lincoln still believed the navy planned to run into the harbor. Annoyed at the thought that the plans may have changed and now included a siege, Lincoln suggested that Fox travel to Port Royal and discuss the operation with Du Pont. Welles disapproved of Fox's visit, believing that it would "touch Du Pont's pride . . . and do more harm than good." The secretary also knew he could not order an attack because of the "contingencies" that Du Pont had to judge. Welles also knew that if he failed after being ordered to attack, the blame would be solely on the department.[22]

Fox steadfastly tried to poison Du Pont's views against army cooperation. He warned Du Pont not to take "soldiers too closely into your counsels in a purely naval matter." Fox continued to show that he was unable or unwilling to understand the difficulties in the Charleston attack. More importantly, he continued to insist it be entirely a naval operation regardless of the outcome and the risk to the naval forces. He persisted, and despite the differences in his and Du Pont's opinions, he never attempted to digest the concerns of the flag officer. Just a day after the meeting he suggested that Du Pont "go in and demand a surrender of the forts or the alternative of destruction to their city."[23]

Feeling pressure from Lincoln, Welles vented his frustrations in his diary. Weary of the perceived delays by the flag officer, he wrote that Du Pont "shrinks from responsibility, dreads the conflict he has sought, yet is unwilling that any other should undertake it, is afraid the reputation of Du Pont will suffer." Welles also felt that Du Pont should be "circumspect and vigilant" and regretted the "signs of misgiving and doubt which have recently come over him."[24]

Meanwhile, Fox continually interjected himself between Du Pont and Welles so that neither of the latter men fully understood the other's situation. Fox, meanwhile, continued his campaign for a wholly naval operation. Five days after General Foster's proposal, Fox wrote Du Pont a letter which showed two things: first, that he completely failed to understand the difficulties of an attack on Charleston and, second, his passionate commitment to an all-naval affair. He once more asked Du Pont not to let the army "spoil" the attack. He also wrote, "I hope you will hold to the idea of carrying in your flag supreme and superb, defiant and disdainful, silent amid the 200 guns until you arrive at the centre of this wicked rebellion and there demand the surrender of the Forts, or swift destruction." While claiming that both Lincoln and Welles supported this, he told Du Pont that the "sublimity of such a silent attack is beyond words to describe . . ."[25]

Uncertainty and Confusion

Fox continued to promise Du Pont additional monitors for the attack. Du Pont, however, became concerned about rumors that refuted the need for more force to attack the city. Foster, still interested in attacking Wilmington, reportedly told Fox that Du Pont would be "perfectly satisfied" with only two more monitors. The flag officer denied this and wrote the assistant secretary that his "wants in ironclads was limited to the capacity of the Department to supply them." Probably in an effort to goad Du Pont into action, Fox reminded the admiral that the department still had plans to attack Wilmington. He told Du Pont that the *Keokuk* and one other ironclad would be held to strengthen Admiral S. P. Lee in this effort. Du Pont, however, tried to discourage this. He wrote, "I trust in God you are not going to let Foster inveigle you into any Wilmington operation until we are through here."[26]

While the discussions continued between Washington and Port Royal, the likelihood of army cooperation crumbled. Foster presented to Hunter his plans to make simultaneous landings on Morris and Sullivan's islands and to construct breeching batteries to attack Fort Sumter. Hunter, who had earlier quieted Seymour concerning a similar plan, called Foster insubordinate. This controversy caused Foster to leave the army's Department of the South. In early March, the disharmony in the army reached a crescendo when Hunter also alienated Brigadier General Henry M. Naglee. Naglee earlier complained of Hunter's ineptness and the confusion within the command. Eventually, Hunter accused Naglee of insubordination and relieved him. With the army command now in complete disarray, Du Pont's chance to get army support appeared dim. This turn of events played right into the hands of Fox.[27]

As Du Pont made his final preparations for the attack, General Hunter threw another problem at him. Hunter, with neither advance notice nor real justification to Du Pont, decided to use Jacksonville, Florida, as a base of operations. On 10 March, he pushed army forces up the St. John's River with the naval support of the *Uncas* and the *Norwich* to occupy the town for a third time during the war. The senior naval officer present, Charles Steedman, reported that the army had not sent enough troops to hold the town. As Steedman predicted, on 27 March, army orders to evacuate the town arrived by steamer. Hunter really had never intend to hold the town, but sent troops there mainly to look for plunder, collect black recruits, and perhaps build a base of Union support in Florida. After a few skirmishes, and with Union sentiment almost nonexistent outside of Jacksonville, the "impulsive" Hunter decided to withdraw the troops. While the *Uncas* and *Norwich* covered the withdrawal, Steedman wrote Raymond Rodgers that the abandonment of the town was "one of the most ill-ordered and ill judged affairs which have occurred during the war." The withdrawal particularly upset Steedman, who witnessed the "grief and despair of the loyal inhabitants." Du Pont pointed to Fox that this evacuation ran counter to everything the Navy Department had ordered him to do—to take as many ports as possible. As the final troops embarked on the twenty-ninth, they finished their task with an exclamation point by sacking and burning the greater part of the town, the churches, and the warehouses. This prompted a national newspaper to query "Was Gen. Hunter crazy?"[28]

Hunter continued to keep the admiral ill at ease. While Hunter had his troops make their short and ill-conceived expedition to Jacksonville, he also mentioned that he needed additional naval protection on Hilton Head and in the Savannah River. Additionally, he mentioned that he might abandon Beaufort and maybe North Edisto Island. This latter proclamation forced Du Pont to realize he could not depend on Hunter's troops to be part of the proposed attack on Charleston. It also caused him to reflect that the navy might be tasked with resecuring the possessions now in Union hands. Du Pont wrote that Hunter's unrealistic suggestion of abandoning Beaufort was both "painful" and "an act of folly and humiliation."[29]

The Doubts Mount

As Du Pont continued his preparations, particularly stockpiling ammunition, both Fox and Welles persistently encouraged him to act, reminding him of the great need to send the monitors to other ports. Du Pont delayed and continued his insistence on getting more ironclads. Fox, meanwhile, gloated that the army would certainly be spectators. The admiral, under a great deal of pressure to begin the operation, knew the department was acting out of an "impatience of ignorance" and essentially the department was asking him to "relieve the national heart." The high political stakes with this operation compounded his personal dilemma. The expectations of the department and the public for him to attack and succeed were immense. To cancel the attack now was virtually out of the question. Although he felt that the attack could not succeed, he never specifically told his officers or the department this. He lamented to his wife, "[S]uccess is not in my hands, to do my duty is . . ."[30]

Nevertheless, advice and reservations came to both Fox and Welles from other sources. Fox had heard similar arguments from the designer of the monitors, John Ericsson. He warned Fox numerous times of the folly of an attack on Charleston. In February, Stimers and Ericsson both warned Fox. Stimers believed that the monitors could not get close enough to fight the forts effectively. Fox certainly knew that rapidity of fire against earthworks was more desirable than weight of metal. Ericsson tried to dissuade Fox from attacking and recollected years later that most of the military leaders laughed at the scheme. He wrote Fox, "Your confidence in the great naval attack astounds me—you have not turrets enough . . . you have not guns enough." Yet, these warnings never altered Fox's opinion. In April, before news of the attack reached the North, Ericsson wrote again, "A single shot will sink a ship, while a hundred rounds cannot silence a fort, as you have proved on the Ogeechee. The immutable laws of force and resistance do not favor your enterprize [sic]—chance therefore can only save you."[31]

By early March two additional *Passaic* class monitors and the iron-clad *Keokuk*, with two fixed and armored towers, traveled south to augment the forces at Charleston. Du Pont's fighting force of seven monitors, the *Keokuk*, and the seagoing broadside ironclad *New Ironsides* all carried heavy armament, but they could boast only thirty-two guns. Additionally, according to John Dahlgren, the 15-inch guns that Du Pont would rely upon to batter down Sumter's walls had a service life of only about three hundred rounds. These guns demonstrated during the attacks on Fort McAllister that they needed repairs after a day's firing. These perceived limitations would all but prevent a deliberate bombardment by the fleet. With a long bombardment no longer an option, Du Pont believed he would have to run by the batteries into the harbor. Raymond Rodgers wrote about this disparity in firepower. "Twenty guns afloat attacking hundreds in battery on shore will be a novel and grand spectacle to which . . . the world will look with profound interest as an epoch in naval history."[32]

The three different classes of ironclads sent to attack Charleston had varying strengths and weaknesses. The *Passaic* class monitors were an improvement over the original *Monitor*. Ericsson increased the turret armor from eight to eleven inches and moved the pilothouse from the deck to the top of the turret. Ericsson had designed them to carry two 15-inch Dahlgren guns, but delays in the gun's development and slow production caused them to fit all the vessels with one of the larger guns and an 11-inch gun. The muzzle of the 15-inch gun, however, would not pass through the opening in the turret. Ericsson had to design a "smoke box" to fit against the opening to keep most of the muzzle exhaust outside the turret when firing the gun. This worked well but easily broke after a few firings. While heavily armored and capable of much more punishment, they still could not lay down a rapid fire. The twin-towered *Keokuk*, armed with two 11-inch Dahlgren guns, was an experimental vessel. She had a turtle-backed deck and advantages of light draft (9′ 3″) and greater speed (10 mph), good stability, and seaworthiness. Her positive attributes, however, were more than compromised by her light armor. She carried an alternating iron and wood system of armor laid vertically to the ship's inner skin. The total thickness including the inner skin was just under five and a quarter inches. The armored nonrotating towers had an additional half-inch iron plate. She was not built to withstand armor-piercing projectiles and Du Pont considered her "weak." The last of the ironclads, *New Ironsides*, was the strongest ship in the navy. She carried fourteen 11-inch smoothbores and two 150-pounder Parrott rifles on her gun deck and thus, carried half of the guns in the ironclad fleet. She could throw nearly two thousand pounds of metal with each broadside. Yet with these strengths, she had an armored belt that varied in thickness and she had unarmored ends. Her helm, situated behind her stack, likewise limited the helmsman's vision. Her slow six-and-one-half knot speed and a draft of nearly sixteen feet also limited her actions.[33]

The Navy Department had provided the most powerful attacking force available, yet doubts of success began to mount in the minds of some of the officers in the squadron. Percival Drayton, one of the most skilled officers in the navy, believed the rate of fire would be too slow, that the 15-inch guns did not prove themselves effective against earthworks fortifications, and the obstructions would be a problem. Charles Steedman wrote, "We are not very sanguine of the attack being successful, the enemy has had such a long time at his command to make the most extraordinary preparations for defense . . ." The torpedo obstructions had Steedman wishing for more monitors and claiming that they had only half of those needed for the attack.[34]

Welles had one final warning before Du Pont gathered the attacking force. In mid-March Alban Stimers reported at the Navy Department that the attack would be delayed until April. Welles became increasingly apprehensive, comparing this operation with the Peninsula Campaign and its delays. Stimers had just returned from Port Royal, having delivered extra armor for the monitors. In the meeting Welles, Fox, and Secretary of the Treasury Salmon P. Chase listened as Stimers recounted a council held on board *Wabash* with senior army and naval officers. The minutes of the meeting plainly showed the army hindering the operations. Just as Fox and Welles began to discuss Du Pont's original thoughts of a joint operation, President Lincoln walked in and, after getting briefed on the earlier discussions, he stated that Du Pont must press on without delay. According to Welles, the President "wanted positive orders given how to make the attack . . ." The President again suggested Fox go to Charleston to consult with Du Pont. Fox, however, "slided out of it." After the meeting, Welles spent a restless and nervous night thinking that Du Pont had lost his enthusiasm for the attack because of the great responsibility of the venture. He also believed that the flag officer sought to preserve his reputation rather than to make one. Welles' opinions, however, were likely created by Stimers' silence in the meeting. Du Pont later suspected that Stimers did not let the men know the real difficulties and the limitations of the ironclads in making the attack. Du Pont theorized that when Stimers found out "how the tide was running" he told the secretary and president what they wanted to hear. Without the facts known by the department, Du Pont's situation later would be almost hopeless.[35]

The Charleston attack was now set in stone. Nevertheless, without the support of the army it was like a crap shoot. Under Fox's lead, the department was playing to win all or nothing. Politics certainly influenced the decision process. Welles reportedly said that "the attack must be made whether successful or not, the people would not stand it and would 'turn us all out'." Welles, and particularly Fox, had staked the reputation of the department on the success of the monitors. Some of these warships, with their alterations, would eventually cost over $1,000,000 each. This represented a huge portion of the Navy Department's budget. Should these warships fail or not be used Welles would have much to explain.[36] In addition, the great sums of money vested in the industrial complex that built these warships was at stake. Success meant more contracts to ship builders, engine manufacturers, and dozens of other smaller contractors who all stood to gain on the building of additional vessels or lose money should the monitors fail.

Plans, Preparations and Problems

Toward the end of March, Du Pont began to make some final preparations for the battle. The squadron's mechanics and machine shop in Port Royal worked at capacity to make alterations, adjustments, and repairs to the monitors for the attack. Since they had all been rushed to completion, they arrived on station needing some work. Alban Stimers brought a crew of mechanics, and one of John Ericsson's assistants was also there on "special service" at Port Royal to assist making repairs and alterations. After a mortar shell had pierced the deck of the *Passaic* at Ft. McAllister, Ericsson had suggested the monitors receive an additional twelve inches of pine timber covered with three-eighth-inch iron plating. He hoped this would reduce the force of a falling shell and keep penetrations to a minimum. Acknowledging the vulnerability of the decks, the department sent down iron plates to cover the most vulnerable parts. Enough iron to provide these areas up to two inches of extra protection arrived at the end of March. Working in the North Edisto River, work-men fitted the iron plates over the magazine, shell rooms, boilers, and engines only days before the attack. As there was a lack of armor or time, the workmen laid logs over the berth deck of *Patapsco*. The com-manding officer of the *New Ironsides*, Captain Thomas Turner, pro-tected the unarmored ends of his ironclad with a layer of sandbags. Green rawhides were laid the entire length of the spar deck "making a carpet of them from one end of the ship to the other." On top of these, he laid sandbags. He also placed sandbags on the powder decks and in cabins and staterooms to protect the lower decks from shot—a total of six thousand sandbags, moistened by a steady stream of moisture. In this configuration she was described as the "personification of ugliness."[37]

Admiral Porter's success with a tallow coating on his ironclads in the Mississippi had Du Pont trying the same procedure. All the ironclad crews slushed the decks, turrets, and pilothouses. The *New Ironsides* likewise received a coating of slush an inch thick. The substance made life on board "disagreeable." The officers and men had it on all their clothing and they tracked it below. John Sanford Barnes called the *New Ironsides* a "slippery, dirty, and a foul-smelling iron floating box." Ad-ditionally, the night before the attack, the *New Ironsides* received spe-cial preparations. Her masts and upper tackle were sent down and her boats removed.[38]

Du Pont also made preparations to deal with the obstructions they might encounter. He began this project, however, without knowing their specific nature. This was, without doubt, a major mistake. Though Welles had stressed the importance of determining just how extensive they were, Du Pont never had a complete reconnaissance made. On the nights of 24 and 30 January, he sent Boutelle and other men from the Coast Survey into the harbor at night to mark the channels, but they did not make a close examination of the obstructions. Boutelle made a final night survey on 5 April to reconfirm and buoy the newly found Pump-kin Hill Channel, discovered during the earlier surveys. Raymond Rodgers later admitted that the knowledge of these obstructions was only "vague and indefinite." To overcome this obstacle and avoid any more delays, John Ericsson designed an obstruction-clearing raft to be fitted to the bow of monitors. The department built four of these rafts. Only two of the four safely arrived at Port Royal.[39]

The rafts were built of heavy timbers crossing at right angles and bolted together. Fifty feet in length and weighing ninety tons, they re-sembled a bootjack as a result of the notch in one end to fit to the bow of a monitor. Chains secured them to the bow of their host. The rafts carried grapples beneath them to snag obstructions and had been designed by Ericsson to carry a seven-hundred-pound torpedo to blow a hole in any obstructions they may encounter. None of the captains were openly willing to use one of these contraptions. John Rodgers, however, agreed to fasten one to the *Weehawken*. He refused, however, to carry a torpedo "unless ordered to do so." He feared that the raft might collide with another Union vessel or flip over the bow of the *Weehawken*, causing the torpedo to destroy his own warship. Despite Stimers' insistence of the raft's value and his constant appeals to the admiral to use the torpedo, Du Pont never had faith in the devices. He remarked, "I have no more idea that we can use them than we can fly."[40]

Du Pont chose to move against the Confederates during the first week in April. A full moon on the second would give the ironclads between one and two feet more water to operate. On 3 April, Du Pont held a conference with the ironclad captains on the *James Adger* to discuss the final details of the attack. Before this meeting, Du Pont "exhibited a studied silence" regarding his plans. The officers offered their opinions for various subjects. They discussed the distance the vessels should remain apart, the possibility of having to anchor, the distance to engage the forts, the role that the "elephant of strength and yet great weakness," the *New Ironsides*, should play, the targets of the gunners, and other important topics. All during the meeting Du Pont thought to himself how "stupid" the attack was and how little there was to gain while a defeat would "add a thousandfold to the strength of the rebellion . . ."[41]

The attacking monitors would face a number of special problems, most related to vision during the attack. Once the battle was joined, signaling would be difficult. Not adapted to either sending or acknowledging the receipt of flag signals, this particular difficulty concerned Du Pont who referred to these warships as "blind giants." The captain and pilot's visions were limited to the small openings in the pilothouse. In the smoke of the battle, the poor vision could complicate conning the vessel down an unknown channel. The ironclads' poor maneuverability and slow speed would compound this problem. The commanding officers would also not have any soundings because while under fire the leadsman would not be able to take his station. A tiny peephole in the side of the turret served as the sighting station for the gun captain. During normal conditions this presented a challenge, but the smoke from the battle would make sighting the guns nearly impossible. With the turret in motion the gun captain's job became more difficult and was considered by some as "practically useless." Getting the turret to stop at the right point to fire the guns was also problematic. The gun captain had to work with the engineer who worked the turret machinery. The order "stop, ready, fire" was spoken in quick order once the object came in sight. If the turret turned too far, it had to be worked back in the opposite direction. The gun captain could sight the 11-inch gun over the barrel, but could not sight the 15-inch gun because of the smokebox attachment. In all cases elevation or depression was a "matter of chance."[42]

While the monitors were designed to fight other ships bows on, John Downes, captain of the *Nahant*, believed they should be fought broadside to the fort to decrease the strike zone. Fought in this manner, enemy gunners would find it more difficult to strike the decks by shot falling short or over reaching. Welles posed this question to John Ericsson, who believed that attacking bows on would give the enemy gunners a smaller target to either side of the ship.[43]

The monitors had faced so little testing prior to this operation that no one knew at what range the ironclads should attack the forts. Du Pont believed that the 15-inch Dahlgren guns could breech the walls of Fort Sumter, but he did not know the effective distance. The shells had a low initial velocity and a short range. John Rodgers and Du Pont discussed this topic some months before the attack. They sought to determine the area in which the 15-inch guns would be effective against the enemy fort, but conversely the fire from the fort would be ineffective against the ironclad's armor. They had to determine this by guesswork because the department had not tested these shells against masonry. Still unknown within days of the attack, Welles asked for Ericsson's opinion. Ericsson believed that the armor would be pierced at 400 yards. John Rodgers believed a farther distance necessary and suggested that the vessels anchor in an arc of about 1,250 yards from Fort Sumter. He felt this would be a safe distance and the ironclads would lie over 1,700 yards from both forts Moultrie and Johnson. He also suggested that the warships anchor during the attack. This would improve the Union gunner's aim and the warships would be less likely to run afoul of torpedoes.[44]

On 4 April Du Pont prepared an order of battle. He instructed Rhind and Boutelle to take the *Keokuk* and buoy the bar. The prescribed order ahead consisted of *Weehawken* in the van pushing the torpedo raft, followed by *Passaic*, *Montauk*, *Patapsco*, *New Ironsides*, *Catskill*, *Nantucket*, *Nahant*, and *Keokuk*. The order of advance was by seniority, the only exception being that *Weehawken* had to lead because of the bootjack. This placed John Rodgers in line ahead of Drayton, who was his senior. Du Pont believed this decision relieved Drayton, who did "not want to be the first to attack his native city . . ." The *New Ironsides* would serve as the flagship. This ironclad was better suited for sending signals and would allow Du Pont to pass his signals to both ends of the line. He instructed the captains to steam up the main ship channel at cable's length (six hundred yards) and to ignore the batteries on Morris Island unless a signal from Du Pont ordered them to commence action. Against Rodgers's advice, Du Pont decided the ironclads would attack Fort Sumter's northwest face at a distance between six hundred and eight hundred yards with precision firing to avoid wasting shot. Should the ironclads successfully silence Fort Sumter, he anticipated attacking the batteries on Morris Island next. A reserve squadron consisting of five wooden steamers commanded by Captain Green would form outside the bar near the entrance buoy. These vessels would remain ready to support, if necessary, the ironclads' attack on the batteries on Morris Island.[45]

The plan of attack offered by Du Pont had little detail, with the exception that he wanted his ironclads to remain in motion. He envisioned passing the obstructions into the harbor, but he gave his officers no further instructions beyond this. He evidently planned to rely on the improvisation of his excellent captains to carry the fight, hoping that something positive might happen. He certainly planned the attack so that his ironclads would be in a better position to retreat. The high tide for 7 April was about 10:30. Attacking on the ebbing tide rather than the flood tide would better allow a damaged ironclad to get to safety. The Union officers felt that if a disabled monitor fell into the hands of the enemy, the maintenance of the blockade at Charleston would be impossible. Attacking on the ebb tide, however, would frustrate any efforts to advance to the middle of the harbor, should the warships breech the obstructions. The ebb tide would give the pilots and commanding officers a better view of the navigational aids in the harbor.[46]

At 7:00 A.M. on Sunday, 5 April, the monitor fleet weighed anchor in the North Edisto. The *James Adger,* with Du Pont on board, left the ironclads behind and steamed ahead. The *James Adger* arrived among the blockading fleet off Charleston and anchored beside the *New Ironsides,* a "massive, graceless barren hull, with its tier of huge guns, . . . strikingly like a great swimming castle." The ironclads, under tow, arrived about two o'clock that afternoon and anchored off the harbor. The garrison at Fort Sumter hoisted flags and fired a salute to hail their arrival, giving notice that the fort was ready for an attack. The *Keokuk* moved in with the *Bibb* and the buoy schooner *Admiral Du Pont,* and under the direction of Charles Boutelle easily buoyed the channel before sunset. At dusk the *Patapsco* and *Catskill* entered the Main Ship Channel and anchored near the inner buoy.[47]

On the morning of the sixth, Flag Officer Du Pont shifted his flag onto the *New Ironsides*. The weather remained hazy and at 7:00 A.M. the ironclads stood into the channel. The warships anchored in line near and above the buoys to wait for the weather to clear. The flag officer realized that if he could not see landmarks clearly for bearings, an attack under these conditions would complicate further the sighting of the guns and steering the monitors into the channel. The day remained hazy and Du Pont postponed the attack until the next day. He called the captains on board *New Ironsides* for another discussion. During the meeting, Turner voiced "strong objections" to the proposed plan of attacking the northwest corner of the fort. The other officers talked about attacking Sumter by steaming farther into the harbor at a point where fewer forts could fire on the ironclads. Here there was more room to maneuver and less chance of grounding. Du Pont's greatest fear was losing the *New Ironsides* should she become disabled. Yet, if he kept her outside the harbor, he would leave half of his firepower behind and defeat might be pinned on this single decision. Worden also showed opposition to the attack, believing the army should be part of a joint operation. John Rodgers, on the other hand, was more sanguine of success.[48]

Du Pont retired that evening less positive than before. Before turning in he wrote to his wife, Sophie, that he should have put his reservations of the attack clearly in writing to the department but "No one would have believed it." He lamented to her that he had mistakenly hoped that the testing of the ironclads on Fort McAllister might have given the department the information necessary to understand the limitations of the ironclads and the strength of the defenses. He realized though that neither Fox, nor Welles, could be swayed to see anything but the capture of Charleston. He felt that honesty would have resulted in his relief. While he feared defeat more than an end to his command, the night before the attack he felt that his forces would not succeed and looked to God for "wisdom and direction."[49]

The Attack

On 5 April, the lookouts on Fort Sumter watched as one ship after another appeared over the horizon. As they hove to outside the bar, the commander of Fort Sumter, Colonel Alfred Rhett, ordered his men to prepare for battle. The defenders watched and waited nervously the next day as the ironclads remained outside the channel buoys. On the seventh a "veil of mist hung over the horizon" but by 10:00 A.M. it cleared away and the ironclads got underway. Rhett telegraphed the city, "The turrets are coming!" With these words, houses emptied as the citizens of Charleston heard the news. Women wore their "gala costumes" to witness the attack from the battery promenade, others climbed the steeples and rooftops and throngs lined the shore to witness the upcoming battle.[50]

At about noon the preparatory signal to get underway rose from the deck of *New Ironsides* and ten minutes later the signal to get underway started the ironclads in motion. The *Weehawken,* in the van, had Robert Platt of the Coast Survey on board to conn the vessel into the channel. The raft on the lead ironclad proved to be unwieldy as predicted and as the *Weehawken* hove up her anchor one of the raft's grapnels entangled the anchor chain. Unfouling the grapnel from the chain took an hour and the entire line remained motionless. This delay upset the timetable slightly. Since Du Pont planned the attack on the ebb tide, this would place the attacking force trying to steam into the harbor under a stronger ebb current and give them a shorter time to remain under fire before the tide would turn.[51]

At 1:15, John Rodgers in *Weehawken* made the signal "all clear" and the vessels again began to move. The *Weehawken,* her bottom foul, and pushing the raft against the ebbing tide, kept the entire column proceeding at about three knots and soon the line of battle became disorganized. The flagship's flawed design, sporting her stack forward of the helm, not only blocked the vision of the helmsman so that he steered "blind" but the smoke pouring aft added to the poor visibility. The *New Ironsides* began experiencing great difficulty trying to keep her station in the shallow and narrow channel and the swift currents. This would have an important impact on the battle.[52]

The Confederates in Fort Sumter watched from their guns as the ironclads began their movement. Their progress was so slow that the men went to dinner. At 2:30, the long roll recalled the garrison of 550 to their posts when the ironclads neared the opening range. Minutes before 3:00 P.M. the fort's band struck up national airs. The Palmetto flag was hoisted over the western corner of the fort; a garrison flag flew from the principal staff on the northern salient, and on the eastern corner of the fort flew the flag of the First Regiment South Carolina Artillery. Following a thirteen-gun salute, the garrison was ready for action.[53]

Just before 3 o'clock, as the *Weehawken* came abreast of Fort Sumter, a shot from Fort Moultrie at fifteen hundred yards distant broke the silence and struck squarely on the lead monitor's turret. The *Passaic*, second in line and flying a pennon, created confusion among the Confederate gunners who mistook her for the flagship.[54]

Rodgers and Platt, meanwhile, peered through the narrow slits in the pilothouse of *Weehawken* as she advanced down the channel. They began to notice colored buoys in the fairway and passed between them and Morris Island. They then observed a line of obstructions looming ahead and believed they could see several rows of casks, but did not know if these supported ropes and netting to foul propellers or if they marked torpedoes. Platt found it difficult to steer the vessel at the mouth of the harbor. Here the tide became strong, and both Platt and Rodgers worried about their ability to keep away from the rope obstructions. Contemporaries felt there was no officer "cooler, more gallant, more judicious" than Rodgers. After seeing the casks he reportedly said, "Torpedoes! Well, heaven help us if they are, for I am going over them." A few moments later an explosion occurred alongside *Weehawken*. It lifted the vessel up slightly and threw a column of water onto the warship, but did no serious damage. With limited visibility, Rodgers thought a torpedo had caused the explosion and apparently slowed or stopped briefly. This must have been a shell burst under the vessel, as the Confederates had deployed no torpedoes in this area.[55]

This explosion, however, may have changed Rodgers' mind. Feeling that the raft could not neutralize the torpedoes or clear the obstructions, he turned *Weehawken* toward Fort Sumter with *Passaic* and *Montauk* in her wake. Should his ironclad become tangled in the mass of obstructions she would surely be sunk by the Confederate gunfire. Rodgers wrote afterwards that he believed the obstructions too formidable and had not "felt authorized" to force his ironclad through them. This decision would doom any prospect of Union success.[56]

On board the flagship, Du Pont, Raymond Rodgers, and the fleet pilot all peered out of the armored pilothouse of the *New Ironsides* for a view of the battle. The small pilothouse could accommodate only three men and prevented Turner or his ship's pilot from remaining inside. This was unfortunate, since the ship had helm peculiarities that required the knowledge of both these men. Before the battle even opened, the flagship with her flat bottom became unmanageable in the channel. Because of the ignorance of the fleet pilot, he was compelled to stop the ironclad.

At 2:40, Du Pont had hoisted the signal "I have stopped." The delay of the flagship confused the after part of the battle line.[57]

As the lead ironclads steamed farther into the harbor, the *Weehawken* passed one of the range-marking buoys and nearly all the guns that could be brought to bear from Moultrie, Batteries Bee and Beauregard, and Cumming's Point opened fire on *Weehawken*. Initially, the Confederates fired all the guns in each battery simultaneously and as rapidly as possible in the belief that the ironclads planned to run by the forts into the harbor. When the Confederates fired at *Weehawken* in this way, she seemed to disappear from sight with water thrown into the air from the misses. Union army officers observing the battle from outside the bar believed her sunk, but as the water settled, she could be seen passing through the hail of shot and shells.[58]

Passaic, Montauk and *Patapsco* joined Rodgers before the obstructions. The Confederates kept up such an intense fire that the shot passing overhead "sang like a swarm of bees." As the Union ships replied, it appeared to the Confederates that the monitors fired, and then backed to reload, and then steamed forward again—doing this to prevent them from becoming stationary targets. In reality, the appearance of the ship reversing course was caused by a loss of steam to the main engines. After firing the guns, steam was diverted from the main engines to run the blowers at high speed in order to clear the smoke from the turrets. With a loss of steam pressure, the vessels slowed or may have even lost headway in the tide. This gave the enemy gunners the impression that the vessels moved in reverse.[59]

As the four monitors in the van passed through the gunfire and stood toward the northeastern face of Fort Sumter, the *New Ironsides*, in the center of the line, continued to be unmanageable. At 3:25, Du Pont signaled the rest of the attacking force to "disregard motions of Commander-in-Chief." Five minutes later, the huge ironclad vessel anchored to avoid going aground. Minutes later, Acting Master John W. Godfrey, the fleet pilot, again found deep water for the *Ironsides*. As the crew hove up anchor again to try to work up the channel, a shot took the armored shutter off the number five gun port.[60]

The signal from Du Pont to disregard the flagship's motion prompted the ironclad captains in the rear of the line to push forward and around the flagship to get within range of the forts. As they moved to pass the unmanageable flagship, both the *Catskill* and the *Nantucket* collided with the *New Ironsides*, and the *Patapsco* avoided her only "with difficulty." These collisions prompted the flag officer to signal the others to give his ship "more room." Fifteen minutes elapsed before the *Catskill* and *Nantucket* could clear the flagship. The four ironclads in the rear of the line eventually joined the other four monitors at the throat of the harbor. The flagship, however, remained behind and once again anchored, unable to cope with the conditions in the channel.[61]

The *New Ironsides* lay directly off Battery Wagner and at a distance that left her effectively out of the battle. Nevertheless, the ship was in grave danger. Unknown to those on board, she lay directly over a torpedo containing three thousand pounds of powder. The Confederates had placed the electrically detonated torpedo in the channel only days before the attack. The Confederates now tried repeatedly to set it off. One theory for its failure to explode was that the Confederates later found that an ordnance wagon had driven over the wires and severed them. It is more likely that the charge never reached the torpedo in sufficient strength to set it off. The Confederates had mistakenly laid out twice as much cable as was necessary to reach the weapon.[62]

As the last four ironclads steamed farther into the harbor, the first four monitors came under a tremendous fire. The water around them was a "seething cauldron," so many shells struck near *Weehawken* that sheets of water splashed over the top of the turret, wet the crews, and risked wetting the ready service powder and priming. The torrents of water also prevented Rodgers and the pilot, as well as the gunner inside the turret, from getting a clear view to steer or fire the guns. When the monitors did not advance past the obstructions, however, the defenders realized that the enemy did not intend to run by the forts and their fire became more "deliberate, accurate, and effective."[63]

The monitors first in line received a tremendous punishment. The *Weehawken* advanced to within about 350 yards of the obstructions and began to fire on Fort Sumter. She remained for about forty minutes under this heavy fire, getting off only two shots from each gun, while being struck fifty-three times during the battle. Rodgers claimed the armor was "beaten off the sides" and that in one place five inches of armor "crumbled into powder." These shots broke plates and pierced the deck, leaving the wood backing showing. A shell fragment also lodged in the seam between the turret and the pilothouse, causing the turret to revolve with difficulty. *Passaic,* commanded by Drayton, followed close aboard. The Confederate gunners aimed at the joint where the turret met the deck and the pilothouses. After the fourth shot from the *Passaic's* 11-inch gun, two heavy shots struck quickly in succession on the lower part of the turret. One broke off a piece of metal that wedged between the turret and the deck, causing it to work poorly. Another dented in a plate enough to damage the rails for the 11-inch gun's carriage, effectively putting this gun out of action for the remainder of the afternoon. A third shot, minutes later, struck the upper edge of the turret, broke eleven plates, and ricocheted into the pilothouse, lifting it off its foundation three inches and exposing the inside. *Weehawken* experienced a similar shot on her pilothouse, which gave Platt a concussion and required John Rodgers to hold Platt up until the latter could recover from the shock. Under this massed fire, the *Passaic* managed to return only four 9-inch shells and nine 15-inch shells while being struck thirty-five times. At 4:20 she had to drop down toward Fort Moultrie to anchor and repair her damage.[64]

Montauk joined the other two monitors about seven hundred yards from the fort, but Worden had a difficult time controlling his vessel with limited vision and the strong tide. He had to maneuver his ironclad to avoid the other monitors and delivered his fire when possible. Engaging the eastern face of Fort Sumter, *Montauk* managed to fire ten 15-inch cored shot, sixteen 11-inch solid shots, and one shell and was struck fourteen times with minor damage.[65]

The *Patapsco*, Daniel Ammen commanding, opened fire with her 150-pound Parrott rifle at 3:10 at a distance of about 1,400 yards. At 1,200 yards the 15-inch gun fired for the first time. Ammen placed his warship about 600 yards from Fort Moultrie and twice that distance from Fort Sumter. After the fifth shot from his rifled gun, the bolts holding the gun to the carriage broke and, despite the efforts to make repairs, the gun remained out of action for the rest of the battle. The Confederates began striking the ironclad regularly and, after several heavy blows on the turret, Ammen found that, like both the *Weehawken*'s and the *Passaic*'s, it would not turn well. This further complicated his maneuvering and the aiming of his remaining gun. *Patapsco* received forty-seven hits and returned only ten shots.[66]

By now the *Catskill, Nantucket, Nahant,* and *Keokuk* had steamed around the flagship and entered the fray. The first shot struck *Catskill* at 3:35 and, four minutes later, she replied. Commander George W. Rodgers pushed his ironclad towards Fort Sumter rather than the obstructions and approached to within 600 yards of the fort. Caught in a severe crossfire she was struck twenty times and managed to fire only fifteen 11-inch and eleven 15-inch shells during the battle. Minutes later the *Nantucket,* next in line, entered the melee and began a deliberate fire on

Fort Sumter from 750 yards. Like the other commanders, the water and smoke obscured Commander Donald Fairfax's vision. The Confederates repeatedly hit the *Nantucket* in quick order. After the third shot from her 15-inch gun, the port stopper jammed when several enemy shots dented and drove in the plating around the opening. This effectively took this gun out of action for the remainder of the fight. Fairfax managed to fire his 11-inch gun only twelve times. Confederate gunners struck this ironclad fifty-one times in forty-five minutes. The enemy shots that struck the turret broke off bolt heads that fell into the space at the bottom of the turret ring. This caused the turret to become jammed for some time. They could only get it moving again by raising the turret higher to clear the bolt heads.[67]

The *Nahant* and *Keokuk* brought up the rear. Both of these vessels took positions close to Fort Sumter and received the hottest fire from the forts. The *Nahant* received two shots at the base of the pilothouse; one of these shots broke off a large piece of iron and sent it flying across the pilothouse. It damaged the steering gear and struck Commander Downes in the foot. This missile caused a painful bruise that kept Downes limping about with a cane for several days after the attack. Despite canvas curtains in the pilothouse to contain flying bolts, one shot sent the head of a bolt flying and fatally injured the helmsman, then struck the pilot. At this point Commander Downs took the helm. During the battle Downes reportedly called down to his gun captain, Acting Ensign Charles E. Clark, and said, "Mr. Clark you hav'n't hit anything yet." Whereby Clark responded, "We ain't near enough Captain Downes." Downes replied, "Not near enough! God damn it, I'll put you near enough! Starboard your helm, quartermaster." By 4:30 the monitor's turret would no longer turn, damaged by the heavy shots that struck at the base of the pilothouse. *Nahant* had to retire in order to try to repair these damages. Thirty-six shots struck the ironclad—nine struck the turret and six struck the pilothouse. These shots broke and indented many plates, pierced the smokestack, cut through the deck, and broke away eighty-three bolts. The *Nahant* managed to return only seven 15-inch and eight 11-inch projectiles.[68]

Keokuk's aggressive commander, Alexander C. Rhind, passed *New Ironsides* shortly after 3:20 and stood towards a position in advance of the *Weehawken* to avoid getting foul of her in the strong currents and narrow channel. Rhind, advised by his pilot Robert Smalls, however, had difficulty turning his ironclad around in these currents and she remained for thirty minutes under a tremendous fire. At about 4:00 P.M.

she "advanced, bow on, gallantly, to within 900 yards of Fort Sumter and about 300 yards from the obstructions. At this point, she received the rebels' "undivided attention . . ." Colonel Rhett asked Lieutenant Colonel Joseph A. Yates to direct the rebel fire on *Keokuk* from one of the Brooke rifles. Firing a square-headed bolt weighing 119 pounds, the first two shots went through one of the turrets, the third struck the pilothouse, and the fourth struck the hull abaft amidships. The firepower from this and the other guns was too much for the thinly armored *Keokuk*. She managed to fire only three shots while the rebels pounded and pierced her armor. This was all she could take and at about 4:10 she withdrew. The Confederates shot away the forward port shutters and disabled her forward gun. So many men lay wounded in the after turret that she could no longer return fire. Shots struck her ninety times and pierced the hull nineteen times at and below the waterline.[69]

At 4:20, shortly after *Keokuk* withdrew, the *New Ironsides* finally entered into the battle half-heartedly by firing a broadside at Fort Moultrie. For about ninety minutes she had lain about fifteen hundred yards from Sumter in a position whereby smoke obscured her view of the fort and any attempt to use her guns would have endangered the monitors more than Fort Sumter. She remained under fire from the forts and suffered more than fifty hits. The shots, however, "dropped from her sides like boys' brickbats from the roof of a house." At 4:25, the anchor on *New Ironsides* was hove up as evening approached. Du Pont considered taking the flagship closer and ordered the signal hoisted "follow motions of commander-in-chief." Du Pont, though, quickly changed his mind. When the pilot reminded him of the tide and after realizing the time of day, he said, "Make signal to the ships to drop out of fire; it is too late to fight this battle tonight; we will renew it early in the morning." The monitors began to retire past the flagship, signaling their disabilities as they passed.[70]

The battle that the Union forces hoped would decisively give them control of the harbor ended after a brief and poor showing by the ironclads. The vessels were under fire for only about two hours and experienced only forty minutes of the most severe fire. The *Keokuk* did not encounter fire for much longer than thirty minutes. During the fight, the ironclads managed to fire only 154 shots. Even less impressive was the minor damage inflicted on the main target, Fort Sumter. Most of the Union fire aimed at the fort was ricochet fire and not accurate. Nearly all of it passed over the fort or fell to either side. Confederate engineers concurred that projectiles struck the fort only thirty-six times. Nineteen other shells burst in front of the walls, doing only superficial damage. The shells that struck the walls did some serious damage to the fort. Some of the shells penetrated the walls and the remaining projectiles left large cracks and craters in the masonry. The Union naval fire killed five and wounded eight. The Confederates fired just over 2,200 shots from 76 guns and struck the Union ironclads 520 times. Despite the incredible pounding the ironclads received, the Union navy lost only one killed and twenty-one wounded.[71]

The Aftermath

After the recall the ironclads steamed back down the channel and anchored out of range. The commanders met on the flagship to report in person to the flag officer. They gathered in the large cabin on the *New Ironsides* and sat at a table where Du Pont had already taken his seat. Each officer in turn gave an account of his ship's part in the battle and the injuries received. Five of his ironclads had received injuries serious enough to limit their fighting capabilities. The *Keokuk*, "riddled like a colander," would never fight again. Brought into smooth water, she remained afloat, but the next morning the wind freshened and became so rough that the water began to pour into her wounds. At 7:30, after all her injured men were safely removed, she disappeared rapidly below the waters outside Charleston Harbor.[72]

On the flagship, the men discussed the battle with Du Pont. As a body, their doubts of renewing the fight left Du Pont with the conviction that the fight could not be resumed. Du Pont's ironclad officers were carefully picked for this attack and represented the best in the navy. The admiral had always relied on his officers' opinions and counsel for making his decisions. Du Pont went to bed on the night of the seventh leaving his officers in the wardroom of *New Ironsides* without giving them a decision. He awoke at 3:00 A.M. to give the matter more thought. At this point, he became even surer that he had made the proper decision. In the morning, he announced that he would not renew the fight, feeling that it would turn a "failure into a disaster." He received unanimous support from his senior officers.[73]

Shortly after his ironclads steamed out of danger, Du Pont wrote his wife, "We have failed as I felt sure we would . . ." Du Pont made the correct decision. His failure to renew the attack, however, caused great discontent in Washington. Du Pont considered some of the following points. Not including the *New Ironsides*, which did not effectively enter the battle, his attacking force managed to deliver in about two hours less than 150 shots from sixteen guns. During the battle the ironclads had to establish their range under a terrific fire in poor visibility. Under this tremendous enemy fire the Union officers were never able to determine the effectiveness of their shots. Despite the effort, the damage inflicted on Fort Sumter was minimal, in part as a result of the slow velocity of the Dahlgren shells. The ironclads' slow rate of fire and their inability to engage any single battery within the forts and silence them independently had also limited their success. Even if they had been able to disable several Confederate guns, the rebels well might have put them back in action the next day. Du Pont also knew that he lost one of his ironclads to battle damage and several others would not be battle-ready for days and some for weeks. Last, and most important, the objective given him by the department was not obtainable by the force under his command.[74]

The attack was designed to reduce Fort Sumter, yet the real problem was much more complicated. Du Pont, the Navy Department, and even the president himself never fully understood the complexity of the problem to be solved at Charleston. Neither Welles nor Fox communicated their perceptions of the objective of the attack. Their correspondence served only to add to Du Pont's confusion. The admiral repeatedly warned the department of the limitations of a naval force attacking alone and pleaded for a combined operation in order to gain some hope of success. The flag officer, however, was sent to solve an "insoluble problem,"—to take Charleston without army cooperation. A general staff-type organization would later prevent this type of mistake. In 1863 there was no similar staff in Washington to prevent Du Pont from being thrust under the Confederate guns with virtually no chance of success. After the war David Porter wrote that the defenses were so extensive that "it would have been little less than a miracle for a hostile fleet to reach the city."[75]

Du Pont's limited instructions to the captains of the ironclads had only added to this tactical problem. He gave them, in effect, no directions for the battle. Had Du Pont taken the lead position in the line on board the *Weehawken*, he might have led by example. This would have, however, reduced his ability to control all the ships by signal. John Rodgers carried the burden of success because the only possible formula for victory was for the ironclads to force their way past the obstructions and into the harbor. It is questionable whether the Union navy could have accomplished its goals even if the ironclads had gotten into the harbor. Even if the fleet had successfully run past the obstructions, its ammunition would have been insufficient to take the city or reduce the batteries. The warships also would have been cut off from coal and supplies. Furthermore, Hunter was not prepared to or capable of garrisoning the city. Fox's hope that temporary control of the harbor would force the Confederates to evacuate the city was not only a leap of faith, but ignorantly optimistic. In reality, the Union warships risked much more given the firepower of the remaining forts and the Confederate ironclads there to bar the way. Once the *Weehawken* turned away from the obstructions, the attack should have been abandoned. Du Pont gave his officers no real plan of attack. Du Pont probably had the best officers in the service. In fact, over a dozen of these men later obtained flag rank. Du Pont's faith in his commanding officers' tactical improvisation under fire, however, did not succeed.

The blame for defeat can be shared. To Du Pont's discredit, he failed to reconnoiter the obstructions as well as the defensive works of the harbor. Those who laid the sole blame on Du Pont and the ironclads, however, steal credit from the Confederates who designed and built an incredible defensive network. The ironclads reached only the gorge of the harbor, never beyond the first circle of fire. The heaviest batteries were never even employed against the Union forces. The department erred in sending ironclads that had largely been untested. The attacks on Fort McAllister could hardly apply and were not comparable to what the navy faced at Charleston. On 7 April, Du Pont thoroughly tested his defense-oriented monitors against superior firepower. In this test they showed they could withstand a great deal of punishment, but they could not return a large enough volume of fire to silence successfully an enemy in well-built defensive positions. Du Pont knew that a continuous fire from many vessels simultaneously was the only way to silence the forts. The admiral's decision not to renew the attack was based on his understanding of the monitors' limitations and their slow rate of fire against a greatly superior number of guns. Unlike the department, Du Pont viewed this contest as an experiment; in this case, the power of the larger number of guns was greater than the endurance of the ironclads. Fox and Welles must also bear blame for the repulse. They were intent on showcasing the monitors in a battle in which they could gain a political victory as well as a strategic one. Despite Du Pont's advice for joint operations and more force, the department never showed any hesitation to put Du Pont into a position in which he could not succeed.[76]

Despite the flawed strategic objectives and the limitations of this class of vessel against a massed fire, final responsibility for this repulse fell squarely on Du Pont's shoulders. His reputation as an aggressive commander was lost in the smoke of battle. He had fought the most important battle in his career, but it would pale in comparison with the battle he would now fight with the press and the department regarding his reputation and that of his officers.

– 7 –

"To the Perpetual Disgrace
of Public Justice"

The Aftermath

Once the smoke cleared on 7 April, the citizens of Charleston rejoiced. The Savannah *Republican* wrote, ". . . The sword of Damocles, has at length fallen . . ." and the Charleston *Mercury* proclaimed with characteristic hyperbole that the city had been delivered from the "most formidable Armada that the hands of man had ever put afloat." Northern papers initially reported that the repulse was due to the fact that the ironclads were "of insufficient strength for the work expected of them" and speculated that this was only a reconnaissance in force to probe the Confederate obstructions. Most gave Du Pont credit for bringing his fleet out of harm's way. The New York *Tribune* wrote that Du Pont was "second to no officer in the Navy in experience, ability, and determined courage . . ."[1]

The day after the battle Du Pont sat in his stateroom on board *New Ironsides* to write the most difficult report of his long career—a summary of his fleet's repulse. He kept it short, promising to send a more detailed version. In his dispatch he mentioned the difficulties of the channel and obstructions which "compelled the attack from the outside." He apprised Welles that he did not intend to renew the attack because he did not want to convert "a failure into a disaster." He added that the city could not be taken by a purely naval attack and the army at this time could not cooperate. Commander Alexander C. Rhind per-

185

sonally took this dispatch to the capital in order to answer fully any questions the secretary might have.[2]

Orders from Welles written five days before the attack arrived on the ninth. John Hay, an assistant secretary to the president, acted as a courier and carried the orders by steamer to Port Royal. The fact that Hay brought them down would give them additional importance in Du Pont's mind. The orders instructed the flag officer, once he attacked the defenses of Charleston, to send all his ironclads fit to move to New Orleans, keeping only two. Included in the packet was also a private letter from Fox reiterating this message and stressing the importance of sending the monitors south. This communication from the department made it necessary for the monitors to get to the workshops in Port Royal for the necessary repairs to put them once again in fighting trim. On 11 April, the monitors crossed the bar, and steamed to Port Royal while the *New Ironsides* resumed her station on the blockade outside Charleston. Du Pont issued orders to the captains of the *Patapsco, Weehawken, Nahant, Catskill,* and *Nantucket* to prepare them for sea.[3]

In Washington Welles and Fox remained anxious for news. Welles brooded while Fox continued to be optimistic. One Washington socialite thought Fox looked "thinner in two weeks & I never saw him look as anxious as now . . ." Welles privately did not believe the ironclads "impregnable," nor did he believe they would accomplish their mission without great sacrifice. When Fox and Welles learned of the attack on 10 April, they believed it was "merely a reconnaissance" and awaited the details. On the afternoon of 12 April, Commander Rhind and Lieutenant Commander John H. Upshur reached the capital with the dispatches and proceeded to Welles's house. As the Secretary read the report, he became extremely disappointed with the lack of detail. Rhind answered many of the secretary's questions, but Rhind, whose vessel was shot to pieces under the guns of Fort Sumter, proved to be an unwise bearer of the news. Welles realized that his experience under fire had unnerved him and had turned Rhind from an ardent advocate of ironclads to a man who had little faith in any vessel.[4]

Welles decided that the president should hear Rhind's story and also have an opportunity to question him. Welles, Rhind, and Upshur traveled to the White House and, while talking to the president, both Fox and Senator Charles Sumner joined the meeting. As Rhind spoke to the president, his disillusion with the monitors was evident. Fox could not idly stand by while Rhind denounced the navy's greatest weapon. He interrupted Rhind and pointed out that the monitors were not designed to engage heavily armed forts and that Du Pont had been expected to run by the Charleston Harbor fortifications. Rhind responded that this could not be done because of the obstructions and torpedoes. Sumner broke in at this point and asked why these had not been removed. "I cannot answer for the others; I did not remove any simply because I could not," snapped Rhind. Sumner sneered, "Well, Joe Hooker will have to take Charleston!" And Rhind brusquely replied, "Is he going down in an ironclad?" Welles, sensing the increasing tension, ended the discussion. Lincoln, however, had made a decision.[5]

Recently Major General Joseph Hooker had suggested to Lincoln that he lead a force to outflank Robert E. Lee's army on the Rappahannock River in order to sever his connections with Richmond. Knowing that the campaign was about to begin, Lincoln decided to telegraph Du Pont with instructions. He told him to keep his monitors within the bar at Charleston, but that, if his vessels had left their stations, to return them there until further orders. Lincoln hoped this would mask any real Union intentions and thereby pose a continued threat to the city and thus tie up more Confederate troops and prevent Beauregard from sending troops to Lee. The telegram, however, contradicted the order of 2 April instructing the flag officer to send all but two of his ironclads to the Gulf. Despite the fact that Welles sent a more conciliatory letter on the eleventh, followed by a telegram from the President on the thirteenth, neither arrived until 16 April.[6]

Du Pont expected a "howl" from the monitor interests, but not from the commander in chief. When Du Pont received the president's telegraph he perceived it as a rebuke and he became depressed and defensive. This telegram deeply affected Du Pont's mental state. In his mind the telegram indicated that Washington did not concur with his decision not to renew the attack. He believed that his prestige was being "robbed" despite this being his "first reverse after a long life of successful service . . ." He wrote to Henry Winter Davis, the Congressman from Maryland, that should anyone try to treat him unfairly that he would "certainly not lamely submit."[7]

Lincoln communicated with Du Pont a second time, sending a more conciliatory letter to clear up inconsistencies in the telegram of the thirteenth. But this missive did not arrive until 24 April. The president sent a copy to both Du Pont and Hunter acknowledging the contradiction contained in the department's instructions on 2 April, which ordered all but two of the ironclads south. Lincoln wrote that he meant no censure toward either Hunter or Du Pont. His chief interest was for the army

and navy to take the batteries on Morris and Sullivan islands, to capture Fort Sumter, and to keep pressure on the enemy forces. This activity was to be "real" but not "desperate."[8]

All this added to the flag officer's already wounded ego. In addition,
Du Pont experienced some dissatisfaction among the men on the *New
Ironsides*, stemming from the fact that before the battle Du Pont had
brought his staff from the *Wabash*. Despite Turner's objections, the
Wabash's officers commanded the guns during the battle, replacing
the *New Ironsides'* officers. When he left the *New Ironsides* for the
Wabash on the twelfth, Turner had all his men mustered at the gangway
and ordered them twice to "cheer ship." The crew, however, felt bitter
and shamed, having their guns appropriated and then firing only eight
shots during the battle. With a hurt pride and no confidence in Du Pont,
"not a 'jack tar' opened his mouth" as he left the ship.[9]

The Screw Tightens

After the 7 April attack Hunter congratulated the admiral on the "magnificent manner in which the vessels fought." Du Pont blamed the inadequacy of the monitors to fight fortifications and stressed that the navy
alone could not carry the harbor. He wrote "I attempted to take the bull
by the horns, but he was too much for us."[10]

At the beginning of April, Hunter wrote Halleck that he intended to
cooperate with the navy in the attack on the harbor. Inexplicably, he
never let Du Pont know this! While the ironclads engaged the Confederate forts, Hunter instructed General Seymour to land a brigade on
Folly Island. With a battery of two guns and the 100th New York Regiment, the brigade crept to the northern end of the island. They learned
that the works on Morris Island were not finished and Seymour asked
for permission to attack. Hunter refused Seymour's request, having no
orders from the War Department to support the navy. The Confederates
learned of the Yankee presence and sent a force across Lighthouse Inlet
to drive them off. On the night of the ninth, Major James C. Duane,
Hunter's chief of engineers, and Seymour, his chief of staff, approached
Du Pont to ask for naval cooperation for an assault on Morris Island.
The flag officer then showed his orders of 2 April ordering him to send
the monitors south, thus ending any possibility of a joint movement.[11]

More interesting than the lack of communication and cooperation
with the army was Hunter's attempt six weeks later to blame Du Pont
for non-cooperation. In a letter to Lincoln, he claimed that his forces

were in "complete readiness" to cross Lighthouse Inlet and land on Morris Island whereby "the fall of Sumter would have been certain." He laid the entire blame at Du Pont's feet and asked the president to "liberate" him for orders to "cooperate with the navy." This rift, made known to the president, further weakened Du Pont's credibility with the White House.[12]

Du Pont's poor relationship with Hunter, never effective, could not be repaired. His credibility with the Navy Department, however, was waning. Du Pont's pride remained wounded by the perceived criticism in Lincoln's telegram of the thirteenth. Welles, meanwhile, believed that Du Pont had failed to provide the department, in a timely fashion, with detailed reports of the attack. When the secretary did receive the details, which included the reports of the ironclads' captains, the secretary immediately became defensive. Welles became critical of the "tone, language, absence of vitality and vigor, and want of zeal" in the letters from Du Pont's captains. He directly blamed Du Pont for this language and became convinced that he had both "discouraged" and "depressed" his junior officers.[13] Du Pont had made it clear that he had little confidence in the attack, but his officers, while loyal, were not sycophants. The truth is that Du Pont relied greatly on the advice of these men and it was due to their opinions that he had cancelled the attack on the eighth.

Du Pont penned his detailed report of the 7 April attack on the fifteenth. In this fourteen-page letter, he laid out in detail the operations from the morning of 2 April, when he left Port Royal for the North Edisto. Attached were the reports of his officers, providing further detail and supporting the conclusions of the flag officer. He reiterated the severity of the fire, the obstructions that could not be passed, and the five disabled ironclads and their injuries. He further wrote that an attempt to pass through the obstructions he feared would trap his warships and expose them to continuous and destructive fire. He had hoped that the "endurance of the ironclads would have enabled them to have borne any weight of fire," but found this was not the case. He believed that the inability to fire at a sufficient rate to occupy the enemy batteries was crucial in the defeat. Interestingly, an earlier draft of this letter still exists. In the final letter sent to the department he omitted one paragraph. This paragraph stated that he had to abandon the attack, "having thus been made aware of the severe injuries . . . and having ascertained that the obstructions could not be passed or removed until the forts were reduced and not being able to effect the latter object by a naval force alone . . ."[14]

The following day Du Pont answered Welles's letter of the eleventh in which the secretary had urged the flag officer to continue to menace the Confederate forces. Unfortunately, he sent it before Lincoln's conciliatory letter arrived on 24 April and the timing of this dispatch further damaged his relationship with Welles. Du Pont wrote that he currently had his ironclads in the North Edisto River for repairs and stated that he would repair his ironclads as soon as practical and send them inside the bar again despite the risks at this "insecure anchorage." Du Pont offered several excuses as to why he could not cooperate with the army on Morris Island and promoted an attack by way of the North Edisto River. He reminded the department that he never advised the attack on the forts and made an issue over the censure he felt from the president's telegram. Despite his claims that he would "obey all orders with the utmost fidelity" he also let Welles now that he knew how best to carry out the instructions of the department. He concluded by writing that the department should "not hesitate to relieve me by any officer who is more able to execute that service in which I have had the misfortune to fail—the capture of Charleston."[15]

This letter caught Welles by surprise and probably represented the point of no return in the relationship between the two. He wrote in his diary that the letter was "not worthy of Du Pont." While the flag officer's tone concerning the president's telegram of the thirteenth bothered Welles, Du Pont's claims that he had not advised the attack infuriated him. He wrote in his diary, "If he never advised the attack, he certainly never discouraged it . . ." He privately wondered how he had misjudged Du Pont.[16]

The Press Enters the Controversy

On 15 April, the Baltimore *American and Commercial Advertiser* published a long article that placed the failure at Charleston squarely on the shoulders of Du Pont. Written by Charles C. Fulton, it essentially charged Du Pont with cowardice and blamed him for not renewing the fight the next day. Fulton wrote that the damage to the ironclads was not severe and gave detailed examples—information Fulton received from Alban Stimers. The paper served as the chief political organ of Montgomery Blair, a political ally of Welles, but an enemy of one of Du Pont's closest friends, Henry Winter Davis. Fulton had arrived at Port Royal as part of the corps of reporters, at the request of Blair, and with Fox's approval. It is possible that Fulton's animosity toward Du Pont had begun during the battle. The flag officer allowed journalist Henry Villard sole access on the *New Ironsides* while Fulton and the rest of the newsmen remained on a vessel outside the bar. With Fulton's connection to Fox, Du Pont at first mistakenly believed that Fox had been deceitful. Unfortunately, Du Pont also initially believed that Fulton's article was an effort by the department to censure him using the press as a weapon.[17]

Du Pont's initial conclusions, however, were not completely unrealistic. Fox had been by far the most outspoken proponent of the monitors. The apparent failure of this class of vessels at Charleston left the assistant secretary exposed. Fulton claimed that he had filed a copy of each of his stories at the department before publication, thus giving Fox a chance to censor any material not appropriate for public knowledge. Charles Boutelle even reported to Du Pont that Fulton showed him envelopes with Fox's name and address already printed on them. Fox maintained he never saw the noncensored story and, although Du Pont publicly stated that he believed this statement, privately he remained skeptical. Henry Winter Davis advanced the theory that the Assistant Secretary of the Navy might have allowed publication, knowing that it would relieve pressure on him and make Du Pont the scapegoat rather than expose the limitations of the monitors. It would also serve as a barometer of public opinion for the department and the monitor interests. With the public's reactions to this issue known, it might be possible to sacrifice Du Pont for the "safety" of Fox. Du Pont later concluded that Fulton never bothered sending his story to the department, knowing that it would never have been accepted.[18]

General opinion in the fleet was that Fox was up to some "mischief." Fox certainly remained busy after the attack trying to shore up the reputation of the monitors. It is clear that the assistant secretary began to retreat from his earlier opinions. Fox's discussions with Admiral Dahlgren within weeks after the battle had the latter confused. Fox had "changed his views of the Charl[eston] business. He says now it could not be expected that Sumter could be taken with so few vessels." When he met others, he likewise had only kind things to say about Du Pont. Fox and Du Pont had been close friends before the attack and had regularly exchanged letters. Yet the last letter ever written between the two was on 2 April. Additionally, Fox seemed desperate to find evidence against Du Pont and visited Ann Rodgers twice trying to locate letters that her husband, John, might have written about the ironclads. Rodgers wrote back to Ann, "I do not care to have my letters shown at the Dept. Mr. Fox is no Daniel; and he does not know sound opinions when he sees them . . ." Rodgers added, "he wished to see in my careless letters something contrary to the tenor of those dispatches to be used and quoted on the other side."[19]

After Du Pont's detailed report of the 7 April attack reached Washington, Welles had to make a decision whether to publish the documents. He held on to them for some time before making any reply to Du Pont. Within the reports he read not only a well written defense of Du Pont, but, distressingly, an indictment against the *Monitor* class penned by the commanding officers. If made public, these reports would place the department in a precarious position, having just signed or preparing to sign contracts for twenty-four more ironclads. Not only was Fox's professional reputation at stake, but the government had just obligated millions of dollars to build these warships. Should the public or Congress question the value of this weapon, the department, already under scrutiny, might be forced to defend its decisions in congressional hearings. The fact that Du Pont had political influence was worrisome, but even more so was the fact that the admiral's officers, the best in the service, supported his unfavorable opinion of the monitors. With these reports in hand, Welles became much less ardent that the navy should expend a great deal of effort against Charleston.[20]

While these letters certainly served to polarize the department, Du Pont made another significant mistake by writing a lengthy diatribe against Fulton and the paper. At the end of his communication he indicted Stimers for passing on the information to Fulton. More damaging was Du Pont's insinuation that the department was indirectly censuring him by withholding his official reports of the battle. He believed that the suppression of these documents allowed him to be censured indirectly by Stimers and the press. When Welles received this letter on 30 April, he concluded that the Admiral was thinking more of himself than of his duty. He believed that Du Pont no longer had confidence or zeal for his command. He wrote in his diary, "I fear he [Du Pont] can no longer be useful in his present command, and am mortified and vexed that I did not earlier detect his vanity and weakness."[21]

The admiral's largest concern throughout this controversy was the lack of support from the department. In order to bolster a defense for his actions, he began to collect affidavits from the ironclad captains so that he could answer the newspaper charges. On 27 April the Baltimore *American*, however, shifted its attack from Du Pont to his officers. It carried a story that Du Pont wished to renew the attack, but that he "unfortunately afterwards yielded to the timorous advice of those from whom better things were expected . . ."[22]

On 24 April, almost in anticipation of this article, six of Du Pont's ironclad captains wrote a lengthy joint letter to the department in response to the newspaper attacks. In this letter they answered many of the accusations in an attempt to correct some of the "false statements, coming from irresponsible parties through the public prints." The officers claimed that the vessels had been "very much injured" before passing the first of three rings of defenses. They wrote that during the battle the ironclads had inflicted little damage to Fort Sumter and would still need to steam three miles under a tremendous fire to reach the city. The officers likewise reminded Welles that a single shot might disable the turret and that the pilothouse of the *Passaic* class monitors was extremely vulnerable. If the pilothouses were made "untenable, as two of them to a great extent had been," then they could not steer the vessels. The officers also debunked the use of the torpedo raft as having "a theoretical reputation for removing obstacles, never having been tried . . ." Included with the letter was a list of the damage to their warships that prevented them from getting into action the following day. The men concluded by confirming Du Pont's long-standing major reservations about the class—that their slow rate of fire limited their effectiveness against heavily armed fortifications. This letter confirmed Welles's suspicions that Du Pont had greatly influenced his officers.[23]

The Controversy Broadens

While the commanding officers defended Du Pont's decision and criticized the offensive power of the monitors, Chief Engineer Alban Stimers gave the department a different impression. Stimers wrote Welles that he had urged the use of two rafts carrying their shells and grapnels, insisting that these had been shown to be completely safe in the tests in New York Harbor. While witnessing the fight from the deck of the Coast Survey vessel *Bibb,* he observed the terrific fire on the ironclads. After the battle, he expected to find extensive damage when the ironclads returned. He wrote that he was "agreeably disappointed" to find the warships unpenetrated, with the exception of *Keokuk,* in which he had little faith.[24]

Stimers talked to a number of officers after the fight. Those on Du Pont's staff realized that he "represented the interests of an influential body of men who were concerned in building monitors." In a conversation with Ericsson's "high priest," Du Pont told Stimers that he hoped that those persons building monitors would not place themselves "in opposition to those who had to fight them." Even before the controversy broke, Du Pont knew Stimers had an agenda that supported the ironclad interests. Before Stimers sailed north, Du Pont told him that, if the newspapers made any disparaging remarks concerning the captains of the ironclads to enhance the reputation of the latter, he would let the public know about the defects in order to protect the reputations of his men. Stimers even tried to curry favor by reportedly telling Du Pont that John Ericsson had instructed him to convince Du Pont not to make the attack until he could get all the monitors available and "if possible . . . prevent it being made at all."[25]

The chief engineer, though, did not sway from his views. On his trip back to Washington on board the steamer *Arago*, Stimers talked freely to the reporters on board. He told the newsmen that he heard from the officers commanding the ironclads that the battle should have been renewed and that the monitors were fit to go into battle the following day. Furthermore, he reportedly criticized Du Pont and said that the admiral was "too much prejudiced against the monitors to be willing to give them a fair trial."[26]

When the Fulton article broke, Du Pont immediately suspected that Stimers was partially responsible. Du Pont asked that Stimers return to Port Royal for trial. Welles would not let this happen. Welles's perception was that Du Pont was "deranged" and wanted a victim. The secretary believed Du Pont wanted to blame his failure at Charleston on the ironclads. But Welles also knew and feared that Du Pont would expose to the public the weaknesses of the ironclads if given the chance. Du Pont could not understand why the department did not support him and silence Stimers. Welles ordered the court of inquiry to meet in Brooklyn, New York, where he believed the facts could be ascertained without "prejudice or partiality." Yet the presiding officer was Rear Admiral Francis Gregory, Stimers' boss.[27]

The court martial of Stimers only added to the controversy, because in many ways Du Pont was also on trial. During the proceedings, Du Pont's officers defended him to a man. They all testified that Du Pont had never shown any prejudice towards the ironclads. Indeed, according to Raymond Rodgers, Du Pont had been "prejudiced in their favor" prior to the attacks on Fort McAllister. All these men likewise refuted Stimers' claim that the monitors were, as a group, ready to fight the next day. Stimers held that the monitors could have gone into battle, but never claimed they would be one hundred percent efficient. He also claimed that, despite the damage to their armor, it was unlikely that any of the monitors would be struck in the exact spot where the armor had been weakened the day before. During his testimony Stimers told the court that it was Du Pont's officers who had influenced the admiral not to renew the fight on the eighth. The testimony from even disinterested persons clearly pointed to Stimers having stated the attack was not a "fair test of the monitors and was not made in earnest." The court, however, after over three months, adjourned without feeling it necessary to pursue the matter further.[28]

On the heels of this trial came another incident that also assailed Du Pont's reputation and further alienated him from effective command and the good graces of the department. Dr. Edward Kershner of the *New Ironsides* wrote an unsigned letter to the Baltimore *American*. Published on 11 May, it blamed Du Pont alone for the defeat. He wrote that two or three ironclads could have done the work if "properly managed" and that the government did not need to send more monitors to Charleston, "but a man to take Charleston." Du Pont immediately dismissed Dr. Kershner and held a court-martial on the *Vermont* for violating a general order. This particular order forbade naval personnel to write letters "liable to publication" that would "censure any person in naval service." Charles Fulton wrote Montgomery Blair and asked him to intercede on behalf of Kershner. Blair told Fulton that Kershner would be "taken care of." The court-martial in Port Royal found him guilty and dismissed him from service. Du Pont seemingly won a small victory, but Welles later remitted the findings of the court after Du Pont was relieved.[29]

Du Pont increasingly became consumed with trying to defend his actions of 7 April. The attacks by the press and other naval officers caused him great anxiety. In January, Welles had promised that the department would share in the responsibility if Du Pont attacked. The fact that the department continued to allow him to take the blame for the defeat rather than disparage the monitors brought out the worst in him. Du Pont believed the only course of action that would prevent the department from making him the scapegoat and then relieving him was to "assure the highest possible bearing just short of defiance." In every letter he wrote he defended his decisions and attempted to defend his honor. His overwhelming pride and vanity only caused him to lose his perspective on the issues to such a degree that he no longer had any fundamental contact with the army and had no operation pending along the entire South Atlantic coast.[30]

While Du Pont seethed in Port Royal, his close friend Henry Winter Davis, who rarely supported Lincoln in Republican Party issues, visited the president on 3 May. The visit was orchestrated in order for Davis to find out the thoughts of Lincoln about the Charleston attack and for the Congressman to show support for Du Pont's decision. Davis believed he might obtain some executive action and possibly vindicate Du Pont, thereby forcing Welles to back down. The meeting uncovered a number of interesting revelations. Davis wrote to Du Pont that the president still had confidence in the admiral, but that he had expected Du Pont to attack the forts forcefully for days and even weeks. It was the brevity of the attack that took the president by "surprise." During the meeting, Lincoln again reiterated that the telegram of the thirteenth was not meant as a censure, but as direction to continue the pressure on Charleston. Davis did relate that Lincoln began to suspect that the whole Charleston project was a "Department pet" for the navy alone. Davis suggested to Lincoln that Fox "managed matters to suit himself and his speculative friends." Additionally, according to the congressman, the president showed "complete ignorance" that Du Pont had insisted on a joint operation and believed all along that the admiral supported the attack and expected to succeed. Davis concluded that the president's "disappointment of the result was the necessary sequel to his confidence in Fox's representation" and "his ignorance of . . . [Du Pont's] views." Davis then added, "Fox was the victim of his own hallucination."[31]

The information that Davis provided Du Pont only made him more confident of his position. Lincoln, however, merely told Davis what he wanted to hear; he had no desire to antagonize the congressman. Davis left the meeting believing that Lincoln would intercede for Du Pont, but the president instead let Welles continue to manage his department. While Du Pont received assurances from Davis, the visit had in reality further damaged the admiral's relationship with the department and widened the gap between the two. Welles realized at this point that Du Pont, with the help of his political friends, would go to any length to discredit the department by attacking its policies and criticizing the monitors. Welles had no choice but to begin gathering information to defend the Navy Department against a political investigation of its ironclad policy.[32]

Welles sought the opinions of officers other than Du Pont. He had a deep and abiding respect for John Rodgers and had interviewed him. Welles believed that Rodgers would defend the monitors since the *Wee-*

hawken survived under a terrific fire off Charleston and was struck fifty-three times. But instead of telling Welles what he wished to hear, he fully supported Du Pont's views. Rodgers suggested that the department should admit there were some "little things to be remedied for it cannot be denied." He further suggested the navy experiment with the monitors to test their defects before sending them into battle again. Rodgers then attempted to mend the fence between Du Pont and Welles. He wrote, "If public opinion backed by all ironclad captains, in a solid body, would sustain the Admiral, for Heavens sake let the Dept. shake hands with him rather than quarrel." Percival Drayton was also in Washington during May. But Drayton's friendship with Du Pont was no secret. Drayton reiterated the difficulties of the department's reliance on the ironclads for offensive movements and their weaknesses. Drayton visited Welles, Fox, and the president, and all left him with the impression that everything was fine. He left believing that all were satisfied with Du Pont and he wrote him to this effect. Welles, who had not written the admiral for weeks, was now ready to communicate.[33]

Welles Responds

Du Pont sat in Port Royal for nearly a month, uncertain how the department viewed his reports. During this period of "unprecedented silence" he received only a solitary letter. Welles penned a letter to the flag officer earlier in May, but withheld it partly on the advice of Fox and also with hope of receiving more information from Port Royal. The information that arrived from Du Pont and his supporters forced Welles to respond. He wrote two letters a day apart. The first letter, written on 14 May, began in a conciliatory manner. He wrote positively about the April attack. He emphasized his regrets that the department's letters and the president's telegram were misunderstood and that neither intended any censure. Welles did mention the fact that he was not aware of Du Pont's reservations concerning the attack, though these might have been raised when he visited Washington in the fall. He regretted that Du Pont had not been candid in his opinions and expressed disappointment in not receiving any updates on projected movements on the port city. He concluded on a graver note. Welles let Du Pont know that he withheld the reports because they had detailed the weaknesses of the monitors. In his opinion these could not be published without compromising national security issues. The department could not afford to inform the enemy of the imperfections of these warships.[34]

The letter of 15 May served as a reprimand and laid the foundation for Du Pont's relief. Welles pointed to the admiral's inactivity since the 7 April attack, which was contrary to his orders from the department and the president. He berated Du Pont for "controverting, commenting on, and refuting the criticism of the Baltimore *American* . . ." He reiterated that nothing could have been gained by publishing his report because no "public benefit" would be arrived at the enemy knowing that a "purely naval attack" could not succeed. He explained that he did not publish Du Pont's reports because "duty to the country forbade it." He also pointed out that, though the press might make negative comments, it would be an "exposition of the weakness" of the monitors if the department published the reports. More serious, Welles believed that the charges made by Du Pont against Fox and Stimers were an "injustice of . . . suspicions . . ." Welles enclosed a copy of the letter from Fox that denied that he had ever seen the Fulton article nor that Fulton was under any obligation to forward his articles to the department for approval.[35]

Du Pont received both of these letters on the twenty-first. They only added to his bitterness. Ready to be relieved of command, he wrote to his wife that Welles had treated him "as a pedagogue would address . . . a refractory (pupil), or rather a pupil that had made him, in some unconscious way, feel badly about himself." He answered the department that he always believed that Fox had never seen the article, but that the author had "openly declared" that he submitted it for Fox's censorship. The admiral claimed that Fulton had therefore lied. Du Pont took offense at the statement Welles made in the letter on the fifteenth that he had "precipitately withdrawn from the harbor of Charleston, abandoning the great object for which we had labored so many months." He once again defended his decision to withdraw as due to the lateness of the day and the fact that the monitors had not passed the obstructions. He also argued that his force could not resume operations the next day because of the injuries sustained in the fight. More important, he had received President Lincoln's 2 April order to prepare these ships for the Gulf. He closed by saying he was not trying to "depreciate" the ironclads, but to report their "obvious defects" to the department.[36]

On 23 May, Welles made his decision about Du Pont's relief known. He and Fox met with President Lincoln, Stanton, and Halleck. Fox and Halleck both favored a renewal of the naval attack on Charleston. Believing now that the city had only political value but no strategic importance, Welles privately did not believe it "wise or best to commence immediate operations upon Charleston." Welles had no confidence in Du Pont and realized that he would be hesitant to do anything. Welles recognized that in order to proceed, he would need to relieve Du Pont. The men decided to wait until they could replace Hunter with Brigadier General Quincy A. Gillmore who had views similar to those of the leaders in Washington.[37]

Welles still had quite a decision to make regarding a replacement. This would not be an easy task. Du Pont enjoyed popularity within his command and possessed political influence. The flag officer's pride would prevent him from willingly stepping down. The secretary, though, had no readily available replacement. He thought that Farragut would be a natural successor if he did not have another command. He believed the "age and standing" of David Porter, who had been only a commander seven months before, would be "objectionable to many." Andrew Hull Foote would also be a good choice, but he might be "overshadowed by Du Pont." Welles also considered Admiral Francis H. Gregory, but the secretary thought his advanced age would likely prevent his active service and give Du Pont supporters an "opportunity to cavil." Finally, he knew Dahlgren wanted the position. But Welles realized that his lack of service afloat and the fact that he was junior to many officers would cause discontent from within the ranks.[38]

A week after initially answering the department and with further thought, on 3 June, Du Pont responded at length to Welles's communications of 14 and 15 May. He was deeply hurt by the stinging criticism of Welles and thought that some of the points were both "ugly and wounding." His lengthy and quarrelsome letter was written to support earlier contentions of the hopelessness of attacking a well-defended harbor with ironclads. Many of his points were identical to those he made in earlier letters to the department. He reiterated the vulnerability of the monitors and their defects and the need of troops to attack the city. He maintained that he had not only kept the department informed, but that on several occasions he had given his views on the proposed attack to Fox, whom he blamed for not keeping the department informed. He reminded Welles that as early as January, after the attacks on Fort McAllister, he expressed his views on the limitations of the monitors. He blamed the department for not answering his reports of 8 and 15 April for six weeks as the reason for not communicating further. He told Welles that the best opportunity to capture Charleston vanished when the Union forces withdrew from James Island. He closed his letter telling Welles again that the ironclads could not lie within the bar because they needed smooth water for an anchorage. He believed that ironclads were not suitable to serve as blockading vessels.[39]

On 3 June, the same day Du Pont wrote this spiteful letter, and before it reached the department, Welles sent a letter relieving the admiral of his command. For three months Du Pont had done little except bicker with the department. The secretary also reasoned that Du Pont had failed to make any suggestions for "active operations" against Charleston, that his views did not concur with the views of the department, and the admiral opposed a renewed attack on Charleston. Three days after his notice of relief, Welles sent the admiral an order to give General Gillmore assistance in his operations. Both Gillmore and Du Pont, however, believed it necessary to wait for the admiral's successor.[40]

The *Atlanta*

Even though Du Pont's command now lay idle, the Confederates never lost their desire to strike at the Union naval forces. Weeks before the 7 April attack, the Confederates made plans to carry the war once more to the Union vessels. In January, once the ironclads arrived at Port Royal, the Confederate leaders began to devise plans to board these warships at night from small boats. In February the Confederate Navy Department formulated a plan to attack the Union monitors off Charleston. The department selected Lieutenant William A. Webb to lead the expedition. Webb envisioned a boarding operation using small rowboats, barges, small steamers, and a single decked vessel protected by cotton bales to carry boarders. He hoped to fit the latter vessel with a scaffold to allow the men easy access to the turrets of the monitors. The plan likewise called for several boarding parties of between ten and twenty men. One party would use iron wedges to be driven between the deck and turret to keep it from turning. A second group intended to throw wet blankets over the pilothouse and a third party of twenty men was organized to throw powder down the smokestack. A fourth group would throw a flammable liquid on the turret and the last group of twenty men planned to stand by to watch all the openings on deck and keep the enemy below.[41]

Webb, accompanied by thirty officers and men, traveled to Charleston and began collecting the necessary boats and began to arm them with torpedoes carrying sixty pounds of powder. He procured, with difficulty, the small steamer *Sumter* to lead the boats. Major Francis D. Lee of the Confederate Torpedo Service supplied the torpedoes. The torpedoes were placed in the small boats with poles that projected twenty feet. A detachment of sailors from Wilmington, North Carolina, traveled down to man the boats.[42]

On 9 April, with the ironclads still off Charleston, Beauregard, Commodore Tucker, and Lieutenant Webb met to put the boarding plan into action. On 10 April, on the fantail of the *Chicora*, Commodore Tucker approached William Parker and asked him to take six of the torpedo boats to attack the monitors. They planned to strike the monitors anchored closest to the mouth of the harbor off Morris Island. As Parker set the plan in motion, it was decided to use all the boats then available. In boats "half full of water," he instructed the men to start from Morris Island in pairs or singly and, on the ebb tide, attack the upper three monitors just as the flood tide began at midnight. Feeling his men and boats unprepared, he changed the night of the expedition to the twelfth. That day the officers met with Parker in the large cabin on the *Stono*, the ex-*Isaac Smith*. Fifteen boats armed with torpedoes lay concealed beside the gunboat. Parker, who never was confident of success, continued with his briefing until Tucker interrupted the meeting with the news that the monitors had sailed.[43]

Beauregard, not willing to concede just yet, suggested an attack on the *New Ironsides*. The general believed this ironclad to be the most dangerous naval foe. Using harbor steamers and blockade runners burning anthracite coal, these vessels would each tow four of the torpedo bearing boats out near the ironclad. Attacking from the bow and stern simultaneously, he thought aggressive maneuvers by the boats could sink the armored warship. Beauregard also envisioned the ironclads following the torpedo boats to break the blockade.[44]

Realizing that an attack on *New Ironsides* bordered on desperation, the Confederate leaders eventually abandoned this idea in favor of attacking the monitors as they lay in the North Edisto for repairs. Lookouts could see the monitors from a church steeple in the town of Rockville on Wadmelaw Island. By this time both Tucker and Parker had torpedo "on the brain" and decided to strike the monitors here. Parker planned to make an attack from Bohicket Creek, taking four of his best boats and one each from the *Chicora* and the *Palmetto State*. On Sunday, 10 May, after drilling his crews on the method of attack, a tug towed the boats most of the way to the staging area. Parker took the boats from Charleston up the Ashley River to Wappoo Creek into the Stono River, then through Church Flats, and into the Wadmelaw River.[45]

Parker had Lieutenant William T. Glassell, well-known to this type of operation, as his second in command. During the day on the eleventh, the boats and men remained out of view. About 10:00 P.M., with muffled oars, they headed down the North Edisto River toward the monitors. With an experienced pilot the boats managed to get into Bohicket Creek without being seen by the Union lookouts. Parker had his men haul the boats close under the bank of the creek and he quartered his men in a deserted mansion for the night.[46]

After daybreak on the twelfth, Glassell discovered one of his men missing. A search by the Confederates failed to find him. Parker became suspicious when one of the monitors got underway and moved to a point off the mouth of the creek and began shelling the shore. Indeed one of the men had deserted to the Union forces by swimming to the monitors. A picket soon confirmed that he had seen a deserter being pulled from the water. Knowing now that the enemy knew their intentions, they scrubbed the mission.[47]

The Confederate Navy Department also envisioned again using its ironclads as offensive weapons. The department hoped to use the iron-clad *Atlanta* to strike at the Union fleet. The iron-hulled merchant steamer *Fingal* looked far different than she had when she ran into Savannah with a load of munitions in November 1861. Converted into an ironclad bearing the name *Atlanta* she was 204 feet long with a 41-foot beam. Her draft of nearly 16 feet would be her greatest limitation, given the area in which she was built to operate. The armor consisted of two layers of two-inch iron plate secured to oak three inches thick backed with pine fifteen inches thick. A sloping casemate slanted at about 30° protected her two 7-inch Brooke rifles carried as bow and stern pivots and her two 6.4-inch Brooke rifles carried in broadside. She carried a spar torpedo as an added threat, but her slow speed of between six and seven knots would make it difficult for her commanding officer to use this weapon effectively against an enemy warship.[48]

In January, at the same time the ironclad attack at Charleston was being planned, Commodore Tattnall prepared to attack the Union fleet with the *Atlanta*. Leaking sponsons delayed her commissioning and Tattnall hastily had the ironclad finished. He hoped to deploy her against the wooden vessels then in Wassaw Sound before the arrival of more monitors. At this point she had merely served as a floating battery moored in a log crib near Elba Island. By warping the warship around, the gunners could control both channels. In early January, during a spring tide, she got underway and steamed several miles down the Savannah River. Her commanding officer, Commander William McBlair, hoped to get to St. Augustine Creek and then steam to the Wilmington River and into Wassaw Sound, but this plan was stopped by Confederate laid obstructions in the south channel of the river.[49]

Confederate Army engineers claimed they could clear these obstructions in two hours, but the men making this statement had to be unaware of the complexity of the obstructions. The obstructions consisted of large pens of heavy timber filled with brick and stones connected together with chains. It took nearly a month of hard work to make a passage large enough for the *Atlanta* to pass. On 4 February, the ironclad, in company with the armed side-wheel steamers *Savannah* and *Resolute*, moved below the obstructions.[50]

The *Atlanta* went no farther. The Union monitor *Montauk* and several other gunboats lay in Wassaw Sound to attack Fort McAllister. Toward the end of February, four monitors were in the sound preparing to attack the fort. Tattnall did not order the *Atlanta* into Wassaw Sound, knowing she was no match for a Union monitor in the close quarters and shoal waters of the sound. Keeping her with a draft light enough to negotiate these waters left her in no condition to fight the Union monitors. Tattnall wrote that "two feet of her hull below the knuckle were exposed" to the enemy. This part of the hull was covered with only two inches of iron. When Du Pont contemplated the attack on Charleston, he withdrew his ironclads and Tattnall believed this was his chance. A mid-March reconnaissance reported the monitors gone. On 19 March, the *Atlanta*, now under the command of Commander Arthur Sinclair, steamed below the obstructions with plans to strike the wooden Union warships in Wassaw Sound. The ambitious plans also included a trip to Port Royal or even to Key West.[51]

Atlanta, however, was delayed again. The ironclad, cursed by her deep draft, had to wait again for high tide at the head of Wassaw Sound. Du Pont knew that Tattnall was ready to order a sortie against his fleet. Tattnall's plans to attack the Union forces were revealed by five foreign deserters from the CSS *Georgia*. The deserters indicated that the *Atlanta* was nearly ready to strike the Union vessels in Wassaw Sound. Du Pont, however, was preparing his ironclads for the attack on Charleston. All of them were receiving additional iron plates and other repairs in the North Edisto River. He could not release any at this time to watch the *Atlanta*.[52]

Tattnall lost his chance for glory. Had the ironclad survived the sea journey, Port Royal might have proved an easy target. Damage to the ships and facilities here could have set back the blockade and damaged the operations of the squadron for many months. Before he could get the ironclad into action, however, Mallory relieved him of command afloat and placed him in charge of the Savannah Naval Station. Commander Richard L. Page succeeded Tattnall as the squadron commander. He was no more successful than Tattnall getting the ironclad into action. *Atlanta* could not move down river because of problems with her steering gear. This became a missed opportunity when Du Pont withdrew his monitors for the Charleston attack in April. By telegram Mallory pleaded with Page to attack while the ironclads were off Charleston. He wrote, "Can you not strike the enemy a blow . . . " Page became restless and, seeing little prospect of combat, requested a transfer. In mid-May Commander William A. Webb hoisted his flag on *Atlanta*, replacing both Page as squadron commander and Sinclair as captain of the ironclad.[53]

Webb had a reputation as an aggressive commander. A Virginian, he commanded the *Teaser* during the *Virginia–Monitor* fight. Mallory asked Webb to operate against the monitors jointly, with the ironclad *Savannah* scheduled to be completed any day. Webb, however, had his hands full with repairs to the *Atlanta*'s troublesome machinery. Once he had these repairs made he could wait no longer for *Savannah* and wrote Mallory that at the next spring tide he would sortie to meet the enemy. Webb's daring plans included breaking the blockade between Savannah and Charleston. He hoped to steam back into the Savannah River and interrupt communications at Fort Pulaski. He optimistically believed that he might strike as far south as Fernandina. He never mentioned how he would deal with the entire South Atlantic Blockading Squadron and the monitors that would likely challenge his venture.[54]

As Webb sent his plans to Richmond, Du Pont learned of Webb's scheme through deserters from Savannah. Du Pont wrote his wife that "we have a ram fever on again. *Fingal* ready to pounce on *Cimarron* at Wassaw and *Dawn* at Ossabaw . . . Sending off *Weehawken*, John Rodgers immediately. Sending up Edisto for *Nahant* and *Montauk* . . ." Du Pont relieved Rodgers from his duty as a member of a court-martial and sent *Weehawken* immediately to Wassaw Sound. "Fighting John" Rodgers was described by his contemporaries as a "glorious old man, with a great head, perfectly white hair, and a very serious countenance." The flag officer had great respect for Rodgers and wrote, "I feel comfortable where he is . . ." John Downes, in command of the *Nahant*, arrived in Wassaw Sound a couple of days later under tow of the *Prometheus*. One of his peers viewed Downes as "polished in manners, and somewhat of a dandy." The Confederates kept the *Isondiga* at the head of the sound for two days watching the Union blockaders in order to inform Webb of the arrival of additional Union warships.[55]

At 6:00 P.M. on 15 June, *Atlanta, Isondiga,* and *Resolute* got underway from their Thunderbolt moorings. Webb moved his flotilla downriver knowing that the Union monitors had arrived in the sound. At 8:00 P.M., Webb stopped to fill his coal bunkers, thereby increasing his draft. On the evening of 16 June, he steamed downriver to within about five miles of the monitors and remained out of sight. Webb readied his warship for battle at dawn the next morning. Webb's decision to attack the two heavily armored monitors was both daring and desperate. His hopes lay in deploying his spar torpedo against the lead vessel and taking her out of action early. Then he must have believed that his rifled guns at short range could deal with the second monitor and deliver disabling blows before his warship could be put out of action.[56]

At 4:10 A.M., in the "grey of the morning" while riding the flood tide with banked fires, the *Weehawken*'s officer of the deck observed the approach of the *Atlanta* and her two consorts. The *Weehawken*'s crew was beat to quarters and they cleared the ship for action, spread the fires to raise steam, struck the awnings, and moored the boats with a kedge anchor. At 4:20 Rodgers had the cables slipped and headed downstream. On the flood tide, both ironclads' sterns had pointed upstream and the pilot advised the commanding officers not to attempt to turn in the narrow channel. The *Weehawken* thus turned toward deeper water and ten minutes later stood up the sound toward the *Atlanta.* The *Weehawken* took the lead position because she had the Wassaw Sound pilot on board. The *Nahant,* after weighing anchor, followed in *Weehawken*'s wake.[57]

Atlanta came down "bold as a lion" toward the monitors under full steam. *Isondiga* and *Resolute,* crowded with women spectators, remained a safe distance behind. Webb, conversing with his pilot, believed that he had enough room to pass a sandbar southeast of Cabbage Island. As the *Atlanta* approached the monitors she grounded. Webb ordered his engines reversed and after fifteen minutes worked the ironclad off the bar. Free again, Webb ordered his engines ahead but found the helm would not respond because the flood tide was pushing against his starboard bow. While the helmsman tried to steer her farther into the channel she ran aground again.[58]

The *Weehawken* continued to close rapidly on the grounded ironclad. Rodgers believed that Webb, an acquaintance of his from the old navy, had intentionally halted across the channel to await his adversaries. At 4:55 Webb ordered Lieutenant Alphonse Barbot to open fire at about twenty-eight hundred yards hoping to stop the *Weehawken* and force Rodgers to fight at a greater distance. If successful, this might allow Webb to extract his warship from the bar. Since the *Atlanta* lay at a slightly careened angle, the shot passed over *Weekawken's* stern and splashed beside *Nahant*. *Atlanta* temporarily became free again from the bottom, only to be pushed aground a third time by the tide.[59]

As the *Weekawken* bore down on the enemy and closed the distance rapidly, the *Atlanta* fired four more shots, but all missed. Rodgers reserved his fire until only three hundred yards separated him from his enemy. At 5:15 Rodgers ordered the 15-inch gun into action. He held the initial fire of his 11-inch gun believing it to be ineffective at this range. The 400-pound cored shot from the 15-inch smoothbore struck above the port shutter abreast the pilothouse. Rodgers observed the "splinters fly as it struck . . ." It shattered the armor but did not pass through. The force of the shell caused a three-foot section of the *Atlanta's* wooden backing to disintegrate, sending splinters through the ship. The force of the blow also sent airborne all the solid shot in the racks as well as all the other loose gear in the vicinity. It disabled the entire port broadside gun crew and half of those at the bow gun, about forty men in all. After reloading, Rodgers fired both guns. The 11-inch shell struck at the knuckle and did little damage. The 15-inch shell struck the ironclad's pilothouse, tearing it off and wounding the pilot and helmsmen. The concussion from this shot incapacitated these two men, and the Confederate ironclad was now not under anyone's control. The pilothouse had only one way in and the prostrated men lay on top of the door, preventing anyone access to conn the vessel.[60]

Webb knew that the situation was hopeless and sent a man to climb on the casemate to send a signal of surrender. Webb, however, had not come prepared to surrender and had carried no white flag in the flag locker. The man therefore had to climb outside and onto the casemate and run aft to the flagstaff. Here he tore off the square canton and fastened the remaining portion of the flag back onto the flagstaff by its two corners.[61]

Rodgers, though, could not tell whether the *Atlanta* had surrendered because of the smoke that hung over her. As he peered through the slit in the pilothouse, he could not discern whether the flag flying was blue or white. Unsure that the *Atlanta* surrendered, he scrambled outside onto the deck to have a clear look. The pilot reported the flag blue and Rodgers gave the order to fire. The 11-inch shot missed, but the heavier shell tore away part of one of the armored gun shutters, ripped away a section of the armor, and disabled more men inside. Moments later the breeze freshened and the flag of truce became visible. At 5:30 Rodgers ordered a cease-fire. The battle ended with the *Weehawken* firing only five shots.[62]

The battle was so brief that Confederate authorities surmised that the crew mutinied and overpowered the officers. The Savannah papers later dispelled this, relating how the crew fought nobly at their posts. *Nahant* did not even have a chance to fire. Downes followed the *Weehawken* into battle and held his fire with intentions of getting close aboard and sending his shots into the enemy from abeam. After the surrender, Downes was "mortified that he did not get a shot" and later protested to both Du Pont and Welles that he and his men felt slighted since all the credit seemed to have fallen on *Weehawken*.[63]

Webb came on board *Weehawken* and tendered his sword in resignation. Rodgers wrote his wife that the victory did not excite him and that he felt sorry for the enemy's "humiliation." Additionally, Rodgers did not allow his men to cheer the victory, telling them the "poor devils they feel badly enough without our cheering." This victory might be viewed as hardly a notable feat. Two superior vessels captured this warship manned by landsmen while it lay grounded. The capture, however, elated Du Pont. Despite his imminent relief, it served to accentuate his positive contributions. Du Pont wrote Rodgers that the capture "must have been your intention to make me a farewell present and I accept it with many thanks long to be remembered and cherished."[64]

The Controversy Continues

Less than two weeks after Welles wrote a congratulatory letter to Du Pont concerning the capture of *Atlanta*, he wrote a scathing censure in response to the Du Pont's 3 June tirade. Welles told Du Pont that he delayed his report after the April attack because he daily expected to receive an official report relative to the president's orders. Du Pont's report did not reach Washington until 20 April. Welles refused to discuss the "demonstration of the 7 of April" and regretted that Du Pont had not understood the department's wishes. He wrote that initially when Dahlgren asked to make the attack he had refused him because he "supposed what he sought as a privilege you claimed as a right." He pointed out to Du Pont that he had been given the opportunity to make his reservations known when he visited to discuss the attack. Welles concluded by apologizing for any portion of the correspondence the department believed caused "dissatisfaction" or "pain."[65]

This exchange cut Du Pont to the quick, as evidenced by the notes made in the margins of the original letter. In Welles's letter he was not clear why he blamed his delayed response on Du Pont or why he connected this with the president's order. These points also confused Du Pont who wrote in the margins, "What connection?" He believed Welles's contrasting "Dahlgren's ardor" with his was a "personal insult." He noted Welles's remark about making his reservations known to the department. Du Pont wrote in the margin, "I did but Department would not appreciate—though experience proved, the Department relieved me to cover its blindness." Welles's remark about being compelled to write these letters and not wishing to cause Du Pont any "pain" or dissatisfaction elicited this response. "Compelled by what? . . . Not a sense of justice, but to shield itself from a foolish imagination that monitors [are] omnipotent."[66]

Before this letter had even reached Port Royal another bitter exchange between the two began concerning the loss of the *Keokuk*'s guns to the Confederates. Shortly after the sinking of *Keokuk*, Adolphus W. LaCoste, a civilian rigger by trade, was hired by the Confederate government to salvage the two 11-inch Dahlgren guns. He picked a crew of special men and within two weeks, working at night under the guns of the Union blockaders, cut through the turret with chisels. Using the old Rattlesnake Shoal Lightship, LaCoste and his men were able to hoist the guns out by 6 May. Du Pont had evidently not been aware of the activity until Welles sent him a clipping from the Charleston *Mercury*.[67]

This note took Du Pont by surprise. The guns were to have been salvaged by Stimers and Chief Engineer Edward D. Robie. They planned to use Ericsson's raft with the torpedoes attached to blow up the wreck, but believed it too dangerous to use. John Rodgers had also tried using the torpedo and the raft. During his attempts the weather was too boisterous and waves breaking over the *Keokuk* delayed his efforts. When he finally managed to get the tank down on the wreck the fuse failed. Again, Du Pont had sent one of his best officers to oversee the project. When Rodgers told him it was too dangerous and impracticable, Du Pont deferred to his judgment and the guns were not recovered. If Rodgers believed the guns unsalvageable, then the fact that the Confederates had found a way to do so without notice was truly astounding.[68]

On 27 June, five days after receiving the clipping, Welles sent another letter of censure. This letter blamed Du Pont for allowing the guns to fall into enemy hands and also for laying the blame of the failure on Chief Engineer Robie. Welles reminded Du Pont that the responsibility fell on the admiral's shoulders. This letter reached Port Royal on the day that Du Pont relinquished his command. The admiral wrote what he thought might be a parting shot at Welles that he was "not prepared for a continuance of that censure from the Department which has characterized its letter . . . since the monitors failed to take Charleston." He concluded that he believed that in his forty-seven years of service "without a word of reproof" that the "censures of the Navy Department would be keenly felt, if I did not know they were wholly undeserved."[69]

This battle between Du Pont and the department, however, would spill over into the political arena and continued for a couple of years, until his death in 1865. In retirement, Du Pont became an outspoken critic of the department and with his connections to Congressman Davis also a force to be reckoned with. Welles's friendship with the Blairs would only make the division sharper. The controversy also migrated into the newspapers for months afterwards, both positively and negatively. In July, after his relief, two articles appeared in the New York papers favorable to Du Pont.[70]

The first shot came from Du Pont in a long complaining letter dated 22 October 1863. The admiral reiterated much that had been said before but laid the blame on the department and asked for the record to be corrected. Yet, even when he wrote the letter, he knew that his last "hope of justice" was "extinguished." Welles quickly wrote an artful and restrained reply. Welles's editorial skills produced a letter that would serve two purposes. It would stop Du Pont's letters, and also, if necessary, be publishable. Welles wrote that he did not have time to enter a controversy, but would answer his "wholly imaginary personal grievances." Again the Secretary of the Navy reiterated many of his past points, pointing out Du Pont's "prompt" abandonment of the harbor after a "brief attack" and his "assaults against editors instead of assaults upon rebel batteries." Welles closed his five-thousand-word letter by stating that Du Pont's accusations and complaints were "as unworthy of you as they are unjust to the Department."[71]

In Congress, Davis attempted to vindicate his friend and simultaneously attack the "Monitor Lobby." Davis believed that there had been graft and gross management in the acquisition of the monitors. Davis defended Du Pont's actions at Charleston and criticized the Navy Department. He claimed that the attack was "devised" in the department without consulting Du Pont. He singled out Fox and claimed that the department had deferred to the judgement of a "cotton spinner" to plan and execute the attack rather than Du Pont, who had a more thorough knowledge. Welles was forced to defend himself and the department in his Annual Report. In the document he mentioned the failure of the flagship to get into action and he disparaged the Du Pont's decision not to run by the obstructions, his failure to attack the following day because of the "slight injury" to the monitors, and his withdrawal of the monitors outside the bar. He also put a positive spin on everything that Rear Admiral Dahlgren had done since the change of command. Senator Benjamin Wade also joined the crusade against Welles, in part because of his dislike of the Blairs. Welles was continually pressured by Wade and Davis to submit all the material that related to the ironclads. Welles worked for months to gather the documents and have them published. The final project spanned more than six thousand pages. It defended the department's ironclad policy and at the same time served to silence both Du Pont and Davis. By stopping Davis and Wade's attacks, however, it sacrificed Du Pont and his reputation in the interest of national security.[72]

The Tally

The aborted attack on Charleston had several consequences. The immediate and conspicuous, besides the repulse of the ironclad force, was the relief of Du Pont. The Navy Department also lost prestige and suffered from a hostile Congress and waning support of public opinion. But in truth there are three men who should share the responsibility of failure—Fox, Welles, and Du Pont.

The attack on Charleston was supposed to showcase the strength of the monitors. The department's commitment to this class of vessel was immense. At the time of the attack, the department had made an enormous investment in this weapon system and had already spent a fortune on the monitors. The navy had recently signed contracts for the *Kalamazoo* and *Casco* class monitors—twenty-four in all. The department hoped the attack would vindicate the building of these ships, but instead, Du Pont's failure to push into the harbor at Charleston represented a severe blow to their usefulness as warships. Dahlgren, who eventually replaced Du Pont, firmly believed that the financial interests that stood to gain from the contracts also had a stake in the public's opinion and therefore had an interest in Du Pont's removal.[73]

Welles and Lincoln were both under political pressure for a victory. Feeling that the public needed to be satisfied, these two men pushed Du Pont to attack without regard to military reality. Du Pont wrote the department and particularly Fox that the capture of the city would require troops. Fox was never willing to listen, not wanting the army to "spoil" an all navy effort. With no staff organization at the Navy Department there was no mechanism in place to prevent Du Pont from being put into this impossible situation. Stephen B. Luce wrote years later that Du Pont was "called upon to solve an insolvable problem, viz.: the capture of Charleston without adequate cooperation by the army."[74]

But Fox's distaste for joint operations and his jealousy and suspicions of the army were only part of the problem. Fox had been the greatest promoter of the ironclads and had even convinced the cabinet members that the ironclads could steam into the harbor. He staked his professional reputation on their impregnability and their ability to do the job at Charleston. Du Pont clearly let Fox know his reservations, particularly after the attacks on Fort McAllister, yet Fox had unwillingly acknowledged the warnings and did not pass along these concerns to Welles. Fox kept these communications private and when the attack failed he laid the paternity of the operations on Du Pont and adeptly covered his tracks. The man who had been so outspoken and had so much confidence in these vessels virtually dropped out of sight for months. He did work behind the scenes to gather information to discredit Du Pont. He even went so far as to claim that Du Pont had never been directed by the department to attack, that the monitors were never constructed to fight forts, and that he had "advised" against the attack. Fox continued to coach Ericsson afterwards and tried to keep the inventor from getting embroiled in the monitor dispute. But Ericsson knew the real story. After the war he wrote, "The whole scheme of capturing Charleston originated with Fox but it was laughed at by most military men."[75]

Du Pont also must share in the responsibility. Du Pont claims that he early believed the monitors would not be able to take Charleston. His protests became weaker as the department continued to add more monitors to the operation. If Du Pont truly believed that the attack was hopeless, he should have either offered his resignation or threatened to resign. His officers believed that this course of action might have forced the department to deal with the Du Pont's judgment rather than with the negative press it would have received. Du Pont's fears of being superseded and his concerns for his reputation clouded his judgment.[76]

Du Pont, while not outspoken, had been completely honest with the department regarding the attack and the limitations of the monitors. The department, on the other hand, had been far from sincere with Du Pont or the public. Welles and Fox continually deceived him after the attack. While Du Pont showed a willingness to accept some responsibility for the defeat, he did not intend to shoulder it all. He did expect the navy to share part of this responsibility. Du Pont's greatest error may have been his failure to be candid with Welles in October 1862, when he visited Washington to discuss the attack. During the visit, he later admitted, they had not discussed details, but at this point the monitors were not complete. The monitors sailed south without the department testing them. The Dahlgren guns also had never been tested on masonry fortifications. After the bombardments of Fort McAllister, Du Pont's concerns went directly through Fox. The flag officer had no reason to believe that Fox was not passing on his concerns to Welles. Du Pont therefore found himself in a difficult situation after learning that Welles had not been apprised of his reservations and that Fox had essentially been running the show behind the secretary's back.

Other historians have blamed Du Pont for being "inflexible" for failing to use the wooden vessels in the attack and for "having a known prejudice against monitor type vessels." Du Pont, though, realized that wooden vessels would have been destroyed quickly under the intense bombardment of these forts. These were not the same forts that he had defeated at Port Royal. The charge that he was prejudiced is also flawed. Initially he had a positive, but reserved, view of the monitors. After the attacks on Fort McAllister had little or no result, he not only judged that similar actions would not be successful at Charleston, but wrote the department with this prediction. He eventually made the attack with the ironclads at his disposal, but not with the number he claimed would succeed.[77]

Du Pont sailed north with his reputation ruined. He continued to maintain that he had used the means at his disposal for this single brief effort and, despite the beliefs of the department, it was "conclusive." After the battle, the department had virtually silenced the admiral. It admitted its fears that Du Pont's revelations about the ironclads' weaknesses would hurt the war effort. But it might have also brought about criticism of the enormous expenses of these warships from both the public and Congress. In January 1863 Welles had promised to "share the responsibility imposed upon the commanders who make the attempt" to capture Charleston. Welles did not keep his word. Instead, it seems that Welles wished to let the press have their day, even at the expense of Du Pont, and allow the controversy to pass. Fox's refusal to take any of the blame left Du Pont feeling that he alone endured all the negative charges. Given his personality he would not let the issue rest, because he believed that it was not only his reputation at stake but that of his men. This controversy was contrary to the wishes of Welles and it only created problems at a time when Welles wanted none. Afraid that Du Pont would embarrass the department by making his plight known by both political means and the court of public opinion, Welles had no choice but to relieve him.[78]

Welles also likely knew that Fox had orchestrated and manipulated Du Pont's removal. After this controversy Fox rarely became involved so personally with any other operation. Welles knew that Fox could be abrasive and "rough and sailorlike in manner," but he was always "true to his chief." Welles needed Fox to help run the department and could not afford to lose him. It seems that Fox realized he had gone too far and he would never go so far again.[79]

Welles received no satisfaction in Du Pont's relief. When he selected him, he recognized his abilities and realized that he had greater personal influence than any man did in the service. This controversy left Welles believing Du Pont selfish and a "courtier, given to intrigue." He recognized Du Pont's pride, but thought he lacked courage.[80] Welles, though, blamed the failure of the attack on the admiral's personal inadequacies rather than a lack of support. Despite any personal flaws Du Pont may have had, these flaws did not cause a failure at Charleston.

During his fight with the department and into retirement, Du Pont sympathized with Vice Admiral John Byng. In 1756 the British Navy, due to political pressure, executed Byng for failing to do his utmost to relieve the besieged British forces at Port Mahon. In Du Pont's papers is a copy of the words chiseled into Byng's monument at his burial site. In part it reads, "To the perpetual disgrace of public justice, the honourable Jno. Byng . . . fell a martyr to Political Persecution . . . when bravery and Loyalty were insufficient securities for the life and honour of a Naval Officer."[81]

— 8 —

"I Do Not Think the Game Is Worth the Candle"

The Change of Command

On the morning of 6 July 1863, Du Pont's barge cast off from the flagship *Wabash*, anchored in Port Royal. The craft made a short trip to the unarmed and newly acquired screw steamer *Augusta Dinsmore*. The oarsmen carefully kept the barge beside the small steamer as Rear Admiral John A. Dahlgren climbed down to be taken to the flagship. Arriving at the *Wabash*, Dahlgren found the decks crowded with "neatly attired" seamen, and a full guard of Marines stood at attention on the quarterdeck. Standing opposite the Marines were the officers. Among all these men the foremost figure of this striking pageant was the stately veteran Du Pont . . . his majestic form towered above all near him." The drum played a ruffle and the Marines presented their arms. After a brief ceremony Du Pont's blue flag was retired from the main and Dahlgren's red pennant was hoisted at the mizzen, signaling the change in command. As Admiral Du Pont climbed over the side, a salute of thirteen guns boomed across the water. The departing admiral and his staff boarded the *Augusta Dinsmore* and when his pennant reached the top of the yard a fifteen-gun salute was fired. The *Augusta Dinsmore* got underway and when she passed *Wabash*, the men in the frigate manned the rigging and cheered Du Pont. The crew of the *Augusta Dinsmore* answered the cheer and she proceeded to sea.[1]

The man left in command was born in Philadelphia, Pennsylvania, in 1809 and received a midshipman's appointment in 1826. He made his first cruise on the frigate *Macedonian* and was later attached to the sloop *Ontario*. Commissioned a lieutenant in 1837 he served in the Coast Survey for six years and then cruised in the frigate *Cumberland* in 1844 and 1845. After this cruise he performed ordnance duty and designed the heavy guns and howitzers that bore his name. The only contact that he had with ships in the sixteen years before the war was his command of the ordnance practice ship *Plymouth* in 1856–1858. Commissioned captain in 1862, he shortly thereafter was appointed chief of the Bureau of Ordnance, which post he held until Welles appointed him to command the squadron. The men believed that Dahlgren was not approachable and he would certainly not be as well liked as Du Pont. One officer wrote of him, "over six feet in height, very slender, severe and sallow visage, wearing an old-fashioned black stock necktie, he looked more like a minister of the Gospel than a Naval officer."[2]

The day that John Dahlgren took command of the South Atlantic Blockading Squadron was the day he had dreamed about for many years. The glory and prominence he desired were now within his grasp. Dahlgren's thirst for a combat command manifested itself nine months earlier when an immediate attack on Charleston looked positive. Welles turned down Dahlgren's request to lead the attack and instead offered him positions of less responsibility. Since these positions did not offer Dahlgren the prominence he sought, he continued his position as chief of the Bureau of Ordnance. His bold and aggressive attempts to get this appointment had raised concerns and distrust from Du Pont, who called Dahlgren a "diseased man on the subject of preference & position." His actions also raised suspicions in Welles.[3]

Dahlgren saw another chance for action after Du Pont's failure before Charleston. Officers throughout the service anticipated Du Pont's replacement. Welles discussed the operations at Charleston with Dahlgren in the middle of May 1863 in an effort to determine if he was still interested in command. At this point Welles did not know whether he had the skill or ability to do the job. The secretary also realized that assigning him this command would cause much discontent within the ranks. Du Pont was not only an extremely popular officer, but also, more importantly, Dahlgren was junior to many of the officers in the squadron and did not have the sea service of officers junior to him. Du Pont and others thought that Dahlgren should have never made admiral. He summed up what many other officers in the squadron thought when he wrote his wife, "His elevation shows two things clearly—that a naval officer who stays on shore is better off than if he went to sea, and that a man who invents a gun is better than the man who fights it."[4]

Welles had several officers that could replace Du Pont, including flag officer Porter and rear admirals David Glasgow Farragut, Gregory, and Foote. Welles carefully weighed all the choices and finally picked Foote for the job. Welles met with Foote on 29 May to discuss his new command. During the meeting the secretary told Foote that Dahlgren would be offered a position as second in command. Fox left the department to inform Dahlgren of the offer and the possibility for him to take an "active part against Charleston." Dahlgren, however, told Fox he would not volunteer to go unless he could command both the naval and the land forces. Yet, he would go if ordered. Fox returned to the department with the negative answer. This answer surprised Welles, who believed Dahlgren would regret this decision, calling him "very proud, selfish and aspiring." Foote, Welles, Fox, and Gillmore then met to discuss the future movements against Charleston. Poring over maps and charts, they shaped the course of the combined operations before the city.[5]

Foote, a friend of Dahlgren's for twenty years, showed a willingness to work with Dahlgren. He believed Dahlgren would be helpful and told Welles that he would try to convince him to go south with him. On 2 June, Welles and Fox again chatted with Dahlgren about him taking a role in the leadership of the squadron. Dahlgren proposed making two commands, one for the squadron and a second for the attacking force. Both Welles and Fox assented if Foote would concur. Dahlgren travelled to New York to discuss this with Foote and he agreed.[6]

Foote was appointed to command of the squadron on 4 June 1863. Four days later Welles received a letter from Foote informing him of an illness that would prevent him from immediately leaving to relieve Du Pont. On 9 June, Foote visited Welles at the department to tell him he would sail on the fifteenth for South Carolina. Foote left again for New York to make preparations to take command, but his health began to deteriorate rapidly. Welles followed Foote's declining health by telegrams from his physician. By 21 June, Welles realized that Foote would not be able to relieve Du Pont and sent a messenger to Dahlgren, who was in church. Dahlgren must have thought his prayers answered when he learned he would get the command.[7]

Foote died at the Astor house on 26 June, as Dahlgren made his final preparations to travel south. The Secretary of the Navy candidly told Dahlgren that his appointment had been in part made as a result of the wishes of the president. Fox also likely had some input into the decision. Whereas Fox did not particularly like Dahlgren, he certainly was disgusted with Du Pont. Fox probably also believed that Dahlgren, who had longed for this command, would be aggressive and take Charleston. Welles advised Dahlgren that relieving Du Pont under these circumstances "involved some risk and responsibility to both the Department and the recipient" because this promotion would cause discontent and would not be "lessened by this command."[8]

Welles had several frank discussions with Dahlgren before he sailed. Not wishing to repeat the same mistakes he had with Du Pont, Welles directed him to keep the department informed of his views and that at no time should his views be "different in any respect" from the department's or from that of the department's policy. He told him that the relationship between them must remain frank and sincere and that he must inform the department " . . . what he was doing, what he proposed doing, and have his frank and honest opinions at all times."[9]

Dahlgren left for Port Royal on 30 June in the *Augusta Dinsmore*. He hurried off without a fleet captain, flag lieutenant, secretary, ordnance office or an experienced clerk. The *Augusta Dinsmore* hove to in Port Royal on the morning of 4 July. The officers in the squadron had anticipated Du Pont's removal, but never expected an officer so junior to replace him. To avoid potential problems with officers with more time in service than Dahlgren, all these men were transferred to other commands. Some did not believe that Dahlgren had the administrative ability, because he had never commanded so many men before. He certainly would be received as an upstart. John Rogers wrote to his wife the thoughts shared by many of these men: "He has seen but little sea service, and as far as I know has never heard a shot fired in anger." He added that he would now command those who have "far more experience . . . as goes the world."[10]

Plans for Joint Operations

Dahlgren's army counterpart would also be new. Brigadier General Quincy A. Gillmore replaced Hunter only a couple of weeks before Dahlgren's arrival. He graduated first in his West Point class in 1849. He served as the chief engineer during the Port Royal expedition and planned the attack on Fort Pulaski. This short siege, using rifled guns to destroy the masonry fortification, earned him recognition as the foremost expert in artillery and engineering in the Union Army. After the fall of Pulaski, he received a promotion to brigadier general of volunteers and transferred to the Department of the Ohio. In May 1863, Gillmore learned that he was being considered to lead a new attack on Charleston. He quickly let a friend on Major General Henry W. Halleck's staff know he was interested in the job. On 12 June, Gillmore relieved Hunter and assumed command of the Department of the South.[11]

In late May Gillmore visited Washington and stopped by the Navy Department to discuss future operations. Chatting with Welles, Fox, and Dahlgren, he set forth a general plan to destroy Fort Sumter and capture Charleston. Gillmore projected several ways to approach the city. All these men knew that another purely naval attack would be impracticable. Gillmore suggested that a force might be landed on James Island. If it could fight across the island to the harbor, it could with deliberation destroy the forts and the city. With a Union force in this position, supplying Fort Sumter would be difficult and a naval force could enter the harbor should the fort surrender. This particular approach was Beauregard's greatest fear, but the federal defeat at Secessionville had intimidated army forces from operating beyond the range of naval gunfire. Gillmore also suggested that troops could land either far south or north of the city. Again, without naval fire support, neither of these plans looked as desirable, since Gillmore did not have a large number of troops to support this type of operation. The last two choices involved an invasion by way of the barrier islands north and south of the harbor. An invasion from Sullivan's Island or Long Island did not look promising because Union forces would have to strike at several strong fortifications and cross several easily defended waterways. Arriving before the city, they finally would have to cross the Cooper River. During most of this approach the troops would be beyond the support of naval gunfire. Yet, Gillmore held this as a possibility into early July.[12]

The War Department, however, never envisioned a siege. With the Army of the Potomac in active operations against Lee, and Ulysses S. Grant at Vicksburg, the War Department could not readily spare troops for an attack on Charleston. According to Halleck, the purpose for troops at Charleston was merely to support naval operations. Gillmore claimed the Navy Department agreed on this four-phase plan. Dahlgren, however, says that this plan never existed except in the mind of the War Department. Dahlgren's only orders were to cooperate in a combined operation.[13]

Gillmore preferred an attack by way of Morris Island on the south side of Charleston Harbor. The island stretched nearly four miles north-

east to southeast. Low, narrow, and sandy for its entire length, it was separated from James Island by Vincent's Creek to the northward and by
soft deep marshes varying from one to three miles wide. A ridge of sand
hills also ran parallel with the beach and sloped into the marshes. At a
few spots, the island lay low enough that high tide broke across the island. Because of the island's narrowness, the guns of the naval vessels
could infilade the entire island. Gillmore proposed first to take possession
of the southern end of the island, then lay siege and reduce Battery Wagner on the northern third of the island. When this fort fell, the works on
Cumming's Point would also fall. Gillmore would move up his artillery
and build breaching batteries. These siege guns and the fleet could destroy Fort Sumter. The last phase was a naval affair. With Sumter silenced
the fleet could take the initiative and remove the obstructions at their
leisure and run by the batteries into the harbor forcing the surrender of
the city.[14]

On the afternoon of his arrival, Dahlgren visited Gillmore on Hilton
Head Island to discuss future joint operations. Gillmore immediately
pressured Dahlgren to give his support for immediate operations against
the forts. Gillmore had also approached Du Pont for similar assistance,
but Du Pont declined stating that once the operations began they could
not be stopped. Du Pont told Gillmore that in fairness to his successor,
and without instructions from the Navy Department, he believed that
he could not thrust Dahlgren into the midst of these operations without
his input.[15]

Dahlgren arrived feeling his primary mission was to support army
operations on Morris Island. The admiral disagreed with Gillmore's approach, but it is doubtful that he ever confronted him. Dahlgren believed
that the narrowness of the island would allow a capable defense by the
enemy and that they would oppose the landings and retire only after
each successive line of works was taken. The enemy would be able to
easily build strong defenses from the island's sand. In Dahlgren's opinion these defensive positions would make the flanking fire of the vessels
"uncertain." He finally believed that a naval attack alone would be successful against Charleston with an additional four or five monitors.
These, however, would not be ready for some five or six months.[16]

Landings on Morris Island

On 5 July, Dahlgren and Gillmore worked out specific details for an attack on Morris Island. The admiral agreed to send five ironclads to

"clear the ground" on the island so that the army could cross Light House Inlet, which separated Morris from Folly Island. To facilitate the landing Gillmore instructed Brigadier General Israel Vogdes to construct batteries on the northern side of Folly Island. Beginning on 15 June, the Union soldiers began in darkness to secretly build twelve batteries. In addition to the assault across Light House Inlet, part of the plans included a diversion to draw enemy troops from Morris Island to James Island. Before the Union troops landed, a contingent of naval vessels would move up the Stono River and land troops on James Island.[17]

The army successfully moved its forces and built batteries to support a move across the inlet. Screened by thick underbrush, the army had forty-seven guns in place. Gillmore had about 10,000 effective soldiers, 600 engineers, and 350 artillerists to use in the attack. Opposing him Beauregard had only 5,860 troops in the entire Charleston area, and only 663 infantry, 248 artillerists, and 11 cavalrymen on Morris Island. Beauregard intentionally left few troops on Morris Island, believing that the Union forces would land on James Island. While General Vogdes made his final preparations, Gillmore quietly put Brigadier General Alfred H. Terry's division of about 4,000 effective men on James Island as a diversion and Brigadier General George C. Strong's 2,500 man brigade landed on Folly Island to prepare to cross over to Morris Island.[18]

Gillmore planned to attack early on the morning of the ninth. On the eighth, Strong's men embarked in the boats and awaited the order to move. That night Dahlgren sent officers and approximately twenty boats to Folly River towed by the tug *Dandelion*. A rain squall caused the men to lose their bearings and the boats did not arrive off the Stono River until the morning of the ninth. The boats laid beside the *Canandaigua* during the day in order not to give their presence away. At 9:00 P.M. that night the boats left again and were towed by the tug *O. M. Pettit* and crossed the bar into Folly River. Gillmore, though, had canceled the assault for the ninth on account of the delay of the naval boats and because his engineers had not finished cutting through obstructions in Folly River.[19]

On the evening of 9 July, Strong's men again embarked in boats in Folly River on the sound side of Folly Island. Lieutenant Commander Francis M. Bunce, in the *Pawnee*'s launch, commanded six launches and an army lighter, most armed with Dahlgren boat howitzers. By daybreak the force reached Lighthouse Inlet and halted at 4:30 A.M. under the cover of marsh grass. The boats waited here for the bombardment to begin. Once they made the commitment to land on Morris Island, they would have to pass several hundred yards under the full view of the enemy's guns.[20]

Dahlgren departed Port Royal on 8 July in the *Augusta Dinsmore*. He left his flag flying on the *Wabash* in order to conceal his departure. He boarded the *New Ironsides* that evening. At 4:00 A.M. on the tenth, Dahlgren hoisted his flag on the *Catskill*, under the command of Commander George Rodgers. The flagship, followed by the *Nahant*, *Montauk*, and *Weehawken*, stood over the Charleston Bar, steaming southwest toward Lighthouse Inlet.[21]

Shortly after 5:00 A.M. Strong's batteries opened on the Confederate positions on the southern end of Morris Island. The day broke with no breeze blowing and became hot and "oppressive." About an hour later the monitors entered the fray. In preparation for extended operations against Confederate forts, the *Weehawken*, *Nahant*, and *Montauk* had all been in Port Royal being fitted with extra armor protection. All had partially received portions of this protection, which included an extra sleeve of iron on their pilothouses and heavy circles of armor at the bases of the turrets and pilothouses. Yet, since all had not received their final alterations, Dahlgren instructed the ironclads to remain at a greater distance and to avoid the fire of the heavier batteries. The fire of the monitors was focused on the concentrations of enemy troops and artillery positions. The Union fire caught the rebels by surprise, but the fire of the monitors made them particularly uncomfortable. The duel between the artillery on both sides of the inlet continued for an hour without either side able to silence their opponent. The Confederate artillery kept up a steady fire at first, but after two hours it gradually withered under the intense bombardment from the monitors.[22]

At 8:00 Strong received his signal to cross the 400-yard wide inlet. As the boats worked their way toward the inlet, shells burst around the boats and the men in the craft returned a rapid fire with the boat howitzers. Shrapnel struck several of the barges, but only one sank. Strong's men landed above the Confederate batteries on the southwest corner of the island and a single regiment of Connecticut troops swung farther toward the ocean, landing on the southern end of the island. As the Union soldiers advanced toward the enemy guns, the Confederates discovered that their eleven pieces of artillery could not be depressed far enough to take them under fire. Strong's men fought through Confederate rifle pits and stormed into the works at about 9:00.[23]

The troops did not halt for long and continued up the island. The monitors maintained their fire in advance of the troops as the men swarmed beyond the fortifications. Confederate reinforcements arrived minutes after their compatriots abandoned the works and all reformed in Battery Wagner. The monitors followed the channel "pouring" into Confederate positions a steady fire of shell and grapeshot.[24]

Just after 9:00 Dahlgren pushed his monitors abreast of Battery Wagner. This irregular sand fort extended from the oceanfront to the sound, stretching just less than 250 yards. Three heavy guns, one 10-inch Columbiad, and two 32-pounder rifled guns protected the sea face that extended a mere 135 yards. The remaining four or five guns in the fort were light guns, chiefly howitzers to prevent the approach of infantry. The ironclads passed the wreck of the *Keokuk* and opened fire at 9:30. Dahlgren planned to fight this fort at a closer range whereby grapeshot could be effective. The pilot, however, could not put the vessels any closer than 1,200 yards from the beach due to shoal water. Colonel Charles H. Olmstead, an officer in the fort, remarked that the first monitor's approach looked "deliberate" yet "insignificant." His curiosity was satisfied when the monitor began to turn her turret to fire. With a "cloud of smoke, a deafening roar, and then, with the rush and noise of an express train, the huge fifteen-inch shell visible at every point of its trajectory passed overhead and burst far in the rear. The next shell exploded in the parapet covering several of us with dirt. The introduction was complete." The fort's defenders returned the monitors' fire briskly until noon when Dahlgren signaled a withdrawal. The monitors dropped down to allow the men dinner and then, at about 2:00 P.M., Dahlgren resumed the action and continued firing at the fort until dusk.[25]

The four monitors fired 534 shell and shrapnel charges during the day. *Catskill*, wearing the Admiral's flag, received most of the enemy's attention, being struck over sixty times. The *Nahant* received six hits; the *Montauk* only two and the *Weehawken* came through the battle without a mark. Most of the shots that struck *Catskill* were light to medium shells fired at long range. She did come out of the battle with some damage, but was able to return to action the next day. One of the shells struck the pilothouse and sent a bolt flying that just missed the flag officer. With the exception of the injury to the *Catskill's* armor and pilothouse, the monitors came through the battle with only slight injuries. The Union sailors also suffered few casualties. The most common malady was men collapsing at their battle stations from the intense heat in the ironclads.[26]

The attack succeeded even though the Union forces only managed to capture about three-quarters of the island. The coordination between the army artillery and naval forces had been nearly flawless. Union casualties for the entire day amounted to 15 killed and 91 wounded. The Confederates lost, in addition to their 11 guns, 17 killed, 112 wounded, and 67 missing.[27]

The lodgment elated Fox, who wrote directly to Gillmore and congratulated him. Fox wrote "The stirring events around us and on the Mississippi do not take my attention from following your movements with the deepest interests, for my mind has from the first centered upon that city, and until you appeared I have not found a person with sufficient faith." Thinking that Gillmore would make quick work of capturing Charleston, he wanted from Gillmore a plan for the capture of Wilmington. He wrote Gillmore "when you get the flag down in Sumter give me a programme [sic] . . . and I will have it ordered."[28]

The following morning Gillmore decided that he could take Battery Wagner. Without considering naval support, and never letting Dahlgren know until afterwards, he instructed Strong to assault the works. At daybreak on the eleventh, three regiments rushed the fort without covering fire. General Strong urged the men in the lead regiment, "Aim low, and put your trust in God." But this attack was doomed from the beginning. The alerted Confederates easily repulsed the attack with a "murderous" volley. Trading blows from the day before, they inflicted 339 casualties and only suffered six dead and six wounded.[29]

At about nine that morning Gillmore sent a note explaining the attack. Gillmore now expected the rebels to reinforce Battery Wagner and asked if Dahlgren would move his monitors to intercept the enemy and "sweep the ground above Wagner." After 9:00 A.M. Dahlgren proceeded up to the fort in the *Catskill* with the *Nahant*, *Montauk*, and *Weehawken* in company. At about 10:00 A.M. the ironclads "peppered away" at Wagner and the neck of land between the fort and Cumming's Point. Wagner replied only infrequently to the gunfire of the monitors. At noon the monitors hauled off with only minor damage compared to the day before. Enemy shots struck *Nahant* eleven times and *Catskill* eight times.[30]

General Gillmore now realized that the Confederates intended to hold tenaciously to Battery Wagner. Any thoughts that the fortification could be taken by an easy assault were gone. He therefore began making preparations to bring up his breaching batteries. On the twelfth, Gillmore boarded the *Augusta Dinsmore* to discuss the future movements with Dahlgren. During the meeting neither agreed how they should proceed and Gillmore left without a decision. Dahlgren now feared the operation might stall before the Confederate earthwork. Mounting Union losses combined with Gillmore's fears of counterattacks spurred the admiral into action. Dahlgren decided to organize three naval battalions, one of Marines and the other two with sailors to serve ashore to assist with the operations.[31]

Diversions, Delays, and Defeat

The diversionary movement up the Stono and the landing of troops on James Island did not draw off troops from Morris Island, but it did draw the attention of the enemy. On the afternoon of the 9th, the *Pawnee*, *C. P. Williams*, *Nantucket* and *Commodore McDonough* convoyed the troops up the Stono River. General Terry's men disembarked at Stevens' Landing. On the eleventh the rebels moved into a position to fire on the army steamer *General Hunter*. The *Commodore McDonough* immediately returned the enemy fire and Commander George Balch, the senior officer present, sent the *C. P. Williams* to drive the Confederates away. That afternoon Balch took the *Pawnee* upriver, anchored off Grimball's Plantation, and opened fire toward Secessionville in order to clear ground for the Union troops to move forward. The *Nantucket*, meanwhile, recrossed the Stono Bar and proceeded back to sea to operate against the enemy on Morris Island.[32]

Little occurred until the sixteenth, when the Confederates advanced from Secessionville and drove in the Union pickets far enough to flank the Union position. Two columns of Confederates drove in the Union left, pushing it back toward the river. The *Pawnee* and *Marblehead* lay at anchor near Tom Grimball's Plantation. Lieutenant Colonel Delaware Kemper brought up four Napoleon 12-pounder guns and began firing on *Pawnee*. Neither the *Pawnee* nor the *Marblehead* could bring her guns to bear in the narrow channel. Escape was also difficult because they could not move out of danger quickly for fear of running aground. The river was so narrow in some places that the *Pawnee* "made almost a connecting bridge from bank to bank." The naval vessels were thus conspicuous targets. Both gunboats eventually dropped downriver and began returning the fire briskly. The *Huron* also came up to take part in the engagement. Kemper's gunners concentrated their fire on the *Pawnee* striking her thirty-three times in the hull and twelve more in the stack, rigging, and boats. The boiler was saved from injury by chain cable the crew hung over the side of the ship to protect this vital area. During the firefight the *Pawnee*'s crew suffered four wounded, one mortally.[33]

Balch received a telegraph from General Terry at 5:50 that evening to fire across the causeway to stop the enemy's advance. The *Pawnee*,

Marblehead, *Huron*, and *Commodore McDonough* provided a covering fire for over an hour and forced the Confederates to retreat under the tremendous barrage. The Confederate forces under Brigadier Generals Johnson Hagood and Alfred H. Colquitt continued to pressure the Union positions. Fearful of being overwhelmed, the Union forces evacuated James Island that evening. This evacuation unquestionably helped the Confederates, who could now focus solely on the defense of Morris Island.[34]

Gillmore was now ready to try Wagner again. On the morning of the sixteenth, Gillmore came out to the flagship to discuss operations. Dahlgren found Gillmore "not too sanguine" about the impending attack. Gillmore told Dahlgren that he would attack the following morning, but during the night of the sixteenth heavy rain delayed the construction of Gillmore's siege batteries and he postponed the assault until the next day. The night of the seventeenth rain again came down in torrents and flooded the army siege batteries, postponing the attack until later that morning. While the army awaited better weather, the naval vessels bombarded the fort with slow deliberate firing from about 10:00 A.M. to 5:00 P.M. each day, throwing about three hundred projectiles into the works to disrupt the Confederates' preparations.[35]

From the tenth through the seventeenth, the wooden gunboats *Wissahickon*, *Chippewa*, *Paul Jones*, and *Ottawa* also engaged Wagner at long range. For additional firepower Dahlgren added the *New Ironsides* to the attacking force. Her deep draft delayed her crossing the Charleston Bar for two days, but she arrived off Morris Island on the fifteenth. Dahlgren directed the ironclad captains to attack from the closest range that the draft of the vessels would allow. He also directed the gun crews to fire as rapidly as possible. He ordered the smooth bore guns to be laid level so that the projectiles could reach the fort by ricochet firing, while the rifled guns were to fire directly into the fort.[36]

On the eighteenth, with wet powder and flooded batteries, Gillmore telegraphed Dahlgren that he would not be ready until about noon. Dahlgren sent word to the gunboats *Paul Jones*, *Ottawa*, *Seneca*, *Chippewa*, and *Wissahickon* under command of Commander Rhind to get underway. These warships opened fire at about 9:00 A.M. and Gillmore's men fired their first shot at about 10:00. At 11:30 Dahlgren boarded the *Montauk* and hoisted his flag. Immediately making a signal to get underway, *Montauk* followed by the *New Ironsides*, *Catskill*, *Nantucket*, *Weehawken* and *Patapsco* all stood toward Battery Wagner to join in the bombardment.[37]

The ironclads arrived off Battery Wagner at about 12:30. Fifteen minutes later *Montauk* fired the first shot from the attacking column of ironclads. The other ironclads joined in as they closed to within twelve hundred yards of the fort. The *Patapsco* was disabled at the second discharge of her gun when two teeth on her pinion wheel broke as well as one on the main wheel that turned the turret. *New Ironsides,* flying the pennant of the sunken *Keokuk,* moved "slowly and majestically" toward Wagner and unleashed broadside after broadside against the fort. The Confederates inside Wagner found the fire from this vessel "exceedingly demoralizing." The large shells from the monitors were also effective against the defenders.[38]

Around 4:00 P.M. the tide rose and the ironclads weighed anchor and closed to within three hundred yards of the fort. By this time the "unusually severe" bombardment silenced the guns of Battery Wagner. Under the tremendous fire of the guns from both the navy and army, the defenders could not leave their bombproofs without risking their lives. This silence of the fort fooled Gillmore, who believed the severe bombardment reduced the garrison. At sunset, Dahlgren received a note in pencil from Gillmore that he had ordered an assault.[39]

Gillmore's decision to attack at twilight would prevent the naval component of the forces from participating and, thereby, should the fort fall, it would give all the glory to the army. The naval vessels on the eighteenth had fired for about eight hours and poured in about nineteen hundred shot and shell into Battery Wagner. The *New Ironsides* alone fired nearly half of this number. Had the attack been made earlier, or the next day, the naval guns might have provided covering fire for the army units making the assault. Instead Dahlgren watched as it became too dark to discern friend from foe and he suspended the fire of the fleet. Brigadier General Truman Seymour and 5,000 men, spearheaded by the Fifty-fourth Massachusetts, a black infantry regiment under the command of Colonel Robert Shaw, were repulsed with heavy loss of life. A second attack that night only added to the carnage. The Union forces suffered a shattering 1,515 casualties and the Confederates only 222.[40]

Gillmore's desire for an army victory stimulated by overconfidence caused his command to suffer one of the greatest repulses of the war. The general would now become extremely conservative and cautious in his approaches to the fort. A well-coordinated joint operation whereby the infantry was covered by naval fire probably would have succeeded. The bombardment of the eighteenth had considerably damaged the fort and the naval gunfire could have kept the Confederates in their bombproofs until the Union soldiers had nearly entered the fort. Yet after this disastrous defeat the Union forces would not make another all-out assault. Dahlgren immediately realized that this meant that the work before him would be undertaken with "patience and perseverance."[41]

The Siege Begins

Fulfilling Dahlgren's worst fears, the campaign seemed to be grinding to a halt and he became increasingly frantic for action. Gillmore, though, realized that he did not have enough men for another frontal assault. Dahlgren earlier considered forming a naval assaulting force but he found the naval forces could not supply the deficiency because the crews in the squadron were already understrength. Additionally, his men were overworked, carrying out the duties of the blockade, fighting Confederate fortifications, and providing men for picket duty in boats at night. He realized that with each day the enemy used their resources to improve the harbor's fortifications. Able to see this progress from the flagship, he lamented to Welles the shortage of men in both service branches and their inability, even with the combination of forces, to assemble enough men to assault the works successfully. Dahlgren must have believed that if the Confederates had enough time to perfect their defenses, he might never get a chance to advance his monitors into Charleston Harbor.[42]

This latest repulse and the possibility of delay, however, stirred the Navy Department into action. After receiving Dahlgren's reports, Welles sent Fox with Dahlgren's dispatches to request reinforcements for Charleston from the army's General in Chief, Major General Halleck. Fox was anxious for the operation to succeed but Halleck "rebuffed" him. Halleck told Fox that Gillmore had not requested reinforcements and if Fox would take care of naval matters that he would care for the army. Welles believed that an operation might succeed with additional troops and on 26 July went directly to the president. This was quite a turn, considering that four months earlier he would not even discuss combined operations with Du Pont. The secretary met with the president in the White House library and shared Dahlgren's reports. He told Lincoln that the army force at Charleston was insufficient and that it would be unwise to wait for Gillmore to be defeated. He suggested the War Department send ten thousand additional troops. Lincoln agreed but could not offer any suggestions whereby the army could secure additional men to send south. Welles spoke up and said he would strengthen Dahlgren with additional seamen and Marines. With this news the president said he would see Halleck. Two days later the secretary of war promised to send Gillmore five thousand men.[43]

On 19 July, the squadron spent a quiet Sunday while the wounded were removed from the field of battle around Battery Wagner. The following day, at 11:30, the army batteries opened again on the Confederate earthwork. Dahlgren ordered *Montauk* and *Weehawken* to move inshore to bring the fort under fire and at noon they broke off the action. After dinner the *Catskill, Nantucket, New Ironsides,* and three gunboats raised anchor and steamed into position to bombard Wagner. At 1:30 that afternoon *Catskill* stood to within 100 yards of Wagner and tried her 11-inch Dahlgren gun at close range. The flagship signaled the vessels to retire at 4:20. During the day's fight, at a distance of fourteen hundred yards, the 10-inch Columbiad in the fort struck the *New Ironsides* fourteen times, but she suffered no serious damage. The *Montauk* was the only other ironclad struck by enemy fire during the day. The next day rough seas prevented the ironclads from getting into action, but Dahlgren sent up two wooden gunboats to annoy the rebel working parties.[44]

Dahlgren discussed further operations with Gillmore and proposed attacking Battery Wagner by pushing his naval vessels close to the fort and maintaining an intense fire to keep the Confederates in their bombproofs. He suggested a frontal assault combined with a simultaneous advance by a picked column of three hundred to four hundred men from the best regiment. He suggested that these men should attack the Confederate defenses from the rear at Vincent's Creek, on the northwest side of the island. Gillmore liked the plan, except he preferred a landing on the east side of Morris Island. He could not, however, spare the men for a second attacking column and he asked Dahlgren to supply the sailors and Marines. The flag officer regrettably declined, explaining that he could not spare a large contingent for service ashore. He also had only 280 Marines and could not find the requisite number from this group either. As a token, Dahlgren did offer the services of 125 officers and men to man four rifled guns ashore.[45]

The Confederates, however, had no intention of easily conceding Battery Wagner or the northern end of the island to the Union forces. Every day that Wagner held allowed Beauregard to further strengthen his works in the harbor. Brigadier General William B. Taliaferro, the Virginia-born, Harvard-educated lawyer, arrived on 13 July, and between bombardments kept his men busy strengthening the works. The Confederates also sent in six more guns along with several regiments of re-inforcements.[46]

Confederate naval forces were also asked to cooperate in the defense of the island. Beauregard suggested to Flag Officer Tucker that one of the Union ironclads might be sunk at night. For this mission, he proposed using the ironclads and the blockade runner *Juno* armed with a spar torpedo. Beauregard also asked that Tucker's ironclads take a position off Cumming's Point to operate against Gillmore's forward siege batteries. Realizing that the Union monitors would likely be able to drive the Confederate ironclads away, Beauregard hoped to get the enemy vessels under the fire of his heavy guns at Battery Greg, Fort Sumter, and Sullivan's Island. Even if they could not damage the monitors, they would serve as a "diversion." But Tucker knew that his two ironclads would be no match for the Union fleet and he refused to commit them against the monitors. Using the Confederate ironclads against the Union siege batteries was also problematical because of shallow water northwest of the island and the fact that the guns could not be elevated through the small gun ports of the ironclads. This left Beauregard helpless to neutralize the gunfire of the Union ironclads or Gillmore's batteries.[47]

While Gillmore continued to prepare his siege positions, Dahlgren awaited anxiously. By 22 July, the operations against Wagner had extended beyond Dahlgren's expectations. Afraid that the continued firing might wear out the guns of the monitors, Dahlgren tentatively ordered that only two at a time would fire on the enemy, supported by the *New Ironsides* and any wooden gunboat that could be used. In the forenoon he sent in the *New Ironsides*, *Weehawken*, and *Montauk* to engage Wagner. At 1:00 P.M. that afternoon, under a cloudy sky and a moderate wind, the ironclad *Nantucket* and the gunboat *Ottawa* hove up their anchors and stood toward the fort. It was not until 2:23 that the *Nantucket* fired the first shot. Thirty minutes later, when a heavy rain began to fall, Dahlgren hoisted the recall signal.[48]

The progress of Gillmore's siege periodically changed the roles of the naval vessels. By the third week in July, Gillmore's men had finished the first parallel. On the moonlit night of the twenty-third, a second parallel was opened using a flying sap. About five hundred men using spades, axes, and gabions moved earth to form a zigzagging trench 175 yards long with a parapet ten feet thick and advanced to within 600 yards of the fort. They also mounted a battery of six guns, constructed palisades, and wire entrenchments and began building a bombproof. This second parallel, however, was extremely vulnerable until the Union forces mounted siege guns forward to protect it.[49]

To keep the Confederates from interfering with the work, Dahlgren brought up his ironclads the next day. At 4:15 A.M. Dahlgren hoisted his flag on *Weekawken* and at about 5:00 A.M., the monitors and *New Ironsides* weighed anchor and got underway. *Weehawken* took the van followed by *New Ironsides*, *Montauk*, *Nantucket*, *Catskill*, and *Patapsco* in the rear. Around 5:30, at approximately 1,400–1,800 yards, the monitors began shelling Battery Wagner. Battery Gregg at Cumming's Point also received some attention, while Battery Bee and Fort Sumter entered the fray and fired mainly on the *Weehawken* and *New Ironsides*. Late that afternoon, the *Paul Jones*, *Seneca*, *Ottawa*, and the screw steamer *Dai Ching* cleared for action and got underway. At about 6:30 these warships added to the fire of the ironclads on Battery Wagner and Battery Bee. The severe bombardment at Battery Wagner went virtually unanswered because the 10-inch Columbiad lay useless at the beginning of the bombardment and the 32-pounders were believed useless against the ironclads. The garrison, therefore, remained in their bombproofs.[50]

The ironclads had fared well against the Confederate forts during the previous weeks. Most suffered some minor injuries, bent and fractured plates, and problems with the guns, but they remained capable of cooperating with Gillmore's forces ashore. Despite the problems with the guns, the ironclads managed to continue service off Morris Island but in a reduced capacity. In order to keep a force continually prepared, Dahlgren constantly had at least two monitors in Port Royal for repairs and alterations. The most serious damage suffered by the monitors during the first month was shots through the decks and broken bolts. As a means to prevent this, the department planned to put an additional one inch of iron plate over the decks to protect them. But to complete the work to all the ironclads would take time. As an interim measure, Dahlgren concluded that sandbags placed on the decks could limit the damage from plunging shot. Dahlgren had William Reynolds use every free hand in Port Royal to fill over ten thousand bags with sand for the naval vessels. Placed on the decks of the ironclads, this layer of sandbags provided some protection. The engineers concluded, however, that the sand weighed more and offered less protection than the one inch plates sent down to be put on the decks. Despite this precaution the decks remained one of the most vulnerable portions of these warships.[51]

The gunfire of the Union fleet proved more troublesome to the Confederates in Wagner than the army siege batteries. The fort, built only to resist an attack by a land approach, could not reply to the tremendous firepower of the ironclads. Beauregard pleaded with Lieutenant Colonel David B. Harris, the chief engineer, to hold out as long as possible. He told him he must "fight the fleet with sand . . ." The great nemesis of the fort was the *New Ironsides*. With four and one-half inches of armor about her load line she could close on the rebel batteries and take direct hits with little or no damage. Her broadside of seven 11-inch guns and one 150-pounder could fire over three hundred rounds an hour. During five sorties in July, she fired nearly eighteen hundred rounds and was struck only forty times. The enemy shots did little damage. They tore away port shutters and when the shots struck the sandbags that protected her decks, the shot merely scooped the bag off and the shot glanced upwards and overboard, shattering but leaving intact the one inch plate underneath.[52]

With practice, the naval gunners became experts at laying down an accurate fire. The explosion from a15-inch shell threw sand high in the air and created a hole "big enough to put a horse and cart in." Brigadier General Taliaferro claimed the monitors looked like "huge water dogs, their black sides glistening in the sun." Since the Confederate gunners did not reply regularly, the shells could be carefully placed nearly anywhere in Battery Wagner, except in the center. This problem, however, the naval gunners solved by ricocheting the shells off the water into the fort. It could only be done on smooth water and shells landing in the fort in this manner caused havoc among the defenders. One of the Union shells ricocheted into a school of mullet, throwing one of the fish nearly in the lap of Captain Robert Pringle, the fort's chief of artillery. He "politely thanked the gunners for sending him such an appetizing breakfast."[53]

This accurate fire virtually gave the Union navy complete control over the fort's defenders and made the lives of these men miserable. The heat intensified by the white sand made the bombproofs nearly unbearable. In addition, an "intolerable stench from the half-buried dead," only made worse by "the swarm of flies attracted by the smell . . ." nearly drove the crowded men in the unventilated bombproofs insane. Parts of the garrison were exchanged every few days throughout the siege to prevent wholesale disability. It had some risking the shot and shell rather than remaining in the shelters. The bursting shells interfered with the men's sleep and added to their misery. Another source of complaint was the men's food. After a trip of forty-eight hours from Charleston it arrived unfit to eat. Lastly, one soldier claimed that water in the fort "was scarcer than whiskey."[54]

Even with this vast superiority over the Confederate defenders, Dahlgren continued to augment his firepower. He instructed Commander George Balch to prepare the *Pawnee* for service off Morris Island. To protect her from enemy fire, he was to protect the boilers with sandbags. Also the flag officer asked Balch to make his broadside as heavy as possible while keeping his draft as light as he could. Balch reconfigured his battery to give the *Pawnee* ten broadside guns—eight 9-inch Dahlgren rifles, one 100-pound Parrott rifle, and a 50-pounder Dahlgren rifle. Balch used 270 fathoms of chain cable to protect his boilers and machinery.[55]

As the Union forces continued to extend their lines toward Battery Wagner, Gillmore became increasingly worried about Confederate counterattacks on his forward trenches. Dahlgren, in the spirit of cooperation, deployed near the advanced lines at night four boats armed with howitzers and two more ready to support these at daybreak. He also detailed an ironclad to move close to shore at daybreak. This warship would sweep the ground should the rebels decide to attack the forward Union trenches.[56]

While the army pushed forward slowly, Dahlgren continued his pressure on the Confederate forces. On the morning of 25 July, he sent in the gunboats *Ottawa, Dai Ching,* and *Paul Jones* to annoy the inhabitants of the fort until late that afternoon. The wooden gunboats frequently participated in the bombardments at long range throughout the rest of the campaign. From 28 July to 1 August, several monitors and the *New Ironsides* took turns firing at the fort. On the twenty-ninth and thirtieth, the gun fire was severe between the navy and Confederate forces ashore at Wagner, Sumter, and Battery Gregg. During these engagements, the *New Ironsides* singularly fired nearly 550 projectiles.[57]

Anxious for an operation that could end the siege, Dahlgren never relinquished his thoughts of a landing behind Wagner or attacking Fort Sumter at night. For this purpose and possibly to ease Gillmore's increasing manpower concerns, he put together a regiment of Marines under the command of Major Jacob Zeilin. The department sent Dahlgren about 260 men and he then stripped as many from the ships as possible to form a regiment. The sole purpose of this five-hundred-man force was to make quick amphibious landings. He instructed Zeilin to clothe his men comfortably for the hot climate, to divest them of extra baggage, and to carry cooked rations and charges of buckshot for close action. Dahlgren provided a detail of boats to land the regiment and four boats armed with a howitzer and a field carriage for covering the landings.[58]

After only a week ashore Zeilin wrote to Du Pont that the plan to forge a coherent fighting force from this Marine unit was not progressing well. Zeilin reported that his men were only accustomed to being organized as small detachments on board ship and had not participated in large unit maneuvers. Many of his men were raw recruits having been stripped off the northern receiving ships and sent south. During the week ashore he had not had the opportunity to drill his men because of the heat and the collateral duties of soldiering ashore, such as cooking. He admitted his men were "very bad at caring for themselves . . ." Zeilin thought it would be hazardous to use his men in an assault until they learned discipline and could be drilled extensively. Only then did he feel that under fire they could perform with "coolness and promptness." This news distressed Dahlgren, who wrote with despair in his diary, "Rather hurtful. What are marines for?"[59]

Hoping to use the Marines once Zeilin thought his men were ready, Dahlgren sent boats nightly on reconnaissance missions to determine the nature of the defenses. The monitors serving as the guard ships anchored within one-half mile of Battery Wagner. Dahlgren also kept picket boats out to protect his fleet. On the night of 5 August, a launch from the *Powhatan* with two officers and twenty-four men spotted what they thought was a blockade runner lying near Cumming's Point. Acting Master Edward Haines, in charge of the boat, opened fire. Thinking he would get the support of the other picket boats in the area, he headed toward the steamer, ordered her to surrender, fired his 12-pounder howitzer, and boarded her. The Union tars, however, got quite a surprise when they discovered that they had boarded the CSS *Juno*, an ex-blockade runner converted into a picket boat and under the command of Lieutenant Philip Porcher. The *Juno* carried no large guns, but had on board a crew about double that in the Union launch. After a short battle the Union sailors surrendered. Haines and twelve men were captured, eight others got away, and several were reported missing.[60]

The Reduction of Fort Sumter

On 14 August, the Union soldiers completed the third parallel about 750 feet in advance of the second parallel and about 500 yards from Battery Wagner. Gillmore, now with several thousand additional troops, felt more secure and he and Dahlgren agreed on a joint operation. Gillmore's men constructed, forward of his original lines, twelve batteries mounting thirty-eight guns including a naval battery ashore. The naval battery consisted of two 8-inch Parrott rifles and two 80-pound Whitworth rifles manned by sailors from the *Wabash* under the command of Commander Foxhall A. Parker.[61]

The Confederates, meanwhile, continued their repairs and even found time to strengthen the works. The sea face now included two 10-inch Columbiads and a 32-pounder. Battery Wagner proved to be much more difficult to take than Gillmore initially envisioned. He realized that this well-defended fort could still cost him time and many casualties in the continuing siege and assault. Gillmore decided that, if he fired over Wagner and destroyed Sumter, then there would be no impediment to the naval forces to move into the harbor and he might take Morris Island without the necessity of directly attacking Battery Wagner. At this point Gillmore's siege guns were closer and in position to fire over Wagner and directly into Fort Sumter. His tremendous array of firepower, he believed, would allow an orderly destruction of both Wagner and Sumter.[62]

The Confederates early perceived the danger to Fort Sumter, and after the Union forces landed on Morris Island, prepared for its potential destruction. The defensive stand at Wagner made this possible. Du Pont's attack in April did little damage to the fort and, importantly for the Confederates, revealed unknown weaknesses. In order to correct these, Beauregard and the district engineer, Colonel David B. Harris, discussed and formulated plans to strengthen the fort. The casemates and weaker parts of the masonry structure were reinforced with wet sand bags and wet bales of cotton. The defenders filled the casemates by placing sand on the floors two feet deep. On top of this the men positioned cotton bales two feet apart and then filled the spaces between them with wet sand. The men replaced the sallyport that faced Morris Island and constructed a new wharf on the west side of the fort so that supplies could be landed once the bombardment began. The Confederates also reconfigured the fort's magazines so that a chance shot would not destroy the fort. A total of twenty thousand bags of sand reinforced the casemates. To prepare the fort quickly, the work progressed day and night under the labor of between 300 and 450 men. Knowing that the fort would likely be reduced to rubble, Beauregard ordered most of Sumter's guns to be removed to James Island and other forts in the harbor. To mask the lack of firepower, Quaker guns now pointed toward the enemy.[63]

With the third parallel advanced, Gillmore scheduled an attack for the fourteenth, but had to postpone it because the Union powder supplies were found to be defective. The navy landed sufficient powder to begin the bombardment on the sixteenth. Gillmore, however, became bedridden and the attack was again postponed until Monday the seventeenth. At the hint of dawn on this day, an 8-inch shell from Battery Brown on the Union right broke the silence. As this shell arced toward its target, the rest of the Union guns belched more than three thousand pounds of metal toward the Confederates in Fort Sumter.[64]

Dahlgren instructed his naval vessels to take positions off Wagner and Sumter. About the time the bombardment began, the naval vessels got underway and stood toward their prospective targets. *Weehawken* flew the admiral's flag and steamed in the van. *Catskill, Nahant, Montauk,* and *New Ironside*s took station farther down the channel off Battery Gregg in order to fire on both Confederate earthworks on Morris Island. At about 6:40 the monitors began to heave to off Battery Wagner. At 6:45 the *Weehawken* fired the first shot at about 1,000 yards. The monitors' main role was to keep the Confederates from interfering with the army's bombardment of Fort Sumter. The Confederates returned the naval fire rapidly and used "every conceivable form of projectile imaginable . . ." The tide had been low earlier that day, but as it rose, the monitors were able to close the fort. *Weehawken* and the other three monitors steamed to within 450 yards of the earthwork and laid down a devastating fire. In support the side-wheel double-ender *Mahaska* led a contingent of wooden vessels including the *Ottawa, Wissahickon, Dai Ching, Conemaugh, Cimmarron,* and the screw gunboat *Lodona* to attack Battery Wagner. The *Seneca* and the *Canandaigua* later joined these vessels. The monitors *Passaic* and *Patapsco* positioned themselves off Wagner, but stood in reserve to attack Fort Sumter later in the day. Additionally, Dahlgren kept the Marine Battalion, with the boats and howitzers, ready to land should it appear the fort could be stormed.[65]

Dahlgren's chief of staff, Captain George W. Rodgers, anxious to take part in the action, asked for a temporary command of one of the attacking vessels. Dahlgren offered him command of the *Catskill*. Rodgers gratefully accepted and transferred to the monitor on the morning of the seventeenth. He took the *Catskill* abreast of Battery Wagner and at 7:30 opened fire. At 8:20 a shot from one of Wagner's 10-inch Columbiads struck the top of the pilothouse, fractured the outer plate and shattered the inner plate. Metal splinters turned the pilothouse into a "bloody shambles." Inside were Captain Rodgers, Paymaster Jesse G. Woodbury, Pilot Abner C. Penton, Acting Master Peter Truscott and Helmsman Oscar Farenholt. A metal splinter struck Rodgers in the head and killed him instantly; a second splinter nearly cut the paymaster in two. The blast prostrated the other three and the wheel of the ship lay shattered. Farenholt managed to take control of the remnants of the wheel. The *Catskill's* anchor was hove up and she flew the signal "Captain is disabled" and steamed toward the tug *Dandelion* to transfer the dead and wounded. Shortly after 10:00 A.M. the crew finished some temporary repairs and she was again off Battery Wagner. As news spread around the fleet that Rodgers died, the warships set their colors at half-mast.[66]

The *New Ironsides* opened fire at 7:00 A.M. on Battery Gregg. Her gunners fired only an occasional shot toward Gregg and spent most of the day firing on Battery Wagner. At 10:15 she opened fire on Fort Sumter, but the shot fell short because the gunners could not elevate the guns sufficiently. During the day, the *New Ironsides* was struck over thirty times, principally from Battery Wagner, with no serious damage. The *New Ironsides* alone fired over four hundred shells at the enemy fortifications.[67]

The other monitors took positions directly off Battery Wagner. As the enemy replied, the *Catskill* fared the worst with seven shots striking her deck and the most crucial shot damaging her pilothouse. *Montauk* suffered little damage with the exception of the trunnion of her 11-inch gun breaking, disabling the gun for the remainder of the day. The *Nahant's* 15-inch gun also suffered a temporary disability. These three ironclads, however, fired nearly 200 shells into the fort.[68]

The *Patapsco* and *Passaic* also took part in the bombardment of Wagner early in the morning. These ironclads arrived off the earthwork fortification around 8:00 A.M. At 10:30 both hoisted their anchors and withdrew out of danger. Dahlgren stepped from the deck of the *Weehawken* to the *Passaic* and hoisted his flag on the latter. He then ordered the *Passaic* and *Patapsco* to get underway and they steamed slowly toward Fort Sumter. Both of these monitors had rifled guns, which could deliver punishing blows to the masonry structure of the fort. At the throat of the harbor these monitors were fired upon from forts Moultrie and Sumter and batteries Gregg and Wagner. Battery Gregg kept up the most effective fire on the two monitors. At 12:10 the monitors again got underway and moved out of range to give the men dinner and to let the guns cool. The admiral left *Passaic* at 12:30 and hoisted his blue flag at the main on the *Augusta Dinsmore*. After lunch the two monitors dropped back down to Battery Wagner and shelled it from about 3:30 until nearly 6:00.[69]

During the day's bombardment, the Confederates in Battery Wagner successfully returned the fire of the Union vessels during the first few hours. But as additional naval vessels joined the battle and opened on the fort, the rebels found it impossible to reply to the massed fire of the army and navy guns. On the seaface the Confederates' two 10-inch Columbiads and the single 32-pounder could not be depressed to fire on some of the ironclads once they closed the fort. In the face of this tremendous volume of fire, the Confederates found it necessary at times to seek the shelter of their bombproofs. This incredible Union fire power several times put the guns out of action and killed and wounded the gunners at their posts. But each time other men replaced the decimated gun crew and made repairs to the guns until the warships ceased fire. At the end of the day one of the 10-inch Columbiad carriages lay in ruins and the following day the 32-pounder was put out of action, leaving Captain Robert Pringle with a single gun to fight the ironclads.[70]

While the naval vessels held down the fire at Battery Wagner, Gillmore's batteries worked on the gorge wall of Fort Sumter. The defenders were so overwhelmed by the army's siege guns that they scarcely replied to the two monitors. During the day nearly seven hundred shells struck the fort. The combined army and naval batteries "knocked one side of the fort into a perfect mass of bricks." The ferocity of the attack on Fort Sumter thoroughly surprised the Confederates. They believed that the Union ships' real objective was to steam past the obstructions into the harbor. During the day Flag Officer Tucker readied his ironclads and torpedo steamers thinking this would happen.[71]

On the evening of the seventeenth, Gillmore telegraphed Dahlgren that he feared an attempt by the enemy to reinforce Fort Sumter. He asked Dahlgren to position his monitors to prevent any enemy troop movements. At 5:15 on the morning of 18 August, the *Passaic*, *Weehawken*, and *New Ironsides* steamed off Battery Wagner to prevent any reinforcements from reaching the fort. From this position the ironclads could watch the fort and bombard it from a distance of between one thousand and fourteen hundred yards. Dahlgren also called up his wooden vessels to attack Battery Wagner at long range. During the day the army batteries continued their fire on Fort Sumter. The ironclads engaged the fortification until after 10:00 A.M. and then withdrew. During the engagement, a 10-inch shot struck the viewing slit of the *Passaic*'s pilothouse from a distance of 900 yards. The force of the blow pressed lead from between the pilothouse and the armored sleeve added in New York to better protect the men inside. This lead struck Lieutenant Commander Edward Simpson in the face and arm and also injured the pilot.[72]

Gillmore's fear of a Confederate counterattack did not abate. As he pushed his approaches toward Wagner he continually requested the navy's presence to cover his troops and to prevent the enemy from repairing the fort. He also asked Dahlgren if he could lay his monitors within four hundred to five hundred yards of Fort Sumter day and night. Dahlgren assented to both, telling Gillmore that he could depend on the fire of the monitors "any time you want it."[73]

Dahlgren, however, realized that keeping the ironclads so close to the throat of the harbor posed a threat to his warships. He ordered that the lead monitor in the channel be vigilant in order to detect the movements of the enemy ironclads. Torpedoes and even fire ships were considered possible dangers, but the real threat would come from torpedo craft, a weapon that Dahlgren never initially considered would be the greatest threat to his ships. These craft would strategically change the method of the Union blockade and create caution in the movement and anchorage of warships during the dark hours.[74]

The small, fast, low profile torpedo boats built by the Confederates were an enormous step in the strategic thinking of the day. With little capital or industrial infrastructure, they could build vessels that could sink the largest Union warship. Lacking the means to build a navy on the scale of the Union, the Confederates actively experimented and built small craft capable of destroying Union ships. Initially, the rebels experimented with the ex-blockade runner *Juno*, fitted with a spar torpedo. Her large size, however, would make her impracticable because she could be detected at great distances and she could be heavily damaged before reaching her foe, or she could be avoided. Enterprising adventurers were promised large sums of money if they could sink the *New Ironsides*, *Wabash*, or any monitor. Captain Francis D. Lee of Beauregard's engineering staff worked on his own design and produced and tested a torpedo to be deployed from a spar on a moving vessel. This project interested Beauregard, who endorsed the transfer of an unfinished floating battery to Lee. Lee managed to obtain a well-worn engine from Savannah and built a torpedo vessel to test his principle. Almost entirely submerged, the vessel carried an unusual triple-headed torpedo. Each warhead weighed one hundred pounds. Painted a light gray like a blockade runner, she was made ready by August and named the *Torch*.[75]

The Confederate authorities perhaps thought that a strike on the fleet would slow down the destruction of Fort Sumter, and sent the *Torch* to attack the *New Ironsides*. Captain James Carlin, a blockade running captain, took command of this "tub-like" ship. On the extremely dark night of 20 August, she got underway and at 10:00 P.M. picked up eleven men at Fort Sumter. Steaming from an anchorage off Morris Island, Carlin spotted the *New Ironsides* and five monitors just before 1:00 A.M. on the twenty-first. As the *Torch* crept to within 450 yards of his objective, Carlin had his spar lowered in the water. Because of the size of the Confederate torpedo boat, the lookouts on *New Ironsides* spotted the steamer at one o'clock coming up fast from astern. Ensign Benjamin H. Porter hailed "ship ahoy" and Carlin answered "Hello" as the *Torch* bore down on *New Ironsides*. Porter hailed again, "What ship is that?" Evasively Carlin answered, "the Live Yankee from Port Royal." *New Ironsides*, swinging at the ebb tide, swung across the path of *Torch*, causing her anchor chain to block the torpedo craft. Carlin ordered the engine stopped while the *Torch* drifted around the chain. Once clear of the anchor chain Carlin ordered the engine restarted, but unfortunately the engine had stopped on dead center and it could not be turned over for two minutes. The *Torch*, meanwhile, grazed the bow and drifted beyond the *New Ironsides*, all the while being hailed by the watch on board. During the confusion, Porter ordered his crew beat to quarters, and the anchor slipped. *Torch* glided by the large ironclad as she fired several guns, but the torpedo craft slipped away in the darkness.[76]

The Navy Strikes at Fort Sumter

The severe pounding that Fort Sumter received during the first days of the bombardment dispelled any hope for Beauregard and his staff that the fort might be held as an artillery platform. Since the Confederate leaders foresaw this, during the siege of Battery Wagner they sent working parties to Fort Sumter to remove all the ordnance, ammunition, and powder. But the Confederates did not plan to give up the fort as a post, and decided to keep infantry stationed there. They believed that within the rubble these men would have great protection and that holding the fort would keep the Union forces from using it as a base to remove the harbor obstructions at their leisure. This small garrison would indeed create difficulties for the Union forces disproportionate to their numbers.

On the afternoon of 20 August, Dahlgren and Gillmore decided to meet to discuss future operations. Dahlgren though was too ill to come ashore and Gillmore met him on the flagship *Philadelphia*. During the discussions both men felt satisfied at the progress of the bombardment on Fort Sumter. The siege was progressing well and the next night the army engineers would open the fourth parallel partly with a flying sap and partly with a full sap. The Confederates in Battery Wagner knew that they had little time left, but continually annoyed the federal work parties when they were not under fire from the fleet.[77]

Dahlgren, looking for a greater role for his warships, decided to lead a naval attack on Fort Sumter. After carefully evaluating the damage to the fort, Dahlgren believed that he would try his hand at "completing the work" using his ironclads. Gillmore wrote the admiral that he believed that there would be little to interfere with the monitors getting close to the fort. With this endorsement, Dahlgren assembled the captains to discuss a night operation. About 10:00 P.M. on the twenty-first, Dahlgren, feeling better, boarded the *Weehawken* to lead the monitors in battle. The *Passaic* took the van without her pilot, who had refused to conn the vessel. Well ahead of the other ironclads she ran aground one-half mile from Fort Sumter. By the time she freed herself of the bottom Dahlgren thought there would be too little time before daylight to attack. With great anguish he postponed the attack until the next night.[78]

The next morning the Confederates in Battery Wagner opened a heavy fire on the Union positions. Gillmore telegraphed Dahlgren for covering fire, fearing that gunfire from Battery Wagner might dismount his siege guns. Dahlgren had already sent *Patapsco* and *Weehawken* to bombard the fort. These warships opened fire at 5:30 A.M. and sustained a slow bombardment for about two hours. Just as they withdrew Dahlgren sent the *New Ironsides* up, and she stood in shore opposite Battery Wagner and maintained a rapid fire. *Nahant* and *Montauk* also cleared for action and joined the fight and by 2:00 P.M. all the warships withdrew. During the day the fort's commanding officer did not reply to the naval fire, thinking it unnecessary to engage the warships at such long range.[79]

Dahlgren remained determined to carry out his night attack on Sumter and assembled the ironclads on the twenty-second. Dahlgren boarded the *Weehawken* at 11:00 P.M. and the "turrets" began moving up the channel in a strong tide. It was nearly 3:00 A.M. before the *Weehawken*, *Montauk*, *Passaic*, *Patapsco*, and *Nahant* arrived to within eight hundred yards of the fort. The monitors began the action with a deliberate fire on Fort Sumter. The fort, though, hardly answered, sending only six shots in reply. During the attack a fog obscured the vision of both sides. The lack of visibility caused some of the monitors to cease firing, but others fired their guns at the fort by using the stars. Fort Moultrie did not respond until about 4:00 A.M., but opened with a heavy fire on the ironclads when they could be seen. The naval gunfire did not severely damage Fort Sumter even at this close distance. But three shells struck near the western magazine, giving the defenders great anxiety. Three hundred loaded shells stored in the adjoining room were rolled into the water to keep another lucky shot from igniting them. The *Weehawken* fired 33 shots; nearly half of the 71 total fired by all five monitors.[80]

At 6:10, when it appeared the fog would not lift, Dahlgren got the *Weehawken* underway. At about 6:30 he ordered the ironclads to withdraw. During the withdrawal, the *Patapsco* grounded about one thousand yards from Fort Moultrie. Fortunately, the fog continued to shroud the ironclad for some time. But before she could get free, the fog cleared for several minutes around her. While she was visible the Confederates kept up a constant fire on *Patapsco* until fog enveloped her again. The monitor escaped with little damage besides a few dented and broken plates.[81]

The attack did not have the results Dahlgren anticipated. Despite the fact that the commanding officers had met beforehand to discuss the night attack, Dahlgren believed that some of his captains still did not "have a clear idea of the purpose." The officers certainly did not show much initiative during the bombardment. The flag ship alone fired nearly half the ammunition expended and *Nahant* fired only a single round, having had trouble with the smokebox around her 15-inch gun. More puzzling to Dahlgren was the absence in the fight of the *New Ironsides*. Dahlgren had expected this vessel to get into action quickly. Captain Stephen C. Rowan though, had problems maneuvering his deep draft vessel through the fog. The *New Ironsides* never entered the fray and at 7:30 that morning steamed toward the fort after the monitors withdrew. This prompted Dahlgren to remark in his diary, "I met the '*Ironsides*' no great way from her berth, coming up as if she really meant to do something. Rowan is terribly careful about that vessel." Nevertheless, Dahlgren himself knew that the *New Ironsides* was restricted by her draft to midchannel. Furthermore, since her ends were not armored and her rudder and screw were vulnerable, she had to attack broadside to her target.[82]

There may have been a more personal side to this story than the unwieldy limitations of the *New Ironsides*. Dahlgren was suspicious about the loyalty of some of his officers. He frequently mentioned Rowan in his diary for his lack of aggressiveness. Rowan must have been jealous and resentful of Dahlgren and let it show. Only two weeks junior to him, Rowan had spent his entire career at sea and certainly viewed Dahlgren as an upstart technician. Dahlgren's lack of command experience did not prepare him to deal with this type of problem or personality and so he never confronted Rowan.[83]

The following two days a southeast gale blew through the area and suspended operations. It came at an opportune time, for the men were exhausted. Since the seventeenth, the naval vessels had engaged the enemy every day and the heat and exertion had left the men worn out. During the eight days between 16 and 23 August 4,424 shots struck Sumter, reducing it to a shapeless ruin. The nearly continuous use of the monitors likewise had begun to show. By the twenty-third only the *Weehawken* and *Passaic* could use both their guns. More critical was the fact that the monitors' daily firefights with the enemy continued to diminish the service life of their guns. Dahlgren believed the service life of the guns currently stood at fifty percent, yet he revised these numbers upward as he continued to use them. Still, any long-term or active campaign to attack into the harbor would quickly wear out the guns.[84]

It was at this point that the relationship between Gillmore and Dahlgren went beyond the normal strain and the spirit of cooperation ceased. With Sumter silenced and no longer a threat to naval operations, Gillmore believed that the navy should have entered the harbor on the twenty-third. At this point batteries Wagner and Gregg served merely as outposts to Sumter. Gillmore believed that the failure by the Union forces to press forward at this time only allowed the Confederates to strengthen their inner harbor defenses. He later maintained that it was at this point that the navy was responsible for steaming past the obstructions and into the harbor. Dahlgren, on the other hand, denied this premise and claimed that the department had committed him and his forces only to joint operations.[85]

Dahlgren faced a dilemma regarding his attacks on Fort Sumter. He realized that he had emasculated the fort's offensive powers. The Confederates' defense, however, was not diminished. The Confederates mounted a great number of the guns from Sumter in Fort Moultrie and the other forts across the channel. With the defense of the channel not appreciably weakened, Dahlgren could not decide whether to attack Sumter again at night or to attack in the daylight when both sides would have equal visibility. He also queried Gillmore to determine whether his ironclads would be used to help finish Battery Wagner, to complete the destruction of Sumter, or were "to be otherwise employed" in other operations against Charleston. He lamented that he faced the same dilemma as Du Pont, that the number of enemy guns had not been appreciably diminished, and that he had fewer ironclads to force an entry into the harbor.[86]

Now that Fort Sumter's offensive capacity lay in ruins, Dahlgren considered the removal of the obstructions. Even though the obstructions had a passage for the blockade runners, the navy could not afford for an ironclad to get tangled in them. This would mean certain destruction under the enemy's guns. Earlier Dahlgren explored this possibility and asked Welles to send explosives experts to help him remove the obstructions. Dahlgren suggested that an explosive device be created using a Francis Life Boat. These eleven-foot enclosed metal boats were used by life-saving organizations to haul people from disabled ships offshore. Since these boats had metallic covers he believed that, if they could be made waterproof and filled with a quantity of powder, the boats might be submerged near the Confederate obstructions, and exploded, creating a hole to allow his warships to pass through. The flag officer also had thoughts of sending men in boats to open holes in the obstructions large enough for the ironclads to pass and requested "intelligent, cool and brave" volunteers. Ensign Benjamin Porter selected men from the various ships in the squadron. Plans called for the men to destroy the obstructions with saws, augers, chisels, hammers, and other equipment. During this operation Dahlgren asked Gillmore to keep up a heavy fire on Sumter until dark. Gillmore offered the services of his calcium lights to illuminate the water between Cumming's Point and Fort Sumter in order to keep enemy boats from disrupting the work. Dahlgren declined the offer, telling Gillmore "I shall need all the darkness I can get—if you light up you will ruin me."[87]

On 26 August, Dahlgren made the final arrangements for this assault while he was ill. He was so weak that he "could hardly rise from the chair and walk across the room." He called the ironclad captains on board the flagship *Philadelphia* to explain the plans. Rowan, whose vessel was to provide covering fire for the boat parties, as usual made objections and showed little interest in the operation. The current bad weather with its high wind and violent rain also bode cancellation. By the time the force arrived off Fort Sumter the flood tide was "setting in like a sluice." Dahlgren feared that, should one of the monitors be disabled, the tide would carry her into the harbor where the enemy would capture her. Since he had the most reliable pilot on board, Dahlgren gave Lieutenant Commander Simpson, in the *Passaic,* the authority to make the decision of whether to continue or to cancel the enterprise. At 2:30 the admiral called off the attack and the Union warships returned to their anchorages.[88]

Dahlgren was again so ill on the twenty-eighth that he found it difficult to even sit in a chair. With the admiral incapacitated, the project was delayed another day. On the morning of 29 August, Dahlgren sent a telegram to Gillmore with the news that Fort Sumter fired several shots that morning. Dahlgren had based his plans to remove the obstructions on the supposition that the fort had no operable artillery. A single gun, in his opinion, could wreak havoc among his boat crews. Gillmore disagreed with the report, arguing that there were no guns operable in the fort. Dahlgren's plans only included protecting his men from the batteries on Sullivan's Island. He believed that he could not protect them from two sides. The following day Gillmore's batteries fired over six hundred shots at the fort in an attempt to silence the last guns.[89]

Once the weather moderated, Dahlgren remained determined to operate against the obstructions. During the morning of the thirty-first, Dahlgren sent his ironclads forward to probe the enemy defenses. The monitors *Passaic*, *Patapsco*, *Nahant*, *Weehawken*, and *Montauk* all cleared for action and steamed toward Fort Moultrie and Sumter. The *Weehawken* opened fire at 10:00 A.M., and the others joined her during the day. A brisk fire was exchanged between the monitors, Fort Moultrie, and batteries Greg and Wagner. The monitors returned the fire and sent an occasional shot into Fort Sumter. During the afternoon the *Passaic* went aground. Lieutenant Commander Simpson floated his warship free in twenty-five minutes by having his powder division pass shot from the forward magazine aft. *Passaic* received the most punishment, being struck nine times, three of these shots going through her deck.[90]

On the morning of 1 September, Dahlgren called his ironclad captains again on board the flagship. During the meeting Commander Thomas Stevens proposed that the *New Ironsides* run the obstructions down under a full head of steam. Rowan, however, had "no taste for that." With no real consensus of the action to be taken, the flag officer determined to try another night attack and maybe to "feel" around the obstructions. Dahlgren held this meeting despite being ill once again. The meeting lasted much longer than he anticipated and left him weaker.[91]

Dahlgren ordered the ironclads to assemble for the attack punctually at 9:30 P.M. Boarding the *Weehawken* at 10:00, the flag officer signaled the warships to get underway. The *Weehawken*, *Nahant*, *Patapsco*, *Montauk*, *Passaic*, and *Lehigh* stood slowly up toward Fort Sumter in close order. The ironclads arrived off the fort before midnight just before the flood tide ceased, thus it was about 11:30 before any of the monitors began firing at the fort at about eight hundred to fifteen hundred yards distant. In the darkness Fort Moultrie's gunners opened fire when the ironclads came within range. Moultrie's gunners "blazed away in full style" as the monitors pounded Fort Sumter. But the aim of the Confederate gunners was spoiled by the "obscurity of the night."[92]

The monitors engaged the fort for two hours before Rowan brought up the *New Ironsides*. Asked later by Dahlgren why his vessel entered the battle so late, Rowan blamed it on the dark night and questioned the value of the attack. The ironclads fired a total of 245 shots at Sumter, Cumming's Point, and Moultrie and received 71 in return. The Confederate fire broke and cracked the armored plates and several passed through the decks of the monitors. One of the enemy projectiles struck the base of *Weehawken*'s turret and drove a piece of iron off the inside. The fragment struck Fleet Captain Oscar C. Badger and broke his leg. This was the third flag captain lost to Dahlgren in two months.[93]

The ironclads' fire on Fort Sumter was again designed to reduce its defensive capabilities. The fifty shells fired into the fort destroyed casemates on the east wall and others passed through to strike the west wall, adding to the destruction. The most serious threat came from three or four shells that struck near the fort's only remaining magazine on the western side, which held several thousand pounds of powder. During the battle Colonel Rhett crossed the parade ground and nearly became a casualty when a shell burst nearby. Dahlgren claimed that Fort Sumter fired two shots during the engagement. Gillmore again disagreed and claimed that none came from the fort. Overall, Gillmore believed that the navy accomplished nothing with this attack and according to one officer on his staff "pooh-poohed it to everyone who would listen." Dahlgren must have also privately held that he had gained nothing, for his plans to deal with the obstructions were temporarily dismissed.[94]

The Fall of Morris Island

On 2 and 3 September, Gillmore and Dahlgren concluded to finish off Battery Wagner before attempting another the operation. They agreed to an amphibious landing at Battery Gregg and envisioned forming a combined navy and army force to seize the battery and spike the guns. The capture of Cumming's Point would effectively cut off Battery Wagner's garrison. To protect this landing, Gillmore requested that a monitor steam to the channel between Cumming's Point and Fort Sumter. Dahlgren, however, thought this channel was too shallow and agreed only to provide two monitors to lie off Cumming's Point during the attack to cover the troops. Initially Gillmore did not feel that a combined force would work and wanted to use only an army force. But he did not have a sufficient number of boats and oarsmen to carry out the attack and approached Dahlgren for these assets. Despite the short notice, the naval party assembled with the army units on the night of 4 September. The operation began well, but as the boats approached the fort, the men spotted a Confederate boat pulling away from Cumming's Point. Instead of letting the boat go, however, the men tried to capture it. In a hail of gunfire, they captured the boat, but also alerted the Confederates ashore and had to cancel the attack.[95]

After the failure of the night landing, it was clear that a frontal assault would be quicker and surer. The final push toward Battery Wagner began on the morning of 5 September. By this date, Gillmore's sappers had completed the 5th parallel, placing them within one hundred yards of the fort. Light mortars mounted in these advanced positions could now effectively drop shells into the fort. With this additional firepower arrayed toward the Confederate positions, the Union guns opened at 5:15 A.M. The guns fired over the heads of the sappers, who rapidly pushed the sap forward to Wagner's moat.[96]

As a prelude to the planned assault, the Union forces kept up a continuous bombardment for forty-two hours. Additionally, in an attempt to keep the Confederates in their bombproofs, the *New Ironsides* hove up anchor and stood up the main channel. At 5:45 she opened fire about thirteen hundred yards from Battery Wagner. With her eight-gun broadside Rowan kept the guns firing in a deliberate rotation in order to keep the fort under continuous fire. Gillmore was impressed by the fire power of this ironclad. He wrote that she fired "with the most admirable regularity and precision, kept a continuous stream of 11-inch shells rolling over the water against the sloping parapet . . . whence deflected upward with a low remaining velocity they dropped vertically, exploding in and over the work, mercilessly searching every part of it except the subterranean shelter."[97]

The other monitors also moved up and fired an occasional shell at Wagner and Moultrie while the *New Ironsides* kept up her relentless attack. In all she fired 488 shells into the fort. That night the Union forces turned calcium lights toward the fort to illuminate the works so that the bombardment could proceed. The sappers, meanwhile, continued to move forward, getting so close that many of the Confederate guns on Sullivan's and James islands could no longer take part in the defense without the risk of putting their shots into the fort.[98]

Gillmore delayed the assault planned for the sixth for one more day. The intense bombardment thus far had not only done great damage to the fort, but it had, more importantly, kept the defenders from rebuilding it. The *New Ironsides* continued firing at the rate of one shot every ten minutes. Dahlgren and Gillmore agreed to assault the work at 9:00 A.M. on the seventh. Thirty minutes before the troops moved forward, the monitors would simultaneously engage Battery Gregg and Fort Moultrie. Rowan was instructed to hoist a red flag prior to the movement of the infantry and open a rapid fire on the fort. At 9:00, he would haul down this flag and cease fire. This would also signal the *Weehawken*, *Passaic*, and *Montauk* to direct all their fire on Battery Gregg to keep the guns at this fort from interfering with the assault.[99]

As the sixth waned, the Confederates in Battery Wagner knew they faced an increasingly impossible situation. Gillmore's sap was within forty yards of the salient and the engineers had widened the trenches to allow the storming parties to quickly get into the fort. During the past forty-two hours the Union had fired more than 3,700 projectiles into the fort, killing and wounding about 100 of the garrison of 900 men. Nearly 1,200 of the shells struck the roof of the bombproof with no effect. With no prospect of his exhausted troops holding the fort, Colonel Lawrence M. Keitt finally received word to evacuate during the afternoon of the sixth. That evening, after dark, the men of the garrison quietly spiked the guns, abandoned the earthworks, and took with them as much as they could of the fort's equipment. The Confederates also withdrew from Cumming's Point and spiked the guns. The rear guard departed Morris Island at 1:30 A.M. on the seventh.[100]

The Union forces, however, never realized that the Confederates were abandoning the fort. Confederate deserters entering the Union lines told the unbelieving Union soldiers about the withdrawal. The Union troops quickly occupied the works and managed to capture some of the rear guard departing in the last boats that left the island. The evacuation was a tremendous Confederate success and deprived the Union forces of nearly one thousand prisoners. Some of the soldiers that had suffered the bombardment never expected to live. After escaping, one North Carolinian remarked, "I have heard the preachers talk about Hell, a great big hole, full of fire and brimstone . . . and I will allow it used [sic] to worrie me at times, but Gentlemen Hell can't be worse than Battery Wagner. I have got out of that, and the other place ain't going to worrie me any more!"[101]

As the Union soldiers crept into the fort, word of the evacuation reached Gillmore who telegraphed Dahlgren, "The whole of Morris Island is ours, but the enemy have escaped." Thus ended this phase of the campaign to take Charleston. This entire operation, however, had differed from earlier assaults such as Port Royal and Hatteras. This time the army landed and took a key role in the entire campaign. Without the navy's support during the operations, however, it is doubtful that the campaign could have even been undertaken. The naval forces played an essential role by keeping forces from counterattacking the Union positions. They also added substantially to the bombardments.[102]

Nevertheless, the purpose of the campaign was to allow the navy to force its way into the harbor. Yet, after the Union forces neutralized Fort Sumter, Dahlgren delayed any attempt to do this. He had numerous reasons for avoiding this action and even admitted that Du Pont's attack five months earlier had revealed the weaknesses of the monitors. He argued that the monitors needed repairs as a result of the "incessant battering" they received during the two months prior. He also believed that he could not move because their bottoms were so foul and their speeds so reduced that it would compromise their battle worthiness. Additionally, he believed that all the monitors required further strengthening and improvements before they made an attempt to strike into the harbor. Dahlgren had also expected more monitors for an attack on the city. He maintained that his "seven battered monitors" were too weak to do anything but perform a raid into the harbor. If he chose this course he believed he would risk losing part of his ironclad force. Furthermore, he not only feared torpedoes, but also, without knowing the full nature of the obstructions, would not pass into the harbor.[103]

This extensive campaign accomplished its goals but did not leave the Union forces in a much stronger position. The Union forces did now occupy Morris Island and controlled half of the entrance to Charleston Harbor. Additionally, Fort Sumter now lay in ruins, served only as an infantry outpost, and anchored one end of the obstructions. The capture of Morris Island, however, did not really place the Union forces much closer to Charleston. For over eight weeks the incredible firepower of both the army and navy was never able to breach Battery Wagner's magazine or to knock out the guns permanently. The navy alone fired over eight thousand shot and shell, over half of these from the *New Ironsides*. The naval vessels, in turn, received 882 hits. Despite the fact that the navy allowed the army to land troops and supplies "as if the enemy were not in sight," Gillmore eventually captured the enemy works not by overwhelming the garrison, but by threatening to cut off his retreat. Gillmore had both an overwhelming advantage of cannon and men during the fifty-seven-day siege, yet the naval forces were expected to engage batteries vastly superior to these and reduce them in order to capture the city of Charleston. The difficult and lengthy Morris Island operations virtually vindicated Du Pont's earlier decision not to run into the harbor. John Rodgers, some months after the Morris Island Campaign, wrote that he could not see any reason to risk an attack on Charleston unless "it be in satisfying the national mind that retributive justice has been done against the city of Charleston, the nursery of the rebellion. In a word, I do not think the game is worth the candle."[104]

~ 9 ~

"Tell Admiral Dahlgren to Come and Take It"

Probing the Defenses

The abandonment of Morris Island and the destruction of Fort Sumter might have opened a new vista for the Federal forces. Gillmore delivered to Dahlgren what he had promised, the reduction of Fort Sumter as a threat to his naval vessels. The single fort, earlier thought to be the key to the defenses, now lay in ruins. The general believed that it was now the navy's turn to move into the harbor. Dahlgren's greatest concern, however, was the unknown nature of the obstructions. He continued to maintain that even though Fort Sumter could no longer threaten his fleet, the small garrison that occupied the ruins could cover the obstructions with light guns and small arms fire.

Dahlgren hoped that the abandonment of Morris Island would cause the Confederates to quit Fort Sumter. Within minutes of learning that the Confederates abandoned Morris Island, Dahlgren sent a flag of truce to demand the surrender of the fort. The Confederates, though, recognized the value of this rubble. Slowly they had formed the fallen walls into a powerful defensive work, often while under fire. Using brick, mortar, and boatloads of sand brought "painfully" from the adjoining islands, the Confederates prepared their positions to repulse a Union boat attack. Dahlgren's demand for surrender and his threat to move his monitors up to engage the fort must have elicited a chuckle from the new commanding officer, Major Stephen Elliott. Elliott and three hundred infantry re-

251

placed Colonel Rhett and his artillerymen. Elliott, who did not have a single large gun mounted, referred Dahlgren's message to Beauregard's headquarters. He received the reply "Tell Admiral Dahlgren to come and take it."[1]

Dahlgren already had this in mind. He knew Fort Sumter maintained only tenuous communications with the mainland and he decided to cut this completely. He instructed Commander Edmund R. Colhoun to take *Weehawken* through the narrow and shallow channel between Cumming's Point and Fort Sumter. While *Weehawken* moved through this channel, Dahlgren planned to take the *New Ironsides* and the other monitors and attempt to pass the obstructions north of Fort Sumter. On the morning of 7 September, Colhoun began to buoy a channel as he carefully sounded his way toward the harbor. Later that morning, when the ironclad swung to the flood tide, she grounded about two thousand yards from Fort Moultrie. Dahlgren ordered tugs up to help her off and during the day the crew removed shot and coal. The men worked all night, but could not refloat her.[2]

Later that afternoon, the *New Ironsides, Passaic, Nahant, Lehigh, Montauk,* and *Patapsco* stood toward Fort Moultrie to reconnoiter the obstructions. *New Ironsides* steamed to within 400 yards of Sumter and 150 yards of the obstructions. In a short but spirited fight lasting less than two hours, the Confederate batteries on Sullivan's Island and the ironclads fired at each other. While the other ironclads covered the *Patapsco,* at 150 yards she fired grape and canister on the obstructions to test their make-up and their strength.[3]

Despite the activity around the *Weehawken,* the Confederates never realized that she was stranded. At high tide on the morning of the eighth, she still lay aground. Major Elliott finally realized her plight and at 7:00 A.M. sent a telegram to district headquarters. Soon all the forts that could bear on the hapless ironclad began to attack her. With several feet of hull exposed, the ironclad might have been severely damaged, but the Confederates did not keep up a continuous fire as they had a shortage of ammunition. The *Weehawken* returned a steady fire, which only helped to lighten her further. During the morning of the eighth, *Weehawken's* second shell from her 15-inch gun struck the muzzle of one of Fort Moultrie's 8-inch Columbiads. It glanced off the gun's muzzle and fell into a supply of ammunition behind a traverse. The resulting explosion killed sixteen men and wounded another dozen. This explosion caused confusion within the Confederate forts and silenced the guns long enough for Colhoun to send his men to breakfast. Dahlgren, impressed by *Weehawken*'s firing, sent the signal "Well done *Weehawken*. Do not give up the ship."[4]

To protect *Weehawken*, Rowan, the senior officer present, earlier brought up the ironclad force to cover her. The *New Ironsides* did not come up immediately because she was replenishing her ammunition. Nevertheless, at 9:30 she hove up her anchor and steamed towards Fort Moultrie. Nearly at flood tide, the ironclad had to pause until the ship could swing around and present her broadside. The *New Ironsides* steamed into a position to interpose herself between the fort and the *Weehawken* and, at 10:15, at a distance of fifteen hundred yards, opened a "very heavy fire." The *New Ironsides* maintained a rapid fire and effectively kept the fort firing only an occasional gun. When Rowan ordered a more economical fire, the fort reopened a heavy fire. Rowan then instructed his gunners to increase the rate of fire to silence the Confederate batteries. During the day *New Ironsides* fired nearly five hundred shells and was hit at least seventy times. Many shots either broke up on the side of the ironclad or bounded a hundred feet or more into the air. The woodwork on the spar deck, described as "a complete mass of ruin," was damaged so severely that the carpenter estimated that as many as one hundred shots hit the ship. The damage to the ironclad was mainly to the rails, bulwarks, and plating. Enemy shots also caused the loss of one gun shutter and damage to two others. She withdrew at 1:20 P.M., having expended all her 11-inch ammunition.[5]

The monitors moved towards Fort Moultrie and Battery Bee just before 9:00 A.M. While at anchor near Fort Moultrie, they maintained a deliberate fire on the earthworks and received a pounding from the Confederate gunners. The *Passaic*, ordered to "go well up and engage Battery Bee," went into battle with a jury-rigged helm and the captain conning the ship from the turret. This disability caused Commander Simpson to fight his monitor in a stationary position so that he could frequently pass orders from the pilothouse to his temporary helm below. She took the van and came under an incredible fire. About 10:40 a shot from Battery Bee struck one of the sliding hatches on top of the *Passaic*'s turret. The hatch fell down into the turret and injured one of the gun crewmen. Fifty-one shots hit the *Passaic*; twenty-nine hit the turret and three passed through the deck. Other shots broke plating and damaged the ring round the base of the turret. It required thirty-two pounds of steam and liberal amounts of melted tallow squirted around the turret's base to make it revolve.[6]

Montauk opened fire at 10:30, anchoring about five hundred yards from Moultrie. She shifted anchor closer to the fort at noon. She was struck forty-three times with no serious damage. The *Patapsco* anchored within eight hundred yards of Fort Moultrie and opened fire on Battery Bee. In this position, *Patapsco* attracted a great deal of enemy fire. Rowan signaled Commander Thomas Stevens to "Drop down below." Stevens instead, in the midst of the battle, climbed into his boat and pulled over to the *New Ironsides*. On board he pleaded with Rowan to let his monitor remain, and said "Wait a moment and see how completely my guns command Bee." The next two shots from *Patapsco* fell so perfectly within the works that Rowan replied, "Captain Stevens, stay where you are; you seem to have taken Battery Bee under your exclusive charge."[7]

At 1:30, while under this "very brisk fire," the *Patapsco* swung her turret around to discharge her guns, but the gun captain failed to clear the stack before giving the order to fire. One of the shells penetrated the stack and burst on the other side, causing the stack to fall over. The stack, disabled in this way, cut off the draft to the boilers and the engines became useless. *Nahant*, which had been hit only three times, withdrew and took the *Patapsco* under tow. *Patapsco* left the battle, having been struck twenty-three times; some of the shots caused "considerable wounds" to her deck plating and one crushed the top of the pilothouse. After dropping *Patapsco* off near the *New Ironsides*, *Nahant* then steamed over and anchored near *Weehawken* to cover her. *Lehigh,* already by her side, took this position after suffering over twenty-nine hits during the engagement. Around 1:45 Rowan signaled the ironclads to withdraw. By this time the tide had risen to protect the hull of the *Weehawken*, and she floated free about 4:00 P.M.[8]

This two-day engagement was fought by thirty Confederate guns against ten on the monitors and the eight-gun broadside of the *New Ironsides*. *Weehawken* was struck twenty-five times. Twelve shots struck her deck and eight passed through into the vital parts of the ship. Other projectiles loosened plates, broke bolts, and broke the turret in two places. The Confederates suffered nineteen killed and twenty-seven wounded. Despite the debilitating damage to some of the warships, the crews suffered only a few injuries and no deaths. This engagement once again proved that the ironclads did not have sufficient firepower to silence the Confederate forts.[9]

Boat Attack on Fort Sumter

While this battle took place Dahlgren had begun to gather a force for a boat attack on Sumter. Unknown to the Admiral, Gillmore had organized a similar attack for the same night. Despite frequent conversation between the two, neither knew of the other's specific designs until Dahlgren telegraphed Gillmore asking him to return four navy launches being used by the army for amphibious operations in Lighthouse Inlet. Gillmore told Dahlgren his plans and revealed he had assembled two regiments for his assault. He then asked if the navy would cooperate with his force, under army command. Dahlgren not only would not consent to put his men under anyone but a naval officer, but signaled Gillmore that he would send the highest ranking naval officer necessary in order for the navy to lead the attack. Dahlgren knew that this would end any chance for a cooperative effort and assumed that the services would launch their own assaults independently. Dahlgren did ask for a watchword so that both groups would avoid shooting at each other.[10]

Gillmore, irritated that Dahlgren would not cooperate, signaled "You decline to act in concert with me or allow the senior officer to command the assault on Sumter, but insist a naval officer must command the party." The rest of the message came by messenger. It read, "Why this should be so in assaulting a fortification, I can not see. I am so fearful that some accident will take place between our parties that I would recall my own if it were not too late."[11]

Since Gillmore and Dahlgren could not mutually agree to act in concert, they continued their preparations independently. The commander of the naval assault, Commander Thomas H. Stevens of the *Patapsco*, was brought in late in the process to complete the organization of his four hundred sailors and Marines into five divisions. During the afternoon, the boats assembled at the flagship *Philadelphia* and the officers all gathered on board to make the final arrangements. At 10:30 that evening all the planning and arrangements seemed to be firm. The boats pulled to the tug *Daffodil* and passed lines to the tug so that she could pull them to a staging position off Fort Sumter.[12]

Yet, as the boats pulled to the *Daffodil*, Dahlgren was still trying to negotiate a combined assault. Samuel Preston, Dahlgren's Chief of Staff, went ashore to confer with the general because normal communications with army headquarters had failed. At 11:30, unable to reach an agreement with the general, Dahlgren sent a message to Stevens to proceed.[13]

Stevens opposed the attack from the beginning. He believed that he did not have reliable information about the fort and did not know if the walls could be scaled. The landing force was not provided any equipment or ladders to do this. He also pointed out that the force had been organized quickly and the enemy knew that the fort would be the objective since they had seen boats gathered around the flagship in broad daylight. Stevens likewise knew the enemy would defend the fort "to the last extremity." Additionally, he feared that, even if his men successfully made a lodgement, they could not hold the fort. Since the obstructions had not been removed, the enemy ironclads and batteries above and below the fort would disrupt his communications and eventually starve his men into surrender. After he informed Dahlgren of these reservations, he asked permission to decline the command. Dahlgren merely said, "You have only to go and take possession. You will find nothing but a corporal's guard to oppose you."[14]

Major Elliott and his men were prepared for an assault and did know the Union tars were coming. The Confederates, since mid-April, had been reading the Union telegraphic signals sent to and from ship to shore by flag signals. This was made possible by two events. The major incident was the discovery on the beach of the signal book from the ironclad *Keokuk*. Even with this signal book in hand, however, there were essential parts of the code that could not be deciphered. So when the Confederates captured a signalman in Florida, they placed an officer disguised as another Union prisoner in his cell to draw out the necessary information to break the code.[15]

Elliott and his three-hundred-man garrison had prepared the fort for a boat attack. He had additionally procured a supply of hand grenades and "fire-balls" from the city to deal with such an assault. Elliott had expected the assault after the fall of Morris Island and kept about one-third of his garrison under arms at the parapet at night. The signals sent by the Union ships foretold the attack and the gathering of boats confirmed it. The *Palmetto State* and *Chicora* were ordered to be poised to steam to the north of the fort to lend fire support. In addition, the nearest batteries in the harbor had practiced daily, firing at the foot of the fort's debris so that the range of the guns would be correct.[16]

Lieutenant Commander Edward P. Williams; Lieutenants George C. Remey, Samuel Preston, and Francis J. Higginson; and Ensign Charles H. Craven each led a division of boats. At about midnight, eight hundred yards from the fort, they struck out in the calm, clear starlight night. Three of the divisions made up the landing party. The fourth division, led by Craven, would either give covering fire or land. The fifth, Higginson's division, was to move toward the northwest face of the fort to make a diversion while the other three divisions attacked the southeast front. The attack was to be supported by the protective gunfire of *New Ironsides*, *Lehigh*, and *Montauk*.[17]

The expedition began badly. The *Daffodil* unexplainably made three passes off Fort Sumter before letting the boats adrift. This maneuver made it "impossible" to coordinate the movement of the different divisions. Some of the boats left in great confusion toward the fort. Unfortunately, other divisions mistook these boats as the main assault and in the confusion began pulling toward the fort. It happened so quickly that Stevens could not recall the men and had to give the order to advance.[18]

As the boats neared the fort, a sentry on the wall hailed them three times and then fired a shot. Williams shouted back the word "passing." With this, a rocket from Fort Sumter lit the sky. This was the signal for the batteries and Confederate naval vessels to open on the advancing boats with grape and canister. The men of the garrison likewise opened fire, giving the Union tars a warm and deadly reception. One officer in the initial wave described the situation as "all the powers of hell and destruction seemed to be let loose, howling and shrieking for our annihilation."[19]

With the tide in their favor, the tars reached the wall rapidly. But when they arrived under the tremendous fire, some found that they could not get beyond the rubble at the foot of the wall and others, who made it to the second tiers of casemates, could not go farther without scaling ladders. Men who remained in the boats attempted to provide a covering fire, but only succeeded in striking some of the men who had climbed halfway up the walls. Other men took refuge in the shell holes made by the numerous bombardments, but the incredible fire power from the Confederates on Sullivan's Island, the *Chicora*, the grenades, fire bombs, small arms, and even brickbats began striking down the gallant tars.[20]

For about twenty minutes, the officers tried to find some way to close with the enemy. Meanwhile the Confederate fire also began disabling the boats at a rapid rate. The officers had to choose whether to remain and suffer capture or to withdraw. The attack began and ended so quickly that the supporting ironclads never got into position to cover the landing. The overall situation was hopeless and the men who landed were forced to surrender. The Union loss was 6 killed, 15 wounded, and 106 prisoners, 11 of whom were officers including Dahlgren's chief of staff, Preston. A special prize of the Confederates was the capture of five stand of colors, reportedly including the flag flying when the fort was surrendered in April 1861.[21]

The army expedition never materialized. Gillmore claimed that low tide at the army rendezvous delayed his attacking force and it was canceled. In truth, his men had set his part of their plan in motion. After the delay, the army contingent moved into position off the fort and, when the firing began, Colonel Francis A. Osborn halted his barges. Gillmore had issued strict orders to the colonel to abandon the operation if the navy landed first. Within sight of the navy's boats, his men turned back and returned to Cumming's Point. It is, however, fortunate that the army expedition did not join the naval contingent. It is unlikely that these additional men could have carried the fort.[22]

The whole attack had been poorly planned and executed. Inexplicably, Stevens did not participate in the organization and did not receive command until virtually all the preparations were made. Dahlgren was greatly disappointed in the failure and believed that the assault had not been "vigorous."[23] The failure of this attack certainly damaged any hopes of future interservice cooperation and served as an encumbrance between Gillmore and Dahlgren. The relationship between the military branches only grew worse. Gillmore had already faulted the navy for not passing into the harbor after the reduction of Fort Sumter. At this point, each man realized he could not trust the other. The failed effort stands out in contrast to the close cooperation that marked the Morris Island Campaign. It was the huge egos of both men that made cooperation difficult and prescribed failure. The prize was too great for men who were looking for glory and headlines. Neither officer was willing to share in the capture of the fort—a success that would have marked one of the greatest exploits of the war.

Logistical Concerns

Dahlgren had two major concerns about an attack into the harbor, other than the obstructions and enemy torpedoes: one was the condition of his monitors and the second the condition of their guns. Each of the monitors had been under fire repeatedly for several months during the day and performed picket duty at night. During the Morris Island operations, the enemy had struck each monitor an average of nearly ninety times. Their guns had fired over three thousand shots and now some of the guns had served well beyond their rated service life. Dahlgren feared that a prolonged attack into the harbor and against the Confederate defenses would completely wear the guns out before the operations could be completed. The Bureau of Ordnance could not furnish replacements; therefore, if the guns failed it might be necessary to cancel the operation in the midst of the campaign.[24]

Immediately after Du Pont's 7 April repulse, Fox and Stimers decided to make improvements on the monitors. The main deficiencies identified were the weak pilothouses, the small clearance between the turret and the deck and between the turret and the pilothouse, and the vulnerability of the decks to plunging fire. These modifications, however, would take some time. The monitors were crucial to the operations at Charleston, so Dahlgren believed that he could not withdraw them from this service. The modifications, therefore, had to be made in Port Royal.[25]

To supervise the modifications slated for the monitors, Welles appointed Patrick Hughes as Assistant Inspector of Ironclads in mid-April. Stimers thought highly of Hughes, calling him "one of the greatest drivers I know . . ." Hughes took forty men and tools down to Port Royal in mid June. Preceding Hughes were four steamers carrying extra armor for the decks of the monitors. To expedite the work, Admiral Gregory sent twenty-four men to accompany the precut and numbered iron plates to allow for easy installation. Yet, when Hughes arrived with his men and specific instructions for further modification, it was clear that the department had failed to inform Du Pont, who claimed he had "no instructions about the work . . ."[26]

Before most of the modifications could be completed, Dahlgren had his vessels in action. During the attacks on Battery Wagner, Dahlgren witnessed Confederate fire causing similar damage to the monitors that Du Pont had experienced just a couple of months before. During the early stages of the Morris Island operations, Dahlgren thought that he could not even spare a single monitor. Nevertheless, had he made the modifications in Port Royal, his warships would have held up better against the enemy fire. Dahlgren instead asked for more monitors, giving Welles feelings of déjà vu.[27]

These modifications required a great deal of work. Workmen began to install three inches of additional laminated iron around the pilothouses and on top of this structure. The additional ten tons of weight fit loosely like a sleeve over top and the vacant space was filled with lead to steady the covering sleeve. The sleeves were designed to prevent bolts from flying off on the inside of the pilothouse by absorbing extra shock from a direct hit on this prominent target. The limitation was that the lead filler tended to be forced out on impact. Lead sometimes shot through the viewing slits of the pilothouse and threw a "shower of lead" into the face of anyone unfortunately looking through the slit at the time. The workmen also chiseled out the decks beneath the lower edge of the turrets, creating a channel eight inches deep. They filled this channel with hemp packing and covered it with a sheet of iron. This served as a pressure plate against the bottom of the turret to prevent water from entering the ship in heavy weather. The workmen added a five-inch thick, fifteen-inch tall band around the base of the turret. A similar but smaller version was fitted around the base of the pilothouse. These bands prevented shells from striking the base of either of these structures and prevented fragments from wedging between the turret and the deck and between the pilothouse and turret. The band for the turret added an additional nine thousand pounds of weight. Some of the modifications required that tremendously heavy objects be lifted. This became problematic. In order to make some of the alterations, the workers had to lift the pilothouses. They found that the derricks on hand could not handle these twenty-four-ton objects. Eventually, with the proper purchases and blocks, they were able to use the foreyard of the *Vermont* to do this work.[28]

The working party could barely keep up with the repairs and alterations as Hughes worked his men night and day. By August, he was beginning to make real progress with the alterations, but Hughes was not a well man and had to be invalided north for several weeks to recover. During his absence, Dahlgren asked that only necessary repairs be made on the monitors and work was to be "pressed with all expedition." Hughes returned in September and by 2 October, he wrote Stimers that all the "additions" on the monitors were complete except on the *Nantucket*.[29]

By November, Stimers believed that the original working party should be replaced with a group about half the size but more skilled in making repairs. Assistant Inspector Thomas J. Griffin would supervise the new group. Griffin had earlier that September traveled to Port Royal to assist in making repairs to *Passaic*'s turret. The turret at the time turned in tandem with the pilothouse and the workmen had not been able to repair it. Griffin's quick diagnosis of the problem, which had stymied all the other mechanics, likely helped him to get his appointment. Griffin and his party of twenty men left for Port Royal on 4 December and Hughes' group left to go north two days before Christmas.[30]

Griffin's working party remained busy repairing the damages that the monitors received during their active operations off Charleston. The workmen continued to add iron plates to the decks, particularly over the boilers, magazines, and around the base of the turret, generally covering the deck over the wardroom to abaft the engines. The plates replaced sandbags that had been placed over the same areas to protect the decks from plunging fire. Interestingly the sand actually weighed more than the one-inch armor replacing it. The *Passaic* at the time had an additional wooden deck over her most vulnerable areas. The one-and-one-quarter-inch-thick wood, however, had been destroyed by the blast of her own guns and only about one-third of the decking remained on the monitor to protect her. Additionally, while in Port Royal, the work crews also helped to install wire rope fenders to protect the ships from torpedo boats.[31]

Other problems plagued the monitors. The boiler tubes built up scale to such an extent that it severely compromised the performance of the engines. Initial efforts to scale the boiler tubes caused many to leak, and the men stopped the cleaning for a short time until they could improve the procedure. Nevertheless, it never became a quick or easy process. The monitors had 1,040 tubes in each boiler. The working party could clear only an average of thirty tubes a day, requiring thirty-five days to finish a single boiler. Griffin considered replacing the tubes rather than cleaning them.[32]

Another problem that affected the performance of the ships was their fouled bottoms. The monitors, with this extra impediment, could make only three to three-and-one-half knots and often off Charleston could barely stem the tide. Dahlgren hired divers to clean the grasses, sometimes three inches long, and the barnacles and oysters from the hulls. The process of cleaning the hull of a monitor could yield about 250 bushels of oysters. It normally took well over fifty hours to clean one hull. Griffin suggested that the monitors be beached and cleaned and the divers be used to remove only the growth on the bottom of the hull. His men successfully beached and cleaned the *Passaic* without straining her hull; all the future jobs were similarly treated.[33]

By the beginning of 1864, active operations off Charleston had begun to wane. By that May, the alterations being performed at Port Royal by the working party had nearly ceased. On 24 May, the working party was discharged and Griffin and his men sailed north.[34]

Another major logistical concern for Dahlgren was getting coal to his warships. Coaling the blockaders off Charleston remained a problem throughout the war. The senior officer here directed all these activities. The vessels at this station used more coal because of the tides and the fact that they moved about to enforce the blockade and to cooperate in combined operations. The heavy swells and rough weather, however, prevented coaling on most days. The alternative was to coal at Port

Royal, but this normally would take the vessel away from her station for at least a day, usually two days.[35] A particular problem for the colliers delivering coal to the ships on station is that they could disperse only so much coal without adding ballast. The colliers often returned to Port Royal with portions of their cargo to finish unloading before traveling north.[36]

The labor required to coal and ballast these vessels was immense and Reynolds used the extra men on the depot ship *Vermont* for this duty. These men were also detailed to fill bags of coal so that it could be delivered to the vessels in bags. Bagged coal allowed for easier delivery of coal at Charleston's rough anchorage. Reynolds thought that filling the bags and hoisting them into another schooner to be delivered was too tedious and not practical. He suggested that it was better in the long term for the vessels to leave their stations and either steam to Port Royal or fill up from a collier farther south.[37]

Once Dahlgren began to use the monitors for daily operations off Morris Island and Fort Sumter, the need for coal for the vessels became more critical. The monitors could not leave their stations and steam to Port Royal for coal. They had to be refueled at their stations. In this rough water, coming alongside an ironclad inevitably caused damage to the colliers, particularly in the winter months. The *New Ironsides* was known as the "terror of the colliers." With any sea running, none of the masters wished to coal this warship. One officer likened it to " being thrown against a rock to touch her rolling, and many were the anathemas hurled against the 'd____d iron box' by the impatient and irate skippers." Despite the damage to the colliers, the blockaders received their coal at their stations. The colliers that went to Charleston were given good terms. They received fifteen cents a day per ton until discharged; the government assumed marine and war insurance, and the government paid for all damage, plus demurrage fees until all the repairs were complete. The continuous complaints about the damages and the fact that the awards for the repairs usually fell far short of the final bill created a situation whereby the masters refused to come to the anchorage. In January 1864, the situation became critical. There was no coal off Charleston and one monitor had only ten tons on board. Reynolds had to forcibly send two colliers off Charleston to keep the warships from drawing their fires. After the occupation of the southern end of Morris Island coaling could be done in Lighthouse Inlet. Dahlgren requested a large amount of coal to be landed here. In addition whenever possible, coal arrived off Charleston in bags so that it could be rowed over to the ironclads.[38]

Colliers arriving off Charleston usually fulfilled the needs of the monitors, tugs, and the vessels on the outside blockade first. After unloading a portion of their cargo into these vessels, the colliers anchored inside Lighthouse Inlet to discharge their remaining coal. This was done because it was easier to refuel the vessels off Charleston from full colliers and no coal vessel with a draft of more than fourteen feet could pass over the bar at Lighthouse Inlet. Colliers also anchored in the North Edisto and Stono rivers to service the outside blockaders. Sidewheel warships and tugs used the Stono River, and propeller vessels used the North Edisto River.[39]

Getting coal to the more southern points of the blockade also provided a challenge. On a frequent basis, gunboats going to other portions of the command would take extra coal in bags or tow colliers. Because of the nature of the duty of an inside blockade, most of the vessels did not burn large amounts of coal and could remain at their stations for long periods of time because they did not move much. Fernandina, at the extremity of the squadron's boundaries, was recognized as a possible intermediate coaling station for all the vessels as far north as St. Simon's and Doboy sounds. A wharf here could accommodate one steamer at a time. The greatest limitation here was the bar. Only colliers and blockaders with light drafts could use the wharf. A wharf in the St. John's River accommodated gunboats with deeper drafts.[40]

Keeping an adequate supply at the different stations, particularly at Port Royal, proved to be difficult, and misfortunes interrupted the supplies. By August 1864, the squadron required as much as 4,500 tons of coal a week. This figure was four times greater than the squadron's needs in March 1862. Floods in the mining areas and ice blocking the rivers kept the coal barges from delivering the coal from the mines. Strikes also played a hand in the shortages. The navy tried to keep a stock on hand. Dahlgren preferred this cushion to be about a two-week supply, but estimating the amount necessary was a complex problem. Daily consumption rose when the vessels began to cruise more at night to avoid the torpedo craft. Another factor was that Port Royal served as a public depot for vessels going south, particularly those that could not coal at Key West because of their deep drafts. When the navy's supply was exhausted, the army quartermaster could loan coal from his supply at Bay Point. This supply was ashore and was not convenient for the navy; access was only by scow and at high tide. Despite the frequent competition between the services, the army readily loaned fuel to the navy and was paid back promptly when the navy's colliers arrived.[41]

Clearing the Obstructions

The improvements to the monitors gave Dahlgren a weapon much more capable of dealing with the Confederate batteries. With Morris Island and Fort Sumter no longer a threat, the obstructions and the possibility of torpedoes posed the only obstacle that remained in Dahlgren's path to glory. Dahlgren, though, reminded the department that should the navy force its way into the harbor, the battle would be "decisive in its character." He felt that the warships should not pause at the first obstructions encountered, but should push to those farther into the harbor under the guns of the numerous batteries and forts Johnson and Ripley, and Castle Pinckney. He also thought the monitors should engage the Confederate ironclads. Dahlgren believed that ten monitors would be necessary for this attack. If given this force, he planned to commit fully to the operation and not withdraw unless his ships sustained "considerable loss." The public remained anxious for the navy to move into the harbor. Most of the papers criticized Dahlgren for failing to force his way in. *The Army and Navy Journal*, however, broke with the other papers, stating that despite the delays the "result will justify the delay."[42]

Dahlgren laid out the five steps he believed necessary to take Charleston. Initially, the warships had to pass the obstructions between forts Sumter and Moultrie. Once past these defensive works, the warships had to withstand the firepower of forts Moultrie, Johnson, and Ripley as they steamed farther into the harbor. The third step required both passing through the obstructions above Fort Ripley and neutralizing or subduing the Confederate ironclads. The fourth step would be an attack on Fort Ripley. The final measure would be to pass any obstructions beyond Fort Ripley, and attack Castle Pinckney and the batteries in Charleston.[43]

The day after writing the department with the outline of this proposed attack, Dahlgren wrote Fox. In his letter, he asked if the department would give him any help in removing the obstructions. He also wondered if he would be expected to "make the final attack" with only seven monitors or if the department intended to send him more.[44]

Rather than removing the obstructions, the flag officer proposed to breach them. Dahlgren procured the schooner *Shark* to be used as a powder vessel. He proposed to sail her into the obstructions and set off the powder, hoping to clear a hole large enough for his ironclads to easily steam through. Not wishing to risk his ironclads in a mission to clear the obstructions, he also asked both Gillmore and Welles for a shallow-draft and powerful side-wheel steamer that could run through the obstructions without getting tangled. Dahlgren asked the army for the eleven-hundred-ton side-wheel steamer *Ben De Ford.* Gillmore, however, could not spare her without a replacement. On 12 September Welles authorized Dahlgren to take "all measures" to remove the obstructions, reminding him that he alone could make the decision. Four days later the secretary authorized Dahlgren to use the *Ben De Ford* or another steamer that might be useful to force a gap in the obstructions. Welles also passed the request to Rear Admiral Francis H. Gregory, Superintendent of Ironclad Construction, to charter a steamer suitable for this work.[45]

But all these proposals did not account for the lack of knowledge of the nature of the obstructions. Since the boat expedition failed to capture Fort Sumter, the Union forces could not leisurely remove them as hoped. Almost nightly "scout" boats made reconnaissance missions into the harbor, but never reconnoitered the obstructions. Dahlgren tasked Daniel Ammen with this mission because of his experience on hydrographic duty here in 1851. On 22 September, Ammen took a six-oared boat with muffled oars and after midnight he and his men pulled to the obstructions. A fixed light on Cummings Point gave Ammen his bearings. He found, using a grapnel, that the lines making up the obstructions were rotten and would present no difficulty for a steamer to clear away. Ammen's scouts also found large gaps in the pilings. In addition, the interrogation of prisoners confirmed during the fall of 1863 the existence of only the rope obstructions. Despite the evidence, Dahlgren though still maintained that heavy obstructions barred his way into the harbor.[46]

Still convinced that the obstructions were more extensive than Ammen found, Dahlgren hoped to use divers to reexamine them. He contemplated using the civilians hired to clean the fouled bottoms of the monitors. He brought the divers to Charleston from Port Royal in October, but was not able to use them because of the engagements with the Confederate defenses. He decided therefore to return the men to their work and sought other means to accomplish his reconnaissance and their removal.[47]

Realizing that the obstructions were problematic, the department approached John Ericsson for his ideas. Ericsson designed an iron basket to be fitted over the propellers to prevent them from fouling the rope obstructions. He also implored Fox to use the rafts he designed. Dahlgren did test the "obstruction remover" designed by Ericsson. John Rodgers had refused to carry the explosive portion of this device during the April 1863 attack on Charleston. The appliance consisted of two cast iron shells each 11′ 6″ long and 10″ in diameter and held six hundred pounds of powder. A trigger board that extended the entire length of the device set off the torpedoes. Attached were four copper air chambers, designed to force the explosion forward. Bad weather and heavy ground swells delayed the tests. Later in calm weather, the *Patapsco* pushed the raft with the device suspended thirteen feet below the water. The trial, witnessed by Dahlgren on 6 November, did not seem to impress him. Though he expected a gigantic explosion, the blast only threw up a column of water about forty-five feet in the air; it raised the raft about two feet but did no injury to the *Patapsco* or the raft. Despite Dahlgren's reserved opinion of the test, others believed it would be completely successful.[48]

Dahlgren also wrote Gillmore to ask for army cooperation for the navy's movement into the harbor. Unwilling to try any of the methods at his disposal for removing the obstructions, he asked that the army batteries on Cumming's Point complete the reduction of Sumter. The flag officer insisted that he needed to eliminate the threat of musketry fire before he could attempt to remove the obstructions. Dahlgren asked this favor because he believed that the ironclads' offensive powers had been "expended" on the Morris Island operations. He did not want his naval force to finish the reduction of Fort Sumter, desiring to save his warships for attacking the works farther into the harbor. He suggested that the possession of Fort Sumter would allow the complete removal of the obstructions. Gillmore, however, felt his men had already carried the brunt of the fighting and believed the navy should now take the lead. He believed that Dahlgren's insistence on the occupation of Sumter was "newly imposed and somewhat grave in character." Gillmore also felt that he had completed his part of the campaign by removing Fort Sumter as a threat to the ironclads. He told Dahlgren he would rather remove the obstructions himself than risk another assault on Fort Sumter while the guns across the channel protected it.[49]

Gillmore's answer deeply disturbed Dahlgren. The admiral was already sensitive about the army getting the sole credit for the Morris Island operations and, therefore, he was incensed with this reply. He did not intend to share this operation with the army, yet he also would not commit his forces fully. He wrote in his diary that the general's four-page reply "has no more to do with my request than Greek." He added that his forces had for sixty days helped the army clear Morris Island, yet "he demurs at the first step in help of me!"[50]

The papers had carried numerous stories about the poor relationship between the two branches of the service. Dahlgren contended these were lies and even wrote his son that he and Gillmore were "on the most cordial terms." Nevertheless, the last exchange of correspondence soured the relationship more than Dahlgren would admit and he could not contain his displeasure in his reply to Gillmore. With an air of contempt, Dahlgren reminded the general that if the threat of musket fire was abated then the obstructions might be removed by boat with the ironclads covering Fort Moultrie. He then launched into a tirade, telling the general he had "not the slightest idea of imposing any new condition" on the army. He also stated that he never asked for the army's help to remove the obstructions as he had never "proposed to work the trenches" during the bombardment of Morris Island. These words certainly drove a larger wedge between these two officers and likely spoiled any chance they had of close cooperation in an attack on the city.[51]

Despite Dahlgren's harsh words, Gillmore wrote that he planned to open on Fort Sumter as soon as his guns were ready. He felt that his batteries could keep musket fire down while the navy worked on the obstructions. He reminded Dahlgren that he had always given the ironclads credit in his operations and that these operations had in mind the goal of the passage of the ironclads into the harbor. Gillmore stated that now it was time for him to "play a subordinate part, and all the means under my control are at your disposal . . ."[52]

In Dahlgren's mind Gillmore's assistance seemed questionable. Therefore, he began to lay the groundwork with the Navy Department to back off from his original plans to attack the city. On the twenty-ninth he wrote Welles that, since Fort Sumter's guns now pointed into the harbor from forts Moultrie and Johnson, the works assumed "quite formidable proportions." He also claimed that once the monitors arrived in the harbor, they could not attack these batteries because they could not elevate their guns sufficiently and would be under a plunging fire. Furthermore, under this destructive fire the pilings in the second row of obstructions would have to be removed. Additionally, as a result of her deep draft, the *New Ironsides* could only offer covering fire from a position near the throat of the harbor. He felt that one or two monitors might be disabled and "compel a withdrawal." Dahlgren, in short, told Welles that with seven monitors he could not assure a successful operation.[53]

Dahlgren though, was not a well man. Almost daily he had complained of illness and at times was so weak and feeble that he could not walk across the cabin. The illness manifested itself in his stomach and head. His officers claimed him seasick. Dahlgren's illness was also common news back in Washington, where discussions of his delicate constitution flourished. Rumors even suggested that Dahlgren "lost caste with the sailors for being seasick." His illness affected his short-term ability to command, making him too ill at times to run the squadron.[54]

Privately Dahlgren was anxious for action. He wanted two more monitors and told Drayton that with these he would "go in, neck or nothing . . ." At the beginning of October, Dahlgren suggested to the department that he would be ready for operations to begin in the middle of the month. He reminded Welles that he would have only five monitors in good repair and that the *Passaic* would still be under repair and perhaps the *Patapsco*. In a timely letter Stimers informed Dahlgren that the *Canonicus* and *Tecumseh* were nearly ready; Dahlgren asked if they could be added to his forces. Welles, however, dispelled the thoughts of getting the two additional ironclads before December. He did, however, mention the possibility of adding the double-turreted *Onondaga* and the *Sangamon* to the operation. Yet, despite this news, Welles told Dahlgren that the department could not risk the ironclads in an assault on the city as there were other pending operations. He reminded Dahlgren that he still knew little about the obstructions and the risks might be too great. He told Dahlgren that it would be better to work with Gillmore to reduce the Confederate defenses. He reminded the flag officer not to let the "public impatience . . . hasten your movements into immature and inconsiderate action . . ." This departmental policy is in stark contrast to the course of action suggested to Du Pont just six months earlier. It also reinforced Dahlgren's cautious and noncommittal strategy for attacking the Confederate defenses.[55]

Infernal Machines, the *David*, and the Blockade

While the Union naval forces paused before the harbor, the Confederate forces continued to work diligently to perfect the defenses and add another dimension to their offensive capabilities. The Confederate high command much earlier realized that the obstructions were too extensive and could never be maintained properly to keep the Union warships at bay. With this in mind, the Confederates began to add torpedoes to the harbor defenses. By September 1863, they had laid down electrical torpedoes in the Hog Island Channel on the western end of Sullivan's Island and others in limited number protected channels into the harbor. The knowledge that these passive weapons even existed paralyzed Union naval operations. The Confederates, however, introduced the Union navy to an even greater threat in October—the steam driven torpedo boat *David*.[56]

Plans to place torpedoes on small moving craft to attack the Union warships became a more viable opportunity after the Confederate ironclad attack in January 1863. The wooden vessels, more capable of dealing with small torpedo craft, necessarily moved to sea while the ironclads moved nearer the harbor's opening. Captain Francis Lee busied himself building torpedoes for passive use in the harbor. He also experimented with torpedoes attached to a spar propelled by a small boat. Testing this principle, he had this boat drawn toward a hulk until the torpedo touched the hull and exploded. The explosion destroyed the hulk and left the small boat intact. With this success, Lieutenant Glassell advanced the creation of a small flotilla of these craft to attack the Union vessels. He approached his friend, merchant and financier George A. Trenholm, who provided the boats and the outfits for this experiment.[57]

Earlier Glassell made three attempts and Tomb made two to reach the ironclads in small rowboats to no avail. The last occurred in March 1863, when Glassell and a crew of six men ventured on an expedition to attack the side-wheel frigate *Powhatan*. Commodore Ingraham allowed only Glassell to go on this mission, refusing other officers who volunteered. During the ebb tide on the night of the eighteenth, Glassell readied his boat, carrying a ten-foot spar and a torpedo armed with fifty pounds of rifle powder. In smooth seas and no moon, the boat approached the frigate. Lookouts on board *Powhatan* spotted the boat about 250 yards away and hailed it to stop. While continually pulling toward the warship, Glassell gave "evasive and stupid" answers. Despite the sentries' threats to shoot, Glassell continued toward the warship. Without a shot being fired and within forty feet of the ship, one of Glassell's men backed his oar, stopping the boat's headway. The other men also stopped and the boat drifted past the ship's stern, all the while being questioned by the officer of the deck. Glassell abandoned the attempt and the men escaped without a shot being fired.[58]

After this failure, it was clear that only a small, steam-propelled, lightly armored torpedo boat would be effective. When the *Torch* successfully closed on the *New Ironsides* in August, it gave some hope. She had been too large and was easily spotted. This near success encouraged several other men working on a torpedo boat project at a site thirty miles above Charleston up the Cooper River. Their invention would change the complexion of the war off Charleston.

A small steam vessel capable of delivering an explosive charge to the side of a Union ship was the brainchild of Dr. St. Julien Ravenel and Theodore Stoney. Both contributed large sums of money and raised money from local merchants to build a prototype craft. What took shape was a cigar-shaped vessel built from a discarded locomotive boiler. About 50 feet long, 6 feet wide and with a draft of only 5 feet, the craft could make about 7 knots. Her builders armed her with a spar that projected fourteen feet ahead and carried a torpedo 6' 6" below the water, armed with approximately 65 pounds of rifle powder. Dubbed the *David*, she was completed about the same time that Lieutenant Glassell returned to Charleston from duty in Wilmington, North Carolina. Glassell immediately volunteered for command and was promoted to Lieutenant Commander. For one week Glassell tested the boat and then was ready to make a sortie.[59]

On 5 October, shortly after dark, with a slight haze over the harbor, the *David* left a wharf in Charleston and proceeded toward the harbor's mouth on the ebb tide. Glassell's intention was to make an attack on one of the blockading vessels at about 9:00 P.M. at the change of the tide. In smooth water, with a slight wind, he maneuvered quietly past Fort Sumter and just before 9:00 P.M., the *New Ironsides* loomed in the dark. At full speed, he steered towards the most powerful ship in the United States Navy.[60]

As he approached, Glassell ordered his engineer, and fireman to remain below. With the pilot Walker Cannon at his side, he conned the vessel with his feet and sat on the deck. Glassell and Cannon each carried double-barreled shotguns loaded with buckshot. He believed that if he took the first shot at the officer of the deck he might cause enough confusion to strike the warship and escape without injury. Glassell aimed *David* at the gangway, but the tide was still running out and it carried him toward the starboard quarter.[61]

The craft's low profile and her bluish color prevented lookouts from spotting her until she had steamed to within three hundred yards of the Union ironclad. When the lookout shouted, "Boat ahoy! Boat ahoy!" several times, Glassell kept his speed, remained quiet and cocked both barrels of his gun. In the commotion on the deck, Acting Ensign Charles W. Howard came to the rail and shouted, "What boat is that?" At this point, the *David* had steamed to within forty yards of the *New Ironsides* and Glassell opened the fight. He discharged both barrels of his gun, and Howard fell mortally wounded. Glassell then quickly ordered the engines stopped, thinking he had plenty of momentum for the *David* to reach her objective. Moments later the torpedo struck the side of the ironclad.[62]

A tremendous explosion rocked both the *New Ironsides* and the torpedo boat. The *New Ironsides* shook from "rail to keelson." The torpedo boat rode a large wave as an enormous column of water shot sixty feet into the air over both vessels. The falling water fell down the stack and the hatchway of *David*. Glassell shouted to the engineer, James H. Tomb, to reverse the engine, but Tomb shouted back that the water had extinguished the fires and that the blast had thrown the iron ballast into the machinery, stopping it.[63]

The beat to quarters brought the crew of *New Ironsides* to their battle stations. With rifles and pistols, the Marine guard and crew poured a hail of gunfire down upon the helpless craft. Fortunately for Glassell and his men, part of the crew of the *New Ironsides* mistook an iron buoy off the bow of the *New Ironsides* as his craft and a portion of the small arms fire struck the buoy rather than *David*. With the engines stopped and under fire, Glassell and his crew thought their only chance of escape was to abandon ship and swim to shore. Glassell and the fireman, James Sullivan, each took a cork life vest and swam away from the vessel. Tomb also jumped in the water, but looked back and saw Cannon, who could not swim, still clinging to the craft. Tomb decided to try one last time to save *David*, swam back, and boarded her. Tomb and Cannon managed to restart the engines and Cannon took the wheel. They steamed back up the channel through the fleet, passing within a few feet of a monitor, all the while under continuous small arms fire, but the *David* escaped. A coal schooner rescued Glassell, and Sullivan was picked up later; both spent time in a Union prison before being exchanged.[64]

The damage to *New Ironsides* after the initial examination appeared minor. Several weeks later, however, when the coal was removed from the bunkers, the seriousness of the damage was exposed. The explosion

started and broke knees and strakes. It parted and carried away stan-
chions; and pushed in the side of the ship about five inches for a length
of nearly forty feet. Seven weeks after the attack divers examined the
outside and found shattered planking six feet by nearly twelve feet.
Rowan's carpenter called the injuries serious and suggested the ship be
docked as soon as she could be spared from the blockade. The injuries,
while serious, were not critical. She managed to remain throughout the
winter storms at her station off Charleston and did not leave north for
repairs for about eight months.[65]

This attack had important ramifications on the blockade. Dahlgren
had not appreciably changed the deployment of the blockaders after replacing Du Pont, with the exception of moving the ironclads into the
main ship channel. Once the ironclads moved to this position, it virtually closed the port of Charleston. Dahlgren kept the majority of his
blockading vessels off this port to maintain the blockade and to assist in
operations against the Confederate defenses. Du Pont found it necessary
to keep his blockaders near the main channels. The vessels under Dahlgren continued to move about during the day and took their blockading stations at night. The New Ironsides took a central position forward
whereby her guns could control a major portion of the throat of the harbor. This gave the Union forces a great deal of fire power to deal directly
with either blockade runners or the Confederate ironclads, but it also
put her, as Dahlgren found, in a vulnerable position to be attacked by
small torpedo craft.[66]

The David's attack affected all the strategic positions of the blockading ships. The monitors now needed to remain together for mutual support. Two served as pickets and two others took positions at anchor
near the New Ironsides. Each of the monitors and the New Ironsides
also received some protection against torpedo craft. Within about two
weeks, the New Ironsides was surrounded by a "stout netting of rope,
rigged out from the ends of fenders, several feet from the sides . . ." A
calcium light mounted on the pilothouse revolved at night and boats
also rowed around the vessels as picket guards. The protective netting
around the ironclads made the vessels look "like women in hoop-skirt
petticoats of netting . . ."[67] The wooden vessels were particularly at risk
and would have to keep moving at night.

This mobile and lethal weapon impressed Dahlgren so highly that
he predicted correctly that this "element" would now be "part of warfare." He requested from Welles similar craft as well as a number of the
fastest pulling boats and several fast tugs. From the prospective of an in-

ventor and scientist, Dahlgren wrote, "among the many inventions with which I have been familiar, I have seen none which have acted so perfectly at first trial." For several nights after the attack on the *New Ironsides*, long low craft were reportedly spotted by the picket boats protecting the fleet—perhaps caused by vivid imaginations or the *David* again making sorties. The Confederates, likewise, tried to exploit this fear and on the night of 22 October launched a sham torpedo boat on the ebb tide. The fifteen-foot-long raft with a stovepipe funnel, however, never reached the forward picket monitor. Union sailors spotted it the next day and broke it apart.[68]

The mobility of the torpedo craft also put Dahlgren's logistical center at Port Royal at risk. Many of the vessels there lay under repair with no steam and were extremely vulnerable to attack, as were the ordnance and store vessels. Reynolds quickly had a boom manufactured to stretch across Station Creek. A tug pulled this across the creek at dusk and did not open it until daylight. Reynolds also kept a tug and a picket boat with a howitzer underway at night to watch the approaches to the facility.[69]

Moving Beyond Sumter

Only days after the attack on *New Ironsides*, Dahlgren, still suffering his illness, asked for leave to come north for about a week. He hoped a respite from his duties would restore his health. His closest friends believed Dahlgren not "up to the command" of the squadron and felt that, if he came north, the department would not send him back. By the eighteenth, before he could receive an answer, Dahlgren's health was "entirely restored" and he was once again "gritting his teeth" and ready to attack Charleston.[70]

A visit by Gillmore on 15 October also infused new hope in Dahlgren. While the two men discussed future operations, Dahlgren observed that the general seemed nervous. Gillmore suggested operations on Fort Johnson and other "interior works." This movement, however, would involve the monitors entering Charleston Harbor. Dahlgren promised to support army operations, but indicated that the monitors, still under repair, could not be immediately utilized. Gillmore insisted that the navy as a "fulfillment . . . of the original programme . . ." remove the obstructions He believed that his batteries could suppress the enemy fire enough so that the inner obstructions could be removed and passed. The outer obstructions, he believed, could be removed at night. Crucial to an agreement for combined operations were Dahlgren's earlier instructions from the department to avoid risks with the ironclads. These instructions would require the department to authorize a move into the harbor.[71]

Two days later Dahlgren wrote the department to obtain authorization for this cooperative venture and sent it by special messenger, asking for an immediate reply from Welles. In his letter he lamented that his monitors would not be ready until the first week in November. He could not account for the lengthy repairs, which required an average of thirty days. Dahlgren seemed certain about the obstructions. He related that the rope obstructions between forts Sumter and Moultrie could be removed and the "impediments" farther into the harbor could be overcome. His greatest concerns at this moment were the torpedoes. He could not confirm whether the Confederates had placed any torpedoes in the harbor, had no way of reconnoitering to find them, and would not know until they were deployed.[72]

Dahlgren gave Welles three approaches for an attack on the Confederate positions. First, the ironclads could enter the harbor by passing the forts and obstructions. They would defeat or drive back the Confederate ironclads, silence Castle Pickney and Fort Ripley, and "take possession of Charleston." Second, the navy could assist an army movement on James Island. A third option was to operate with the army against Sullivan's Island. Dahlgren's greatest fear was leaving the army's communications exposed should the forces afloat be defeated. Because of the tremendous risks involved, Dahlgren did not wish to shoulder any of the responsibility. Fearing repercussions similar to those Du Pont faced, Dahlgren asked Welles to relieve him of "the responsibility of such a result . . ."[73]

Gillmore again visited the flagship on 19 and 20 October, each time staying for several hours to consider these potential operations. During one of the meetings, he and Dahlgren discussed the rumored disagreements between them. Neither man was forthcoming about the soured relationship. Gillmore "good-naturedly disclaimed any idea of disagreement" and blamed it on the reporters and discontented officers. Dahlgren maintained that he was somewhat suspicious of the general but trusted him. Gillmore said he would handle the press and Dahlgren wrote the department to dispel the concerns of a dispute between them.[74]

The relationship between the two was far from perfunctory. Dahlgren was perhaps naïve and did not wish to confront the general. Gillmore, though, had no intention of working with Dahlgren and attempted to have him replaced. The general acted sincere in the presence of Dahlgren, but sent two of his officers to visit Welles. On 24 October, these men described Dahlgren as "incompetent, imbecile, and insane." They claimed he was "totally unfit for his position . . ." Welles realized that Gillmore had sent these men and dismissed most of their remarks. Welles also knew that Dahlgren's long-term illness had likely influenced some of these observations. Yet he indicated in his diary that he did not absolve him from all of the claims.[75]

Welles, meanwhile, had already exhibited concerns over Dahlgren's judgement of the strategic situation at Charleston. To get a better idea, the Secretary of the Navy asked him to poll his officers. On 22 October, Dahlgren held a council of war on board the flagship *Philadelphia*. During the six hour session the admiral posed several questions and discussed the options of attacking the enemy to the attending eight ironclad captains and two staff officers. In attendance were Dahlgren, Rowan, Dahlgren's new Fleet Captain George F. Emmons, and Ammen, the latter the only officer that had participated in the attack with Du Pont. The monitor captains present were Commander Andrew Bryson of *Lehigh*, Commander Stevens of *Patapsco*, Commander Colhoun of *Weehawken*, Lieutenant Commander Edward Simpson of *Passaic*, Lieutenant Commander John L. Davis of *Montauk*, Lieutenant Commander Greenleaf Cilley of *Catskill*, and Lieutenant Commander John J. Cornwell of *Nahant*.[76]

Dahlgren asked five questions to give the department a broader strategic viewpoint. The first question inquired if there would be "extreme risks incurred without adequate results" by entering the harbor— 4 voted no, 6 voted yes. Question Two concerned Welles's letter of 9 October in which he instructed Dahlgren not to risk the ironclad force. The question asked if the flag officer would be justified with his present force to attack the inner defenses, destroy the rebel ironclads, and shell the city—2 voted yes, 8 voted no. Question Three was, Should the *New Ironsides* enter the harbor with the monitors? The officers remained divided on this question: 4 voted yes, 4 voted no, and 2 remained undecided. Question Four: If the present naval force was not sufficient to attack Charleston directly, should the navy cooperate with the army to attack Sullivan's Island and gradually reduce the defenses and remove the obstructions? Overwhelmingly the officers believed cooperation necessary, 9 voting yes and only 1 voting no. Question Five: Could fort Moultrie or Johnson be reduced with the ironclads at hand, unassisted by the army? All voted no.[77] Clearly, the most senior officers in the squadron were concerned that the naval force had no chance of success except in a combined operation. It is also evident that no one at the meeting had a clear concept of the problem to be solved. Dahlgren forwarded the notes of this discussion to the department for comment.

Gillmore continued to believe that success lay in the naval vessels being able to pass into the harbor. The general likewise intended to do everything in his power to end Fort Sumter's ability to support the Confederate defenses. Since the fall of Morris Island Gillmore's men had steadily toiled to convert the captured Confederate works on the island into siege batteries. By 26 October, Gillmore's guns were ready to begin firing. Around 12:30 that afternoon the gunners began firing ranging shots on the gorge wall of Fort Sumter. Gillmore planned to cut the face of this wall down so that the casemates in reverse could be opened for easier access to bombardment. This army bombardment would last day and night for forty-one days. The heaviest bombardment occurred during the first ten days when 1,000 shells each day pounded the gorge and sea face walls.[78]

Gillmore also asked for naval assistance to occupy Fort Sumter. This request arrived one day before the bombardment began. Dahlgren still felt that he had fully committed his forces to cooperate with the army, but privately felt that Gillmore had not shown a similar effort to work with his forces to achieve a common objective. When Dahlgren earlier asked army assistance to occupy Fort Sumter, Gillmore had showed little interest in cooperation. Dahlgren felt the army had failed him and he wrote in his diary that the general had been, "Rather singular . . . [and] much exercised because I asked him to do that very thing in order to enable me to go in!"[79]

Dahlgren did send his ironclads to help with the further destruction of Fort Sumter. On the twenty-sixth, *Patapsco* moved up to augment the army bombardment of the fort from a position off forts Wagner and Gregg, now renamed forts Strong and Putnam, respectively. *Lehigh* did not participate as planned as there was some unfinished work on board. The *Patapsco* moved up within eighteen hundred yards. In the flood tide she fought while underway, but managed to fire only eighteen shots. These shells, however, did effective work both inside and outside the works.[80]

Later on the twenty-sixth, Dahlgren directed Captain Rowan to send the *Lehigh* and *Patapsco* to bombard Fort Sumter the following day. He instructed the commanding officers to maintain a deliberate fire from a range of two thousand yards. Because of the fragile status of his ironclads, he also asked that the officers not expose their warships to "effective fire" of the batteries on Sullivan's Island. On the twenty-seventh and twenty-eighth both the *Lehigh* and *Patapsco* moved up and opened on the northeast bastion of the fort. With the army fire pouring in from the south, the huge shells from the monitors displaced large sections of masonry, threw into the air pieces of heavy timber, and opened casemates. The monitors fired 111 shots and the army over 700. This destructive fire soon crumbled the walls on this part of the fort.[81]

The bombardment continued for weeks as the monitors took turns helping to reduce the works. The Union forces together fired over one thousand shells at the fort on 31 October. While a couple of his ironclads daily helped with the destruction, Dahlgren took this opportunity to make repairs, clean his ships' bottoms, and replace the guns of the other monitors in order to prepare for a possible attack on the city. Dahlgren almost daily steamed up the channel to observe personally the damage to the fort. During the first two weeks of the bombardment the monitors fired over twelve hundred shells at the fort. Dahlgren wrote in his diary, "The only original feature is the northeast face; the rest is a pile of rubbish."[82]

On 8 November Dahlgren received an answer from the department commenting on the findings of the council of war held on the flagship over two weeks earlier. Commander Daniel Ammen delivered the message to Welles and returned with the answer. Dahlgren had candidly submitted his reservations in his letter and Welles answered each in turn. The secretary's answer sent mixed signals. Welles began by telling the flag officer that the obstructions consisting of the double line of hawsers could be removed and that torpedoes, thus far, had not been "dangerous or serious preventatives to naval operations." He wrote that the Confederate ironclads were "much inferior" and could probably be "disabled before they could close." Welles's major concern was the timber obstructions across the channel. Nevertheless, he reminded Dahlgren that the department had sent a side-wheel steamer that could be sacrificed to pass the obstructions. Welles asked Dahlgren to consult Gillmore and ask the general whether he believed an advance by the monitors into the harbor would cause the rebels to evacuate their seaward defenses. He promised the *Onondaga*, *Canonicus*, and *Tecumseh* within six weeks, as well as the *Sangamon*. This promise of reinforcements seemed to dispel all of Dahlgren's concerns. Confusingly, he closed the letter by telling Dahlgren that success against the city was paramount, but it would be better to delay operations to insure success.

He wrote that the department would acquiesce to any delay because, whereas a "delay is annoying, failure would be more so."[83]

On the eleven Gillmore and Dahlgren met and walked on the beach to discuss the Navy Department's answer regarding the council of war. Two days later the general boarded the flagship to continue the talks. Gillmore favored Dahlgren's idea of waiting for the monitors scheduled to arrive in December. By "attacking in force," Gillmore saw an opportunity to also strike with his troops. Gillmore believed that, if the navy could advance into the harbor, Sullivan's Island would be abandoned, but not James Island. They agreed to discuss this program at length later. The entire move, however, hinged on the addition to Dahlgren's forces of four more monitors.[84]

As a follow-up, Welles wrote another letter to Dahlgren and accentuated the need to determine the nature and extent of the obstructions. He urged Dahlgren to make this examination. During the month of November, Dahlgren sent in scouting parties at night to probe the rope obstructions between Fort Sumter and Battery Bee. None of the missions, however, found any torpedoes.[85]

The shore batteries meanwhile continued their deliberate bombardment of Sumter. The ten-day heavy bombardment by the army batteries left many of their guns worn out. The artillerists then shifted to firing mainly mortars in order to keep the men in the fort from repairing their protective works. During the lull, on the evening of 15 November, the Confederate batteries in Fort Moultrie opened an unexpected heavy fire on the Union batteries on Morris Island. At about 10:00 P.M., fearing an enemy attack by boats on Cumming's Point, General Gillmore telegraphed Dahlgren to move his vessels up to cover the batteries. The admiral ordered the monitors on picket duty to advance and cover the army positions. The Lehigh steamed to the most forward position and anchored. During the night the Lehigh swung on the flood tide and settled on a "lump" about twenty-three hundred yards from Fort Moultrie. At daylight Commander Bryson tried to get his warship underway and discovered that she would not move.[86]

The Confederates did not realize the plight of the Lehigh until 7:15, at which point they immediately opened fire. Shots from nine different batteries began striking the unfortunate ironclad. The Lehigh immediately sent signals asking for help and the Montauk, Passaic, and Nahant all moved up to assist her. Admiral Dahlgren boarded the Passaic at 7:55 and then took his barge over to Nahant to direct personally the effort to get her off the bar. It was imperative that she get off at high tide, otherwise she would sit under the fire of the forts for another twelve hours and likely be destroyed. That the *New Ironsides* was delayed getting into the fight was due to her torpedo netting. It required some time before the crew could stow it in order for the ironclad to get underway.[87]

Nahant, being the closest monitor at the time, steamed up to *Lehigh* and anchored nearby to pass a towline. She suspended her fire as the crew brought a hawser from below and worked it through the turret to pass it to *Lehigh*. At 8:00 A.M., in a "rain of shot, shell, and grapeshot," Assistant Surgeon William Longshaw, gunner's mate George W. Wineland, and coxswain Thomas Irving, in a small boat, carried the hawser to *Lehigh*. Unfortunately, the men on *Lehigh* could not make it fast. A second trip succeeded in passing the line, only to have a shell cut it in two. At 8:03 a third try, made this time by two landsmen and a seaman, again succeeded in passing the line successfully, only to have another shell cut the line again. The fourth try was successful.[88]

While this occurred, the Confederate batteries and the other two Union monitors had quite a battle. The army artillery positions on Morris Island might have materially added to the fight, but fired a paltry twenty-one shots in the defense of the *Lehigh*. The Confederate gunners fired over three hundred shot and shell, concentrating on the grounded monitor. She "got pretty well hammered," being struck twenty-two times. Eleven shots passed through her deck while others broke and started plates, broke bolts and caused a major leak near the bow. These injuries forced her to undergo over ten days of repairs in Port Royal. The other monitors suffered only slight damage.[89]

The prolonged army and naval bombardment reduced the profile of Fort Sumter to such a degree that it led Gillmore to test the fort's defenders. On the night of 19 November, without informing Dahlgren, he sent two hundred men in boats to "reconnoiter" the defenses. It is probable that he thought that his bombardment had weakened the defenses enough that he could capture the fort and the laurels as well. Gillmore's men got to within thirty yards of the works but a dog barked and aroused the garrison. Small arms fire wounded two men as the boats withdrew without attacking. Gillmore's officers concluded that at least two hundred men still occupied the works.[90]

Awaiting Reinforcements and the New Year

During the last several months the navy had continually augmented the bombardment of Fort Sumter as well as supported every request by Gillmore for fire support and cover for his artillery positions. Despite these efforts, the newspapers had not favorably reported Dahlgren's accomplishments. Gillmore, however, had more access to the press, and supplied the reporters information slanted toward his operations. Unknown to Dahlgren, though, Gillmore had been leaking information that showed him in an unfavorable light. Dahlgren now found himself in a position similar to that of Du Pont. Dahlgren had continually used his monitors in support of army operations. The Morris Island Campaign and the fights with the Confederate forts left his warships continually needing repairs. Limited by the operational capabilities of the monitors, he could not relate their limitations or their dire need of repairs to the press. This would explain his delays, but it would also give the enemy important information. The newspapers reported naval inactivity when Dahlgren merely was both trying to save his vessels for an advance into the harbor and to make repairs on the others.[91]

While Dahlgren waited for the additional monitors, he maintained an optimistic view that he would enter the harbor as soon as the these ironclads arrived. While waiting for these ships and continually harassing Fort Sumter, he sent expeditions to probe other areas. On 28 November, a combined operation pushed up Skull Creek on the northwestern side of Hilton Head Island to determine if the rebels had erected batteries nearby. *Chippewa*, in company with the army transport steamer *Monohassett*, and the army's armed transport *Mayflower* got underway at about 8:45. Off Pinckney Island, the *Chippewa* began clearing the woods with canister fire. Army troops began landing without opposition at 10:30. Finding no enemy, they reembarked at noon.[92]

On 5 December, Dahlgren received the distressing news that *Weehawken* sank at her anchorage. This would decrease his forces should he try to advance into the harbor. The ironclad had recently received a full load of ammunition and was riding out a moderate gale at anchor. The crew, however, neglected to place a gasket in the hawsehole and the hatch over the windlass room. Water accumulated so fast in the forward compartments that by the time the crew reacted, the vessel was so far down by the head that she was doomed. The pumps of the monitor lay aft, and as the forward part of the vessel filled, the water could not flow aft to the pumps. At 2:25, about the time the water reached the berth deck, the *Weehawken* signaled for assistance. The other vessels nearby began launching boats and, only fifteen minutes after signaling, she rolled over and sank, carrying with her four officers and twenty men.[93]

On Christmas Day, the Confederates opened a surprise attack on the naval forces in the Stono River. Dahlgren kept the gunboats deployed in the river to protect the army positions ashore. The rebels intended to cripple the naval vessels and drive them off. They then planned to attack an army work party engaged in pulling down houses in Legáréville for wood to build houses for the Union troops on Kiawah Island. The Confederates secretly built two gun platforms about seventy-five yards apart about three-quarters of a mile below Legareville. Another battery about three hundred yards downstream put the gunboats in a crossfire. On the twenty-fifth, the Confederates moved two 30-pounders and two 8-inch guns in the upper battery and another howitzer and three field pieces in the lower position. Infantry moved to the woods near Legareville hoping to charge into the town after the shelling began and capture the Yankee work party.[94]

At 6:00 A.M. the Confederate batteries opened on the screw steamer *Marblehead*. The gunboat slipped her cable but could not move quickly because the engineers had hauled the fires in the starboard boiler to repair a leak. Slowly the *Marblehead* moved to present her broadsides, and at one thousand yards, she kept up a tremendous fire on the rebel batteries. The *Pawnee* lying around a bend in the river, moved up to infilade the batteries and the *C. P. Williams* slipped her cable and dropped down the Folly River under sail and also opened fire. The *Pawnee*'s flanking fire was particularly damaging and the firepower from three vessels was too hot for the Confederate gunners who at 7:30 retreated so quickly that they had to abandon two of their 8-inch howitzers. The rebels, however, managed to strike the *Marblehead* thirty times, killing three and wounding four. The corresponding attack on the army working party never developed. The Confederates lost three killed and nine wounded.[95]

As the year wound down, Gillmore pressed the War Department for ten thousand to twelve thousand additional troops to assault Charleston via James Island. He favored this route because he felt it had several advantages: (1) the garrison on Folly Island could assist, (2) the troops could be landed from the Stono at all stages of the tide, and (3) the Union forces already held the southern end of the island. He suggested a second operation might advance from Bull Bay to Charleston. Additionally, he proposed a surprise attack on Savannah. Gillmore, however, had over thirty-three thousand men in his command, nearly all of whom were in the Charleston area. Halleck wrote the general on 22 December that he had the department's authorization to undertake any operations that he wished but that he would not be given any reinforcements.[96]

Despite the written hopes and optimism of Dahlgren, he showed that he was unlikely to make a move into the harbor even with a larger ironclad force. He never could overcome his fear of the unknown nature of the obstructions. In addition to the information gathered from reconnaissance missions and deserters, he likewise engaged an engineer, Benjamin Maillefert from New York, to determine if the obstructions could be removed. Maillefert recommended a series of 150 underwater charges be exploded at several depths to remove the obstructions. Each charge would contain 110–125 pounds of powder and be set off by clockwork devices. Grapnels would hold the charges in place by snagging anything they met. The department, however, never felt the plan feasible. Dahlgren had torpedoes shipped to Port Royal in case he wished to try them against the obstructions. In late December heavy weather swept through Charleston and washed a large section of the obstructions outside the harbor. To Dahlgren's surprise it consisted of twenty-two sections united with railroad bars and sections of wood fifteen inches square. The substantial nature of these obstructions surprised Dahlgren, who believed his intelligence would have informed him of these. These obstructions, though, were from the Hog Island channel and would not have interfered with Union forces entering the harbor.[97]

As the year closed it appeared that the movement that began in July with so much hope had permanently stalled. From October to December, the Union forces fired nearly twenty thousand projectiles at Fort Sumter. Reducing it to rubble, according to Dahlgren, had not ended its value as an anchor for the obstructions. The incredible firepower massed against the fort managed to kill only thirty men and wounded another seventy. It became clear that Dahlgren would not risk a single vessel on an enterprise to pass or breech the obstructions—fearing failure and a fate similar to that of Du Pont. Welles, however, had also given Dahlgren orders not to take any risks, thereby putting him in an awkward position. Dahlgren managed to stall any movement while he awaited the arrival of the new monitors. On the last day of the year, Dahlgren lamented his lack of accomplishment during the previous year. He wrote in despair, "Thus endeth the old year 1863—one that had witnessed my highest advancement, but not my happiness, for I have been loaded with responsibilities that no one could hope to lead to a favorable issue; the best possible result of which would ruin the reputation of any man. And now what is there to look forward to?"[98]

— 10 —

"He Could Only Expect Me
to Hold On"

Stalemate in the New Year

"What record shall this year bear for me?" are the first words in Dahlgren's journal for 1864. Clearly, Dahlgren began the New Year with the anxiety of the old weighing heavily on his mind. His apprehension stemmed mainly from "slander and base abuse" he had received from the press and others whom he believed had ruined his good reputation. He also faced gloomy prospects of a combined operation. Yet Dahlgren still believed that if he could get the monitors repaired as well as add a few more to his command, he might "get a chance to try an entrance to Charleston."[1]

Dahlgren knew that while Gillmore remained in command he had little prospect of army support in a campaign. This was confirmed on 16 January, when he and Gillmore met on board the flagship to discuss operations. During a lengthy conversation Gillmore related that he had asked for additional troops to operate against Charleston, but the War Department refused his request. The general now had abandoned all hope of attacking the city. Gillmore did not believe he could make a successful attack even if the navy captured and controlled the upper portion of the harbor. Gillmore still maintained that he and Dahlgren had agreed to silence Fort Sumter and afterward the navy would be responsible for leading the attack into the harbor. With confirmation that the "operations became purely naval" Gillmore asked the admiral what he would do. Dahlgren said he would attack "unless otherwise instructed." Once reinforced, he would "silence Johnson, knock down Fort Ripley, shut up Pickney, and engage the city batteries, [as well as] capture or drive back the ironclads."[2]

On 12 January, both Fox and Welles wrote Dahlgren "prodigiously flattering" letters requesting his input on the character of the ironclads. The request resulted from the department's battle with Du Pont. Welles believed he could discredit Du Pont's attacks on the Navy Department by not only publishing the latter's reports, but also the reports and opinions of others who defended the monitors. Both Welles and Fox appealed to Dahlgren's ambition, vanity, and his desires of being a hero. Dahlgren also viewed this as an opportunity to defend and vindicate himself against the earlier slanders of Gillmore and the press. Within a week, the admiral had penned a fifty-four-page report. The first part blamed the army for its inept frontal attacks on Battery Wagner. The second part related the severe pounding the monitors took during the siege operations. Dahlgren asserted that while the monitors had limitations due to their slow rate of fire, they were good warships for shallow draft operations.[3]

In addition to flattering Dahlgren, Fox's letter also relayed the severe delays in the completion of the monitors. The assistant secretary did not believe that the *Onondaga*, *Tecumseh*, *Canonicus*, or the *Manhattan* could be completed before March. Fox told Dahlgren that the "work at Charleston is done" yet, he wrote "politically and morally, we ought to enter far enough to burn the city by naval fire and accomplish the destruction of their naval force . . ." Fox, however, advised Dahlgren not to attempt anything unless he could guarantee success.[4]

Dahlgren realized that Fox's letter concerning an attack on the city was merely window dressing. But he had received a letter just days before from Welles that repeated his orders from 12 September authorizing him to remove the obstructions and silence or pass the batteries—essentially to do what was necessary to take Charleston. In Dahlgren's answer to Fox, he asked that the department "modify that condition of success as indispensable." Dahlgren proclaimed that he could not guarantee success given the unknown nature of the obstructions and torpedoes. What he could promise was to attack with vigor. Not wishing to repeat the mistakes of Du Pont, he also insisted that the department issue him orders to attack. He similarly wrote Welles that this would be an experiment and that he believed that he could push to the throat of the harbor, but that "there should be some modification of the injunction, that it must be successful." He wrote his son Ulric that the department had affirmed for him to *"go in if you can be successful*—but do not lose." In despair he told his son that he could not do this under these terms and it "would be a bold man who could."[5]

His answer to Welles had essentially laid the foundation for exoneration should an attack fail. In it he hedged on the success of any enterprise to attack the city. But he wrote Lincoln also to cover himself farther. The letter to the president stated that once he received the additional ironclads he would be "able to do more without the risk of advantages so great . . ." He continued, "no man in the country will be more happy than myself, to plant the flag of the Union where you most desire to see it."[6]

Dahlgren's long hours of work each day, conducting the business of the squadron, began to reveal an ailing man. Throughout his tenure he suffered bouts of seasickness and exhaustion. At the end of January, he wrote Fox, "I am weary, very weary dear Fox." Dahlgren likewise remained on an emotional roller coaster, feeling little support from anyone. Despite his efforts to fit in, he had never been able to get close to his subordinates nor did they fully accept him. These relationships might have helped to sustain him in his everyday problems. At the beginning of February, he learned that throughout the squadron he was not well liked or supported. He wrote in his diary, "I never felt so pained. I had been working every moment and never spared myself and yet here was a set of treacherous officers . . ."[7]

Despite the personal disappointment and isolation, Dahlgren continued to appeal to Gillmore to assist with some combined operation on the city and informed the general about the delays of the monitors. On 3 February he suggested striking Charleston by landing on Long Island and operating against the Confederate defenses on Sullivan's Island. Gillmore, though, would not be moved. Dahlgren, still concerned with a frontal attack through the harbor, continued to collect information on the obstructions. From observations, the obstructions near Fort Sumter appeared to be disintegrating because of freshets. But deserters provided good descriptions of the torpedo boats and the torpedoes, only adding to Dahlgren's fears. That January, reports began to surface of a new Confederate vessel, the *American Diver*, which could submerge to attack her enemy.[8]

The Blockade

With the army idle, Dahlgren focused his attentions more on the blockade. Beginning in 1863, the port of Charleston experienced a revival in blockade running. During the first half of the year more would enter this port than the entire number the year before. The vessels that now plied to and from the supply entrepôts to the Confederacy, however, were faster, had shallower drafts, and had features that made them difficult to spot at sea. The squadron enjoyed a six-month hiatus, but in the spring of 1864, the trade began to revive.[9]

During 1861 virtually any vessel might be used as a blockade runner, but gradually the steamships evolved to meet the challenge of the naval vessels. These new, specially designed steamships constructed expressively for speed usually displaced between four hundred and six hundred tons.[10] Most often built of iron or steel, they sat low in the water, had extremely narrow beams, had rakish designs, and sometimes had turtleback forward decks to help these ships to drive through heavy seas. Builders constructed both screw and side-wheel vessels, each having its advantages. Twin-screw steamers became common toward the war's end, perhaps because they made little noise, were more maneuverable, and were less vulnerable to gunfire. The paddle-wheel steamers, on the other hand, could operate in shallower water, were easier to extract from shoals, and were slightly faster than screw-propelled vessels.

Avoiding detection was singularly the most important characteristic necessary for the success of the blockade runners. In many cases these ships carried only a light pair of lower masts, with no yards. A small crow's nest on one of the masts often appeared as the only alteration from the ship's sharp outline. The hull showed little above the water and was usually painted dull gray to camouflage the vessel. The captain kept the ship's boats lowered to the gunwales and some steamers had telescoping funnels that could be lowered to the deck to maintain a low profile. English engines became more powerful as the war progressed, and the boilers normally burned semibituminous English coal, but the blockade runners used anthracite coal whenever possible because it made little or no smoke. When approaching the shore, these vessels blew their steam off under water, showed no lights, and sometimes muffled their paddle wheels with canvas, all to avoid detection. Some captains even insisted that their crews wear white clothing, believing that one black figure could reveal the position of a vessel.[11]

The blockade of the port of Charleston was a challenge because of the geography of the entrance. The Charleston Bar extended six miles to sea south of the harbor and nearly three miles beyond the throat on the northern end. Four major channels intersected the bar and further dissected the blockaders. While the Confederates maintained control of

Morris Island, they kept the blockading fleet at a greater distance and forced the Union vessels to maintain an extended perimeter to watch the harbor.[12]

The blockade runners had several distinct advantages. The blockade runners could choose the best time to run from the port. The blockaders also had larger profiles, and could be spotted at greater distances and be avoided. There were also other things that betrayed the blockader to the enemy. For example, the *Housatonic*'s donkey pumps made a noise similar to that of paddle-wheels in motion. This noise could be heard more than one mile away. A careful master on a blockade runner could avoid this large sloop.[13]

The most important change made during the war to stop the blockade runners at Charleston was the use of the monitors as blockading vessels. Shortly after taking command, Dahlgren placed his ironclads inside the bar as close to the harbor as he dared. This was thought to be impractical by the ironclad captains under Du Pont. These men advised him that their ground tackle was inadequate in heavy seas to hold the monitors in place off Morris Island. While this was true, Dahlgren solved this problem by placing nine-thousand pound mooring anchors in the main ship channel to allow the ironclads to ride out bad weather. With the monitors anchored safely in the main ship channel and able to sink any ship that tried to run past, the blockade-running activity of the port virtually came to a standstill.[14]

Initially Dahlgren stationed the most advanced monitor in the channel about three miles south of Battery Wagner. *New Ironsides* took her station one-half mile south and two other monitors were stationed at intervals of one third of a mile below the *New Ironsides*. Two other monitors remained at their moorings. At night one of these monitors, with the aid of a tug and with picket boats as protection, took station above the most advanced monitor to watch the Swash Channel, which intersected the main ship channel about two miles outside the harbor's mouth. The monitor captains directed the movement of the tugs and boats. Positioning a monitor here had a dual purpose. It discouraged the use of the Swash Channel by blockade runners and it dissuaded the Confederate ironclads from attacking Union positions ashore. At this point Dahlgren was confident that this would virtually close the port. He wrote to Fox, "The Blockade if not entirely certain must be nearly so."[15] With the fall of the batteries on Morris Island, the monitors were able to push nearer the throat of the harbor without danger. The forward-most monitor now could position herself in full view of the channel between Sumter and

Moultrie, but remained far enough southward to be out of range of the rebel guns. Here the picket monitor, protected by tugs and picket boats, could both control the channel and keep a lookout for the Confederate ironclads.

While the occupation of the main ship channel by the monitors helped strangle blockade running, the Union blockade also benefited from the fall of Morris Island. When the Union forces occupied this island, the line of blockade was now nearly halved because the forts also commanded the main ship channel. Any vessel trying to enter Charleston not only passed the naval vessels, but a potential barrage from the army batteries. In addition to the monitors, beginning in July, Dahlgren also placed most of his blockading force at Charleston inside the bar. This had an immediate and devastating impact on the blockade. From January to the end of July 1863, forty-five steamers arrived and forty-four cleared Charleston. During the eight months from August 1863 until March 1864 only a single steamer arrived and five cleared. None arrived after 16 August 1863 nor cleared the port after 18 September until March 1864.[16]

By December 1863, the picket ironclads moved up every evening and lay about one thousand yards from Fort Sumter and left at daylight. Four monitors performed picket duty, two for each night. One took an advanced position and the second anchored in a supporting position. The deployment of the ironclads in these positions exposed them to attack by torpedo craft because getting the ironclads underway quickly was impossible. They likewise could not get underway to capture a blockade runner. One of the officers on the *New Ironsides* wrote, "The spectacle of the 'Ironsides' slipping her cable and starting after a swift blockade-runner would have been as absurd and useless as the efforts of an elephant in pursuit of a camelopard."[17]

Picket boats and tugs served as the eyes and ears of the monitors. They prevented surprises by the enemy and warned of blockade runners trying to escape. The tugs moved in front of the monitors like sentries on a beat. The other blockading vessels supplied the boats and a tug towed these craft into place at night so that they would not be seen getting to their stations. At least two of the boats carried howitzers and the remaining crews carried rifles, bowie knives, and other weapons to fend off Confederate picket boats. All boats were instructed to have muffled oars, carry night glasses, and the crews to be served hot coffee upon both leaving and returning from their patrols. The duty in these boats was harsh and grueling. The swift current in the harbor never allowed the men to rest; therefore, the crews changed daily to keep fresh. Bad weather limited nighttime operations, but the boat crews could take shelter on the decks of the monitors when the water became too rough for their deployment.[18]

Small boat operations may have been one of the most important aspects of the blockade off Charleston. The use of small craft was essential because the bar was so far from the mouth of the harbor. There was not much room, therefore, for the large ships to maneuver if they spotted a blockade runner heading to sea. The support of the boats by as many as six picket tugs gave the blockade here in effect three to four lines of defense.

About eight boats performed this service each night. Three classes of vessels were used. Boats of the first class were called scout boats. These craft had sharp lines and were finely built. Single banked, they carried five oarsmen, one coxswain, and an officer. Usually only one of these boats deployed each night. Used only in calm weather, the scout boat's main duty was to get behind the enemy's picket boats. These craft often carried the men who examined the obstructions and took soundings in the harbor. The second class of picket boats were cutters that carried nine men. These boats patrolled in front of the enemy's lines and either ran or fought with the enemy picket boats. The third class comprised larger craft, usually described as launches. These craft carried fourteen or sixteen men and often a boat howitzer. They supported the other boats and sometimes attacked the blockade runners. Dahlgren, however, found his fastest boats to have inadequate speed to elude the rebel picket boats and to penetrate the harbor. He asked the Bureau of Construction and Repair to build him boats with the "greatest possible speed." The New York Navy Yard built special boats for the squadron, but they did not perform well and the men performing the reconnaissance work asked for their old boats back.[19]

Generally, the vessels off Charleston remained at anchor blocking the channels and rarely moved. The senior officer off Charleston, Captain Green, preferred a blockade maintained by anchored vessels. This type of blockade required that Green know exactly which vessels he would have to assign to this duty each night. Dahlgren, however, failed to keep Green informed and the warships in many cases failed to report to the senior officer to let him know whether they were under his command or not. Green questioned the command structure and begged to have direct communication with Dahlgren to relieve him of "a great deal of embarrassment."[20]

The largest warships, because of their drafts, could not operate inshore and maintained the outside blockade. These ships laid about five miles from the inner vessels and four miles apart. Keeping these stations posed an interesting problem when the blockade runners were inwardbound. The deeper-draft vessels could not pursue the fleeing ship over the bars and had to rely on the inner line of shallow-draft vessels or picket boats to stop them. With the southern side of the harbor virtually shut by the ironclads, the blockade runners had no choice but to use the northern channels, particularly Maffit's Channel. Dahlgren hoped to strengthen the northern part of the blockade by adding tugs that could operate in the shallow areas and close to shore. But the vessels continued to remain at anchor, making them less effective blockaders. In the fall of 1863, the outside vessels lay mainly off the northern approaches to the harbor in a double line guarding the channels. Despite the fact that they lay about a mile from their nearest consort, blockade runners continued to elude the Union ships on extremely dark nights. On 22 August, the side-wheel steamer *Fannie* managed to run directly between six blockading vessels on this side. The *Fannie* ran so close to the Union ships that the blockading vessels could hear the orders given to the *Fannie*'s helmsman as she escaped.[21]

The *Hunley*

The attacks by the Confederate torpedo boats alerted Dahlgren to the vulnerability of his blockaders. The ironclads that took their stations near the entrance to the harbor were the most exposed. To help deal with this threat he had equipped the ironclads with fenders and nets kept in place with shot to keep a torpedo boat at a distance. Calcium lights lit the darkness and boats and steam tugs constantly patrolled around the monitors to warn of an approaching enemy. Through interviews with Confederate deserters, Dahlgren learned that the enemy had a torpedo vessel that could dive. He knew that this introduced a completely new variable to underwater warfare and suggested that the monitors anchor in shallower parts of the channel so that it would be more difficult for this vessel to operate. Writing Fox, he claimed that these threats "keep all eyes open."[22]

Dahlgren's fears were realized on 17 February 1864. Early that evening on the ebb tide the submarine *Hunley* slipped out of Breach Inlet. The Confederates developed this weapon in Mobile, Alabama. It consisted of a cylindrical boiler cut in two with a 12-inch inset of boiler iron to give the craft a more oval shape. Bow and stern castings gave the *Hunley* tapered ends. In all, she measured about forty feet long, four feet wide, and five feet deep. The vessel could be raised or lowered in the water with ballast tanks fitted in either end. Two hatches on top of the craft gave access to the crew of seven and a helmsman. Powered by hand cranks attached to the propeller, the *Hunley* could make between three and four knots in smooth water.[23]

Dahlgren's intelligence-gathering was extremely accurate. He and his officers had carefully interviewed deserters and prisoners to gather information. She was indeed originally developed to tow a torpedo and to dive under vessels and drag her torpedo against the ship's hull. The torpedo, however, had a tendency, when the *Hunley* was laying on the surface, to drift down upon her. To prevent the torpedo from potentially destroying the submarine, the torpedo was fastened to a spar. After the loss of several crews in testing the vessel she left on her first mission with Lieutenant George E. Dixon and his seven-man volunteer crew.[24]

The blockaders on the north side of the harbor lay at anchor during this calm night in the North Channel under a three-quarter moon. At 8:45 Acting Master John K. Crosby, the officer of the deck on the blockader *Housatonic*, spotted an object moving in the water about one hundred yards away. At first, it appeared to be a plank but when it continued directly toward the ship, Crosby ordered the *Housatonic*'s chain slipped, the engines backed, and all hands called to quarters. Within two minutes the *Hunley* closed the distance to the ship to the point where the Union gun crews could not depress the large guns sufficiently to fire. Thus the craft met only some random small arms fire. Dixon and his crew struck *Housatonic* forward of the mizzen mast on the starboard side. About a minute later a tremendous explosion ripped the large sloop of war apart. Timbers and splinters filled the air, followed by rushing water and dense black smoke that settled on the deck. She sank quickly stern first as she heeled over to port and settled on the bottom.[25]

Despite the intensity of the explosion, the attack cost the lives of only five Union officers and men. Most of the crew managed to climb into the rigging, still above the water. The *Hunley*'s crew, however, did not live to enjoy a hero's welcome. She was to return by way of Breach Inlet and reportedly exchanged signals with the beach, but never arrived.[26]

Dahlgren wrote his son after the attack, "Well I have cried 'Wolf! Wolf!' until tired and no one but a few seem to regard the danger as real. *Now* it has come and a heavy blow it is. Yet if the Rebs had been wise they might have made it almost irreconcilable by striking at several vessels . . ." This attack demonstrated the vulnerability of all the warships and forced Dahlgren to make changes to the blockade. He realized that the waters might be "infested with these cheap, convenient and formidable" craft. He asked the department for torpedo boats that could steam around the monitors at night. Almost a month earlier he had made a similar request to the Bureau of Construction and Repair and made a second request within days of the loss. Dahlgren also instructed Rowan to provide outriggers and netting that would protect all the inside blockaders. Those on the outside would now keep underway for the rest of the war. Until the vessels on the inside blockade could be fitted with their torpedo boat protection, they were to anchor outside the bar at night. The calcium light on the *New Ironsides* was always in operation. Placing a similar light on the monitors was considered but never implemented. The Confederates demonstrated that lone warships were particularly vulnerable. Dahlgren believed the exposed position of the *Patapsco* in Wassau Sound imperiled her to a boarding attempt. Dahlgren instructed two gunboats to remain nearby and sweep the decks of the monitor with grape or canister should boarders gain the deck of the *Patapsco*.[27]

The loss of *Housatonic* also had a detrimental effect on the men. Blockading duty was grueling and vigilance now became even more important. The officers and men were already exhausted by the responsibilities of the blockade, manning the boats, in addition to the normal watches and work on the ships. Commanding officers often slept in their clothes and some remained awake all night to ensure that the watches were maintained with vigor. One man wrote that after the loss of *Housatonic* "our nights were thereafter made miserable by the fear that we might, at any time, wake up and find ourselves overboard."[28]

Frequent alarms on the vessels during the night revealed these fears of torpedo craft and submarines. Often men would awaken hearing the cry, "Slip the cable! Slip the cable." Men sprang to their feet and ran to their battle stations. In one instance, an officer reported that as he arrived on deck he saw "bearing down upon us a floating object that filled every soul with dread." As the broadside gun was cast loose, the boatswain cried, "Back her! Back her! For God's sake back her; she is right under our bows." As the ship responded and began to reverse course, the gunners fired and cut the object in two. But it turned out to be only a mass of floating seaweed. Everyone on ship, relieved of the danger, began to take notice of the lack of clothing on deck and the large number of men in their nightshirts. The greatest joke was on the master at arms, who in his haste to get to the deck had run his legs through the sleeves of his pea jacket and had buttoned it around his body.[29]

The Blockade of the Secondary Waterways

The early successes of Du Pont virtually sewed shut the smaller inlets and harbors north and south of Charleston. The vessels that blockaded these waterways maintained their vigilance on stations inside. This was a much more effective blockade because the vessels usually could control the entire navigable channel with their guns. The Confederates virtually conceded the small and less used entrances to the Union forces. Rarely during the war was the Union blockade challenged by blockade runners in these waters. More importantly, the rebels rarely contested the presence of the gunboats or harassed them to complicate the enforcement of the blockade.

Most of the attention of blockade running was focused on Charleston, but the squadron still had to watch the ports north and south of the city. Dahlgren kept a minimal force to blockade these entrances. At Georgetown, Bull Bay, and at St. Catherine's, Doboy, Sapelo, St. Andrew's, Altamaha, and St. Simon's sounds and Mosquito Inlet, a single vessel at each usually maintained the blockade. Dahlgren also kept some of his vessels cruising between the smaller entrances. But small sailing vessels carrying between three hundred and four hundred bales of cotton managed to escape from Savannah periodically throughout the war. Fewer ran into the city; the *Rebecca Hertz*, being the last to run through the blockade, arrived in late December 1864 from Nassau.[30]

Despite the appearance of easy duty, the warships did face certain inherent problems. The ships could not watch all the waterways, particularly in the large bays and sounds. For example, in May 1863 only the 1,165-ton ex-merchant screw steamer *South Carolina* watched Bull Bay. She anchored on the southern side of the bay near the main ship channel. The Cape Romain River on the north side of the bay, ten miles away, though, remained unwatched. This vessel could not simultaneously watch and protect both. The commanding officer, by necessity, had to occasionally leave his post on the south side to reconnoiter the other side.[31] This problem was repeated frequently by warships in the squadron, but was also never corrected given the dearth of vessels to watch the long expanse of coastline.

Small boat operations served as a force multiplier for the navy. Picket boat operations allowed the navy to watch more areas of the interior waterways. Boats and launches, usually armed with boat howitzers, under the command of an ensign or other junior officer, provided mobility. These men also conveniently provided a striking force to burn small vessels capable of running the blockade, destroy saltworks, accommodate the escape of refugees, destroy or carry off produce, and disrupt enemy operations.[32] These small boats, however, were extremely vulnerable to surprise attack and at all times the crews had to be vigilant.

Anchoring in the interior waters also posed imminent dangers. The threat of a Confederate attack always existed and the crew had to watch for both blockade runners and enemy attacks. Sailing vessels stationed in some of these waters were extremely vulnerable to boarding parties and torpedo boats. They, likewise, had no chance of catching steam blockade runners. The commanding officers had boarding nets triced up at dusk, posted lookouts around the ship, and sent boats to reconnoiter the water around the vessel. Steam gunboats usually kept the boilers producing steam so that the vessel could move quickly if necessary. When the blockading ships operated near army forces, the nighttime routine became more strained by the occasional army vessel and small craft passing by. The interior blockaders had to deal with passwords and signals by lantern in order not to impede army activity.[33]

As the war progressed, the dangers gradually increased for the Union vessels. The growing threat of torpedoes and torpedo craft created an increasingly dangerous situation and caused the Union officers to change their methods of blockade. With these threats, vessels on the inside blockades of the sounds could generally not remain at anchor any longer. Lone sailing vessels were the most vulnerable. In St. Helena Sound it was reported too dangerous to keep underway at night because of the roughness of the water and the tides. On 28 March 1864, while moving to an anchorage not threatened by torpedoes, the bark *Kingfisher* ran aground, and become a total loss.[34]

At the extreme boundary of the squadron's limits lay Murrell's Inlet near the North and South Carolina boundary. Blockaders from the South Atlantic Blockading Squadron visited this far north only periodically. A substantial trade began to develop out of this small inlet by the spring of 1863. An expedition that May, by the screw gunboat *Monticello* of the North Atlantic Blockading Squadron, destroyed a schooner and injured four other vessels there. Trade continued and, in July, the *Seneca* observed four schooners lying within sight of the inlet. That October, the Union mortar schooner *T. A. Ward* arrived off the inlet and observed a schooner lying about eight hundred yards from the inlet. At

8:15 P.M. the *Ward* put two boats in the water and they pulled toward the schooner. The sailors boarded the schooner, which turned out to be the 50-ton *Rover*, an ex-Charleston pilot boat. Loaded with a full cargo of cotton, she lay fast aground and the navy tars found her impossible to get afloat. The sailors set her afire and returned to the *T. A. Ward*.[35]

Three days later Acting Master William L. Babcock took the *T. A. Ward* to within easy range of the beach and at 1:30 that afternoon put a boat ashore armed with a howitzer. Babcock placed the *Ward* about five hundred yards off the beach to give cover to the men should they find it necessary to retreat to the beach. Lying to off the beach, the *Ward* began shelling one of the nearby buildings. Babcock sent ashore a second boat after 2:00 P.M. to cut out or destroy the schooner *Cecilia* about a mile and a half up the inlet. Without instructions to the contrary, Acting Ensign Myron W. Tillson landed and decided to examine the surroundings to see if his men could obtain water. Leaving the boats on the beach, he took ten men with him. Around 3:15, near the schooner, they were surprised by an overwhelming number of cavalry and all but one were captured.[36]

On 5 December, the men from the brig *Perry* tried to finish the job of burning *Cecilia*. Acting Master Samuel B. Gregory sent two boats ashore with twenty-two men. Starting for the schooner, they proceeded only a short distance when enemy cavalry came bearing down on them. The men retreated to a knoll. But the *Perry*, lying head on to the beach in this position, could not protect the men. When a second company of cavalry attacked the sailors from the rear, they surrendered after a short fight. Three officers and twelve men were captured, including Gregory's son.[37]

This loss infuriated Dahlgren and he remained unsatisfied with the officers' accounts of the mission. Dahlgren thought it was a "blundering affair" caused by the poor judgment of the commanding officer and the disobedience of those sent ashore. To ensure that this did not happen a third time, Dahlgren ordered Captain Green, the senior office off Charleston, to send four gunboats, as well as the bark *Ethan Allen* and schooner *George Mangham* to deal with the rebels. Green was also to supply 100 Marines and 4 howitzers for the expedition. He gave the captain great latitude on how to attack, but wished him to capture as many of the cavalry and other rebels as he could and to destroy the schooner.[38]

On 29 December, Green's force, consisting of the steamers *Nipsic* and *Mary Sanford*, the steam tug *Daffodil*, and bark *Ethan Allen*, left

Charleston and anchored fifteen miles from the inlet the following afternoon. The schooner *George Mangham* joined the flotilla from Murrell's Inlet. As the warships made their final preparations to land the following day, the wind began to freshen and a heavy swell developed. On the thirty-first, in a secure anchorage, Green had the launches transferred to the *Daffodil* and the boat howitzers removed from the launches and placed on the *Mary Sanford* and *Nipsic*. By 4:00 A.M. on the first, the weather had deteriorated to such a degree that it threatened the launches in tow of the *Mary Sanford* and the *Nipsic*. Green had to abandon the attempt and sent *Ethan Allen* back to Charleston and, the *Mangham* back to blockade Murrell's Inlet. The remaining vessels sought a safe anchorage about ten miles from the Georgetown Light. On the second, Commander James H. Spotts returned to Murrell's Inlet with the *Nipsic*. The *Nipsic*'s heavy armament of one 150-pounder, one 30-pounder, two 9-inch Dahlgrens, and two 24-pound howitzers opened fire to "scour the woods" and to destroy the schooner. Intervening hills, however, prevented the shells from reaching the vessel. Thirty Marines under the command of Lieutenant Louis E. Fagan landed and deployed as skirmishers. A party of sailors in a launch, armed with a howitzer, took a position to enfilade any advance by rebel cavalry. Another party of seamen landed a boat howitzer on a field carriage and positioned themselves to fire on the schooner. On the fifth shot they set the schooner ablaze. The party all returned to the *Nipsic* without any casualties.[39]

Logistical Concerns

While these small sorties occupied Dahlgren's mind, he had a number of major concerns on the overall efficiency of the blockade. Despite the convenience of repair facilities and a machine shop nearby, the mechanics could not keep ahead of the repair work. The monitors, which regularly received a pounding by Confederate gunners, took an immense share of the shop's manpower and consumed its capacity to make needed repairs for the other ships. By fall 1863 this had become a problem of epidemic proportions. That October Dahlgren had a total of six ships in Port Royal and another four at northern yards for repairs. The absence of this number of warships had a great impact on the blockade. It reduced his outside blockading force at Charleston to only five warships, seven less than when he took command. He wrote Welles that this "embarrasses me exceedingly." In November he wrote the secretary, "It is notorious that since my taking command, the disability of vessels has increased to such an extent as to render the blockade nearly inefficient in some places." By December this number increased to twelve ships at Port Royal and six away north for repairs. Others, handicapped for lack of speed, needed engine repairs and careening to clear their hulls. Desperate, Dahlgren was willing to do almost anything. He even asked Welles if he could use vessels "unfit to send north" to put a couple of guns on and use these vessels in smooth water. It would, however, only get worse.[40]

The Port Royal facilities served the squadron well for a couple of years. Station Creek was rather narrow and always crowded with ships awaiting attention. It served well as a careenage, where the naval vessels could be beached so that their bottoms and rudders could be repaired. A wharf was later constructed that jutted out into the creek near the machine shop hulks and expedited some of the work. On average, over twenty-three percent of the vessels attached to the squadron were constantly away for repairs. About two-thirds (sixty-one percent) of the squadron's repairs were made at Port Royal. Without this facility the squadron's warships would have remained absent for tremendous amounts of time going to and from repair facilities and awaiting their turns for repairs in the overcrowded northern yards. Though the hulks served well, they were not as efficient as shore facilities. The workmen had to pass back and forth between the ships as well as to take supplies, tools, etc. between them. Interestingly, the army steamers also received repairs at the machine shop. Du Pont complained about this relationship, pointing out that not only did it interfere with the work on his warships, but the army had "every facility in workmen, timber + in establishing a machine shop of its own. There is an Engineer regiment filled with artisans."[41]

Eventually the squadron completely outgrew the floating facilities. There was a small dry piece of ground off the creek suitable to place buildings. In early 1864 it was suggested that some of the lathes and other work be moved ashore. The shops remained afloat, however, until the spring tides in the middle of August 1864. These tides nearly carried all the work afloat to a halt. The extremely high tides carried *India* (blacksmith shop) off her "bed" of piles that kept her in place. She floated down the creek and went ashore on the other side. She was towed back and beached, but she could not be placed back in her bed because she now had water in her hold. Stranded, the iron, copper, and engineers' stores were removed ashore. Reynolds ordered her to be broken up as quickly as possible. The *Edward* faired only slightly better. She righted herself in the tides and was pumped out. The tug *Pettit* forced her aground but she ended near the wharf. By December everything had been removed (boiler, engines, tools, etc.) and carried ashore. Because of fear that the same would happen to the *Ellen* and suspend the crucial carpentry work, the carpenters on board were instructed to build a new shop on shore.[42]

Since the floating store ships and repair hulks could never be as efficient as facilities ashore, in 1863, Du Pont began the construction of a logistical facility at Bay Point. It was to have four cranes for hoisting coal and a railway that ran one-half mile from the wharf inland to the site of the storage houses. Framed shop buildings fitted with glazed windows and with offices were likewise envisioned. Delays started from the beginning. The contract for the wharf was signed in January 1863, but problems with the carpenters impeded the project. At times there were less than two dozen men working. They also at least once refused to work and procrastinated throughout the project. This delay cost the government substantial sums of money for demurrage costs as well as inconvenience and inefficiency of keeping the logistical facilities afloat.[43]

By April 1864, the Bay Point wharf was still not complete. Reynolds eventually fired the contractor and it was finally finished during the summer of 1864. Yet the site of this new facility was not chosen well. The wharf, with a perpendicular dock, could accommodate only one vessel in good weather. Also, southwest or northwest breezes exposed the vessels lying at the dock. Though designed to accommodate a fleet of eighty to ninety vessels, inside the "T" there was not enough room for a small schooner to tie up without grounding at low water. The facility was designed to be used as a coaling wharf, but most of it still needed to remain afloat to accommodate the needs of the squadron. Since the wharf remained busy with other business, three prefabricated storehouses were added ashore in May. These building accommodated provisions, ordnance, and engineers' stores, allowing some of the chartered vessels to be discharged. Much of the ordnance stores continued to remain afloat.[44]

Interestingly, after the navy worked on this project for over a year, at its near completion the army also claimed use of the land, not realizing it was "purely naval jurisdiction." Dahlgren was livid. He wrote the army that he did not know of any formal arrangements between the services about the land. Dahlgren not only asked for the document that gave the army authority over the land but also reminded the commanding general that it was the navy that captured Port Royal. Lastly he said, "I, myself, am unwilling to tolerate for a moment the right of any military authority to march a guard upon ground or ships belonging to the navy." The matter was closed.[45]

Operations in Florida

With offensive operations at a standstill off Charleston, Gillmore was desperate to get involved with another project. When control of Florida became a Union priority again, Gillmore and his troops became a potential political tool. Unionists in Florida, acting on Lincoln's Amnesty Proclamation in late 1863, approached Secretary of the Treasury Salmon P. Chase to help bring the state back into the Union fold and to reconstruct a loyal state government. Chase, wishing to be nominated as the Republican candidate for President in 1864, thought that if a government could be formed in Florida, the quasi-state delegates would support him. Chase's friends began to urge Gillmore to undertake an expedition to help the Florida Unionists and to recruit black soldiers from the interior as he swept through the state. Additionally, a successful campaign would open up a market for cotton, turpentine, lumber, and other products as well as prevent the Confederacy from utilizing the state's large cattle herds to feed troops.[46]

The army envisioned an advance by Brigadier General Seymour up the St. John's River to establish small depots on the west bank. Union leaders hoped this would give the Union forces control of the northeastern part of Florida. Part of the operation involved an elaborate feint on John's Island. Brigadier General Alexander Schimmelfennig was ordered to make this diversion. His instructions included transporting troops from Kiawah Island to Seabrooks Island on the night of 8 February in order to attack Confederates on John's Island on the morning of the ninth. Schimmelfennig's men crossed over to John's Island and drove in the enemy pickets. On the eleventh, they pushed forward three miles and then withdrew that night. Schimmelfennig's movement was designed to keep the Confederate troops in the Charleston area from being sent to Florida to operate against General Seymour's forces. *Nipsic* and the screw tug *Iris* steamed to Edisto to cooperate with this diversionary movement.[47]

Gillmore requested two or three gunboats to assist landing troops on the west bank of the St. John's River. Dahlgren, who also longed for action, took an interest in this expedition and left to direct his forces personally. General in Chief Halleck attached "very little importance" to military operations of this nature, but he approved the quest for recruits and agricultural products. Yet it seems as though the entire campaign was designed from start to finish to secure "booty from within enemy lines."[48]

Dahlgren ordered the small screw steamers *Ottawa* and *Norwich*, already stationed at the mouth of the St. John's River, to convoy army troops to Jacksonville. He also dispatched *Mahaska, Dai Ching,* and *Water Witch* to the St. John's. On the morning of 6 February, the army transport *Island City* arrived carrying Gillmore and his staff. *Norwich* guided *Island City* over the bar and just after 7:00 A.M., anchored. The senior officer, Lieutenant Commander S. Livingston Breese, suggested *Norwich* be sent up river to cut off the escape of the steamer *St. Mary's,* a blockade runner waiting in the river to run past the blockaders. The army opposed this sortie believing it would inform the rebels of the Union intentions.[49]

The next morning army transports began to arrive and *Maple Leaf* and *General Hunter* steamed over the bar. At 10:10 *Norwich* stood up the river ahead of the transports. The piebald collection of transports carrying cavalry, artillery, and infantry followed at a distance. *Norwich* arrived at Jacksonville at 3:20 that afternoon with the transport *Maple Leaf,* Seymour's flagship, close astern. Federal troops began landing at 3:40 as the other transports arrived at the wharf. Jacksonville was for a fourth time under Union occupation. Since the Confederates did not contest the landing, the *Norwich* moved farther up the river to block the escape of the *St. Mary's.* Acting Master Frank B. Meriam of *Norwich* placed a picket boat at the mouth of McGirt's Creek to keep the *St. Mary's* from escaping. *Ottawa* came up later that night and remained in Jacksonville to protect the transports. [50]

On the ninth the Union forces continued to arrive. *Water Witch, Mahaska, Dai Ching,* and the tugs *Oleander* and *Dandelion* came up to support the operation. The naval forces did not pursue the *St. Mary's,* learning that the rebels sank her. Dahlgren reached Jacksonville later that day and conferred with Gillmore to determine the needs of the Union forces ashore. When Seymour's fifty-five hundred troops advanced inland, Dahlgren departed, feeling his presence no longer necessary. He left *Mahaska, Ottawa,* and *Norwich* at anchor off the town.[51]

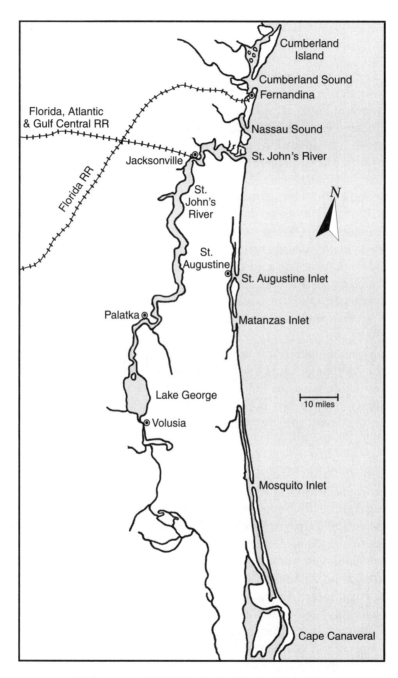

MAP 10.   NORTHEAST COAST OF FLORIDA

The army troops departed Jacksonville and moved west with plans to destroy the bridges of the Florida, Atlantic and Gulf Central Railroad passing over the Suwanne River. On 20 February, marching through low flat pine forests, Seymour was met near Olustee by about five thousand troops under Brigadier General Joseph Finegan. In a sharp fight that lasted several hours the Confederates overwhelmed the Union forces at dusk. Seymour, thinking fifteen thousand men had attacked him, left Olustee in full retreat having suffered 1,861 casualties, about one-third of his force. The Confederates might have won a major victory had they pursued the Union forces. The Confederates had suffered about 750 casualties and were content to let Seymour's forces retreat back to Jacksonville.[52]

The Battle of Olustee would be the largest battle in Florida during the war. Once Seymour arrived back at Jacksonville, the gunboats remained in the river as a force multiplier and to keep communications open as Seymour fortified the town. The gunboats remained active for some time patrolling the waters above Jacksonville and destroyed boats and flats that might aid the Confederates wishing to cross the river in force.[53]

Combined operations along the St. John's River as far up river as Palatka continued. On 11 March, about seventy-five miles upriver on the west bank, the army landed forces at Palatka in an attempt to make this area another strong point. Naval forces kept communications open and secure from enemy troops along this one hundred miles of the St. John's River. During this campaign, however, the Confederate forces demonstrated the vulnerability of ships to torpedoes in confined waters. In April, the army lost both the transports *Maple Leaf* and *General Hunter* in the St. John's River to torpedoes. During this time, Seymour's officers continually besieged the navy for more force in the St. John's. But the entire campaign would be short-lived. A skirmish on 27 March convinced the Union leaders it would be difficult to keep garrisons on the west bank without a large expenditure of men and assets. The army withdrew from Palatka on 4 April, having accomplished little but tying up the naval forces unnecessarily.[54]

This movement into northeast Florida was made possible solely by naval support. The Union forces again moved into the state with little or no planning, nor did they attempt to coordinate the efforts with other forces. This operation was carried out without consulting the commander of the East Gulf Blockading Squadron. Rear Admiral Theodorus Bailey wrote that not only would he have wished to cooperate, but he could also have supplied an additional fifteen hunded men to make a diversionary attack to pull troops away from the northeastern part of the state.[55]

A Trip North

Despite the delays, Dahlgren remained anxious to attack Charleston, and asked the department's permission to visit the capital to discuss future operations. Before receiving his answer, he wrote again on 18 February to inquire if the department still wished him to attack and, if so, what the department expected of him. He reiterated his concern of the earlier proviso that stated he should attack Charleston only if he could guarantee success. Dahlgren believed that this stipulation would keep him from making an attempt. He wrote, "It rarely happens that a commander can promise even to himself an absolute certainly of success unless his advantage of numbers or position are decided." He reiterated that he could not guarantee success without complete knowledge of the nature of the torpedoes and the obstructions. He believed that the department had minimized the dangers, particularly of the torpedoes, to an attack. Dahlgren received a reply on 22 February from Welles, stating that he would "be glad" to see him for a few days. Dahlgren met with Captain Rowan and left him in command of the squadron. Boarding the *Harvest Moon*, Dahlgren crossed the Charleston bar on his way to Washington after midnight on 27 February.[56]

Leaving the burdens of command behind, Dahlgren wrote in his diary that the cold northwester that drove against the *Harvest Moon* invigorated him. On 2 March, he arrived in Washington and visited Welles and then Fox. The following day he dropped in to visit the president, but missed him. Dahlgren's earlier visit with Fox left him despondent. Despite the department's hearty approval of Dahlgren's activity, the Assistant Secretary of the Navy related the department's views of a renewed attack on Charleston. He told the admiral that an assault would have to be successful or that it should not be undertaken. Fox told Dahlgren that the government could not afford a defeat with the presidential reelection coming soon. More distressing to the admiral was the department's plans to send the new monitors to Farragut at Mobile. Dahlgren now fully realized the operations were to be suspended indefinitely. He wrote that he was "averse to holding a command when I was expected to do something yet could do nothing."[57]

Early in the day on 4 March, Lincoln sent Dahlgren a message that his son, Ulric, was missing in action after a raid on Richmond. Troubled by this news and the department's decision to maintain the status quo at Charleston, Dahlgren, on 5 March, asked to be relieved of command. This news "astonished" Welles. Both Fox and Welles tried to change his mind and told the admiral that they were satisfied with his efforts. Welles pondered this request for a day and then told Dahlgren that he wanted him to remain in command and that he would not assent to his request to be relieved.[58]

On 8 March, Dahlgren received word of Ulric's death. This was a crushing blow to his psyche. He spent over a week at Fort Monroe hoping to recover his son's body and sadly returned to Washington without his son. On 21 March, he made another short trip to Fort Monroe and remained for two days, again hoping to retrieve his son's remains. Dahlgren, though, once again returned to Washington without Ulric.[59]

On 25 March, the department sent for the admiral to talk about future operations at Charleston. Speaking to Fox first, Dahlgren reminded the assistant secretary that the new monitors had been promised to him for six months and to send these warships farther south would be unjust. Dahlgren asked for a temporary addition of ten thousand to fifteen thousand troops, the monitors *Onondaga*, *Tecumseh*, *Canonicus*, and *Manhattan* and the screw sloop *Brooklyn*. With twelve ironclads and the frigate *New Ironsides* he believed he could take Charleston. Fox told Dahlgren that Lieutenant General Ulysses S. Grant's proposed campaign in eastern Virginia would now take precedence. Fox, showing much more reserve than he had with Du Pont, continued to doubt that an attack would succeed. But Dahlgren insisted that a "trial should be made," whereby Fox answered that "everyone considered the project abandoned." For the next couple of weeks Dahlgren continued to meet with Fox and Welles while he waited for his son's remains to arrive. Dahlgren, realizing that the department did not favor a purely naval attack, suggested the navy pursue combined operations on the north side of the harbor at Long Island. The goal of this combined venture would be the capture of the works on Sullivan's Island. Welles agreed with this plan and forwarded it to Stanton.[60]

During Dahlgren's trip north, the Confederates sent the *David* on another sortie. Since her attack on the *New Ironsides* she had been improved and now carried quarter-inch boiler iron above the waterline to protect the vessel and crew from small arms fire. Workmen also changed her spar torpedo arrangement so that it not only could be lowered to the desired depth, but it could also be deployed from the conning station. In addition, a shield protected the top of the stack to prevent water from dousing the boiler fires as had happened during her attack of the *New Ironsides*.[61]

General Beauregard, anxious for more success with this craft, requested Flag Officer John Tucker send her to attack Union vessels in the Stono River. Tucker ordered the *David*, under command of Lieutenant James Tomb, to sortie against the Union ships. On the night of 4 March, he steered the little craft down the North Edisto River. When he approached close enough to see the lights on the closest vessel, the *David's* pumps failed and he abandoned the attack. A second attempt the next night was a repeat of the night before. Again the pumps failed at nearly the same spot at the same time. Calmly Tomb guided the *David* into the nearby marsh and made repairs and then got her underway at about midnight. At 12:30 A.M. on the sixth, he approached the blockader *Memphis* and steamed within hailing distance before the watch spotted the craft. The officer of the deck ordered the crew on *Memphis* beat to quarters and the chain slipped as the *David* rapidly approached. Small arms fire began to pepper the torpedo craft and within moments the torpedo struck the *Memphis* under her port quarter. The torpedo armed with 95 pounds of powder, 30 more than had been used on the *New Ironsides*, however, failed to explode. Tomb veered off to port and turned around to try again. The *Memphis*, now underway, became a more difficult target. Tomb aimed the *David* at the blockader and "at good speed" he struck the *Memphis* a glancing blow on the starboard quarter; once again the torpedo failed to explode. Tomb realized that he could do nothing more and took *David* back up the river.[62]

After returning to Church Flats, Tomb examined the warhead and it was found defective. Had it exploded, it would likely have blown the stern entirely off the *Memphis*. In April, fitted with a new torpedo, Tomb took the *David* out once more, this time to attack the *Wabash* off Charleston. Ensign Charles Craven, the officer of the deck, spotted *David* 150 yards away from the frigate, but she never got much closer. A heavy swell rolling over the little craft forced her to turn back three times as *Wabash* slipped her anchor chain and got underway. Thwarted once again, Tomb abandoned his attack.[63]

On 23 April, Welles ordered Dahlgren back to Port Royal. Dahlgren's hopes of a prompt attack on Charleston were dashed with the certain news that the next two ironclads finished would go to support operations in Virginia. General Halleck had also cast doubts that the iron-clads could take Charleston or make enough difference to aid an army attack. Dahlgren, wishing to recover his son's remains, had by this time become "inconsolable." On 28 April, before boarding the *Harvest Moon* to sail south, he made one last visit to the Navy Department. He told Welles that without more monitors the department could not ex-pect any results and that the secretary "could only expect me to hold on." Since the immediate efforts of both the army and navy would be to support Grant's move on Richmond, Welles told Dahlgren that this "was all he expected" from him.[64]

The Bad News Gets Worse

The *Harvest Moon* dropped anchor in Port Royal on 2 May. The fol-lowing day Rowan hauled down his broad pennant when Dahlgren re-sumed command of the squadron. During Dahlgren's two-month ab-sence, Rowan essentially maintained the status quo within the entire command. The day before Dahlgren returned, Gillmore relinquished his command of the Department of the South. He left on a steamer heading north as Dahlgren entered Port Royal Harbor. Gillmore would take with him his Tenth Corps, constituting twenty thousand men, to augment the Army of the James. This was bittersweet news to Dahlgren. While he de-spised Gillmore, this served another blow to the admiral, who realized there was no hope of immediate operations against Charleston. During a 4 May meeting with Gillmore's replacement, Brigadier General John P. Hatch, Dahlgren learned firsthand that Gillmore had indeed been the source of the newspaper attacks and had used him as a scapegoat for the failures off Charleston. Dahlgren wrote the somber note in his diary, "Here is patriotism for you and honor, & honesty!"[65]

With the knowledge that no joint action would be likely at Charles-ton, Dahlgren decided to gather his ironclad captains together to discuss options for operations. On 9 May, at the point of convening the meet-ing, however, Rowan sent him a note claiming that Dr. Marius Duvall, the surgeon of the *New Ironsides* reported to the Navy Department that both Rowan and his executive officer, George E. Belknap, had made "disparaging remarks" about the flag officer. Duvall, a continuous mal-content, had alienated many on board the *New Ironsides*. A subsequent Court of Inquiry concluded that no one had spoken in a disrespectful manner. Yet, this was another instance of division within the ranks. Rowan later court-martialed Duvall for conduct unbecoming an officer, but Welles and Fox interceded to keep him from being dismissed from service.[66]

Dahlgren again called his ironclad captains for a conference. The next day at 11:00 A.M. he convened a Council of War on the flagship. Concluding nothing the first day, the officers met again on the twelfth. During the meetings the men seemed to have had no clear conception of the problem to be solved, other than the ironclads making some attempt to force their way into the harbor. The goals beyond this step seemed obscured. On the afternoon of the twelfth, the men discussed whether to attack Fort Sumter and reduce all its offensive and defensive capabilities. Seven of the officers voted no and only two voted yes. This vote convinced Dahlgren that with the ironclads at hand, he could not attack. It was clear that all concerned believed any attack would be ill advised and would accomplish little or nothing. The department had already made its policy clear in letters to Dahlgren in October and November—he was not to take any risks because the country could not afford a defeat.[67]

Yet the overall problem was more comprehensive than this. The department had clearly stated that it desired the squadron to operate against Charleston, but it complicated the situation by weighing all the risks on the political scale. The officers, however, believed they were "groping in the dark." Writing years later, then-Admiral Stephen Luce stated, "There was no one there that seemed to understand the problem to be solved and able to state it in precise terms." Just like Du Pont, Dahlgren was being asked to solve an insolvable problem—the capture of Charleston without the cooperation of the army. Additionally, the department had instructed Dahlgren he was not to fail.[68]

On the fourteenth, Dahlgren relayed the information of the Council of War to the department. He also reported that the army had only 14,500 men and would now be capable only of defensive operations. With this knowledge, the known improvements to the Confederate defenses, and the department's desires to support operations along the James River and afterwards against Mobile, Dahlgren expressed his apprehensions. It appeared that he would have no opportunity to operate actively against the rebels. Dahlgren's sole purpose for accepting command of the squadron was for some grand action that would satisfy his quest for glory. Without any prospect of quenching this need he asked once again to be relieved.[69]

While awaiting an answer, Dahlgren sent his ironclads to keep Fort Sumter under fire. He hoped to demolish the improvements made by the Confederates during the winter. They had strengthened the walls by adding ten feet of pine timber, palmetto trees, and ballasted debris to cushion enemy shell fire. Dahlgren tested this material in March. For four days, beginning on the thirteenth of May, he sent two monitors each day off the sea face to fire in conjunction with the batteries on Morris Island. The monitors fired from a position that did not fully expose them to the guns of Fort Moultrie. During these four days the Union forces fired over eleven hundred shots at the fort and did relatively little damage. Dahlgren concluded that the monitors were really receiving more damage than they inflicted. With enemy shots scoring the armor, striking under the overhangs, and causing leaks, he called off the naval attacks. These would be the last shots fired at Fort Sumter by the navy during the war.[70]

Further Defeat

On 24 May, the naval vessels were asked to cooperate in a combined movement designed to cut the Charleston and Savannah Railroad. A diversionary move by the navy up the South Edisto River was designed to mask the real thrust up the Ashepoo River. Dahlgren sent the side-wheel ferryboat *Commodore McDonough*, the screw steamers *Chippewa* and *E. B. Hale*, and the Coast Survey steamer *Vixen* to assist. Charles Boutelle boarded *Vixen* to sound the narrow and twisting channel as they ran upstream. These warships steamed up the South Edisto as a diversion. Here the naval force landed Marines and two howitzers and to make the feint more convincing, they marched inland. At 7:35 on the morning of the twenty sixth, the landing party opened fire on Willstown, South Carolina. At 11:30 the *McDonough* and the *Hale* also opened fire for a couple of hours to support the men ashore. That afternoon the Marines and howitzers fell back and were reembarked.[71]

The *Dai Ching* accompanied the army portion of the expedition up the Ashepoo. The army transports arrived piecemeal and without the proper pilots. To make matters worse, Brigadier General William Birney failed to coordinate the action of his transports, and two of them headed upstream rather than waiting for the naval force. Around midnight, the transport *Boston* ran aground well above her naval support. In the morning, with a pilot on board, the *Dai Ching* steamed up the Ashepoo River to the sounds of gunfire. She found the *Boston* under a brisk fire with nearly all the troops ashore. Lieutenant Commander James C. Chaplin brought his guns to bear on the rebel battery and drove the gunners away. The transport *Plato* arrived to bring off the army troops with General Birney on board. Chaplin asked Birney if the *Dai Ching* might try to save the transport. Birney, however, had already decided to burn her and retire. The transport *Plato* reembarked the "panic-stricken" soldiers while the *Dai Ching* covered the retreat. The expedition failed miserably and left the naval officers "galled at the business."[72]

Farther south in the St. John's River, the navy continued its support of army operations. The warships escorted and ferried troops on various missions and kept communications open along the river between the different army posts. In early May, a Confederate torpedo again sank another army transport, the *Harriet A. Weed*. Dahlgren, who realized that this might have been one his ships, had his gunboats picket the river to keep the Confederates from putting down any more torpedoes. He later had the river swept with small boats to find and destroy these weapons.[73]

When Gillmore took the Tenth Corps north, the remaining Union troops found themselves on the defensive and continually threatened. The Confederates, now bolder, could with greater hope of success strike any of the detached posts. The rivers and the gunboats served as the only connection between the garrisons stretched along the St. John's River. The Union posts in Florida were the most exposed. Realizing this weakness, the Confederates attacked.

When Union leaders perceived a threat at Volusia, Florida, they sent reinforcements by water to keep the garrison safe. On 21 May, the *Ottawa* and the small side-wheel tug *Columbine* steamed up the St. John's River with the army transport *Charles Houghton*. Carrying nearly seven hundred men, these vessels disembarked the troops below Volusia at Palatka. *Columbine*, with a draft of just under six feet, continued up-river to Volusia; the *Ottawa* anchored and remained behind to protect the *Houghton*. Unexpectedly, four Confederate field pieces, under the command of Captain John J. Dickison, began to fire on *Ottawa* and *Houghton*. Dickison concealed his artillery well and the naval gunners could only return fire, aiming at the flashes of the rebel guns. The large 150-pound rifled gun of *Ottawa* eventually forced the rebels to retreat after a brief engagement.[74]

Columbine, carrying a small detachment of the Thirty-fifth U.S. Infantry steamed fifty miles upriver and arrived at the Volusia Bar at 11:30 P.M. on the twenty-second. Acting Ensign Frank Sanborn sent a boat over the bar the next morning to communicate with the army garrison. At noon on the twenty-third, *Columbine* weighed anchor and steamed back down the river to Welaka. Here Sanborn communicated with the army again, and then continued down river. He called all hands to quarters as the tug approached a landing that he expected would conceal an enemy force. The *Columbine* shelled the woods as she progressed and the Confederates, again under Captain Dickison, returned the fire. *Columbine*, armed with only two 20-pounder guns, fought against two concealed pieces of artillery and sharpshooters. *Columbine*, protected by an addition of fifty sandbags and bales of hay, however, was no match for the field pieces. The second enemy shot cut the wheel chains and at the same time the pilot panicked and jumped off the ship. The *Columbine* swung toward the bank and another enemy shell struck the main steam pipe. The *Columbine*, with no power or means of steering, ran aground. The naval gunners replied to the hail of canister, solid shot, and small arms fire. The infantry on board the *Columbine* began to abandon ship and swim ashore. At this point, the engineer reported to Sanborn that the engines could not be repaired. With no hope of escape, Sanborn surrendered the ship. The gunfire killed Acting Master's Mate John Davis, but the rest of the naval crew survived. Army losses were about twenty-one killed and wounded. The rebels burned the *Columbine* to the water's edge rather than trying to save her.[75]

The loss of *Columbine* distressed Dahlgren. He lamented to Welles the risks that the small lightly armed steamers faced in narrow rivers. They were vulnerable to concealed enemy batteries at all times without warning, and once under fire they could not maneuver to escape. Furthermore, the armament on most of these vessels was usually "too trifling to be of much account." The loss of *Columbine* he believed would be critical, since she had a draft of under six feet, one of only three in the entire squadron of similar draft.[76]

Loss of the *Water Witch*

Despite the inherent dangers of enemy action, torpedoes, and commerce raiders, a large number of the men rarely saw an enemy craft or even spotted enemy soldiers ashore. The warships lay at anchor at day and often at night in the confined waters with little chance of action. The blockading ships off Charleston had the capability of supporting one another. But the blockaders lying in the small inlets and the calm backwater sounds faced complete separation. The 580-ton side-wheel steamer *Water Witch* stationed in Ossabaw Sound was no exception. Usually alone, she watched the water approaches to the back door of Savannah. This isolation, however, spawned Confederate plans to capture this blockader by a boarding party.[77]

Flag Officer William W. Hunter, commanding the Confederate naval forces at Savannah, authorized an expedition to capture the blockader. He assigned the project to Lieutenant Thomas Postell Pelot, the executive officer of the CSS *Georgia*. Pelot assembled 7 boats, 15 officers, and 117 men. Most came from the floating battery *Georgia*, the ironclad ram *Savannah*, and the gunboat *Sampson*. These men appeared to one observer to be "carefully selected for the enterprise."[78]

The group left the *Georgia* on the afternoon of 31 May and dropped down the Vernon River in tow of the steam tender *Firefly*. Casting off from the *Firefly* at 5:00 P.M. the men reached the battery at Beaulieu on the Vernon River at 9:00 that evening. Here they camped for the night. The next day scouts reported a gunboat lying at anchor in the Little Ogeechee River. That night Pelot and seven boats dropped down the river in search for this gunboat. Probing until nearly morning, they found nothing. Realizing that the gunboat had changed her position, Pelot wrote Hunter that the "bird had flown." Pelot asked Hunter for more time, sure that the blockader would return. The next day, 2 June, he sent out scouts to once again locate his prey.[79]

At 8:00 that night the boats pulled away from the battery at Beaulieu in dark squally weather. The boats formed two columns and they proceeded with muffled oars. Pelot picked up his scouts, who had located the Union vessel just off Bradley's River. Waiting until midnight, the boats began pulling cautiously toward the blockader *Water Witch*. The boats advanced in two columns through the rain, which concealed the boats from the deck of the Union ship. Lieutenant Pelot led the port column and Lieutenant Joseph Price led the starboard column. The boarding party managed to pull within about thirty yards of the steamer before lightning betrayed its presence. The watch on the ship hailed the boats. "Ship ahoy! Who goes there?" The Confederate boats were so close by now that they no longer needed to conceal their identity and the reply was, "Go to hell, you sons of bitches."[80]

On deck, the watch sprung the rattle, and the men rushed to their battle stations. The engineers started the engines, but inexplicably shut them down after only one or two revolutions. The rebels grabbed at the bulwarks and climbed over the triced up anti-boarding netting as the Union tars fought back with cutlasses and small arms. Pelot gained the deck first and was instantly killed by a shot in the heart.[81]

Hearing the commotion, Lieutenant Commander Austin Pendergrast, the commanding officer, reached the deck before the Confederates managed to board his ship. He ordered, "Call all hands to repel boarders, slip the chain, and start the engine." He then hurried to his stateroom for weapons and clothing, but was struck senseless by a blow from a cutlass. Minutes later Pendergrast regained consciousness, only to faint from loss of blood. The Union officers resisted desperately and many were wounded in the struggle. Pendergrast, however, claimed that many of his sixty-five enlisted men were "paralyzed with fear" and did not fight back. Thus, the fight began briskly, but ended in about ten minutes.[82]

The Confederates took their prize up the Vernon River to White Bluff. They attempted for some time to get her to Savannah to bolster the defenses there, with no success. The close and intense fight cost the Confederates the life of Pelot, five others killed, and seventeen wounded. The Union suffered two killed and twelve wounded. All the surviving crew was captured, with the exception of a black contraband, Peter McIntosh, who jumped over the side and was rescued from the south end of Ossabaw Island.[83]

This event alarmed Dahlgren and forced him to take stronger measures for the defense of his vessels. He told Welles that the capture of the *Water Witch* was partially due to the fact that she had not been fitted with log outriggers and netting around the vessel. To discourage enemy boarding parties and torpedo boats, he ordered his warships on the inside blockade to take positions on the outside until these could be rigged. These apparatuses, however, made these vessels much less capable of moving after a blockade runner or running from torpedo craft. Fitted with the log outriggers, escape from an attacking Confederate cruiser would be impossible. The commanding officers now had to be careful when investigating suspicious vessels. The gunboats likewise had to take stations where they could support each other. Dahlgren also issued an order warning his officers to "omit no precaution," instructed them to stack arms and boarding pikes on the decks before dark, and ordered each man of the watch to be armed with a bowie knife.[84]

Dahlgren reminded the secretary of the limitations he faced in making the blockade strict while keeping his warships secure. He had sixteen sailing vessels in use as blockaders and he believed these ships could manage well as long as they could remain at anchor. Currently, he also had thirteen vessels under repair, which diminished his force to the point that it compromised the blockade. Additionally, Welles learned that the squadron had a shortage of 1,360 men. The *Water Witch* alone had a deficit of seventeen men at the time of her capture, a hint that she might have been able to defend herself properly had this shortage been remedied. Dahlgren lamented that the loss of the *Water Witch* would force him to remove one of his more powerful vessels from the Charleston Blockade to Ossabaw Sound. He also sent another vessel to aid the monitor at Wassaw, and withdrew all the vessels from the inside blockades south of Ossabaw Sound, "thereby disorganizing the efficiency of the blockade and giving the rebels more scope."[85]

Pendergrast faced a court-martial over the loss of his vessel, the charge "culpable inefficiency in the discharge of duty." The court convicted him of failing to take proper measures to insure the safety of his vessel from attack and leaving the deck in charge of an officer that was neither competent nor vigilant. In the deliberations, the Court of Inquiry also found the acting first and third engineers culpable. Tried in absentia, Pendergrast was found guilty of failing to secure his ship. His sentence was suspension from duty for two years from the date of the sentence on half pay, with loss of rank during the period of his suspension.[86]

New Commander, New Hope

When Gillmore departed, the Department of the South was reorganized. In May Brigadier General Hatch took temporary command, but he was relieved on 26 May by Major General John G. Foster. Foster was considered both competent and aggressive. In mid-June Dahlgren proposed to Foster that a combined force enter the inlet above Sullivan's Island with five thousand men. With the support of the gunboats he believed they could seize a position in the rear of the defenses and possibly force the Confederates to withdraw. In conjunction with this move he suggested a feint up the Stono River to draw away Confederate forces. Foster considered this particular operation too risky and, after pondering other "notions," the discussions ended with no agreement.[87]

The talks between the two continued and, on the twenty-seventh, Dahlgren and Foster agreed to try an expedition up the North Edisto or Ashepoo river to cut the Charleston and Savannah Railroad. Dahlgren was interested in this particular expedition because intelligence gathering reported that the Confederates planned to attack the blockade with both their ironclads, as well as other warships, to protect a large shipment of cotton from Darien, Georgia. Foster convinced Dahlgren to cut the railroad first and then think about securing the cotton. Both eventually settled on a move up the North Edisto and the Stono rivers.[88]

Dahlgren and Foster agreed to send General Schimmelfenning up the Stono River to land at Legareville with one thousand men on the night of 1 July. Another two thousand men would disembark that same night on Cole's Island to advance toward Secessionville. The plan called for General Hatch to land with four thousand men at Seabrook's Island and advance inland. General Birney was to transport his troops up the North Edisto River as far as possible and land them to destroy the railroad. Designed generally as a "demonstration," Dahlgren and Foster planned to exploit any enemy weaknesses.[89]

Dahlgren sent the monitors *Lehigh* and *Montauk*, the gunboats *Pawnee*, and *McDonough*, and the mortar schooner *Racer* to cooperate with army forces in the Stono River. He assigned *Dai Ching*, the screw steamer *Wamsutta* and the side wheel gunboat *Geranium* to support Birney's men up the North Edisto. The scheduled movement of these vessels kept Dahlgren anxious because none of the ships reached their stations on the eve of the operations. Should weather or tides intervene, it could impede the warships and cause a delay in at least the Stono River part of the expedition.[90]

For the Stono operation Dahlgren initially sent the *Dai Ching* there early to send boats in advance to drag for torpedoes. The side-wheel steamer *Oleander* arrived later with a torpedo raft to sweep for torpedoes. The *Winona* towed the *Montauk* and the *Acacia* towed the *Lehigh* to the Stono Bar, but both had to wait for a high tide to get across the bar. On the afternoon of Saturday, 2 July, the *Lehigh* and *Montauk* crossed the Stono Bar with the help of the *Harvest Moon*. General Schimmelfenning's men meanwhile landed on Cole's Island. Dahlgren steamed up the Stono on *Philadelphia* and then transferred his flag to *Montauk* late that afternoon. As the monitors steamed up the narrow channel, the helmsmen found the ironclads difficult to steer. On the flood tide the rudders and propellers lay exposed to enemy fire. In one narrow portion of the channel *Montauk* touched bottom with no harm. The pilot was reluctant to go farther and that night the naval vessels anchored below Grimball's Plantation.[91]

The North Edisto expedition progressed as planned. Birney disembarked his troops at White Point on the evening of the second and his men bivouacked near the Dawho River. Birney's force included thirty-five Marines that manned two howitzers. At 5:15 A.M. the next morning, they began to advance and had not traveled but one thousand yards before Confederate skirmishers began firing at the column. Birney pushed the enemy skirmishers back and drove his men three miles inland. Here, with just over twelve hundred men, he halted in front of an enemy earthwork and probed the defenses in a desultory fashion. Of the three naval vessels assigned to support Birney, only the *Geranium* was able to advance far enough to fire at the rebel batteries. The Union gunboats in the Dawho River made an effort to assist the troops ashore, but generally were out of range. Even the little revenue cutter *Nemaha* was pressed into service to carry General Foster and to land troops. She later provided gunfire support. That afternoon Birney withdrew "leisurely" with only six men wounded. Reembarking his men, he joined the operations in the Stono on the fourth.[92]

On the morning of the third, the warships in the Stono River prepared to move up the river. Dahlgren boarded the *Montauk* at 9:50 and about twenty minutes later the naval vessels began their advance. At 10:40 the *Montauk* fired the first gun, sweeping the ground in front of Schimmelfenning's positions. The *Lehigh, Pawnee,* and *McDonough,* joined by the two mortar schooners *Para* and *Racer,* fired on Battery Pringle. Later that afternoon some of Schimmelfenning's troops embarked in boats. They pulled from the tip of Morris Island to assault Battery Simkins on the extreme right at Lazaretto Creek. Most of the boats, however, ran aground and the men abandoned the assault. Five boats carrying 141 officers and men landed and captured the battery, but surrendered after the remaining force failed to support them. Hatch, who landed on John's Island, meanwhile, marched his troops in a position to hold the left. Hatch, however, never advanced much beyond the covering fire of the naval vessels.[93]

The vessels continued to fire "moderately" at the Confederate positions in support of the operations. Schimmelfenning was particularly complimentary of the naval fire support. He wrote Dahlgren that the gunfire drove the enemy from their rifle pits and prevented the rebels from erecting more earthworks. He thought that he would have to advance later and the fire of the monitors would "undoubtedly save many lives on our side, for which I desire to express to them my thanks."[94]

On Tuesday the fifth Dahlgren accompanied generals Foster and Hatch ashore. About 4:00 P.M. they rode along the southern bank of the Stono River to examine the rebel works. An engineer who rode with them pronounced the defenses too strong to assault. Dahlgren, meanwhile, ordered his warships to continue shelling the Confederate positions. On the seventh *Pawnee, McDonough, Para,* and *Racer* maintained a steady fire, and continued throughout the night. The next day generals Foster and Hatch boarded the *Philadelphia.* They told Dahlgren that the Confederates were too strong and that they would withdraw their forces. This was a bitter pill for Dahlgren to swallow. The admiral believed that the army had made little effort to advance and did not truly test the Confederate defenses. He wrote in his diary, "I am utterly disgusted—the troops will not fight—that is the plain truth—and Foster's a humbug."[95]

The naval vessels, therefore, began their preparations to assist in the withdrawal. After dark on 9 July, the troops began to reembark slowly on the transports. The naval vessels continued their fire fight with Battery Pringle, which during the preceding six days had often seen heavy and accurate exchanges from both sides. By Sunday afternoon all but a few stragglers had embarked on the army transports to be carried down the river. The naval vessels remained in the Stono until Monday morning the eleventh, to allow any stragglers "an opportunity of escaping."[96]

On the heels of the withdrawal, Dahlgren finally received an answer to his 14 May request to be relieved. Welles attributed the two-month delay to "embarrassments to the department in relation to the several commands . . ." Welles closed his letter with an ambiguous statement. It seemed to imply that should another officer come along that could relieve Dahlgren, Welles would replace him. By July Dahlgren was nearly worn out and would have welcomed being relieved. The commanding officer of the *Harvest Moon*, Acting Volunteer Lieutenant Joshua Warren, observed that Dahlgren was always the last to go to sleep and the first to awake. In July 1864 he remarked, "I don't think the Admiral has had his boots off for three weeks."[97] Welles, though, needed Dahlgren to remain off Charleston. The department had in mind two separate attacks, one at Mobile and the other at Wilmington. But neither included Dahlgren. The navy had relegated this part of the coast a low priority. Dahlgren had thus far maintained the status quo and this was sufficient for the department.

Dahlgren's disappointment grew every day. The glory he sought when he accepted this command would probably never be possible. In fact, he had not even come close. Dahlgren, tired of the "public abuse," fully realized that any offensive move within this theatre was "entirely dependent on those of the Army." The army forces, however, did not have the strength for a major offensive thrust against the strong Confederate defenses. Five days after Welles's refusal to accept his resignation, he wrote Dahlgren again. Anticipating using the monitors in the South Atlantic Blockading Squadron for other projects, Welles asked the admiral if he could hold Charleston and maintain the blockade without the ironclads. If so, could the army hold Morris Island with only the wooden vessels protecting them? Dahlgren must have believed that his star had finally set.[98]

— 11 —

"The Rebellion Is Shut Out
from the Ocean"

Blockade Running Revival

Despite the Navy Department's relegation of the South Atlantic seaboard to an area of secondary importance, keeping the status quo at Charleston continued to be exacting. The blockade of this port had virtually shut it off from the outside. The presence of the monitors in the main ship channel and the subsequent placement of picket boats inside the bar, close to the harbor's mouth, made it extremely difficult and risky for the blockade runners to test the blockade. Yet in the spring and summer of 1864, the port of Charleston saw a revival in this trade, renewing a challenge for Dahlgren.

For nearly six months, from 16 August 1863 until 2 March 1864, not a single steam blockade runner managed to make a successful trip into Charleston. But this changed radically that spring. There were four ships in particular that had a large role in reviving the trade—the *Chicora*, *Syren*, *Druid*, and *Fox*. Charleston-based companies owned all four, and for the remainder of the year, these four small but fast blockade runners would make twenty-four successful voyages into Charleston. These trips amounted to sixty-three percent of all successful runs into the port during this period.[1]

The blockade-running trade at Charleston was not nearly as brisk as that at Wilmington, North Carolina, but this renewed activity certainly gained the attention of Dahlgren and Captain Green, the senior officer off Charleston. Green reported the escape or entrance of a single vessel as "unpleasant news." By June 1864 Green's greatest problem was logistical in nature. When the *Fannie* escaped Charleston on the eleventh, only two small steamers and a tug lay on the outside station. The three fastest blockaders, *Canandaigua* (under repair), *Winona* (replaced *Water Witch* in Ossabaw Sound), and *Nipsic* (away for coal), were absent. Dahlgren's forces were spread thin and he had no others to replace these three. He currently had five other ships north for repairs, two cripples awaiting repairs, and three others supporting operations in the St. John's River.[2]

The blockade of Charleston required a large number of ships. Dahlgren's basic tactical configuration by mid-1864 consisted of two lines of blockaders. His five ironclads supported by four tugs anchored within the bar. The monitors' guns commanded a large area and complicated the evasion of the blockade. The four tugs with boats served as pickets for the monitors to give warning of torpedo boats or the approach of the enemy ironclads. The boats took their stations farther into the harbor to give notice of ships running outward. Outside he placed six screw steamers—none, however, with a great deal of speed. At night, three of these sailed off southward to watch the coast for blockade runners. Green was instructed to have the others watch Maffitt's Channel after dark. The success of the Confederate cruisers, however, made it necessary for the weaker warships to remain within signal distance of other Union ships.[3]

By mid-August Dahlgren had an additional three gunboats and five tugs to augment the blockade. On 29 August, Green stationed the relatively small screw steamers *Azalea*, *Acacia*, and *Sweet Brier* off Maffitt's Channel, a thoroughfare that Green suspected accommodated many of the blockade runners. He also dispatched the screw steamer *Laburnum* to Bull Bay to watch for ships trying to violate the blockade in the inlets north of Charleston. The additional ships allowed Green to send two of his faster ships off shore during the day, one to the north and the other southward. These vessels returned to their inshore stations at dark. At night, because of the threat of torpedo boats, Green kept all his vessels moving when the weather permitted.[4]

On 3 September, the escape of the large side-wheel steamer *General Whiting* had the Union officers looking for more answers. Seven warships lay at their stations along the route of the escape. Lookouts on six of the blockaders never reported seeing anything, even when signals alerted them of the presence of an escaping steamer. Had some of the warships been in position to chase the blockade runner it would have made little difference, because none of the ships were well-suited for blockade duty. *Sweet Brier*, one of the ships, could make only three knots. And *Acacia*, while faster than most of the warships off Charleston, had a draft of eleven feet, which limited her ability to maneuver and chase across the shoal areas. Captain John De Camp of *Wabash* pointed out that the blockade runners had every advantage and the campfires on Morris Island and the Charleston Lightship aided their navigation.[5]

Dahlgren admonished Green on 7 September. This was the second incident of this nature in a week. The blockade runner *Mary Bowers* had successfully run by the same vessels on the night of 31 August, only to become impaled on the wreck of the *Georgiana*. Dahlgren believed that this looked "very unpromising for the efficiency of the blockade . . ." The admiral blamed it on a "lack of vigilance . . . which I trust will be arranged."[6]

With nearly all the fast and light-draft steamers at his command, Green shifted his vessels to the north to cover Swash and Maffit's channels. He instructed his officers to form two lines: the light draft steamers to take their stations inside and the larger warships to patrol outside. The outside blockaders were ordered to keep underway with the exception of the gunboats watching Breach Inlet. Green allowed these ships to anchor for two or three hours and shift their positions to best enforce the blockade. Several days later he shifted the *Canandaigua* farther to sea, giving him better coverage. The blockading forces off Charleston did enjoy some success in the fall of 1864. In the span of three months, the squadron was credited with stopping four blockade runners. Interestingly, the *Flora*, *Prince Albert*, *Constance*, and *Mary Bowers* were all inward bound and ran aground or snagged other wrecks on their way in.[7]

When a lookout spotted a blockade runner, chaos erupted. The officer of the watch called the crew to quarters as steam was raised and the ship turned toward the enemy. A complicated system of signaling the nearby vessels, using guns and rockets, added to the confusion. Along the northern boundary of the blockade of Charleston, the concentration of so many vessels only ensured that this chaos reached epic proportions. Scores of rounds from the ships and boats might fill the air, all aimed in the direction of the intruder. Additionally the Confederate forts opened in the direction of the blockaders and picket boats. This rarely had any impact on the blockade runner at this point because she was almost at her destination. The shells seemed to have hit the Union vessels more frequently.[8]

In mid-September Dahlgren formalized his blockading instructions for the monitors watching the southerly approaches. He stationed the picket boats in the mouth of the harbor in the direction of Sullivan's Island. The picket monitor anchored about twenty-two hundred yards from Fort Moultrie. The tugs and cutters on picket duty reported to the commanding officer of this monitor. By general order these cutters and tugs were instructed to patrol toward the northerly channels and between forts Moultrie and Sumter. A second monitor took her station five hundred yards south and two other monitors supported these farther down the channel. Despite this fine tuning, the blockade runners seemed to come and go at will. Between September and the end of the year, twenty-one successful runs were made by blockade runners; twenty of these ships successfully cleared the port.[9]

Dahlgren's and Senior Officer Joseph Green's positioning of his blockaders remained extremely inefficient. These warships were placed much too close to the harbor's mouth to be effective. By the time the blockade runners were spotted, it left too little time for the anchored blockading vessels to react. It was reported that at times a vessel could not move more than a hundred yards before the chase would be out of sight. Frequently the blockade runners were not sighted at all because, after seeing the signals of the picket boats or other blockading vessels, the blockade runners could steer to avoid the Union forces. Rear Admiral Samuel Phillips Lee of the North Atlantic Blockading Squadron placed his warships off Wilmington in several lines extending far outside the inlets. This allowed each successive line to warn the next line of vessels in time for these vessels to react and cut off the blockade runners whether entering or clearing the port. Dahlgren's blockaders were comparatively much slower than Lee's, which made this type of positioning even more necessary. Dahlgren, however, may have feared Confederate cruisers. Given the slowness and weakly armed vessels under his command, few of his blockaders could have successfully fought a Confederate raider.

Some of Dahlgren's problems with the blockade can be directly attributed to other factors. Better positioning of his gunboats might have improved the efficiency of his blockade, but he never had enough warships to cover the port adequately. Additionally, many of his ships were crippled, operated on faulty boilers, or were just plain slow. Constant repairs also kept nearly twenty-five percent of the squadron in the hands of the mechanics in Port Royal and in northern yards. At the end of October, he had twenty-nine vessels away for repairs; eight of these were blockaders.[10]

There is also another factor that may have played a large role in successful blockade running at Charleston. Only months before the war ended, the firms running the blockade began to build "trifling draft" vessels. These ships had drafts of about seven feet or less. Most were specifically built to run into the ports in the Gulf of Mexico. It appears that the blockade running interests might have used at least a half a dozen for the Charleston trade. These vessels would have a superior advantage off Charleston, being able to navigate anywhere off the port without concern of running into shoals. In the final month of 1864, Dahlgren acknowledged that this "special class of vessels" could be a problem to stop. *Syren*, though not part of the class being specially built for the trade, could be classified as a trifling draft blockade runner, having a draft of only about seven feet. Her thirty-three successful trips are a partial testimony to her attributes.[11]

The picket boats stationed in the throat of the harbor offset somewhat the inefficient positioning of the blockaders. These boats were extremely valuable in warning the fleet of blockade runners clearing the harbor. Yet, even a warning did not aid the blockaders that remained at anchor. After slipping their cables, they did not have much hope of capturing a speedy blockade runner. In the fall of 1864, Dahlgren had as many as a dozen launches and boats as well as tugs detached for this duty. Armed with howitzers, the small craft frequently spotted the blockade runners and drove them back into the harbor. In a couple of cases, they caused the blockade runners to alter their course and run aground or to snag earlier wrecks.[12]

The picket boats also captured a blockade runner. On the night of 27 November, the side-wheel steamer *Beatrice* made land south of Charleston. Steering toward the Charleston Lightship, she passed around this beacon and steered for Maffit's Channel. One of the blockaders watching the bar spotted the *Beatrice* and fired at her repeatedly, but she escaped unharmed. Under a full head of steam, another blockader managed to get several shots at her and struck her twice. Still unhampered, she sped down Maffit's Channel toward Charleston. *Beatrice* then struck a shoal, backed her engines and started off once again. By this time, however, the picket boats had spotted her and surrounded the *Beatrice*. Under a heavy fire she ran on a shoal again and the boat crews boarded the *Beatrice* before she could escape. The tars destroyed the *Beatrice* because they could not extract her from the shoals. Dahlgren praised these men and recommended they be given a month's pay.[13]

In January, the fall of Fort Fisher in North Carolina closed Wilmington, the South's leading port. Additional gunboats arrived off Charleston, making it extremely difficult for the blockade runners to use this

portal to the Confederacy. Once the Federal forces cut the railroad connections in February, the port became obsolete. The last blockade runner
to arrive, the *Syren*, passed over the bar on 16 February. This was her
thirty-third trip. The *G. T. Watson* was the last to escape. She managed
to steam past the blockaders on the seventeenth, as the Confederate
troops evacuated the city.[14]

Manpower

From the beginning of the war, manpower problems persistently troubled the navy. The deficiency of enlisted men, however, became worse as
the war continued. The navy's expansion created the need for thousands
of additional men. But, beginning in 1863, the enlistments began to expire as many of the new ships were ready to be put to sea. The expiration
of enlistments became the Navy Department's single greatest worry during the war. By 1864 it became a navywide crisis. Dahlgren was permitted to grant a one-month furlough and an extra month's pay to the men
willing to reenlist for one year. Competition with the army for men was
also fierce. Sailors who reenlisted in their home states received a bounty
of three months' pay and a one-month furlough. The navy was afraid of
these men joining another branch or sitting out the war. It was not until
that September that sailors received the same bounties for reenlisting that
they could receive at the naval rendezvous. Men also received extra
bonus money based on the number of years for which they reenlisted.[15]

The South Atlantic Squadron continually had a large deficiency of
men. When Dahlgren took command in July 1863, the squadron was
one thousand men short. This never improved. By spring 1864 nearly
one-third of all the sailors in the navy were entitled to their discharge.
The vessels on the Atlantic coast had only half of their complements and
thirty-five ships awaited crews. The men who remained continued holding watches and manning boat crews; they were expected to report for
action during the day and maintain the blockade by night. Manning the
picket boats put an additional strain on the men. For duty night and day
it required three hundred men to man the numerous boats required for
patrols off Charleston. Gustavus Fox wrote to Lincoln that "All the anxieties and panics of this war I have passed through without a feeling of
trouble until the present moment." Enlistments fell so low that rebel
prisoners began to fill the vacancies. Although an extreme measure, after
an oath of allegiance they were distributed within the South Atlantic
Blockading Squadron.[16]

Welles approached the president to solve the manpower problem. He suggested the transfer of twelve thousand men from the army for naval service. The lack of men was accentuated when Grant began his Petersburg Campaign in the spring of 1864. This campaign occurred at the same time that the navy's three-year enlistments had ended that March. To help the navy with recruiting, the War Department allowed any man who could furnish proof that he was a "mariner by vocation, or an able seaman, or ordinary seamen" to transfer to the navy. Secretary of War Stanton directed General Gillmore to transfer one thousand of these men to the South Atlantic squadron. Not a man had been received by that May, but by August a large influx came into the squadron.[17]

The manpower crisis continued and throughout the rest of the summer Dahlgren begged for men. In May he had a deficiency of 1,400 men. As the squadron's complement was 6,200 men, this represented a deficiency of nearly twenty-three percent. In June the squadron was deficient 1,360 men, in August 600, and by November the deficit had grown again to about 1,500 men. This shortage had such a great impact on operations that it forced Dahlgren to hold his men beyond their terms of enlistment by an average of over thirty days. By June, not a man was discharged who had not served a month over his term and some as many as three months over. Dissatisfaction among the crews was widespread and provoked a demonstration. A group of dissatisfied men on the *New Ironsides* burned a figure of Dahlgren in effigy from the rigging. The men, however, went unpunished because Rowan could not identify the individuals. While expressing his disappointment in his men, he also sympathized with them. The South Atlantic Blockading Squadron still had a dire need for additional men, but in August, Welles wrote in his diary with some relief that "A desire to enter the navy to avoid the draft is extensive, . . . so that our recruiting rendezvous are, for the time being, overrun."[18]

Seamen with acute medical cases traveled north on the supply steamers for better treatment. This situation nearly drove Dahlgren to despair. The process of getting the men a medical survey, then issuing a sick ticket, the time spent traveling north, and the treatment time could take a while. Many of the men who went north for treatment beginning in 1863 had their enlistments expire and Dahlgren had no way of getting his men back. Dahlgren even suspected that some officers used medical surveys as a leave of absence. In September 1863, he refused to approve medical surveys requiring treatment in a northern port when it could be accomplished at Port Royal. Naval or marine hospitals in Portland, Maine; Portsmouth, New Hampshire; Chelsea, Massachusetts; New York, New York; Philadelphia, Pennsylvania; and Washington D.C. provided beds for most of the men. There were also small facilities in Port Royal and a small house at Fernandina. The army facility at Beaufort allowed the admittance of officers and men as a "courtesy."[19]

Once the men enlisted, they usually found the navy far different than they had imagined. Although the navy had changed little in decades, some joined for adventure, others for prize money, but most found the service monotonous. Life at sea, though, varied depending on the gunboat's station and the vessel itself. Some of the ex-merchantmen were commodious and others were cramped; those ships built for the navy were generally less spacious. In comparison to the enlisted men, officers often had pleasant, comfortable, and well-furnished quarters. The most uncomfortable experience by far was service on a monitor. These warships were hot in the summer and cold in the winter. Off Charleston the heavy swells left the decks awash and only about once every three weeks could the air scuttles be kept open to provide ventilation below. These conditions caused many officers and men to report sick. The sailors were said to look "forlorn and sad" in these "floating penitentiaries." The summer months seemed to elicit the worst complaints. In the engine rooms men "fainted, others lost their minds, while many others weakened from the heat." In the officers' staterooms, it was so hot that when writing letters home one officer tucked a towel under his chin to absorb the perspiration. The terrible conditions had the old sailors accustomed to wooden ships complaining. One commented, "Them newfangled iron ships aint fit for hogs to go to sea in, let along honest sailors!"[20]

The health of the men on the ironclads was important to Dahlgren. The daily use of these warships to bombard the Confederate fortifications required a great effort from the crews. If substantial numbers of these men reported to the daily sick call, then it affected operations. Dahlgren attempted to improve the health of these men in particular. After only two weeks of command, he requested a hulk be sent south so that he could rotate men between the monitors and this hulk for rest. The department sent the 725-ton screw steamer *Home* to serve as a place of relief to the crews.[21]

The conditions in the engine rooms prompted Dahlgren to ask for more coal heavers and firemen since these men faced such severe duty. Additionally, the flag officer requested a whiskey ration, an increase in pay of twenty-five percent for enlisted men, an extra allowance of clothing, and ice for the ironclad sailors. The department, with the exception of the whiskey ration, which the Bureau of Medicine and Surgery vetoed, granted these. Interestingly, these benefits did not extend to the *New Ironsides*. Rowan pointed out that his vessel was not unlike the monitors. The berth deck could reach over 100 degrees in warm weather and it was wet in stormy weather. Welles denied the request, arguing that should it be extended to the *New Ironsides* it might as well be extended to all the ships.[22]

The seamen and, to a lesser extent, the officers felt powerless to change their circumstances. The men on board the ships continued through the war to live with their depravations, monotony, and restlessness. Most of the men longed for the day that their enlistments expired. One officer stationed on the bark *Fernandina* in St. Catherine's Sound expressed his despair, and probably those of his shipmates, when he wrote in his diary, "Dull! Dull! Dull! Is the day. Nothing to do."[23]

Interior Operations

These feelings of restlessness only increased because throughout the war the ships of the squadron rarely participated in small or single-vessel raids along the coast. This was particularly due to the fact that raids of this nature could do little but annoy the enemy along the sparsely populated coastline. Expeditions into the interior served to keep the Confederate forces on guard. These missions also tied up a disproportionate number of Confederate troops to watch the coastal areas. Within a one-month period during the summer of 1864, several landing parties went ashore to annoy and disrupt local affairs.

The first sortie began at 2:00 A.M. on the morning of 30 July. Acting Volunteer Lieutenant Robert P. Swann of the screw gunboat *Potomska* took two cutters, one officer, and seventeen men to destroy two saltworks near the Back River in Georgia. The cutters advanced six miles up the river and landed at the first saltwork just before daylight. The naval force wrecked salt pans, burned buildings, and destroyed wagons and 150 bushels of salt. Swann ordered his men to return to the ship at 9:30, but their escape was slow because low tide forced them to drag the boats for some distance. At 10:00 A.M. the Confederates managed to muster a local force and fired a surprise volley into the boats, mortally wounding one man and wounding four others less severely. The tars, armed with Spencer rifles, returned such a rapid fire after being surprised that the Confederates, though determined, could not effectively pursue them afterwards. The raiding party arrived back at the *Potomska* with no further casualties.[24]

A more remarkable expedition began three days later. Commander George M. Colvocoresses of the sloop *Saratoga*, lying in Doboy Sound, received a copy of a newspaper published in Savannah. The article called for a meeting at the McIntosh County Courthouse to form a coast defense unit. Since Colvocoresses considered himself and his men as "interested parties" in this meeting, he decided to attend. Taking with him eight officers and one hundred seven sailors and Marines, he left the *Saratoga* on the afternoon of 2 August. In seven boats the men reached the mainland just before 9:00 that evening. After landing, Colvocoresses sent the boats back to the ship with instructions to later meet him at a predetermined place. The commander threw out a skirmish line and advanced toward the main road leading to Savannah. When his party arrived at a bridge, he left a boatswain and seven men to guard it and to capture anyone coming from McIntosh County. He ordered the bridge to be burned at 11:00 A.M. the next morning, the time of the meeting. He hoped that burning the bridge would make it difficult for anyone to escape and might prevent cavalry in the area from attacking his rear.[25]

The remaining officers and men continued toward the courthouse. He arrived without being seen and divided his forces in the woods on both sides of the building. At 11:00 A.M. the following morning, after the local inhabitants began to arrive, Colvocoresses and his men attacked. They completely surrounded the courthouse and captured all but three men, who escaped. The party from the bridge arrived shortly thereafter, bringing with them eleven more men, as well as some horses and buggies. On the way back to the ship the tars captured an additional three men, making a total of twenty-six prisoners. Colvocoresses' force destroyed a second bridge and a large encampment on the way back to the spot where he asked the boats to meet him. His instructions, however, were misunderstood and the boats arrived late. Colvocoresses and his crew, along with his prisoners, did not reach the *Saratoga* until noon the following day.[26]

This entire episode caused quite a bit of consternation on both sides. The men captured by the Union navy were mostly over the age of 50 or under 20. A few were considered important local officials. Dahlgren proposed to hold these men to be exchanged with naval officers being held in captivity. Dahlgren maintained that these men were legitimate prisoners of war; the Confederates claimed they were citizens who had not borne arms. Welles upheld Dahlgren's views.[27]

Before the controversy ended on the first raid, however, Colvocoresses made another. On the night of 16 August, he landed again, this
time with a force of 10 officers and 120 men at South Newport, McIntosh County, Georgia. During this sortie he captured a lieutenant and
twenty-eight privates of the Third South Carolina Cavalry along with a
cache of small arms. He also burned their encampment, a bridge, and
destroyed two saltworks. He brought back to the ship six overseers of
the saltworks, seventy-one slaves, and twenty-nine soldiers.[28]

Colvocoresses' success also spawned other efforts. On 22 August,
Acting Volunteer Lieutenant Swann took *Potomska* up the Satilla River
in southeast Georgia. Steaming thirty-one miles to Penniman's Landing,
he launched two cutters, each under the command of an ensign. Row-
ing up White Oak Creek with a scow in tow, Swann's men found a turpentine still and burned twenty-five hundred barrels of rosin and
turpentine. They carried thirty-one barrels back downstream as a prize.
His men also captured one cavalryman and transported seventeen
refugees. The boats returned to the ship on the twenty-third. The following day Swann sent out another expedition. After reconnoitering for
several hours, the men brought more refugees to the *Potomska*. Swann
then ordered his ship back down to Doboy Sound.[29]

The final substantial missions occurred at the end of August. Acting
Master William Gillespie sent armed boats from the bark *Braziliera* on
sorties to annoy the enemy in the St. Simon's Sound area. For the next
four weeks his men made several "excursions" up the rivers and creeks
that emptied into the sound. The sailors burned cotton, destroyed boats,
wrecked saltworks, and ruined hundreds of bushels of salt. They brought
back to *Braziliera* prisoners, slaves, and refugees.[30]

Schemes and Dreams

While these missions demonstrated an active command, Dahlgren continued to seek alternatives to attack Charleston. At times, it seemed that
a joint operation might develop, because his relationship with Major
General Foster was much more cordial. Dahlgren and Foster collabo-
rated on several torpedo experiments, hoping that they might somehow
accomplish the removal of the obstructions. Unfortunately, all these
mechanisms proved to be failures or showed too little promise while
Confederate batteries and naval vessels could protect these defenses.[31]

Part of these experiments included powder rafts. Both Foster and
Dahlgren hoped that an explosion of a large quantity of powder near

Fort Sumter might bring down some of the remaining walls. This joint effort, though, did not proceed as planned. The first trial was scheduled for the night of 21 July. Dahlgren assigned *Nahant* to tow a powder-laden scow to within one thousand yards of the fort. The powder, not stowed on the scow in time for the test, caused Dahlgren to postpone it. On the night of 28 July, Foster decided to start the raft from shore, and the scow floated near the fort and exploded, but with no effect. A second trial near the end of the month using two tons of powder had similar results and this particular experiment was abandoned. The trials with smaller explosive devices continued through October with encouraging results. Dahlgren, however, never tested them on the obstructions.[32]

The two officers also discussed battering down the remnants of Sumter's walls with more conventional means. Foster wanted the monitors to lay in the channel and pound down the walls as they had done earlier. Dahlgren, though, believed that this was not feasible. His monitors were nearly worn out and he believed that earlier trials proved that these warships would be disabled first by enemy fire from the forts on Sullivan's Island. With hopes that the further destruction of Fort Sumter would allow an assault on the city, Dahlgren offered to lend the army some 11-inch guns, men, and ammunition to help in this work. By the end of August, he determined to land six of the large caliber pieces, but had carriages for only four. These guns would augment the army's seven large guns and fourteen mortars already in place on Morris Island.[33]

Welles and the department, though, had no thoughts of operating against Charleston at this time. Wilmington, North Carolina, would be the next point of attack. On 20 July, Welles asked Dahlgren to confer with General Foster to determine if the withdrawal of the monitors from Charleston would endanger the forces afloat and ashore. Before providing a complete answer, Dahlgren tried to recycle the old proposal of an attack on the Confederate defenses via James Island. He believed that ten thousand more troops would be sufficient to turn the defenses of Charleston. Foster did not concur with Dahlgren and considered it unfeasible.[34]

Welles ultimately decided to leave the ironclads with Dahlgren. In September he told him that Farragut would be in Port Royal at the end of September with a force to attack Wilmington. Welles placed Dahlgren under Farragut's orders and instructed him to work on the impression that Charleston would be the next port to be attacked. Dahlgren, however, did not get this message until 21 October, long after David Dixon Porter had replaced Farragut in command. The plan to strike Wilmington should have finally convinced Dahlgren that the department was only interested in him keeping the status quo along the South Atlantic coast. Dahlgren, however, continued to embrace the hope that he would lead a climactic attack on the city. This misunderstanding may have resulted from Welles's request on 3 October, for detailed information on the defenses of Charleston. Dahlgren quickly wrote an extensive report, but never thoroughly discussed the character of the obstructions or the known locations of torpedoes.[35]

Continually driven by false hope, in November, Dahlgren again proposed two more movements. One was to occupy territory between the Peedee and Santee rivers as a base for further operations. A second, more ambitious plan called for still another attack on the defenses of Charleston via Sullivan's Island. This proposition called for between thirty thousand and fifty thousand troops.[36]

The unknown character of the obstructions and the absence of information on the enemy torpedoes certainly did not help Dahlgren's proposals gain acceptance. The only known obstructions were a series of log, raft, and rope obstructions extending from Fort Sumter to Battery Bee. Unknown to Dahlgren, the Confederates had been laying down three lines of torpedoes between Fort Sumter and Fort Moultrie. By 1865, the Confederates would have sixteen torpedoes placed along this line, each anchored with a mushroom anchor. These devices lay between five and six feet below the waterline at low tide, completely out of view. A few large torpedoes made from boilers filled with powder and electrically detonated completed this portion of the defenses.[37]

Sherman's March to the Sea

Events ending the war progressed so rapidly in the fall and winter of 1864 that Dahlgren's opportunities for glory before Charleston by now had nearly ended. Fighting through Georgia, Major General William Tecumseh Sherman reached an evacuated Atlanta on 2 September. For ten weeks he rested his army and left Atlanta on 15 November en route to Savannah. Dahlgren knew that the navy's next major effort would be to capture Wilmington, yet he must have held some hope for himself since the department did not take his ironclads.

On 22 November, Welles wrote Dahlgren that Sherman left Atlanta with intentions of marching to the coast near Savannah. He directed Dahlgren to cooperate closely with Sherman's sixty thousand veteran troops who departed the city with twenty days' worth of rations and planned to forage on their way to Savannah. Dahlgren immediately issued a general order sending his gunboats up the rivers and estuaries to report contact with Sherman's troops.[38]

Naval cooperation with Sherman's movement would be difficult at best. The Georgia coastline, though intersected with navigable waters, was well-defended. Heavily armed earthworks and obstructions prevented Union naval vessels from operating too far up these waterways. Fort McAllister serves as a prime example of one of these heavy fortifications. Though this fort lay outside the main Savannah defenses, it had proven to be too strong to be reduced by naval gunfire. The Confederate navy and army had also worked together to continue to lay additional obstructions and mines in the channels to further discourage naval movements.[39]

The Confederate naval vessels in these waters, although no match for their Union counterparts, still had the capability to make any movement up the rivers difficult. Flag Officer William W. Hunter had the ironclads *Savannah* and *Georgia* and the steam gunboats *Isondiga*, *Macon*, and *Sampson*. Two other small side-wheel steamers, the *Resolute* and the *Firefly*, served as tenders. The *Savannah* was a formidable warship, mounting two 7-inch single-banded Brooke rifled guns and two 6.4-inch double-banded Brooke rifled guns. The *Georgia*, on the other hand, was merely a floating battery; she could move if necessary, but she was mainly used to protect the obstructions near Fort Jackson.[40]

On the afternoon of 24 November, Dahlgren received a note from General Foster requesting naval cooperation to assist Sherman. Envisioned was an expedition against the Charleston and Savannah Railroad to serve as a diversion to aid Sherman's march to the sea. If the Union forces could sever the Charleston and Savannah Railroad near Grahamville, they might prevent rebel reinforcements from reaching Savannah to oppose Sherman. Bringing "all the disposable" troops in his department, General Foster arrived with about five thousand men, but delegated command of the expedition to Brigadier General John P. Hatch. Dahlgren jumped at this opportunity and, before he turned in, issued orders to collect light artillery, sailors, and Marines.[41]

Dahlgren had given much thought to operations such as this during his career. He had even designed a boat howitzer to be used ashore for operations of this nature. Nearly four months before this particular call to action, Dahlgren had issued an order to his commanding officers to exercise and drill their men with small arms. He also prescribed for the use of the sailors, a short rifled musket (Plymouth musket). Designed by

Dahlgren, this gun fired a .69 caliber bullet and was specially fitted with a short, broad bladed, bowie-type bayonet. The gun could also be fitted with a sword bayonet, depending on the circumstances of its use.[42]

Dahlgren had specific views on the use of his boat howitzers. He designed the howitzers to be used in batteries of three sections of two guns each. Four smoothbore and two rifled 12-pounders would compose each battery. Dahlgren organized two batteries, but during the engagements only landed the necessary number of guns for the specific operations. He never foresaw that these guns would be used massed in large numbers. Rather, he believed that, if the guns remained mobile, they could be better served. He also believed that, if he dispersed his guns in combat, it exposed his men less to the enemy's guns.[43]

As a force, this body of men was called the Fleet Brigade. Commanded by Commander George Henry Preble, it consisted of 29 officers, 145 men in the naval artillery, 156 in the naval infantry, 156 rank and file from the Marine battalion, and 6 black hospital stewards and nurses—a total of 492 officers and men. Dahlgren prescribed that twenty men would be attached to each howitzer—thirteen to service the gun and another seven armed with the Plymouth muskets. Additionally, four pioneers would be attached to each howitzer to level space for the guns or to throw up breastworks as needed in the field. He divided the Marines into companies of fifty men; they served as skirmishers to protect the artillery during engagements. He planned to have other men detached to form fatigue parties to cook, pitch camp, etc. To ensure his force could move quickly, each seaman in the naval artillery sections carried a round of ammunition. Reserve ammunition would follow in small hand wagons under the fatigue parties. Since the navy did not have the wherewithal to supply horses, forage, and rations ashore, the army quartermaster fulfilled the Fleet Brigade's needs.[44]

This project had Dahlgren as excited as a schoolboy. On the day after Thanksgiving, at 3:00 A.M., he had the flagship *Harvest Moon* picking up Marines gathered from the various ships. On the twenty-sixth, and for the next two days, he personally helped to organize the seamen and Marines. Dahlgren had his men, gathered at Bay Point, hold a drill in which they "scampered through the bushes and over sand-hills with howitzers." On the afternoon of the twenty-eighth, the men were ready to embark. The *Pontiac* carried the artillery, the *Mingoe* the infantry, and the *Sonoma* the Marines. Foster earlier requested the navy provide six howitzers and a force to move on the night of the twenty-eighth.[45]

Dahlgren and Hatch planned to land their force up the Broad River at Boyd's Landing, thirty-five miles northeast of Savannah. The navy provided the tugs *O. M. Pettit* and *Daffodil*, which led the way, followed by the *Pontiac*, *Mingoe*, *Sonoma*, *Harvest Moon* (flag), *Pawnee*, *Winona*, and *Wissahickon*. Fog delayed the expedition and the *Wissahickon* ran aground on her way up river. The naval contingent did not begin landing until 9:00 A.M. on the twenty-ninth, several hours behind schedule. Within thirty minutes, all of the seamen, the guns, and the Marines had come ashore. Dahlgren landed on the ruins of a wharf, walked a mile with the advance units of his brigade, and remained ashore until 11:00 A.M. Because of the fog, the army transports did not begin arriving until noon and the troops did not land until that afternoon. The fog caused some of the transports to run aground; others sailed up the wrong river. Dahlgren returned to Port Royal, taking with him the *Winona*, *Wissahickon*, and *Harvest Moon*.[46]

The Fleet Brigade, the first organized body of troops that landed, "pushed to the front to occupy a cross-roads two miles in advance of the landing." The artillery battalion, commanded by Lieutenant Commander E. Orville Matthews, dragged the guns up the road, supported on the right by the battalion of sailors commanded by Lieutenant James O'Kane and on the left by the battalion of Marines under the command of First Lieutenant George G. Stoddard (USMC). At the fork of a road the men halted and Preble placed the artillery in a defensive position.[47]

Without a proper map to guide him, Preble began to feel that he halted his men at the wrong crossroads. Taking his adjutant, Lieutenant Commander Alex F. Crossman, and fifteen men, they reconnoitered to the right two miles in advance of the column. After exchanging shots with rebel pickets, he returned and decided to move his men to another crossroads, one and a half miles to their north. Brigadier General Edward E. Potter rode up later that afternoon and informed Preble that neither of the crossroads he had visited was the one intended for his men to defend. Once again Preble moved his "tired and hungry" men. They finally made camp that night at their initial site.[48]

At 7:00 A.M. on the thirtieth, Preble had his men moving once again. Reporting to General Hatch, Preble was ordered to send his two lightest guns back to the crossroads. The rest of the guns and the brigade joined Hatch's move toward the Grahamville depot, about a mile east of the railroad. The confusion of the Union forces alerted the Confederates, who by now had managed to assemble a small force of Georgia militia reinforced by South Carolina artillery and cavalry units to oppose Hatch and the Fleet Brigade. Beginning about 10:00 A.M. the Union forces pushed the Confederates back toward an earthwork on Honey Hill. A marsh and dense woods prevented a flank attack and two frontal attacks were repulsed easily by the rebels, who inflicted severe losses on the advancing Union troops. At noon a third charge, supported by the Marine battalion, was also thrown back, and Hatch decided to withdraw. The Naval Brigade played a reserve role with the exception of two howitzers that were called into the line late in the afternoon and fired about three hours at the enemy. The Fleet Brigade retired in good order and took a position at the crossroads to cover the withdrawal of Hatch's forces until the morning of 31 November. In the battle of Honey Hill, the navy suffered trifling casualties of 2 killed, 7 wounded, and 1 missing. The army suffered about 750 killed, wounded, and missing while the Confederates returns reported only 50 casualties.[49]

Dahlgren and Foster agreed to try a similar advance towards Tulifinny Crossroads in order to cut the Charleston and Savannah Railroad here. On 4 December, Dahlgren sent the *Pawnee* and *Sonoma* to the Coosawatchie River and Foster sent steamers with a regiment on board up Whale Branch. To mislead the enemy, boats from the *Pontiac* reconnoitered up the creek from Boyd's Landing. The *Pawnee* and *Sonoma*, meanwhile, engaged two enemy guns placed in a position to bar the passage of the gunboats up the Coosawatchie River. When Dahlgren arrived, the two warships were "busy pounding" this small battery. Unable to reply effectively or damage the naval vessels, the Confederate battery withdrew.[50]

The Fleet Brigade had remained in a defensive position along the Grahamville Road. The men entrenched here from 1 December until the evening of 5 December. Receiving orders to withdraw to Boyd's Landing, the Fleet Brigade embarked for the expedition up the Tulifinny River and on 6 December disembarked at Gregory's Landing. The naval infantry landed with army units and advanced to support the troops already ashore. The Marines and guns came ashore at a lower landing. This spot proved to be a poor choice as it was marshy terrain. Once landed, the guns had to be dragged through a swamp with "great labor." Preble hurried his men to the firing, but as the main body of the naval brigade reached an open field, an enemy field piece began raking their position. With rebel musket fire also pouring in from the nearby woods, Preble wheeled the howitzers into position, drove the infantry back, and silenced their gunfire.[51]

During the night the Fleet Brigade slept on the battlefield and, on the morning of the seventh, the Confederates renewed a skirmish fire.

Preble ordered his howitzers to open fire and dispersed the skirmishers with artillery and musket fire. Preble was later ordered to move his command back and entrench. He left two heavy howitzers at the front, and spent the remaining portion of the seventh, and the entire day of the eighth, improving his entrenched position. On the ninth, his men again were ordered forward on the right. He placed four guns in a position to shell the woods in front of a column of advancing Union troops. A Union regiment forged into the woods with axes to clear a road one hundred feet wide so that the railroad would be vulnerable to artillery fire. The naval guns maintained a continuous fire into the woods on both flanks to discourage any enemy movements that might disrupt the axe men. With this road complete, the army withdrew without successfully cutting the rail lines. During the engagements of the sixth, seventh, and ninth, the Naval Brigade suffered about three dozen casualties.[52]

This movement by the Union forces had little impact on the war effort. Neither of the two probes successfully cut the railroad. They did, however, draw away troops that might have opposed Sherman's march to the sea. The Marines and seamen behaved well and were extremely disciplined. But this was not a sufficient test for Dahlgren's idea of a naval landing force. The concept, though, was the model for later landing force operations, but it lay unused for nearly fifty years. Hatch held the Fleet Brigade in high esteem. He commended their "gallantry and action and good conduct during the irksome life in camp . . ." He believed any "jealousy" that existed between the branches of the service disappeared after they fought in harmony, which allowed them to gain a better knowledge of each other.[53]

On the ninth, Dahlgren received word from a deserter that Sherman was within fifteen miles of Savannah. The admiral, anxious to make contact with the Union advance, began sending his gunboats on scouting missions to open communications. Sherman reached the outskirts of Savannah on 12 December and on the same day established communication with Dahlgren when the *Flag* picked up an officer and two of Sherman's scouts.[54]

Dahlgren moved his flagship *Harvest Moon* to Wassaw Sound to oversee operations in case the ironclad *Savannah* tried to sortie rather than suffer capture or destruction. He also moved five other vessels, including the monitor *Sangamon*, here to support both the *Passaic* in Wassaw Sound and Sherman's troops, should it be necessary. On 13 December, Dahlgren sent a note to Sherman to let him know how he had deployed his naval forces and suggested that Sherman attack the Confederate lines via the Ogeechee, reducing Fort McAllister from the rear. Since McAllister lay outside the main network of fortifications around Savannah, it could not be fully supported. He convinced Sherman of the soundness of this approach by relating that no enemy forces "of consequence" lay south of McAllister, or near the Vernon River.[55]

On 14 December, Dahlgren learned that Sherman's men had carried Fort McAllister by assault. The fall of this fort allowed Sherman's troops to be resupplied by water from the Ogeechee River. Dahlgren ordered his flagship to Ossabaw Sound by way of Wassaw and, when he reached the latter body of water, Foster's steamer stood toward the *Harvest Moon*. Signals from this vessel indicated that Sherman was on board. The *Harvest Moon* anchored immediately and, when the army steamer came alongside, Dahlgren jumped on board. He found the cabin filled with officers discussing the next objectives of the campaign. Sherman instantly showed a liking for Dahlgren, calling him "kind and courteous." Dahlgren and Sherman became "personal friends and faithful and indefatigable coajutors . . ."[56]

After some discussion Sherman and Dahlgren decided that the general would return to Fort McAllister on board the *Harvest Moon* rather than with Foster. On the fifteenth the admiral went ashore with Sherman to look at the fort. Dahlgren was impressed by the strength of the fortification. The tug *Dandelion* began removing the pilings and the torpedo defenses in the river. This opened the Ogeechee River, allowing naval support in Sherman's rear.[57]

The probing activities continued as the warships pushed several miles up the Vernon River. The side-wheel gunboat *Sonoma* arrived below Fort Beaulieu on the afternoon of the fourteenth. Coming within range at 1:30, she opened fire. Finding the works strongly defended and the Confederate gunner's aim good, she continued a deliberate fire until the seventeenth, when the mortar schooner *John Griffith* joined her. The *Winona* came up on the twentieth to assist her two consorts. At 6:00 A.M. on the twenty-first, having heard from a deserter that the rebels were evacuating the works, Lieutenant Commander Robert W. Scott ordered *Sonoma* and *John Griffith*, and the newly arrived *Germanium*, upriver. Scott called away six boats and armed them for assaulting the works. When the men rowed ashore they found Fort Beaulieu abandoned. At 10:05 the American ensign was hoisted above the fort. Scott quickly sent *Winona* up the Little Ogeechee River to Battery Rosedew and, ninety minutes later, the Union flag was flying over this battery as well.[58]

The fall of Fort McAllister created an impossible situation for Lieutenant General William J. Hardee, who decided he could no longer hold Savannah. This circumstance left the Confederate warships pinned between the advancing army and the overwhelming force of the Union navy. After dark on 20 December, the Confederate army spiked the guns defending the city and withdrew over pontoon bridges. Flag Officer Hunter had instructions from the Confederate Navy Department to save the *Savannah*, *Isondiga*, and *Macon*. Mallory optimistically believed that these warships might fight their way past the naval vessels on the Savannah River, rush past Fort Pulaski, and then steam to Charleston, Wilmington, or Georgetown. In any event, Mallory preferred the warships to "fall in the conflict of battle, taking all the risks of defeat and triumph, than that they be tamely surrendered to the enemy or destroyed by their own officers."[59]

The Confederate gunboats *Macon* and *Sampson* earlier received one last mission. Flag Officer Hunter took these two warships and the small steam transport *Resolute* up the Savannah River to burn the Charleston and Savannah Railroad bridge to delay Sherman's move across the river. During the night of 11 December, Confederate tars in armed boats succeeded in placing combustible material at the bridge and destroyed it. As the flotilla returned downstream the next day, Union artillery awaited it. In a gauntlet of fire, Hunter, standing on the hurricane deck of *Sampson*, directed the two naval vessels downstream. Under a tremendous fire, the Confederate gunboats continued downstream until gunfire disabled the transport steamer *Resolute*, forcing her to surrender. Hunter concluded he could not escape and turned back upriver with all speed. Hunter managed to get his gunboats over obstructions below Augusta, and arrived there safely on Christmas Day. *Macon* and *Sampson* were the only two vessels of his command that escaped.[60]

Hunter now knew the instructions to fight his way through the Union forces were unrealistic. The small vessels had virtually no chance of making it downriver without being disabled before they got to sea. The *Savannah* might fight her way past the ships at the mouth of the Savannah River, but because of her slow speed she would be subjected to a devastating fire from all the Union vessels on her way to another open Confederate port.

Despite the odds, Hunter ordered the *Savannah* readied for sea and instructed that the torpedoes be removed from the Wilmington River. The officer who put the torpedoes down found it impossible to remove them with a few men and grapnels. The obstructions in the Savannah

River were also much too extensive to remove. Hunter thus had no choice but to destroy the remaining ships in his command. The *Water Witch* was burned on the nineteenth and the *Isondiga* and *Firefly* were also destroyed. The unfinished ironclad *Milledgeville* was burned to the water's edge and sunk in the middle of the Savannah River. The ironclad *Georgia*, which "laid practically useless for any purpose of war," spent most of her career as a floating battery moored in a log crib near Elba Island. She could move only with the assistance of tugs and her battery could only be brought to bear on either channel by warping her into position. On the twentieth, the Confederate sailors spiked her guns, and the warship called a "marine abortion" was scuttled at her moorings. On the twenty-first, the Union soldiers began entering the city. The *Savannah* was set on fire at about 11:30 that night. The demise of this vessel could be seen for miles. At Fort Pulaski onlookers saw a "dull red flame," then a "red light suddenly shot up into a brilliant fiery column, shone brightly for a few seconds and disappeared." Soon afterward the explosion was heard; it reportedly shook windows as far away as Hilton Head.[61]

On 22 December, Sherman wrote Lincoln, "I beg to present you as a Christmas-gift the city of Savannah . . ." Dahlgren joined Sherman the next day at the general's headquarters. The two spent the next few weeks discussing the future movements of the army. Sherman, however, had already decided his course of action. On his march from Atlanta he had purposely avoided Augusta, because he thought that this would create indecision on the part of the Confederates when he crossed the Savannah River. This course of action would force the Confederates to divide their forces, not knowing whether to defend Augusta or Charleston. Instead, he planned to move toward Columbia, South Carolina. He concluded that Charleston was a "mere desolated wreck" and not worth attacking or spending the time to starve the defenders out. Sherman told Lieutenant Commander Stephen B. Luce, the captain of the *Pontiac*, "You navy fellows have been hammering away at Charleston for the past three years. But just wait till I get into South Carolina; I will cut her communications and Charleston will fall into your hands like a ripe pear."[62]

The Fall of Charleston

The war along the South Atlantic seaboard was rapidly coming to a close. Dahlgren retained hope that the navy would be given some chance to operate against the Confederate forces in Charleston. Dahlgren believed that Sherman's approach into South Carolina would make the Confederates here desperate. He warned his senior officer off Charleston to be more vigilant in case the ironclads sortied from the harbor. Dahlgren had seven monitors at the Charleston anchorage to prevent their escape, but feared that the Confederate ironclads still might attack the most advanced picket monitor. He issued explicit instructions to keep the Confederate warships from successfully making a surprise attack. He actually hoped to lure the enemy out far enough so that he could put his monitors between the enemy ironclads and the harbor, preventing them from retreating to safety. He also asked Brigadier General Alexander Schimmelfennig to keep his guns pointed seaward and loaded with grapeshot to destroy torpedo boats that might venture out with the ironclads.[63]

On 3 January, Sherman began moving his troops from the Savannah area. At Thunderbolt, Dahlgren met with Sherman and Major General and Chief Engineer John G. Barnard on board the *Bibb*. Sherman greeted Dahlgren in a faded and unkempt uniform. As they spoke, he observed a gunboat firing at a Confederate battery. Sherman watched as the gunboat's shells consistently fell short of their mark. Curiously, Sherman asked, "Admiral, what is that fellow trying to do?" Dahlgren replied, "He is reducing that battery General." Where upon Sherman reportedly replied, "If I were you Admiral, I would order him up where he would get hurt."[64]

Sherman now hoped to shift rapidly the right wing of his army to continue his campaign northward, but lacked transports to do this. On 4 January, Dahlgren lent his flagship *Harvest Moon* to carry eight hundred troops from Thunderbolt to Beaufort as Sherman transferred the right wing of his army to operate from this base. By 7 January, Dahlgren knew that Sherman's plans did not include an attack on Charleston. Dahlgren wrote Welles of his disappointment, lamenting, "It is with great regret that the conclusion is forced on me that the work marked out here will not include Charleston."[65]

On 9 January, Secretary of War Edwin M. Stanton arrived in South Carolina to talk with Sherman about the next portion of his campaign. On the twelfth, Dahlgren dined on board the army transport *Nevada* with Stanton and generals Sherman, Foster, Montgomery C. Meigs, Barnard, and their staff officers. These men hammered out some final arrangements before the two wings of Sherman's army left their coastal bases. During a meeting the following day, Sherman told the admiral that his final plan did not include any work against Charleston, but an advance along interior lines, destroying the railroads as he proceeded. During the meeting Dahlgren must have pleaded for some part in the campaign and probably urged the general to take Charleston, but Sherman insisted that Dahlgren not place his vessels under fire at Charleston.[66]

On the thirteenth, Dahlgren learned that he would receive ironclads and other warships as soon as Porter finished at Wilmington. Porter and Dahlgren had asked each other for ironclads for their particular operations. On the morning of the fifteenth, Dahlgren summoned the monitors' captains on board the flagship. Realizing that the war was about to end without his ambitions of glory being met, he held a council of war to determine their views on a possible attack. Dahlgren proposed three options: (1) attack Sullivan's Island, (2) pass in and attack Fort Johnson, and (3) run into the harbor and attack the city. After a "full and unreserved discussion" the captains showed interest in only the first option. Dahlgren believed his officers timid, remarking in his diary "Not a fire eater among them . . ."[67]

Several days earlier Sherman had asked Dahlgren to make demonstrations against Charleston to draw the enemy's attention away from the movements of the army. The admiral, however, may have been a bit more ambitious than providing a mere diversion. On the night of 15 January, hours after the council of war, he sent *Patapsco* and *Lehigh* forward to examine the obstructions. The *Patapsco* got underway and proceeded up the harbor to serve as the picket monitor. *Lehigh* anchored nearby to serve as a reserve. This night three scout boats equipped with grapnels and drags and covered by the *Patapsco*'s guns were sent forward to search for obstructions and torpedoes. The ironclad, with her torpedo fenders deployed, drifted to a position nearly between Forts Sumter and Moultrie when she struck a torpedo about thirty feet from her bow on the port side. The ironclad sank so quickly that only a few men below, at the time of the explosion, safely abandoned ship. The scout and picket boats rescued five officers and thirty-eight men; sixty officers and men perished. This ended Dahlgren's hopes of getting into the harbor by force.[68]

Dahlgren still maintained hope of attacking Sullivan's Island, but Sherman was adverse to this. Sherman continued to urge Dahlgren not to risk his vessels against the guns and torpedoes of Charleston. Instead, he suggested that Dahlgren move on Mount Pleasant by way of Bull Bay. Bull Bay lay over twenty miles north of Charleston. Sherman hoped to "embarrass the rebel general" to his true designs as he moved northward. He believed a landing of a small force at Bull Bay would give the enemy the impression he was headed toward Charleston instead of Columbia and later toward Wilmington.[69]

On 24 January, Sherman also asked if the gunboats could make a diversion up the Edisto or Stono rivers to make the rebels "uneasy on that flank." Dahlgren sent the *Sonoma* up the North Edisto and the *Pawnee* up the South Edisto River. Dahlgren ordered his vessels as far up the rivers as they could operate. The Union warships protected Sherman's troops ashore, particularly at the river crossings. The warships also reconnoitered Confederate positions, annoyed the enemy, kept communications open, and ferried troops.[70]

One of the gunboats actively operating on the flanks of the Confederate forces was the *Dai Ching*. She proceeded up the Combahee River, in company with the screw tug *Clover*, to operate with the left flank of Sherman's troops. On the morning of 26 January, Lieutenant Commander James C. Chaplin learned that a small schooner loaded with cotton lay about five miles above them. Getting underway, both vessels steamed up the river. Within two miles of Confederate earthworks, the Union warships spotted the schooner *Coquette*. Chaplin sent an armed crew to capture her and ordered the *Clover* to take her in tow as a prize. With the schooner secured Chaplin decided to learn if the battery above the ships was occupied.[71]

Dai Ching and *Clover* approached the rebel battery carefully. Chaplin ordered his 20-pounder rifled gun cast loose and trained it on the works. As the *Dai Ching* closed to within a mile of the fortifications, three guns opened on her. One shot fell short and the other two whistled over the deck. Chaplin ordered his engines reversed so that he could position his vessel in a bend in the river below. Here his steamer would be less exposed to the fort's gunfire. As the *Dai Ching* turned sharply in the strong ebb tide, Chaplin noticed his vessel steering toward a bank. He turned to his pilot, but found that he had abandoned the bridge and fled below. Chaplin rang three bells to reverse his engines, but the little steamer forged ahead and ran aground.[72]

The gunners on board quickly got the guns that could bear turned toward the enemy. They managed to swing the four 24-pound howitzers and the after 20-pound rifle towards the earthworks. Others in the crew began cutting away the main rail so that the 100-pounder could also be trained toward the enemy. Chaplin ordered the *Clover* to come up and assist. As the gun crews exchanged fire with the fort, *Clover* came up and, with great difficulty, passed a line to *Dai Ching*. When the line parted, instead of returning to pass a second hawser, the *Clover* unexplainably stood back down the river.[73]

Dai Ching was now alone. Chaplin sent a boat to communicate with the *Pawnee* and *Stettin* and repeatedly sent signals recalling *Clover* to the action. Acting Ensign Frank S. Leach of *Clover* ignored the pleas, and when Chaplin sent a boat to communicate with him, he withdrew his tug farther downriver.[74]

The *Dai Ching* was in a difficult position: the tide continued to fall, there was no help in sight, and the enemy gunners maintained a scathing fire. The enemy struck the *Dai Ching* more than thirty times. The naval gunners replied with vigor until the ammunition for the smaller guns was exhausted. Rather than exposing his men, Chaplin instructed most of his crew to jump into the marsh under the bow of the vessel. Here they lay protected from the enemy's fire. The gun crew at the 100-pounder continued defending the ship until a shot disabled this gun and wounded four men. After a seven-hour defense, Chaplin concluded he could no longer defend his wrecked ship, and he decided to destroy the *Dai Ching* and escape downriver. At 3:00 P.M. the ship was set ablaze. The only remaining usable boat carried the wounded, and the remaining men escaped in the marsh toward the mouth of the river. Nine of Chaplin's men suffered wounds, but the rest escaped, with the exception of five men captured trying to take a message to the *Clover*.[75]

A Court of Inquiry exonerated Chaplin for the loss of his gunboat and praised him and his men for the "spirit and bravery" they showed defending the vessel. The black pilot, Stephen Small, was to be punished for deserting his post. Acting Ensign Leach was charged with disobeying orders and deserting his post. He was put under arrest, and a naval general court martial found him guilty of these offenses. Leach was dismissed from the service and given five years of confinement at hard labor for his cowardice.[76]

On 28 January, in similar operations, the *Commodore McDonough* probed the Stono River and exchanged shots with Battery Pringle. On the twenty-ninth and thirtieth, the *Sonoma* and *Pawnee* helped General Potter change his base of operations from Edisto Island to White Point, the point of land between the North Edisto and Dawho rivers. On the thirtieth the gunboats supported the movement of the troops from the North Edisto and sent ashore a 12-pound rifled gun from *Sonoma*. Finding the Confederate positions well-defended, the two ships covered the embarkation of the soldiers and moved back downriver to their original anchorage.[77]

These "diversions" continued for several weeks, until 10 February, along the North Edisto, Wadmalaw, Folly, Combahee, and Stono rivers and Toogoodoo Creek. On the ninth, at Toogoodoo Creek, two miles above White Point off the North Edisto River, the *Pawnee*, *Sonoma*, and *Daffodil* engaged nearby Confederate batteries. *Pawnee* expended nearly four hundred shells and rebel gunners struck *Pawnee* ten times and the others twice each. The following day, in a diversion in the Stono, *Wissahickon*, *Commodore McDonough*, *Dan Smith*, *Geranium*, *Azalea*, and *C. P. Williams*, as well as the monitor *Lehigh*, shelled the Confederate works and protected the flanks and front of the troops ashore. Cooperating with General Schimmelfennig, the navy transported troops, horses, and guns, and steamed up narrow and winding waterways. Schemmelfinnig's troops landed on James Island under the covering fire of the naval vessels. While this landing took place, *Commodore McDonough* and the mortar schooner *Dan Smith* ascended Folly River near Secessionville as a further diversion. By the tenth, though, Sherman had firmly established his army's presence in South Carolina and was feinting toward Branchville, sixty miles west of Charleston.[78]

A shadow was cast on the operations when Gillmore returned to Charleston on 6 February to replace the ailing Foster. Foster went north, reportedly to have an old wound treated, but others surmised it was to save face. This substitution caught Dahlgren by surprise, but surprise turned into astonishment the following day. One of Dahlgren's officers brought a copy of General Gillmore's recently published book regarding the operations against the defenses of Charleston. Throughout the pages, Dahlgren's name was mentioned and at each citation he could see that the book was a "vindication" of Gillmore's actions at Dahlgren's "expense." This was more than the admiral could take. He knew that this destroyed any potential working relationship that the two might have and for a third time he asked to be relieved.[79]

On 11 February the two officers met for the first time since Gillmore's return. Gillmore decided to visit Dahlgren and boarded the flagship. Dahlgren had no intention of pretending that the relationship was cordial. When the general crossed the deck to shake Dahlgren's hand, the admiral bowed, directed him to his cabin, but did not take his hand. No one, however, seemed to notice Dahlgren's snub. In the cabin, they briefly discussed the upcoming Bull Bay demonstration and Gillmore left without mentioning the incident.[80]

Using his overwhelming numbers and control of the sea, Sherman directed a feint at Bull Bay to again try to draw off Confederate troops from the Charleston area. A landing here would threaten the back door of Charleston via the Wando River. Dahlgren's warships convoyed a force under the command of General Potter to the landing site. On 12 January the larger warships remained outside while *Pawnee, Sonoma, Ottawa, Winona, Potomska,* the side-wheel steamer and ex-blockade runner *Wando,* and schooner *James S. Chambers* and the tugs *Geranium, Iris,* and *Catalpa* entered the bay, under the command of Commander Fabius Stanly.[81]

The naval vessels and transports arrived at the bay with no clear idea of where to land. A gale and shallow water complicated the efforts to find a suitable site. The larger gunboats could not approach close enough to shore to provide covering support, so for the remainder of the day the naval forces sounded into Sewee Creek looking for a channel to Sewee Bay off the southwest corner of Bull Bay. Soundings through Sewee Bay on the thirteenth did not progress any faster because the boat crews came under fire from Confederate artillery. Confederate fire and bad weather stalled the Union forces for a couple more days. On the seventeenth, the naval forces managed to land about 750 men on the northern side of Bull Bay at Owendaw Creek. The remaining troops landed the following day with little or no effect on the Confederates and their deployments around Charleston.[82]

By the time these troops landed, the Confederate high command had already decided to abandon Charleston. The city was becoming increasingly isolated as Sherman advanced inland. By 14 February, General Beauregard determined that the garrison in the city was more important than the city itself. He realized that it would be only a few days before he abandoned the city, and began making plans for the orderly withdrawal of his forces.[83]

The situation, though, deteriorated more rapidly than the Confederates wished. On the thirteenth, Dahlgren received a cipher letter from Sherman that indicated he might have to turn back to Charleston. This turn of events and the note that Dahlgren received from Sherman on the thirteenth, caused the admiral to change his mind about his earlier request to be relieved. Now, with another chance to take part in an attack, and at the very least to enter the conquered city, he fired off a letter to the Navy Department withdrawing his 7 February request. It was clear that Dahlgren did not wish to command unless his reputation would benefit. His search for glory continued to overwhelm his sense of duty.[84]

The Evacuation

Rumors that the rebels planned to evacuate Charleston began to spread rapidly. Anticipating that the Confederates might evacuate some of the outer works first, Dahlgren instructed *Lehigh*, *Wissahickon*, and other gunboats to keep advancing up the Stono in order to cover the Union troops. By the seventeenth, the Confederates had withdrawn most of men from James Island and the Union forces easily took possession of the works along the Stono River. The navy, though, advanced with caution after discovering torpedoes in the river. The remaining rebels evacuated their positions on the night of the seventeenth. At dusk on the seventeenth, the *Lehigh* and *Wissahickon* began a steady covering fire for the Union troops ashore. These warships maintained this fire from 8:00 P.M. until 2:00 A.M. The following day the *Nahant* arrived in the afternoon to bolster the naval force.[85]

By the night of the seventeenth, the evacuation in Charleston was full-scale. The Confederate naval forces, however, had no way to escape. Flag Officer John Randolph Tucker, commanding the forces afloat at Charleston, ordered his ironclads destroyed. On the morning of the eighteenth, the three commissioned ironclads were set on fire. This destruction created a "magnificent spectacle." The *Palmetto State* exploded first, followed by the *Chicora* at 9:00 A.M. The *Charleston*, the newest of the ironclads, blew up two hours later. Her red-hot plates fell on the wharves of Charleston and set them on fire. A witness recalled that "the whole upper works and decks were blown upward into the air, when they appeared to float for an instant . . . then fall into the shallow water of the harbor."[86]

On the eighteenth, the monitors on picket duty at the entrance of the harbor had no idea that the Confederate ironclads no longer existed. During the mid and morning watches the men spotted large fires and an occasional heavy explosion came from the direction of Charleston. At daylight the monitor *Canonicus*, a new addition to the squadron, got underway and steamed toward Fort Moultrie, but thick haze prevented lookouts from seeing anything until 7:00 A.M. At 7:45, the haze cleared, lookouts could see the rebel flags still flying on Fort Moultrie, Castle Pickney, and Battery Bee, as well as in the city. The *Canonicus* threw two shells into the fort and received no response. Lieutenant Commander Belknap immediately sent a tug to the sloop *John Adams* to inform the senior officer. These two shots by the *Canonicus* were the last two shots fired at Charleston after nearly eighteen months of continuous bombardment.[87]

With the fate of the *Patapsco* in mind, Belknap did not risk taking his ironclad farther into the harbor. As the Confederate demolition crews finished their work, the magazine at Battery Bee exploded. Knowing that the enemy still had small parties of men in the forts destroying stores, magazines, and armaments, the Union officers could not risk sending a boat ashore to reconnoiter. Later that morning the monitor *Mahopac*, another new addition to the squadron, weighed anchor and steamed up near the *Canonicus*. Belknap then moved *Canonicus* near the Wagner Buoy. Here he spotted a Union army boat showing a white flag pulling away from Cumming's Point toward Fort Sumter. Minutes later another boat began pulling for Sullivan's Island. Realizing that the enemy had abandoned their works, he put his ship about and sent ashore an armed boat to land at Fort Moultrie, but the army boat arrived first. At 9 A.M., Belknap boarded the blockade runner *Celt* loaded with cotton. She ran aground near Fort Moultrie on the fourteenth and never got off. When the American flag was hoisted over Fort Sumter, the crews of *Mahopac* and *Canonicus* gave "nine rousing cheers" to indicate their delight with the capture of the symbol of secession.[88]

The word of the evacuation spread fast through the fleet and warships began to steam to the entrance of the harbor. Dahlgren also learned and brought the *Harvest Moon* from the Stono River that morning, crossing the bar at Charleston at 1:00 P.M. He arrived off Fort Moultrie an hour later. With the threat of torpedoes still substantial, Dahlgren made up his mind "to go in, torpedoes or not." With the mate of a blockade runner guiding him in, Dahlgren, his staff, and several of his officers "quietly steamed up to the wharves and walked through the town."[89]

With the abandonment of Charleston common news about the squadron, small boats and naval vessels began racing into the harbor. Sailors from the tug *Gladiolus* boarded the burning blockade runner *Syren* at the docks on the Ashley River. The seaman found a group of blacks on the ship loading their boats with *Syren*'s cargo. Organizing the men into a bucket brigade, the crew managed to save the vessel. The war's most successful blockade runner was sent north as a prize. Meanwhile, Belknap went ashore on Sullivan's Island and kept the blockading running signal lights trimmed. At 9:00 that evening a steamer stood down Maffitt's Channel toward the harbor, but ran aground near Fort Beauregard. She proved to be the blockade runner *Deer*. The officers on board the *Deer*, despite noticing incorrect signals, proceeded anyway. The federal forces also captured the unfinished ironclad *Columbia*, which ran aground near Fort Moultrie on 12 January. Other Confederate warships captured included three torpedo boats, the transport *Queen Mab*, the hulk *Lady Davis*, and the tug *Transport*.[90]

Finis

As the Confederate forces withdrew up the coast before the advance of Sherman's army, the Union vessels continued probing up the rivers to disrupt enemy movements and to preserve the bridges and railroad trestles. Northward, at Georgetown, Dahlgren quickly ordered vessels up the North Santee and to the harbor of Georgetown. The shallow water on the bar at the Santee prevented all but the shallowest draft vessels from proceeding. The tug *Geranium* and the ferry boat *Commodore McDonough* both explored this waterway. On George Washington's birthday, while the fleet celebrated, the Confederates evacuated Georgetown. On the twenty-third, *Pawnee*, *Mingoe*, and *Nipsic* stood up Winyah Bay toward Georgetown. These ships captured Fort White on the Pee Dee River and then steamed to the town. After the Marines landed, the naval officers accepted the surrender of Georgetown from the local officials.[91]

Other gunboats cooperated with army forces up the Cooper River. On 25 February the side-wheel steamers *Sonoma* and *Chenango* accompanied the armed transport *Savannah* carrying one hundred troops. These warships crept up the Cooper River to "follow up" Confederate forces, hoping to reach the head of navigation of the Cooper River at the Santee Canal. This canal connected the Cooper to the Santee River. Their real objective was to save a trestle of the North Eastern Railroad that crossed here. When the Union force arrived they found that the Confederates had already crossed the river and burned the trestle. With no further need for the navy, the two gunboats returned to their anchorages in Charleston.[92]

Despite the close cooperation and success of his forces, an article that appeared in the New York *Herald* on 22 February soured Dahlgren. The article, written by a correspondent attached to Gillmore's headquarters, pointed out that it was "not likely a chance will be afforded to the squadron to emulate the actions of Porter's and Farragut's brilliant organization." This statement, Dahlgren pointed out, was "unjust personally and so hurtful to the discipline of my command." Yet the article really struck at Dahlgren's ego because in essence it summed up his deepest regret—his personal failure to achieve a glorious victory. Gillmore denied any responsibility, but it intensified the feud between them. Dahlgren maintained that the general was responsible for the article since a correspondent attached to his command wrote it.[93]

The squadron's most daunting task after the Confederate evacuation was clearing the harbors and rivers of torpedoes and obstructions. These weapons and obstacles posed a serious threat to shipping; it would be months before normal trade could resume. On the morning of 1 March, the *Harvest Moon* weighed anchor and stood down Winyah Bay en route to Charleston. At 7:45 A.M., Dahlgren, pacing in his cabin, heard a loud explosion. The admiral witnessed the bulkhead separating his cabin and the wardroom shatter and fly toward him. Unhurt, Dahlgren thought that either the ship's boiler or a magazine had exploded. Instead, a Confederate torpedo struck under the starboard quarter, blasting a large hole in the hull and tearing up the deck over it. The *Harvest Moon* immediately began to sink and within five minutes settled on the bottom with her upper decks above the water. The tug *Clover* removed Dahlgren and his staff. The explosion killed one of the wardroom stewards. Five days later *Jonquil* struck a torpedo in the Ashley River and, less than three weeks later, another torpedo damaged the Coast Survey steamer *Bibb* in Charleston Harbor.[94]

For the next two months Dahlgren spent most of his time and energy reducing his command. He worked with the Navy Department to return north the men and ships no longer necessary for the blockade and other military actions. He discharged the chartered vessels and transferred their cargoes to other ships or ashore. He also stopped all the extra work at the shops in Port Royal and sent unneeded hands north. The remaining warships in the squadron continued their blockade and performed reconnaissance missions up the rivers between Charleston and Georgetown. On 11 April Lincoln proclaimed all the major ports within the squadron closed to all traffic except those with supplies for the army and navy.[95]

On the fourth anniversary of Sumter's surrender, the victorious Union forces held a ceremony to celebrate this anniversary and the approaching end of the war. The day before the ceremony, the news of Robert E. Lee's surrender reached Charleston, adding to the festivities. At 8:00 A.M., Dahlgren ordered his ships dressed and they fired a twenty-one-gun salute. Soldiers and sailors lined the wharf and walls of Fort Sumter as dignitaries came to participate in the celebration. Amidst "great cheering" Brigadier General Robert Anderson raised the same flag he had hauled down four years earlier. After a one-hundred-gun salute, the Reverend Henry Ward Beecher gave a speech and a prayer that ended the ceremony. At sunset the ships fired another salute to conclude the remembrance.[96]

On 17 June, with all the major Confederate commands surrendered, Dahlgren made his final preparations to turn the squadron over to Acting Rear Admiral William Radford and sail north. Many of his officers boarded the flagship *Philadelphia* to bid him a final farewell. His last official act was to issue a general order to his officers and men recalling their important accomplishments. At 3:30 P.M., he transferred to the *Pawnee* for the trip north. She hoisted her anchor at 4:00 P.M. and, as she got underway, fired a thirteen gun salute. On 12 July, three weeks after Dahlgren arrived in Washington, D.C., he hauled down his flag during a thirteen-gun salute, ending his two years of command afloat.[97]

CONCLUSION

"The Fall of Satan's Kingdom"

The defining moment of the Civil War for the South Atlantic Blockading Squadron was the 7 April 1863 attack on Charleston. All the efforts of the squadron before this date were aimed at controlling the coast and capturing Confederate-held port cities. After the capture of key points along the South Atlantic coast, the Navy Department determined that it must strike Charleston. Despite warnings that this venture would be both difficult and risky, events seemed to accelerate headlong toward this attack. Union leaders held that Charleston was the keystone of the Confederate psyche. They believed the enemy's loss of the cradle of the rebellion would certainly spell ruin to the Confederate cause. Furthermore, Fox was convinced that a naval victory would showcase the monitors as invulnerable warships capable of taking any defended port. But, with a Union defeat, Charleston retained its importance as a symbol of the rebellion. It was not only a military defeat, but also a political reversal. All the Union naval actions after the April 1863 attack were intrinsically tied to this failure. It left a legacy that not only influenced all the strategic decisions on both sides of the harbor but also ruined Du Pont's reputation and left the subsequent commanding officers fearful of failure.

The navy began its activity on the South Atlantic seaboard with the establishment of a blockade. The institution of a blockade was an attack on the economic infrastructure of the South. When Du Pont sailed with a large attacking force and instructions to capture as many ports as possible, this economic warfare was carried farther. The capture of coastal towns made the interruption of trade more certain and it allowed the naval forces to more thoroughly watch the remaining ports. Du Pont's gunboats, furthermore, carried the war into the interior. The sorties in the interior often destroyed the Confederates' means of making a living and disrupted the local economy. Just the presence of the gunboats was enough to throw the local populace into a panic and often stopped the tending, harvesting, and movement of cotton to market. This naval activity actually accomplished more than designed.

Charleston, a major Southern port, enjoyed early success as a center for blockade runners. Its value to the Confederacy, however, gradually diminished. By the beginning of 1863, Wilmington, North Carolina, became the major port of entry in the Confederacy. Both ship owners and the Confederate government shifted their operations to this port for several reasons. Charleston was farther to the front than Wilmington. Supplies coming into Charleston had to travel an extra two hundred miles over an already burdened rail system to get to Virginia. Wilmington was also more difficult to blockade because of the Cape Fear River's two widely separated entrances. But Charleston's usefulness or viability as a port of entrance all but ceased when Dahlgren stationed his monitors in the main ship channel. This deployment prevented virtually all but the fast and medium- to shallow-draft runners from using the port with a good chance of success.

The blockade of twenty-one ports maintained by the squadron may be considered effective. Although steamers arrived and cleared over 120 times, this represents only about half as much trade as that which ran into Wilmington. The squadron also captured and destroyed over 150 vessels, both coastal and inland. These were mainly small trading schooners used in the interior waterways. The squadron captured or destroyed only 28 steamers along the coast. This figure is low because the capture of the port towns and entrances virtually stopped Southern trade. The Confederates did not try to contest this control and for the most part conceded these entrances to the Union forces.

The Confederates realistically did not have the means to oppose the Union navy. The weak and quickly built defenses that the Union forces encountered early in the war proved no match for the naval forces. Nevertheless, once the weak forts and the smaller undefended port towns fell, the Confederate leaders concentrated on building strong defensive works at Charleston and Savannah. The Confederacy's hopes lay in a long-term and patient approach of disrupting and annoying the Union vessels when they lay in vulnerable positions. Early in the war the blockaders anchored along most of the coast with little fear of Confederate reprisal. As the Confederates built ironclads to contest the blockade and to protect the interior waters, the Union countered by building numerous and more powerful monitors to negate the threat of the Confederate ironclads.

The success with the blockade enjoyed by both Du Pont and Dahlgren can be partially attributed to the fact that both men were able to keep their ships operational. The logistical problems of the squadron were not as severe as those suffered by other commands. The first-rate repair facility located at Port Royal was conveniently placed nearly equidistant from the operational limits of the squadron. Additionally, the blockade for most of the war was carried out from stations inside the numerous sounds and waterways. This created less coal consumption and less wear and tear on the machinery of the warships. All these factors contributed materially to the overall readiness of the squadron to undertake additional operations when needed.

By operating along the South Atlantic coastline with superior forces both ashore and afloat, the United States posed a continuous threat. Despite the overwhelming superiority of the Union forces and the mobility they enjoyed, this advantage went largely unused, untried, or ignored. After the initial capture of the major port towns, the combined forces made only several minor attempts, but made no earnest effort to move into the interior to disrupt Confederate activities, logistical bases, railroads, or any other communications. In part, this was due to a lack of transportation for interior operations. The army garrisoned the towns and merely denied the Confederates their use. Holding these towns forced the Confederates to keep troops nearby, but the demands of keeping idle garrisons along the coast denied a larger fighting force to the Union war effort. When these men remained inactive, they contributed little to the war while consuming immense amounts of supplies.

Du Pont arrived with instructions to capture and hold as many ports as he could. The capture of Port Royal, Fernandina, Beaufort and other points were purely naval victories. But once the armies landed there was no real continuing strategy. The Union forces had no plans to consolidate or follow these conquests with thrusts into the interior. The War Department never made any commitment to large campaigns with broad reaching goals. When the Union forces captured Fort Pulaski and James Island in 1862, they might have developed either of these campaigns to include larger objectives. The failure to exploit the landings on James Island stands out as a tremendous mistake. The Morris Island campaign in 1863 had similar shortcomings. Misunderstandings and false expectations of long-range goals crippled any continuing strategy.

The ease of the early naval victories may have influenced the Navy and War departments as well as the public. Some Union leaders had an inflated perception of the capability of naval gunfire to reduce fortifications. In 1863 Du Pont, in particular, found the army unable and unwilling to support a combined effort to take Charleston. This lack of cooperation, however, did not relieve the Navy Department's pressure on Du Pont. Both Welles and Fox made it abundantly clear that they wanted Du Pont to make something happen at Charleston. After the ironclads sailed south, the department, and particularly Fox, believed these warships were the solution to attacking this heavily defended harbor, despite Du Pont's cries for more force and a combined operation. When this attack failed, no one had an alternate plan and the finger pointing began.

Yet, the six-month delay in building and delivering the monitors to Du Pont altered the strategic circumstances. It allowed the Confederates time to strengthen their defenses. Du Pont realized this, but Fox became so emotionally attached to the Charleston project that he lost all his objectivity. The department viewed Du Pont as relcaltricant and Fox turned a blind eye to the reservations that Du Pont pointed out. Maybe Fox believed that the capture of the port would somehow serve as revenge for his failed attempted to relieve Fort Sumter in 1861. The Navy Department, so confident of a quick success, issued orders on 2 April to send the ironclads to the Gulf Theatre after the attack. In the battle, Du Pont proved that invulnerability could not overcome a greater volume of fire, a cardinal rule of naval gunnery. Failure fell on Du Pont's shoulders alone, despite the department's promise to share in this defeat. The department deflected the political ramifications of the defeat by allowing Du Pont to shoulder all the blame. The public viewed it as a military setback. Du Pont, a somewhat tragic figure, spent the remaining two years of his life trying to exonerate himself.

Du Pont's failure at Charleston did not sway the department's quixotic vision of taking the port. Additionally, Fox believed a naval victory outweighed the need of a combined operation. His personal goals ran counter to those that might have led to a successful campaign at Charleston and other strategic points. The department never did formulate a viable strategy to make use of the monitors. The department never withdrew them to operate at either Wilmington or Mobile until late in the war. Politically, this was not feasible in 1863. To withdraw the ironclads after the Charleston fight would have admitted defeat.

Dahlgren arrived to take command of the squadron virtually on the eve of the defeat. Dahlgren's deep desire for a glorious climactic battle, whereby he would emerge as a victorious leader, only made him more cautious. During his entire career Dahlgren had never experienced a command where he had to take risks. He showed immense personal bravery and seemed willing to risk his life but not his reputation. Had he lost in a climactic battle like Du Pont, it would have ended his quest for glory.

Dahlgren thought that his prime mission was to cooperate with the army and with some luck he would get his chance for glory. With about the same number of ironclads as Du Pont had he did an excellent job. His warships made the capture of Morris Island by the army possible. Without naval support, General Gillmore's force could not have landed nor remained there. The Union forces seemed to move closer to taking Charleston in the fall of 1863, when the combined army and naval forces pounded Fort Sumter into rubble. Dahlgren, who had a better prepared ironclad force than Du Pont, however, refused to commit to any naval sortie into the harbor. Dahlgren's ironclads were greatly strengthened by the addition of armor on vulnerable parts of the warships. Additionally, he had a special working party to make repairs. Du Pont had neither, and he was held accountable for pointing out that a purely naval attack could not succeed. Dahlgren, in a stronger position than his predecessor, believed that a naval attack would not be successful. If this was so, then Du Pont was correct; his forces never stood a chance.[1]

Dahlgren, though, suffered through attacks not from the department but from the press. But it is no small wonder that Gillmore appeared less culpable to the public than Dahlgren. Gillmore's access to the press only aided his cause. The public read how he had captured Morris Island and deprived Fort Sumter of its offensive powers in September 1863. During 280 days of bombardment, Fort Sumter endured over forty-six thousand projectiles weighing in excess of more than seven million pounds of metal. There was no other bombardment during the war that could compare. He fully believed the navy capable of passing the batteries, because Fort Sumter gave, in Gillmore's mind, no advantage to the Confederate defense. As an engineer he did not fully understand naval matters, but he blamed the navy for not moving forward, having done his job within the parameters of his profession. Dahlgren, though, blamed Gillmore for not assaulting Battery Wagner when it might have been taken with little effort. Dahlgren maintained that he used up his ironclads against the defenses of Morris Island. He believed that by the time Fort Sumter was no longer a threat, his worn-out ironclads were in no position to pass into the harbor against better prepared defenses. Within the confines of the harbor, the navy would face fortifications stronger than Fort Sumter. The naval vessels had no way of delivering a fire that could destroy or silence these guns. Unless he had an inflated perception of naval gunfire's capabilities, this was a premise that Gillmore the engineer could certainly understand, but failed to acknowledge.[2] The public certainly never could understand the delays and viewed the navy as dilatory. Again, the lack of a continuing strategy or a sense of realistic goals set down by the leaders in Washington is evident.

In August 1864, Rear Admiral David Glasgow Farragut was asked to solve a similar problem—to force his way into the harbor at Mobile, Alabama. This battle immortalized his name and earned him enduring fame and distinction. Yet this attack was not nearly as risky or were the defenses as difficult to overcome. Farragut's warships had only to pass eighteen guns to reach the harbor. Once past these guns the warships were safe from the shore batteries and had only to contend with the ironclad *Tennessee*. In contrast, Du Pont's warships faced seventy-six guns at the throat of the harbor and similar defenses within the harbor. There was virtually no place for Du Pont's warships to anchor safely out of the range of the enemy's guns. He also had two ironclads to deal with. Dahlgren faced a similar number of guns and an additional ironclad. Furthermore, Du Pont and Dahlgren faced the dilemma of losing an ironclad to the enemy if she became disabled. Finally, at Charleston the strategy promoted by the Navy Department was flawed and the political stakes were much higher than those faced by Farragut.

The heavy armament of the forts did not by itself keep the ironclads at bay. It was also the unknown character of the obstructions and the knowledge that torpedoes might bar the way. Here both admirals failed either to acquire fully the necessary information to deal effectively with these weapons, or to test their capabilities. Both men knew that these weapons might influence an attack and cause failure, but neither did the necessary reconnaissance work to learn the nature of the obstructions and torpedoes. Both assumed that the defenses were too formidable. This fear of the unknown stopped Du Pont's attack and influenced Dahlgren never to undertake one. But the Confederate officers never believed that the obstructions were "formidable" or that they effectively blocked the harbor. The Confederates only maintained the appearance that they were formidable. The obstructions were designed merely to slow down an enemy so that the fire from the forts could damage or sink vessels trying to force the harbor. Torpedoes augmented the obstructions and, by 1865, included 123 in Charleston and the Stono River. Yet, like the obstructions, the Confederate authorities did not feel that the torpedoes could effectively keep the Union ships out of the harbor.[3]

With Fort Sumter reduced to an infantry outpost, it is puzzling that Dahlgren did not at least make some effort to examine the obstructions throughly. The blockade runners were passing in, so there was an opening. Had Dahlgren pressed for a thorough examination of the obstructions, however, he then had no excuse for not forcing his way into the harbor. Dahlgren realized that, even if his warships passed into the harbor, they faced Confederate defenses as strong as those Du Pont encountered in April 1863. Dahlgren did not commit his forces because he feared defeat.

It is ironic that after Morris Island fell Dahlgren soon found himself in a position similar to that of Du Pont. Dahlgren, as squadron commander, accomplished little other than cooperating with the army forces to capture Morris Island and reduce Fort Sumter. He lost two ironclads, the *Housatonic*, and several other blockaders. His boat attack on Fort Sumter failed miserably and torpedo attacks plagued his command. The loss of *Water Witch* was particularly embarrassing. Despite this seemingly poor record Welles never mentioned the removal of Dahlgren and kept him in command in spite of his repeated requests to be relieved. This might be explained several ways. Welles needed someone at Charleston who could keep the status quo. Dahlgren was not a great commanding officer but he managed to do this. During the latter part of the war, Welles and the department had several controversies brewing—the trouble with Du Pont, the shortcomings of the *Casco* class ironclads, and repeated attacks by members of Congress. The department could not afford to enter any more disputes. Lastly, and extremely important, Dahlgren was Lincoln's favorite naval officer and his removal might invite questions and maybe the displeasure of the president.

Both admirals, though, found it difficult to coordinate any activity because the command structure created a situation that complicated cooperation between the armed forces. Personalities, egos, and misunderstandings continually strained the relationship between the services. Du Pont managed to overcome the ego problems to some extent but neither he nor Dahlgren had anywhere to appeal any disagreement other than to Welles and Fox. Since Welles and Fox did not work particularly well with the secretary of war, any conflicts that could not be resolved were appealed directly to Lincoln. When solutions to problems needed attention at this level, the petty differences between the commanders went unsolved. When the large egos of Dahlgren and Gillmore became engaged, a larger wedge was driven between the army and navy in the South Atlantic Theatre of operations. Dahlgren conceded much more in the relationship than Gillmore, but the structures of inter-service cooperation were already dysfunctional and could not be repaired to help these men.

The lack of any inter-service cooperation before the war laid the groundwork for the problems. The failure began at the top and trickled down. Both services remained hamstrung because of separate service traditions, organization, doctrine, and the lack of unified command. Without a general staff type of organization, these problems could not be hammered out. There was no one person responsible for overall command decisions. Had there been a greater understanding and more cooperation in planning and strategy, the forces along the South Atlantic seaboard would have made a much larger contribution to the war effort.

The army certainly should have been more active. It had a large number of troops available to attack Confederate positions. Nevertheless, until Sherman swept through the area in 1865, the naval vessels virtually defined the reach of the Union forces along the South Atlantic coast. Not until November 1864 did the Union forces make an attempt to cut one of the railroads leading from Charleston. There were several places along the coast where, with naval support, the Union forces might have accomplished this strategic goal. The Charleston and Savannah Railroad should have been attacked repeatedly. There were no orders from Washington to this effect and the leaders in the Department of the South showed little initiative. The army was more active during the first two years of the war. When Gillmore took command this changed. Gillmore, the engineer, understood siege warfare, but had little knowledge of field operations. He failed to utilize his large force effectively after the capture of Morris Island. The War Department never considered the operations in this theatre to be essential until 1865. After 1863, it rarely pressured any of the commanding officers or gave them the resources to aggressively attack the enemy.[4]

The possession of an overwhelmingly superior naval force gave the Union a much greater control over its actions and movements. Yet, after the initial ports were captured, the Union leaders failed to exploit this advantage. The presence of the naval force made it mandatory for the Confederates to disperse their forces to protect vulnerable targets and to maintain a defensive perimeter. The army nevertheless failed to fully use the naval assets to pressure the Confederate defenses, to land troops, project their power, or make the Confederate defense bend and stretch to parry continuing thrusts.

The Union's military superiority might have been even larger. Dahlgren continually waited for the new *Casco* class monitors, scheduled to be ready in the fall and winter of 1863. Their design problems prevented the department from putting these warships into service as intended and most lay unfinished until after the war. Had the *Casco* class monitors been available, Dahlgren may have made the grand attack he envisioned. Their delayed procurement altered Union naval strategy at Charleston and likely altered the army's strategic thinking. Increasingly, the Navy Department's view of the situation at Charleston was tied to the success of the ironclads.

After Morris Island fell, the navy made no real effort to utilize the monitors for a full-scale offensive movement. These warships represented the greatest expenditure of the department during the war, and yet they lay idle much of the time off Charleston. The Navy Department did not wish to send the ironclads elsewhere for other operations. The department was not ready to attack any of the Gulf ports or Wilmington. Fox and Welles had made an immense political and military commitment at Charleston, from which they could hardly retreat. The ironclads were also physically able to remain there. The facilities at Port Royal facilitated easy repairs and maintenance. Both Fox and Welles realized that at any moment the army might agree to cooperate and, once transferred to other commands, it would be problematic to recall these warships. The greatest symptom that this points to, however, is again the lack of continuing strategy. The Union leaders had no strategic progression to utilize their naval resources, no prioritized goals. They had no long-term strategy formulated and seemed to plan strategy as a reaction to a particular crisis.

Since the Union forces failed to utilize their large force, one might argue that this worked in the favor of the Confederacy. A large number of ironclads and gunboats lay off this coast and in the waters to protect army positions and to perform blockade duty. The garrisons did little during the war except hold these small bits of territory. The garrisons that held the coastal areas did effectively limit blockade running, but added little else to the war effort. The blockade likely would have been just as airtight with the naval vessels that were required to protect the troops ashore at sea instead.

The greatest error by the Union forces was their failure to change the center of gravity in the theatre. After the initial victories along the coast, virtually the entire effort by both the army and navy along the South Atlantic coast was aimed at Charleston. The city of Charleston, however, had less military value after the summer of 1863. The rise of Wilmington as the major port of the blockade runners had Charleston contributing less to the war effort. Both sides continued to fight for control because this city had great political value. Even though its downfall would have done little to change the war in the East, both Du Pont and Dahlgren became entangled in the Navy Department's narrow vision and a lack of continuing strategy. Attacking into the harbor and the capture of the city, however, would have required a combined operation. The stalled operations at Charleston delayed attacks at Wilmington and Mobile until the end of the war. The incredible resources spent on the combined operations against Morris Island and the destruction of Fort Sumter led to nothing strategic. Neither branch of the service nor the leaders in Washington projected a strategy beyond the capture of the port. Gaining access to the harbor without capturing Charleston had little or no continuing military value. Yet the Navy Department asked both admirals to risk everything for an objective that they could not clearly understand.

This defective strategy led Du Pont and Dahlgren down a chute to certain failure. The reason that Fox and Welles never focused on a more far-reaching plan was their faith in the ability of the monitors. Du Pont's failure in his coup de main in April 1863 did not deter the department. Dahlgren, however, also failed without trying. The difference between Dahlgren and Du Pont was the latter's outspoken criticism of the lack of the department's foresight. Dahlgren was a less capable leader than Du Pont, but kept quiet and maintained the status quo. Dahlgren realized that he "acted strictly under the views of the department." Dahlgren did not earn the laurels that he sought, but he did keep his warships actively engaged against the Charleston defenses. Both men failed to achieve the department's defective goals. Neither Welles nor Fox seemed to have any real understanding of the intrinsic value of capturing the city other than making banner headlines, which would blunt some of the criticism aimed at the department. Whereas Dahlgren grudgingly accepted the reproach of the papers as a consequence of the public's misunderstanding, he still believed the department should have come forward to claim the responsibility for the policy. Du Pont, however, could not accept this reproach and tried to force the department to acknowledge its failed policy and its shortcomings.[5]

The South Atlantic Blockading Squadron seemingly had little effect on the national war effort. Overall, the effect is perhaps slight. The blockade was effective in keeping out only about one in five attempts by steam blockade runners. Still, not a large number of vessels even ran the blockade of the South Atlantic seaboard after 1863. The department provided this command the most powerful warships in the navy. Yet with the exception of Du Pont's 7 April 1863 attack and the Morris Island campaign, it could be claimed that the ironclads were never fully utilized for the purpose the department sent them. Once the Union forces occupied Morris Island, the ironclads virtually sat out the rest of the war. These warships might have been better used strategically to capture Wilmington or Mobile and end the war quicker. The navy force, however, was not diminished because it protected the Union positions and kept the status quo. Political considerations kept the monitors and a strong naval force off Charleston, and influenced naval operations, particularly during the last two and one half years of the war.[6]

The capture of Charleston clearly became a political goal and nothing more. Neither of the branches of the service found it useful to work together to accomplish this objective. The lack of cooperation resulted, in part, because the army and navy's goals were different. In the Eastern Theatre, the army concentrated early in the war on the capture of Richmond. Lincoln later consistently urged his generals to make Lee's army rather than Richmond their target. General Lee, however, used the Confederate capitol to anchor his defensive lines. Thus, the Union army's goal did not change appreciably. The navy aided when it could, but remained focused at Charleston. This polarization of goals diminished the possibility of a joint movement. Both Du Pont and Dahlgren insisted that cooperation was necessary to capture Charleston, but the leaders in Washington never agreed to organize a combined operation for this purpose. Sharing a political victory seemed undesirable. Thus, both the Navy and War departments underutilized a large number of resources during the last half of the conflict.

Although most of the South Atlantic coastline was in Union hands by spring 1862, Charleston and Savannah did not fall until the last months of the war. It might be asserted that the Confederates won the campaign along the South Atlantic seaboard until Sherman's soldiers marched to the sea and then moved northward. In 1865 Gustavus Fox finally witnessed the "fall of Satan's Kingdom." But one must question how the Navy Department's desires for a victory at Charleston affected the war effort. Although the South Atlantic Blockading Squadron played an active role along the South Atlantic seaboard and contributed to Confederate defeat, it was a failure in the Union's leadership that kept the armed forces from making a quicker and more substantial contribution to this defeat

NOTES

Introduction

1. W. F. G. Peck. "Four Years Under Fire at Charleston," *Harper's New Monthly Magazine,* vol. XXXL (August 1865), p. 358.

2. The screw steamer *Pochantas* was also sent to relieve the fort, but arrived only in time to evacuate the troops.

3. Fox to Du Pont, 6 January 1863, 3 April, 3 June 1862, Gustavus Vasa Fox, *Confidential Correspondence of Gustavus Vasa Fox: Assistant Secretary of the Navy, 1861–1865,* 2 vols., Robert Means Thompson and Richard Wainwright, eds. (New York: De Vinne Press, 1918–1919), 1:114–15, 126–28, 172–73.

Chapter 1

1. Lincoln's proclamation did not in reality establish a blockade. The blockade of each port had to be established by written notification sent ashore from a naval vessel. Abraham Lincoln to William Seward, 19, 27 April 1861, eds. Richard Rush et al., *Official Records of the Union and Confederate Navies in the War of the Rebellion,* 31 vols. (Washington, D.C.: Government Printing Office, 1894–1927), ser. 1, 5:620–21 (hereafter cited as *ORN*); *Report of the Secretary of the Navy,* Sen. Ex. Doc. 1, 36th Cong., 2d sess., 1 December 1860, 5; U.S. Congress, House, *Number of Vessels in the Navy,* H. Ex. Doc. 159, 40th Cong., 2d sess., 1868; James Russel Soley, *The Navy in the Civil War: The Blockade and the Cruisers* (New York: Charles Scribner's Sons, 1883), 12; "Statement of the Number and Names of Vessels Belonging to or Connected With the Navy on the First of April 1861." Mobilization and Demobilization, Subject File OL, Naval Records Collections of the Office of Naval Records and Library, Record Group 45, National Archives, Washington, D.C. Hereinafter all references to Record Groups will be simply RG and to the National Archives NA.

2. John Lenthall to Gideon Welles, 8 November 1861, Letters Sent to the Secretary of the Navy From the Bureau of Construction and Repair, Letters Sent to the Secretary of the Navy, Entry 49, The Records of the Bureau of Ships, RG 19, NA.

3. The commanding officer of any group of ships was generally known as a flag officer because he was allowed to display a broad pennant or flag from the mast. Pendergrast To All Whom It May Concern, 30 April 1861, *ORN*, ser. 1, 4:356; Pendergrast File, ZB Collection, Naval Historical Center, Washington, D.C. Hereinafter all references to the Naval Historical Center will be NHC.

4. Soley, *The Blockade and the Cruisers*, 87.

5. Ibid., 88; A. D. Bache, "Notes on the Coast of the United States June 1861," Du Pont Family Papers, Hagley Museum and Library, Wilmington, Delaware, hereinafter cited as Du Pont Papers, Hagley; Du Pont et al., 13 July 1861, eds. R. N. Scott et al., *The War of the Rebellion: A Compilation of the Official Records of the Union and Confederate Armies*. 70 vols. (Washington, D.C.: Government Printing Office, 1880–1901), ser. 1, 53:67 (hereinafter cited as *ORA*); "The Southern Harbors of the United States," *The Merchants' Magazine and Commercial Review*, XLV (no. 1 July 1861):18.

6. Ibid.; First Report of Blockade Strategy Board, Du Pont, et al., 5 July 1861, *ORN*, ser. 1, 12:195–98.

7. Ibid., 88.

8. Tables of distances vary widely within the sources but I used figures from Department of Commerce, *Distances Between United States Ports* (Washington, D.C.: Government Printing Office, 1929).

9. The *Macedonian* was a frigate razeed into a sloop between 1852 and 1853. Pendergrast to Stringham, 14 May 1861, Pendergrast Papers, Entry 395, RG 45, NA. Pendergrast at this time referred to Stringham's command as the U.S. Blockading Squadron. Stringham's command also included the Potomac Flotilla. In a letter to S. Lee on 15 July 1861. Letters Sent by Flag Officer Garrett J. Pendergrast, Letter Books of Officers of the United States Navy at Sea, Entry 395, RG 45, NA; Stringham to Welles, 4 July 1861, *ORN*, ser. 1, 5:764–65; Welles to Stringham, 4 April, 17 May 1861, *ORN* ser. 1, 5:617, 621, 635; Welles to Pendergrast, ibid., 636; Stringham to Welles, 4 July 1861, ibid., 764–65; Welles to J. Smith, 30 May 1861, Subject File OL, Entry 464, RG 45, NA.

10. Stuart L. Bernath, *Squall Across the Atlantic: American Civil War Prize Cases and Diplomacy* (Los Angeles: The University of California Press, 1970), 8; Du Pont to Welles, 23 December 1861, *ORN*, ser. 1, 12:426–27. It was not until December 1861 that Du Pont modified the rules and allowed the seizure of all suspicious vessels.

11. *The Charleston Mercury*, 13 May 1861; *The Charleston Courier*, 13, 14 May 1861; The *Ella Warley* is given the distinction of the first vessel to run out with a load of cotton. E. Milby Burton, *The Siege of Charleston 1861–1865* (Columbia: University of South Carolina Press, 1970), 243; William W. McKean to Welles, 12 May 1861, *ORN*, ser. 1, 5:629.

12. The *Harriet Lane* was transferred to the Navy in September 1861. When the *Wabash* arrived she collided with the *Seminole*, thinking her a block-

ade runner. Roswell Lamson to Flora, 3 August 1861, Roswell Lamson to Katie, 10 July 1861, *Lamson of the Gettysburg: The Civil War Letters of Lieutenant Roswell H. Lamson, U.S. Navy,* eds. James M. and Patricia R. McPherson (New York: Oxford University Press, 1997), 23–24; Daniel Ammen, *The Old Navy and the New* (Philadelphia: J. B. Lippencott Co., 1891), 344.

13. Supplying water to the ships was also a major concern. A. D. Bache, Memoir Showing Locations for Fresh Water, Fuel and Water, Subject File, XF, RG 45, NA; Stringham to Paulding, 30 May 1861, *ORN,* ser. 1, 5:683; Charles Cowley, *Leaves From A Lawyer's Life Afloat and Ashore* (Lowell, Mass.: Penhallow Printing Company, 1879), 12–13; Stringham to Welles, 19, 30, May 1861, *ORN,* ser. 1, 5:648, 682; Mercer to Stringham, 10 July 1861, Transportation of Passengers and Supplies, Subject File OX, RG 45, NA; Welles to Stringham, 5 June 1861, *ORN,* ser. 1, 5:702–703.

14. International Law (nd), Subject File, VL, RG 45, NA; By 4 July, the navy had only twenty-two vessels in service off the Atlantic coast. Daniel Ammen, *The Navy In The Civil War: The Atlantic Coast* (New York: Charles Scribner's Sons, 1898), 11; Bunch to Lyons, 4, 5 June 1861, Great Britain, Foreign Office, *Papers Relating to the Blockade of the Ports of the Confederate States, Presented to Both Houses of Parliament by Command of Her Majesty 1862,* North America, No. 8, London: Harrison, 1862, 10–11.

15. Welles to Stringham, 21 May, 5 June 1861, *ORN,* ser. 1, 5:660–61, 701–702; Stringham to Welles, 24 May, 11 June, 1861, ibid. p 664, 714; Letters From Commandants of Navy Yards and Shore Stations, Entry 34, RG 45, NA; *Report of the Secretary of the Navy,* S. Ex. Doc. 1, 37th Cong., 1st sess., 4 July 1861; Purchases, Sales and Final Dispositions of Naval Vessels, Subject File AY, RG 45, NA.

16. Pendergrast to Stringham, Pendergrast Papers, 14 July 1861, Entry 395, RG 45, NA; Welles to Pendergrast, 29 August 1861, *ORN,* ser. 1, 6:145–46.

17. Dana, Charles A. *Recollections of the Civil War With the Leaders at Washington and in the Field in the Sixties* (New York: D. Appleton and Company, 1898), 170.

18. Paullin, "President Lincoln and the Navy," *The American Historical Review* XIV (January 1909), 286, 290.

19. Samuel Francis Du Pont to Sophie Du Pont, 28 June 1861, John D. Hayes, ed., *Samuel Francis Du Pont: A Selection From His Civil War Letters,* 3 vols. (Ithaca: Cornell University Press, 1969) 1:85–86, hereafter cited as Du Pont, *Letters.*

20. Notes of the Blockade Strategy Board, 13 July 1861, Strategy and Tactics, Subject File ON, RG 45, NA; James M. Merrill "Strategy Makers in the Union Navy Department 1861–1865," *Mid-America: An Historical Review* 44 (January 1962) 23; Du Pont, *Letters,* 1:lxviii; Charles Oscar Paullin, *Paullin's History of Naval Administration 1775–1911* (Annapolis: United States Naval Institute, 1968), 263–64.

21. Du Pont, *Letters*, 1:lxvii–ix; Paullin, *Naval Administration*, 263–64; Charles Henry Davis, *Life of Charles Henry Davis, Rear Admiral, 1807–1877* (Boston: Houghton, Mifflin and Company, 1899), 134.

22. Blockade Strategy Board Minutes (n.d.), 13 July 1861, Subject File ON, RG 45, NA.

23. Blockade Strategy Board to Welles, 13 July 1861, ibid.

24. Ibid.

25. Ibid.

26. McClellan also had ideas of attacking along the seaboard and issued a memorandum to Lincoln in August. George B. McClellan, *McClellan's Own Story* (New York: Charles L. Webster and Company, 1907), 103, 204–205; Blockade Strategy Board to Welles, 13 July 1861, Subject File ON, RG 45, NA; Blockade Strategy Board Memoranda, ibid.

27. Blockade Strategy Board Memoranda, 26 July 1861, Subject File ON, RG 45, NA.

28. Stephen B. Luce, "Naval Administration II," *Proceedings of the United States Naval Institute* XXVII (December 1902), 843.

29. Pendergrast to Stringham, 14 July 1861, *ORN*, ser. 1, 5:792; U.S. Navy, Naval History Division, *Dictionary of American Naval Fighting Ships*, 8 vols. (Washington, D.C.: Government Printing Office, 1959–1981), vol. VII, 407; Hereinafter cited as *DANFS*; Paul H. Silverstone, *Warships of the Civil War Navies* (Annapolis: Naval Institute Press, 1989), 112; J. R. Goldsborough to Stringham, 18 July 1861, *ORN*, ser. 1, 6:11; J. W. Livingston to Stringham, ibid., 86–87; P.F. Watmough et al. to Stringham, 9 August 1861, ibid., 81–82; L. C. Sartori to Stringham, 7 August 1861, ibid., 15–16, 65.

30. Samual Mercer to Stringham, 19 July 1861, *ORN*, ser. 1, 6:13–14; Pendergrast to Stringham, 22 July 1861, ibid., 25–26; Stringham to Fox, 10 September 1861, ibid., 192.

31. Pendergrast to S. Lee, 20 August 1861, ibid., 96; Hugh Dunlop to Mercer, 14 September 1861, ibid., 215; Regis A. Courtemanche, *No Need of Glory: The British Navy In American Waters 1860–1864* (Annapolis: United States Naval Institute, 1977), 17.

32. S. P. Lee later became the flag officer of the North Atlantic Blockading Squadron. Lee to Henry D. Grant, 28 September 1861, *ORN*, ser. 1, 6:294; Courtemanche, *No Need of Glory*, 29–31.

33. Marcus W. Price, "Blockade Running as a Business in South Carolina During the War Between the States, 1861–1865," *The American Neptune* IX (January 1949): 53–54; Soley, *Blockade and the Cruisers*, 89; *Daily Intelligencer* Atlanta, 18 September 1861.

34. International Law (n.d.), Subject File, VL, RG 45, NA.

35. Scharf, Thomas J. *History of the Confederate States Navy From Its Organization to the Surrender of Its Last Vessel* (New York: Rodgers and Sherwood, 1887, reprint Fairfax Press, 1977), 656, 658.

36. Scharf, *History of the Confederate States Navy*, 658; James D. Bulloch, *The Secret Service of the Confederate States in Europe or How the Confederate Cruisers Were Equipped*, 2 vols. (New York: Thomas Yoseloff, 1959), 1: 143–44; William Harwar Parker, *Recollections of a Naval Officer 1841–1865* (Annapolis: U.S. Naval Institute Press, 1985), 292.

37. *The Charleston Mercury*, 26 August 1861; see William Morrison Robinson, *The Confederate Privateers* (New Haven, Conn.: Yale University Press, 1928), passim.

38. Stringham to Fox, 10 September 1861, *ORN*, ser. 1, 6:192; Stringham to Welles, 16 September 1861, ibid., 217; Welles to Du Pont, 12 October 1861, ibid., 12:213–14; William Seward to Welles, 19 October 1861, ibid., 222.

39. Welles to Du Pont, 3 August 1861, *ORN*, ser. 1, 12:207; Blockade Strategy Board Minutes, Subject File ON, RG 45, NA; Du Pont, J. G. Barnard, A. D. Bache, C. H. Davis to Welles, 5 July 1861, *ORN*, ser. 1, 12:195–98; Du Pont, Bache, Barnard, Davis to Welles, 26 July 1861, ibid., 202–206.

40. J. T. Headley, *Farragut and Our Naval Commanders* (New York: E. B. Treat and Co., 1867), 122; Merrill, "Hatteras Expedition, August, 1861," *The North Carolina Historical Review* 29 (April 1951), 219; Gideon Welles, "Admiral Farragut and New Orleans, With an Account of the Origin and Command of the First Three Naval Expeditions of the War," *The Galaxy* 5 (July 1871), 671–72; Samuel Du Pont to Sophie Du Pont, 17 September 1861, Du Pont, *Letters*, 1:149; Stringham became the first naval victim of the press during the war. Naval officers often took much undeserved criticism because the army had a greater influence over the press. The small number of officers in the navy as compared to the large number in the army along with the press's greater access to army headquarters caused the navy to receive less attention. Some army officers curried favor with the press because they were already politicians or were looking for postwar political careers. Richard West, "The Navy And The Press During The Civil War," *United States Naval Institute Proceedings* 63 (January 1937), 36–38.

41. The Strategy Board actually considered splitting it into more than two commands, Strategy Board Memorandum to Welles, 16 July 1861, Subject File ON, RG 45, NA; Stringham to Welles, 16 September 1861, *ORN*, ser. 1, 6:217; Rowena Reed, *Combined Operations in the Civil War* (Annapolis: Naval Institute Press, 1978), 19; Welles to Stringham, 18 September 1861, *ORN*, ser. 1, 6:231–32; Richard S. West Jr., *Mr. Lincoln's Navy* (New York: Longmans Green and Company, 1957), 82.

42. Just over two weeks before, Welles disestablished the West India Squadron, ending the confusing and overlapping authorities of the commands. Welles to Pendergrast, 29 August 1861, *ORN*, ser. 1, 6:145–46; Du Pont had actually learned that he would get command of the squadron a day earlier. Neither flag officer was next in line to command according to the system of seniority. Goldsborough was placed over thirteen of his seniors and Du Pont over

eighteen of his seniors. Du Pont, *Letters*, 1:156n; Welles to Goldsborough, 18 September 1861, *ORN*, ser. 1, 6:233–34; Welles to Du Pont, 18 September 1861, Du Pont Papers, Hagley.

43. Lincoln to Welles, 18 September 1861, Roy Basler, *The Collected Works of Abraham Lincoln*, 9 vols. (New Brunswick, N.J.: Rutgers University Press, 1953–55), 4:528.

Chapter 2

1. Welles to Du Pont, 18 September 1861, Letters Received by the Secretary of the Navy From Commanding Officers of Squadrons, Entry 30, RG 45, NA, Microfilm Publication Number M89, hereinafter cited as M89, RG 45, NA.

2. In contrast to other members of his immediate family, Frank chose to capitalize the particle of his name. H. A. Du Pont, *Rear Admiral Samuel Francis Du Pont United States Navy: A Biography* (New York: National Americana Society, 1926), 3–4, 11, 15, 19; Du Pont, *Letters*, 1:xlvi–passim; Headley, *Farragut And Our Naval Commanders*, 124–25; Thomas F. Bayard, *Oration Delivered by the Hon. Thomas F. Bayard . . .* (Washington, D.C.: Government Printing Office, 1885), 10–passim; David Dixon Porter, *The Naval History of the Civil War* (Sherman Publishing Company, 1886, reprint Secaucus, N.J.: Castle Books, 1984), 61; Ammen, *The Atlantic Coast*, 123.

3. Ammen, *The Atlantic Coast*, 13; L. H. Pelouze, General Orders No. 15, 17 October 1861, *ORA*, ser. 1, 6:179–80.

4. Gideon Welles, *Diary of Gideon Welles*, Entry for 23 August 1864, ed. Howard K. Beale, 3 vols. (New York: W. W. Norton & Company, Inc., 1960) 2:118; Daniel Ammen, "Du Pont and the Port Royal Expedition," *Battles and Leaders of the Civil War* 4 vols. (New York: Thomas Yoseloff, 1956) 1:691; Welles to Goldsborough, 12 October 1861, *ORN*, ser. 1, 6:313.

5. Du Pont to Sophie, 8 September 1861, Du Pont, *Letters*, 1:146; as quoted in Ammen, "Du Pont and the Port Royal Expedition," *Battles and Leaders*, 1:674; Du Pont to Welles, 18 September 1861, M89, RG 45, NA.

6. Thornton A. Jenkins to Du Pont, 9 August 1861, Du Pont, *Letters*, 1: 130–31.

7. Testimony of Thomas W. Sherman, *Report of the Joint Committee on the Conduct of War*, Part 3, 37th Cong., third sess., Senate Report No. 108, 292; Du Pont to Sophie, 25 July 1861, Du Pont, *Letters*, 1:116.

8. Du Pont to Sophie, 15 September 1861, Du Pont, *Letters*, 1:147.

9. Lincoln to Welles, 18 September 1861, *ORN*, ser. 1, 12:208; Du Pont to Henry Winter Davis, 8 October 1861, Du Pont, *Letters*, 1:162–64.

10. Ibid.

11. Du Pont to Henry Du Pont, 15 October 1861, Du Pont, *Letters*, 1:165; Testimony of Thomas Sherman, *Conduct of War*, 3:293; Du Pont to Fox, 24

December 1861, Gustavus Vasa Fox Papers, New-York Historical Society, hereinafter cited as NYHS.

12. Charles Boutelle, Coast Survey Assistant, spent six years making hydrographic surveys in the Port Royal vicinity. Welles to Du Pont, 12 October 1861, *ORN*, ser. 1, 12:214–15; Du Pont to Sophie, 17, 26, 27 October, 1861, Du Pont, *Letters*, 1:170, 188–91.

13. T. W. Sherman to Adjutant General U. S. Army, 8 November 1861, *ORN*, ser. 1, 12:288; Davis, *Life of Charles Henry Davis*, 170; Du Pont to Sophie, 20 October 1861, Du Pont, *Letters*, 1:192; Du Pont to Fox, 27 October 1861, Fox, *Correspondence*, 1:59–60; Albert Bigelow Paine, *A Sailor of Fortune: Personal Memoirs of Captain B. S. Osbon* (New York: McClure, Phillips and Co., 1906), 135–36; Joseph R. Hawley to Welles, 28 October 1861, Gideon Welles Papers, Library of Congress Manuscript Division, Washington, D.C., hereinafter cited as LCM.

14. On the 25th, as the final plans were discussed, Du Pont and Sherman instructed the men to practice amphibious operations with the ferryboats and the surfboats. During the exercises they discovered a number of problems that they could avoid during the assault. *Civil War Naval Chronology 1861–1865*, U.S. Navy, Naval History Division, 6 vols. (Washington, D.C.: Government Printing Office, 1971), I: 30; Du Pont to Fox, 25, 27 October 1861, Fox, *Correspondence*, 1:59–60; Davis, *The Life of Charles Henry Davis,* 166–70; Du Pont to Welles, 6 November 1861, M89, RG 45, NA; Testimony of Thomas Sherman, *Conduct of War*, 3:293; Fox to Welles, 22 October 1861, Welles Papers, LCM; Egbert Viele, "Port Royal Expedition, 1861," *Magazine of American History* XIV (October 1885), 333–34; "Succinct Military History of Brigadier General T. W. Sherman," U. S. Army Generals Reports of Civil War Service 1864–1883, Entry 160, Records of the Adjutant General's Office, RG 94, NA; Darwin H. Stapleton, "Assistant Charles O. Boutelle, of the United States Coast Survey, With the South Atlantic Blockading Squadron 1861–1863," *The American Neptune* XXXI (October) 1971, 253–54.

15. Ibid.

16. Du Pont to Fox, 29 October 1861, Du Pont Papers, Hagley; John Sanford Barnes Journal, Entry for 30 October 1861, John Sanford Barnes Papers, NYHS; *National Intelligencer*, 8 November 1861; *Times* (New York), 26 October 1861; Du Pont to Fox, 28 October 1861, Fox, *Correspondence*, 1:63; Instructions to Captains, Masters, (n.d.) Du Pont Papers, Hagley.

17. Ammen, *The Old Navy and the New*, 346; Du Pont to Sophie, 31 October 1861, Du Pont, *Letters*, 1:203; Ammen, "Du Pont and the Port Royal Expedition," *Battles and Leaders*, I: 675; Barnes Journal, Entry for 30, 31 October 1861, Barnes Papers, NYHS.

18. Barnes Journal, Entries for 31 October, 1, 2 November 1861, NYHS; Ammen, *The Atlantic Coast*, 15; Ammen, "Du Pont and the Port Royal Expedition," *Battles and Leaders*, 1:675.

19. Welles to Son, 3 November 1861, Gideon Welles Papers, LCM; Du Pont to Welles, 6 November 1862, *ORN*, ser. 1, 12:259–60; Journal of *Augusta*, 3 November 1861, Correspondence of Enoch G. Parrott, Entry 392, RG 45, NA.

20. Edward S. Philbrick to Mrs. Philbrick, 7 March 1862, Elizabeth Ware Pearson, ed., *Letters from Port Royal 1862–1868* (New York: Arno Press, 1969), 5.

21. Du Pont to Sophie, 31 October 1861, Du Pont, *Letters*, 1:205; J. R. Goldsborough to Welles, 5 November 1861, *ORN*, ser. 1, 12:256; J. W. A. Nicholson to Du Pont, 4 November 1861, ibid., 245–46; Ammen, *The Atlantic Coast*, 18; R. Saxton to M. C. Meigs, *ORA*, ser. 1, 6:186.

22. Hog braces are part of a trussing system to support the ends of shallow draft vessels in order to keep the ends from sagging. John George Reynolds to Du Pont, 8 November 1861, *ORN*, ser. 1, 12:233–35; For a complete account of the heroic rescue see John H. Magruder's "The Wreck of the Governor," *Leatherneck* XXXVIII (November 1955), 74–77.

23. Magruder, T. Tileston to Ringgold, 28 February 1862, *ORN*, ser. 1, 12:249.

24. Du Pont to Ringgold, 8 November 1861, *ORN*, ser. 1, 12:238; Reynolds to Du Pont, 8 November 1861, ibid.; Du Pont to Sophie, 18 February 1862, Du Pont, *Letters*, 1:331.

25. The expedition sailed with hopes of attacking on 2 November, the date of the predicted spring tides. Du Pont to Welles, 6 November 1863, Du Pont Papers, Hagley; Ammen, *The Atlantic Coast*, 18; Robert Chisolm, "The Battle of Port Royal," *Under Both Flags: A Panorama of the Great Civil War* (Philadelphia: Peoples Publishing Company, 1896), 255; Lamson to Flora, 4 November 1861, *Lamson of the Gettysburg*, 40.

26. Jones, *Tattnall*, 131; *Savannah Republican*, 12 November 1861.

27. Ammen to Du Pont, 15 November 1862, Ammen Letter Book, Entry 395, RG 45, NA; Scharf, *Confederate Navy*, 664; Charles C. Jones Jr., *The Life and Services of Commodore Josiah Tattnall* (Savannah Ga. Morning News Steam Printing House, 1870), 135; John Rodgers to Du Pont, 4 November 1861, *ORN*, ser. 1, 12:255–56; Lamson to Flora, 4 November 1863, *Lamson of the Gettysburg*, 40.

28. John Rodgers to Ann, 5 November 1861, Rodgers Family Papers, LCM; Stephen Elliot Jr. to William H. Talley, 13 November 1861, *ORA*, ser. 1, 6:27.

29. Ammen, *The Old Navy and the New*, 349; Ammen to Du Pont, 15 November 1861, *ORN*, ser. 1, 12:78; Ammen, *The Atlantic Coast*, 20; Alexander A. Lawrence, *A Present for Mr. Lincoln: The Story of Savannah from Secession to Sherman* (Macon, Ga.: Ardivan Press, 1961), 38; Royce Shingleton, *High Seas Confederate, The Life and Times of John Newland Maffitt* (Columbia: University of South Carolina Press, 1994), 36–37; *The Charleston Daily*

Courier, 11 November 1861; John Newland Maffitt to Florie, 5 December 1861, John Newland Maffitt Papers, Southern Historical Collection, University of North Carolina, Chapel Hill, hereinafter cited as SHC.

30. Barnes Journal, Entry for 5 November 1861, Barnes Papers, NYHS.

31. The *Ocean Express* arrived just before the attack began. John E. Wool to Simon Cameron, 28 October 1861, *ORA*, ser. 1, 6:184; Viele, "Port Royal Expedition," 336–37; Shearon to Adjutant General's Office, 8 November 1861, *ORA*, ser. 1, 6:4.

32. Alfred Roman, *The Military Operations of General Beauregard In the War Between the States, 1861–1865*, 2 vols. (New York: Harper & Brothers, 1884), 1:51.

33. Du Pont, however, thought the works "scientifically constructed." This judgment only perpetuated the belief that batteries could be taken by naval bombardments. Du Pont to Fox, 9 November 1861, Fox, *Correspondence*, 1: 65; there were guns in each fort that were unmounted or unusable. Barnes claims there were 20 guns at Fort Beauregard and 23 guns a Fort Walker. Barnes to Rodgers, 9 November 1861, *ORN*, ser. 1, 12:270; Samuel Jones, *The Siege of Charleston and the Operations on the South Atlantic Coast in the War Among the States* (New York: Neal Publishing Company, 1911), 51; Drayton to Walker, 24 November 1861, *ORN*, ser. 1, 12:301, 304; C. R. P. Rodgers to Du Pont, 8 November 1861, ibid., 269; F. D. Lee to H. E. Young, 4 December 1861, *ORA*, ser. 1, 6:1–19.

34. Du Pont to Sophie, 6 November 1861, 5 May 1862, Du Pont, *Letters*, 1:220; 2:32; Davis, *Life of Charles Henry Davis*, 185; T. W. Sherman to Adjutant-General U. S. Army, 8 November 1861, *ORN*, ser. 1, 12:288–89; James H. Wilson, *Under the Old Flag: Recollections of Military Operations in the War for the Union, the Spanish War, the Boxer Rebellion, Etc.* 2 vols. (New York: D. Appleton and Company, 1912), 70–71; Testimony of Thomas Sherman, *Conduct of War*, 3:294.

35. Du Pont to Sophie, 5, 6 November 1861, Du Pont, *Letters*, 1:216, 220; Ammen, *The Old Navy and the New*, 349–50; Davis, *Life of C. H. Davis*, 163–64; Barnes Journal, Entry for 5 November 1861, Barnes Papers, NYHS.

36. Davis, *Life of Charles Henry Davis*, 183–84; Robert Erwin Johnson, *Rear Admiral John Rodgers: 1812–1882* (Annapolis: United States Naval Institute, 1967), 175; Du Pont claimed the idea of moving while firing was his. Otherwise, he threw away the advantage of his steam warships if they anchored. Du Pont to Sophie, 5 May 1862, Du Pont, *Letters*, 2:32.

37. Chisolm, "Battle of Port Royal," 256; Ammen, *The Atlantic Coast*, 21; Log of *Wabash*, 7 November 1861, Ship's Logs, Stations, and Miscellaneous, Entry 118, Bureau of Naval Personnel, RG 24, NA.

38. Ammen, *The Old Navy and the New*, 350; ibid., "Du Pont and Port Royal Expedition," 1:679; Paine, *A Sailor of Fortune*, 141; Barnes Journal, 9 November 1861, Barnes Papers, NYHS; Log of *Augusta*, 7 November 1861,

Entry 118, RG 24, NA; Du Pont to Welles, 11 November 1861, Du Pont Papers, Hagley.

39. Log of *Wabash*, 7 November 1861, Entry 118, RG 24, NA; Ammen, *The Atlantic Coast*, 23; Chisolm, "The Battle of Port Royal," 256; Du Pont to Welles, 11 November 1861, Du Pont Papers, Hagley; Jones, *Tattnall*, 137–38; Scharf, *The Confederate States Navy*, 665; *World* (New York), 12 November 1861; Frank Moore, ed., *The Rebellion Record: A Diary of American Events*, 11 vols. (New York: G. Putnam, 1861–1862), 3:306: "Reminiscences and Journal of Francis Thornton Chew, Lieutenant, C.S.N." 15, Francis Thornton Chew Papers SHC; Marlinspike (pseud), *Abstract of the Cruise of U. S. Steam Frigate Wabash, Bearing the Flag of Rear-Admiral S. F. Du Pont, 1861, '62 & '63* (New York: Edward O. Jenkins, 1863), 11.

40. Ammen, *The Old Navy and the New*, 351; Welles, *Diary*, Entry for 30 September 1867, 3:217; Du Pont to Sophie, 7 November 1861, Du Pont, *Letters*, 1:222; Charles Steedman, *Memoir and Correspondence of Charles Steedman Rear Admiral, United States Navy with His Autobiography and Private Journals, 1811–1890*, ed. Amos Lawrence Mason (Cambridge, Mass.: The Riverside Press, 1912), 292; Welles, *Diary*, 30 September 1867, 3:216–17.

41. Ammen, *The Atlantic Coast*, 26; Francis McCarten, *Description and Cruise of the USS Augusta, South Atlantic Blockading Squadron*, (s.1:2n, 1876) 7; E. G. Parrott to Du Pont, 27 August 1861, ORN, ser. 1, 12:284; Thomas Budd to Du Pont, 8 November 1861, ibid., 280; Parrott, Journal of *Augusta*, 7 November 1861, Entry 392, RG 45, NA; Log of *Augusta*, 7 November 1861, Entry 118, RG 24, NA.

42. Du Pont never mentioned this failure by his officers to obey the orders. He perhaps felt it would open a futile controversy. Not until 1883 when Daniel Ammen wrote *The Atlantic Coast* did one of his officers tell the story. C. H. Wells to Steedman, 15 June 1883, Steedman, *Memoirs*, p. 297; Du Pont to Welles, 11 November 1861, ORN, ser. 1, 12:263; Du Pont to Sophie 7 November 1861, Du Pont, *Letters*, 1:222–23.

43. Du Pont always blamed Godon for breaking the line and had nothing but praise for Commander Charles Steedman of the *Bienville*. It did not hurt Godon's career. He retired as a Rear Admiral. Du Pont to Welles, ibid.

44. Scharf, *The Confederate Navy*, 665; Ammen, *The Old Navy and the New*, 351; Paine, *A Sailor of Fortune*, 142; Log of *Seneca*, 7 November 1861, Entry 118, RG 24, NA.

45. Rodgers reported an 80-pound shot hit the mainmast but the only gun mounted in the fort that could throw a shot of this size was the Columbiad and its projectile weighed 86 pounds. Raymond Rodgers to Du Pont, 8 November 1861, Raymond Rodgers Papers, Entry 395, RG 45, NA; John Rodgers to Anne, 8 November 1861, Rodgers Papers, LCM; Drayton to Wise, 30 November 1861, ORN, ser. 1, 12:272–74; John A. Wagener to H. E. Young, 11 November 1861, ORN, ser. 1,12:308–309; John Sanford Barnes, "My Ego-

tistigraphy," Barnes Papers, NYHS, 167–68; Chilsolm, "The Battle of Port Royal," 257.

46. Du Pont to Welles, 8, 11 November 1861, Du Pont Papers, Hagley; Letter of John Rodgers, 9 November 1861, *The Rebellion Record*, 3:112; Ammen, *The Atlantic Coast*, 23–24; Marlinspike, *Abstract of the Cruise of U.S. Steam Frigate* Wabash, 12.

47. Tattnal landed Marines from his ships to augment the defenders. Reinforcements arrived from Savannah on the afternoon of the sixth but remained outside Fort Walker. Extract from the *Savannah Republican*, 12 November 1861, ORN, ser. 1, 12: 297; Ripley to Cooper, 5 November 1861, *ibid*, p. 828; *The Charleston Daily Courier*, 19 November 1861; Thomas F. Drayton to L. D. Walker, 24 November 1861, ORA, ser. 1, 6:7.

48. Drayton to Walker, 24 November 1861, ORA, ser. 1, 6:8.

49. This is Steedman's version of the event. John Sanford Barnes claimed that Stedman received a "dressing" on the bridge of the *Wabash* after the battle for cutting ahead of the *Mohican*. Stedman, *Memoirs*, 292; Barnes Journal, Entry for 9 November 1861, Barnes Papers, NYHS; Du Pont served with Godon on the Ship-of-the-Line *Ohio*. Du Pont blamed Godon for the unauthorized movement which ended their friendhip. Welles, *Diary*, 30 September 1867, 3:217; Marlinspike, *Abstract of the Cruise of U.S. Steam Frigate* Wabash, 13.

50. Drayton to Walker, ORA, ser. 1, 6:8–9; Drayton to Wise, 30 November 1861, ORN, ser. 1, 12:272; William H. Summers to James L. Lardner, 7 November 1861, ibid., 276; C. R. P. Rodgers to Du Pont, 10 November 1861, ibid., 267–68.

51. Du Pont to Welles, 11 November 1861, Du Pont Papers, Hagley; Xanthus Smith to Mother, 6 April 1863, Smith Family Papers, Archives of American Art, Smithsonian Institution, Washington D.C. Hereinafter cited as AAA.; Drayton to Du Pont, 9 November 1861, ORN, ser. 1, vol. 12, 272; Owen to Father, 8 November 1861, *Rebellion Record*, 3:114.

52. Ibid., Du Pont to Welles, 11 November 1861, Du Pont Papers, Hagley; Barnes Journal, 9 November 1861, Barnes Papers, NYHS; *Charleston Mercury*, (n.d.) cited in the *Rebellion Record*, 3:116.

53. Drayton to Walker, 24 November 1861, ORA, ser. 1, 6:10–11; R. G. M. Dunovant to H. E. Young, 16 November 1861, ORN, ser. 1, 12:314–16.

54. Du Pont to Welles, 11 November 1861, Du Pont Papers, Hagley; Log of *Augusta*, 7 November 1861, Eugene Whittemore Papers, SHC; Daniel Ammen, "Du Pont and the Port Royal Expedition," *Battles and Leaders*, 1:686.

55. Charles Lafundy to his sister, 15 November 1861, Charles Lafundy Papers, Manuscript Collection, Fort Pulaski National Monument; Barnes Journal, Entry for 9 November 1861, Barnes Papers, NYHS; Du Pont to Welles, 11 November 1862, Du Pont Papers, Hagley; Log of *Seneca*, 7 November 1861, Entry 118, RG 24, NA; Boutelle to Bache, 8 November 1861, U.S. Department of

Commerce, *Military and Naval Service of the United States Coast Survey 1861–1865* (Washington, D.C.: Government Printing Office, 1916), 50.

56. Davis, *Life of Charles Henry Davis*, 179; Du Pont to Sophie, 7 November 1862, Du Pont, *Letters*, 1:222; Du Pont to Welles, 8 November 1862, M89, RG 45, NA; Welles to Du Pont, 15 November 1862, *ORN*, ser. 1, 12:294; Drayton to Walker, 24 November 1861, ibid., 308.

57. Welles to Du Pont, 30 July 1862, *ORN*, ser. 1, 12:291.

58. Louise to Mrs. C. L. Pettigrew, 18 November 1861, Pettigrew Family Papers, SHC; Du Pont to Fox, 6 December 1861, Fox Papers, NYHS.

59. Du Pont used up most of his ammunition during the attack and waited for some time before it could be replenished. The army had also consumed much of its food and water. Both the men and animals had consumed supplies while the expedition was delayed during the initial staging and while it regrouped off Port Royal after the storm. By December, Sherman still did not have sufficient field artillery and no cavalry to move beyond Hilton Head. Sherman to Cameron, 21 December 1862, *ORA,* ser., 1, 6:209.

Chapter 3

1. *Charleston Daily Courier*, 8, 9, 11, 12 November 1861; *Charleston Mercury*, 8, 9, 11, 12 November 1861; *Savannah Republican*, 8 November 1861; *Central Georgian* (Sandersville), 13 November 1861.

2. Also the army did not have the small steamer for interior operations promised by the War Department. Testimony of Thomas Sherman, *Conduct of War*, 3:294; Ammen, *The Old Navy*, 359; Ammen to Du Pont, 9 November 1861, Correspondence of Danniel Ammen, Entry 395, RG 45, NA; Charles Boutelle to Du Pont, 7 November 1861, J. Glendy Sproston to Ammen, Boutelle to Du Pont, 7 November 1861, *ORN*, ser. 1, 12:332, 337–38; Ammen, *The Atlantic Coast*, 33.

3. Villard, *Memoirs*, 14; Ammen to Du Pont, 9 November 1861, Ammen Correspondence, Entry 395, RG 45, NA; Ammen, *The Atlantic Coast*, 33; Napoleon Collins to Du Pont, 11 November 1861, *ORN*, ser. 1, 12:339; Gillis to Du Pont, ibid., 351; Charles Nordhoff, "Two Weeks at Port Royal," *Harper's New Monthly Magazine* XXVII (June 1863), 116, June 1863, vol. XXVII; Note Placed in Beaufort by Captain Bankhead, (n.d.) Du Pont Papers, Hagley.

4. Du Pont to Sherman, 18 November 1861, Fox, *Correspondence*, 1:70.

5. Du Pont to Welles, 17 November 1861, Du Pont Papers, Hagley.

6. Testimony of Sherman, *Conduct of War*, 3:295–97; Sherman to Adjutant-General, U.S. Army, 15 November 1861, *ORA*, ser. 1, 6:188.

7. According to Sherman's later testimony Du Pont's responsibility was only for the landing of troops, not their later transportation. Testimony of Sherman, *Conduct of War*, 3:294; Sherman to Du Pont, 6 December 1861, *ORN*, ser. 1, 12:390; Sherman to General Meigs, 10 December 1861, *ORA*, ser. 1, 6:201–203.

8. By December the navy became occupied with the sinking of hulks along the coast. Sherman to Du Pont, 6 December 1861, *ORN*, ser. 1, 12:390; Sherman to Cameron, 21 December 1861, *ORA*, ser. 1, 6:209; Sherman to McClellan, 19 December 1861, ibid., 208; Ammen, *The Old Navy*, 359; Roswell Lamson to Flora, 24 November 1861, Lamson, *Lamson of the Gettysburg*, 45; Du Pont to Grimes, 2 December 1861, Du Pont, *Letters*, 1:269.

9. With the exception of the pending Port Royal Ferry Expedition, Sherman never mentioned any other operations in writing. Sherman to Simon Cameron, 26 December 1861, *ORN*, ser. 1, 6:211; Sherman to General McClellan, ibid., 211–12; Quincey A. Gillmore to Sherman, 25 December 1861, ibid., 212–13.

10. Ammen, *The Old Navy*, 354.

11. T. Conn Bryan, *Confederate Georgia* (Athens, Ga.: University of Georgia Press, 1964), 66–70; Gilbert Sumter Guinn, "Coastal Defense of the Confederate Atlantic Seaboard States, 1861–1862: A Study of Political and Military Mobilization." Unpublished Ph.D. dissertation, University of South Carolina, 1973, 26.

12. Confederate troops withdrew from the island on 10 October. *Savannah Morning News*, 13 November 1861; Du Pont to John Rodgers, 19 November 1861, *ORN*, ser. 1, 12:324; Du Pont to Sherman, 23 November 1861, ibid.; Du Pont to Welles, 25 November 1861, ibid., 325–26.

13. The tower had an earthwork battery at its base. Logs of *Seneca, Augusta*, 24 August 1861, Entry 118, RG 24, NA; Ammen, *The Atlantic Coast*, 35; Abstract Log of *Flag*, 24 November 1861, *ORN*, ser. 1, 12:26–27; Abstract Log of *Pocahontas*, 24 November 1861, ibid., 327; J. S. Missroon to Du Pont, ibid., 326.

14. R. E. Lee to J. P. Benjamin, 29 November 1861, ibid., 328; Journal of *Augusta*, 27, 29 November 1862, Entry 392, RG 45, NA; Du Pont to Welles, 27 November 1861, *ORN*, ser. 1, 12:364; Sherman to Du Pont, 27 November, 2 December 1861, ibid., 364, 383–84; Du Pont to Sherman, 2 December 1861, ibid., 384.

15. Rodgers to Du Pont, 6 December 1861, C. R. P. Rodgers Papers, Entry 395, RG 45, NA.

16. Drayton protected the *Pawnee*'s machinery with cotton bales. Du Pont to Sophie, 21 November 1861, Du Pont, *Letters*, 1:255; Drayton to Du Pont, 28 November 1861, ibid., 321–23; Boutelle to Bache, 30 November 1861, *Military and Naval Service of the Coast Survey*, 54–55.

17. Drayton to My dear Hoyt, 30 November 1861, Percival Drayton, *Naval Letters of Captain Percival Drayton, 1861–1865 Printed From the Original Manuscripts Presented to The New York Public Library by Miss Gertrude L. Hoyt* (New York: The Library, 1906), 10.

18. John Withers, Special Order No. 206, 5 November 1861, *ORA*, ser. 1, 6:309; *Charleston Mercury*, 12 November 1861; Lee to Cooper, 21 November 1861, 8 January 1862, *ORA*, ser. 1, 6:327, 367.

19. George W. Davis to Welles, 14 October 1861, *ORN*, ser. 1, 6:322.

20. *News* (Savannah), 27 November 1861; Tattnall's biographer Charles Jones claims the date was 26 December, yet the official documents do not bear this out. Jones, *Tattnall*, 143; J. R. Goldsborough to Du Pont, 26 November 1861, *ORN*, ser. 1, 12:362–63; Scharf, *Confederate Navy*, 630–31.

21. Sherman to Du Pont, 30 November, 2 December 1861, *ORN*, ser. 1, 12:371, 383–84; Du Pont to Sherman, 1 December 1861, ibid., 371; Du Pont to Fox, 6 December 1861, Fox, *Correspondence*, I:77; Du Pont to Welles, 4 December 1861, *ORN*, ser. 1, 12:382; Ammen, *The Atlantic Coast*, 37.

22. Drayton to Du Pont, 9 December 1861, *ORN*, ser. 1, 12:388–90.

23. Captain Boutelle of the Coast Survey was a tremendous help in the reconnaissance of these shallow and poorly charted waters. Drayton to Du Pont, 21 December 1861, *ORN*, ser. 1, 12:405–406; Ammen, *The Atlantic Coast*, 39–40.

24. Rodgers to Du Pont, 6, 12 December 1861, *ORN*, ser. 1, 12:385–86, 396–97; Du Pont to Rodgers, 10 December 1861, ibid., 392; Ammen, *The Atlantic Coast*, 38–39.

25. Sherman to Thomas, 14 December 1861, *ORA*, ser. 1, 6:203–204.

26. Davis to Wife, 2 December 1861, Davis, *Life of Charles Henry Davis*, 193; Du Pont to Sophie, 5 December 1861, Du Pont, *Letters*, 1:272; Du Pont et al. to Fox, 5 September 1861, Subject File ON, RG 45, NA.

27. Welles to Morgan, 17 October 1861, *ORN*, ser. 1, 12:416; Welles to Du Pont, 7 November 1861, ibid., 417; Arthur Gordon, "The Great Stone Fleet: Calculated Catastrophe," *U.S. Naval Institute Proceedings* XLIV (December 1968), 77; Undated Memo in Subject File AY, RG 45, NA.

28. Gordon, ibid., 79; *Daily News* (Savannah), 5, 6 December 1861, passim.

29. *Savannah Republican*, 7 December 1861; Du Pont to Welles, 25 November 1861, *ORN*, ser. 1, 12:325–26; Du Pont to Fox, 6 December 1861, Fox, *Correspondence*, I:77–78.

30. Du Pont to Fox, 6 December 1861, Fox, *Correspondence*, I:77–78; Missroon to Du Pont, 5 December 1861, *ORN*, ser. 1, 12:419–20; *DANFS*, 5:433; Du Pont to Sophie, 5 December 1861, Du Pont, *Letters*, 1:275.

31. Davis to his family, 2 December 1861, as cited in Sidney Withington, *Two Dramatic Episodes of New England Whaling* (Mystic, Conn.: The Maritime Historical Association Inc., 1958), 51.

32. Fourteen of these were from Savannah and two were early arrivals from the second contingent. Davis to Du Pont, 21 December 1861, *ORN*, ser. 1, 12:422–23; Gordon, *The Great Stone Fleet*, 81; "Operations of the Stone Fleet," Moore, *The Rebellion Record*, 3:508.

33. George Balch to Dahlgren, 26 January 1862, George Beall Balch Papers, SHC; Gordon, *The Great Stone Fleet*, 82; Lee to Benjamin, 20 December 1861, *ORN*, ser. 1, 12:423; Du Pont to Fox, 16 December 1861, Fox, *Corre-*

spondence, I:79; John E. Woodman, "The Stone Fleet," *The American Neptune* XXI (October 1961), 254; *Times* (New York), 26 November 1861.

34. Ammen, *The Atlantic Coast*, 42.

35. W. T. Truxton to Du Pont, 27 December 1861, *ORN*, ser. 1, 12:436.

36. Budd to Du Pont, 14 January 1862, ibid., 463.

37. Sherman to McClellan, 26 December 1861, *ORA*, ser. 1, 6:211–12.

38. The *Hale* was added to the expedition after they sailed. Du Pont to Sophie, 21 January 1862, Du Pont Papers, Hagley; Du Pont to Welles, 4 January 1862, M89, RG 45, NA; Sherman to Du Pont, 5 December 1861, *ORN*, ser. 1, 12:386–87.

39. Barnes Journal, 5 January 1862, Barnes Papers, NYHS; Isaac I. Stevens to L. H. Pelouze, 3 January 1862, *ORA*, ser. 1, 6:47; Rodgers to Du Pont, 3 January 1862, C. R. P. Rodgers Papers, Entry 395, RG 45, NA; Hazard Stevens, "Military Operations in South Carolina in 1862, Against Charleston, Port Royal Ferry, James Island, Secessionville." *Operations of the Atlantic Coast 1861–1865, Virginia 1862, 1864, Vicksburg*, Papers of the Military Historical Society of Massachusetts, IX, Boston, 1912, 119.

40. This was the first use of Meyer's signals to direct naval gunfire. Rodgers to Du Pont, 3 January 1862, C. R. P. Rodgers Papers, Entry 395, RG 45, NA; Tafft to Stevens, 3 January 1862, *ORA*, ser. 1, 6:63–passim; Stevens, "Military Operations," 121.

41. Ammen to Du Pont, 3 January 1861, *ORN*, ser. 1, 12:450–51.

42. Sherman to Thomas, 4 January 1862, *ORA*, ser. 1, 6:46–47; Rodgers to Du Pont, 3 January 1862, *ORN*, ser. 1, 12:448–50; Ammen, *The Atlantic Coast*, 43–45; J. C. Pemberton to T. A. Washington, 10 January 1862, *ORA*, ser. 1, 6:67–68;William Thompson Lusk, *War Letters of William Thompson Lusk* (New York: privately printed, 1911), 113–14.

43. Sherman to Thomas, 4 January 1862, *ORA*, ser. 1, 6:46–47.

44. Du Pont to Welles, 8 February 1862, Samuel F. Du Pont, *Official Dispatches and Letters of Rear Admiral Du Pont, US Navy, 1846–48, 1861–63* (Wilmington, Del.: Ferris Brothers, 1883), 98–99; Rodgers to Du Pont, 18 January 1862, *ORN*, ser. 1, 12:492–93; Sherman to McClellan, 27 December 1861, *ORA*, ser. 1, 6:214; Gillmore to Sherman, 30 December 1861, Fox, *Correspondence*, 1:92–93; Du Pont to Fox, 11 November 1861, ibid.; Testimony of Sherman, *Conduct of War*, 3:306.

45. Testimony of Sherman, *Conduct of War*, 3:298.

46. James Russell Soley considered the channels dangerous because the Confederates had removed the channel markers. Soley, *Blockade and the Cruisers*, 109; Sherman to Du Pont, 16 January 1862, *ORN*, ser. 1, 12:485–86; Thomas W. Sherman, "Succinct Military History," 47–48, RG 94, NA.

47. Rodgers to Du Pont, 8 January 1862, *ORN*, ser. 1, 12:469–70.

48. Rodgers to Du Pont, 18 January 1862, ibid., 492; Du Pont to Rodgers, 17 January 1862, ibid., 491–92; J. H. Wilson to Louis H. Pelouze, 2 January

1862, *ORA*, ser. 1, 6:215; Scharf, *Confederate Navy*, 632; Quincey A. Gillmore, *Official Report to the United States Engineer Department of the Siege And Reduction of Fort Pulaski, Georgia, February, March, and April 1862* (New York: D. Van Nostrand, 1862), 16; Horace Porter to Father, 16 February 1862, Horace Porter Papers, LCM; *Express* (New York), reprinted in Moore, *Rebellion Record*, 4:56.

49. Herbert M. Schiller, *Sumter is Revenged: The Siege and Reduction of Fort Pulaski* (Shippensburg, Pa.: White Mane Publishing, 1995), 34, calls the navy's efforts "dilatory." Neither Schiller nor the army, however, understood the limitations of shallow water on the operations of the gunboats and their complete helplessness should they get aground. Du Pont to Rodgers, 17 January 1862, *ORN*, ser. 1, 12:491–92; Rodgers to Du Pont, 18 January 1862, ibid., 492–93; Wilson to Pelouze, 18 January 1862, *ORA*, ser. 1, 6:219; Barnes, "My Egotistigraphy," Barnes Papers, NYHS, 171; Gillmore, *Siege and Reduction of Ft. Pulaski*, 16; Horace Porter to Mother, 3 February 1862, Horace Porter Papers, LCM; Du Pont to Fox, 2 January 1862, Du Pont Papers, Hagley.

50. Fox to Du Pont, 4 January 1862, Du Pont Papers, Hagley; Du Pont to Fox, 2, 11 January 1862, ibid.; Du Pont to Welles, 11 January 1862, ibid.

51. Sherman to McClellan, 26 March 1862, *ORA*, ser. 1, 6:253–54; Du Pont to Fox, 11 January 1862, Fox, *Correspondence*, 1:100–101; Sherman, in his memoirs, laid the blame squarely on the navy for the failure. Sherman, "Succinct Military History," 50–53, RG 94, NA; Sherman to Hunter, 31 March 1862, *ORA*, ser. 1, 6:257; Du Pont to Welles, 8 February 1862, Du Pont Papers, Hagley; Testimony of Sherman, *Conduct of War*, 3:296–300.

52. Du Pont's decision to give these missions to the Rodgers cousins and Davis had Commander John B. Marchand brooding. He was jealous of his three fellow officers and wrote in his journal "The selfishness on the whole party to monopolize all the honor has given me a most thorough disgust for Commodore Du Pont's administration of affairs here." John M. Marchand, *Charleston Blockade: The Journals of John B. Marchand U.S. Navy 1861–1862*, ed. Craig L. Symonds (Newport, R.I.: Naval War College Press, 1976), Entry for 24 January 1862, 85; Sherman, "Succinct Military History," 50, RG 94, NA; Davis to Du Pont, 1 February 1862, *ORN*, ser. 1, 12:523–24; Du Pont to Welles, 8 February 1862, Du Pont Papers, Hagley.

53. Ammen, *The Atlantic Coast*, 46; Scharf, *Confederate Navy*, 633.

54. Ammen, *The Old Navy*, 358–59.

55. Davis to Du Pont, 1 February 1862, *ORN*, ser. 1, 12:524–25; Scharf, *Confederate Navy*, 633–34.

56. Davis to Du Pont, *ORN*, ser. 1, 12:524–25; Rodgers to Du Pont, 28 January 1862, ibid., 494; *Savannah Republican*, 29 January 1862.

57. The Confederate transport *Leesburg* passed down river to Fort Pulaski and returned unmolested just after the engagement of the 28th. *Savannah Republican*, 31 January 1862.

58. Rodgers to Du Pont, 28 January, 4, 18 February 1862, *ORN*, ser. 1, 12:496–97, 502–503.

59. Sherman to Adjutant General, U.S. Army, 15 February 1862, *ORA*, ser. 1, 6:226; Scharf, *Confederate Navy*, 634–35; Bankhead to Rodgers, 19 February 1862, M89, RG 45, NA; Testimony of Sherman, *Conduct of War*, 3:301.

60. Sherman to Du Pont, 17 February 1862, *ORN*, ser. 1, 12:500; Viele to Pelouze, 16 February 1862, ibid., 500–501; Gillmore, "Siege and Capture of Fort Pulaski," *Battles and Leaders*, 2:6; Charles H. Olmstead, "Fort Pulaski," *The Georgia Historical Quarterly* 1 (March 1917) 101; Sherman to Du Pont, 19 February 1862, *ORN*, ser. 1, 12:555; Du Pont to Sherman, 19 February 1862, Du Pont Papers, Hagley.

61. Collins to Lardner, 19 March 1862, *ORN*, ser. 1, 12:641; Lardner to Du Pont, 20 March 1862, ibid., 641–42; C. H. Wells to Lardner, 21 March 1862, ibid., 653–54.

62. McClellan to Sherman, 12, 14 February 1862, *ORA*, ser. 1, 6:224–25; Fox to Du Pont, 4 January 1862, Du Pont Papers, Hagley.

63. Du Pont to Fox, 10 February 1862, Du Pont Papers, Hagley; Welles to Stringham, 14 June 1861, *ORN*, ser. 1, 5:719.

64. Benjamin to Lee, 24 February 1862, *ORA*, ser. 1, 6:398; Trapier to Washington, 28 March 1862, *ORN*, ser. 1, 12:617–18.

65. Du Pont, Journal Letter 31, 22–26 February 1862, Du Pont Papers, Hagley; Du Pont to Sherman, 24 February 1862, *ORN*, ser. 1, 12:569; McBlair to Buchanan, 24 February 1862, ibid., 840–41.

66. Some of the vessels were left behind in Wassau Sound for the blockade. Circular, Du Pont 1 March 1862, Du Pont Papers, Hagley; Du Pont to Welles, 4 March 1862, Du Pont Papers, Hagley; Du Pont to Sherman, 25, 27 February 1862, *ORN*, ser. 1, 12:569–70; Du Pont to Gillis, 28 February 1862, ibid., 570; *Times* (New York), 15 March 1862; Du Pont to Sophie, 2 March 1862, Du Pont, *Letters*, 1:347.

67. Memorandum of Instruction regarding plans of Operations, *ORN*, ser. 1, 12:572.

68. Du Pont to Welles, 4 March 1862, ibid., 53–74; Ammen, *The Old Navy*, 360; Circular, 1 March 1862, Du Pont Papers, Hagley; Du Pont to Sophie, 3 March 1862, Du Pont, *Letters*, 1:349; Memorandum from Du Pont to Lardner, (n.d.) *ORN*, ser. 1, 12:572.

69. Drayton to Du Pont, 4 March 1862, *ORN*, ser. 1, 12:576.

70. Ibid.

71. Rodgers to Wm. Marvin, 17 March 1862, C. R. P. Rodgers Papers, Entry 395, RG 45, NA; Stevens to Du Pont, 7 March 1862, *ORN*, ser. 1, 12:584.

72. Drayton to Du Pont, 4 March 1862, *ORN*, ser. 1, 12:577; Marchand, *Charleston Blockade*, Entry for 4 March 1862, 126.

73. Ibid.; Memorandum, Percival Drayton, 4 March 1862, *ORN*, ser. 1, 12:578–79; R. M. Goldsborough to L. M. Goldsborough, 10 March 1862,

Du Pont Papers, Hagley; Drayton to Dahlgren, 29 March 1862, John Adolphus Dahlgren Papers, LCM; Louis M. Goldsborough to Mother, 10 March 1862, Goldsborough Papers, Hagley.

74. T. H. Stevens to Du Pont, 13 March 1862, *ORN*, ser. 1, 12:599–600; Trapier to Washington, 20 March 1862, *ORA*, ser. 1, 6:414–15; Du Pont to Welles, 13 March 1862, *ORN*, ser. 1, 12:598.

75. Du Pont to Welles, 13 March 1862, *ORN*, ser. 1, 12:598; T. H. Stevens to Du Pont, 28 March 1862, ibid., 638–39.

76. Du Pont to Welles, 13 March 1862, *ORN*, ser. 1, 12:598; Godon to Du Pont, 10 March 1862, ibid., 607.

77. Godon to Du Pont, 10 March 1862, *ORN*, ser. 1, 12:607–08; Balch to Godon, ibid., 591; Godon to Du Pont, 13 March 1862, ibid., 609–10; Balch to Godon, 11 March 1862, ibid., 610–11. Godon found the area was not completely secure. On the eleventh, the *Pocahontas* landed a boat crew to procure beef for the ships. Having secured the beef, the boat began its trip back to the *Pocahontas*. When only twenty yards from shore, enemy soldiers asked the men in the boat to surrender. When they refused and began to pull for the safety of the naval vessels, about forty troops fired a volley, killed two, and wounded six more men. Both the *Mohican* and the *Potomska* opened fire on the enemy and drove them off.

78. Godon to Du Pont, 16 March 1862, ibid., 613–14.

79. For a complete discussion of St. Augustine during the war see: Jacqueline K. Fretwell, ed., *Civil War Times in St. Augustine* (St. Augustine, Fla.: St. Augustine Historical Society, 1988); Rodgers to Du Pont, 12 March 1862, ibid., 595–96; Du Pont to Welles, 13 March 1862, ibid., 598–99; P. J. Staudenraus, A" War Correspondent's View of St. Augustine and Fernandina 1863," *The Florida Historical Quarterly* 41 (July 1962), 61; Omega G. East, "St. Augustine during the Civil War," *The Florida Historical Quarterly* XXXI (October 1951), 76, 78–79, 82.

80. The Marine battalion consisted of just under three hundred officers and men. Welles to Du Pont, 6 March 1862, *ORN*, ser. 1, 12:583; Du Pont to T. H. Stevens, 21 March 1862, *ORN*, ser. 1, 12:615; Du Pont to Reynonds, 17 March 1862, ibid., 631; Du Pont to Welles, 15 March 1862, ibid., 604.

81. Du Pont to Sophie, 19 March 1862, Du Pont, *Letters*, 1:372–74.

82. Du Pont to Sophie, 23 March 1862, Du Pont, *Letters*, 1:377, 377n; Du Pont to Welles, 25 March 1862, *ORN*, ser. 1, 12:657–58.

83. The "town" of Smyrna had three houses. Located nearby were supposed to be 40,000 board feet of live oak timber and 2,000 board feet of cedar. Du Pont to Mather, 19 March 1862, ibid., 647; Du Pont to Budd, ibid., 646; Du Pont to Welles, 24 March 1862, ibid., 655.

84. Some of the casualties occurred as the other boats passed down the river. Du Pont to Welles, 24, 25 March 1862, ibid., 645–46. 648; Dilwork to Washington, 4 April 1862, ibid., 646–51; Du Pont to Sophie, 23 March 1862,

Du Pont, *Letters*, 1:379–82; Williamson to Du Pont, 29 March 1863, *ORN*, ser. 1, 12:649.

85. Bulloch mounted four guns in the *Fingal* in case they met a blockading vessel. Bulloch, *Secret Service*, 1:112, 121; *Charleston Mercury*, 18 November 1861; Du Pont to Welles, 21 November 1861, M89, RG 45, NA; Welles to Du Pont, 23 November 1861, *ORN*, ser. 1, 12:360; Du Pont to Welles, 21 November 1861, ibid., 358–59; Lardner to Du Pont, 26 November 1861, ibid., 361.

86. Du Pont to Sophie, 24 December 1861, Du Pont, *Letters*, 1:286; Du Pont to Welles, 1 December 1861, ibid., 1:267; Du Pont to Welles, 6 December 1861, *ORN*, ser. 1, 12:384–85; Welles to Du Pont, 25 January 1861, ibid., 522.

87. Missroon to Du Pont, 21 November 1861, ibid., 355–56; Missroon to J. R. Goldsborough, 16 November 1861, ibid., 348–49; Du Pont to Godon, 18 November 1861, ibid., 351; Du Pont to Lardner, 17 December 1861, ibid., 403.

88. Drayton to Dahlgren, 10 January 1862, Dahlgren Papers, LCM; Du Pont to Welles, 1 April 1862, Du Pont Papers, Hagley.

89. Du Pont to Thornton A. Jenkins, 9 November 1861, *ORN*, ser. 1, 12:335; Welles to Du Pont, 16 November 1861, ibid., 348.

90. Missroon to Du Pont, ibid., 348–39; Du Pont to Missroon, 20 December 1861, ibid., 415.

91. Du Pont to Fox, 10 February 1862, ibid., 541; Barnes, "My Egotistigraphy," Barnes Papers, NYHS, 147; Du Pont to Welles, 25 January 1862, *ORN*, ser. 1, 12:490; Du Pont to Purviance, 19 December 1861, ibid., 411; Du Pont to Welles, 25 January 1862, ibid., 490; Du Pont to Fox, 11 November 1861, Fox, *Correspondence*, I:68; Du Pont to Fox, 24 December 1861, Fox Papers, NYHS.

92. Entry for 12 March 1862, Marchand, *Charleston Blockade*, 136.

93. General Order Number 5, 1 January 1862, Du Pont, *Dispatches*, 92–94; L. C. Sartori to Marston, 16 October 1861, *ORN*, ser. 1, 6:326; Entry for 25 December 1861, Marchand, *Charleston Blockade*, 69; F. W. Seward to Welles, 6 November 1861, *ORN*, ser. 1, 12:330; Missroon to J. R. Goldsborough, 16 November 1861, ibid., 348–49.

94. Hansard's Parliamentary Debates, 3rd series, vol. CLXV, 1862, 1193–94, 1240; *Philadelphia Daily Evening Bulletin*, 17 February 1862; Hale to Welles, 3 April 1862, *ORN*, ser. 1, 12:720; Stephen R. Wise, *Lifeline of the Confederacy, Blockade Running During the Civil War* (Columbia: University of South Carolina Press, 1988), Appendices 7 and 8; *Times* (New York), 28 April 1862; Du Pont to Goldsborough, 21 March 1862, *ORN*, ser. 1, 12:645.

95. Godon to Welles, 2 October 1862, M89, RG 45, NA; Du Pont to Fox, 4 January 1862, Fox, *Correspondence*, 1:87; Du Pont to Fox, 14 March 1862, Fox, *Correspondence*, 1:113; Du Pont to Welles, 1 December 1861, Du Pont to Sophie, 8 July 1862, Du Pont, *Letters*, 1:267, 2:155; Du Pont to Fox, 16 De-

cember 1863, Fox, *Correspondence*, 1:79–81; Watmough to Welles, 21 November 1861, Correspondence of Penrod G. Watmough, Entry 395, RG 45, NA; T. H. Stevens to Du Pont, 14 November 1861, *ORN*, ser. 1, 12:343; L. C. Santori to Du Pont, 10 November 1861, ibid., 339.

96. Du Pont to Fox, 12 November 1861, M89, RG 45, NA.

97. Welles to Du Pont, 16 November 1861, *ORN*, ser. 1, 13:348; Lenthall to Du Pont, 18 November 1861, Letters Sent to Officers, Entry 51, RG 19, NA; Withington, *Two Dramatic Episodes*, 45–47; Gordon, "The Great Stone Fleet," 78.

98. Gordon, ibid.; Du Pont to Sophie, 24 December 1862, Du Pont, *Letters*, 2:317; Daniel Eldredge, *The Third New Hampshire Regiment and All About It* (Boston: E. B. Stillings and Company, 1893), 273.

99. Contrabands were employed on the *Edward* to carry out some of the menial tasks required around the shop. Returns from the *Edward*, Records of the United States General Accounting Office, RG 217, NA; *Herald* (New York), 14 April 1863; Frederick C. Russel Papers, Entry for 9 June 1864, Fort Sumter National Monument; Elbridge J. Copp, *Reminiscences of the War of the Rebellion 1861–1865* (Nashua, N.H.: Telegraph Publishing Co., 1911), 211–12.

100. Cogswell to Du Pont, 29 October 1862, Enclosure to Du Pont to Lenthall, 31 October 1862, Letters Received From Officers, Entry 62, RG 19, NA; Du Pont to Lenthall, 14 May 1863, ibid.; Reynolds to Du Pont, 17 May 1864, Correspondence of William Reynolds, Entry 395, RG 45, NA.

101. A lack of tools seemed to delay the work more than a lack of manpower. Lenthall to Dahlgren, 4 October 1864, Entry 51, RG 19, NA; Du Pont to Lenthall, 25 November 1862, ibid.; Du Pont to Sophie, 30 December 1863, Du Pont, *Letters*, 2:329; Lenthall to Du Pont, 11 May 1862, *ORN*, ser. 1, 12: 813–14; *DANFS*, 2:341; Cosby to Rowan, 22 April 1864, Entry 62, RG 19, NA; Lenthall to Du Pont, 22 June 1863, Entry 51, RG 19, NA.

102. Du Pont to Sophie, 5 January 1863, Du Pont Papers, Hagley.

103. Welles to Du Pont, 27 January 1862, *ORN*, ser. 1, 12:529; Du Pont to Fox, 21 August 1862, Fox, *Correspondence*, 1:152; Du Pont to Sophie, 16 June 1862, Du Pont, *Letters*, 2:117.

104. This practice was instituted by the navy in the 1880s. Du Pont to Lenthall, 1 September 1862, Du Pont, *Letters*, 2:214, 214n.

105. Du Pont to Sophie, 1 May 1862, Du Pont, *Letters*, 2:23; White to Luce, 21 November 1863, Stephen B. Luce Papers, LCM; Rodgers to Fox, 10 November 1861, *ORN*, ser. 1, 12:340; Du Pont to Welles, 7 March 1863, M89, RG 45, NA.

106. Le Roy to Du Pont, 1 November 1862, William E. Le Roy Papers, Entry 395, RG 45, NA; Budd to Welles, 30 September 1862, *ORN*, ser. 1, 13:339; Du Pont to Sophie, 21 December 1862, Du Pont, *Letters*, 2: 308; Du Pont to Gillis, 13 January 1862, *ORN*, ser. 1, 12:482.

107. Du Pont to Upshur, 22 January 1862, *ORN*, ser. 1, 12:518–19; Du Pont to Fox, 10 February 1862, ibid., 540–41; Parrott to Du Pont, 23 February 1862, ibid., 549; Certificate issued by Du Pont, 17 December 1861, *ORN*, ser. 1, 12:421; Withington, *Two Dramatic Episodes*, 45, 47; Du Pont to Boggs, 24 February 1862, *ORN*, ser. 1, 12:561.

108. Du Pont to Fox, 25 November 1861, Fox, *Correspondence*, 1:74; Du Pont to Bridge, 13 May 1862, Du Pont, Papers, Hagley.

109. Du Pont to Baldwin, 2 June 1862, Du Pont, *Letters*, 2:53n.

110. It was not clear whether this was ever rectified. It is doubtful given the formal traditions of the navy regarding senior officers. Du Pont to Baldwin, 29 August 1862, *ORN*, ser. 1, 13:295; Horace R. Barnes, "Rear Admiral William Reynolds: A Distinguished Lancastrian 1815–1879," *Papers Read Before the Lancaster County Historical Society*, XXXVIII No. 2, 61–66; Lewis Randolph Hamersly, *Record of Living Officers of the U.S. Navy and Marine Corps* (Philadelphia: L. R. Hammersly and Company, 1870), 60; Reynolds to Dahlgren, 19 September, 20 November 1863, Correspondence of William Reynolds, Entry 395, RG 45, NA.

111. The average number of sick on board was over two dozen men. Reynolds to Dahlgren, 20, 24 October 1863, Correspondence of William Reynolds, Entry 395, RG 45, NA; Lenthall to Du Pont, 3 July 1862, Entry 51, RG 19, NA.

112. Reynolds to Du Pont, 16 February 1863, E72, Entry 395, RG 45, NA; Reynolds to Dahlgren, 24 October 1863, ibid.; Dahlgren to Welles, 14 July 1863, Dahlgren Papers, LCM.

113. Du Pont to Harwood, 9 June 1862, Du Pont Papers, Hagley; Du Pont to Harwood, 13 June 1862, *ORN*, ser. 1, 13:94–95; Reynolds to Dahlgren, 8 December 1863, Correspondence of William Reynolds, Entry 395, RG 45, NA; Dahlgren to Fox, 22 July 1863, Fox Papers, NYHS; Du Pont to Dahlgren, 2 January 1863, *ORN*, ser. 1, 13:495.

114. Alvah Folsom Hunter, *A Year on a Monitor and the Destruction of Fort Sumter*, ed. Craig L. Symonds (Columbia: University of South Carolina Press, 1991), 30; Reynolds to Dahlgren, 18 August 1863, Correspondence of William Reynolds, Entry 395, RG 45, NA; Reynolds to CRP Rodgers, 17 August 1863, ibid.; Dahlgren to Welles, 14 July 1863, Dahlgren Papers, LCM; Reynolds to Dahlgren, 21 August 1863, Repair Subject File, AR, RG 45, NA; *Valparaiso* Returns 1861–1863, RG 217, NA.

115. They considered converting the sloop *John Adams* into a store ship but Reynolds believed she could not serve well and the conversion would be too difficult. Reynolds to Dahlgren, 29 October, 8 December 1863, Correspondence of William Reynolds, Entry 395, RG 45, NA; Reynolds to Dahlgren, 20 December 1864, ibid; Reynolds to Dahlgren, 31 August 1863, *ORN*, ser. 1, 14:527.

116. Welles to Samuel Breese, 11 July 1861, Subject File OX, RG 45, NA.

117. J. Smith and C. H. Davis to Welles, 1 June 1861, Letters from Bureaus of the Navy Department, Entry 32, RG 45, NA; Minutes of the Board of Bureau Chiefs, Subject File OL, Entry 464, ibid.; Charles B. Boynton, *The History of the Navy During the Rebellion* 2 vols. (New York: D. Appleton & Co., 1867–1868), 82.

118. Paullin, *Naval Administration*, 291–92.

119. Welles to Stringham, 16 July 1861, *ORN*, ser. 1, 27: 357; Maxwell Woodhull to Gideon Welles, 4 October 1861, ibid., 367–68.

120. Bridge to Welles, 29 July 1861, Entry 32, RG 45, NA; Wodhull to Welles, 19 February 1862, *ORN*, ser. 1, 27: 417; Woodhull to Welles, 21 June 1862, ibid., 446.

121. List of Cargo of the *USS New Berne*, passim, Samuel Phillips Lee Papers, LCM; Welles to J. B. Montgomery, 9 May 1863, Letters From the Secretary of the Navy to Boston Navy Yard, Entry 319, RG 45, NA.

122. Du Pont to Welles, 4 March 1862, *ORN*, ser. 1, 12:575.

123. Drayton to Dahlgren, February (n.d.) 1862, Dahlgren Papers, LCM.

Chapter 4

1. South Carolina troops seized Fort Johnson in Charleston Harbor the day before. The garrison of the fort was intended to be eight hundred men. *Forts, Arsenals, Arms*, H. Rept. 85, 36th Cong., 2d sess., 26–27; Olmstead, *Fort Pulaski*, 98, 101, 102; Charles H. Olmstead, *The Memoirs of Charles H. Olmstead*, ed. Lilla Mills Hawes, Collections of the Georgia Historical Society Series XIV (Savannah, Ga.: Southern Printing and Publishing Co., 1961) 79–81; W. H. Andrews, *Footprints of a Regiment: A Recollection of the 1st Georgia Regulars 1861–1865* (Atlanta: Longstreet Press, 1992), 7.

2. *The Civil War Naval Chronology* 1:4 states that Tattnall brought his flotilla down the river on 26 December, and attacked the Union blockaders. The Union reports mention no action on this date; "34 Years in the United States Navy: Life and Correspondence of Captain C. Marius Schoonmaker United States Navy." Unpublished manuscript, LCM, 92–93, 100; *News* (Savannah), 27 December 1861.

3. Gillmore, "Siege and Capture of Fort Pulaski," in *Battles and Leaders*, 2:1; Olmstead, "Fort Pulaski," 102; Montfort to Mother, 18 February 1862, Theodorick W. Montfort, "Rebel Lawyer: The Letters of Lt. Theodorick W. Montfort, 1861–1862," ed. Spencer Bidwell King Jr., *Georgia Historical Quarterly* (March 1965): 95, 84.

4. Scharf, *Confederate Navy*, 636; Edward C. Anderson, *Confederate Foreign Agent: The European Diary of Major Edward C. Anderson*, ed. Stanley Hoole (Tuscaloosa: University of Alabama, Confederate Publishing Company, 1976), 117–18; Olmstead, *Memoirs*, 92.

5. Gillmore, *Official Report*, 22.

6. "Sketches of Army Life: Siege of Fort Pulaski," by T. Y. T, unpublished manuscript; Civil War (Federal, Miscellaneous) Papers, SHC; Du Pont to Hunter, 6 April 1862, *ORN*, ser. 1, 12:717–18; Du Pont to Sophie, 30 March 1862, Du Pont, *Letters*, 1:394–95.

7. It is possible that the vessel they spotted was the unfinished CSS *Georgia*. She was not completed until that fall and in March did not even have her armor. She may have been on a trial to test her machinery. Viele to Sherman, 28 March 1862, *ORN*, ser. 1, 12:669; Sherman to Commanding Officer U.S. Naval Forces Port Royal, 28 March 1862, ibid. 669–70; Collins to Lardner, 27 March 1862, *ORN*, ser. 1, 12:662–63; Gillis to Collins, 27 March 1862, ibid., 663; Du Pont to Sherman, 28, 29 March 1862, Du Pont Papers, Hagley.

8. William N. Still Jr., *Savannah Squadron* (Savannah, Ga.: Coastal Heritage Press, 1989), 4–passim; Du Pont to Fox, 21 August 1862, *ORN*, ser. 1, 13:269.

9. The text referred to a Wither's Island but, since there is no island by this name, the reference is probably to Whitmarsh Island. Gillis to Du Pont (circa March 1862), Du Pont Papers, Hagley; Sherman to Du Pont, 29 March 1862, *ORN*, ser. 1, 12:673–74; Du Pont to Welles, 3 April 1862, ibid., 706–7; Du Pont to Godon, 29 March, 3 April 1862, ibid., 672–704 Gillis to Collins, 30 March 1862, ibid., 680–81; *Times*, (New York), 14 April 1862; Du Pont to Sophie, 25, 30 March 1862, Du Pont, *Letters*, 1: 385, 393–95.

10. Abraham J. Palmer, *The History of the Forty-eighth Regiment New York State Volunteers in the War for the Union 1861–1865* (New York: Veterans Association of the Regiment, 1885), 34.

11. Sherman to Hunter, 31 March 1862, *ORA*, ser. 1, 6:257; Du Pont to Sophie, 4 April 1862, Du Pont, *Letters*, 1:400; Ezra J. Warner, *Generals in Blue, Lives of the Union Commanders* (Baton Rouge: Louisiana State University Press, 1964), 244; Du Pont to Sophie, 14 April 1862, Du Pont to Gerhard, 27 May 1862, Du Pont, *Letters*, 2:9, 75.

12. *Times* (New York), 19 April 1862; Du Pont to Hunter, 8 April 1862, *ORN*, ser. 1, 12:722; Olmstead, *Memoirs*, 96.

13. Du Pont to Irwin, 9 April 1862, *ORN*, ser. 1, 12:731; Rodgers to Du Pont, 13 April 1862, ibid., 731–32; Du Pont to Sophie, 12 April 1862, Du Pont, *Letters*, 1:421; Herbert M. Schiller, *Sumter is Avenged: The Siege and Reduction of Fort Pulaski* (Shippensburg, Pa.: White Mane Publishing Company, Inc., 1995), 105.

14. Gillmore, "Siege and Capture of Pulaski," 9; Rodgers to Du Pont, 13 April 1862, *ORN*, ser. 1, 12:93; Olmstead, "Fort Pulaski," 104.

15. Horace Porter to Father, 11 April 1862, Horace Porter Papers, LCM; Bryan, *Confederate Georgia*, 71; Tattnall to Pelot, 3 November 1862, *ORN*, ser. 1, 13:815.

16. Du Pont to Fox, 8 October 1862, Du Pont, *Letters*, 2:243; Ammen to Du Pont, 5 August 1862, Ammen Correspondence, Entry 395, RG 45, NA; Du Pont to Sophie, 3 August 1863, Du Pont Papers, Hagley.

17. Benham to Wright, 2 April 1862, *ORA*, ser. 1, 6:127–28; Du Pont to Fox, 3 April 1862, Fox, *Correspondence*, I:115–16.

18. *Press* (Philadelphia), n.d., Moore, *Rebellion Record*, 4:443; John E. Johns, *Florida During the Civil War* (Gainesville: University of Florida Press, 1963), 66.

19. The Union's policy was that of noninterference with property and the officers were instructed to return all slaves to their owners before leaving in order not to offend Southerners who are sympathetic to the Union cause. The Confederate forces never kept a garrison in the town and only visited Jacksonville to gather intelligence. Nicholson to Du Pont, 27 June 1862, *ORN*, ser. 1, 13:147; Hately to Nicholson, 27 June 1862, ibid., 147; Nicholson to Hately, ibid., 148; W. S. Dilworth to T. A. Washington, 15 April 1862, *ORA*, ser. 1, 6:131–32. Du Pont to Drayton, 5 April 1862, *ORN*, ser. 1, 12:717; Nicholson to Du Pont, 17 April 1862, ibid., 753–74; Ammen to Hopkins, 28 April 1862, Entry 395, Ammen Correspondence, RG 45, NA; Sprotson to Ammen, 28 April 1862, *ORN*, ser. 1, 12:750–51; Stevens to Drayton, 13 April 1863, ibid., 739–40. Johns, *Florida During the Civil War*, 68.

20. Benham to Du Pont, 21 April 1862, *ORN*, ser. 1, 12:766; Rodgers to Du Pont, 12 March 1862, ibid., 595–96; Johns, *Florida During the Civil War*, 68–69; Thomas Graham, "The Home Front: Civil War Times in St. Augustine," *Civil War Times in St. Augustine*, ed. Jacqueline K. Fretwell (St. Augustine, Fla.: St. Augustine Historical Society, 1988), 3.

21. Welles to Du Pont, 25 September 1861, *ORN*, ser. 1, 12:210; Beaumont to Du Pont, 21 November 1862, Beaumont Correspondence, Entry 395, RG 45, NA; Ammen, *The Old Navy and the New*, 357; Ammen to Du Pont, 29 December 1861, 3 January 1862, M89, RG 45, NA; Villard, *Memoirs of Henry Villard*, 22; Rhind to Du Pont, 7 February 1862, *ORN*, ser. 1, 12:520–21; Goldsborough to Du Pont, 16 July 1862, *ORN*, ser. 1, 13:195; Baxter to Du Pont, 15 July 1862, ibid., 192–93; Du Pont to Balch, 21 July 1862, ibid., 203–204.

22. The story of the free blacks on these islands is much more complex and could be the subject of a book-length study. Destitute whites also came out to the squadron looking for food. Woodhull to Du Pont, 7 November 1862, *ORN*, ser. 1, 13:436; Du Pont to Gerhard, 27 May 1862, Du Pont, *Letters*, 2:75–76; Du Pont to Fox, 10 February 1862, Fox Papers, NYHS; Balch to Du Pont, 25 July 1862, *ORN*, ser. 1, 13:213; Willie L. Rose, *Rehearsal for Reconstruction; The Port Royal Experiment* (Indianapolis: Bobbs-Merrill Inc., 1964), 24, 47; Du Pont to Gerhard, 27 May 1862, Du Pont, *Letters*, 2:75; Proclamation, Lincoln, 19 May 1862, *ORA*, ser. 3, 2:42–43.

23. Rhind to Du Pont, 3 April 1862, *ORN*, ser. 1, 12:676; Semmes to Goldsborough, 30 April 1862, Watmough Correspondence, Entry 395, RG 45, NA;

Rhind to Du Pont, 30 April 1862, *ORN*, ser. 1, 12:790–91; Ammen, *The Atlantic Coast*, 63–64; Stevens to Du Pont, 28 March 1863, *ORN*, ser. 1, 12:638–39.

24. Rhind to Du Pont, 30 April 1862, *ORN*, ser. 1, 12:790–91; Du Pont to Welles, ibid., 789; Du Pont to Sophie, 1 May 1862, Du Pont, *Letters*, 2:27.

25. This was part of General R. E. Lee's plan to abandon the weak defenses along the coast and move them farther to the interior. Pemberton to Cooper, 27 March 1862, *ORA*, ser. 1, 6:420.

26. Ravenel to Ripley, 13 May 1862, *ORN*, ser. 1, 12:825; E. Milby Burton, *The Siege of Charleston*, 94–95; Du Pont to Welles, 14 May 1862, *ORN*, ser. 1, 12:821; Du Pont to Sophie, 11 May 1862, Du Pont Papers, 2:50; Edward A. Miller, Jr., *Gullah Statesman: Robert Smalls From Slavery to Congress, 1839–1915* (Columbia: University of South Carolina Press, 1985), 2.

27. Smalls and other men divided in unequal portions $4,584 in prize money for the *Planter*, Welles to Du Pont, 15 July 1862, *ORN*, ser. 1, 12:823; Nickels to Parrott, 13 May 1862, ibid., 822; Du Pont to Marchand, 15 May 1862, *ORN*, ser. 1, 13:4–6.

28. Pemberton to Cooper, 27 March 1862, *ORA*, ser. 1, 6:420; Washington to Pemberton, 2 April 1862, ibid., 423–24; Jones, *Siege of Charleston*, 196–97; Marchand, Charleston Blockade, Entry for 20 May 1862, 170–73; Marchand to Du Pont, 19 May 1862, *ORN*, ser. 1, 13:13–14; Boutelle to Du Pont, 22 May 1862, ibid., 16–17.

29. Welles promised Flag Officer Louis M. Goldsborough of the North Atlantic Blockading Squadron the same monitors for a move on Wilmington, North Carolina. Neither flag officer, however, would be able to use *Galena* for some time. During the battle of Drewry's Bluff on the 15th the *Galena* was severely damaged and would not be ready for service for some months later. Welles to Du Pont, 13 May 1862, *ORN*, ser. 1, 12:820.

30. Benham to Meigs, 23 May 1862, *ORA*, ser. 1, 14:345; Rodgers to Du Pont, 22 May 1862, C. R. P. Rodgers Correspondence, Entry 395, RG 45, NA; Rodgers to Benham, 22 May 1862, ibid.; Du Pont to Fox, 31 May 1862, Du Pont, *Letters*, 2:92; Stevens, "Military Operations," 133.

31. Rodgers to Benham, 22 May 1862, C.R.P. Rodgers Correspondence, Entry 395, RG 45, NA.

32. Rodgers to Du Pont, 20, 22 May 1862, ibid.; Du Pont to Hunter, 24 May 1862, *ORN*, ser. 1, 13:27–28.

33. Rodgers to Marchand, 27 May 1862, C.R.P. Rodgers Correspondence, Entry 395, RG 45, NA; Du Pont to Drayton, 28 May 1862, *ORN*, ser. 1, 13:51–52.

34. Collins to Marchand, 25 May 1862, *ORN*, ser. 1, 13:37; Gist to Walker, ibid., 37–38.

35. Du Pont to Welles, Du Pont, *Dispatches*, 182–83; Drayton to Du Pont, 30 May 1862, *ORN*, ser. 1, 13:55–56; Du Pont to Sophie, 29 May 1862, Du Pont, *Letters*, 2:79.

36. Ely to Stevens, 31 May 1862, Christ to Stevens, 30 May 1862, *ORA*, ser. 1, 14:20, 22–24; Moore, "Operations in South Carolina," *Rebellion Record*, 9: 238; Stevens, "Military Operations," 134–36.

37. Du Pont to Sophie, 3 June 1862, Du Pont, *Letters*, 2:97–98; Marchand had several months earlier had a petty quarrel with the flag officer. After the attack on Fernandina, Marchand asked Charles Davis to send a letter to his wife informing her of his well being. Du Pont's policy was to allow only official letters to go north with the first ship so that no inaccurate accounts of the attack would reach the press. After a "sharp conversation" with Davis, Du Pont "shoved a sheet of note paper" to Marchand and told him to write a note which he would mail. Marchand wrote four lines and handed it to Du Pont. Marchand, *Charleston Blockade*, Entry for 5 March 1862, 127–28; Du Pont to Marchand, 10 June 1862, *ORN*, ser. 1, 13:56–57.

38. J. B. Creighton to Du Pont, 6 June 1862, *ORN*, ser. 1, 13:79; Du Pont to Sophie, 7 June 1862, Du Pont, *Letters*, 2:107–109.

39. D. H. Howard to Samuel T. Cushing, 23 June 1863, *ORA*, ser. 1, 14:27–28; Jones, *Siege of Charleston*, 97; Beauregard, "The Defense of Charleston," in *Battles and Leaders*, 2:21.

40. Hunter to Benham, 10 June 1862, *ORA*, ser. 1, 14:46; Jones, *Siege of Charleston*, 98; Drayton to Du Pont, 10 June 1862, *ORN*, ser. 1, 13:88–89.

41. Benham to Drayton, 10 June 1862, *ORN*, ser. 1, 13:87; Drayton to Du Pont, 13 June 1862, ibid., 98.

42. Drayton to Du Pont, 13, 17 June 1862, ibid., 104–105; Drayton to Du Pont, 14, 15, June 1862, ibid., 100–102; Du Pont to Sophie, 13 June 1862, Du Pont, *Letters*, 2:113.

43. Benham to Drayton, 17 June 1862, *ORN*, ser. 1, 13:105; Drayton to Du Pont, 17 June 1862, ibid., 104; Beauregard, "Defense of Charleston," 21.

44. Hunter General Order Number 14, 10 June 1862, *ORN*, ser. 1, 13:57–58; Du Pont to Drayton, 18 June 1862, ibid., 112–13; *Times* (New York), 28 June 1862; Drayton to Du Pont, 23 June 1862, *ORN*, ser. 1, 13:133; Hunter to Stanton, 23 June 1862, *ORA*, ser. 1, 14:43.

45. Marchand, *Blockade of Charleston*, Entry for 29 June 1862, 230; Charles Steedman to Sally, 4 July 1862, Steedman Papers, Duke University Manuscript Collection, Perkins Library, Durham, N.C., hereinafter cited as DUM. This letter mirrors the sentiments and similar words of Drayton in a letter he wrote to Du Pont on 2 July 1862, *ORN*, ser. 1, 13:165; Du Pont to Whetten, 18 April 1863, Du Pont Papers, Hagley; Du Pont to Fox, 30 June, 2 July, 31 August 1862, Fox Papers, NYHS.

46. Du Pont to Welles, 8 February 1862, *ORN*, ser. 1, 13:651; Welles to Du Pont, 17 April 1862, ibid., 755.

47. Welles to Du Pont, 28 March 1862, *ORN*, ser. 1, 12:671; Du Pont to Sophie, 10 April 1862, Du Pont, *Letters*, 1:408.

48. Du Pont to Fox, 10 February 1862, Fox Papers, NYHS; Du Pont to Welles, 23 April 1862, *ORN*, ser. 1, 12:772–73.

49. Du Pont to Sophie, 19, 29 April 1862, Du Pont, *Letters*, 2:17, 21; Du Pont to Welles, 27 April 1862, *ORN*, ser. 1, 12:782–83.

50. John P. Hale to Welles, 3 April 1862, *ORN*, ser. 1, 12:720; Du Pont to Lardner, 19 April 1862, *ORN*, ser. 1, 12:759–60.

51. *Times* (New York), 4 April 1862.

52. At this point in the war most of the blockade running had been performed by small coastal vessels. Along the entire South Atlantic coast, steam blockade runners had successfully run into port only fourteen times and run out nineteen. Welles to John P. Hale, 9 May 1862, *ORN*, ser. 1, 13:8–9; Wise, *Lifeline*, Appendices 7–10, 251–261.

53. Mullany to Steedman, 26 August 1862, *ORN*, ser. 1, 13:290–91; Marchand, *Charleston Blockade*, Entries for 27, 28 April 1862, 151–52; J. D. Dexter to J. F. Green, 12 April 1862, Joseph F. Green Papers, LCM; Parrott to Du Pont, 11 May 1862, M89, RG 45, NA; Marchand to Du Pont, 25 May 1862, *ORN*, ser. 1, 13:31.

54. Du Pont to Welles, 9 May 1862, M89, RG 45, NA; Parrott to Du Pont, 11 May 1862, ibid.

55. Du Pont to Sophie, 19 May 1862, Du Pont, *Letters*, 2:58–59.

56. The blockaders' distance from shore depended on the draft of the vessel and the particular station. Marchand to Du Pont, 25 June 1862, *ORN*, ser 1., 13:138–39; Marchand Circular, 16 June 1862, ibid., 119; Marchand Circular 21 June 1862, ibid., 131; Map of Charleston Harbor 11 May 1862, enclosure to Du Pont to Welles, 14 May 1862, *ORN*, ser. 1, 12:816; Marchand to Du Pont, 3, 25, June 1862, *ORN*, ser. 1, 13:73, 138–39; Steedman to Hazard, 21 August 1862, ibid., 270–71.

57. Le Roy blamed the loss on a poor quality coal. Le Roy to Du Pont, 28 June 1862, enclosure to Du Pont to Lenthall, Entry 62, RG 19, NA; Wise, *Lifeline*, 251, 255; Le Roy to Du Pont, 25 June 1862, *ORN*, ser. 1, 13: 136–37.

58. Du Pont to Welles, 27 June 1862, *ORN*, ser. 1, 13:134–35.

59. Marchand to Du Pont, 30 June 1862, ibid., 157.

60. Du Pont to Gerhard, 19 February 1863, Wells to Du Pont, 28 July 1862, Du Pont, *Letters*, 2:174–75, 445–46; Du Pont to Sophie, 5 March 1863, ibid, 2:469; James Iredell Waddell, Diary, entry for 29 August 1863, Waddell Collection, U.S. Naval Academy Library, Annapolis, Md.; Harriot to Middleton, 2 March 1862, Isabella Middleton Leland, ed., "Middleton Correspondence, 1861–1865," *The South Carolina Historical Magazine* 63 (January 1962), 40.

61. Du Pont to Welles, 23 July 1862, *ORN*, ser. 1, 13:206; Mullany to Steedman, 25 August 1862, ibid., 289–90; Rodgers to Mullany, 29 August 1862,

ibid., 293; Du Pont to Welles, 25 August 1862, Du Pont, *Dispatches*, 283; Marchand to Du Pont, 2 August 1862, *ORN*, ser. 1, 13:240–41; Du Pont to Le Roy, 10 August 1862, ibid., 247.

62. Du Pont to Sophie, 31 August 1862, Du Pont, *Letters*, 2:209; Ammen to Bache, 8 July 1862, *ORN*, ser. 1, 13:184–85; Rodgers to Mullany, 29 August 1862, ibid., 280–81; General Instructions regarding Signals, 25 August 1862, ibid., 280–81; Du Pont to Welles, 2 September 1862, Du Pont, *Dispatches*, 294–54; Circular J. F. Green, 17 October 1862, *ORN*, ser. 1, 13:393–94; Albert Warren Kelsey, *Autobiographical Notes and Memoranda By Albert Warren Kelsey 1840–1910* (Baltimore, Md.: Munder-Thomsen Press, 1911), 38.

63. Downes to Wise, 11 September 1862, *ORN*, ser. 1, 13:324.

64. Du Pont felt it crucial to keep the vessels in commission while under repair. The normal procedure called for a vessel to be put out of commission and her crew dismissed, accounts settled, etc. Du Pont insisted the navy should not break up this "internal organization . . ." He argued the vessels should remain in commission, their crews remain with the ship to expedite repairs, and be ready to sail once the repairs were complete. Fox to Du Pont, 31 July 1862, Fox Papers, NYHS; Du Pont to Sophie, 9 July 1862, 6 August 1862, Du Pont, *Letters*, 2:157–58, 180; Du Pont to Fox, 21 August 1862, Du Pont Papers, Hagley; Welles to Paulding, 27 August 1862, *ORN*, ser. 1, 13:285–86; Du Pont to Welles, 18 August 1862, ibid., 265.

65. Du Pont to Welles, 8 January 1862, M89, RG 45, NA.

66. Welles to Breese, 2 August 1861, Letters Sent by the Secretary of the Navy to Officers, Entry 1, RG 45, NA. The *Arkansas* and the *Blackstone* had made irregular stops off Wilmington with supplies. Ship's Log of *Cambridge*, Entry 118, RG 24, NA; Welles to William H. West, 18 July 1863, *ORN*, ser. 1, 27:518; Thomas H. Lookes to Lee, 15 September 1862, ibid., 462–63; Welles to Goldsborough, 18 April 1862, ibid., 428; Welles to Du Pont, 17 April 1862, ibid., 428; Du Pont to Sophie, 29 April 1862, Du Pont, *Letters*, 2:21; Du Pont to Sophie, 16 December 1862, ibid.

67. Cunningham Memo, 1 May 1863, *ORN*, ser. 1, 14:170; Du Pont to Kasson, 8 May 1862, *ORN*, ser. 1, 12:803; Welles to Woodhull, 10 May 1862, *ORN*, ser. 1, 12:808; Welles to Trenchard, 2 June 1862, *ORN*, ser. 1, 13:69; Du Pont to Lenthall, 24 April 1862, Entry 62, RG 19, NA; Du Pont to Sophie, 1 January 1863, Du Pont to Welles, 27 February 1863, Du Pont, *Letters*, 2:332, 457; Du Pont to Sophie, 26 February 1863, Du Pont Papers, Hagley; Steedman to Rockwell, 8 April 1863, *ORN*, ser. 1, 27:492–passim; Du Pont to Fox, 22 December 1862, Fox Papers, NYHS; Journal of S. B. Luce, 8 September 1864, Luce Papers, LCM.

68. Welles to West, 4 March 1863, *ORN*, ser. 1, 27:485–86; Dahlgren to Welles, 21 January 1864, Dahlgren Papers, LCM; Abstract Log of *Arkansas*, 29 June–29 August 1863, *ORN*, ser. 1, 27:671–72.

69. Du Pont used these sailing vessels to carry supplies because he needed the steam vessels for the blockade. Also ton for ton they could carry more supplies than steamers. Du Pont to Welles, 2 February 1862, ibid., 406; Mullany to Du Pont, 24 April 1862, *ORN*, ser. 1, 12:774–75; Du Pont to Welles, 22 December 1862, *ORN*, ser. 1, 13:484.

70. General Order No. 23, Du Pont, January 8, 1863, Subject File OX, RG 45, NA; Dahlgren to Reynolds, 7 August 1863, Dahlgren Papers, LCM; Regulations for Supply Steamers, 19 October 1863, ed. Magnus S. Thompson, *General Orders and Circulars Issued By the Navy Department from 1863 to 1887* (Washington, D.C.: Government Printing Office, 1887), 11; Reynolds to Dahlgren, 10 November 1863, Reynolds Correspondence, Entry 395, RG 45, NA; Dahlgren to Green, 6 September 1864, Dahlgren Papers, LCM; to Ammen, 6 May 1862, *ORN*, ser. 1, 12:751; Log of *Oleander*, 12 March 1864–passim, Entry 118, RG 24, NA.

71. Marchand to Adger, 22 June 1862, *ORN*, ser. 1, 13:132; Rowan to Dahlgren, 5 November 1863, passim, Naval Stores Afloat, Subject File XN, RG 45, NA; Lenthall to Dahlgren, 21 November 1863, 17 March 1864, 30 April 1864, Entry 51, RG 45, NA; Reynolds to Welch, 17 February 1865, Reynolds Correspondence, Entry 395, RG 45, NA; Dahlgren to Reynolds, 7 January 1865, Dahlgren Papers, LCM.

72. Reynolds to Dahlgren, 7 August 1864, Reynolds Correspondence, Entry 395, RG 45, NA; Isherwood to Dahlgren, 5 December 1864, Letters Sent to Naval officers, Entry 966, RG 19, NA.

73. Du Pont to Fox, 22 December 1862, *ORN*, ser. 1, 13:486; Du Pont to Fox, 23 October 1862, ibid., 409; Dahlgren to Welles, 29 December 1863, *ORN*, ser. 1, 15:211–12.

74. Welles to Bridge, 3 June 1861, Letters to Bureaus of the Navy Department, Entry 13, RG 45, NA; Aubrey Henry Polser Jr., "The Administration of the United States Navy 1861–1865," Ph.D. dissertation, University of Nebraska, 1975, 26; Paullin, *Naval Administration*, 250; U.S. Congress, House, *Report of the Secretary of the Navy*, H. Ex. Doc. 1, 39th Cong., 1st sess., 4 December 1865, XXXIII.

75. U.S. Congress, House, *Report of the Secretary of the Navy*, H. Ex. Doc. 1, 37th Cong., 1st sess., 7 December 1863, XXVI.

76. Francis P. B. Sands, "Lest We Forget: Memories of Service Afloat from 1862 to 1866," *Military Order of the Loyal Legion of the United States Commandery of the District of Columbia*, War Papers 73 (Washington, D.C.: The Commandry, 1894), 4; *Report of the Secretary of the Navy*, 1865, XIII; Soley, *The Blockade and the Cruisers*, 4–5, 7–9; William S. Dudley, *Going South: U. S. Navy Officer Resignations & Dismissals on the Eve of the Civil War*, Naval Historical Foundation, Washington, D.C., 1981.

77. Breese to Welles, 11 May 1861, Letters Sent by the Commandant, New York Navy Yard, Entry 332, RG 45, NA; Welles to Stringham, 31 July 1861,

ORN, ser. 1, 6:45; Paulding to Welles, 22 December 1861, Entry 34 (New York), RG 45, NA; Circular, Gideon Welles, 9 August 1864, Enclosure; Lee to Welles, 20 August 1864, S. P. Lee Collection, LCM.

78. Reuben Elmore Stivers, *Privateers and Volunteers: The Men and Women of Our Reserve Naval Forces 1776–1866* (Annapolis: U.S. Naval Institute, 1975), 203; John A. Dahlgren, *Memoirs of John A. Dahlgren Rear Admiral United States Navy*, ed. Madelein Dahlgren (Boston: J. R. Osgood, 1882), 10 December 1863, 429–30.

79. Du Pont to Davis, 4 January 1863, Du Pont Papers, Hagley; Dahlgren to Welles, 14 June 1864, *ORN*, ser. 1, 15:524; Dahlgren to Welles, 24 July 1863, *ORN*, ser. 1, 14:389–90; Du Pont to Sophie, 28 August 1862, 28 January 1863, Du Pont, *Letters*, 2:204, 389–90; Du Pont to Welles, 26 September 1862, M89, RG 45, NA; Drayton to Du Pont, 28 December 1861, *ORN*, ser. 1, 12:442–43.

80. Stringham to Welles, 15 August 1861, *ORN*, ser. 1, 6:83; Welles to Stringham, 3 September 1861, ibid., 163; Davis to Du Pont, 15 June 1861, Area 7, Area File, Entry 463, RG 45, NA; Dahlgren to Welles, 23 February 1864, Dahlgren Papers, LCM.

81. Stringham to Welles, 18 July 1861, *ORN*, ser. 1, 6:8; Welles to Stringham, 22 July 1861, ibid., 10.

82. Welles to Dahlgren, 25 September 1861, Letters Received From the Secretary of the Navy by the Commandant, Entry 346 (Philadelphia Navy Yard), RG 45, NA; Circular, Gideon Welles, 18 December 1862, S. P. Lee Collection, LCM.

83. General Order No. 11, 15 May 1862, Ammen Correspondence, Subentry 49, Entry 395, RG 45, NA; Welles to Dahlgren, 28 July 1863, *ORN*, ser. 1, 14:401; Fox to Dahlgren, 5 August 1863, Fox Papers, NYHS; Meade to Paulding, 24 December 1862, Entry 34, RG 45, NA; Dahlgren to Welles, 6 August 1863, Dahlgren Papers, LCM.

84. Dahlgren, *Memoirs*, 10 December 1863, 430.

85. Samuel Pellman Boyer, *Naval Surgeon: The Diary of Dr. Samuel Pellman Boyer*, eds. Elinor and James A. Barnes (Bloomington: Indiana University Press, 1963), 14–passim; Case Book, Edward Kershner Papers, DUM.

86. Reynolds to Rowan, 19 March 1864, Reynolds Correspondence, Entry 395, RG 45, NA; Reynolds to Rant, 4 May 1864, ibid.; Hunter, *A Year on a Monitor*, 103.

87. Du Pont to Lenthall, 13 December 1862, Entry 62, RG 19, NA; Welles to Smith, 2 November 1863, Letters Sent by the Secretary of the Navy to Commandants and Navy Agents 1808–65, Entry 13, RG 45, NA, Microfilm Publication Number M480; Du Pont to Welles, 26 September 1862, M89, RG 45, NA; Dahlgren to Reynolds, 15 January 1864, Dahlgren Papers, LCM; Reynolds to Dahlgren, 16 October 1864, Reynolds Correspondence, Entry 395, RG 45, NA; Reynolds to Welch, 2 January 1865, ibid.

88. Dahlgren to A. N. Smith, 6 October 1863, Dahlgren Papers, LCM; Reynolds to Chief of Staff, 23 August 1863, Reynolds Correspondence, Entry 395, RG 45, NA; Reynolds to Dahlgren, 19 November 1864, ibid.; Reynolds to Du Pont, 20 October 1984, ibid.

89. Du Pont to Lenthall, 13 June 1863, Entry 62, RG 19, NA; Reynolds to Chief of Staff, 25 September 1863, Reynolds Correspondence, Entry 395, RG 45, NA; Reynolds to Dahlgren, 19 November 1864, ibid.

90. Marchand to Du Pont, 22 June 1862, *ORN*, ser. 1, 13:132; Du Pont to Sophie, 24 August 1862, Du Pont, *Letters*, 2:198; Parrott, Journal of the *Augusta*, February 1862, passim, Parrott Correspondence, Entry 392, RG 45, NA.

91. Du Pont to Foote, 13 December 1862, *ORN*, ser. 1, 13:479–80; These figures are for average use. If all have been moving constantly, Du Pont would have needed another two hundred tons. Average consumption of coal per day of the steamers belonging to the South Atlantic Blockading Squadron March 1861 [1862], Du Pont Papers, Hagley. It dipped to as low as eight hundred tons a week in January 1863. Du Pont to Foote, 13 January 1863, Du Pont, *Letters*, 2:359; Du Pont to Welles, 27, 28 March 1862, M89, RG 45, NA.

92. Du Pont to Fox, 18 February, 14 March 1862, Fox Papers, NYHS; Du Pont to Welles, 27, 28 March 1862, M89, RG 45, NA; Du Pont to Sophie, 25 March 1862, Du Pont, *Letters*, 1:383.

93. Du Pont to Sophie, 12 September 1862, Du Pont, *Letters*, 2:225; Tyler Stone & Co. to General Montgomery C. Meigs, 30 March 1863, Records of the Quartermaster General's Department, Record Group 92, Consolidated Correspondence File, Entry 225, NA; F. Charles Petrillo, *Anthracite and Slackwater: The North Branch Canal 1828–1901* (Easton, Pa.: Center For Canal History and Technology 1986), 203; Manville B. Wakefield, *Coal Boats To Tidewater: The Story of the Delaware and Hudson Canal* (South Fallsburg, N.Y.: Steingart Associates, Inc., 1965), 59; Adams to Du Pont, 31 March 1863, Du Pont Papers, Hagley.

94. Chester Lloyd Jones, *The Economic History of the Anthracite-Tidewater Canals*, Publications of the University of Pennsylvania Series in Political Economy and Public Law 22 (Philadelphia: University of Pennsylvania, 1908), 142; S. F. Du Pont to Sophie, 29 June 1863, Du Pont, *Letters*, 3:188–89; Dahlgren to Lenthall, 9 June 1862, Entry 62, RG 19, NA; Dahlgren to Reynolds, 21 September 1862, Dahlgren Papers, LCM; Dahlgren to Smith, 3 August 1863, ibid.; Dahlgren to Welles 9 August 1863, *ORN*, ser. 1, 14:431; Beaumont to Reynolds, 7 August 1863, Beaumont Letters, Beaumont Correspondence, Entry 395, RG 45, NA; Reynolds to Beaumont, 9 August 1863, ibid.; General Letter to Commanders Southward, 3 August 1863, ibid.

95. Ammen, *The Atlantic Coast*, 65–67; Prentiss to Du Pont, 25 May 1862, *ORN*, ser. 1, 13:22–23.

96. Ammen to Du Pont, 21 May 1862, Ammen Correspondence, Entry 395, RG 45, NA; Ammen to Du Pont, 8 June 1862, *ORN*, ser. 1, 13:83–84;

Du Pont to Sophie, 13 June 1862, Du Pont, *Letters*, 2:111; Ammen, *The Atlantic Coast*, 69.

97. Rhind to Du Pont, 23 June 1862, *ORN*, ser. 1, 13:126–27.

98. The *Western World* grounded on the way in and detained the expedition for two tides. Then the *Henry Andrew* got ashore and the passage to the North Santee was not reached until the evening of the 25th. During the expedition a plantation was plundered and a great many articles were brought back on the steamers Du Pont had returned. Prentiss to Du Pont, 2 July 1862, *ORN*, ser. 1, 13:122; Du Pont to Welles, 2 August 1862, ibid., 230.

99. Truxton to Du Pont, 20 July 1862, *ORN*, ser. 1, 13:199–200; Nichols to Du Pont, 4 August 1863, ibid., 220; Goldsborough to Du Pont, 13 August 1862, ibid., 251; Hunter to Du Pont, 30 June 1862, ibid., 156–57; Du Pont to Welles, 3 July 1862, ibid., 166–67.

100. Du Pont to Fox, 21 August 1862, Fox, *Correspondence*, I: 150; Balch to Du Pont, 15 August 1862, *ORN*, ser. 1, 13:257–59.

101. Ammen, *The Atlantic Coast*, 70; Crane to Du Pont, 9, 11 September 1862, *ORN*, ser. 1, 13:324–25.

102. Steedman to Du Pont, 17 September 1862, *ORN*, ser. 1, 13:329–30; Finegan to Cooper, 19 September 1862, ibid., 331; Steedman to Mrs. Steedman, 17 September 1862, Steedman, *Memoir*, 328–29.

103. Ammen, *The Atlantic Coast*, 70; Jones, *The Siege of Charleston*, 124–25; Steedman to Du Pont, 14 October 1862, *ORN*, ser. 1, 13:362–63; Woodhull to Steedman, 3 October 1862, ibid., 356; Brannan to Prentice, 13 October 1862, *ORA*, ser. 1, 14:129–30.

104. Woodhull to Steedman, 7 October 1862, *ORN*, ser. 1, 13:367–68; Abstract Log of *E. B. Hale*, ibid., 370.

105. Williams to Steedman, 9 October 1862, ibid., 366–67.

106. The naval vessels operating in the interior waters faced an interesting dilemma. They had to keep enough fuel and supplies for extended operations yet too much could create draft problems. The *Cimarron* had to keep one hundred tons of "something or other to keep her steering trim." Woodhull to Steedman, 11 October 1862, *ORN*, ser. 1, 13:360–61; Woodhull to Godon, 21 October 1862, ibid., 398; Woodhull to Du Pont, 3 November, 1 December 1862, ibid., 428, 466–67; Beard to Saxton, 22 November 1862, Moore, *Rebellion Record*, 6:200–201; Hughes to Du Pont, 11, 23 November 1862, *ORN*, ser. 1, 13:442–43; Du Pont to Sophie, 2 May 1862, Du Pont, *Letters*, 2:29.

107. The army, unable to use the transport *Cosmopolitan* and a tug, required the use of the naval vessels to transport troops. Mitchel to Godon, 15 October 1862, *ORN*, ser. 1, 13:399; Steedman to Du Pont, 27 October 1862, ibid., 402.

108. Ammen, *The Atlantic Coast*, 71; Steedman to Du Pont, 27 October 1862, *ORN*, ser. 1, 13:400–401.

109. Steedman to Du Pont, 27 October 1862, *ORN*, ser. 1, 13:400–401; Phoenix to Steedman, 24 October 1862, ibid., 402–403; Brannan to Prentice, 24 October 1862, Moore, *Rebellion Record*, 6:34; Eldridge, *3rd New Hampshire*, 223; U.S. Navy, Bureau of Navigation, *Record of the Medals of Honor: Officers and Enlisted Men of the United States Navy, Marine Corps, and Coast Guard 1862–1923* (Washington D.C.: Government Printing Office, 1924), 94; Adams to Corbin, 21 June 1863, Correspondence of Thomas G. Corbin, Entry 395, RG 45, NA.

110. Steedman to Du Pont, 27 October 1862, *ORN*, ser. 1, 13:400–401.

111. Brannan to Prentice, 24 October 1862, ibid., 404; Du Pont to Fox, 23 October 1862, Du Pont Papers, Hagley; Du Pont to Sophie, 23 October 1862, Du Pont, *Letters*, 2:262.

Chapter 5

1. Congress had created the rank of Rear Admiral on 16 July 1862. Du Pont to Sophie, 9, 10 August 1862, Du Pont, *Letters*, 2:185–87.

2. Fox to Du Pont, 3 June 1862, Fox Papers, NYHS.

3. Rodgers to Fox, 3 September 1862, Fox Papers, NYHS; Du Pont to Sophie, 23 September 1862, Du Pont, *Letters*, 2:235; Gideon Welles, *The Diary of Gideon Welles*, ed. Howard K. Beale, 3 vols. (New York: W. W. Norton, 1960), Entry for 2 October 1862, 1:160; Welles to Du Pont, 10 September 1862, *ORN*, ser. 1, 13:322; Du Pont to Whetten, 8 October 1862, Du Pont, *Letters*, 2:244.

4. Du Pont to Sophie, 18, 22 October 1862, Du Pont, *Letters*, 2:258–59; Du Pont to Davis, 25 October 1862, Copy of Mr. Davis' Sketch (circa 27 July 1863), Du Pont Papers, Hagley.

5. Dahlgren to Lincoln, 1 October 1862, Dahlgren Papers, LCM; Fox to Du Pont, 7 October 1862, Du Pont to Grimes, 8 August 1863, Du Pont, *Letters*, 2:242; Du Pont to Fox, 8 October 1862, Fox, *Correspondence*, 1:160–61; Du Pont to Davis, 25 October 1862, Du Pont Papers, Hagley.

6. Welles to Dahlgren, 8 October 1862, *ORN*, ser. 1, 13:376–77; Welles, *Diary*, 9 October 1862, 1:163–65; Dahlgren to Welles, 10, 11 October 1862, *ORN*, ser. 1, 13:353–54, 377–78; Du Pont to Fox, 8 October 1862, Fox, *Correspondence*, 1:160–61; Robert J. Schneller, Jr. *A Quest for Glory, A Biography of Rear Admiral John A. Dahlgren* (Annapolis, Md.: Naval Institute Press, 1996), 233–34.

7. Du Pont to Sophie, 16, 17, 21, 22 October 1862, Du Pont, *Letters*, 2:245–48, 251–52, 258; Du Pont to Davis, 25 October 1862, Du Pont Papers, Hagley.

8. Du Pont to Sophie, 18, 20, 22 October 1862, Du Pont, *Letters*, 2:248–49, 258–59; MacBeth to Beauregard, 17 October 1862, *ORA*, ser. 1, 14:642; Beauregard to Cheves, 17 October 1862, ibid., 642; Beauregard to Randolph, 17 October 1862, ibid., 642.

9. Robert M. Browning Jr. *From Cape Charles to Cape Fear, The North Atlantic Blockading Squadron During the Civil War* (Tuscaloosa: University of Alabama Press), 1993, 275–83.

10. Du Pont to Sophie, 22, 23 October 1862, Du Pont, *Letters*, 2:261–62; Roman, *Beauregard*, 2:60; Report of John McCrady, *ORA*, ser. 1, 14:222–23; George B. Davis et al., *Atlas to Accompany the Official Records of the Union and Confederate Armies* (Washington, D.C.. Government Printing Office, 1891), Reprint entitled *The Official Military Atlas of the Civil War* (New York: The Fairfax Press, 1978), plate LXX.

11. Memorandum of Napoleon Collins, 24 July 1862, Steedman, *Memoir*, 315–16; Du Pont to Steedman, 9, 25 July 1862, *ORN*, ser. 1, 13:186–87, 212; Steedman to Du Pont, 29 July 1862, ibid., 221.

12. After this attack, at 11:30 on 7 November, Lieutenant Commander John Davis ordered the *Wissahickon* and *Dawn* to steam up the Little Ogeechee River. He hoped to destroy or capture a schooner lying under Coffee Bluff awaiting a chance to run the blockade. As the schooner tried to escape upriver, the guns of Fort McAllister opened fire on the naval vessels but the shots fell short. The two naval vessels successfully destroyed the schooner and left her on flames from stem to stern before retiring downstream. Davis to Du Pont, 19 November 1862, *ORN*, ser. 1, 13:454; Abstract Log of *Dawn*, 19 November 1862, ibid., 454; Abstract Log *Wissahickon*, 19 November 1862, ibid., 454–55.

13. Browning, *From Cape Charles to Cape Fear*, 277–83; Du Pont to Sophie, 25 January 1863, Du Pont, *Letters*, 2:379; Welles, *Diary*, 5 January 1863, 1:216.

14. Samuel L. Browne, "First Cruise of *Montauk*," *Soldiers and Sailors Historical Society of Rhode Island, Personal Narratives of Events in the War of the Rebellion*, 2nd ser., no. 1 (Providence: The Society, 1879), 15, 20.

15. Green to Du Pont, 16 January 1863, *ORN*, ser. 1, 13:514; Du Pont to Green, 17 January 1863, ibid., 514; Du Pont to Worden, 20 January 1863, ibid., 520.

16. Du Pont to Welles, 28 January 1863, Du Pont, *Letters*, 2:286–87; Du Pont to Worden, 20 January 1863, *ORN*, ser. 1, 13:520.

17. Worden to Du Pont, 27 January 1863, *ORN*, ser. 1, 13:544.

18. Worden to Du Pont, 27 January 1863, ibid., 544; Brown, "First Cruise of the *Montauk*," 35.

19. Worden to Du Pont, 27 January 1863, *ORN*, ser. 1, 13:544–45; Abstract Log of *C. P. Williams*, 27 January 1863, ibid., 549; Abstract Log of *Dawn*, 27 January 1863, ibid., 548; Browne, "First Cruise of the *Montauk*," 41.

20. The shock from the guns when they were fired on the *Montauk* caused the deck and the boilers aft to "spring up an inch or more . . ." Abstract Logs of *Montauk, Seneca, Dawn, Wissahickon, C. P. Williams*, 27 January 1863, *ORN*, ser. 1, 13:547–49; Du Pont to Sophie, 28 January 1863, Du Pont to Gerhard, 30 January 1862, Du Pont, *Letters*, 2:390–91, 394; Thomas A. Stephen

to Worden, 27 January 1863, *ORN*, ser. 1, 13:546; Beauregard to Cooper, 28 January 1863, ibid., 550.

21. Jones, *Tattnall*, 224–25.

22. Du Pont to Welles, 28 January 1863, *ORN*, ser. 1, 13:543; Du Pont to Worden, 28 January 1863, ibid., 547; Du Pont to Welles, 28 January 1863, Du Pont, *Letters*, 2:387.

23. Brown to Nance, 1 February 1863, *ORN*, ser. 1, 13:568–69; Gary to Nance, 1 February 1863, *ORA*, ser. 1, 14:203; Yates to Nance, 1 February 1863, ibid., 567.

24. Gary to Nance, 1 February 1863, *ORA*, ser. 1, 14:203; Conover to Welles, 7 May 1863, *ORN*, ser. 1, 13:563–64.

25. Conover to Welles, 7 May 1863, *ORN*, ser. 1, 13:563; Parker, *Recollections*, 326.

26. Bacon to Du Pont, 31 January 1863, Du Pont Papers, Hagley; Conover to Welles, 7 May 1863, *ORA*, ser. 1, 13:563–64; *Charleston Daily Courier*, 2 February, 3 March 1863.

27. Du Pont believed that these ironclads had six inches of armor. It is likely that the *Charleston* was the "Ladies Gunboat" but the *Palmetto State* went by the nickname. Du Pont to Wise, 16 January 1863, Du Pont, *Letters*, 2:359; Scharf, *Confederate Navy*, 670–71; Silverstone, *Warships*, 205; William N. Still Jr., *Iron Afloat, The Study of Confederate Armorclads* (Nashville, Tenn.: Vanderbilt University Press, 1971), 81; Marguerite Couturier Steedman, "The Ladies Build a Gunboat," *Sandlapper* 1 (September 1868), 57–63.

28. The information regarding the building of these vessels and their armament is confusing and conflicting. Some sources give the *Chicora* four broadside guns. Parker, *Recollections*, 308; Scharf, *Confederate Navy*, 671; Still, *Iron Afloat*, 82.

29. Beauregard, "Defense of Charleston," *Battles and Leaders*, 4: 6; Scharf, *Confederate Navy*, 676; Du Pont to Welles, 5 September 1862, Du Pont, *Letters*, 2:216; Memoranda Concerning Charleston Harbor, 14 January 1863, Du Pont Papers, Hagley.

30. Scharf, *Confederate Navy*, 674–75n.

31. Henry James Rochell, *Life of Rear Admiral John Randolph Tucker* (Washington, D.C.: The Neale Publishing Company, 1903), 24–passim; Richard N. Current, *Encyclopedia of the Confederacy*, 4 vols. (New York: Simon and Schuster, 1993), 4:1623–24.

32. Parker, *Recollections*, 308, 314–15, 317; Ingraham to Mallory, 2 February 1863, *ORN*, ser. 1, 13:617–18.

33. Stellwagen to Du Pont, 31 January 1863, Du Pont Papers, Hagley; Parker, *Recollections*, 316; Proceedings of the Naval Court of Inquiry, Record Number 3181, Records of General Courts Martial and Courts of Inquiry of the Navy Department, 1799–1867, RG 125, NA (Microfilm Publications Number M273).

34. The *Mercedita* carried eight 32-pounders and one 20-pound rifled gun. Ingraham to Mallory, 2 February 1863, *ORN*, ser. 1, 13:617; Stellwagen to Du Pont, 31 January 1863, ibid., 579; Parker, *Recollections*, 316; Stellwagen to Du Pont, 31 January 1863, *ORN*, ser. 1, 13:579; *Charleston Mercury*, 2 February 1863; Proceedings of the Court of Inquiry, Record Number 3181, M273, RG 125, NA.

35. Thirteen Union sailors also put a boat over the side and deserted the *Mercedita*. They were later held in confinement by the U.S. Navy. Du Pont to Welles, 18 February 1863, *ORN*, ser. 1, 13:613; Stellwagen to Du Pont, 31 January 1863, ibid., 579–80; Abbot to Stellwagen, 31 January 1863, ibid., 580–81; Proceedings of the Court of Inquiry, Record Number 3181, M273, RG 125, NA.

36. Du Pont to Sophie, 19 May 1862, Du Pont, *Letters*, 2:59–60; Hammersly, *Records of Living Officers*, 430; Proceedings of the Court of Inquiry, Record Number 3181, M273, RG 125, NA.

37. Le Roy to Du Pont, 31 January 1863, *ORN*, ser. 1, 13:581–82; Abstract Log *Keystone State*, 31 January 1863, Du Pont Papers, Hagley; Le Roy Correspondence, Entry 395, RG 45, NA.

38. Scharf, *Confederate Navy*, 677; Xanthus Smith, "Confederate Ram Raid off Charleston, S.C." in George M. Vickers, ed., *Under Both Flags A Panorama of the Great Civil War* (Philadelphia: People's Publishing, 1896), 239; Abstract Log of *Keystone State*, Du Pont Papers, Hagley; Le Roy to Du Pont, 31 January 1862, Le Roy Correspondence, Entry 395, RG 45, NA.

39. Scharf, *Confederate Navy*, 677–78; Le Roy to Du Pont, 31 January 1863, Le Roy Correspondence, Entry 395, RG 45, NA; A. K. Eddowes to Le Roy, 31 January 1863, ibid.; Letter of James H. Tomb, 30 January 1863, *ORN*, ser. 1, 13:622–23. D. W. Grapley Diary, as cited in Still, *Iron Afloat*, 122.

40. Tucker to Ingraham, 31 January 1863, *ORN*, ser. 1, 13:619–20; Le Roy to Du Pont, 31 January 1863, Le Roy Correspondence, Entry 395, RG 45, NA; T. H. Eastman to Mrs. Eastman, 3 February 1863, *ORN*, ser. 1, 13:586.

41. Neither the *Powhatan* nor *Canandaigua*, two of the heaviest armed warships in the squadron, even participated. Both had been in Port Royal for coal and repairs. The captain of *Housatonic* claimed to have shot away the pilot house and flag staff of one of the rams. Taylor to Du Pont, 31 January 1863, *ORN*, ser. 1, 13:587. Ingraham to Mallory, 2 February 1863, ibid., 618; Parrott to Du Pont, 31 January 1863, Du Pont Papers, Hagley; Edward A. Butler, "Personal Experiences in the Navy 1862–1865," *War Papers Read Before the Commandery of the State of Maine, Military Order of the Loyal Legion of the United States*, 2 vols. (Portland, ME: Lefavor-Tower Company, 1902), 191.

42. Ingraham to Mallory, 2 February 1863, *ORN*, ser. 1, 13:618; *Charleston Daily Courier*, 2 February 1863.

43. Nine of the deaths on *Keystone State* were caused by scalding from the steam escaping from the boiler. Mason to Stellwagen, 31 January 1862, *ORN*,

ser. 1, 13:581; T. H. Eastman to Mrs. Eastman, 3 February 1863, ibid., 586; George Farrer to J. M. Frailey, 2 February 1863, ibid., 594.

44. Benjamin to George Moore, 31 January 1863, *ORN*, ser. 1, 13:620–24; Jordan to Baron De St. Andre, 31 January 1863, ibid., 620–24; Benjamin to Moore, 31 January 1863, ibid., 620–21; Extract of *Republican* (Savannah), 2 February 1863, ibid., 617; Godon to Du Pont, 8 February 1863, ibid., 600–601, Freeman Snow, *International Law: A Manual Based Upon Lectures Delivered At the War College* (Washington, Government Printing Office, 1898), 157.

45. *Savannah Republican*, 2 February 1863; Munez De Moncada to Jordan, 1 February 1863, *ORN*, ser. 1, 13:621–22; Scharf, *Confederate Navy*, 683.

46. Statement of William Rodgers Taylor, et. al., 10 February 1863, *ORN*, ser. 1, 13:605–607; Parker, *Recollections*, 321–23.

47. Letter of James H. Tomb, 30 January 1863, *ORN*, ser. 1, 13:623.

48. Stellwagen to Du Pont, 2 February 1863, ibid., 611; Le Roy to Du Pont, 5 February 1863, ibid., 612; Du Pont to Le Roy, 6 February 1863, ibid., 612; Du Pont to Welles, 12 February 1863, ibid., 660–61.

49. Du Pont to Welles, 18 February 1863, ibid., 613; Welles to Shubrick, 3 March 1863, ibid., 614; Shubrick, Davis, Totten to Welles, 12 March 1863, ibid., 614.

50. Du Pont to Welles, 3 February 1863, ibid., 577; Du Pont to Gerhard, 19 February 1863, Du Pont, *Letters*, 2:448; Fox to Du Pont, 12 February 1863, Fox, *Correspondence*, 1:178; Du Pont to H. A. Wise, 16 January 1863, Henry Augustus Wise Papers, NYHS.

51. Welles to Du Pont, 6 January 1863, Du Pont, *Letters*, 2:352–53.

52. Du Pont to Welles, 24, 28 January 1863, ibid., 2:377, 386–87; Welles to Du Pont, 31 January 1863, ibid., 2:399–400.

53. Du Pont to Drayton, 26 January 1863, *ORN*, ser. 1, 13:536–37; Edgar Holden, "First Cruise of the Monitor *Passaic*," *Harper's New Monthly Magazine* XXVII (October 1863): 581.

54. Du Pont to Gerhard, 30 January 1863, Du Pont, *Letters*, 2:394.

55. Worden to Du Pont, 2 February 1863, *ORN*, ser. 1, 13:628; Du Pont to Fox, 25 February 1863, Fox Papers, NYHS; Du Pont to Sophie, 26 February 1863, Du Pont Papers, Hagley.

56. Worden reports the distance at 600 yards but Confederate reports put it at between 700 and 800. Worden to Du Pont, 2 February 1863, *ORN*, ser. 1 13:628; Worden to Du Pont, 1 February 1863, Du Pont, *Letters*, 2:400–401.

57. Worden to Du Pont, 2 February 1863, *ORN*, ser. 1 13:628; Worden to Du Pont, 1 February 1863, Du Pont, *Letters*, 2:400–401.

58. Telegram Brigadier General Mercer, 1 February 1863, *ORN*, ser. 1, 13:633; Anderson to Mercer, 2 February 1863, ibid., 635–36; Henry Bryan to Jordan, 1 February 1863, ibid., 635.

59. A cored shot was a XV-inch shell with a six-inch sphere removed from the middle. This hollow shell weighed 32 pounds less than a solid shot. Wor-

den to Du Pont, 2 February 1863, ibid., 628. U.S. Congress, House, *Report to the Joint Committee on the Conduct of War: Heavy Ordnance*, S. Rept. 121, 38th Cong., 2d sess., 1865, 72.

60. Worden to Du Pont, 2 February 1863, ibid., 628, 630–31; Osbon, *A Sailor of Fortune*, 236; the guns which fired directly above the boilers vibrated them so badly that the joints in the boiler tubes were damaged. This would become a major problem once the guns were fired regularly off the Charleston forts.

61. Anderson to Mercer, 2 February 1863, *ORN*, ser. 1, 13:635 37; Henry Bryan to Jordan, 1 February 1863, ibid., 634–35.

62. Worden to Du Pont, 28 February 1863, ibid., 697.

63. Worden to Du Pont, 28 February 1863, ibid., 697–98; Browne, "First Cruise of the *Montauk*," 54.

64. Gutta-percha is a rubber-like substance that is obtained from the Gutta-Percha tree and used at the time for waterproofing items. Du Pont to Sophie, 1 March 1863, Du Pont, *Letters*, 2:458; Thomas Stephens to Worden, 28 February 1863, *ORN*, ser. 1, 13:700–704; Barnes, "My Egotistigraphy," NYHS, 183; George W. Anderson to George A. Mercer, 28 February 1863, *ORN*, ser. 1, 13:708–709; Browne, "First Cruise of the *Montauk*," 57–58.

65. Du Pont to Sophie, 1 March 1863, Du Pont, *Letters*, 2:458; John Rodgers to Du Pont, 7 February 1863, *ORN*, ser. 1, 13:653–54; Ammen to Du Pont, 16 February 1863, Ammen Correspondence, Entry 395, RG 45, NA; Downes to Welles, 20 February 1863, *ORN*, ser. 1, 13:682.

66. Du Pont to Beaumont, 27 February 1863, *ORN*, ser. 1, 13:693; Du Pont to Upshur, 27 February 1863, ibid., 693; Du Pont to Worden, 27 February 1863, ibid., 694; Drayton to Hoyt, 4 March 1863, Drayton, *Letters*, 30–31.

67. Du Pont to Drayton, 27 February 1863, *ORN*, ser. 1. 13:694–95; Abstract Logs of *Seneca*, *Wissahickon*, *Dawn*, *C. P. Williams*, *Para*, *Norfolk Packet*, 3 March 1863, ibid., 723–25; *Herald* (New York), 18 March 1863.

68. Kelsey, *Autobiographical Notes*, 33–34; Ammen to Drayton, 3 March 1863, *ORN*, ser. 1, 13:720–21; Drayton to Dahlgren, 8 March 1863, ibid., 725; Downes to Drayton, 4 March 1863, ibid., 721; Drayton to Hoyt, 4 March 1863, Drayton, *Letters*, 30; Report of John McCrady, 8 March 1862, *ORN*, ser. 1, 13:730–33.

69. Drayton to Hoyt, 4 March 1863, Drayton, *Letters*, 30–31; Report of John McCrady, 8 March 1863, *ORN*, ser. 1, 13:732.

70. The mortar schooners continued firing for some time after the monitors withdrew. Drayton to Dahlgren, 8 March 1863, *ORN*, ser. 1, 13:726; Downes to Drayton, 4 March 1863, ibid., 722; Ammen to Drayton, 3 March 1863, ibid., 721; Ammen to Drayton, 3 March 1863, ibid., 720–21; Drayton to Du Pont, 4 March 1863, ibid., 717–19; Report of John McCrady, 8 March 1863, ibid., 732.

71. The *Wissahickon* was struck by an errant shot entering her coal bunkers. A patch applied on the hull from the outside allowed her to get to Port Royal for repairs. Drayton to Du Pont, 4 March 1863, *ORN*, ser. 1, 13:717;

Captain Drayton's Report of Practice of Ironclads at Fort McAllister, March 3rd 1863, Dahlgren Papers, LCM; Drayton to Dahlgren, 8 March 1863, *ORN*, ser. 1, 13:728; Hunter, *A Year on a Monitor*, 39–40; Kelsey, *Autobiographical Notes*, 34; Report of John McCrady, 8 March 1863, *ORN*, ser. 1, 13:730; J. N. Miller to Drayton, 4 March 1863, Dahlgren Papers, LCM; Drayton Report of Practice of Ironclads, 3 March 1863, ibid.

72. Dahlgren to Du Pont, 12 March 1863, Dahlgren Papers, LCM; Du Pont to Fox, 4 March 1863, Fox Papers, NYHS.

73. Drayton to Hoyt, 4 March 1863, Drayton, *Letters*, 617; Drayton to Du Pont, 8 March 1863, *ORN*, ser. 1, 13:727; Rodgers to Dear Sir, 10 March 1863, Rogers Papers, LCM.

74. Du Pont to Sophie, 4 March 1863, Du Pont, *Letters*, 2:466–67; Rough Notes by J. Rodgers, Circa 3 March 1863, Du Pont Papers, Hagley; Du Pont to Biddle, 25 March 1863, ibid.

75. Stimers to Welles, Telegram 11 March 1863, *ORN*, ser. 1, 13:729; Welles, *Diary*, 17 March 1863, 1:249.

76. Welles, *Diary*, ibid; Harris to Jordan, 9 March 1863, *ORN*, ser. 1, 13:729–30.

Chapter 6

1. Special Orders No. 216, 1 September 1862, *ORA*, ser. 1, 14:380; Mitchel to Halleck, 20 September 1862, ibid., 383; Warner, *Generals in Blue*, 327.

2. Special Order No. 352, E. D. Townsend, 18 November 1862, *ORA*, ser. 1, 14:389; T. Seymour, Memorandum Concerning Charleston Harbor, January 14, 1863, *ORN*, ser. 1, 13:510–11; Hunter, General Order No. 3, 20 January 1863, *ORA*, ser. 1, 14:392.

3. Hunter to Halleck, 7 February 1863, *ORA*, ser. 1, 14:396–passim–410.

4. Beauregard, Ingraham, Minutes of Meeting 29 September 1862, *ORN*, ser. 1, 13:808–809; Samuel R. Bright, "Confederate Coast Defense", Unpublished Ph.D. diss., Duke University, 1961, 52–54.

5. Roman, *Beauregard*, 2:4–6.

6. Du Pont, through the interrogation of deserters, knew the nature of the armament. Statement of Thomas Carnes, January 1863, *ORN*, ser. 1, 13:531–2; Richard Wainwright, "The Naval Attack on Charleston, South Carolina," *The United Service*, New Series IV (November 1890), 434; John Johnson, *The Defense of Charleston Harbor Including Fort Sumter and the Adjacent Islands, 1863–1865* (Charleston, S.C.: Walker Wvans and Cogswell Co., 1890), 41; Victor Ernest Rudolph von Scheliha, *A Treatise on Coast Defense: Based on Experiences Gained By Officers of the Corps of Engineers of the Army of the Confederate States* (London: E. & F.N. Spon, 1868), 8; Ripley Circular, 26 December 1862, *ORA*, ser. 1, 14:732–35.

7. Johnson, *Defense of Charleston*, 17–38.

8. Beauregard to Ripley, 8 February 1863; Roman, *Beauregard*, 2:61–62; Beauregard and Ingraham, Minutes of Meeting, 29 September 1862, *ORN*, ser. 1, 13:809.

9. Parker, *Recollections*, 327; Memo G. T. Beauregard, 14 November 1863, cited in Johnson, *Defense of Charleston*, cxliv–cxlv; Beauregard to Pickens, 8 October 1863, *ORN*, ser. 1, 13:811; Beauregard to Cooper, 13 October 1862, ibid., 812.

10. Scharf, *Confederate Navy*, 686; Wainwright, "Naval Attack Upon Charleston," 437.

11. Johnson, *Defense of Charleston*, 29–30; von Scheliah, *Coast Defense*, 199–200; plate IV; Beauregard, "Defense of Charleston," 2; Jordan to Echols, 1 October 1862, Roman, *Beauregard*, 2:439–40; Boynton, *History of the Navy*, 2:447; Pierre G. T. Beauregard, "Torpedo Service in Charleston Harbor," *The Annals of the War Written by Leading Participants North and South* (Philadelphia: Times Publishing Co., 1879), 147–48; Ripley to Gillmore, 17 July 1865, Dahlgren Papers, LCM; Beauregard to Miles, 14 March 1863, *ORA*, ser. 1, 14:826; U.S., Congress, House, *Report of the Secretary of the Navy*, H. Ex. Doc. 1, 39th Cong., 1st sess., 4 December 1865, 253–300,

12. De Lisle to Beauregard, 25 May 1863, *ORA*, ser. 1, 14:950; R. O. Crowley, "The Confederate Torpedo Service," *Century Illustrated Monthly Magazine* (June 1898), 298; Johnson, *Defense of Charleston*, 30–32; Cheves to Beauregard, 9 December 1862, *ORA*, ser. 1, 14:706; Beauregard, "Torpedo Service," 147–154.

13. Du Pont to Sophie, 22 June 1862, Du Pont, *Letters*, 2:129; Du Pont to H. A. Wise, 16 January 1862, *ORN*, ser. 1, 13:513; Marchand to Du Pont, 25 June, 2 August 1862, ibid., 140–41, 240; Du Pont to Godon, 22 January 1862, ibid., 534.

14. Du Pont to Fox, 25, 31 May, 20 September 1862, Fox, *Correspondence*, I:120, 122–23, 156; Davis, *Life of Charles Henry Davis*, 133; Fox to Welles, 24 February 1865, *ORN*, ser. 1, vol. 4, 245.

15. Fox to Porter, 14 October 1862, Fox, *Correspondence*, 2:138–39; Welles, *Diary*, 26 September 1862, I: 153; Du Pont to Sophie, 25 January 1863, Du Pont, *Letters*, 2:379.

16. Fox to Du Pont, 13 December 1862, Fox Papers, NYHS; Browning, *From Cape Charles to Cape Fear*, 278–83; Welles, *Diary*, 5 January 1863, 1:216.

17. Fox to Du Pont, 23 January 1863, Du Pont Papers, Hagley; Fox to Du Pont, 6 January 1863, Fox Papers, NYHS; Welles, *Diary*, 6 January 1863, I: 217; Welles to Du Pont, 6 January 1863, Du Pont Papers, Hagley.

18. Du Pont to Rodgers, 6 January 1863, John Rodgers Papers, LCM; Du Pont to Davis, Du Pont Papers, Hagley.

19. Du Pont to Welles, 24 January 1863, Du Pont Papers, Hagley; Copy of Davis's Sketch, circa 27 July 1863, ibid.

20. Welles to Du Pont, 31 January 1863, *ORN*, ser. 1, 13:571; John Niven, *Gideon Welles Lincoln's Secretary of the Navy* (New York: Oxford University Press, 1973), 429; Copy of Davis's Sketch, c. 27 July 1863, Du Pont Papers, Hagley.

21. Fox to Du Pont, 12 February 1863, Fox Papers, NYHS; Du Pont to Biddle, 25 March 1863, Du Pont Papers, Hagley.

22. Foster's plan was later implemented after April 1863. Fox to Du Pont, 16 February 1863, Fox Papers, NYHS; Welles, *Diary*, 16 February 1863, 1:236–37.

23. Fox to Du Pont, 16 February 1863, Fox Papers, NYHS; Welles, *Diary*, 16 February 1863, 1:236–37.

24. Welles, *Diary*, 16 February 1863, 236–37.

25. Fox to Du Pont, 20 February 1863, Fox Papers, NYHS.

26. Fox to Du Pont, 16, 20, 26 February 1863, ibid.; Du Pont to Fox, 2 March 1863, ibid.

27. Hunter to Halleck, 11 February 1863, *ORA*, ser. 1, 14:396–passim; Naglee to Halpine, 1 March 1863, ibid., 415–16.

28. Steedman to Wife, 20 March 1863, Steedman, *Memoirs*, 361; Steedman to Du Pont, 20 March 1863, *ORN*, ser. 1, 13:777; Steedman to Rodgers, 29 March 1863, Steedman, *Memoirs*, 364; Rust to Halpine, 2 April 1863, *ORA*, ser. 1, 14:232–passim; Du Pont to Fox, 2 April 1863, Fox Papers, NYHS; Duncan to Du Pont, 30 March 1863, *ORN*, ser. 1, 13:794; Moore, *Rebellion Record*, vol. 6, 444–45, 483–84; Thomas Wentworth, "The Reoccupation of Jacksonville in 1863," *Civil War Papers Read Before the Commandry of the State of Massachusetts, Military Order of the Loyal Legion of the United States* (2 vols.), Boston: The Commandry, 1900, 474.

29. Du Pont to Biddle, 25 March 1863, Du Pont Papers, Hagley; Du Pont to Davis, 31 March 1863, ibid.; Du Pont to Sophie, 27 March 1863, Du Pont, *Letters*, 2:520–21; Du Pont to Fox, 2 April 1863, Fox Papers, NYHS.

30. Du Pont to Biddle, Du Pont Papers, Hagley; Du Pont to Fox, 25 February 1862, ibid.; Welles to Du Pont, 6 March 1863, *ORN*, ser. 1, 13:736–37; Fox to Du Pont, 6 March, 11 March, 2 April 1863, Fox Papers, NYHS; Du Pont to Fox, 2 March 1863, ibid.; Du Pont to Sophie, 10 March 1863, Du Pont, *Letters*, 2:484.

31. Stimers to Fox, 28 February 1863, Fox Papers, NYHS; William Conant Church, *The Life of John Ericsson* 2 vols. (New York: Charles Scribner's Sons, 1891), 2:45–46, 124–25; Ericsson, "The Early Monitors," *Battles and Leaders*, 4:30; Ericsson to Fox, 22 February 1863, Fox Papers, NYHS; Ericsson to Axel Aldersparre, 6 March 1868, Ericsson to Fox, 10 April 1863, Ericsson Papers, American Swedish Historical Museum; hereinafter cited as ASHM.

32. Rodgers to Le Roy, 24 March 1863, Steedman, *Memoirs*, 362–63.

33. The *Keokuk*'s inner skin was seven-sixteenth boiler plate. The *Commanche*, completed after the war, had two XV-inch guns. *Herald* (New York), 23 April 1863; Du Pont to Biddle, 25 March 1863, Du Pont Papers, Hagley.

34. Drayton to Hamilton, 11 February 1863, Drayton Papers, New York Public Library; Steedman to wife, 3 April 1863, Steedman, *Memoirs*, 366; Xanthus Smith to Mother, 9 January 1863, Smith Family Papers, Archives of American Art, Smithsonian; John Irwin to J. S. Barnes, 25 December 1862, John Irwin Papers, NYHS.

35. Entry for 12 March, 2 April 1863, Welles, *Diary*, 247, 259; Du Pont to Sophie, 27 March 1863, Du Pont, *Letters*, 2.518 19.

36. U.S. Congress, House, *Naval Vessels*, H. Ex Doc No. 280, 40th Cong., 2nd Sess., 7 May 1868; Du Pont to Sophie, 27 March 1863, Du Pont, *Letters*, 2:519; the Navy Department's budget for 1862 was $42,668,227 and for 1863, $63,221,968. U. S. Department of Commerce, *Historical Statistics of the United States 1789–1945* (Washington, D.C.: Government Printing Office, 1949), 300.

37. Du Pont shifted his flag from the *Wabash* to the *James Adger* in order that the frigate could protect Hilton Head. Du Pont also moved the *Vermont* to the Hilton Head side of the harbor to protect army positions during the attack. Four other gunboats were also stationed either as added protection or as a reserve in case the Confederates attacked while the main force was off Charleston. Belknap and Turner contradict each other concerning whether the hides were on the top or the bottom. Ericsson to Welles, 15 March 1863, Letters Received by the Secretary of the Navy: Miscellaneous Letters 1801–84, Entry 21, RG 45, NA, Microfilm Publication Number M124, hereinafter cited as M124, RG 45, NA; Du Pont to Steedman, 1 April 1863, *ORN*, ser. 1, 13:802–803; Du Pont to Fox, 19 March 1863, Du Pont Papers, Hagley; Drayton to Alex Hamilton Jr., 16 December 1862, Drayton, *Letters*, 22; Turner to Du Pont, 10 April 1863, *ORN*, ser. 1, 14:26; Stimers to Du Pont, 31 March 1863, *ORN*, ser. 1, 13:800; Edward Simpson, "The Monitor Passaic," *The United Service* 2 (April 1880), 420; *Tribune* (New York), 14 April 1863; George E. Belknap, "Reminiscent of the '*New Ironsides*' off Charleston," *The United Service* (January 1879), 166; Villard, *Memoirs*, 35; Alban Stimers Court Martial #3251, RG 125, NA, Microfilm Publication Number M273, hereinafter cited as M273, RG 125, NA; George E. Belknap, "Reminiscent of the Siege of Charleston," *Publications of the Military Historical Society of Massachusetts Naval Actions and History* 14 vols. (Boston: The Society, 1902), 2:162–64; Logs of *Catskill, Nantucket, Nahant, Patapsco*, 27 March–3 April 1863, Entry 118, RG 24, NA.

38. Barnes, "My Egotistigraphy," Barnes Papers, NYHS, 185–86; Porter to Welles, 12 January 1863, copy in Du Pont Papers, Hagley; Log of *Patapsco*, 5 April 1863, Entry 118, RG 24, NA; Oscar Walter Farenholt, "The Monitor *Catskill*: A Years Reminiscences! 1863–1864," *Civil War Papers of the California Commandery of the Military Order of the Loyal Legion of the United States*, War Papers, No. 23 (San Francisco: Shannon-Conmy, 1913), 383; Smith to Mother, 26 March 1863, Smith Family Papers, AAA, Smithsonian.

39. Despite the fact that Du Pont had Boutelle going in at night to buoy channels, he did not utilize his expertise to go farther into the channel. Du Pont to

Bache, 29 January 1863, Du Pont Papers, Hagley; F. H. Gregory to E. D. Robie, 20 January 1863, *ORN*, ser. 1, 13:519–20; Du Pont to Welles, 18 February 1863, ibid., 669; Testimony of C.R.P. Rodgers in the Court of Inquiry, *Report of the Secretary of the Navy in Relation to Armored Vessels* (Washington, D.C.: Government Printing Office, 1864), 158–59.

40. After the battle, Rodgers cut the boot jack adrift after it loosened the *Weehawken*'s armor plates. Rodgers to Dear Sir [Hodge], 23 April 1863, Rodgers Papers, LCM; *Times* (New York), 8 November 1863; Rodgers claimed they weighed 90 tons but Francis Gregory reported the weight double, at 180 tons this seems too high. Records of the Office of the General Superintendent of Ironclads, Entry 1235, RG 19, NA; Ammen, *The Atlantic Coast*, 92n; Du Pont to Sophie, 15 February 1863, Du Pont, *Letters*, 2:439; Rodgers to Du Pont, 20 April 1863, *ORN*, ser. 1, 14:43.

41. Steedman to wife, 10 May 1863, Steedman, *Memoirs*, 373; Du Pont to Sophie, 3 April 1863, Du Pont, *Letters*, 2:540–41; Moore, *Rebellion Record*, 6:504.

42. Du Pont to Hunter, 4 February 1863, Du Pont to William Whitten, 17 March 1863, Du Pont, *Letters*, 2:413, 490; Davis, *Life of Davis*, 137–38; B. W. Loring, "The Monitor *Weehawken* in the Rebellion," *Proceedings of the United States Naval Institute* XII (1886): 117; Hunter, *A Year on a Monitor*, 15, 89.

43. Downes to Du Pont, 18 March 1863, M89, RG 45, NA; Ericsson to Welles, 29 March 1863, Ericsson Papers, ASHM.

44. Du Pont to Sophie, 22 October 1862, Du Pont, *Letters*, 2:258–59; Du Pont to Grimes, 8 August 1863, ibid., 3:224 John Rodgers to Du Pont, 29 October 1863, *ORN*, ser. 1, vol. 13, 421–23; Ericsson to Welles, 29 March 1863, Ericsson Papers, ASHM.

45. Order of Battle and Plan of Attack Upon Charleston, South Carolina, n.d. (4 April 1863), Rodgers Papers, LCM; Du Pont to Sophie, 6 April 1863, Du Pont, *Letters*, 2:551.

46. According to the Bureau of Ordnance and Hydrography, *Almanac For The Use Of Navigators From the American Ephemeris and Nautical Almanac for the Year 1863* (Washington, D.C.: Government Printing Office, 1861), the high tide was at 10:39 that morning and the low tide at 4:46 that afternoon. Miller's *Almanac* as cited in Johnson, *The Defense of Charleston*, p. 46n puts the high tide at 10:20. According to Captain Worden, the flood tide began about 3:30 that afternoon. Worden to Du Pont, 8 April 1863, Du Pont Papers, Hagley. Confederate Secretary of the Navy Stephen Mallory was particularly critical of Du Pont for selecting the ebb tide to attack, "showing thereby that he was thinking more of the discomfiture of his ships and their drifting safely away from the works than he was of pushing by the forts and entering the harbor . . ." He continued, "If Du Pont had possessed a spark of flame . . . he might have failed but he could not have been disgraced." Mallory to Bulloch, 7 May 1863,

ORN, ser. 1, vol. 2, 418; Testimony of CRP Rodgers in the Court of Inquiry of Alban C. Stimers, *Armored Vessels*, 159.

47. Villard, *Memoirs*, 33–34; Johnson, *Defense of Charleston*, 44; Ripley to Trapier, 5 April 1863, *ORN*, ser. 1, 13:823; Du Pont to Welles, 15 April 1863, Du Pont, *Letters*, 2:551; Abstract Log of *Keokuk*, 5 April 1863, *ORN*, ser. 1, 14:24.

48. Du Pont to Sophie, 6 April 1863, Du Pont, *Letters*, 2:550–52; Abstract Log *Keokuk*, 6 April 1863, *ORN*, ser. 1, 14:24.

49. Du Pont to Sophie, 6 April 1863, Du Pont, *Letters*, 2:553.

50. Peck, *Four Years Under Fire at Charleston*, 368; *Times* (New York); Moore, 6: 505; Frank Vizetelly, "When Charleston Was Under Fire," *The New Age Magazine* XV (September 1911): 222; Villard, *Memoirs*, 38.

51. Rodgers writes in one letter that it took two hours before she could proceed but other accounts seem to confirm that it was only one hour. Du Pont, *Dispatches*, 448; Loring, "*Weehawken*," 113; Rodgers to Du Pont, 8 April 1862, Du Pont Papers, Hagley.

52. The raft pounded the *Weehawken* even in the moderate sea and sprung plates in the forward overhang. Du Pont, *Dispatches*, 448; Du Pont to Boutelle, 29 January 1863, Du Pont Papers, Hagley; Du Pont to Welles, 8 April 1863, *ORN*, ser. 1, 14:3.

53. Rhett to Nance, 13 April 1863, *ORN*, ser. 1, 14:95–98; Johnson, *Defenses of Charleston*, 44, 46–47; *Mercury* (Charleston), 11 April 1863.

54. The Union and Confederate sources differ on times by a few minutes. The report of the pennon is curious. Du Pont may have allowed Drayton to fly a divisional flag to denote his seniority over Rodgers, who took the position ahead of him in the line of battle. Johnson, *Defense of Charleston*, 48; Drayton to Du Pont, 8 April 1863, Du Pont Papers, Hagley; Roman, *Beauregard*, 2:468; *Register* (Mobile) and *Mercury* (Charleston), n.d. as cited in Moore, *Rebellion Record*, 6:513, 516.

55. Johnson, *Defense of Charleston*, 46; These buoys were range markers for the Confederate gunners. Loring, "*Weehawken*," 113–14; John Rodgers, "Du Pont's attack at Charleston," *Battles and Leaders*, 4:36; Ammen, *The Atlantic Coast*, 93; Log of *Passaic*, 7 April 1863, Entry 118, RG 24, NA.

56. Johnson, *Rodgers*, 243; Ammen, *The Atlantic Coast*, 93–94; Stimers Court Martial #3251, M273, RG 125, NA.

57. Turner to Du Pont, 10 April 1863, *ORN*, ser. 1, 14:25; Du Pont, Notes on the Attack of Fort Sumter, Du Pont, *Dispatches*, 448; Belknap, "Reminiscent of the Siege of Charleston," 170.

58. Rodgers to Du Pont, 8 April 1863, Du Pont Papers, Hagley; Johnson, *Defense of Charleston*, 49, 51.

59. Echols to Harris, 9 April 1863, Roman, *Beauregard*, 2:468; Ericsson to Fox, 17 December 1862, Fox Papers, NYHS; Anonymous, "Charleston Under Fire," *The Cornhill Magazine* X (1864): 103; Rodgers to Hodge, April (n.d.) 1863, Rodgers Papers, LCM.

60. Notes on the attack on Fort Sumter, April 7th, Du Pont, *Dispatches*, 448.

61. Ibid., 448–49; Rodgers to Du Pont, 8 April 1863, C. R. Rodgers Correspondence, Entry 395, RG 45, NA; Fairfax to Du Pont, 8 April 1863, Du Pont Papers, Hagley; Moore, *Rebellion Record*, 6:508; Stimers Court Martial #3251, M273, RG 125, NA.

62. Interestingly, Du Pont had been warned about this torpedo by deserters shortly before the attack. Du Pont to Davis, 1 April 1863, Du Pont, *Letters*, 2:533. One deserter claimed the torpedo was sabotaged by the officer that had deployed it. He believed it "not Christian" to kill men this way. Statement of John B. Patrick, 26 June 1864, *ORN*, ser. 1, 9: 770; Scharf, *Confederate Navy*, 758; DeLisle to Beauregard, 25 May 1863, *ORA*, ser. 1, 14:950.

63. In heavy weather water pouring into the turret wet the blower belts threatening to "stop the breath and kill the steam of the vessel." The water pouring into the top of the turrets had to create similar concerns during the attack. Downes to Du Pont, 18 March 1863, M89, RG 45, NA; Vizetelly, "When Charleston Was Under Fire," 224; Loring, "*Weehawken*," 114; Johnson, *Defenses of Charleston*, 51.

64. The *Passaic* arrived at the Brooklyn Navy Yard on 4 May for repairs. She did not leave until 20 July. Rodgers to Hodge, 23 April 1863, Rodgers Papers, LCM; Stimers Court Martial #3251, M273, RG 125, NA; Log of *Passaic*, 7 April–20 July 1863, Entry 118, RG 24, NA; Drayton to Du Pont, 8 April 1863, Du Pont Papers, Hagley; Rodgers to Du Pont, 8 April 1863, ibid.; Loring, "*Weehawken*," 114; Ammen, *The Atlantic Coast*, 94–95; Drayton to Alex Hamilton Jr., 15 April 1863, Drayton, *Letters*, 34; Despite the fact that *Weehawken* did not get extremely close to the obstructions, when she arrived back in Port Royal 150 feet of 2-inch manila rope was unwound from the propeller shaft and some 3-inch line taken off the raft. Rodgers to Hodge, 23 April 1863, Rodgers Papers, LCM; "Appointment of Robert Platt to the Rank of Commander," U.S., Congress, Senate, 54th Cong., 1st sess., S. Rept. No. 1114, 3.

65. Worden to Du Pont, 8 April 1863, Du Pont Papers, Hagley; Cushman to Worden, n.d., *ORN*, ser. 1, 14:14.

66. Ammen to Du Pont, 14 April 1863, Ammen Correspondence, Entry 395, RG 45, NA; Log of *Patapsco*, 7 April 1863, Entry 118, RG 24, NA.

67. Rodgers to Du Pont, 8 April 1863, C. R. Rodgers Correspondence, Entry 395, RG 45, NA; Fairfax to Du Pont, 8 April 1863, Du Pont Papers, Hagley; Ammen, *The Atlantic Coast*, 97; Log of *Catskill*, 7 April 1863, Entry 118, RG 24, NA; Beardslee to Fairfax, 8 April 1863, Du Pont Papers, Hagley.

68. The *Nahant* was unable to turn her turret for twenty-four hours and then only with difficulty. Downs to Du Pont, 13 April 1863, Du Pont Papers, Hagley; Stimers Court Martial #3251, M273, RG 125, NA; Belknap, "Reminiscent of the Siege of Charleston," 169.

69. Rhind to Du Pont, 8 April 1863, Du Pont Papers, Hagley; Rhett to Nance, 13 April 1863, *ORN*, ser. 1, 14:96; *Register* (Mobile), 8 April 1863; Miller, *Gullah Statesman*, p. 19; Roman, *Beauregard*, 2:71.

70. Major William Echols placed the *New Ironsides* seventeen hundred yards from Moultrie and two thousand from Fort Sumter. Echols to Harris, 9 April 1863, *ORN*, ser. 1, 14:86; Turner to Du Pont, 10 April 1863, ibid., 26; Notes on the Attack on Fort Sumter, Du Pont, *Dispatches*, 449; Villard, *Memoirs*, 44; Stimers Court Martial #3251, M273, RG 125, NA: Log of *New Ironsides*, 7 April 1863, Entry 118, RG 24, NA.

71. The 520 hits represented an incredible pounding. A smaller number of hits produced problems during the attacks on Fort McAllister. But the guns at Fort McAllister were not as heavy and were fought at greater ranges. The ironclads in later operations off Morris Island in a period of about two months would suffer only 882 hits. These ironclads were also strengthened and rotated into repair facilities at Port Royal where "special working parties" expedited their repairs. "Service of Ironclads So. At. Block. Squadron Shots fired & hits received by them," n.d., Dahlgren Papers, LCM; Beauregard to Cooper, 24 May 1863, *ORN*, ser. 1, 14:75; Alfred Roman claims only sixty-nine guns participated in the battle. Roman, *Beauregard*, 2:73, 77; Beauregard, "Defense of Charleston," *Battles and Leaders*, 4:10–11; Table of Effects on Projectiles on Walls of Fort Sumter, William H. Echols, *ORN*, ser. 1, 14:95; Vizetelly, "Charleston Under Fire," 99–100; Echols to Harris, 9 April 1863, *ORN*, ser. 1, 14:85; Jones, *Siege of Charleston*, 178; Rodgers to Smalley, 25 April 1863, as cited in Villard, *Memoirs*, 50.

72. Du Pont to Welles, 15 April 1863, *ORN*, ser. 1, 14:5–6; A. C. Rhind to Du Pont, 8 April 1863, Du Pont Papers, Hagley; Rogers, "Du Pont's Attack at Charleston," 37.

73. Du Pont to Sophie, 10 April 1863, Du Pont Papers, Hagley.

74. Du Pont to Sophie, 8 April 1863, Du Pont, *Letters*, 3:3.

75. Ammen, *The Atlantic Coast*, 102–103; Luce, "Naval Administration II," 818–19; Porter, *Naval History of the Civil War*, 769.

76. John Rodgers faulted the department for not testing the ironclads before sending them south. He pointed out that the European countries all performed trials before sending them into battle. Roman, *Beauregard*, 74–75; Rodgers to Hodge, 23 April 1863, Rodgers Papers, LCM.

Chapter 7

1. C. L. Burckmyer to wife, 17 April 1863, *Cornelius L. Burckmyer Letters, March 1863–June 1865*, ed. Charlotte R. Holmes (Columbia, S.C.: The State Company, 1926), 49; *Savannah Republican*, 7 April 1863; *Charleston Mercury* (n.d.); Press Scrap Book, George Anderson Mercer Papers, DUM; *Herald* (New York), 11 April 1863; *Times* (New York), (n.d.) cited in Moore, *Rebellion Record*, 6: 502; *Tribune* (New York) 14 April 1863.

2. Du Pont to Welles, 8 April 1863, Du Pont Papers, Hagley.

3. Hay to Lincoln, 10 April 1863, John Hay, *Lincoln and the Civil War in the Diaries and Letters of John Hay*, ed. Tyler Dennett (New York: Dodd, Mead and Company, 1939), 75–78; Welles to Du Pont, 2 April 1862, Du Pont Papers, Hagley; Fox to Du Pont, 2 April 1863, ibid.; Du Pont to Sophie, 10 April 1863, Du Pont, *Letters*, 3:15; Du Pont to Rodgers, 13 April 1863, ORN, ser. 1, 13:131–32. This order originated from President Lincoln, who had a great desire to open the Mississippi River. The idea of using monitors was quickly dropped.

4. Welles, *Diary*, Entries for 9, 10, 12 April 1863, 1: 264–65, 267–68; Lizzie to Phil, 28 August 1863, Elizabeth Blair Lee, *Wartime Washington: The Civil War Letters of Elizabeth Blair Lee*, eds. Virginia Jean Laas and Dudley Cornish (Urbana: University of Illinois Press, 1991), 256.

5. Welles believed that Du Pont sent Rhind to give the report in order to diminish the reputation of the monitors. As cited in Niven, *Welles*, 436; Du Pont to Sophie, 25 April 1863, Du Pont, *Letters*, 3: 59–60; Welles, *Diary*, entry for 12 April 1863, 1: 267–69.

6. Lincoln to Du Pont, 13, 14 April 1863, Du Pont Papers, Hagley; Welles to Du Pont, 11 April 1863, ibid.; Du Pont to Welles, 16 April 1863, ibid.

7. Du Pont to H. W. Davis, 8, 14 April 1863, Du Pont to Sophie, 17 April 1863, Du Pont, *Letters*, 3: 11, 27, 40–41; Du Pont's letter of 16 April to Welles was not answered until 14 May.; Hay to Lincoln, 16 April 1863, Hay, *Letters*, 60–61.

8. Lincoln to Du Pont and Hunter, 14 April 1863, Du Pont, *Letters*, 3: 30; Du Pont to Welles, 16 April 1863, ORN, ser. 1, 14:139–40.

9. U.S. Navy, *Armored Vessels*, 276; Turner to Du Pont, 19 May 1863, Du Pont Papers, Hagley; Butler, "Personal Experiences in the Navy," 193.

10. Hunter to Du Pont, 8 April 1863, ORN, ser. 1, 14:31–32; Du Pont to Hunter, 8 April 1863, ibid., 30–31.

11. Hunter to Halleck, 3 April 1863, ORA, ser. 1, 14:436–37; Stephen R. Wise, *Gate of Hell, Campaign for Charleston Harbor, 1863* (Columbia: University of South Carolina Press, 1994), 31; Rodgers, "Du Pont's Attack at Charleston," 41; entry for 7 April 1863, Arthur Brailsford Wescoat Diary, Arthur Brailsford Wescoat Papers, DUM; Du Pont to Sophie, 10 April 1863, Du Pont, *Letters*, 3: 15; William Reynolds—Memorandum of Conversation between Gen. Seymour, Capt. Rodgers, Major Duan, and Col. Balch, n.d., Du Pont Papers, Hagley.

12. Hunter to Lincoln, 22 May 1863, ORA, ser. 1, 14:455–57.

13. Welles, *Diary*, entry for 20 April 1863, 1: 276–77.

14. Du Pont's officers all supported him both publicly and privately. Steedman to Sally, 10 May 1863, Steedman Papers, DUM; Dahlgren Diary, 6 May 1863, John A. Dahlgren Papers, Special Collection, Syracuse University; Du Pont to Welles, 15 April 1863, Du Pont Papers, Hagley.

15. Du Pont to Welles, 16 April 1863, Du Pont Papers, Hagley; Du Pont to Whelan, 18 April 1863, ibid.

16. Du Pont, of course, felt that he had kept the department informed of his reservations of the attack and of the limitations of the ironclads through Fox. Fox, though, had not passed the information to Welles. Du Pont also felt that his attacks on Fort McAllister should have made it clear that ironclads could not, because of their slow rate of fire, fight well-built and heavily armed fortifications. Welles, *Diary*, 21 April 1863, 1: 277.

17. Du Pont had never trusted the press and called them a "gang of thugs" who "mutilate" reports. Du Pont to Fox, 7 July 1862, Fox, *Correspondence*, 1:130; *American and Commercial Advertiser* (Baltimore) 15 April 1863, Niven, *Welles*, 436–37; Villard, *Memoirs*, 48.

18. Drayton, one of Du Pont's closest friends, also believed that Fox never saw the article and talked to Fox about this. Sophie Du Pont to Davis, 25 May 1865, Du Pont Papers, Hagley; Boutelle to Du Pont, 22 April 1863, ibid.; Du Pont to Welles, 27 May 1863, ibid.; Davis to Sophie Du Pont, 15 May 1863, ibid.; Du Pont to Sophie, 5 June 1863, Du Pont, *Letters*, 3:119, 161.

19. Steedman to wife, 3 May 1863, Steedman, *Memoirs*, 371–72; Ann Rodgers to John, 16, 18 April 1863, Rodgers Family Papers, LCM; John Rodgers to Ann, 26 April, 1863, ibid.; Dahlgren Diary, 3 May 1863, Dahlgren Papers, Syracuse; Drayton to Du Pont, 12 May 1863, Du Pont, *Letters*, 3:110–111.

20. These were the *Casco* and *Kalamazoo* classes. "List of Contracts of Iron Clad Steamer Batteries," Entry 50, RG 19, NA; Welles to Fox, 20 April 1863, *ORN*, ser. 1, 14:45; Du Pont to Welles, 15 April 1863, ibid., 5–8, passim; Welles, *Diary*, 20 April 1863, 1:276.

21. Du Pont to Welles, 22 April 1863, Du Pont Papers, Hagley; Welles, *Diary*, 30 April 1863, 1:288.

22. G. W. Rodgers to Du Pont, 23 April 1863, G. W. Rodgers Correspondence, Entry 395, RG 45, NA; *American and Commercial Advertiser* (Baltimore), 27 April 1863.

23. Drayton, J. Rodgers, Ammen, G. W. Rodgers, Fairfax and Downes to Welles, 24 April 1863, *ORN*, ser. 1, 14:45–48.

24. Stimers to Welles, 14 April 1863, ibid., 41–43.

25. Drayton also believed that those interested in promoting the monitors would try to blame the officers' "want of zeal or energy." Drayton to Hamilton, 15 April 1863, Drayton, *Letters*, 34; Memorandum of conversation between C. R. P. Rodgers and Stimers, 10 April 1863, Du Pont Papers, Hagley; Memorandum of conversation between Du Pont and Stimers, ibid.

26. Du Pont to Welles, 12 May 1863, enclosure, Charges and Specifications of Charges . . . against Chief Engineer Alan C. Stimers, U.S. Navy, *ORN*, ser. 1, 14:59–61; Du Pont to Sophie, 10 April 1863, Du Pont, *Letters*, 3:17.

27. Welles, *Diary*, 20 May 1863, 307; Du Pont to Davis, 26 April 1863, Du Pont, *Letters*, 3:62.

28. Record of the proceedings of a Naval Court of Inquiry, Alban C. Stimers Case #3251, M273, RG 125, NA.

29. *American Commercial Advertiser* (Baltimore), 11 May 1863; Fulton to Blair, 22 June 1863, Fulton to Kershner, 21 July 1863, Welles to Kershner, 28 October 1863, Kershner Papers, DUM; court-martial of Edward Kershner #3253, M273, RG 125, NA.

30. Du Pont to Sophie, 5 June 1863, Du Pont, *Letters*, 3:161.

31. Davis and Du Pont became friends when Davis's first wife, Constance, met Sophie Du Pont. After the Mexican War their friendship grew. Davis followed up his visit with a letter the following day. Davis to Lincoln, 4 May 1863, Abraham Lincoln Papers, LCM; Davis to Du Pont, 3 May 1863, Du Pont, *Letters*, 3:79–84; Gerald S. Henig, *Henry Winter Davis: Antebellum and Civil War Congressman from Maryland* (New York: Twayne Publishers, Inc., 1973), 37, 196; Davis to Lincoln, 4 May 1863, Du Pont Papers, Hagley.

32. Welles, *Diary*, 25 May 1863, I:312.

33. Rodgers to Welles, 2 May 1863, Gideon Welles Papers, The Huntington Library and Art Gallery, San Marino, California; Welles, *Diary*, 8 May 1861, 1: 295–96; Drayton to Du Pont, 12 May 1863, Du Pont Papers, Hagley.

34. John Niven believed that Welles deliberately did not answer Du Pont in order to gather information to damage Du Pont's synopsis of the attack. *Gideon Welles*, 437–38; Du Pont to Biddle, 8 May 1863, Du Pont Papers, Hagley, Memo written by Du Pont circa 19 May 1863, ibid.; Welles, *Diary*, 14 May 1863, 1: 302; Welles to Du Pont, 14 May 1863, *ORN*, ser. 1, 14:61–63.

35. Welles to Du Pont, 15 May 1863, Du Pont Papers, Hagley; Fox to Welles, 13 May 1863, ibid.

36. Du Pont to Sophie, 17, 26 May 1863, Du Pont, *Letters*, 3: 120–21, 137; Du Pont to Welles, 27 May 1863, Du Pont Papers, Hagley.

37. Welles, *Diary*, 20 April, 23, 25, 26 May 1863, 1: 276, 309–14.

38. Ibid., 25, 27 May 1863, 1: 311–13.

39. Du Pont to Welles, 3 June 1863, Du Pont Papers, Hagley; Du Pont to Sophie, 26 May 1863, Du Pont, *Letters*, 3: 135–36.

40. The navy assisted in several minor probing expeditions. At the end of May and the beginning of June, expeditions of the army landed on James Island and at Bluffton, South Carolina. On 11 June, the navy also participated in the expedition that resulted in the burning of Darien, Georgia. Welles to Du Pont, 3 June 1863, *ORN*, ser. 1, 14:230; Welles to Du Pont, 6 June 1863, Du Pont Papers, Hagley; Du Pont to Sophie, 25 June 1863, Du Pont, *Letters*, 3:182–83.

41. Jordan to Ripley, 15 January 1863, *ORA*, ser. 1, 14:749–50; Mallory to Webb, 19 February 1862, *ORN*, ser. 1, 13:820–21.

42. The Confederate Torpedo Service was created by an act of the Confederate Congress in October 1862. Scharf, *Confederate Navy*, 688; Parker, *Rec-*

410 Notes to Pages 201–205

ollections, 332–35; Lee to Jordan, 13, 19 March 1863, ORA, ser. 1, 14:820–21, 837.

43. Tucker had just relieved Ingraham and commanded the vessels afloat. Scharf, Confederate Navy, 689–90; Parker, Recollections, 332–35.

44. Beauregard to Tucker, 13 April 1863, ORN, ser. 1, 14:688–89; Scharf, Confederate Navy, 690–91; Parker, Recollections, 336–37.

45. Parker, Recollections, 336–38.

46. Ibid., 338–39.

47. Ibid.

48. Mallory to Richard Page, 5 April 1863, Savannah Squadron Papers, Special Collections, Emory University; Taylor, Rogers, et. al. to Du Pont, 22 June 1863, ORN, ser. 1, 14:273–76; Scharf, Confederate Navy, 641.

49. McBlair took command on 22 November 1862, Dabney Minor Scales Diary, DUM; Scharf, Confederate Navy, 642; Jones, Tattnall, 223; Still, Savannah Squadron, 12.

50. Dabney Minor Scales Diary, entry for 12 January 3, 4, February 1863, Dabney Minor Scales Papers, DUM.

51. On 16 February, McBlair died while in command. Jones, Tattnall, 224–26; Dabney Minor Scales Diary, entry for 23 February, 20 March 1863, Dabney Minor Scales Papers, DUM.

52. Abstract of Statement of Deserters (n.d.), ORN, ser. 1, 13:767; Rodgers to Du Pont, 19 March 1863, ibid., 767; Still, Iron Afloat, 133; Logs of Catskill, Montauk, Passaic, Nahant, Nantucket, and Patapsco, 15 March–7 April 1863, Entry 118, RG 24, NA.

53. Still, Savannah Squadron, 12–13; Page to Webb, 13 May 1863, ORN, ser. 1, 14:697; Mallory to Page, 5, 6, April 1863, Savannah Squadron Papers, Emory.

54. The Savannah was not complete until 3 August. Webb to Mallory, 1, 10 June 1863, ORN, ser. 1, 14:705, 710–11.

55. Du Pont to Sophie, 10 June 1863, Du Pont, Letters, 3: 170–71; Du Pont to Halpine, 8 January 1864, ORN, ser. 1, 14:282; Du Pont to Downes, 10 June 1863, ibid., 250; Du Pont to Fox, 25 December 1861, Fox, Correspondence, 1:83–84; Downes to Rodgers, 18 June 1863, ORN, ser. 1, 14:267; Rodgers to Davis, 25 June 1863, Davis, Life of Charles Henry Davis, 296; Xanthus Smith to Mother, 6 April 1863, Smith Family Papers, AAA, Smithsonian.

56. Webb to Mallory, 19 October 1864, ORN, ser. 1, 14:290–92; Kennard to Mallory, 17 June 1863, ibid., 288; Jones to Kennard, 17 June 1863, ibid., 289; Kennard to Mallory, 17 June 1863, ibid., 288.

57. According to one participant, the boats were cast adrift when the Weehawken turned back upstream. Loring, "Weehawken," 114–15; Rodgers to Du Pont, 17 June 1863, ORN, ser. 1, 14:265; Downes to Rodgers, 18 June 1863, ORN, ser. 1, 14:2567; Rodgers to Hodge, 18 June 1863, Rodgers Family Papers, LCM.

58. Rodgers to Hodge, 18 June 1863, Rodgers to Anne, 18 June 1863, Rodgers Family Papers, LCM; Scharf, *Confederate Navy*, 644n, Webb to Mallory, 19 October 1864, *ORN*, ser. 1, 14:290.

59. *Inquirer* (Philadelphia), as cited in Moore, *Rebellion Record*, 6:70; Webb to Mallory, *ORN*, ser. 1, 14:290–91; Rodgers to Du Pont, 17 June 1863, *ORN*, ser. 1, 14:265–66; Loring, "*Weehawken*," 114–15; Rodgers to Anne, 18 June 1863, Rodgers Family Papers, LCM.

60. The splinters that Rodgers saw fly were reported to be from a pile of lumber stowed on top of the casemate. Loring on the *Weehawken* describes this and says it "filled the air with flying boards, . . . giving us the flattering impression that the whole institution had 'gone up'!" There is some disagreement over where the third shot struck the *Atlanta*. Webb and Rodgers each describe in reverse order the third and fourth shots. I have relied on Rodgers' sequence since he made his report the day of the battle and Webb's was written sixteen months later. Webb to Mallory, 19 October 1864, *ORN*, ser. 1, 14:290–91; Rodgers to Du Pont, 17 June 1863, ibid., 265–66; Loring, "*Weehawken*," 114–15; Rodgers to Anne, 18 June 1863, Rodgers Family Papers, LCM; Testimony of John Rodgers, *Heavy Ordnance*, 72.

61. The Second National Confederate flag's canton had the St. Andrews Cross and thirteen stars (as per the Confederate battle flag). This flag was easily mistaken as a flag of surrender when it hung limp and a broad red bar was placed on the fly end of the white field in March 1865. Hunter, *A Year on a Monitor*, 79–81; Johnson, *Rodgers*, 255.

62. Rodgers to Hodge, 18 June 1863, Rodgers Family Papers, LCM.

63. The division of the prize money was settled in court; the judge decided that since the two monitors represented a superior force, the proceeds would be split between the officers and crews and the other half to the United States. *Decisions of Hon. Peleg Sprague in Maritime Admiralty and Prize Cases in the District Court of the United States For the District of Massachusetts 1854–1868*, 2 vols. (Boston: Little Brown and Co., 1868), 2: 251–61. Both Rodgers and Downes by Joint Resolution of Congress received a vote of thanks. The appraised value of the ironclad was $350,829.26 which represented a handsome sum of prize money for the officers and crews. W. H. Mercer to Jordan, 17 June 1863, *ORN*, ser. 1, 14:290; *Republican* (Savannah), 27 June 1863; *Daily Morning News* (Savannah), 27 June 1863; Rodgers to Anne, 17 June 1863, Rodgers Family Papers, LCM; Downes to Welles, 8 July 1863, *ORN*, ser. 1, 14:285–86; Downes to Du Pont, 20 June 1863, Downs to Rodgers, 18 June 1863, Du Pont Papers, Hagley; Rodgers to Davis, 25 June 1863, *Life of Charles Henry Davis*, 298.

64. Rodgers to Anne, 18 June 1863, Rodgers Family Papers, LCM; Du Pont to Rodgers, 18 June 1863, ibid.

65. Welles to Du Pont, 26 June 1863, Du Pont Papers, Hagley.

66. Ibid.

67. Johnson, *Defense of Charleston*, 65–passim; Welles to Du Pont, 22 May 1863, *ORN*, ser. 1, 14:212.

68. Du Pont to Welles, 6 June 1863, Du Pont Papers, Hagley; Du Pont to Davis, 14 April 1863, ibid.; Rodgers to Hodge, April (n.d.) 1863, 23 April 1863, Rodgers Family Papers, LCM.

69. Welles to Du Pont, 27 June 1863, Du Pont Papers, Hagley; Du Pont to Welles, 5 July 1863, Du Pont, *Letters*, 3: 195–96.

70. *Times* (New York), 27 July 1863, *Sunday Times* (New York), July 26, 1863; *Tribune* (New York), 11 December 1863.

71. Davis helped Du Pont draft his 22 October letter and Welles knew this. Copy of Mr. Davis's Sketch [c. 27 July 1863], Du Pont Papers, Hagley. For a more detailed view of the political feud see Niven, *Welles*, 472–78 and Reinhard H. Luthin, "A Discordant Chapter in Lincoln's Administration: The Davis-Blair Controversy," *Maryland Historical Magazine* (March 1944) 25–48; Du Pont to Welles, 22 October 1863, Du Pont, *Letters*, 3: 253–57; Welles to Du Pont, 4 November 1863, ibid., 3:257–61; Salmon P. Chase, "The Diary of Salmon P. Chase," *Annual Report of the American Historical Association 1902*, 2 vols. (Washington, D.C.: Government Printing Office, 1903) 13 September 1862, 2:78.

72. In the Navy Department's Annual Report of 1864, Welles continued his belittling of Du Pont regarding the activities of the monitors off Morris Island and their ability to withstand this service. Simpson, *Paper on Armored Vessels Addressed to the Secretary of the Navy*, s.1, s. n, p., 1866, 5; *Report of the Secretary of the Navy 1863*; H. Ex. Doc. 1, 38th Cong., 1st sess., 7 December 1863; ibid., 1864; *The Congressional Globe*, 25 February 1864, 38th cong., 1st sess., 830; Niven, *Welles*, 474; Welles, *Diary*, 26 February 1864, 1: 531.

73. Du Pont to Biddle, 4 May 1863, Du Pont Papers, Hagley; Dahlgren also blamed Welles for the "unworthy treatment" of Du Pont for the 7th April attack. Notes entitled "Naval Administration," circa 1869, Dahlgren Papers, Syracuse.

74. Albert Gleaves, *Life and Letters of Rear Admiral Stephen B. Luce* (New York: G. P. Putnam's Sons, 1925), 91.

75. Fox to Ericsson, 27 February 1864, Fox Papers, NYHS; Fox to Ericsson, 13 January 1864, Ericsson Papers, ASHM; Ericsson to Aldersparre, 6 March 1868, ibid.

76. Barnes, "My Egotistigraphy," 187, Barnes, Papers, NYHS.

77. James M. Merill, "Naval Operations Along the South Atlantic Coast," Ph.D. diss., University of California of Los Angeles, 1954, 301–302; Reed, *Combined Operations*, 295; Copy of Mr. Davis's Sketch [circa 27 July 1863], Du Pont Papers, Hagley.

78. Du Pont to Sir, circa May 1863 (n.d.) draft of letter probably to Welles, W9-2910, Du Pont Papers, Hagley.

79. Welles, *Diary*, 22 February 1865, 2:247; Welles to Du Pont, 31 January 1863, Du Pont, *Letters*, 2:399–400.

80. Welles, *Diary*, 23 June 1865, 2: 320–31.

81. Copy of Epitaph on John Byng, Du Pont Papers, Hagley. This copy varies somewhat in capitalization and style from the real monument. Dudley Pope, *At Twelve Mr. Byng Was Shot* (Philadelphia, J. B. Lippncott Company, 1962), 33–34.

Chapter 8

1. Du Pont, being the senior officer, flew the blue pennant signifying his seniority. The navy had specially chartered the *Augusta Dinsmore* to carry Dahlgren to Port Royal. Dahlgren Diaries, 6 July 1863, Dahlgren Papers, Syracuse; Log of *Wabash*, 6 July 1863, Entry 118, RG 24, NA.

2. Hamersly, *Records of Living Officers*, 417–18; Schneller, *A Quest for Glory*, pg. 5–passim; Farenholt, "The Monitor 'Catskill'", 388.

3. Dahlgren to Lincoln, 1 October 1862, Dahlgren Papers, LCM; Welles to Dahlgren, 8 October 1862, ibid., Dahlgren Diaries, 1 October 1862, Dahlgren Papers, Syracuse; Du Pont to Fox, 8 October 1863, Fox, *Correspondence*, 1:160.

4. Welles, *Diary*, 27, 28 May 1863, I:314–16; Dahlgren Diary, 13 May 1863, Dahlgren Papers, Syracuse; Turner to Du Pont, 24 June 1863, Du Pont Papers, Hagley; Du Pont to Sophie, 7 March 1863, Du Pont, *Letters*, 2:474.

5. Dahlgren wrote in his diary that a dual command would "render collusion of opinion possible + hence dissention." Welles, *Diary*, 28, 29 May 1863, 1:315, 317; Dahlgren Diaries, 28, 29 May 1863, Dahlgren Papers, Syracuse; Welles, *Diary*, 28, 29 May 1863, I:315, 317.

6. Welles, *Diary*, 29 May 1863, 1:317; Schneller, *Quest*, 243–44.

7. Welles, *Diary*, 21 June 1863, 1:336; Dahlgren to Fox, 9 April 1863 [sic], Dahlgren Papers, LCM.

8. Thomas Legg in "Quest for Glory, The Naval Career of John A. Dahlgren, 1826–1870," unpublished dissertation, The College of William and Mary, 1994, 205–206, believes Fox had the most influence in getting Dahlgren the command. John A. Foote, "Notes on the Life of Admiral Foote," *Battles and Leaders*, 1:347; Welles, *Diary*, 21 June 1863, 1:336–37; Fox to Porter, 16 July 1863, Fox, *Correspondence*, 2:185.

9. Welles, *Diary*, 23 June 1863, 1:341.

10. Dahlgren to Fox, 9 April 1863, [sic] Dahlgren Papers, LCM; Drayton to Wise, [September] 1863, Wise Papers, NYHS; J. Rodgers to Anne, 29 June 1863, Rodgers Papers, LCM.

11. Warner, *Generals in Blue*, 176; Wise, *Gate of Hell*, 33–34.

12. Quincy A. Gillmore, "The Army Before Charleston in 1863," *Battles and Leaders*, 4:54–55; Gillmore, *Charleston 1863*, 12–13.

13. Quincy A. Gillmore, *Engineer and Artillery Operations Against the Defenses of Charleston Harbor in 1863* (New York: D. Van Nostrand, 1865), 7, 16–17; Gillmore, "The Army Before Charleston," *Battles and Leaders*, 4:54–55; W. W. H. Davis, "The Siege of Morris Island," *The Annals of the War Written by Leading Participants North and South* (Philadelphia: The Times Publishing Company, 1879), 95.

14. Gillmore, *Engineer and Artillery Operations*, 16–17; Dahlgren to Welles, 16 October 1865, Dahlgren Papers, LCM.

15. Gillmore's rush may have been caused by a report made by Commander Balch. Interviewing deserters he learned that a large force of blacks was deepening Wapoo Cut in order to get their ironclads into the Stono River. Du Pont sent his two most experienced pilots and they found a shorter and straighter channel that carried fourteen feet at the highest spring tide. Du Pont ordered the *Nantucket* into the Stono on 1 June. Du Pont to Welles, 2 July 1862, *ORN*, ser. 1, 14:306; Du Pont did have instructions to cooperate with any joint operations but preferred not to do so. Dahlgren to Welles, 6 July 1863, Dahlgren Papers, LCM; Ammen, *The Atlantic Coast*, 122; Dahlgren, *Memoirs*, 4 July 1863, 396; Du Pont to Gillmore, 29 June 1863, Du Pont Papers, Hagley.

16. Dahlgren, *Memoirs*, 5 June 1863, 393.

17. Dahlgren, Diary, 5 July 1863, Dahlgren Papers, Syracuse; Wise, *Gate of Hell*, 40–41. Jones, *Siege of Charleston*, 208–209. On 30 June Gillmore wrote that his preparations were nearly complete but that he could do nothing more until Du Pont's replacement arrived. Du Pont was later held accountable for these delays yet Gillmore was not ready to move until the tenth of July, four days after Dahlgren relieved Du Pont. When Dahlgren arrived, he did not know whether he should cooperate and wrote the department on the sixth. Welles replied on the fifteenth, after the attack began, that he should not only follow the orders Du Pont had from the department but that he should also use his own judgment. Welles to Du Pont, 15 July 1863, *ORN*, ser. 1, 14:343.

18. Gillmore, "The Army Before Charleston in 1863," 55–57; Johnson, *Defenses of Charleston*, 85; Thomas Harry Williams, *P. G. T. Beauregard; Napoleon in Gray* (Baton Rouge: Louisiana State University Press, 1955) 186; Roman, *Beauregard*, 2:124.

19. A. S. MacKenzie to Parker, 12 July 1863, *ORN*, ser. 1, 14:327–28; Wise, *Gate of Hell*, 65.

20. Gillmore, "The Army Before Charleston in 1863," 57–58; MacKenzie to Parker, 12 July 1863, *ORN*, ser. 1, 14:327–38; Bunce to Balch, 12 July 1863, ibid., 329.

21. The *Patapsco* had to remain behind because of a fractured tooth in the pinion that turned her turret. Dahlgren, General Instruction, 9 July 1863, *ORN*, ser. 1, 14:318; Dahlgren, *Memoirs*, July 8–10 1863, 397–98.

22. Strong to Seymour, 10 July 1863, *ORA*, ser. 1, vol, 28, pt. 1, 354; Dahlgren, *Memoirs*, 10 July 1863, 398; Dahlgren to Welles, 28 January 1864,

Armored Vessels, 580; General Instructions, Dahlgren, 9 July 1863, *ORN*, ser. 1, 14:317; Rodgers to Dahlgren, 10 July 1863, G. W. Rodgers, Entry 395, RG 45, NA; Gillmore, "The Army Before Charleston in 1863," 58; Bunce to Balch, 12 July 1863, *ORN*, ser. 1, 14:329.

23. Bunce to Balch, 12 July 1863, *ORN*, ser. 1, 14:329–30; Wise, *Gate of Hell*, 69–70; Gillmore, "The Army Before Charleston in 1863," 58.

24. R. F. Graham to W. F. Nance, 18 July 1863, *ORA*, ser. 1, vol. 28, pt. 1, 414; Charles Olmstead, *Reminiscences of Service with the First Volunteer Regiment of Georgia, Charleston Harbor in 1863* (Savannah Ga.: J. H. Estill, 1879), 5.

25. Olmstead, ibid., 7; Beauregard, "The Defense of Charleston," *Battles and Leaders*, 4:23; Dahlgren to Welles, 12 July 1863, *ORN*, ser. 1, 14:319; Dahlgren to Welles, 28 January 1864, Dahlgren Papers, LCM; Johnson, *Defense of Charleston*, 81; Eldridge, *Third New Hampshire*, 334; *The Official Military Atlas of the Civil War*, Plate XLIV; Robert C. Gilchrist, "Confederate Defense of Morris Island," *Yearbook 1884* (Charleston, S.C.: City of Charleston, 1884), 355–56.

26. Rodgers noted more hits on *Catskill* than 60, not being able to count those that struck under the water. Dahlgren later wrote that the *Catskill* was struck 68 times. Dahlgren to Welles, 12 July 1863, *ORN*, ser. 1, 14:319–20; Rodgers to Dahlgren, 10 July 1863, G. W. Rodgers Correspondence, Entry 395, RG 45, NA; Dahlgren to Patty Dahlgren, 12 July 1863, Dahlgren Papers, Newberry Library, Chicago; Beauregard to Cooper, 10 July 1863, *ORN*, ser. 1, 14:335; Dahlgren, *Diary*, 10 July 1863, 399; Frederick Stow to Mary, 20 August 1863, Harrisburg Civil War Round Table Collection, U.S. Army Military History Institute, Carlisle Barracks, Pennsylvania.

27. Wise, *Gate of Hell*, Table 6, Appendix, 228.

28. Fox to Gillmore, 16 July 1863, Personal Papers of Quincy A. Gillmore, Generals' Papers and Books, Entry 159, RG 94, NA.

29. Ibid., Table 8, Appendix, 229; Johnson, *Defense of Charleston*, 95; Strong to Seymour, 11 July 1863, *ORA*, ser. 1, vol. 28, pt. 1. 355–56; Grey to Hawley, 13 July 1863, ibid., 360–61.

30. Dahlgren, *Memoirs*, 11 July 1863, 400; Dahlgren to Gillmore, 11 July 1863, *ORN*, ser. 1, 14:319; Abstract Logs of *Montauk, Nahant, Catskill*, 11 July 1863, ibid., 330–32. The *Weehawken* log and report is missing from the *ORN*. Rodgers to Dahlgren, 10 July 1863, G. W. Rodgers Correspondence, Entry 395, RG 45, NA.

31. Dahlgren, *Memoirs*, 12 July 1863, 400; Dahlgren to Parker, 12 July 1863, *ORN*, ser. 1, 14:337.

32. The diversion did not draw troops from Morris Island because there were no troops that could be spared. Jones, *Siege of Charleston*, 208–209; Balch to Dahlgren, 21 July 1863, *ORN*, ser. 1, 14:346–48; Abstract Log, *Nantucket*, 11 July 1863, ibid., 333.

33. Ripley to Jordan, 22 July 1863, *ORA*, ser. 1, vol. 28, pt. 1, 372–73; Balch to Dahlgren, 16 July 1863, 21 July 1863, *ORN*, ser. 1, 14:345, 348; Radcliffe to Molony, 17 July 1863, ibid., 352–53; George Henry Gordon, *A War Diary of Events in the War of the Great Rebellion 1863–1865* (Boston: James R. Osgood and Company, 1927), 200.

34. Balch to Dahlgren, 21 July 1863, *ORN*, ser. 1, 14:348–49; Bacon to Dahlgren, 16 July 1863, ibid., 346; Terry to Smith, 16 July 1863, ibid., 351.

35. Dahlgren, *Memoirs*, 17, 18 July 1863, 401–402; Dahlgren to Welles, 17 July 1863, *ORN*, ser. 1, 14:357–58; Taliaferro to Nance, 21 July 1863, ibid., 369.

36. Dahlgren, *Memoirs*, July 17, 18, 1863, 402; Dahlgren to Welles, 17 July 1863, *ORN*, ser. 1, 14:357–58; Taliaferro to Nance, 21 July 1863, ibid., 369; *Tribune* (New York) cited in Moore, *Rebellion Record*, 7:214.

37. There is some disagreement within the sources concerning the stations held by the ironclads when they got underway. Log *Patapsco*, 18 July 1863, Entry 118, RG 24, NA; Dahlgren Staff Journal, 18 July 1863, Dahlgren Papers, LCM; Dahlgren Diaries, 18 July 1863, Dahlgren Papers, Syracuse; Dahlgren to Welles, 19 July 1863, *ORN*, ser. 1, 14:359.

38. Eldridge, *Third New Hampshire*, 314; Dahlgren to Welles, 19 July 1863, *ORN*, ser. 1, 14:359; Dahlgren, *Memoirs*, 18 July 1863, 402; Circular, Dahlgren, 15 July 1863, *ORN*, ser. 1, 14:357; Olmstead, "Reminiscences of Service in Charleston," 158.

39. Dahlgren to Welles, 19 July 1863, *ORN*, ser. 1, 14:359; Olmstead, "Reminiscences of Service in Charleston," 162; Dahlgren placed his Marines in boats beside the *New Ironsides* in case they might get a chance to assault the fort later in the day. Alvin C. Voris, "Charleston in the Rebellion," *Sketches of War History 1861–1865, Papers Read Before the Ohio Commandery of the Military Order of the Loyal Legion of the United States*, 6 vols. (Cincinnati, Ohio: Robert Clark & Co., 1886), 2:326–27.

40. "Observations on the operations against Morris Isl., July and August 1863," Dahlgren Papers, LCM; Wise, *Gate of Hell*, 92–118; G. W. Rodgers to Dahlgren, 18 July 1863, *ORN*, ser. 1, 14:360–61–passim; The *New Ironsides* fired 805 shells, about 40 tons of metal. Belknap, "Reminiscent of the Siege of Charleston," 180.

41. Dahlgren to Welles, 19 July 1863, *ORN*, ser. 1, 14:359; Taliferro to Nance, 21 July 1863, ibid., 371.

42. Welles, *Diary*, 26, 28 July 1863, 1:382–85; Dahlgren to Welles, 21 July 1863, *ORN*, ser. 1, 14:380.

43. Welles, *Diary*, 26, 28 July 1863, 1:382–85.

44. It is unclear whether *Patapsco* fired on the forts. Her log mentions no firing and mechanics at work on her turret. The log of *Catskill*, however, has her engaging the enemy shortly after noon. Dahlgren, *Memoirs*, July 19–20, 1863, 403–404; Rowan to Dahlgren, 20 July 1863, *ORN*, ser. 1, 14:377; Logs

of *Catskill, Patapsco, Nantucket, Montauk,* 20–21 July 1863, Entry 118, RG 24, NA; Report of Firing by USS *Ironsides,* Quarter ending 30 Sept. 1863, Dahlgren Papers, LCM; Dahlgren, *Memoirs,* 21 July 1863, 404.

45. Dahlgren to Gillmore, 20 July 1863, Dahlgren Papers, LCM; Gillmore to Dahlgren, 20 July 1863, *ORN,* ser. 1, 14:381; Dahlgren to Williams, 21 July 1863, ibid., 379; Dahlgren to Welles, 30 July 1863, ibid., 409.

46. Taliaferro to Ripley, 14, 21 July 1863, *ORA,* ser. 1, vol. 28, pt. 1, 415–16; Ezra J. Warner, *Generals In Gray, Lives of the Confederate Commanders* (Baton Rouge: Louisiana State University Press, 1959) 297–98; Taliaferro to Nance, 23 July 1863, *ORA,* ser. 1, vol. 28, pt. 1, 421.

47. Beauregard to Tucker, 12, 18, 27 July 1863, *ORN,* ser. 1, 14:725, 728, 736; Roman, *Beauregard,* 2:98.

48. Dahlgren, *Memoirs,* 21 July 1863, 404; Abstract Logs of *Nantucket* and *Ottawa,* 22 July 1863, *ORN,* ser. 1, 14:385; Orders J. A. Dahlgren, 22 July 1863, ibid., 384–85; Dahlgren, *Memoirs,* 22 July 1863, 404; Logs of *Montauk, Nantucket, Catskill,* Entry 118, RG 24, NA.

49. Dahlgren to Gillmore, 22 July 1863, *ORN,* ser. 1, 14:383–84; Journal of Major Brooks, 23 July 1863, *ORA,* ser. 1, vol. 28, pt. 1, 274–75.

50. Abstract Logs of *New Ironsides* et al., 24 July 1863, *ORN,* ser. 1, 14:392–94; Dahlgren to Welles, 25 July 1863, ibid., 391; Olmstead, "Reminiscences of Service," 10.

51. Dahlgren to Welles, 29 July, 22 August 1863, *ORN,* ser. 1, 14:406, 470; Hughes to Dahlgren, 23 July 1863, ibid., 388–89; Dahlgren to Reynolds, 26 July 1863, Dahlgren Papers, LCM; Reynolds to Dahlgren, 13 July, 13 August 1863, Reynolds Correspondence, Entry 395, RG 45, NA; Note 10 July 1863 ibid.; Griffin to Stimers, October (n.d.) 1863, Records Relating to Claims in Connection With Civil War Naval Vessels, 1861–1909 [Port Royal Working Party], Entry 186, RG 19, NA.

52. The Marines on board *New Ironsides* manned the aftergun. Beauregard to Harris, 24 July 1863, *ORN,* ser. 1, 14:394; Von Schelina, *Coast Defense,* 32; Belknap, "Reminiscent of the Siege of Charleston," 177, 181; Rowan to Dahlgren, 29 January 1864, Rowan Papers, LCM.

53. John Harleston, "Battery Wagner on Morris Island in 1863," *The South Carolina Historical Magazine* 57 (January 1956) 5; Pringle was later killed by a shell that ricocheted into the fort and burst near him. Robert C. Gilchrist, "Confederate Defense of Morris Island," 384; Eldridge, *Third New Hampshire,* 333.

54. Harleston, *Battery Wagner on Morris Island,* 5; Olmstead, "Reminiscences of Service," 8.

55. The addition of the 50-pounder Dahlgren gun to the broadside made his ship more sluggish at the helm and increased the draft slightly. Dahlgren to Balch, 27 July 1863, *ORN,* ser. 1 14:400; Balch to Dahlgren, 4 August 1863, ibid., 416–17.

56. Gillmore had increasingly become concerned over this base at Hilton Head. He asked Dahlgren to send a vessel there to help protect the base. Dahlgren consented but reminded the general that this was the third vessel sent "to secure points elsewhere." Dahlgren to Gillmore, 21 July 1863, Dahlgren Papers, LCM; Dahlgren wanted to plate the wooden ship with armor around the boilers but would have to remove weight from other parts of the ship. Dahlgren, Orders of 25 July 1863, ORN, ser. 1, 14:396.

57. Dahlgren, *Memoirs*, 536–39; Abstract Logs *Ottawa, Dai Ching, Paul Jones*, 25 July 1863, ORN, ser. 1, 14:397; Abstract Logs of *Catskill, Ottawa, New Ironsides, Patapsco, Passaic, Montauk*, 29 July–1 August 1863, ibid., 404–406; The *Passaic* had arrived on the twenty-fifth and took part in her first engagement on the twenty-ninth. Dahlgren to Welles, 26 July 1863, ibid., 397; Simpson to Dahlgren, 9 October 1863, ibid., 585.

58. Dahlgren to Welles, 29 June 1863, *ORN*, ser. 1, 14:303; Welles to Dahlgren, 3 July 1863, Dahlgren Papers, LCM; Dahlgren to Welles, 6 August 1863, ibid., 428; Dahlgren Instructions, 7 August 1863, ibid., 428–29; Zeilin to Dahlgren, 10 August 1863, ibid., 434; Dahlgren, *Memoirs*, 8 August 1863, 406.

59. Zeilin to Dahlgren, 13 August 1863, ORN, ser, 1, 14:439–40; Dahlgren, *Memoirs*, 13 August 1863, 407.

60. Dahlgren to Gillmore, 10 August 1863, *ORN*, ser. 1, 14:433; Haines to Welles, 29 October 1864, ibid., 425–26; Statement of James H. Tomb, 8 August 1863, ibid., 427; Within a week the Confederates tried to strike again, this time sending torpedoes down the Stono River. In the early morning of 16 August, an explosion occurred within thirty yards of the *Pawnee*. Forty-five minutes later, a lookout in the *C. P. Williams* spotted what he thought were two cans floating towards the vessel. As they got near, they discovered them to be two torpedoes attached to a line. Four others were discovered later and in an attempt to recover them, one destroyed the *Pawnee*'s launch. To prevent a further surprise from drifting torpedoes the sailors stretched a net across the river above the vessels. Balch to Dahlgren, 16, 20 August 1863, ORN, ser. 1, 14:445–46; Dahlgren to Welles, 24 August 1863, ibid., 446; Abstract Log of *C. P. Williams*, 16 August 1863, ibid., 448; George Bacon to wife, 23 August 1863, George Bacon Papers, Fort Sumter National Monument, National Parks Service.

61. Jones, *Siege of Charleston*, 255; Journal of Brooks, 13 August 1863, ORA, ser. 1, vol. 28, pt. 1, 286.

62. Keitt to Nance, 17 August 1863, ORA, ser. 1, vol. 28, pt. 1, 286.

63. Gillmore, *Engineer and Artillery Operations*, 65; Johnson, *Defense of Charleston*, 180–89; Journal of Captain John C. Mitchel, July 22–passim, ORA, ser. 1, vol. 28, pt. 1, 574–79; von Scheliha, *Coast Defense*, 9.

64. The naval battery also took part and in the following week it fired 925 shells at Fort Sumter. Dahlgren, *Memoirs*, 15 August 1863, 407–408; Parker to

Dahlgren, 23 August 1863, *ORN*, ser. 1, 14:471–77; The first shot from the siege batteries was fired on 12 August as a test shot. W. W. H. Davis, "The Siege of Morris Island," 101; Wise, *Gate of Hell*, 156, Table 18, 236–38.

65. Dahlgren, Diary, 17 August 1863, Dahlgren Papers, Syracuse; Dahlgren to Welles, 17 August 1863, *ORN*, ser. 1, 14:453. The *Passaic* was originally to be the flagship. Dahlgren Order No. 24, 14 August 1863, Orders to the South Atlantic Blockading Squadron, 1863–1865, Historical Society of Pennsylvania, Philadelphia, hereinafter cited as HSP; Dahlgren to Welles, 18 August 1863, *ORN*, ser. 1, 14:452, Gibson to Dahlgren, 22 September 1863, ibid., 456; Logs of *Catskill, Patapsco, Passaic*, 17 August 1863, Entry 118, RG 24, NA.

66. Ammen, *The Atlantic Coast*, 131; Carpenter to Dahlgren, 17 August 1863, *ORN*, ser. 1, 14:458; Oscar W. Farenholt, "*The Monitor 'Catskill': A Year's Reminiscences 1863–1864.*" *Civil War Papers of the California Commandry of the Military Order of the Loyal Legion of the United States* (San Francisco: Shannon-Conmy, 1912, reprint edition, Broadfoot Publishing Company, Wilmington, N.C., 1995) 386–87; Oscar W. Farenholt, "*From Ordinary Seaman to Rear Admiral.*" *Civil War Papers of the California Commandry of the Military Order of the Loyal Legion of the United States* (San Francisco: Shannon-Conmy, 1910, reprint edition, Broadfoot Publishing Company, Wilmington, NC, 1995) 375, 386–87; Log of *Catskill*, 17 August 1863, Entry 118, RG 24, NA.

67. Abstract Log of *New Ironsides*, 17 August 1863, *ORN*, ser. 1, 14:474.

68. Abstract Logs of *Montauk, Nahant, Catskill*, 17 August 1863, ibid., 476–79; Danby to Faron, 22 August 1863, ibid., 47.

69. The times differ in the accounts when Dahlgren shifted his flag to the *Dinsmore*. Logs of *Passaic, Patapsco*, 17 August 1863, Entry 118, RG 24, NA; Dahlgren Staff Journal, 17 August 1863, *ORN*, ser. 1, 14:454–55.

70. Keitt to Nance, 17, 18 August 1863, *ORA*, ser. 1, vol. 28, pt. 1, 470–74; Pringle to Bryan, 18 August 1863, ibid., 487–88.

71. Ammen, *The Atlantic Coast*, 131; George Bacon to wife, 23 August 1863, Bacon Papers, Fort Sumter National Monument; Roman, *Beauregard*, 2:126–27; Tucker to Dozier, 17 August 1863, *ORN*, ser. 1, 14:483.

72. Gillmore to Dahlgren, 17 August 1863, *ORN*, ser. 1, 14:451; Dahlgren, Order No. 26, 17 August 1863, Orders to the South Atlantic Blockading Squadron, 1863–1865, HSP; Abstract Logs of *New Ironsides, Passaic* et al. l, 18 August 1863, *ORN*, ser. 1, 14:475–passim; Simpson to Dahlgren, 20 August 1863, ibid., 460–61.

73. Gillmore to Dahlgren, 19 August 1863, *ORN*, ser. 1, 14:462; Dahlgren to Gillmore, 19 August 1863, ibid., 462; Dahlgren, Order No. 28, 20 August 1863, Orders to the South Atlantic Blockading Squadron, 1863–1865, HSP.

74. Order of Rear Admiral Dahlgren, 5 August 1863, *ORN*, ser. 1, 14:420.

75. Bob Holcombe of the Port Columbus Civil War Naval Center believes the *Torch* to be an unfinished *Maury* class gunboat, with a casemate added—

F. M. Jones builder. Augustine T. Smythe, "Torpedo and Submarine Attacks on the Federal Blockading Fleet off Charleston During the War of Secession," *Year Book 1907* (Charleston, S.C.: City of Charleston, 1907), 54; Ripley to Jordan, 23 July 1863, *ORN*, ser. 1, 14:734–35; Beauregard to Tucker, 12 July 1863, ibid., 725; Wagner to Beauregard, 13 August 1863, *ORA*, ser. 1, vol. 28, pt. 2, 280; Pierre G. T. Beauregard, "Torpedo Service in the Harbor and Water Defenses of Charleston," *Southern Historical Society Papers* 5 (1878, no. 4) 148–50.

76. Quincy A. Gillmore, "Operations Against the Defenses of Charleston in 1863" Gillmore Papers, Entry 159, RG 94, NA; Beauregard, "Torpedo Service," 148–50; Porter to Rowan, 28 August 1863, *ORN*, ser. 1, 14:498; Abstract Log of *New Ironsides*, 28 August 1863, ibid., 498; Carlin to Beauregard, 22 August 1983, ibid., 498–99; Smythe, "Torpedo and Submarine Attacks," 55.

77. Gillmore to Cullum, (n.d.), *ORA*, ser. 1, vol. 28, pt. 1, 24; Dahlgren, *Memoirs*, 20 August 1863, 409.

78. The *Catskill*, which had suffered damage in the earlier fight, had steamed to Port Royal for repairs. Dahlgren, *Memoirs*, 21 August 1863, 409; Gillmore to Dahlgren, 21 August 1863, *ORN*, ser. 1, 14:465; Dahlgren to Gillmore, 22 August 1863, ibid., 466–67.

79. Gillmore to Dahlgren, 22 August 1863, *ORN*, ser. 1, 14:468; Dahlgren, *Memoirs*, 22 August 1863, 409; Abstract Logs of *Nahant, Montauk, Patapsco, New Ironsides*, 22 August 1863, *ORN*, ser. 1, 14:475–78; Hagood to Nance, 22 August 1863, ibid., 289–90.

80. *Nahant* and *Montauk* each had one gun disabled. Order J. A. Dahlgren, 22 August 1863, *ORN*, ser. 1, 14:467; Dahlgren, *Memoirs*, 22 August 1863, 409–10; Giraud to Dahlgren, 23 August 1863, *ORN*, ser. 1, 14:503; Colhoun to Dahlgren, 23 August 1863, ibid., 503–504; Forrest to Dahlgren, Notes on engagement night of 22 August 1863, ibid., 504–505; Johnson, *Defense of Charleston*, 129–30; Dahlgren to Gillmore, 24 August 1863, Dahlgren Papers, LCM.

81. Clingman to Nance, 23 August 1863, *ORN*, ser. 1, 14:509; Dahlgren, *Memoirs*, 22 August 1863, 409–10; Downes to Dahlgren, 23 August 1863, *ORN*, ser. 1, 14:502; Colhoun to Dahlgren, 23 August 1863, ibid., 503–504; Giraud to Dahlgren, 23 August 1863, ibid., 503.

82. Years later Dahlgren claimed *New Ironsides* exhausted her ammunition and had to replenish it. Dahlgren to W. W. H. Davis, 28 October 1869, Dahlgren Papers, LCM; Dahlgren, *Diary*, 23 August 1863, Dahlgren Papers, Syracuse; Log of *New Ironsides*, 23 August 1863, Entry 118, RG 24, NA; Jim Dan Hill, *The Civil War Sketchbook of Charles Ellery Stedman, Surgeon, United States Navy* (San Rafael, Calif.: Presidio Press, 1976), 171; Dahlgren to Welles, 28 January 1864, *ORN*, ser. 1, 14:599.

83. Hammersly, *Records of Living Officers*, 14, 16.

84. Gillmore, *Engineer and Artillery Operations, 1863*, 65–66; Dahlgren to Davis, 28 October 1869, Dahlgren Papers, LCM.

85. Dahlgren to Gillmore, 22 August 1863, Dahlgren to Wise, 29 July 1863, Dahlgren Papers, LCM; Dahlgren to Welles, 22 August 1863, *ORN*, ser. 1, 14:470; Roman, *Beauregard*, 2:510; Gillmore, "The Army Before Charleston," 4:62.

86. One was in Wassaw Sound, one in Port Royal for repairs, and another had a gun injured. Dahlgren to Gillmore, 22 August 1863, Dahlgren Letters, LCM; Dahlgren to Welles, 22 August 1863, *ORN*, ser. 1, 14:470.

87. Dahlgren to Welles, 6, 11 August 1863, *ORN*, ser. 1, 14:428, 435–36; Dahlgren, Order No. 33, 25 August 1863, Orders to the South Atlantic Blockading Squadron, 1863–1865, HSP; Dahlgren, Order No. 34, 26 August 1863, *ORN*, ser. 1, 14:516; Dahlgren to Gillmore, 26 August 1863, Dahlgren Papers, LCM.

88. Dahlgren, Diary, 26 August 1863, Dahlgren Papers, Syracuse; Dahlgren, Order No. 34, 26 August 1863, Orders to the South Atlantic Blockading Squadron, 1863–1865, HSP.

89. There appears that at least one 11-inch Dahlgren or a rifle-banded 42-pounder remained operable in the fort. Wise, *Gate of Hell*, 188; Johnson, *Defense of Charleston*, 120–32; On page XXVII, in Johnson's appendix, he claims there were no guns left by the 1st. Dahlgren, *Memoirs*, 28, 29 August 1863, 411–12; Dahlgren to Gillmore, 29 August 1863, *ORN*, ser. 1, 14:524–25; Gillmore to Dahlgren, 29 August 1863, ibid., 524–25; Report of Rhett, 30 August 1863, *ORA*, ser. 1, vol. 28, pt. 1, 618–19.

90. Log of *Passaic*, 31 August 1863, Entry 118, RG 24, NA; Abstract Logs of *Montauk* et al., 31 August 1863, *ORN*, ser. 1, 14:562–64.

91. Dahlgren, Diary, 1 September 1863, Dahlgren Papers, Syracuse.

92. Dahlgren, Order No. 38, 1 September 1863, Orders to the South Atlantic Blockading Squadron, 1863–1865, HSP; Johnson, *Defense of Charleston*, 129; De Treville to Nance, 1 September 1863, *ORN*, ser. 1, 14:569; Dahlgren to Welles, 2 September 1863, ibid., 531–33; Dahlgren to Welles, 28 January 1864, Dahlgren Papers, LCM; Log of *Passaic*, 1 September, 1863, Entry 118, RG 24, NA.

93. Dahlgren to Welles, 2 September 1863, *ORN*, ser. 1, 14:531–33; Dahlgren, *Memoirs*, 1–2 September 1863, 412; Abstract Log of *New Ironsides*, et al., 2 September 1863, *ORN*, ser. 1, 14:559–passim.

94. Johnson, *Defense of Charleston*, xxvii, 141–42; Gordon, *War Diary*, 206.

95. Wise, *Gate of Hell*, 193–94; Dahlgren to Gillmore, 4 September 1863, *ORN*, ser. 1, 14:536; Dahlgren to Reynolds, 4 September 1863, ibid., 537; Gillmore to Dahlgren, 4 September 1863, ibid., 537; Dahlgren to Williams, 4 September 1863, ibid., 537.

96. W. W. H. Davis, "The Siege of Morris Island," 101; Dahlgren, *Memoirs*, 2–3 September 1863, 412.

97. Jones, *Siege of Charleston*, 268; Abstract Log *New Ironsides*, 5 September 1863, *ORN*, ser. 1, 14:559; Gillmore, "Army Before Charleston," 225.

98. William Elliot Furness, "Siege of Fort Wagner," *Military Essays and Recollections: Papers Read Before the Commandry of the State of Illinois, Military Order of the Loyal Legion of the United States* (Chicago: A. C. McClury and Company, 1891) 225; Florance, "Morris Island: Victory of Blunder," *The South Carolina Historical Magazine* 55 (July 1954), 149–50; Jones, *The Siege of Charleston*, 268; Johnson, *Defense of Charleston*, 149.

99. The steering gear of the *Passaic*, however, was disabled and only the *Weehawken* and the *Montauk* could operate against Battery Gregg. Keitt to Nance, 5 September 1863, *ORN*, ser. 1, 14:570–71; Dahlgren, Orders No. 42, 43, 44, 6 September 1863, Orders to the South Atlantic Blockading Squadron, 1863–1865, HSP; Dahlgren to Gillmore, 6 September 1863, *ORN*, ser. 1, 14:-546; Dahlgren Circular, 6 September 1863, Dahlgren Papers, LCM.

100. Ammen, *The Atlantic Coast*, 134; Johnson, *Defense of Charleston*, 143; Keitt to Nance, 6 September 1863, *ORA*, ser. 1, vol. 28, pt. 1, 482–88.

101. Harleston, "Battery Wagner on Morris Island," 13.

102. Gillmore to Dahlgren, 7 September 1863, *ORN*, ser. 1, 14:548; Dahlgren to Welles, 28 January 1864, Dahlgren Papers, LCM.

103. Dahlgren to W. W. H. Davis, 28 October 1869, Dahlgren Papers, LCM; Dahlgren to Welles, 16 October 1865, ibid.; Dahlgren, *Memoirs*, 545–46.

104. Dahlgren was critical of Gillmore. He maintained that if a sufficient number of men had initially assaulted Battery Wagner on 11 July, that forts Greg and Sumter would have fallen as a "matter of course." This would have allowed the ironclads to attack into the harbor against imperfect defenses instead of receiving two months of battering. Dahlgren to Welles, 28 January 1864, Dahlgren Papers, LCM; Dahlgren to Welles, 18 October 1863, ibid.; Report of the Firing by USS *New Ironsides* Quarter ending 30 September 1863, ibid.; Opinion of John Rodgers given before the Committee of the United States Senate, 3 February 1864, as cited in Johnson, *Defense of Charleston*, Appendix F, clii–cliii.

Chapter 9

1. Roman, *Beauregard*, 2:150, 155; Dahlgren to Gillmore, 7 September 1863, *ORN*, ser. 1, 14:548; Dahlgren, *Memoirs*, 7 September 1863, 413.

2. Dahlgren to Welles, 8 September 1863, *ORN*, ser. 1, 14:549; Colhoun to Dahlgren, 9 September 1863, ibid., 550.

3. The *Passaic* did not take part in the bombardment of the forts because she was hampered by a debilitating injury to her turret shaft that brought her pilothouse along with the turret when it turned. Dahlgren Order No. 45, 7 September 1863, Orders to the South Atlantic Blockading Squadron, 1863–1865, HSP; Abstract Logs of *New Ironsides*, *Passaic* et al., 7 September 1863, *ORN*, ser. 1, 14:559–66; Simpson to Dahlgren, 10 September 1863, ibid., 556–57.

4. Elliott to Nance, 8 September 1863, *ORA*, ser. 1, vol. 28, pt. 1, 716; Colhoun to Dahlgren, 9 September 1863, *ORN*, ser. 1, 14:550–51; Butler to White,

12 September 1863, ibid., 577; Staff Journal B, 8 September 1863, Dahlgren Papers, LCM.

5. Dahlgren did not arrive until that afternoon, having spent the day arranging with Gillmore an assault on Fort Sumter. 8 September 1863, Dahlgren, *Diary*, 413–14; Butler to White, 12 September 1863, ORN, ser. 1, 14:577; Rowan to Dahlgren, 10 September 1863, Rowan Papers, LCM; Log of *New Ironsides*, 7 September 1863, Entry 118, RG 24, NA; Belknap, "Reminiscent of the New Ironsides off Charleston," 77–78; Robeson to Rowan, 8 September 1863, ORN, ser. 1, 14:554.

6. Butler to White, 12 September 1863, ORN, ser. 1, 14:577–78; Abstract Logs of *Passaic* et al., 8 September 1863, ibid., 561–66; Simpson to Dahlgren, 10 September 1863, ibid., 556–57; Simpson, "The Monitor Passaic," 415, 418.

7. The distances given by the Confederates range between nine hundred and fourteen hundred yards. Butler to White, ORN, ser. 1, 14:377–78; Cowley, *Leaves*, 106.

8. The distance from Fort Moultrie given by the Union ironclad commanders is substantially less than that given by Confederate sources. Abstract Logs of *Passaic* et al., 8 September 1863, ORN, ser. 1, 14:561–66; Dahlgren, *Memoirs*, 8 September 1863, 413; Hunter, "A Year on a Monitor," 128–29; Log of *Patapsco*, 8 September 1863, Entry 118, RG 24, NA; Dahlgren to Welles, 12 October 1864, ORN, ser. 1, 16:13; Stevens to Dahlgren, 23 September 1863, ORN, ser. 1, 14:665–67.

9. It was estimated that it would take about eighteen days to repair the damage to *Weehawken*. Hughes to Stimers, Sept. (n.d.) 1863, Entry 186, RG 19, NA; Johnson, *Defense of Charleston*, 158.

10. The words relating Dahlgren's insistence on naval command of the expedition was omitted from the ORN, ser. 1, 14:608 citation. The watchword was "Detroit," Dahlgren to Stevens, 8 September 1863, ibid., 610; Dahlgren to Gillmore, 8 September 1863, ORA, ser. 1, vol. 28, pt. 1, 88; Remey to Preston, 8 September 1863, ORN, ser. 1, 14:607; Gillmore to Dahlgren, 8 September 1863, ibid., 608.

11. Gillmore to Dahlgren, 8 September 1863, ORN, ser. 1, 14:608–609, 608n; Staff Journal, September 8–9 1863, Mortimer L. Johnson, ibid., 611–12.

12. Stevens, "The Boat Attack on Sumter," *Battles and Leaders*, 4:49; Staff Journal, September 8–9 1863, Mortimer L. Johnson, ORN, ser. 1, 14:611–12.

13. Staff Journal, September 8–9 1863, Mortimer L. Johnson, ORN, ser. 1, 14:611–12; Dahlgren to Gillmore, 8 September 1863, ibid., 609.

14. Stevens, "The Boat Attack on Sumter," *Battles and Leaders*, 4:49.

15. Beauregard to Seddon, 13 April 1863, ORN, ser. 1, 14:689; Ripley to Jordan, 10 April 1863, ORA, ser. 1, 14:893; Scharf, *Confederate Navy*, 699–700; Olmstead, "Reminiscences of Service in Charleston Harbor," 161.

16. Johnson, *Defense of Charleston*, 160; Roman, *Beauregard*, 2:155; Alfred P. Rockwell, "The Operations Against Charleston," *Publications of the*

Military History Society of Massachusetts 14 vols. (Boston: The Society, 1895–1918) 9:184.

17. Dahlgren to Welles, 11 September 1863, *ORN*, ser. 1, 14:610–11; Jones, *Siege of Charleston*, 281–84; Williams to Welles, 27 September 1863, *ORN*, ser. 1, 14:628; Dahlgren to Rowan, 8 September 1863, ibid., 609; Stevens to Emmons, 21 September 1863, ibid., 626.

18. Stevens, "The Boat Attack on Sumter," 49; Williams to Welles, 27 September 1863, *ORN*, ser. 1, 14:628.

19. Ibid., 628–29; Butler, "Personal Experiences in the Navy," 195.

20. Williams to Welles, 27 September 1863, *ORN*, ser. 1, 14:628–29; Higginson to Dahlgren, 21 September 1863, ibid., 618; Artha Brailsford Westcoat, *Diary*, Entry for 8 September 1863, DUM.

21. This flag was also reportedly raised at the ceremony at the fort after the fall of Charleston. The casualty and POW figures vary slightly between the sources. Elliott to Nance, 9, 12 September 1863, *ORN*, ser. 1, 14:636–39; Beauregard to Bonham, 12 September 1863, ibid., 639–40; Forrest to Stevens, 10 August 1865, ibid., 634.

22. Dahlgren claims that tide delayed the army forces. Dahlgren to Wade, 20 June 1864, Dahlgren Papers, LCM; Jones, *Siege of Charleston*, 282–84; Stevens to Welles, 28 September 1863, *ORN*, ser. 1, 14:633; Wise, *Gate of Hell*, 207.

23. Forrest to Stevens, 10 August 1865, *ORN*, ser. 1, 14:634; Dahlgren, *Memoirs*, 12 September 1863, 414; Gillmore, "The Army Before Charleston," 4:62.

24. In order to collect information to refute charges by Du Pont, Welles had requested a report from the commanding officers of the monitors regarding the number of shots and damage by enemy fire, the number of rounds fired, and the effect of this on the officers and men. Welles to Dahlgren, 11 September 1863, *ORN*, ser. 1, 14:642–43; Dahlgren to Welles, 18 September 1863, Dahlgren Papers, LCM; Giraud to Davis, 18 September 1863, *ORN*, ser. 1, 14:653–54.

25. Fox to Stimers, 24, 25 April 1863, Fox Papers, NYHS.

26. Stimers to Fox, 4 June 1863, ibid.; Stimers to Gregory, 30 September 1863, Entry 186, RG 19, NA; Du Pont to Welles, 15 May 1863, *ORN*, ser. 1, 14:195–96; Gregory to Du Pont, 6 April 1863, Entry 1235, RG 19, NA; Hughes to Stimers, 27 June 1863, Entry 186, RG 19, NA.

27. Dahlgren to Welles, 22 July 1863, *ORN*, ser. 1, 14:382.

28. Clay was later substituted for lead. Hughes to Stimers, 17 September 1863, Entry 186, RG 19, NA; Simpson, "The Monitor Passaic," 422; Dana Wegner, "Port Royal Working Parties," *Civil War Times Illustrated* 15 (December 1976) 26–27; Simpson to Dahlgren, 28 September 1863, *ORN*, ser. 1, 14:685; Griffin to Stimers, 6 February 1864, Journal of Thomas Jefferson Griffin, Volume II, (n.d.), Charles Gideon Dale Collection, American Swedish Historical Museum, hereinafter cited as Griffin Journal, ASHM.

29. Hughes to Stimers, 13, 15 August, 2 October 1863, Entry 186, RG 19, NA; Reynolds to Dahlgren, September (n.d.) 1863, Repair, AR, RG 45, NA.

30. Griffin later received more workmen for his crew. Stimers to Gregory, 21 November 1863, Enclosure Gregory to Lenthall, 22 November 1863, Letters Received by Superintendents Outside of Navy Yards, Entry 64, RG 19, NA; Thomas Griffin Journal passim, ASHM; Reynolds to Dahlgren, 23 December 1863, Reynolds Correspondence, Entry 395, RG 45, NA.

31. Griffin to Stimers, October (n.d.) 1863, 6 January 1864, Entry 186, RG 19, NA; Griffin to Stimers, 16 February 1864, Griffin Journal, Dale Collection, ASHM.

32. Griffin to Stimers, 30 December 1863, Entry 186, RG 19, NA; Memorandum for Consideration, 9 May 1864, Dahlgren Papers, LCM; Dahlgren to Johnson, 24 August 1864, ibid.

33. Griffin Journal, (n.d.), Dale Collection, ASHM; Dahlgren to Welles, 4 November 1963, ibid.; Dahlgren Diary, 18 October 1864, Dahlgren Papers, Syracuse; Reynolds to Dahlgren, 22 October 1863, Reynolds Correspondence, Entry 395, RG 45, NA; Beaumont to Dahlgren, 21 September 1863, John C. Beaumont Correspondence, Entry 395, RG 45, NA.

34. Reynolds to Oliver, 22 May 1864, Entry 186, RG 19, NA; Endorsed by Gregory, 24 May 1864, ibid.; *American* (Baltimore), 29 December 1863, clipping in Dahlgren Papers, LCM.

35. Lanier to Du Pont, 11 November 1861, *ORN*, ser. 1, 12:340; Parrott to Du Pont, 4 March 1862, ibid., 620.

36. Du Pont to Marchand, 24 July 1862, *ORN*, ser. 1, 14:207; Reynolds to Dahlgren, 10 January 1864, Reynolds Correspondence, Entry 395, RG 45, NA.

37. Reynolds to Dahlgren, 28, 29 July 1863, 12 August, 20 October 1864, Reynolds Correspondence, Entry 395, RG 45, NA.

38. Reynolds to Dahlgren, 10 January, 22, 23 October 1864, Reynolds Correspondence, Entry 395, RG 45, NA; Dahlgren to Welles, 7 August 1863, 26 January 1864, Dahlgren Papers, LCM; Dahlgren to A. N. Smith, 4, 31 August 1864, Dahlgren Papers, LCM; Belknap, "Reminiscent of the *New Ironsides* off Charleston," 64; Dahlgren to Welles, 5 August 1863, *ORN*, ser. 1, 14:419; Rowan to Dahlgren, 1 June 1864, Rowan Papers, LCM.

39. The ordnance hulks for the Charleston station were also kept in the Stono River. Green to Thompson, 1 December 1864, Joseph F. Green Journals, Port Columbus Civil War Naval Center, Columbus, Georgia, hereinafter cited as Port Columbus; Green to Johnson, 13, 17 August 1864, ibid; Green to Dahlgren, 25 August 1864, ibid; Green to DeCamp, 31 August, 12 September 1864, ibid; Green to Patterson, 19 September 1864, ibid.

40. Marchand, *Charleston Blockade*, entry for 24 April 1862, 148; Du Pont to Lardner, 19 April 1862, Du Pont, *Letters*, 2:13; Godon to Welles, 3 October 1862, *ORN*, ser. 1, 13:373–74; Reynolds to Dahlgren, 16 November

1863, Reynolds Correspondence, Entry 395, RG 45, NA; Nicholson to Rodgers, 17 June 1862, *ORN*, ser. 1, 13:109; Breese to Dahlgren, 13 December 1863, Dahlgren Papers, LCM.

41. Dahlgren to A. N. Smith, 28 August 1863, 20 February 1864, 23, 31 August 1864, Dahlgren Papers, LCM; Du Pont to Lenthall, 13 April 1862, Du Pont Papers, Hagley; Du Pont to Lenthall, 1 September 1862, Entry 62, RG 19, NA; Du Pont to Fox, 10 February 1862, Fox Papers, NYHS; Reynolds to Dahlgren, 11 August 1863, *ORN*, ser. 1, 14:437.

42. Dahlgren to Welles, 23 September 1863, *Armored Vessels*, 243; Dahlgren to Fox, 24 September 1863, *ORN*, ser. 1, 14:672; Drayton to Henry A. Wise, 6 September 1863, Wise Papers, NYHS; *Army and Navy Journal*, 5 September 1863.

43. Dahlgren to Welles, 23 September, *ORN*, ser. 1, 14:659–660.

44. Dahlgren to Fox, 24 September 1863, ibid., 672.

45. Dahlgren to Welles, 10 September 1863, Dahlgren Papers, LCM; Dahlgren to Welles, 5 September 1863, *ORN*, ser. 1, 14:582; Welles to Dahlgren, 12, 16 September 1863, *ORN*, ser. 1, 14:644, 649; Welles to Gregory, 16 September 1863, *ORN*, ser. 1, 14:649.

46. Ammen, *The Atlantic Coast*, 160; Ammen, *The Old Navy and the New*, 375–76; Reynolds to Dahlgren, 16 September 1863, *ORN*, ser. 1, 14:649–50; Green to Dahlgren, 23 September 1864, Green Journals.

47. Dahlgren to Welles, 10 October 1863, *ORN*, ser. 1, 15:30.

48. Ericsson to Aldersparre, 6 March 1868, Ericsson Papers, ASHM; In Church's biography of Ericsson, he claims the shells held 100 pounds of powder, 2:50; Dahlgren, *Memoirs*, 6 November 1863, 423–24; Griffin to Dahlgren, 7 November 1863, Griffin Journal, Dale Collection, ASHM; Stevens to Dahlgren, *ORN*, ser. 1, 15:102; Griffin to Stimers, 17 October 1863, Entry 186, RG 19, NA.

49. Dahlgren had asked Gillmore to fire on enemy vessels in the vicinity of the obstructions to prevent them from being repaired. Dahlgren to Gillmore, 17, 25 September 1863, Dahlgren Papers, LCM; Gillmore to Dahlgren, 27 September 1863, *ORN*, ser. 1, 14:674–75; Ericsson to Fox, 13 September, 3 October 1863, Ericsson Papers, ASHM; Ericsson to Aldersparre, 6 March 1868, ibid.

50. Dahlgren, *Memoirs*, 27 September 1863, 416.

51. Dahlgren to Gillmore, 29 September 1863, Dahlgren Papers, LCM; Dahlgren to Ulric, 22 September 1863, ibid.

52. Gillmore to Dahlgren, 30 September 1863, *ORN*, ser. 1, 14:684.

53. Dahlgren to Welles, 29 September 1863, ibid., 680–81.

54. Dahlgren, Diary, 11 August 1863–passim, Dahlgren Papers, Syracuse; Dahlgren to Ulric, 22 September 1863, Dahlgren Papers, LCM; John Hay Diary, entry for 20 October 1863, 21 January 1864, *The Letters of John Hay*, 103–104, 156.

55. Dahlgren to Wise, 22 September 1863, Wise Papers, NYHS; Dahlgren to Welles, 2 October 1863, *ORN*, ser. 1, 15:4; Welles talked with Commander Robert W. Shufeldt between 3 and 5 October. Shufeldt believed that the city could not be taken with the force at hand. Welles, *Diary*, 3 October 1863, 1:466–67; Welles to Dahlgren, 9 October 1863, *ORN*, ser. 1, 15:26–27.

56. There is no clear documentation on the number of torpedoes at this time. By 1865 they were in many places throughout the harbor. Jordan to Tucker, 3 September 1863, *ORN*, ser. 1, 14:766; Von Scheliah, *Coast Defense*, Plate Number 1.

57. Glassell, "Reminiscences of Torpedo Service," 226.

58. Ibid., 227; "Memoirs of Chief Engineer James H. Tomb, CSN," Southern Historical Collection, Chapel Hill S.C.; Tomb, "Submarines and Torpedo Boats, C.S.N.," *Confederate Veteran* 22 (1914), 168.

59. Tomb claims in one source the torpedo carried 100 pounds of powder. Herbert R. Sass, "The Story of the Little David," *Harper's Magazine* 186 (May 1943): 621–22; W. T. Glassell, "Reminiscences of Torpedo Service in Charleston Harbor," *Southern Historical Society Papers* 5 (November 1877): 229–30; Tomb, "Submarines and Torpedo Boats," 168–69; Tucker to Glassell, 18, 22 September 1863, *ORN*, ser. 1, 15:12.

60. Glassell, "Reminiscences of Torpedo Service," 230–31; *Charleston Daily Courier*, 7 October 1863; "Memoirs of Chief Engineer James H. Tomb, C.S.N.," James Hamilton Tomb Papers, SHC.

61. Glassell, "Reminiscences of Torpedo Service," 231.

62. Ibid. Howard died several days after the attack and was promoted to Acting Master posthumously. Belknap, "Reminiscent of the New Ironsides off Charleston," 82.

63. Glassell, "Reminiscences of Torpedo Service," 232; Tomb to Tucker, 6 October 1863, *ORN*, ser. 1, 15:20–21; Belknap, "Reminiscent of the Siege of Charleston," 191.

64. Belknap, "Reminiscent of the Siege of Charleston," 191; Rowan to Dahlgren, 6 October 1863, Rowan Papers, LCM; James Lachlison, "Daring Deed in Saving the *David* C. S. Navy," *Confederate Veteran* 16 (February 1908): 78; "Memoirs of Chief Engineer James H. Tomb, C.S.N.," Tomb Papers, SHC; Tomb to Tucker, 6 October 1863, *ORN*, ser. 1, 15:21.

65. Tomb to Tucker, *ORN*, ser. 1, 15:21; Rowan to Dahlgren, 6 October 1863, Rowan Papers, LCM; Bishop to Rowan, 24 November 1863, ibid.

66. Dahlgren to Smith, 21 November 1864, Dahlgren Papers, LCM; Du Pont to Sophie, 18 March 1864, Du Pont, *Letters*, 2: 493; Du Pont to Gerhard, 19 February 1863, ibid., 2: 445–46; Du Pont to Welles, 16 April 1863, 21 May 1863, *ORN*, ser. 1, 14:139–40, 209; Du Pont to Turner, 31 January 1863, ibid., 13:623.

67. The torpedo guard for a monitor required six thousand feet of wire. Simpson to Dahlgren, 11 January 1864, Entry 189, RG 19, NA; Belknap, "Reminiscent of the Siege of Charleston," 198; Glassell, "Reminiscences of Torpedo

Service," 233; Dahlgren Order No. 51, 6 October 1863, Dahlgren Papers, LCM; Dahlgren Order No. 52, 22 October 1863, Orders to the South Atlantic Blockading Squadron, 1863–1865, HSP.

68. Dahlgren to Fox, 7 October 1863, Dahlgren Papers, LCM; Dahlgren to Welles, 9 October 1863, *ORN*, ser. 1, 15:28–29; Phinney to Rowan, 8 October 1863, ibid., 29; Phinney to Dahlgren, ibid., Dean to Dahlgren, 10 October 1863, ibid., 30; Cilley to Dahlgren, 24 October 1863, ibid., 72.

69. Reynolds to Dahlgren, 22 December 1863, Reynolds Correspondence, Entry 395, RG 45, NA; Reynolds to Harrison, 19 March 1864, ibid.; Reynolds to DeCamp, 24 April 1864, ibid.; Reynolds to Rowan, 27 April 1864, ibid.

70. Dahlgren to Welles, 10 October 1863, *ORN*, ser. 1, 15:31–32; Drayton to Wise, [September] 1863 and 21 October 1863, Wise Papers, NYHS.

71. Dahlgren to Welles, 17 October 1863, Dahlgren Papers, LCM; Dahlgren to Gillmore, 18 October 1863, ibid.; Dahlgren, *Memoirs*, 15 October 1863, 418; Gillmore to Dahlgren, 17 October 1863, *ORN*, ser. 1, 15:49.

72. Dahlgren to Welles, 17, 18 October 1863, Dahlgren Papers, LCM.

73. Ibid.

74. "Gen. Gillmore and Admiral Dahlgren," *Army and Navy Journal*, 31 October 1863; Dahlgren to Ulric, 22 September 1863, Dahlgren Papers, LCM; Dahlgren to Welles, 20 October 1863, *ORN*, ser. 1, 15:63.

75. Welles, *Diary*, 24 October 1863, 1: 474–75.

76. Welles, *Diary*, entries for 1, 24 October 1863; Unsigned document, 22 October 1863, Dahlgren Papers, LCM; Belknap, "Reminiscent of the Siege of Charleston," 193.

77. Unsigned document, 22 October 1863, Dahlgren Papers, LCM.

78. Extract of Journal of Operations, 26 October 1863, *ORA*, ser. 1, vol. 28, pt. 1, 149; Johnson, *Defense of Charleston*, 170–71; Dahlgren, *Memoirs*, 26 October 1863, 420.

79. Dahlgren, *Memoirs*, 25 October 1863, 420; Gillmore, "The Army Before Charleston," *Battles and Leaders*, 4: 67.

80. Stevens to Dahlgren, 2 November 1863, *ORN*, ser. 1, 15:76–77; Diary of Stephen Elliott Jr., 26 October 1863, *ORA*, ser. 1, vol. 28, pt. 1, 630; Bunce to Stevens, 2 November 1863, *ORN*, ser. 1, 15:78.

81. Dahlgren to Rowan, 26 October 1863, *ORN*, ser. 1, 15:76; Stevens to Dahlgren, 2 November 1863, ibid., 76–77; Bunce to Stevens, 2 November 1863, ibid., 78; Diary of Elliot, 27–28 October, 1863, *ORA*, ser. 1, vol. 28, pt. 1, 630; Bryson to Dahlgren, 4 November 1863, *ORN*, ser. 1, 15:81–82.

82. Dahlgren to Welles, 4 November 1863, *ORN*, ser. 1, 15:79–80; Diary of Elliot, 31 October 1863, *ORA*, ser. 1, vol. 28, pt. 1, 632; Bunce to Stevens, 2 November 1863, *ORN*, ser. 1, 15:78–passim; Dahlgren, *Memoirs*, 5 November 1863, 423.

83. The *Pawnee* had been damaged by floating mines just three months previous. Balch to Dahlgren, 16 August 1863, *ORN*, ser. 1, 14:445; Welles to Dahl-

gren, 2 November 1863, *ORN*, ser. 1, 15:96–97; Dahlgren, *Memoirs*, 8 November 1863, 424.

84. Dahlgren to Welles, 15 November 1863, Dahlgren Papers, LCM; Dahlgren, *Memoirs*, 11 November 1863, 424.

85. Welles to Dahlgren, 2 November 1863, Dahlgren Papers, LCM; Farenholt, "The Monitor Catskill," 391.

86. Dahlgren to Welles, 15 November 1863, *ORN*, ser. 1, 15:114; Dahlgren to Welles, 17 November 1863, ibid., 117; Jones, *Siege of Charleston*, 293; Bryson to Dahlgren, 17 November 1863, *ORN*, ser.1, 15:119; Valentine to Edgerton, 17 November 1863, *ORA*, ser. 1, vol. 28, pt. 1, 741; Extract of Journal of Operations, 16 November 1863, *ORN*, ser. 1, 15:124.

87. Bryson to Dahlgren, 17 November 1863, *ORN*, ser. 1, 15:119; Abstract Log *Passaic*, 16 November 1863, ibid., 122; Dahlgren, *Memoirs*, 16 November 1863, 425; Hunter, *A Year on A Monitor*, 162–63; Belknap, "Reminiscent of the Siege of Charleston," 194; Log of *New Ironsides*, 16 November 1863, Entry 118, RG 24, NA.

88. Dahlgren writes that chafing caused the line to break twice and a shell cut it the third time. The landsmen were Frank S. Gile and William Williams, and the seaman Horatio N. Young. These three along with Leland and Irving were given the Congressional Medal of Honor for their actions. Assistant Surgeon Longshaw was given the privilege of an examination as soon as his two years of sea service were completed and if he passed he would be made passed assistant surgeon without reference to others of his date or class. Acting Ensign Richard Burke was also promoted to acting master. Abstract Log of *Nahant*, 16 November 1863, *ORN*, ser. 1, 15:121; Dahlgren General Order, 17 November 1863, ibid., 120; *Record of Medals of Honor*, 41, 56, 66, 122, 124.

89. Extract of Journal of Operations, 16 November 1863, *ORN*, ser. 1, 15:124; Valentine to Edgerton, 17 November 1863, ibid., 127; Hughes to Dahlgren, 29 November 1863, ibid., 145–46; Hughes to Stimers, 27 November 1863, Entry 186, RG 19, NA.

90. Dahlgren, *Memoirs*, 20 November 1864, 427; Terry to Gillmore, 20 November 1864, *ORA*, ser. 1, vol. 28, pt. 1, 606.

91. President Lincoln even censured the general for his leaks. Du Pont to Grimes, 11 September 1863, Du Pont, *Letters*, 3: 235–36; Lincoln to Stanton, 21 December 1863, Basler, *The Collected Works of Abraham Lincoln*, 7:84.

92. Dahlgren to Welles, 30 November 1863, Dahlgren Papers, LCM; Harris to Reynolds, 28 November 1863, *ORN*, ser. 1, 15:138.

93. Edmund Colhoun, the captain of *Weehawken*, went north due to sickness only two days before the accident. Dahlgren believed that the sinking may have been caused by the clogging of the apertures that allowed the water to flow aft to the pumps. Dahlgren, Memorandum 2 January 1864, *ORN*, ser. 1, 15:168–69; Ammen, *The Atlantic Coast*, 144–45; Ericsson to Welles, 12 December 1863, *ORN*, ser. 1, 15:166–67; Abstract Logs of *New Ironsides*, *Pat-*

apsco, Montauk, 6 December 1863, ibid., 169–70; Dahlgren, *Memoirs,* 4 December 1863, 429.

94. Edward Manigault, *Siege Train: The Journal of a Confederate Artilleryman in the Defense of Charleston,* ed. Warren Ripley (Columbia: University of South Carolina Press, 1986), Diary entry for 25 December 1863, 101–102.

95. Four enlisted men on *Marblehead* earned the Medal of Honor for their efforts in this battle. Robert Blake was one of these men. He was the first African American to earn the Medal of Honor. *Roll of Honor,* 8, 35, 73, 75; Balch to Dahlgren, 25 December 1863, *ORN,* ser. 1, 15:188–90; Freeman to Balch, 27 December 1863, ibid., 193–94; George Gordon to Turner, 31 December 1863, Scott to Balch, 15 February 1864, Balch Papers, SHC; R. R. Page to Pearce, 27 December 1863, *ORN,* ser. 1, 15:206–207; Meade to Balch, 28 December 1863, ibid., 194–96; Meade to Dahlgren, 25 December 1863, ibid., 190–91; Report of B. H. Kidder, 25 December 1863, ibid., 191; Meade to Dahlgren, 26 December 1863, ibid., 192; List of Casualties, 25 December 1863, ibid., 205.

96. This number represents the aggregate present. The total was over 40,000. Gillmore to Halleck, 17 December 1863, *ORA,* ser. 1, vol. 28, pt. 2, 130; Gillmore to Halleck, 15 December 1863, ibid., 129; Abstract of Return of the Department of the South, October 1863, December 1863, ibid., 116, 136; Halleck to Gillmore, 22 December 1863, ibid., 134.

97. Dahlgren to Welles, 28 November, 21 December 1863, *ORN,* ser. 1 , 15:139, 185; Maillefert to Dahlgren, 27 November 1863, ibid., 140; Cornwell to Dahlgren, 29 December 1863, ibid., 210–11; Griffin to Stimers, 3 December 1863, Entry 186, RG 19, NA.

98. Johnson, *Defense of Charleston Harbor,* 184–85, 280; Dahlgren to Welles, 29 December 1863, *ORN,* ser. 1, 15:213; "Reasons for not taking Charleston with the Naval Force Present from Sept 8 1863 to 1864," Dahlgren Papers, LCM; Dahlgren, *Memoirs,* 15, 31 December 1863, 431, 433.

Chapter 10

1. Dahlgren did not fully understand the delays and logistical problems related to repairs of the ironclads. Dahlgren, *Memoirs,* 1 January 1864, 434; Dahlgren to Fox, 30 January 1864, Fox Papers, NYHS.

2. Dahlgren, Diary, 16, 28 January 1864, Dahlgren Papers, Syracuse; Dahlgren, Notes circa January 1864, Dahlgren Papers, LCM.

3. Welles to Dahlgren, 12 January 1864, Cabinet Members' Letters, Lincoln Museum, Fort Wayne, Indiana; Fox to Dahlgren, 12 January 1864, Fox Papers, NYHS; Schneller, *A Quest for Glory,* 295; Dahlgren to Welles, 28 January 1864, *Armored Vessels,* 579–88; Dahlgren, *Memoirs,* 30 January 1864, 438.

4. Fox to Dahlgren, 12 January 1864, Fox Papers, NYHS; Ericsson had suggested that a 13-inch gun be placed in a monitor that could fire into

Charleston from the mouth of the harbor. Ericsson to Fox, 3 October 1863, Ericsson Papers, ASHM.

5. Welles to Dahlgren, 11 January 1864, *ORN*, ser. 1, 15:236–37; Dahlgren to Fox, 22 January 1865, Dahlgren Papers, LCM; Dahlgren to Welles, 22 January 1864, ibid.; Dahlgren to Ulric, 20 February 1864, Dahlgren Papers, Newberry Library.

6. Dahlgren to Lincoln, 23 January 1864, Dahlgren Papers, LCM.

7. Dahlgren to Gillmore 28 January 1864, Gillmore Papers, Entry 159, RG 94, NA; Dahlgren to Fox, 30 January 1864, Fox Papers, NYHS; Dahlgren, *Diary*, 2 February 1864, Dahlgren Papers, Syracuse.

8. The *American Diver* was built in Mobile, Alabama, and was never made operational as there were flaws in the design. Mortimer Johnson to Dahlgren, 1 January, 1 February 1864, *ORN*, ser. 1, 15:218–29; Dahlgren to Welles, 7 January 1864, *ORN*, ser. 1, 15:225–26; ibid., 13 January 1864, Dahlgren Papers, LCM; A. E. Johnson to Dahlgren, 1 February 1864, ibid., LCM; Information obtained by Deserters, 7–8 January 1864, *ORN*, ser. 1, 15:227–33; Dahlgren to Gillmore, 3 February 1864, Dahlgren Papers, LCM.

9. Wise, *Lifeline*, 251–57.

10. Marcus W. Price, "Ships That Tested the Blockade of the Carolina Ports, 1861–1865," *American Neptune* 8 (July 1948):199. A ton was equal to about forty cubic feet. John Lyman, "Register Tonnage and Its Measurement," *American Neptune* 5 (July 1945):227.

11. Thomas E. Taylor, *Running the Blockade: A Personal Narrative of Risks and Escapes During the American Civil War* (London: Murray, 1912) 17, 29, 33–34, 40–41, 48, 50; Augustus Charles Hobart-Hampton (Roberts), *Never Caught: Personal Adventures Connected with Twelve Successful Trips in Blockade-Running during the American Civil War, 1863–1864* (London: John Camden Holton, 1867), 2–3; John Jay Almy, "Incidents of the Blockade," *Military Order of the Loyal Legion of the United States Commandry of the District of Columbia, War Papers* 9 (Washington, D.C.: Companion, 1892),4; Emma Martin Maffitt, *The Life and Services of John Newland Maffitt* (New York: Neale, 1906), 230.

12. Coast Chart No. 53, 1866, RG 23, NA; Du Pont was severely criticized for his decision not to move the ironclads inside the bar. His decision, however, was based on the advice of his ironclad captains. Dahlgren at first was also somewhat hesitant to leave these vessels so near the shore. Rowan, though, convinced the admiral that the ironclad captains would be the "best judges of how long they can safely remain." *Report of the Secretary of the Navy 1864*, XI; Rowan to Rodgers, 20 July 1863, *ORN*, ser. 1, 14:377–78.

13. Pickering to Green, 30 August 1863, Joseph Green Papers, LCM.

14. John Rodgers, et al to Du Pont, 25 May 1863, Du Pont Papers, Hagley; Du Pont, Hayes, 23n; Dahlgren to Smith, 21 November 1864, Dahlgren Papers, LCM; Observations on the Operations Against Morris Island, July and August 1863, ibid.

15. Dahlgren, Orders 12 July 1863, 22 July 1863, *ORN*, ser. 1, 14:338, 384–85; Dahlgren to Fox, 22 July 1863, Fox Papers, NYHS; Dahlgren to Simpson, 27 January 1864, Dahlgren Papers, LCM; Memorandum for the Government of Monitors, Tugs, and Boats on Picket Duty, (n.d.), Green Papers, LCM.

16. Before the monitors blocked the channel, an occasional small sailing vessel still managed to run the blockade. In certain stages of the weather and the moon, they managed to slip out of Charleston unseen. This activity seemed to cease with the closing of the southern route of escape. Small vessels did continue to run out of Savannah and other small inlets throughout 1864. Small entrepreneurs owned most of these vessels. They did realize some success; no one would have risked their capital on a venture that had a one-hundred percent failure rate. Cressy to Welles, 22 May 1863, *ORN*, ser. 1, 14:200; Johnson to Rowan, 9 April 1864, *ORN*, ser. 1, 15:402; Lawrence, *A Present*, 86; *Republican* (Savannah) 23 November, 30 December 1864; Charles Seton Henry Hardee, *Reminiscences and Recollections of Old Savannah* [s. n] Savannah: 1928; *The Morning News* (Savannah) 21 February 1897; Ammen to Dahlgren, 28 July 1863, Dahlgren Papers, LCM; Observations on the Operations against Morris Island, July and August 1863, ibid.; Distribution of vessels of the South Atlantic Blockading Squadron 16 July 1864–passim, *ORN*, ser. 1, 15:570–71; Wise, *Lifeline*, 252–53, 256–57.

17. Farenholt, "The Monitor *Catskill*," 389; Hunter, *A Year on A Monitor*, 134; Dahlgren Order No. 65, 3 December 1863, Orders to the South Atlantic Blockading Squadron, 1863–1865, HSP; Belknap, "Reminiscent of the *New Ironsides*," 70.

18. Oscar Farenholt participated in these boat crews and claimed that they went into the inner harbor to the wharves of Charleston. Dahlgren, Order No. 65, 3 December 1863, Order No. 10, 18 January 1864, Orders to the South Atlantic Blockading Squadron, 1863–1865, HSP; Dahlgren to Green, 19 July 1863, *ORN*, ser. 1, 14:373; Green to Dahlgren, 3 August 1863, ibid., 414; Farenholt, "From Ordinary Seaman to Rear Admiral," 376; Butts, "A Cruise Along the Blockade," *Personal Narratives of Events in the War of the Rebellion Being Papers Read Before the Rhode Island Soldiers and Sailors Historical Society* (Providence R.I.: N. Bangs Williams and Co., 1881), 22.

19. Within a couple of weeks of this report a boat from *Nipsic* was captured; this was due to inferior speed. Butts, "A Cruise Along the Blockade," 20–21; Brand, "Reminiscences of the Blockade off Charleston," *War Papers Read Before the commandery of the State of Wisconsin Military Order of the Loyal Legion of the United States*, 4 vols. (Milwaukee, Wisc.: Burdick and Allen, 1891–1903), 3:22; Waite, "The Blockade Service," 243; Dahlgren to Lenthall, 16 January, 23 February 1864, Entry 62, RG 19, NA; Lenthall to Dahlgren, 20 January 1864, Entry 51, RG 19, NA.

20. Green to Dahlgren, 28 July 1863, *ORN*, ser. 1, 14:403; Charles Fairchild to Sarah, 5 August 1863, Charles Fairchild Papers, East Carolina University Manuscript Collection, Greenville, North Carolina.

21. Green to Dahlgren, 20, 23, 28 July, 3 August 1863, Dahlgren Papers, LCM; Reynolds to Dahlgren, 28 September 1863, *ORN*, ser. 1, 14:678–79; Dahlgren to Fox, 24 September 1863, Dahlgren Papers, LCM; Instructions For the Commandant of the Picket Tug *Daffodil*, March (n.d.) 1864, ibid.; Dahlgren to Green, 29 January 1864, ibid.; Rowan to Green, 18 March 1864, ibid.; Admiral's Log, June 1864–passim, ibid.; Green to Rowan, 3 March 1864, *ORN*, ser. 1, 15:348–49; Green to Dahlgren, 23 August 1863, *ORN*, ser. 1, 14:500; Whiting to Green, 23 August 1863, ibid., 500–501; Green to Dahlgren, 25 August 1863, ibid., 501.

22. Dahlgren also relayed fears of English rams thought being built by the Confederates in England. Should one appear at Charleston, Dahlgren instructed Captain Green to pull his vessels from the outside over the bar and with coal and provisions they could wait. All vessels with drafts over sixteen feet, though, would steam to Port Royal, where he expected Reynolds to sink obstructions and cover them with the guns of the fleet to keep the ironclad out. Dahlgren to Green, 15 September 1863, *ORN*, ser. 1, 14:648; Order of Dahlgren, 7 January 1864, *ORN*, ser. 1, 15:226–27; Dahlgren to Fox, 22 January 1864, Fox Papers, NYHS.

23. W. A. Alexander, "Thrilling Chapter in the History of the Confederate States Navy: Work on Submarine Boats," *Southern Historical Society Papers* 30 (1902): 165–66, 170; W. A. Alexander, "The Confederate Submarine Torpedo Boat Hunley," *The Gulf States Historical Magazine* 1 (September 1902), 83, 87.

24. Recent scholarship suggests that the torpedo fit loosely on the spar and had a spike that could be driven into the enemy ship. A line fed from a reel and attached to the torpedo would allow the *Hunley* to back away and detonate the weapon at a safe distance. The primary documents, however, do not support this with certainty. The last person intimately involved with the project who lived was William Alexander. In all his recollections, he clearly speaks only of the spar with a fixed torpedo. If the other arrangement was used, it was placed on the *Hunley* less than two weeks before her fateful sortie. The use of the spike was part of the first proposed arrangement and has confused the issue. It is unlikely that the Confederates would have changed their method of delivery of the warhead after so much practice with the fixed warhead. The drawing of the Singer Torpedo in the Papers of Quincy A. Gillmore, Generals Papers, RG 97, NA shows a contact device. In contemporary illustrations, the Confederate ironclads also used a fixed charge similar to the arrangement found on the *Hunley*. Lastly, the officer in charge of torpedoes in Charleston believed that the *Hunley* went down with the *Housatonic*, not having enough power to back away after the explosion. M. M. Gray to Maury, 29 April 1864, *ORN*, ser. 1, vol. 16, 427; Harry Von Kolnitz, "The Confederate Submarine," *U.S. Naval Institute Proceedings*,

October 1937, 1453–57 is the first to suggest the barb type of arrangement from drawings made available to him. Also see Mark K. Ragan's book *The Hunley: Submarines, Sacrifice, & Success* (Charleston, S.C.: Narwhal Press, 1999), 168; and James E. Kloppel's *Danger Beneath the Waves*, (Orangeburg S.C., Sandlapper Publishing Inc., 1992); 92; Maurey to Johnson, 24 August 1863, *ORA*, ser. 1, vol. 26, pt. 2, 180; Alexander, "Thrilling Chapter," 167.

25. The delay in the detonation can be attributed to the fact that the torpedo had a single detonator and might have required several tries by Dixon and his crew to make a good contact with the *Housatonic*. Also Confederate torpedoes were notoriously faulty. Higginson to Dahlgren, 18 February 1864, *ORN*, ser. 1, 15:328; Churchill to Dahlgren, 27 November 1864, ibid., 334; "Loss of the *Housatonic*," Moore, *Rebellion Record*, 8:391; Butler, "Personal Experiences," 198.

26. Higginson to Dahlgren, 18 February 1864, *ORN*, ser. 1, 15:328; Dantzler to Wilson, 19 February 1864, ibid., 335.

27. The requirement to keep underway required coal in greater quantities. Dahlgren to Ulric, 20 February 1864, Dahlgren Papers, Newberry Library; Dahlgren to Welles, 19 February 1864, *ORN*, ser. 1, 15:329–30; Dahlgren to Wise, 23 February 1864, Dahlgren Papers, LCM; Dahlgren to Lenthall, 23 February 1864, ibid.; Dahlgren to Rowan, 19 February 1864, ibid.; Green to Rowan, 3 March 1864, *ORN*, ser. 1, 15:348–49; Dahlgren to Welles, 6 April 1864, Dahlgren Papers, LCM; Dahlgren to Madigan, 6 June 1864, ibid.

28. Corbin, Orders Relating to the Blockade, August 1863, Administration and Organization (Internal), Subject File OA, RG 45, NA; Du Pont to Sophie, 10 March 1863, Du Pont, Letters, 2:484; Steedman to Sally, 20 April 1863, Steedman Papers, DUM; William H. Anderson, "Blockade Life," *War Papers Read Before Military Order of the Loyal Legion of the United States, Maine Commandery* 3 vols. (Portland, Maine: Lefabor-Tower, 1902), 7.

29. Butts, "A Cruise," 14.

30. Dahlgren to Welles, 29 October 1864, *ORN*, ser. 1, 16:35; Dahlgren to Stone, 15 July 1864, *ORN*, ser. 1, 15:569; Dahlgren to Kennison, 13 June 1864, ibid., 522–523; Dahlgren to Gosman, 21 June 1864, Dahlgren Papers, LCM; *Republican* (Savannah) 30 December 1864; Hardee, *Reminiscences of Old Savannah*, 95.

31. Turner to Du Pont, 21 May 1863, *ORN*, ser. 1, 14:21.

32. In Florida the Union forces were continually trying to promote Union sentiment and encouraging refugees to take up arms against the local Confederate forces. Boyer, *Naval Surgeon*, Entry for 23 December 1863, 237; Gibson to Dahlgren, 24 September 1863, *ORN*, ser. 1, 14:669–70; Dahlgren to Breese, 19 November 1863, *ORN*, ser 1, 15:128–29; Dutch to Du Pont, 19 May 1863, *ORN*, ser. 1, 14:205.

33. Balch to Dahlgren, 3 October 1863, *ORN*, ser. 1, 15:9; Reynolds to Dahlgren, 13 October 1863, ibid., 33–34; G. W. Rodgers, General Order, 10 June

1863, G. W. Rodgers Correspondence, Entry 395, RG 45, NA; Gibson to Dahlgren, 19 September 1863, *ORN*, ser. 1, 14:656.

34. Dutch to Rowan, 30 March, 7 April 1864, *ORN*, ser. 1, 15:384–88; Hunter to Pelot, 31 May 1864, William W. Hunter Papers, Howard-Tilton Memorial Library, Tulane University, New Orleans, Louisiana; Pierson to Mallory, 10 September 1864, *ORN*, ser. 1, 15:481.

35. Welles to Du Pont, 15 May 1863, *ORN*, ser. 1, 14:194; Gibson to Dahlgren, 4 August 1863, ibid., 417; Abstract Log of *T. A. Ward*, 17 October 1863, *ORN*, ser. 1, 15:61.

36. Tillson to Welles, 5 November 1864, *ORN*, ser. 1, 15:60; Abstract Log of *T. A. Ward*, 20 November 1863, ibid., 61; Trapier to Jordan, 22 October 1863, ibid., 62.

37. One sailor was reputed to have been mortally wounded by a rebel officer when he could not rise because of a wound he received earlier. The black landsman who went ashore was also reputed to have been hung. Anderson accounted for only fourteen men but was writing nearly nine months after the event. Anderson to Welles, 22 October 1864, *ORN*, ser. 1, 15:159–60; Gregory to Dahlgren, 15 December 1863, *ORN*, ser. 1, 15:153;

38. Dahlgren to Welles, 5 January 1864 *ORN*, ser. 1, 15:155–56; Dahlgren to Green, 23 December 1863, Dahlgren Papers, LCM.

39. Green to Dahlgren, 4 January 1864, *ORN*, ser. 1, 15:156–57; Dahlgren to Welles, 5 January 1864, ibid., 156; Spotts to Green, 1 January 1864, ibid., 157–58.

40. Dahlgren to Welles, 10, 14 October 1863, Dahlgren Papers, LCM; Dahlgren to Meriam, 19 November 1863, ibid.; Dahlgren to Wise, 17 September 1863, Wise Papers, NYHS; Dahlgren to Welles, 31 December 1861, *ORN*, ser. 1, 15:216–17; Dahlgren to Welles, 17 February 1864, Dahlgren Papers, LCM.

41. The percentage of repairing vessels was taken from the dispositions of vessels in the *ORN*. During Du Pont's tenure, he reported only those repairing at Port Royal and did not count those in Northern ports. Dahlgren, however, reported both, so the figures represent from July 1863 until February 1865. For scattered references to the facility at Port Royal see Subject File AR, RG 45, NA; Reynolds to Dahlgren, 25 July, Reynolds Correspondence, Entry 395, RG 45, NA; Reynolds to Dahlgren, 6 October 1863, ibid.; Du Pont to Lenthall, 9 January, 9 February 1863, Entry 62, RG 19, NA; Reynolds to Dahlgren, 17 February 1864, Reynolds Correspondence, Entry 395, RG 45, NA.

42. The full moon occurred on the night of 17 August. Virtual Reality Moon Phase Pictures, Time Service Department, U.S. Naval Observatory, http://tycho.usno.navy.mil/vphase.html. Map enclosure Boutelle to Reynolds, 4 February 1865, Entry 62, RG 19, NA; Dahlgren to Reynolds, 18 February 1864, Dahlgren Papers, LCM; Reynolds to Dahlgren, 19 August, 3 November, 20 December 1864, Reynolds Correspondence, Entry 395, RG 45, NA; Reynolds to Welch, 29

August 1864, ibid.; Dahlgren to Smith, 17 February 1864, Dahlgren Papers, LCM; Dahlgren to Welles, 19 May 1864, ibid.; Dahlgren to Ankers, 17 September 1864, ibid.

43. Lenthall to Du Pont, 27 January, 17 February 1863, Entry 51, RG 19, NA; Du Pont to Welles, 21 May 1863,*ORN*, ser. 1, 14:208–209; Reynolds to Dahlgren, 15 July, 6 August 1863, Reynolds Correspondence, Entry 395, RG 45, NA; Reynolds to Joseph Smith, 17 September 1864, ibid.

44. Dahlgren stated it was complete in May, yet Reynolds in a letter on 28 June 1864 says it will be finished in a couple of days. Reynolds to Dahlgren, 28 June 1864, Reynolds Correspondence, Entry 395, RG 45, NA; Dahlgren to Brisbone, 30 May 1864, Dahlgren Papers, LCM; Reynolds to Rowan, 2 April, 14 April 1862, Reynolds Correspondence, Entry 395, RG 45, NA; Reynolds to Dahlgren, 17 February 1864, 20 December 1864, 21 January 1865, ibid., Dahlgren to Welles, 9 August 1864, Dahlgren Papers, LCM.

45. Dahlgren to Foster, 14 August 1864, Dahlgren Papers, LCM.

46. William Eliot Furness, "The Battle of Olustee, Florida, February 29, 1864," *Operations on the Atlantic Coast 1861–1865, Virginia 1862, 1864, Vicksburg*, Papers of the Military Historical Society of Massachusetts (Boston: By the Society, 1912) X:236–39; *Historical Times Illustrated Encyclopedia of the Civil War*, Patricia L. Faust, ed., "Olustee (Ocean Pond) Fla., Battle of," by Edward G. Longacre (New York: Harper & Row, 1986), s.v., 545.

47. Schimmelfennig to Commanding Officer, 7 February 1864, *ORN*, ser. 1, 15:318; Terry to Dahlgren, 8 February 1864, ibid., 317; Rowan to Dahlgren, 8 February 1864, ibid., 317; Itinerary of Military Operations, January 1–November 13, *ORA*, ser. 1, vol. 35, pt. 1, 30–31.

48. Dahlgren to Gillmore, 5 February 1864, *ORN*, ser. 1, 15:273–74; Gillmore to Halleck, 31 January 1864, *ORA*, ser. 1, vol. 35, pt. 1, 279; Halleck to Gillmore, 22 January 1864, ibid.

49. Dahlgren to Breese, 6 February 1864, *ORN*, ser. 1, 15:274; Meriam to Dahlgren, 11 February 1864, ibid., 280.

50. Meriam to Dahlgren, 11 February 1864, *ORN*, ser. 1, 15:280–81; *Rebellion Record*, 8:394.

51. Gillmore tried to claim the *St. Mary*'s as an army prize when the army had not even been near the vessel when she was scuttled. Meriam to Dahlgren, 11 February 1864, *ORN*, ser. 1, 15:280–81; Gillmore to Dahlgren, 11 February 1864, ibid., 277–78; Dahlgren to Gillmore, 12 February 1864, ibid., 278–79; *Pawnee* arrived on the tenth. As a result of the naval activity in the river, Dahlgren had to order coal brought down under tow to keep the warships supplied. Dahlgren to Reynolds, 14 February 1864, *ORN*, ser. 1, 15:275–76; Dahlgren to Welles, 15 February 1864, ibid., 276–77; Dahlgren, *Memoirs*, 9 February 1864, 439.

52. Samuel Jones, "The Battle of Olustee, or Ocean Pond, Florida," *Battles and Leaders*, 4:76–79; Return of Casualties, 20 February 1864, Seymour, *ORA*, ser. 1, vol. 35, pt. 1, 298.

53. Balch to Dahlgren, 23, 29 February, 6 March 1864, *ORN*, ser. 1, 15:285–86, 289–91; Sanborn to Balch, 23 February 1864, ibid., 286; Berber to Freeman, 22 February 1864, ibid., 284–85; Balch to Breese, 17 March 1864, ibid., 295; Breese to Balch, 21 March 1864, ibid., 295–96.

54. While the Union army confiscated property at will, Rowan asked the senior officer, Commander George Balch, to work with the army in the St. John's River to secure railroad iron and live oak knees if possible. His instructions included the caveat that he should not take anything "without a clear understanding with the army." Balch to Rowan, 24 March 1864, *ORN*, ser. 1, 15:296–97; Breese to Balch, 26 March 1864, ibid., 297–98–passim; Rowan to Balch, 25 March 1864, Balch Papers, SHC; Hatch to Balch, 5 April 1864, *ORN*, ser. 1, 15:312.

55. Bailey to Farragut, 24 March 1864, *ORN*, ser. 1, 17:672.

56. Dahlgren to Welles, 18 February 1864, Dahlgren Papers, LCM; Dahlgren, *Memoirs*, 23, 27 February 1864, 441–42; Dahlgren to Rowan, 27 February 1864, *ORN*, ser. 1, 15:345.

57. Dahlgren, *Memoirs*, 2–4 March 1864, 442–43; Memorandum, March (n.d.) 1864, Dahlgren Papers, LCM.

58. Dahlgren, *Memoirs*, 5, 6, March 1864, 443–44.

59. Ibid., 8–24 March 1864, 444–47.

60. Ibid., 25–29 March, 1864, 447–48; Memorandum, March (n.d.) 1864, Dahlgren Papers, LCM; Dahlgren to Welles, 21 April 1864, *ORN*, ser. 1, 15:409.

61. Tomb, "Submarines and Torpedo Boats," 168–69; Extract from Notebook of First Assistant Engineer Tomb, (n.d.) *ORN*, ser. 1, 15:359; "Memoir of Chief Engineer James H. Tomb, C.S.N.," Tomb Papers, SHC.

62. Tomb, "Submarines and Torpedo Boats," 168–69; Extract from Notebook of First Assistant Engineer Tomb, *ORN*, ser. 1, 15:359; Beauregard to Tucker, 13 February 1864, *ORA*, ser. 1, vol. 35, pt. 1, 603; Patterson to Rowan, 6 March 1864, *ORN*, ser. 1, 15:356–67. After the attack, William Reynolds, the commander of the Naval Depot in Port Royal, realized how vulnerable the vessels there were. He placed a boom above the anchorage with picket boats out to patrol above the boom. Reynolds to Rowan, 19 March 1864, *ORN*, ser. 1, 15:371; Reynolds to Harrison, 19 March 1864, ibid., 371; "Memoir of Chief Engineer James H. Tomb, C.S.N.," Tomb Papers, SHC.

63. Tomb, Extract from Notebook of First Assistant Engineer Tomb, *ORN*, ser. 1, 15:359; DeCamp to Rowan, 19 April 1864, ibid., 405.

64. Welles to Stanton, 21 April 1864, *ORN*, ser. 1, 15:408; Welles to Dahlgren, 23 April 1864, ibid., 412; Halleck to Grant, 24 April 1864, *ORA*, ser. 1, vol. 35, pt. 2, 68; Dahlgren, *Memoirs*, 14–28 April 1864, 449–51.

65. Hatch remained in command of the Department of the South only until General John Foster arrived at the end of May. Welles gave Rowan authority to hoist a pennant on 12 March, Welles to Rowan, 12 March 1864, *ORN*, ser. 1,

15: 1363; Rowan to Welles, 3 May 1864, Rowan Papers, LCM; General Order No. 56, 1 May 1864, *ORA*, ser. 1, vol. 25, pt. 2, 79; Dahlgren, Diary, 4 May 1864, Dahlgren Papers, Syracuse.

66. He did receive a sentence of two months' suspension from duty and a reprimand. William H. Roberts, *USS New Ironsides In the Civil War* (Annapolis, Md.: U.S. Naval Institute Press, 1999), 85–87; Dahlgren, *Memoirs*, 9, 11, 14, 16, 17 May 1864, 452–54; Dahlgren to DuVall, 9 May 1864, Dahlgren Papers, LCM; Dahlgren to Simpson, Gibsen, 14 May 1864, ibid.; Rowan to Dahlgren, 8, 13 May 1864, Rowan Papers, LCM.

67. Dahlgren, *Memoirs*, 10, 12 May 1864, 452–53; Stephen B. Luce, "Naval Administration III," *Proceedings of the United States Naval Institute*, 29 (December 1903), 819; Notes, Council of War 10 May 1864, Dahlgren Papers, LCM; Welles to Dahlgren, 9 October, 2 November 1864, *ORN*, ser. 1, 15:26–27, 96–97.

68. Gleaves, *Luce*, 91.

69. For a complete discussion of this quest see Robert J. Schneller's *A Quest for Glory, A Biography of Rear Admiral John A. Dahlgren*, Dahlgren to Welles, 14 May 1864, Dahlgren Papers, LCM; Entry for 17 May 1864, Dahlgren Diaries, Dahlgren Papers, Syracuse.

70. The Confederates reported striking the pilothouse of one monitor causing it to look like a "damaged umbrella on a stormy day." Johnson, *Defense of Charleston*, 202, 209–10; Dahlgren to Welles, 21 May 1864, *ORN*, ser. 1, 15:438; Bombardment of Fort Sumter by USS *Nantucket*, 13 May 1864, Luce Papers, LCM.

71. Dahlgren to Stone, 24 May 1864, Dahlgren Papers, LCM; Foster to Halleck, 26 May 1864, *ORA*, ser. 1, vol. 35, pt. 1, 7–passim.

72. Dahlgren to Stone, 24 May 1864, Dahlgren Papers, LCM; Foster to Halleck, 26 May 1864, *ORA*, ser. 1, vol. 35, pt. 1, 7–passim; Chaplin to Dahlgren, 26 May 1864, *ORN*, ser. 1, 15:461–62; Chaplin to Dahlgren, 26 May 1864, ibid., 461–62; Dahlgren, *Memoirs*, 27 May 1864, 455.

73. Balch to Dahlgren, 10 May 1864, *ORN*, ser. 1, 15:425–26; Dahlgren to Mitchell, 29 May 1864, Dahlgren Papers, LCM.

74. Gordon to Burger, 27 May 1864, *ORN*, ser. 1, 15:441–44; Breese to Balch, 28 May 1864, ibid., 444–46; Mary Elizabeth Dickison, *Dickison and His Men: Reminiscences of the War in Florida* (1890; reprint, Gainesville, Fla.: University of Florida Press, 1962), 64–65.

75. Edwards to Balch (n.d.), *ORN*, ser. 1, 15:449–50; Sanborn to Dahlgren, 3 September 1864, ibid., 451–53; Breese to Balch, 28 May 1864, ibid., 444; Dickison to Barth, 24 May 1864, ibid., 453–54; Dickison, *Dickison and His Men*, 66, 187.

76. Dahlgren to Welles, 4 June 1864, Dahlgren Papers, LCM.

77. Hunter to Tucker, 15 March 1864, Hunter Papers, Tulane.

78. This number included a contingent of Confederate Marines from the *Georgia*. The numbers of men vary widely between the sources. William

Harden, "Capture of the U.S. Steamer *Water Witch* in Ossabaw Sound Georgia, June 2–3 1864," *Georgia Historical Quarterly* 3 (March 1918), 14; Pierson to Dahlgren, 10 September 1864, *ORN*, ser. 1, 15:482.

79. Pelot to Hunter, 1 June 1864, *ORN*, ser. 1, 15:492; Price to Hunter, 8 June 1864, Hunter Papers, Tulane.

80. Pelot to Hunter, 1 June 1864, *ORN*, ser. 1, 15:492; Kennison to Dahlgren, 4 June 1864, *ORN*, ser. 1, 15:469; John R. Blocker, "Capture of the Blockader *Water Witch*," *Confederate Veteran* 39 (April 1931), 604; other answers were also given, one was reported as "contraband"; West to Dahlgren, 5 June 1864, *ORN*, ser. 1, 15:473–74; *Republican* (Savannah), 4, 7 June 1864; Price to Hunter, 8 June 1864, Hunter Papers, Tulane.

81. The Savannah *Republican* reported that the intense battle on the ship convinced two of the barges full of men not to board the vessel. They returned upriver thinking that all the party had been killed or captured. *Republican* (Savannah), 7 June 1864; Pendergrast to Welles, 22 October 1864, *ORN*, ser. 1, 15:477; Buck to Welles, ibid., 480; Price to Hunter, 8 June 1864, Hunter Papers, Tulane.

82. Pendergrast to Welles, 22 October 1864, *ORN*, ser. 1, 15:477; Buck to Welles, 23 October 1864, ibid., 479–80; Price to Hunter, 8 June 1864, Hunter Papers, Tulane; Pierson to Mallory, 10 September 1864, *ORN*, ser. 1, 15:482–88.

83. Hunter to Mallory, 4 June 1864, *ORN*, ser. 1, 15:498; Scharf, *Confederate Navy*, 649; West to Dahlgren, 5 June 1864, *ORN*, ser. 1, 15:473; Extract from an Appendix to the Report of the Secretary of the Navy dated April 30, 1864, ibid., 506.

84. Dahlgren to Preble, 15 November 1864, Dahlgren Papers, LCM; Dahlgren to Fillebrown, Kennison and Stone, 15 August 1864, ibid.; Dahlgren to Cavendy, 12 July 1864, ibid.; Dahlgren to Gamble, 21 June 1864, ibid.; Dahlgren to Gosman, 21 June 1864, ibid.; Dahlgren to Stone, 18 July 1864, *ORN*, ser. 1, 15:574; Dahlgren to Patterson, 20 July 1864, Dahlgren Papers, LCM; Dahlgren Order No. 41, 21 June 1864, Orders to the South Atlantic Blockading Squadron, 1863–1865, HSP; Dahlgren to Welles, 6 June 1864, Dahlgren Papers, LCM; Dahlgren Order No. 38, 13 June 1864, Orders to the South Atlantic Blockading Squadron, 1863–1865, HSP.

85. Dahlgren to Welles, 12 June 1864, Dahlgren Papers, LCM; Dahlgren, *Memoirs*, 4 June 1864, 457.

86. Welles, Finding of Court-martial 27 January 1865, *ORN*, ser. 1, 15:490–91; Goldsborough, Eastman, Extract of Proceedings in a court of inquiry, 3 June 1864, ibid., 488–89.

87. Frank J. Welcher, *The Union Army 1861–1865: Organization and Operations, Volume I: The Eastern Theater* (Bloomington: Indiana University Press:, 1989), 90; Dahlgren, *Memoirs*, 12 June 1864, 458.

88. Foster envisioned a five-pronged attack, coordinated to take place almost simultaneously. See Burton, *The Siege of Charleston*, 285; Dahlgren, *Mem-*

oirs, 25, 27 June 1864, 459; Foster to Halleck, 23 June 1864, *ORA*, ser. 1, vol. 35, pt. 2, 146–47.

89. Dahlgren to Foster, 1 July 1864, Dahlgren Papers, LCM; Dahlgren to Welles, 11 July 1864, *ORN*, ser. 1, 15:554–55.

90. Dahlgren changed some of the initial dispositions of the vessels during the operation. Dahlgren to Welles, 11 July 1864, *ORN*, ser. 1, 15:554–55; Dahlgren to Foster, 1 July 1864, Dahlgren Papers, LCM.

91. Dahlgren to Chaplin, 1 July 1864, *ORN*, ser. 1, 15:551; Dahlgren, *Memoirs*, 2 July 1864, 460–62; ibid., 2 July 1864, 462; Dahlgren to Schimmelfennig, 3 July 1864, Dahlgren Papers, LCM; Log of *Lehigh*, 2 July 1864, Log of *Montauk*, 2–3 July 1864, Entry 118, RG 24, NA; Joshua Warren Journal, Entry for 2 July 1864, Naval Historical Center, Washington, D.C.

92. Birney to Burger, 13 July 1863, *ORA*, ser. 1, vol. 35, pt. 1, 409; Dahlgren to Welles, 11 July 1864, *ORN*, ser. 1, 15:555; Deck Log of *Nemaha*, 1–3 July 1863, Records of the United States Coast Guard, RG 26, NA.

93. Dahlgren to Welles, 11 July 1864, *ORN*, ser. 1, 15:554–55; Dahlgren, *Memoirs*, 3 July 1864, 464; Hoyt to Jewett, 5 August 1864, *ORA*, ser. 1, vol. 35, pt. 1:87–89.

94. Dahlgren, Diary, 4 July 1864, Dahlgren Papers, Syracuse; Schimmelfenning to Dahlgren, 6 July 1864, *ORN*, ser. 1, 15:557.

95. Dahlgren, Diary, 5–8 July 1864, Dahlgren Papers, Syracuse; Dahlgren to Welles, 11 July 1864, *ORN*, ser. 1, 15:555.

96. Dahlgren Order No. 49, 9 July 1864, Orders to the South Atlantic Blockading Squadron, 1863–1865, HSP; Dahlgren, Diary, 9–10 July 1864, Dahlgren Papers, Syracuse; Dahlgren to Wise, 22 July 1864, *ORN*, ser. 1, 15:357–58; Dahlgren to Welles, 11 July 1864, ibid., 555–56.

97. Welles to Dahlgren, 15 July 1864, Lincoln Library and Museum; Joshua Warren Journal, 8 July 1864, June (n.d.) 1870, NHC.

98. Dahlgren, Diary, 2 July 1864, Dahlgren Papers, Syracuse; Dahlgren to Stone, 15 July 1864, Dahlgren Papers, LCM.

Chapter 11

1. Wise, *Lifeline*, 210, 253–54.

2. Dahlgren to Welles, 12 June 1864, *ORN*, ser. 1, 15:518; Wise, *Lifeline*, 257 relates that the *Fannie* escaped about this date.

3. Dahlgren to Green, 13, 21 June 1864, *ORN*, ser. 1, 15:521, 536–37; Green to Lee, 23 June 1864, Green Journal, Port Columbus; Green to Williamson, ibid.

4. Dahlgren to Welles, 17 August 1864, *ORN*, ser. 1, 15:634–36; Green to De Camp, 29 August 1864, ibid., 651; Green to Williamson, 19 August 1864, ibid., 637–38; Green to Balch, 5 August 1864, Green Journal, Port Columbus; Green to Dahlgren, 30 June 1864, ibid.

5. De Camp to Green, 5 September 1864, *ORN*, ser. 1, 15:660–61.

6. Dahlgren to Green, 7 September 1864, ibid., 667.

7. Ibid.; Green to De Camp, 8, 10, 14 September 1864, Green Journal, Port Columbus.

8. Order of Rear Admiral Dahlgren, 23 September 1864, *ORN*, ser. 1, 15:685–88; Abstract logs of *Potamska, Pontiac, Nipsic, Winona*, 14 September 1864, ibid., 674–75.

9. Dahlgren, Order No. 73, Duties of Inner and Outer Blockade, Charleston 16 September 1864, Orders and Circulars Issued and Received by the South Atlantic Blockading Squadron, Entry 395, RG 45, NA; Wise, *Lifeline*, 253–54, 259.

10. These figures were compiled by the disposition reports throughout *ORN*. Dahlgren to Welles, 25 September 1864, *ORN*, ser. 1, 15:688–89; Dahlgren to Meriam, 19 November 1863, *ORN*, ser. 1, 15:129; Dahlgren to Welles, 29 October 1864, *ORN*, ser. 1, 16:35; Distribution of Vessels . . . October 22, 1864, ibid., 27–28.

11. Dahlgren to Welles, 25 December 1864, *ORN*, ser. 1, 16:147.

12. Dahlgren to Green, 7 November 1864, *ORN*, ser. 1, 16:44; Green to Dahlgren, 21, 31 October 1864, Green Journal, Port Columbus; Dahlgren to Welles, 29 October 1864, *ORN*, ser. 1, 16:34–35.

13. Dahlgren to Welles, 1 December 1864, Dahlgren Papers, LCM.

14. Wise, *Lifeline*, 210–11, 254, 259.

15. Dahlgren was authorized to reenlist them on shipboard for $100 for one year, $200 for two years, and $300 for three years. Order John D. Dahlgren, 15 February 1864,*ORN*, ser. 1, 15:324; Rowan to Welles, 7 March 1864, Dahlgren Papers, LCM; Circular, 22 October 1864, 9 September 1864, Orders and Circulars, Entry 395, RG 45, NA; Circular, John A. Dahlgren, 22 October 1862, ibid.

16. Dahlgren to Welles, 17 July, 26 October 1863,*ORN*, ser. 1, 14:358; 15:75–76; Fox to Lincoln, 26 March 1864, Fox Papers, NYHS; Dahlgren to De-Camp, 18 July 1864, Dahlgren Papers, LCM.

17. General Orders No. 91, Adjutant Generals Office, War Department, 4 March 1864, S. P. Lee Collection, LCM; Welles to Lincoln, 25 March 1864, *ORN*, ser. 1, 15:382–83; Welles to Stanton, 4, 8 April 1864, ibid., 391, 395; Dahlgren to A. N. Smith, 6 May, 8 August, 11 September, 24 September, Dahlgren Papers, LCM; Order No. 66, John A. Dahlgren, 24 August 1864, Orders to the South Atlantic Blockading Squadron, 1863–1865, HSP.

18. Dahlgren to Welles, 17, 26 May 1864, 6 June, 22 November 1864, Dahlgren Papers, LCM; Rowan to Dahlgren, 7 June 1864, Rowan to Welles, 1 July 1864, Rowan Papers, LCM; Entry for 26 August 1864, Welles, *Diary*, 2:121.

19. There was also a marine hospital for merchant sailors at Bay Point. Dahlgren to Fleet Surgeon William Johnson, 26 September 1863, Dahlgren Papers, LCM; Dahlgren to Welles, 29 November 1863, ibid.; Dahlgren to Welles, 4

August 1864, ibid.; Dahlgren to Foster, 13 August 1864, ibid.; Dahlgren to William Johnson, 26 September 1863, ibid.; Dahlgren to Clymer, 17 July 1863, ibid.; Reynolds to Thatcher, 4 July 1864, Reynolds Correspondence, Entry 395, RG 45, NA; Reynolds to Du Pont, 16 July 1864, ibid.; Drayton to Du Pont, 14 May 1862, *ORN*, ser. 1, 13:3; Boutelle to Reynolds, 4 February 1865, Entry 62, RG 19, NA; Dahlgren to Welles, 18 December 1863, *ORN*, ser. 1, 15:181–82.

20. Du Pont to Gerhard, 30 January 1863, Du Pont, *Letters*, 2:395; Du Pont to Davis, 18 May 1863, ibid., 3:129; Paul Henry Kendricken, *Memoirs of Paul Henry Kendricken* (Boston: Privately printed, 1910), 216; Loring, "Weehawken," 116; Hunter, *A Year on a Monitor*, 9.

21. Dahlgren to Welles, 20 July 1863, Dahlgren Papers, LCM; Dahlgren Order No. 37, 31 August 1863, Orders to the South Atlantic Blockading Squadron, 1863–1865, HSP.

22. Dahlgren to Welles, 4 November 1864, Dahlgren Papers, LCM; Dahlgren Order No. 25, 16 August 1863, Orders to the South Atlantic Blockading Squadron, 1863–1865, HSP; Dahlgren to Clymer, 17 July 1863, Dahlgren Papers, LCM; Dahlgren to Bradford, 17 July 1863, ibid.; Whelan to Welles, 4 August 1863, *ORN*, ser. 1, 14:418–19; Rowan to Dahlgren, 2 October 1863, Rowan Papers, LCM; Welles to Dahlgren, 16 October 1863, *ORN*, ser. 1, 15:46–47.

23. *Augusta* Steerage Mess, 25 December 1861, Whittemore Papers, SHC; Boyer, *Naval Surgeon*, Entries for 3 December, 25 December 1862, 26 November 1863, 25 December 1863, 21, 34, 208–209, 242–43.

24. Swann to Dahlgren, 30 July 1864, *ORN*, ser. 1, 15:584–85.

25. Colvocoresses to Dahlgren, 6 August 1864, *ORN*, ser. 1, 15:594–96; Ammen, *The Atlantic Coast*, 150–51; General Order of Dahlgren, 15 August 1864, *ORN*, ser. 1, 15:599–600.

26. Ibid.

27. Dahlgren to Welles, 8 August 1864, Jones to Dahlgren, 16 August 1864, *ORN*, ser. 1, 15:603–604; Welles to Dahlgren, 7 September 1864, ibid., 607–608.

28. Colvocoresses to Dahlgren, 19 August 1864, *ORN*, ser. 1, 15:630; Abstract Log of *Saratoga*, 16 August 1864, *ORN*, ser. 1, 15:633–34.

29. Swann to Dahlgren, 25 August 1864, *ORN*, ser. 1, 15:639; Abstract Log of *Potomaska*, 22–24 August 1864, ibid., 639–40.

30. Gillespie to Dahlgren, 9 September 1864, *ORN*, ser. 1, 15:648; Abstract Log of *Braziliera*, 26 August–6 September 1864, ibid., 649–50; 14–22 September, ibid., 673–74.

31. Foster to Dahlgren, 18 July 1864, *ORN*, ser. 1, 15:575; Schimmelfennig to Dahlgren, 25 July 1864, ibid., 579; Schimmelfennig to Green, 20 August 1864, ibid., 638.

32. Dahlgren to Foster, 22 July 1864, *ORN*, ser. 1, 15:576; Dahlgren, *Memoirs*, 21 July 1864, 470; Johnson, *Defense of Charleston*, 232–34; Dahl-

gren to Welles, 12 September, 13 October 1864, *ORN*, ser. 1, 15:670–72; ser. 1, 16:14; S. B. Luce Letterbook, 30 August 1864, S. B. Luce Papers, LCM.

33. Dahlgren, *Memoirs*, 20 July 1864, 469–70; Luce Letterbook, 30 August 1864, Luce Papers, LCM; Dahlgren to Welles, 23 August 1864, *ORN*, ser. 1, 15:640–41.

34. Foster to Dahlgren, 19 August 1864, *ORN*, ser. 1, 15:662–63; Dahlgren to Welles, 1 August 1864, ibid., 591–93.

35. Welles to Dahlgren, 22 September 1864, ibid., 684; Dahlgren to Wise, September (n.d.) 1864, Wise Papers, NYHS; Welles to Dahlgren, 3 October 1864, *ORN*, ser. 1, 16:6; Dahlgren to Welles, 19 October 1864, Dahlgren Papers, LCM; Dahlgren to Welles, 19 October 1864, Operations of Large Groups of Vessels, Subject File OO, RG 45, NA.

36. Dahlgren to Welles, 2, 10 November 1864, *ORN*, ser. 1, 16:39–40, 49–50.

37. Tuttle to Dahlgren, 2 November 1864, ibid., 41–42; Johnson, *Defense of Charleston*, clxxi–clxxiii; James H. Tomb, "The Last Obstructions in Charleston Harbor, 1863," *Confederate Veteran* 32 (March 1924), 98; Examination of Francis Wood, 28 March 1865, *Report of the Secretary of the Navy, 1865*, 289–90.

38. Welles to Dahlgren, 22 November 1864, *ORN*, ser. 1, 16:57; John A. Dahlgren Order No. 97, 22 November 1864, Orders to the South Atlantic Blockading Squadron, 1863–1865, HSP.

39. Dahlgren to Welles, 21 November 1864, Dahlgren Papers, LCM; McGrady to Hunter, 6 July 1864, Hunter Papers, DUM; Tomb, "Last Obstructions in Charleston Harbor," 98.

40. Hunter to Lee, 14 September 1864, *ORN*, ser. 1, 15:771; Hunter to Gilmer, 12 January 1864, ibid., 702–703.

41. Dahlgren, *Memoirs*, 24 November 1864, 477–78, 608; Ammen, *The Atlantic Coast*, 152; Foster to Halleck, 7 December 1864, *ORA*, ser. 1, 44:420; Hatch to Burger, December (n.d.) 1864, ibid., 421–22.

42. Robert H. Rankin, *Small Arms of the Sea Services* (New Milford, Conn.: N. Flayderman and Co., 1972), 118; John A. Dahlgren, Boat Artillery and Infantry, 8 August 1864, Orders to the South Atlantic Blockading Squadron, 1863–1865, HSP.

43. It appears that only about eight guns landed. Dahlgren, Boat Artillery and Infantry, Orders to South Atlantic Blockading Squadron; Preble to Dahlgren, 5 December 1864, *ORN*, ser. 1, 16:78.

44. The hospital stewards were blacks. These numbers in the Fleet Brigade slightly contradict the ones given on 4 October 1864. Preble to Hatch, 2 December 1864, *ORN*, ser. 1, 16:74; Dahlgren to Preble, 26 November 1864, ibid., 66–67; Hatch to Preble, 4 October 1866, Preble Journal, Operations of the Fleet Brigade, Subject File HJ, RG 45, NA; General Instructions, John A. Dahlgren, 26 November 1864, *ORN*, ser. 1, 16:67–68; William A. Courtney, "Fragments of

War History Relating to the Coast Defense of South Carolina 1861–65 and the Hasty Preparations for the Battle of Honey Hill, November 30, 1864," *Southern Historical Society Papers*, Richmond: The Society 26 (1898), 69.

45. Dahlgren took all the Marines off the outside blockaders. Green to Patterson, 25 November 1864, Green Journals, Port Columbus; Dahlgren, *Memoirs*, 25–28 November 1864, 478; Dahlgren to Reynolds, 25 November 1864, ORN, ser. 1, 16:63; Dahlgren to Preble, 28 November 1864, ibid., 64; Dahlgren to Welles, 26 November 1864, ibid., 65.

46. The tugs *Catalpa* and *Carnation* were also in the river to help with the landing but did not remain. Dahlgren Order No. 101, 28 November 1864, Orders to the South Atlantic Blockading Squadron, 1863–1865, HSP; Dahlgren, *Memoirs*, 28 November 1864, 479–80; Dahlgren to Welles, 30 November 1864, Dahlgren Papers, LCM; Dahlgren to Balch, 29 November 1864, ORN, ser. 1, 16:71; Hatch to Burger, December (nd) 1864, ORA, ser. 1, 421–22.

47. Preble to Hatch, 4 December 1864, ORN, ser. 1, 16:76.

48. Potter was also confused; he took the wrong road and marched his men six miles before returning. Preble to Hatch, 4 December 1864, ORN, ser. 1, 16:76; Preble to Dahlgren, 5 December 1864, ibid., 78–81; Hatch to Burger, December (nd) 1864, ORA, ser. 1, 44:422–25.

49. The Confederate casualties were probably higher since several units made no reports. Preble to Dahlgren, 5 December 1864, ORN, ser. 1, 16:78–81; Smith to Hardee, 6 December 1864, ORA, ser. 1, 44:415–16; Dahlgren to Welles, 1 January 1865, ORN, ser. 1, 16:96.

50. Foster offered scows to land and remove the howitzers and horses to drag them into their positions. Dahlgren to Welles, 7 December 1864, ORN, ser. 1, 16:83; Dahlgren Order No. 106, 5 December 1864, Operations of the Fleet Brigade, Preble Journal, Subject File HJ, RG 45, NA.

51. Preble to Dahlgren, 7 December 1864, Dahlgren Papers, LCM; Preble to Dahlgren, 8 December 1864, 10 January 1865, ORN, ser. 1, 16:84–87, 105–106.

52. Preble to Dahlgren, 10 January 1864, ORN, ser. 1, 16:107–108; Dahlgren to Welles, 1 January 1865, ibid., 97.

53. Hatch to Dahlgren, 7 February 1865, Dahlgren Papers, LCM.

54. Dahlgren, *Memoirs*, 9 December 1864, 483; Dahlgren to Bailey, 10 December 1864, Dahlgren Papers, LCM; *Report of the Secretary of the Navy, 1865*, vi–viii; Dahlgren to Lincoln, 12 December 1864, ORN, ser. 1, 16:127.

55. Dahlgren to Young, 13 December 1864, Dahlgren Papers, LCM; Distribution of Vessels of the South Atlantic Blockading Squadron, 15 November, 12 December 1864, ORN, ser. 1, 16:54–55; 125–26; Dahlgren to Fillebrown, 13 December 1864, ibid., 129–30; Dahlgren to Sherman, 13 December 1864, ibid., 129.

56. Dahlgren, *Memoirs*, 14 December 1864, 485; Cowley, *Leaves*, 143, 181; William T. Sherman, *Memoirs of General William T. Sherman*, 2 vols. (New York: D. Appleton and Company, 1875), 2:203.

57. Dahlgren, *Memoirs*, 15 December 1864, 486.

58. Battery Rosedew was armed with six guns, three of which were 10-inch Columbiads. Dahlgren, *Memoirs*, 21 December 1864, 487; Memorandum of Instructions, 17 December 1864, *ORN*, ser. 1, 16:134; Abstract Log of *Winona*, 20 December 1864, ibid, 137; Dahlgren to Welles, 31 January 1865, ibid., 210; Scott to Dahlgren, 27 December 1864, ibid, 148–49; *The Official Military Atlas of the Civil War*, LXX:2.

59. S. S. Lee to Hunter, 17 December 1864, *ORN*, ser. 1, 16:481.

60. Scharf, *Confederate Navy*, 651–53; Extract from Journal of Flag Officer Hunter, 25 December 1864, *ORN*, ser. 1, 16:488; Winegar to Mickle, 24 December 1864, *ORA*, ser. 1, 44:357.

61. Brent to Hunter, 24 December 1864, *ORN*, ser. 1, 16:483–85; Scharf, *Confederate Navy*, 651–53; John C. Gray Jr. to mother, 25 December 1864, John C. Gray Jr. to John C. Ropes, 7 January 1865, John Chipman Gray and John Codeman Ropes, *War Letters, 1862–1865, of John Chipman Gray and John Codeman Ropes* (Boston: Houghton Mifflin Company, 1927), 431, 434; Scharf, *Confederate Navy*, 641.

62. Sherman to Lincoln, 22 December 1864, Sherman, *Memoirs*, 2: 231; Sherman to Grant, 24 December 1864, *ORA*, ser. 1, 44:797–98; Luce, "Naval Administration," II:820.

63. Dahlgren to Scott, 13 December 1864, Dahlgren Papers, LCM; Memorandum of Instructions from John A. Dahlgren to Captain Scott, 31 December 1864, *ORN*, ser. 1, 16:153–54; Dahlgren to Schimmelfennig, 30 December 1864, Dahlgren Papers, LCM.

64. Dahlgren, *Memoirs*, 3 January 1865, 491; Dahlgren to Welles, 4 January 1865, *ORN*, ser. 1, 16:157; Gershom Bradford, *In With the Sea Wind: The Trials and Triumphs of Some Yankee Sailors* (Barre, Mass.: Barre Gazette, 1962), 187–88.

65. The transfer took two weeks. *Report of the Secretary of the Navy, 1865*, VI–VII; Dahlgren, *Memoirs*, 4 January 1865, 491; Dahlgren to Welles, 4, 7, January 1865, *ORN*, ser. 1, 16:156–58, 161–62.

66. Dahlgren, *Memoirs*, 9, 12, 13 January 1865, 492.

67. Dahlgren to Porter, 21 January 1865, Dahlgren Papers, LCM; Fox to Marston, 10 February 1865, John Marston Papers, LCM; Dahlgren, *Diary*, 13, 15 January 1865, Dahlgren Papers, Syracuse.

68. Instructions Dahlgren, 15 January 1865, *ORN*, ser. 1, 16:169; Dahlgren to Welles, 16 January 1865, ibid., 171–75; Quakenbush to Welles, ibid., 175–76; Sampson to Quakenbush, Ibid.; Edgar K. Thompson, "The U.S. Monitor *Patapsco*," *U.S. Naval Institute Proceedings* 94 (December 1968), 149.

69. Dahlgren, *Memoirs*, 18 January 1865, 493.

70. Sherman to Dahlgren, 17 January 1865, *ORN*, ser. 1, 16:180–81; Johnson, *Defense of Charleston*, 247; Dahlgren to Fillebrown, 24 January 1865, Dahlgren Papers, LCM; Dahlgren to Balch, ibid.; Luce to Dahlgren, 31 January

1865, Luce Papers, LCM; Abstract Log of *Pontiac*, 24 January-8 February 1865, *ORN*, ser. 1, 16:189–90; Dahlgren to Welles, 24 January 1865, ibid., 187.

71. Chaplin to Dahlgren, 28 January 1865, *ORN*, ser. 1, 16:192.

72. Ibid.

73. Ibid.

74. Ibid.

75. Ibid., 192–94.

76. Dahlgren to Welles, 10 February 1865, Copy of the finding of a court of inquiry, *ORN*, ser. 1, 16:198–200; Cowley, *Leaves*, 158.

77. Crosman to Dahlgren, 29 January 1865, *ORN*, ser. 1, 16:204; Johnson, *Defense of Charleston*, 247–48.

78. Several other vessels were in the Stono acting as tenders to the *Lehigh*. Balch to Dahlgren, 9 February 1865, *ORN*, ser. 1, 16:226–27; Schimmelfennig to Dahlgren, 10 April 1865, ibid., 312–13; Schimmelfennig to Scott, 9 February 1865, Dahlgren Papers, LCM; Hayes to Balch, 9 February 1865, *ORN*, ser. 1, 16:227; Parker to Dahlgren, 12 February 1865, ibid., 232; Johnson to Dahlgren, 12 February 1865, ibid., 233; Crosman to Dahlgren, 13 February 1865, ibid., 233–35; Dahlgren to Welles, 13 February 1865, ibid., 242.

79. Dahlgren, Diary, 7 February 1865, Dahlgren Papers, Syracuse; Dahlgren to Welles, 7 February 1865, Dahlgren Papers, LCM.

80. Dahlgren, Diary, 11 February 1865, Dahlgren Papers, Syracuse.

81. Stanly to Ridgely, 19 February 1865, *ORN*, ser. 1, 16:239–40; Dahlgren to Ridgely, 12 February 1865, ibid., 238–39; Dahlgren to Welles, 22 February 1865, ibid., 262.

82. Stanly to Ridgely, 19 February 1865, Ibid.; Johnson, *Defense of Charleston*, 250–51; Ridgely to Dahlgren, 19 February 1865, *ORN*, ser. 1, 16:239; Dahlgren, *Memoirs*, 12 February 1865, 497.

83. Memoranda of Orders for General W. J. Hardee, 14 February 1865, *ORA*, ser. 1, vol. 47, pt. 2, 1179–80.

84. A cipher with this message is somewhat confusing since Sherman had found virtually no serious opposition to his movements. Dahlgren to Welles, 14 February 1865, *ORN*, ser. 1, 16:243–44; Schneller, *Quest for Glory*, 310.

85. The *C. P. Williams* grounded before she could take part in the action. Dahlgren to Scott, 17 February 1865, *ORN*, ser. 1, 16:247; Semmes to Dahlgren, 18 February 1865, ibid., 251.

86. *The Daily Courier* (Charleston), 20 February 1865; Brand, *Reminiscences*, 31; Belknap, "Reminiscent of the Siege of Charleston," 200–201.

87. The last shot fired by the Confederates were ironically fired at the *Canonicus* on 4 February and struck just abaft the smoke stack. Belknap to Dahlgren, 19 February 1865, *ORN*, ser. 1, 16:258–59; Cowley, *Leave*, 165–66.

88. Belknap to Dahlgren, 19 February 1865, *ORN*, ser. 1, 16:258–59.

89. Dahlgren, *Memoirs*, 18 February 1865, 499–500; Dahlgren to Porter, 18 February 1865, Dahlgren Papers, LCM.

90. The engines of the *Lady Davis* provided the motive power for the *Palmetto State*. Cowley, *Leaves*, 170–71; Byram to Boughton, 18 February 1865, *ORN*, ser. 1, 16:252; Belknap to Dahlgren, 19 February 1865, ibid., 253–54; Barrett to Dahlgren, 20 February 1865, ibid., 254–55; Scharf, *Confederate Navy*, 706.

91. Dahlgren to Gillmore, 22 February 1865, *ORN*, ser. 1, 16:261; Creighton to Stellwagen, 24 February 1865, ibid., 268; Dahlgren, *Memoirs*, 22 February 1865, 501; Dahlgren to Welles, 28 February 1865, *ORN*, ser. 1, 16:273.

92. Dahlgren to Fillebrown, 25 February 1865, Dahlgren Papers, LCM; Fillebrown to Dahlgren, 25 February 1865, *ORN*, ser. 1, 16:271; Schimmelfennig to Commanding Officer, U.S. Naval Forces, 25 February 1865, ibid., 269.

93. Dahlgren to Gillmore, 27 February, 11, 27 March 1865, Dahlgren Papers, LCM; Gillmore to Dahlgren, 1, 19 March 1865, Ibid.

94. Dahlgren to Patty Dahlgren, 3 March 1865, Dahlgren Papers, Newberry Library; Dahlgren to Welles, 1 March 1865, *ORN*, ser. 1, 16:282–83; Abstract Log of *Harvest Moon*, 1 March 1865, ibid., 283–84; Boutelle to Dahlgren, 18 March 1865, ibid., 295–96; Hanson to Dahlgren, 4 June 1865, ibid., 408–409.

95. Welles to Dahlgren, 24 February 1865, *ORN*, ser. 1, 16:267; Dahlgren to Welles, 12 March 1865, *ORN*, ser. 1, 16:291, 308–309; Morris to Stellwagen, 9 March 1865, ibid., 288; Swann to Dahlgren, 15 March 1865, ibid., 294; Stellwagen to Dahlgren, 27 March 1865, ibid., 299–300; Dahlgren to Welles, 29 April 1865, ibid., 325; Dahlgren General Orders No. 44, 45, 27, 29 April 1865, ibid., 325–26.

96. This flag was also said to be lost in the naval boat attack on Fort Sumter in September 1863. Dahlgren, *Memoirs*, 14 April 1864, 508–509; Cowley, *Leaves*, 182–85.

97. William Radford assumed command of the newly created Atlantic Squadron in July 1865. It comprised all the vessels that had once been in the North and South Atlantic Blockading Squadrons. Brigadier General Stan Watie did not surrender until 23 June 1865. Dahlgren, General Order No. 65, 17 June 1865, Dahlgren Papers, LCM; Dahlgren, *Memoirs*, 21 June, 12 July 1865, 514–15; Logs of *Pawnee*, *Philadelphia*, 17 June 1865, Entry 118, RG 24, NA.

Conclusion

1. Rodgers, "Du Pont's Attack at Charleston," *Battles and Leaders*, 4:34.

2. Johnson, *Defense of Charleston*, p. 273.

3. Gillmore to Ripley, 17 July, 15 August 1865, Dahlgren Papers, LCM; Ripley to Gillmore, 19 July, 16 August 1865, Dahlgren Papers, LCM; Jefferson Davis, *The Rise and Fall of the Confederate Government 1861*, 2 vols. (New York: D. Appleton and Company, 1881), 2:208.

4. They might have also pushed up the Santee River to cut the North Eastern Railroad.

5. Dahlgren, *Memoirs*, (n.d.), p. 552.

6. Dahlgren, General Order No. 65, 17 June 1865, Dahlgren, *Memoirs*, p. 614.

BIBLIOGRAPHY

Primary Sources

MANUSCRIPT COLLECTIONS

American Swedish Historical Museum, Philadelphia, Pennsylvania
    Charles Gideon Dale Collection, Papers of Thomas Jefferson Griffin
    John Ericsson Papers
Archives of American Art, Smithsonian Institution, Washington, D.C.
    Smith Family Papers
Department of the Interior, National Parks Service
    Fort Pulaski National Monument, Georgia
        Charles Lafundy Papers
    Fort Sumter National Monument, Charleston, South Carolina
        Anonymous, Sargent, Eighth Maine Volunteers
        George Bacon Papers
        Frederick C. Russell Papers
Duke University Rare Book, Manuscript, and Special Collections Library,
    Perkins Library, Durham, North Carolina
    William W. Hunter Papers
    Edward Kershner Papers
    George Anderson Mercer Papers
    William Read, Jr., Papers
    Dabney Minor Scales Papers
    Mary Eliza Schooler Papers
    Charles Steedman Papers
    Arthur Brailsford Wescoat Papers
East Carolina University Manuscript Collection, Greenville, North Carolina
    Charles Fairchild Papers
Emory University, Special Collections, The Robert W. Woodruff Library
    Savannah Squadron Papers
The Hagley Library and Museum, Wilmington, Delaware
    The Du Pont Family Papers
    Louis M. Goldsborough Papers

The Historical Society of Pennsylvania, Philadelphia, Pennsylvania
  Orders to the South Atlantic Blockading Squadron, 1863–1865
The Huntington Library and Art Gallery, Department of Manuscripts, San
  Marino, California
  Gideon Welles Papers
Lincoln Museum, Fort Wayne, Indiana
  Cabinet Member Papers
Library of Congress, Manuscript Division, Washington, D.C.
  John C. Beaumont Papers
  John Adolphus Dahlgren Papers
  Joseph F. Green Papers
  Abraham Lincoln Papers
  Samuel Phillips Lee Papers
  Stephen B. Luce Papers
  John Marston Papers
  Horace Porter Papers
  William Radford Papers
  Rodgers Family Papers
  Stephen Clegg Rowan Papers
  Cornelius Marius Schoonmaker Papers
  Gideon Welles Papers
National Archives, Washington, D.C.
  Record Group 19, Records of the Bureau of Ships
    Entry 49, Letters Sent to the Secretary of the Navy
    Entry 50, Letters Sent to the Secretary of the Navy From the Bureau of
      Construction and Repair
    Entry 51, Letters Sent to Officers
    Entry 58, Letters Sent by the Bureau of Construction and Repair
    Entry 59, Letters Sent
    Entry 61, Circulars by Secretary of the Navy Gideon Welles
    Entry 62, Letters Received from Officers
    Entry 64, Letters Received by Superintendents Outside Navy Yards
    Entry 65, Reports from the Superintendents Outside of Navy Yards
    Entry 68, Reports from Superintendents Outside of Navy Yards
    Entry 71, Letters Received
    Entry 186, Records Relating to Claims in Connection with Civil War
      Naval Vessels, 1861–1909 (Port Royal Working Party)
    Entry 966, Letters Sent to Naval Officers
    Entry 1235, Records of the Office of the General Superintendent of
      Ironclads
  Record Group 23, Records of the Coast and Geodetic Survey
  Record Group 24, Bureau of Naval Personnel
    Entry 118, Ship's Logs, Stations, and Miscellaneous

Record Group 26, Records of the United States Coast Guard
Record Group 45, Naval Records Collection of the Office of Naval
    Records and Library
    Entry 1, Letters Sent by the Secretary of the Navy to Officers
    Entry 13, Letters to Bureaus of the Navy Department
    Entry 21, Letters Received by the Secretary of the Navy: Miscellaneous
        Letters 1801–84, Microfilm Number M124
    Entry 22, Letters from Officers of the Rank Below that of Commander
    Entry 30, Letters Received by the Secretary of the Navy From
        Commanding Officers of Squadrons, Microfilm Number M89
    Entry 32, Letters from Bureaus of the Navy Department
    Entry 34, Letters from Commandants of Navy Yards
    Entry 37, Letters from Rear Admirals, Commodores, and Captains
    Entry 41, Directives
    Entry 43, Directives
    Entry 319, Letters from the Secretary of the Navy to the Boston
        Navy Yard
    Entry 332, Letters Sent by the Commandant, New York Navy Yard
    Entry 346, Letters Received from the Secretary of the Navy by the
        Commandant (Philadelphia Navy Yard)
    Entry 395, Letterbooks of Officers of the United States Navy at Sea
        Correspondence of Daniel Ammen
        Correspondence of John C. Beaumont
        Correspondence of Thomas G. Corbin
        Correspondence of George F. Emmons
        Correspondence of William E. Le Roy
        Correspondence of Garret J. Pendergrast
        Correspondence of William Reynolds
        Correspondence of Cristopher Raymond Perry Rodgers
        Correspondence of George W. Rodgers
        Correspondence of Enoch G. Parrott, Journal of the *Augusta*
        Correspondence of Penrod G. Watmough
        Orders and Circulars Issued and Received by the South Atlantic
            Blockading Squadron
    Entry 463, Area Files
    Entry 464, Subject File
    AR Repair
    AV Miscellaneous
    AY Purchases, Sales, and Final Disposition of Naval Vessels,
        except prizes
    HA Engagement with Enemy War Vessels
    HJ Joint Military-Naval Engagements
    HP Privateer Engagements

452 — *Bibliography*

NH Heroic Acts, Commendation, Honors, Memorials, and Medals
OA Administration and Organization
OL Mobilization and Demobilization
OO Operations of Large Groups of Vessels
ON Strategy and Tactics
OX Lines of Supply and Supply Ships
PS Sites and Boundaries
VL International Law
XF Fuel and Water
XN Naval Stores Afloat
XS Naval Supplies Ashore
Record Group 77, Civil Works Map File
Record Group 92, Records of the Quartermaster General's Department
  Entry 225 Consolidated Correspondence File
Record Group 94, Records of the Adjutant General's Office, 1780–
  1917
  Entry 159 Generals' Papers and Books
  Entry 160 Generals' Reports of Service
Record Group 125, Records of General Courts-Martial and Courts
  of Inquiry of the Navy Department, 1799–1867 Microfilm
  Number M273
Record Group 217, Records of the United States General Accounting
  Office
Naval Historical Center, Operational Archives, Washington, D.C.
  Garrett J. Pendergrast File
  Joshua Warren Journal
Newberry Library, Chicago, Illinois
  John Adolphus Dahlgren Papers
New-York Historical Society, New York, New York, Naval History
  Society Collection
  John Sanford Barnes Papers
  Gustavus Vasa Fox Papers
  John Irwin Papers
  Henry Augustus Wise Papers
New York Public Library, New York, New York
  Percival Drayton Papers
The Southern Historical Collection, Wilson Library, University of North
  Carolina, Chapel Hill, North Carolina
  George Beall Balch Papers
  Francis Thornton Chew Papers
  Civil War (Federal, Miscellaneous) Papers
  John Newland Maffitt Papers
  Pettigrew Family Papers

James Hamilton Tomb Papers
Eugene Whittemore Papers
South Caroliniana Library, University of South Carolina, Columbia,
    South Carolina
Anonymous Journal
George H. Petit Papers
Syracuse University Library, Department of Special Collections, Syracuse,
    New York
John A. Dahlgren Papers
Tulane University, Howard-Tilton Memorial Library, New Orleans, Louisiana
    William W. Hunter Papers (Savannah Squadron Papers)
U.S. Army Military History Institute, Carlisle Barracks, Pennsylvania
    Harrisburg Civil War Round Table Collection
U.S. Naval Academy, Special Collections Division, Nimitz Library,
    Annapolis, Maryland
George E. Welch Papers
James Iredell Waddell Papers
Port Columbus Civil War Naval Center, Columbus, Georgia
Joseph F. Green Journals

GOVERNMENT DOCUMENTS

*Atlas to Accompany the Official Records of the Union and Confederate
    Armies. Washington: Government Printing Office, 1891, reprint entitled
    The Official Military Atlas of the Civil War.* New York: Fairfax Press,
    1978.
Great Britain. Parliament. *Sessional Papers,* Commons.
Hansard's Parliamentary Debates, Lords.
U.S. Bureau of Ordnance and Hydrography. *Almanac for the Use of
    Navigators from the American Ephemeris and Nautical Almanac for the
    Year 1863.* Washington, D.C.: Government Printing Office, 1861.
U.S. Congress. House. *Forts, Arsenals, Arms &c.* H. Rept. 85, 36th Cong.,
    2d sess., 18 February 1861.
U.S. Congress. House. *Letter of the Secretary of the Navy in Answer to a
    Resolution in the House to the Number of Vessels in the Navy.* H. Ex.
    Doc. 159, 40th Cong., 2d sess., 1868.
U.S. Congress. House. *Number of Vessels in the Navy.* H. Ex. Doc. 159, 40th
    Cong., 2d sess., 1868.
U.S. Congress. House. *Report of the Secretary of the Navy.* H. Ex. Doc. 1,
    37th Cong., 3rd sess., 1 December 1862.
U.S. Congress. House. *Report of the Secretary of the Navy.* H. Ex. Doc. 1,
    38th Cong., 1st sess., 7 December 1863.
U.S. Congress. House. *Report of the Secretary of the Navy.* H. Ex. Doc. 1,
    38th Cong., 2d sess., 5 December 1864.

U.S. Congress. House. *Report of the Secretary of the Navy.* H. Ex. Doc. 1, 39th Cong., 1st sess., 4 December 1865.

U.S. Congress. House. *Report of the Secretary of the Navy.* H. Ex. Doc. 1, Vol. 5, 39th Cong., 1st sess., 4 December 1864.

U.S. Congress. Senate. *Appointment of Robert Platt to the Rank of Commander.* Sen. Rept. 1114, 54th Cong., 1st sess., 3 June 1890.

U.S. Congress. Senate. *Certain War Vessels Built in 1862–1865.* S. Rept. 1942, 57th Cong., 1st sess., 1942.

U.S. Congress. Senate. *Operations Against Charleston.* S. Rept. 142, 38th Cong., 2d sess., 1864.

U.S. Congress. Senate. *Report of the Joint Committee on the Conduct of the War.* S. Rept. 108, 37th Cong., 3rd sess., 1863.

U.S. Congress. Senate. *Report of the Secretary of the Navy.* S. Doc. 1, 37th Cong., 1st sess., 4 July 1861.

U.S. Congress. Senate. *Report of the Secretary of the Navy.* S. Ex. Doc. 2, 36th Cong., 1st sess., December 1859.

U.S. Congress. Senate. *Report of the Secretary of the Navy.* S. Ex. Doc. 1, 36th Cong., 2nd sess., December 1, 1860.

U.S. Congress. Senate. *Report of the Secretary of the Navy.* S. Ex. Doc. 1, Pt. 3, 37th Cong., 2nd sess., December, 1861.

U.S. Congress. Senate. *Report to the Joint Committee on the Conduct of War: Heavy Ordnance.* S. Rept. 121, 38th Cong., 2d sess., 1865.

U.S. Congress. Senate. *The Congressional Record.*

U.S. Department of Commerce. *Distances Between United States Ports.* Washington, D.C.: Government Printing Office, 1929.

U.S. Department of Commerce. *Historical Statistics of the United States 1789–1945.* Washington, D.C.: Government Printing Office, 1949.

U.S. Department of Commerce. *Military and Naval Service of the United States Coast Survey, 1861–1865.* Washington, D.C.: Government Printing Office, 1916.

U.S. Department of the Navy. *Record of the Medal of Honor Issued to Blue Jackets of the United States Navy 1862–1888.* Washington, D.C.: Government Printing Office, 1888.

U.S. District Court, Massachusetts. *Decisions of Hon. Peleg Sprague in Maritime Admiralty and Prize Causes in the District Court of the United States for the District of Massachusetts 1854–1868.* 2 vols., Philadelphia: T & J Johnson and Company, 1861; Boston: Little, Brown and Company, 1868.

U.S. Navy. Bureau of Navigation. *Record of the Medal of Honor: Officers and Enlisted Men of the United States Navy, Marine Corps and Coast Guard 1862–1923.* Washington, D.C.: Government Printing Office, 1924.

U.S. Navy. Naval History Division. *Civil War Naval Chronology 1861–1865.* 6 vols. Washington, D.C.: Government Printing Office, 1971.

U.S. Navy. Naval History Division. *Dictionary of American Naval Fighting Ships.* 8 vols. Washington, D.C.: Government Printing office, 1959–1981.
U.S. Navy. *Report of the Secretary of the Navy in Relation to Armored Vessels.* Washington, D.C.: Government Printing Office, 1864.

NEWSPAPERS

Army and Navy Journal
American and Commercial Advertiser (Baltimore)
Central Georgian (Sandersonville)
The Charleston Daily Courier
The Charleston Mercury
The Congressional Globe
Daily Intelligencer (Atlanta)
Daily Morning News (Savannah) (also known as the *Daily News, News,* and *Savannah Morning News* during the war)
Herald (New York)
National Intelligencer
Times (New York)
Tribune (New York)
Philadelphia Daily Evening Bulletin
Republican (Savannah)
Register (Mobile, Alabama)
Sunday Times (New York)
World (New York)

BOOKS

Ammen, Daniel. *The Navy in the Civil War: The Atlantic Coast.* New York: Charles Scribner's Sons, 1898.
Ammen, Daniel. *The Old Navy and the New.* Philadelphia: J. B. Lippincott Co., 1891.
Anderson, Edward C. *Confederate Foreign Agent: The European Diary of Major Edward C. Anderson.* Edited by W. Stanley Hoole. University, Ala.: Confederate Publishing Co., 1976.
Andrews. W. H. *Footprints of a Regiment: A Recollection of the 1st Georgia Regulars 1861–1865.* Atlanta, Ga.: Longstreet Press, 1992.
Basler, Roy P., ed. *The Collected Works of Abraham Lincoln.* 9 vols. New Brunswick, N.J.: Rutgers University Press, 1953–1955.
Blan, Henry. *Reminiscences of My Blockade Running.* Savannah, Ga.: n.p., 1910.
Boyer, Samuel Pellman. *Naval Surgeon: The Diary of Dr. Samuel Pellman Boyer.* Edited by Elinor and James A. Barnes. Bloomington: Indiana University Press, 1963.

Boynton, Charles B. *The History of the Navy During the Rebellion.* 2 vols. New York: D. Appleton & Co., 1867–68.

Bulloch, James D. *The Secret Service of the Confederate States in Europe on How the Confederate Cruisers Were Equipped.* 2 vols. New York: Thomas Yoseloff, 1959.

Burkmyer, Cornelius L. *Burkmyer Letters, March 1863–June 1865.* Edited by Charlotte R. Holmes. Columbia, S.C.: The State Company, 1926.

Caldwalader, John. *Caldwalader's Cases: Being Decisions of the Hon. John Caldwalder.* 2 vols. Philadelphia: Rees Welsh and Co., 1907.

Confederate States of America. Department of South Carolina, Georgia, and Florida. *Report of the Affair at Port Royal Ferry on 1st January 1862, J. C. Pemberton Brigadier General Commanding,* n.p., n.d.

Confederate States of America. *Official Report of the Chief Engineer of the District of Georgia at the Attack by the Enemy's Turreted Iron Clads on Genesis Point Battery March 3, 1863.* n.p., 1863.

Confederate States of America. *Reports of the Military Engineers of the Engagement of the Enemy's Iron-Clad Fleet with the Forts and Batteries Commanding the Outer Harbor of Charleston, on the Seventh April 1863.* Charleston, S.C.: n.p., 1864.

Confederate States of America. Army. Department of South Carolina, Georgia, and Florida. *Report of General G. T. Beauregard of the Defense of Charleston.* Richmond, Va.: R. M. Smith, 1864.

Copp, Elbridge J. *Reminiscences of the War of the Rebellion 1861–1865.* Nashua, N.H.: n.p.,1911.

Cowley, Charles. *Leaves from a Lawyer's Life Afloat and Ashore.* Lowell, Mass.: Penhallow Printing Company, 1879.

Dahlgren, Madeleine. *Memoirs of John A. Dahlgren Rear Admiral United States Navy.* Boston: J. R. Osgood, 1882.

Dana, Charles A. *Recollections of the Civil War with the Leaders at Washington and in the field in the sixties.* New York: D. Appleton and Company, 1898.

Davis, Charles H. *The Life of Charles Henry Davis, Rear Admiral 1807–1877.* Boston: Houghton Mifflin and Company, 1899.

Davis, Jefferson. *The Rise and Fall of the Confederate Government.* New York: D. Appleton and Company, 1881.

Dawson, Francis W. *Reminiscences of Confederate Service 1861–1865.* Charleston, S.C.: The News and Courier Book Presses, 1882.

Drayton, Percival. *Naval Letters of Captain Percival Drayton, 1861–1865 Printed From the Original Manuscripts Presented to the N.Y. Public Library by Miss Gertrude L. Hoyt.* New York: The Library, 1906.

Du Pont, Samuel F. *Abstract of the Cruise of the U.S. Frigate Wabash Bearing the Flag of the Rear Admiral Samuel Francis Du Pont 1861–62 & 63.* New York: Edward O. Jenkins, 1863.

Du Pont, Samuel F. *Samuel Francis Du Pont: A Selection From His Civil War Letters.* Edited by John D. Hayes. 3 vols. Ithaca, N.Y.: Cornell University Press, 1969.

Du Pont, Samuel F. *Official Dispatches and Letters of Rear Admiral Du Pont U.S. Navy 1846–48, 1861–63.* Wilmington, Del.: Ferris Brothers, 1883.

Eldredge, Daniel. *The Third New Hampshire Regiment and All About It.* Boston: E. B. Stillings and Company, 1893.

The Federal Cases, Comprising Cases Argued and Determined in the Circuit and District Courts of the Unites States. 30 vols, St. Paul, Minn.: 1894–1897.

Fox, Gustavus. *Confidential Correspondence of Gustavus Vasa Fox Assistant Secretary of the Navy 1861–1865.* Edited by Robert Means Thompson and Richard Wainwright. New York: The De Vinne Press, 1918.

Gillmore, Quincey A. *Engineer and Artillery Operations against the Defenses of Charleston Harbor in 1862.* New York: D. Van Nostrand, 1865.

Gillmore, Quincy A. *Engineer and Artillery Operations against the Defenses of Charleston Harbor in 1863.* New York: D. Van Nostrand, 1865.

Gillmore, Quincy A. *Official Report To The United States Engineer Department of the Siege and Reduction of Fort Pulaski Georgia, February, March, and April, 1862.* New York: D. Van Nostrand, 1862.

Gleaves, Albert. *Life and Letters of Rear Admiral Stephen B. Luce.* New York: G. P. Putnam's Sons, 1925.

Gordon, George Henry. *A War Diary of Events in the War of the Great Rebellion 1863–1865.* Boston: James R. Osgood and Company, 1882.

Gray, John Chipman and John Codman Ropes. *War Letters, 1862–1865, of John Chipman Gray and John Codman Ropes.* Boston: Houghton Mifflin Company, 1927.

Great Britain. Foreign Office. *Papers Relating to the Blockade of the Ports of the Confederate States, Presented to Both Houses of Parliament by Command of Her Majesty 1862.* North America, no. 8, London: Harrison,1862.

Greene, Albert S. *Organization of the Engineer Corps of the Navy and Education of its Officers.* n.p., 1864.

Hardee, Charles Seton Henry. *Reminiscences and Recollections of Old Savannah.* Savannah, Ga.: [s.n.], 1928.

Hay, John. *Lincoln and the Civil War in The Diaries and Letters of John Hay.* Edited by Tyler Dennett. New York: Dodd, Mead & Company, 1939.

Hobart-Hampton (Roberts), Augustus Charles. *Never Caught: Personal Adventures Connected with Twelve Successful Trips in Blockade-Running during the American Civil War, 1863–1864.* London: John Camden Holton, 1867.

Hunter, Alvah Folsom. *A Year on a Monitor and the Destruction of Fort Sumter.* Edited by Craig L. Symonds. Columbia: University of South Carolina Press, 1991.

Johnson, John. *The Defense of Charleston Harbor Including Fort Sumter and the Adjacent Islands, 1863–1865.* Charleston, S.C.: Walker, Evans and Cogswell Co., 1890

Kelsey, Albert Warren. *Autobiographical Notes and Memoranda By Albert Warren Kelsey 1840–1910.* Baltimore: Munder-Thomsen Press, 1911.

Kendricken, Paul Henry. *Memoirs of Paul Henry Kendricken.* Boston: privately printed, 1910.

Lamson, Roswell. *Lamson of the Gettysburg: The Civil War Letters of Lieutenant Roswell H. Lamson, U.S. Navy.* Edited by James M. McPherson and Patricia R. McPherson. New York: Oxford University Press, 1997.

Lee, Elizabeth Blair. *Wartime Washington: The Civil War Letters of Elizabeth Blair Lee.* Edited by Virginia Jean Laas and Dudley Cornish. Urbana: University of Illinois Press, 1991.

Lusk, William Thompson. *War Letters of William Thompson Lusk.* New York: privately printed, 1911.

McCarten, Francis. *Description and Cruise of the USS "Augusta", South Atlantic Blockading Squadron.* n.p., n.d., 1876.

McCarten, Francis. *In Peace and in War: or Seven Years in the U.S. Navy.* Printed on the USS *Tennessee* 1876–78.

McClelland, George B. *McClellan's Own Story.* New York: Charles L. Webster and Company, 1887.

Mahan, Alfred Thayer. *From Sail to Steam: Recollections of Navy Life.* 1907. New York: Da Capo Press, 1968.

Manigault, Edward. *Siege Train, The Journal of a Confederate Artilleryman in the Defense of Charleston.* Edited by Warren Ripley. Columbia: University of South Carolina Press, 1986.

Marchand, John M. *Charleston Blockade: The Journals of John B. Marchand U.S. Navy, 1861–1862.* Edited by Craig L. Symonds. Newport, R.I.: Naval War College Press, 1976.

Marlinspike (pseud), *Abstract of the Cruise of U. S. Steam Frigate* Wabash, *Bearing the Flag of Rear-Admiral S. F. Du Pont, 1861, '62 & '63,* New York: Edward O. Jenkins, 1863.

Moore, Frank, ed. *The Rebellion Record: A Diary of American Events.* 11 vols. and supplement. New York: G. P. Putnam, 1861–1862. D. Van Nostrand, 1864–1868.

Morgan, James Morris. *Recollections of a Rebel Reefer.* Boston: Houghton Mifflin, 1917.

The Navy in Congress: Being Speeches of the Hon. Messrs. Grimes, Doolittle, and Nye; of the Senate and the Hon. Messrs. Rice, Pike, Griswold, and Blow; of the House of Representatives. Washington, D.C.: Frank Taylor, 1865.

Olmstead, Charles H. *Reminiscences of Service With the First Volunteer Regiment of Georgia, Charleston Harbor in 1863.* Savannah, Ga.: J. H. Estill, 1879.

Olmstead, Charles H. *The Memoirs of Charles H. Olmstead.* Edited by Lilla Mills Hawes. Collections of the Georgia Historical Society Series, vol. XIV, Savannah, Ga.: Georgia Historical Society, 1964.

Paine, Albert Bigelow. *A Sailor of Fortune: Personal Memoirs of Captain B. S. Osbon.* New York: McClure, Phillips and Co. 1906.

Palmer, Abraham J. *The History of the Forty-eighth Regiment New York State Volunteers in the War for the Union 1861–1865.* New York: Veterans Association of the Regiment, 1885.

Parker, Francis E., and John Lathrop, comp. *Decisions of Hon. Peleg Sprague in Maritime, Admiralty and Prize Causes in the District Court for Massachusetts . . .* 2 vols. Philadelphia: T. & J.W. Johnson & Co., 1861–1868.

Parker, William Harwar. *Recollections of a Naval Officer 1841–1865.* 1883. Annapolis, Md.: United States Naval Institute, 1985.

Parrott, Enoch G. *Description and Cruise of the USS Augusta.* New York: McCarten, 1876.

Pearson, Elizabeth Ware, ed. *Letters From Port Royal 1862–1868.* New York: Arno Press, 1969.

Porter, David D. *The Naval History of the Civil War.* New York: The Sherman Publishing Company, 1886.

Roman, Alfred. *The Military Operations Of General Beauregard In The War Between The States 1861–1865.* New York: Harper & Brothers, 1884.

Rush, Richard, et al., eds. *Official Records of the Union and Confederate Navies in the War of the Rebellion.* 31 vols., Washington, D.C.: Government Printing Office, 1894–1914.

Scharf, J. Thomas. *History Of The Confederate States Navy From Its Organization To The Surrender Of Its Last Vessel.* New York: Rodgers and Sherwood, 1887. Reprint. Fairfax Press, 1977.

Scott, R. N. et. al., eds. *The War of the Rebellion: A Compilation of the Official Records of the Union and Confederate Armies.* 70 vols. Washington, D.C.: Government Printing Office, 1880–1901.

Sherman, William T. *Memoirs of General William T. Sherman.* 2 vols. New York: D. Appleton and Company, 1875.

Simpson, Edward. *Paper on Armored Vessels, Addressed to the Secretary of the Navy.* s. l, s.n, 1866.

Soley, James Russel. *The Navy in the Civil War: The Blockade and the Cruisers.* New York: Charles Scribner's Sons, 1883.

Sprague, Peleg. *Decisions of Hon. Peleg Sprague in Maritime Admiralty and Prize Cases in the District Court of the United States for the District of Massachusetts 1854–1868.* 2 vols. Boston: Little, Brown and Co. 1868.

Steedman, Charles. *Memoir and Correspondence of Charles Steedman Rear Admiral, United States Navy, with His Autobiography and Private Journals, 1811–1890.* Edited by Amos Lawrence Mason. Cambridge, Mass.: The Riverside Press, 1912.

Thompson, Magnus S. ed., *General Orders and Circulars Issued by the Navy Department From 1863 to 1887.* Washington, D.C.: Government Printing Office, 1887.

Villard, Henry. *Memoirs of Henry Villard, Journalist and Financier 1835–1900.* 2 vols. New York: Houghton, Mifflin and Company, 1904.

Von Scheliha, Victor. *A Treatise on Coast Defense: Based on the Experience Gained by Officers of the Corps of Engineers of the Army of the Confederate States.* London: E & F. N. Spon, 1868.

Watson, William. *The Adventures of a Blockade Runner on Trade in Time of War.* London: T. Fisher, 1898.

Welles, Gideon. *Diary of Gideon Welles.* Edited by K. Howard Beale. 3 vols. New York: W. W. Norton & Company, Inc., 1960.

Wilkinson, John. *The Narrative of a Blockade Runner.* New York: Sheldon & Co., 1877.

Wilson, James H. *Under the Old Flag: Recollections of Military Operations in the War for the Union, the Spanish War, the Boxer Rebellion, Etc.* 2 vols. New York: D. Appleton & Co., 1912.

ARTICLES

Alexander, W. A. "The Confederate Submarine Torpedo Boat Hunley." *The Gulf States Historical Magazine* 1 (Sept. 1902): 81–91.

Alexander, W. A. "Thrilling Chapter in the History of the Confederate States Navy: Work on Submarine Boats." *Southern Historical Society Papers* XXX (1902): 164–74.

Almay, John Jay. "Incidents of the Blockade." *Military Order of the Loyal Legion of the United States Commandery of the District of Columbia.* War Papers 9. Washington, D.C.: Companion, 1892.

Ammen, Daniel. "Du Pont and the Port Royal Expedition." In *Battles and Leaders of the Civil War,* ed. Robert Underwood Johnson and Clarence Clough Buel, 4 vols. New York: Thomas Yoseloff, 1956, 1:671–90.

Anonymous. "Charleston Under Fire." *The Cornhill Magazine* X (1864): 99–110.

Anderson, William H. "Blockade Life." *War Papers Read Before the Military Order of the Loyal Legion of the United States Maine Commandery.* 3 vols. Portland, ME: Lefabor-Tower, 1902, 2: 1–20.

Bacot, Clara. "Destruction of A Federal Gunboat." *Confederate Veteran* XVI (Jan.–Dec. 1908): 347.

Barnes, James. "The Port Royal Expedition 1861." *Harper's Weekly* LV (Dec. 23, 1911): 9.

Barnes, John S. "The Battle of Port Royal Ferry, South Carolina; With the Entry for New Year's Eve and Day, 1862 from the Journal of John S. Barnes." Edited by John D. Hayes and Lillian O'Brien. *New-York Historical Society Quarterly* XLVII (April 1963): 109–36.

Beauregard, Pierre G. T. "The Defense of Charleston." *Battles and Leaders of the Civil War,* ed. Robert Underwood Johnson and Clarence Clough Buel, 4 vols. New York: Thomas Yoseloff, 1956, 4: 1–23.

Beauregard, Pierre G. T. "Torpedo Service in Charleston Harbor." *The Annals of the War Written by Leading Participants North and South.* Philadelphia: Times Publishing Co., 1879, 514–26.

Beauregard, Pierre G. T. "Torpedo Service in the Harbor and Water Defenses of Charleston." *Southern Historical Society Papers* V No. 4 (1878): 145–61.

Belknap, George E. "Reminiscent of the 'New Ironsides' off Charleston." *The United Service,* I (January 1879): 63–82.

Belknap, George E. "Reminiscent of the Siege of Charleston." *Naval Actions and History Papers of the Military Historical Society of Massachusetts.* 14 vols. Boston: The Society, 1895–1918, XII, (1902): 155–207.

Belknap, George E. "The Home Squadron in the Winter of 1860–61." *Publications of the Military History Society of Massachusetts.* 14 vols. Boston: The Society, 1895–1918. vol. XII: 75–100.

Blocker, John R. "Capture of Blockader, 'Water Witch'." *Confederate Veteran* 17 (December 1909): 604.

Brand, Robert. "Reminiscences of the Blockade Off Charleston, SC." *War Papers Read Before the Commandery of the State of Wisconsin, Military Order of the Loyal Legion of the United States.* 4 vols. Milwaukee: Burdick and Allen, 1891–1903, 3: 14–32.

Browne, Samuel L. "First Cruise of the Montauk." *Soldiers and Sailors Historical Society of Rhode Island, Personal Narratives of Events in the War of the Rebellion.* 2nd ser., no. 1. Providence: The Society, 1879: 7–59.

Butler, Edward A. "Personal Experiences in the Navy, 1862–65." *War Papers Read Before the Commandery of the State of Maine, Military Order of the Loyal Legion of the United States.* 2 vols. Portland, Maine: Lefavor-Tower Company, 1902: 184–200.

Butts, Frank B. "A Cruise Along the Blockade." *Personal Narratives of Events in the War of the Rebellion Being Papers Read Before the Rhode Island Soldiers and Sailors Historical Society.* Second Series No. 12. Providence, R.I.: N. Bangs Williams and Co.,1881: 5–37.

Chase, Salmon P. "*The Diary of Salmon P. Chase.*" *Annual Report of the American Historical Association 1902.* 2 vols. Washington, D.C.: Government Printing Office, 1903.

Chisolm, Robert. "The Battle of Port Royal." *Under Both Flags A Panorama of the Great Civil War*, ed. George M. Vickers, Philadelphia: People's Publishing, 1896: 255–57.

Church, William C. "The Naval Victory at Port Royal, South Carolina, November 7, 1861." *Papers Read Before the Military Order of the Loyal Legion of the United States New York Commandry*, 4 vols. New York: The Commandery, 1891–1892, 2: 55–66.

Courtenay, William A. "Fragments of War History Relating to the Coast Defense of South Carolina 1861–65 and the Hasty Preparations For the Battle of Honey Hill, November 30, 1864." *Southern Historical Society Papers*, Richmond, Va. The Society, XXVI (1898): 62–87.

Crowley, R. O. "The Confederate Torpedo Service." *Century Illustrated Monthly Magazine* (June 1898): 290–300.

Davidson, Hunter. "Mines and Torpedoes during the Rebellion." *The Magazine of History* VIII (November 1908): 255–61.

Davis, W. W. H.: The Siege of Morris Island." In *The Annals of the War Written By Leading Participants North and South.* Philadelphia: The Times Publishing Company, 1879: 95–110.

Drayton, Percival. "What Its Captain Thought of the Monitor Passaic: 'I rue the Day I got into the ironclad Business.'" Edited by Ashly Halsey Jr. *Civil War Times Illustrated* (April 1965): 28–34.

Ericsson, John. "The Early Monitors." In *Battles and Leaders of the Civil War*, ed. Robert Underwood Johnson and Clarence Clough Buel, 4 vols. New York: Thomas Yoseloff, 1956, 4: 30–31.

Farenholt, Oscar W. "From Ordinary Seaman to Rear Admiral." *Civil War Papers of the California Commandry of the Military Order of the Loyal Legion of the United States.* San Francisco: Shannon-Conmy, 1910. Reprint. Wilmington, NC: Broadfoot Publishing Company, 1995.

Farenholt, Oscar W. "The Monitor 'Catskill': A Years' Reminscences 1863–1864." *Civil War Papers of the California Commandry of the Military Order of the Loyal Legion of the United States.* San Francisco: Shannon-Conmy, 1912. Reprint. Wilmington, N.C.: Broadfoot Publishing Company, 1995.

Foote, John A. "Notes on the Life of Admiral Foote." In *Battles and Leaders of the Civil War*, ed. Robert Underwood Johnson and Clarence Clough Buel, 4 vols. New York: Thomas Yoseloff, 1956, 1: 347.

Furness, William Eliot. "The Battle of Olustee, Florida, February 29, 1864." *Operations on the Atlantic Coast 1861–1865, Virginia 1862, 1864, Vicksburg.* Papers of the Military Society of Massachusetts. Boston: By the Society, 1912, 10: 235–63.

Furness, William Eliot. "The Siege of Fort Wagner." *Military Essays and Recollections: Papers Read Before the Commandery of the State of Illinois, Military Order of the Loyal Legion of the United States.* Chicago: A. C. McClurg and Company, 1891: 210–29.

Gilchrist, Robert C. "Confederate Defense of Morris Island." *Yearbook 1884.* City of Charleston, 1884: 350–402.

Gillmore, Quincy A. "Siege and Capture of Fort Pulaski." In *Battles and Leaders of the Civil War,* ed. Robert Underwood Johnson and Clarence Clough Buel, 4 vols. New York: Thomas Yoseloff, 1956, 2: 1–12.

Gillmore, Quincy A. "The Army Before Charleston in 1863." In *Battles and Leaders of the Civil War,* ed. Robert Underwood Johnson and Clarence Clough Buel, 4 vols. New York: Thomas Yoseloff, 1956, 4: 52–71.

Glassell, W. T. "Reminiscences of Torpedo Service in Charleston Harbor." *Southern Historical Society Papers 5* (November 1877) 4: 225–35.

Glassell, W. T. "Torpedo Service in Charleston Harbor." *Confederate Veteran* XXV (March 1917): 113–16.

Grier, John A. "A Sketch of Naval Life." *Military Essays and Recollections: Papers Read Before the Commandry of the State of Illinois Military Order of the Loyal Legion of the United States.* Chicago: The Dial Press, 1899.

Harden, William. "The Capture of U.S. Steamer 'Water Witch' in Ossabaw Sound, Georgia, June 2–3 1864." *Georgia Historical Quarterly* III (March 1919): 11–27.

Harleston, John. "Battery Wagner on Morris Island, 1863." *The South Carolina Historical Magazine* LVII (January 1956): 1–13.

Holden, Edgar. "The First Cruise of the 'Monitor' Passaic." *Harper's New Monthly Magazine* XXVII (October 1863): 577–95.

Jervey, Theodore D. "Charleston During the Civil War." *Annual Report of the American Historical Association for the Year 1913.* 1 (1915): 167–77.

Jones, Samuel. "The Battle of Olustee, or Ocean Pond, Florida." In *Battles and Leaders of the Civil War,* ed. Robert Underwood Johnson and Clarence Clough Buel, 4 vols. New York: Thomas Yoseloff, 1956, 4: 76–79.

Lachlison, James. "Daring Deed in Saving the David—C.S. Navy." *Confederate Veteran* XVI (February 1908): 78.

Leland, Isabella Middleton, ed. "Middleton Correspondence, 1861–1865." *The South Carolina Historical Magazine* 63 (January 1962): 33–41.

Loring, B. W. "The Monitor *Weehawken* in the Rebellion." *Proceedings of the United States Naval Institute* XII (1886): 111–20.

Luce, Stephen B. "Naval Administration II." *Proceedings of the United States Naval Institute* XXVII (December 1902): 839–49.

Luce, Stephen B. "Naval Administration III." *Proceedings of the United States Naval Institute* XXIX (December 1903): 809–21.

Maffitt, John N. "Blockade Running." *The United Service* VI (June 1882): 626–33, VII (July 1882): 14–33.

McNaughton, J. "The Recapture of the Emily St. Pierre." *Blue Peter* XV (January 1935): 10–11.

Montfort, Theodorick W. "Rebel Lawyer: The Letters of Lt. Theodorick W. Montfort, 1861–1862." Edited by Spencer Bidwell King Jr. *Georgia Historical Quarterly* 49 (March, June, September 1965): 82–97, 200–216, 324–34.

Nordhoff, Charles. "Two Weeks at Port Royal." *Harper's New Monthly Magazine* XXVII (June, 1863): 110–118.

Olmstead, Charles H. "Fort Pulaski." *The Georgia Historical Quarterly* 1 (March 1917): 98–105.

Olmstead, Charles H. "Reminiscences of Service in Charleston Harbor in 1863." *Southern Historical Society Papers* XI (1883): 118–25, 158–71.

Peck, W. F. G. "Four Years Under Fire at Charleston." *Harper's New Monthly Magazine* XXXL (August 1865): 358–66.

Rockwell, Alfred P. "The Operations Against Charleston." *Publications of the Military History Society of Massachusetts*. 14 vols. Boston: The Society, 1895–1918. [Vol. IX, pp. 159–95]

Rodgers, C. R. P. "Du Pont's Attack at Charleston." In *Battles and Leaders of the Civil War,* ed. Robert Underwood Johnson and Clarence Clough Buel, 4 vols. New York: Thomas Yoseloff, 1956, 4: 32–47.

Sanders, Robert W. "Efforts to Capture Charleston, S.C. and Evacuation of the City." *Confederate Veteran* XXXIII (April 1925): 142–43.

Sands, Francis P. B. "Lest We Forget: Memories of Service Afloat from 1862 to 1866." *Military Order of the Loyal Legion of the United States Commandery of the District of Columbia,* War Papers 73, Washington, D.C., The Commandery, 1894.

Shanks, W. F. G. "The Brooklyn Navy-Yard." *Harper's New Monthly Magazine* XLII (Dec. 1870): 1–13.

Simpson, Edward. "The Monitor *Passaic.*" *The United Service* II (April 1880): 413–23.

Smith, Xanthas. "Confederate Ram Raid off Charleston, S.C." In George M. Vickers, ed. *Under Both Flags; A Panorama of the Great Civil War.* Philadelphia: People's Publishing, 1896: 236–39.

Smythe, Augustine T. Jr. "Torpedo and Submarine Attacks on The Federal Blockading Fleet off Charleston During the War of Secession." In *Year Book, 1907.* Charleston, S.C.: City of Charleston, pp. 53–64.

Staudenraus, P. J. (ed.) "A War Correspondent's View of St. Augustine and Fernandina: 1863." *Florida Historical Quarterly* 41 (July 1962): 60–65.

Stevens, Hazard. "Military Operations in South Carolina in 1862, Against Charleston, Port Royal Ferry, James Island, Secessionville." *Operations on the Atlantic Coast 1861–1865, Virginia 1862, 1864; Vicksburg.* Papers of the Military Historical Society of Massachusetts IX, Boston: The Military Historical Society of Massachusetts, 1912.

Stevens, Thomas H. "The Battle of Port Royal." *The United Service* 3rd Series IV (Feb. 1904): 175–77.

Stevens, Thomas H. "The Boat Attack on Sumter." In *Battles and Leaders of the Civil War,* ed. Robert Underwood Johnson and Clarence Clough Buel, 4 vols. New York: Thomas Yoseloff, 1956: 4:47–51.

Tomb, James H. "Submarines and Torpedo Boats, C.S.N." *Confederate Veteran* XXII (April 1914): 168–69.

Tomb, James H. "The Last Obstructions in Charleston Harbor 1863." *Confederate Veteran* XXX11 (March 1924): 98–99.

Viele, Egberth. "The Port Royal Expedition, 1861." *Magazine of American History* XIV (October 1885): 329–340.

Vizetelly, Frank. "When Charleston was Under Fire." *The New Age Magazine* XV No. 3 (September, 1911): 217–27; XV No. 4 (October 1911): 341–46.

Voris, Alvin C. "Charleston in the Rebellion," *Sketches of War History 1861–1865, Papers Read Before the Ohio Commandery of the Military Order of the Loyal Legion of the United States.* 6 vols. Cincinnati, Ohio: Robert Clark and Co., 1886.

Wainwright, Richard. "The Naval Attack Upon Charleston, South Carolina." *The United Service* New Series IV (November 1890): 433–41.

Wait, Horatio L. "The Blockading Service." *Military Essays and Recollections; Papers Read Before the Commandery of the State of Illinois, Military Order of the Loyal Legion of the United States.* 4 vols. Chicago: A.C. McClurg and Company, 1891–1912, 2: 211–52.

Welles, Gideon. "Admiral Farragut and New Orleans, With an Account of the Origin and Command of the First Three Naval Expeditions of the War." *The Galaxy* 5 (July 1871): 669–83.

Wentworth, Thomas. "The Reoccupation of Jacksonville in 1863." *Civil War Papers Read Before the Commandery of the State of Massachusetts, Military Order of the Loyal Legion of the United States.* Boston: The Commandry, 1900: 467–74.

Williams, Alonzo. "The Investment of Fort Pulaski." *Providence—Personal Narratives Rhode Island Soldiers and Sailors Historical Society.* Providence, The Society, 1887.

Secondary Sources

BOOKS

Alexander, Kitt H., comp. *Robert Smalls, America's Forgotten Black Naval Hero and the Value of the Steamer* Planter *to the Confederacy and to the Union.* United States: The Author, n.d.

Barnes, James S. *Submarine Warfare Offensive and Defensive.* New York: D. Van Nostrand, 1869.

Baynard, T. F. *Oration Delivered By the Hon. Thomas F. Bayard, U.S. Senator From Delaware at the Unveiling of the Statute of Rear-Admiral Samuel Francis Du Pont, United States Navy at Washington, D.C., December 20, 1884.* Washington, D.C.: Government Printing Office, 1885.

Bernath, Stuard L. *Squall Across the Atlantic: Civil War Prize Cases and Diplomacy.* Los Angeles: University of California Press, 1970.

Black, Robert C. III. *The Railroads of the Confederacy.* Chapel Hill: The University of North Carolina Press, 1952.

Bradford, Gershom. *In With the Sea Wind: The Trials and Triumphs of Some Yankee Sailors.* Barre, Mass.: Barre Gazette, 1962.

Brennan, Patrick. *Secessionville: Assault on Charleston.* Campbell, Calif.: Savas Publishing Company, 1996.

Browning, Robert M. Jr. *From Cape Charles to Cape Fear, The North Atlantic Blockading Squadron During the Civil War.* Tuscaloosa: University of Alabama Press, 1993.

Bryan, T. Conn. *Confederate Georgia.* Athens: University of Georgia Press, 1964.

Burton, E. Milby. *The Seige of Charleston, 1861–1865.* Columbia: University of South Carolina Press, 1970.

Callahan, Edward W. *List of Officers of the Navy of the United States and of the Marine Corps From 1775 to 1900.* New York: Haskell House Publishers, Ltd., 1969.

Canney, Donald L. *The Old Steam Navy.* 2 vols. Annapolis, Md.: Naval Institute Press, 1990, 1993.

Carse, Robert. *Department of the South: Hilton Head Island in the Civil War.* Columbia, S.C.: The State Printing Co., 1961.

Cauthen, Charles C. *South Carolina Goes to War, 1860–65.* Chapel Hill: University of North Carolina Press, 1960.

Church, William C. *The Life of John Ericsson.* 2 vols. New York: Charles Scribner's Sons, 1891.

Courtemanche, Regis A. *No Need of Glory: The British Navy In American Waters 1860–1864.* Annapolis, Md.: United States Naval Institute, 1977.

Current, Richard N., ed. *Encyclopedia of the Confederacy.* 4 vols. New York: Simon & Schuster, 1993.

Dickison, Mary Elizabeth. *Dickison and His Men: Reminiscences of the War in Florida.* 1890. Reprint. Gainesville: University of Florida Press, 1962.

Dudley, William S. *Going South: U.S. Navy Officer Resignations & Dismissals on the Eve of the Civil War.* Washington, D.C.: Naval Historical Foundation, 1981.

Du Pont, H. A. *Rear Admiral Samuel Francis Du Pont United States Navy A Biography.* New York: National Americana Society, 1926.

Faust, Patricia, ed. *Historical Times Illustrated Encyclopedia of the Civil War.* New York: Harper & Row, 1986.

Fretwell, Jacqueline K., ed. *Civil War Times in St. Augustine.* St. Augustine, Fla.: St. Augustine Historical Society, 1988.

Gibson, Charles Dana and E. Kay Gibson. *Assault and Logistics: Union Army Coastal and River Operations 1861–1866.* Camden, Maine: Ensign Press, 1995.

Gibson, Charles Dana and E. Kay Gibson. *Dictionary of Transports and Combat Vessels Steam and Sail Employed by the Union Army, 1861–1868.* Camden, Maine: Ensign Press, 1995.

Goff, Richard D. *Confederate Supply.* Durham, N.C.: Duke University Press, 1969.

Hamersly, Lewis Randolph. *The Records of Living Officers of the U.S. Navy and Marine Corps.* Philadelphia: L. R. Hamersly & Co., 1890.

Hamersly, Lewis Randolph. *The Records of Living Officers of the U.S. Navy and Marine Corps.* Philadelphia: L. R. Hamersly & Co., 1870.

Hamersly, Thomas H. S. *Complete General Navy Register of the United States of America From 1776 to 1877.* New York: T. H. S. Hamersly, Publisher, 1888.

Hamersly, Thomas H. S., ed. *General Register of the United States Navy and Marine Corps.* Baltimore, Md.: William K. Boyle, 1882.

Headley, J. T. *Farragut And Our Naval Commanders.* New York: E. B. Treat & Co., 1867.

Heitman, Francis B. *Historical Register and Dictionary of the United States Army From Its Organization, September 29, 1789 To March 2, 1903.* 2 vols. Washington, D.C.: Government Printing Office, 1903.

Henig, Gerald S. *Henry Winter Davis: Antebellum and Civil War Congressman from Maryland.* New York: Twayne Publishers Inc., 1973.

Hill, Jim Dan. *The Civil War Sketchbook of Charles Ellery Stedman Surgeon United States Navy.* San Rafeal, Calif.: Presidio Press, 1976.

Johns, John E. *Florida During the Civil War.* Gainesville: University of Florida Press, 1963.

Johnson, Robert Erwin. *Rear Admiral John Rodgers: 1812–1882.* Annapolis, Md.: United States Naval Institute, 1967.

Jones, Charles C. Jr. *The Life and Services of Commodore Josiah Tattnall.* Savannah, Ga.: Morning News Steam Printing House, 1878.

Jones, Chester Lloyd. *The Economic History of Anthracite-Tidewater Canals.* Publications of the University of Pennsylvania Series in Political Economy and Public Law 22. Philadelphia: University of Pennsylvania, 1908.

Jones, Samuel. *The Siege of Charleston and the Operations on the South Atlantic Coast in the War Among the States.* New York: Neal Publishing Company, 1911.

Kloppel, James E. *Danger Beneath the Waves: A History of the Confederate Submarine H. L. Hunley.* Orangeburg, S.C.: Sandlapper Publishing, Inc., 1992.

Lawrence, Alexander A. *A Present for Mr. Lincoln: the Story of Savannah from Succession to Sherman.* Macon, Ga.: Ardivan Press, 1961.

Long, E. B. and Barbara Long. *The Civil War Day By Day, An Almanac 1861–1865.* Garden City, N.Y.: Doubleday and Company Inc., 1971.

Maffitt, Emma Martin. *The Life and Times of John Newland Maffitt.* New York: Neale, 1906.

Merrill, James M. *Du Pont: The Making of an Admiral, A Biography of Samuel Francis Du Pont.* New York: Dodd, Mead & Company, 1986.

Miller, Edward A. Jr. *Gullah Statesman, Robert Smalls from Slavery to Congress, 1839–1915.* Columbia: University of South Carolina Press, 1995.

Niven, John. *Gideon Welles: Lincoln's Secretary of the Navy.* New York: Oxford University Press, 1973.

Orvin, Maxwell C. *In South Carolina Waters, 1861–65.* Charleston, S.C.: Southern Printing and Publishing Co., 1961.

Paullin, Charles Oscar. *Paullin's History of Naval Administration 1775–1911.* Annapolis, Md.: United States Naval Institute, 1968.

Perry, Milton F. *Infernal Machines: The Story of Confederate Submarine and Mine Warfare.* Baton Rouge: Louisiana State University Press, 1965.

Peterson, Clarence S. *Admiral John A. Dahlgren, Father of U.S. Naval Ordnance.* New York: Hobson, 1945.

Petrillo, Charles. *Anthracite and Slackwater: The North Branch Canal 1828–1901.* Easton, Pa.: Center for Canal History and Technology, 1986.

Pope, Dudley. *At Twelve Mr. Byng Was Shot.* Philadelphia: J. B. Lippincott Company, 1962.

Powell, William H., comp. *List of Officers of the Army of the United States From 1779 to 1900.* New York: L. R. Hammersly & Co., 1900.

Ragan, Mark K. *The Hunley: Submarines, Sacrifice, & Success in the Civil War.* Charleston, S.C.: Narwhal Press, 1999.

Ragan, Mark K. *Union and Confederate Submarine Warfare in the Civil War.* Mason City, Iowa: Savas Printing, 1999.

Rankin, Robert H. *Small Arms of the Sea Services.* New Milford, Conn.: N. Flayderman and Co., 1972.

Reed, Rowena. *Combined Operations in the Civil War.* Annapolis, Md.: Naval Institute Press, 1978.

Roberts, William H. *USS New Ironsides in the Civil War.* Annapolis, Md.: U.S. Naval Institute Press, 1999.

Robinson, William M. *The Confederate Privateers.* New Haven, Conn.: Yale University Press, 1928.

Rochelle, James Henry. *Life of Rear Admiral John Randolph Tucker.* Washington, D.C.: The Neale Publishing Company, 1903.

Roland, Alex. *Underwater Warfare in the Age of Sail.* Bloomington: Indiana University Press, 1978.

Rose, Willie L. *Rehearsal for Reconstruction; the Port Royal Experiment.* Indianapolis, Ind.: Bobbs-Merrill Inc., 1964.

Schafer, Louis S. *Confederate Underwater Warfare: An Illustrated History.* Jefferson, N.C.: McFarland & Company, Inc., 1996.

Schiller, Herbert M. *"Sumter is Avenged": The Siege and Reduction of Fort Pulaski.* Shippensburg, Pa.: White Mane Publishing Company, Inc., 1995.

Schneller, Robert J. Jr. *A Quest for Glory, A Biography of Rear Admiral John A. Dahlgren.* Annapolis, Md.: Naval Institute Press, 1990.

Shingleton, Royce. *High Seas Confederate: The Life and Times of John Newland Maffitt.* Columbia: University of South Carolina Press, 1994.

Silverston, Paul H. *Warships of the Civil War Navies.* Annapolis, Md.: Naval Institute Press, 1989.

Smith, Myron J. Jr. *American Civil War Navies: A Bibliography.* Metuchen, N.J.: The Scarecrow Press, Inc., 1972.

Snow, Freeman. *International Law: A Manual Based Upon Lectures Delivered at the Naval War College.* Washington, D.C.: Government Printing Office, 1898.

Still, William N. Jr. *Iron Afloat, The Story of Confederate Armorclads.* Nashville, Tenn.: Vanderbilt University Press, 1971.

Still, William N. Jr. *Savannah Squadron.* Savannah, Ga.: Coastal Heritage Press, 1989.

Stivers, Reuben Elmore, *Privateers and Volunteers: The Men and Women of Our Reserve Naval Forces, 1776–1866.* Annapolis, Md.: U.S. Naval Institute, 1975.

Superintendent of Documents. *Checklist of United States Public Documents 1789–1909.* Washington, D.C.: Government Printing Office, 1911.

Taylor, Thomas E. *Running the Blockade: A Personal Narrative of Adventures, Risks and Escapes during the American Civil War.* London: Murray, 1912.

Tucker, Spencer. *Arming the Fleet: U.S. Naval Ordnance in the Muzzle-Loading Era.* Annapolis, Md.: Naval Institute Press, 1989.

Wakefield, Manville B. *Coal Boats to Tidewater: The Story of the Delaware and Hudson Canal.* South Fallsburg, N.Y.: Steingart Associates, Inc., 1965.

Warner, Ezra J. *Generals In Blue, Lives of the Union Commanders.* Baton Rouge: Louisiana State University Press, 1964.

Warner, Ezra J. *Generals In Gray, Lives of the Confederate Commanders.* Baton Rouge: Louisiana State University Press, 1959.

Welcher, Frank. *The Union Army 1861–1865: Organization and Operations, Volume I: The Eastern Theater.* Bloomington: Indiana University Press, 1989.

Werlich, David P. *Admiral of the Amazon: John Randolph Tucker, His Confederate Colleagues, and Peru.* Charlottesville: University Press of Virginia, 1990.

West, Richard S. Jr. *Gideon Welles, Lincoln's Navy Department.* New York: The Bobbs-Merrill Company, 1943.

West, Richard S. Jr. *Mr. Lincoln's Navy.* New York: Longmans Green and Company, 1957.

Williams, Thomas Harry. *P.G.T. Beauregard, Napoleon in Gray.* Baton Rouge: Louisiana State University Press, 1955.

Wise, Stephen R. *Gate of Hell, Campaign for Charleston Harbor, 1863.* Columbia: University of South Carolina Press, 1994.

Wise, Stephen R. *Lifeline of the Confederacy: Blockade Running During the Civil War.* Columbia: University of South Carolina Press, 1988.

Withington, Sidney. *Two Dramatic Episodes of New England Whaling.* Mystic, Conn.:The Maritime Historical Association Inc., 1958.

ARTICLES

Allard, Dean. "Naval Technology during the American Civil War." *American Neptune* 49 (Spring 1989): 114–22.

Allen, Walter "The Defense of Charleston Harbor in the Civil War." *New Englander and Yale Review* 248 (November 1890): 406–10.

Anderson, Bern. "The Naval Strategy of the Civil War." *Military Affairs* 26 (Spring 1962): 11–21.

Anonymous. "The Southern Harbors of the United States." *The Merchant's Magazine and Commercial Review* 45 (No. 1 July 1861): 17–24.

Bakewell, Henry P. Jr. "The USS *Sabine*." *American Neptune* 23 (Oct. 1963): 261–63.

Barnes, Horace R. "Rear Admiral William Reynolds: A Distinguished Lancastrian 1815–1879." *Papers Read Before the Lancaster County Historical Society* 38, No. 2, (1934): 61–66.

Blair, C. H. "Submarines of the Confederate States Navy." *U.S. Naval Institute Proceedings* 78 (September 1952): 1115–21.

Blair, Montgomery. "Confederate Documents Relating to Fort Sumter." *The United Service* 4 (March 1881): 358–84.

Blake, W. H. "Coal Barging in War Times, 1861–1865." *Gulf States Historical Magazine* 1 (May 1903): 409–12.

Bolander, Lewis H. "The Stone Fleet in Charleston Harbor." *Confederate Veteran* 39 (April 1931): 133–36.

Bowman, Berry. "The Hunley—Ill-Fated Confederate Submarine." *Civil War History* 5 (Sept. 1959): 315–19.

Chandler, Alfred D. Jr. "Du Pont, Dahlgren, and the Civil War Nitre Shortage." *Military Affairs* 12 (Fall 1949): 142–49.

Church, Henry F. "The Harbor Defenses of Charleston." *The Military Engineer* 23 (Jan.–Feb. 1931): 11–14.

Durham, Roger A. "Savannah: Mr. Lincoln's Christmas Present." *Blue and Gray* (8 February 1991): 8–18, 42–53.

Earle, Ralph. "John Adolphus Dahlgren." *Proceedings of the United States Naval Institute* 51 (March 1925):424–36.

East, Omega. G. "St. Augustine during the Civil War." *The Florida Historical Quarterly* 31 (October 1952): 75–91.

Florance, John E. Jr. "Morris Island: Victory or Blunder?" *The South Carolina Historical Magazine* 55 (July 1954): 143–52.

Gordon, Arthur. "The Great Stone Fleet: Calculated Catastrophe." *U.S. Naval Institute Proceedings* 44 (December 1968): 72–82.

Graham, Thomas. "The Home Front: Civil War Times in St. Augustine." *Civil War Times in St. Augustine.* Edited by Jacqueline K. Fretwell, St. Augustine, Fla.: St. Augustine Historical Society, 1988: 19–45.

Hagerman, G. "Confederate Submarines." *U.S. Naval Institute Proceedings* 103 (September 1977): 74–75.

Harding, Ursala and James F. "The Guns of the *Keokuk.*" *Civil War Times Illustrated* 1 (November 1962): 22–25.

Hayes, John D. "Captain Fox: He Is the Navy Department." *U.S. Naval Institute Proceedings* 91 (November 1965): 64–71.

Hayes, John D. "Fox versus Du Pont: The Crisis in Civil-Military Relations 7 April 1863." *Shipmate* 26 (April 1963): 10–11.

Hayes, John D. "Lee Against the Sea; Port Royal, South Carolina 7 November 1861." *Shipmate* 20 (June 1957): 20–22.

Hayes, John D. "Samuel William Preston (1841–1865), Flag Lieutenant to Three Admirals and Tragic Example of the Staff Officer in War." *Shipmate* 26 (Jan. 1963): 18–19.

Hayes, John D. "The Battle of Port Royal, S.C., From the Journal of John Sanford Barnes, October 8 to November 9, 1861." *New York Historical Society Quarterly* 45 (October 1961): 365–95.

Henig, Gerald. "Admiral Samuel F. Du Pont, the Navy Department and the Attack on Charleston, April 1863." *Naval War College Review* 32 (February 1979): 68–77.

Holcombe, John L. and Walter Buttgenbach. "Confederate Forts Inadequate to Protect Port Royal From US Navy." *The Artilleryman* (Winter 1998): 28–32.

Luthin, Reinhard H. "A Discordant Chapter in Lincoln's Administration: The Davis-Blair Controversy." *Maryland Historical Magazine* (March 1944): 25–48.

Lyman, John. "Register Tonnage and Its Measurement." *American Neptune* 5 (July 1945): 223–34.

Magruder, John H. "The Wreck of the Governor." *Leatherneck* 38 (November 1955): 74–77.

McClean, Malcolm. "The Short Cruise of the CSS *Atlanta*." *Georgia Historical Quarterly* 40 (March 1956): 130–43.

McKibben. Frank P. "The Stone Fleet of 1861." *The New England Magazine* 18 (June 1898): 484–89.

Melton, Maurice. "The First and Last Cruise of the CSS *Atlanta*." *Civil War Times Illustrated* 10 (Nov. 1971): 4–9, 44–46.

Merrill, James M. "The Hatteras Expedition, August 1861." *North Carolina Historical Review* 29 (April 1952): 204–19.

Merrill, James M. "Strategy Makers in the Union Navy Department 1861–1865." *Mid-America: An Historical Review* 44 (January 1862): 19–32.

Merrill, James M. "The Yankee Blockade of the South Atlantic." *Civil War History* 4 (December 1958): 387–97.

Merrill, James M. "USS Weehawken-Gallant Ironship." *U.S. Naval Institute Proceedings* 86 (October 1960): 162–63.

Neeser, Robert W. "Historic Ships of the Navy—*Montauk*." *U.S. Naval Institute Proceedings* 67 (May 1941): 687–91.

Neeser, Robert W. "Historical Ships of the Navy—*New Ironsides*." *U.S. Naval Institute Proceedings* 52 (Dec. 1926): 2443–51.

Paullin, Charles O. "President Lincoln and the Navy." *The American Historical Review* 14 (January 1909): 284–303.

Powells, James M. "The *Hunley* Sinks the *Housatonic*." *Navy* 8 (Jan. 1965): 23–25.

Price, Marcus W. "Blockade Running as a Business in South Carolina During the War Between the States, 1861–1865." *The American Neptune* 9 (January 1949): 31–62.

Romaine, Laurence B. "A Blockade Runner Who Never Returned: The Story of James Dickson's Diary-Logbook 1861–1862." *Manuscripts* 7 (Spring 1955): 167–72.

Ropp, Theodore. "Anaconda Anyone?" *Military Affairs* 27 (Spring 1963): 71–76.

Sass, Herbert R. "The Story of the Little *David.*" *Harper's Magazine* 186 (May 1943): 620–25.

Seifert, E. M. "The Evolution of the Torpedo." *Ordnance* 39 (March-April 1955): 720–24.

Stapleton, Darwin H. "Assistant Charles O. Boutelle, of the United States Coast Survey, With the South Atlantic Blockading Squadron, 1861–1863." *The American Neptune* 31 (October 1971): 253–67.

Steedman, Marguerite Couturier. "The Ladies Build a Gunboat." *Sandlapper* 1 (September 1968): 57–63.

Thompson, Edgar K. "The U.S. Monitor *Patapsco.*" *U.S. Naval Institute Proceedings* 94 (December 1968): 148–49.

Von Kolnitz, Harry. "The Confederate Submarine." *U.S. Naval Institute Proceedings* 63 (October 1937): 1453–57.

Wegner, Dana. "The Port Royal Working Parties." *Civil War Times Illustrated* 15 No. 8 (December, 1976): 22–31.

West, Richard. "The Navy and the Press During the Civil War." *United States Naval Institute Proceedings* 63 (January 1937): 33–41.

Woodman, John E. "The Stone Fleet." *American Neptune* 21 (October 1961): 233–59.

DISSERTATIONS

Bright, Samuel R. "Confederate Coast Defense." Ph.D. diss., Duke University, 1961.

Griffin, James D. "Savannah Georgia During the Civil War." Ph.D. diss., Emory University, 1963.

Guinn, Gilbert Sumter. "Coast Defense of the Confederate Atlantic Seaboard States, 1861–1862: A Study of Political and Military Mobilization." Ph.D. diss., University of South Carolina, 1973.

Henig, Gerald Sheldon. "Henry Winter Davis: A Biography." unpublished Ph.D. diss., The City University of New York, 1971.

Legg, Thomas James. "Quest for Glory: The Naval Career of John A. Dahlgren, 1826–1870." Ph.D. diss., The College of William and Mary, 1994.

Merrill, James M. "Naval Operations Along the South Atlantic Coast." Ph.D. diss., University of California at Los Angeles, 1954.

Polser, Aubrey Henry Jr. "The Administration of the United States Navy 1861–1865." Ph.D. diss., University of Nebraska, 1975.

Tomblin, Barbara B. "From Sail to Steam: The Development of Steam Technology in the United States Navy 1838–1865." Ph.D. diss., Rutgers University, 1988.

WEB SITE

U.S. Naval Observatory, Time Service Department, Washington, D.C. [http://tycho.usno.navy.mil/vphase.html].

INDEX

ABOUT THE AUTHOR

ROBERT M. BROWNING JR., Ph.D., is the Chief Historian of the U.S. Coast Guard. His previous books include *From Cape Charles to Cape Fear: The North Atlantic Blockading Squadron during the Civil War* and *U.S. Merchant Vessel War Casualties of World War II*. He lives in Dumfries, Virginia.